Ford Focus Automotive Repair Manual

by Jay Storer and John H Haynes

Member of the Guild of Motoring Writers

Models covered:

Focus models
2000 through 2007

Does not include information specific to SVT and rear disc brake models

(1M7 - 36034)   ABCD

Haynes Publishing Group
Sparkford Nr Yeovil
Somerset BA22 7JJ England

Haynes North America, Inc
861 Lawrence Drive
Newbury Park
California 91320 USA

Acknowledgements

Wiring diagrams provided exclusively for Haynes North America, Inc. by Valley Forge Technical Information Services. Technical writers who contributed to this project include R.M. Jex and Peter T. Gill.

© **Haynes North America, Inc. 2002, 2004, 2005, 2009**

With permission from J.H. Haynes & Co. Ltd.

A book in the Haynes Automotive Repair Manual Series

Printed in the U.S.A.

ISBN-13: 978-1-56392-754-6
ISBN-10: 1-56392-754-3

Library of Congress Control Number 2009921721

About this manual

Its purpose

The purpose of this manual is to help you get the best value from your vehicle. It can do so in several ways. It can help you decide what work must be done, even if you choose to have it done by a dealer service department or a repair shop; it provides information and procedures for routine maintenance and servicing; and it offers diagnostic and repair procedures to follow when trouble occurs.

We hope you use the manual to tackle the work yourself. For many simpler jobs, doing it yourself may be quicker than arranging an appointment to get the vehicle into a shop and making the trips to leave it and pick it up. More importantly, a lot of money can be saved by avoiding the expense the shop must pass on to you to cover its labor and overhead costs. An added benefit is the sense of satisfaction and accomplishment that you feel after doing the job yourself.

Using the manual

The manual is divided into Chapters. Each Chapter is divided into numbered Sections, which are headed in bold type between horizontal lines. Each Section consists of consecutively numbered paragraphs.

At the beginning of each numbered Section you will be referred to any illustrations which apply to the procedures in that Section. The reference numbers used in illustration captions pinpoint the pertinent Section and the Step within that Section. That is, illustration 3.2 means the illustration refers to Section 3 and Step (or paragraph) 2 within that Section.

Procedures, once described in the text, are not normally repeated. When it's necessary to refer to another Chapter, the reference will be given as Chapter and Section number. Cross references given without use of the word "Chapter" apply to Sections and/or paragraphs in the same Chapter. For example, "see Section 8" means in the same Chapter.

References to the left or right side of the vehicle assume you are sitting in the driver's seat, facing forward.

Even though we have prepared this manual with extreme care, neither the publisher nor the author can accept responsibility for any errors in, or omissions from, the information given.

NOTE

A **Note** provides information necessary to properly complete a procedure or information which will make the procedure easier to understand.

CAUTION

A **Caution** provides a special procedure or special steps which must be taken while completing the procedure where the Caution is found. Not heeding a Caution can result in damage to the assembly being worked on.

WARNING

A **Warning** provides a special procedure or special steps which must be taken while completing the procedure where the Warning is found. Not heeding a Warning can result in personal injury.

Introduction

The front-drive design features unitized construction and 4-wheel independent suspension. Over the years covered, models have been available in 2-door, 3-door, 4-door, 5-door and station wagon body styles.

The transversely mounted four-cylinder engine drives the front wheels through a five-speed manual, a six-speed manual or four-speed automatic transaxle by way of unequal length driveaxles. The rack-and-pinion steering gear is mounted behind the engine and is available with power assist. Brakes are discs at the front and drum-type at the rear with vacuum assist. Rear disc brakes are available on 2TS and ST models.

Vehicle identification numbers

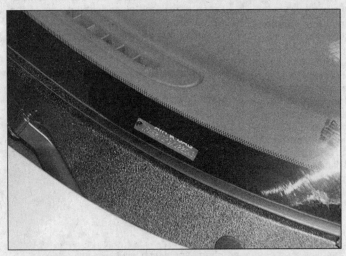

The Vehicle Identification Number (VIN) is visible from outside the vehicle through the driver's side of the windshield

The Certification label is located on the left front door post or door

Modifications are a continuing and unpublicized process in vehicle manufacturing. Since spare parts lists and manuals are compiled on a numerical basis, the individual vehicle numbers are necessary to correctly identify the component required.

Vehicle Identification Number (VIN)

This very important identification number is stamped on a plate attached to the dashboard inside the windshield on the driver's side of the vehicle (see illustration). The VIN also appears on the Vehicle Certificate of Title and Registration. It contains information such as where and when the vehicle was manufactured, the model year and the body style.

VIN engine and model year codes

Two particularly important pieces of information found in the VIN are the engine code and the model year code. Counting from the left, the engine code letter designation is the 8th digit and the model year code designation is the 10th digit.

On the models covered by this manual the engine codes are:

P . . . . 2.0L SPI
3 . . . . 2.0L Zetec
5 . . . . SVT Duratec
N . . . . 2005 and later 2.0L
Z 2.3L

On the models covered by this manual the model year codes are:

2 2002
3 2003
4 2004
5 2005
6 2006
7 2007

Vehicle Certification Label

The Vehicle Certification Label is attached to the driver's side door pillar (see illustration). Information on this label includes the name of the manufacturer, the month and year of production, the Gross Vehicle Weight Rating (GVWR), the Gross Axle Weight Rating (GAWR) and the certification statement.

Engine number

The engine number is stamped onto a machined pad on the external surface of the engine block. There's also an identification label that's usually on the timing belt cover.

Buying parts

Replacement parts are available from many sources, which generally fall into one of two categories - authorized dealer parts departments and independent retail auto parts stores. Our advice concerning these parts is as follows:

Retail auto parts stores: Good auto parts stores will stock frequently needed components which wear out relatively fast, such as clutch components, exhaust systems, brake parts, tune-up parts, etc. These stores often supply new or reconditioned parts on an exchange basis, which can save a considerable amount of money. Discount auto parts stores are often very good places to buy materials and parts needed for general vehicle maintenance such as oil, grease, filters, spark plugs, belts, touch-up paint, bulbs, etc. They also usually sell tools and general accessories, have convenient hours, charge lower prices and can often be found not far from home.

Authorized dealer parts department: This is the best source for parts which are unique to the vehicle and not generally available elsewhere (such as major engine parts, transmission parts, trim pieces, etc.).

Warranty information: If the vehicle is still covered under warranty, be sure that any replacement parts purchased - regardless of the source - do not invalidate the warranty!

To be sure of obtaining the correct parts, have engine and chassis numbers available and, if possible, take the old parts along for positive identification.

Maintenance techniques, tools and working facilities

Maintenance techniques

There are a number of techniques involved in maintenance and repair that will be referred to throughout this manual. Application of these techniques will enable the home mechanic to be more efficient, better organized and capable of performing the various tasks properly, which will ensure that the repair job is thorough and complete.

Fasteners

Fasteners are nuts, bolts, studs and screws used to hold two or more parts together. There are a few things to keep in mind when working with fasteners. Almost all of them use a locking device of some type, either a lockwasher, locknut, locking tab or thread adhesive. All threaded fasteners should be clean and straight, with undamaged threads and undamaged corners on the hex head where the wrench fits. Develop the habit of replacing all damaged nuts and bolts with new ones. Special locknuts with nylon or fiber inserts can only be used once. If they are removed, they lose their locking ability and must be replaced with new ones.

Rusted nuts and bolts should be treated with a penetrating fluid to ease removal and prevent breakage. Some mechanics use turpentine in a spout-type oil can, which works quite well. After applying the rust penetrant, let it work for a few minutes before trying to loosen the nut or bolt. Badly rusted fasteners may have to be chiseled or sawed off or removed with a special nut breaker, available at tool stores.

If a bolt or stud breaks off in an assembly, it can be drilled and removed with a special tool commonly available for this purpose.

Most automotive machine shops can perform this task, as well as other repair procedures, such as the repair of threaded holes that have been stripped out.

Flat washers and lockwashers, when removed from an assembly, should always be replaced exactly as removed. Replace any damaged washers with new ones. Never use a lockwasher on any soft metal surface (such as aluminum), thin sheet metal or plastic.

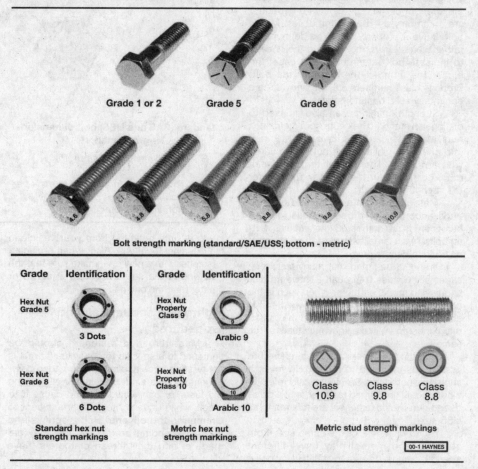

Grade 1 or 2   Grade 5   Grade 8

Bolt strength marking (standard/SAE/USS; bottom - metric)

Grade	Identification	Grade	Identification
Hex Nut Grade 5	3 Dots	Hex Nut Property Class 9	Arabic 9
Hex Nut Grade 8	6 Dots	Hex Nut Property Class 10	Arabic 10

Standard hex nut strength markings

Metric hex nut strength markings

Class 10.9   Class 9.8   Class 8.8

Metric stud strength markings

00-1 HAYNES

Fastener sizes

For a number of reasons, automobile manufacturers are making wider and wider use of metric fasteners. Therefore, it is important to be able to tell the difference between standard (sometimes called U.S. or SAE) and metric hardware, since they cannot be interchanged.

All bolts, whether standard or metric, are sized according to diameter, thread pitch and length. For example, a standard 1/2 - 13 x 1 bolt is 1/2 inch in diameter, has 13 threads per inch and is 1 inch long. An M12 - 1.75 x 25 metric bolt is 12 mm in diameter, has a thread pitch of 1.75 mm (the distance between threads) and is 25 mm long. The two bolts are nearly identical, and easily confused, but they are not interchangeable.

In addition to the differences in diameter, thread pitch and length, metric and standard bolts can also be distinguished by examining the bolt heads. To begin with, the distance across the flats on a standard bolt head is measured in inches, while the same dimension on a metric bolt is sized in millimeters (the same is true for nuts). As a result, a standard wrench should not be used on a metric bolt and a metric wrench should not be used on a standard bolt. Also, most standard bolts have slashes radiating out from the center of the head to denote the grade or strength of the bolt, which is an indication of the amount of torque that can be applied to it. The greater the number of slashes, the greater the strength of the bolt. Grades 0 through 5 are commonly used on automobiles. Metric bolts have a property class (grade) number, rather than a slash, molded into their heads to indicate bolt strength. In this case, the higher the number, the stronger the bolt. Property class numbers 8.8, 9.8 and 10.9 are commonly used on automobiles.

Strength markings can also be used to distinguish standard hex nuts from metric hex nuts. Many standard nuts have dots stamped into one side, while metric nuts are marked with a number. The greater the number of dots, or the higher the number, the greater the strength of the nut.

Metric studs are also marked on their ends according to property class (grade). Larger studs are numbered (the same as metric bolts), while smaller studs carry a geometric code to denote grade.

It should be noted that many fasteners, especially Grades 0 through 2, have no distinguishing marks on them. When such is the case, the only way to determine whether it is standard or metric is to measure the thread pitch or compare it to a known fastener of the same size.

Standard fasteners are often referred to as SAE, as opposed to metric. However, it should be noted that SAE technically refers to a non-metric fine thread fastener only. Coarse thread non-metric fasteners are referred to as USS sizes.

Since fasteners of the same size (both standard and metric) may have different strength ratings, be sure to reinstall any bolts,

Metric thread sizes	Ft-lbs	Nm
M-6	6 to 9	9 to 12
M-8	14 to 21	19 to 28
M-10	28 to 40	38 to 54
M-12	50 to 71	68 to 96
M-14	80 to 140	109 to 154

Pipe thread sizes		
1/8	5 to 8	7 to 10
1/4	12 to 18	17 to 24
3/8	22 to 33	30 to 44
1/2	25 to 35	34 to 47

U.S. thread sizes		
1/4 - 20	6 to 9	9 to 12
5/16 - 18	12 to 18	17 to 24
5/16 - 24	14 to 20	19 to 27
3/8 - 16	22 to 32	30 to 43
3/8 - 24	27 to 38	37 to 51
7/16 - 14	40 to 55	55 to 74
7/16 - 20	40 to 60	55 to 81
1/2 - 13	55 to 80	75 to 108

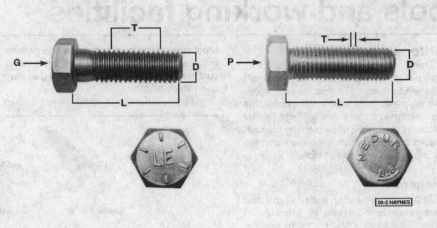

Standard (SAE and USS) bolt dimensions/ grade marks

G   Grade marks (bolt strength)
L   Length (in inches)
T   Thread pitch (number of threads per inch)
D   Nominal diameter (in inches)

Metric bolt dimensions/grade marks

P   Property class (bolt strength)
L   Length (in millimeters)
T   Thread pitch (distance between threads in millimeters)
D   Diameter

studs or nuts removed from your vehicle in their original locations. Also, when replacing a fastener with a new one, make sure that the new one has a strength rating equal to or greater than the original.

Tightening sequences and procedures

Most threaded fasteners should be tightened to a specific torque value (torque is the twisting force applied to a threaded component such as a nut or bolt). Overtightening the fastener can weaken it and cause it to break, while undertightening can cause it to eventually come loose. Bolts, screws and studs, depending on the material they are made of and their thread diameters, have

specific torque values, many of which are noted in the Specifications at the beginning of each Chapter. Be sure to follow the torque recommendations closely. For fasteners not assigned a specific torque, a general torque value chart is presented here as a guide. These torque values are for dry (unlubricated) fasteners threaded into steel or cast iron (not aluminum). As was previously mentioned, the size and grade of a fastener determine the amount of torque that can safely be applied to it. The figures listed here are approximate for Grade 2 and Grade 3 fasteners. Higher grades can tolerate higher torque values.

Fasteners laid out in a pattern, such as cylinder head bolts, oil pan bolts, differential cover bolts, etc., must be loosened or tightened in sequence to avoid warping the com-

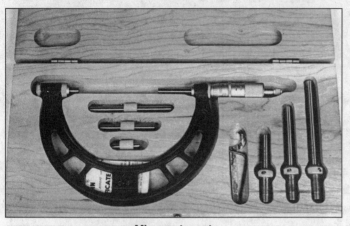

Micrometer set

Dial indicator set

ponent. This sequence will normally be shown in the appropriate Chapter. If a specific pattern is not given, the following procedures can be used to prevent warping.

Initially, the bolts or nuts should be assembled finger-tight only. Next, they should be tightened one full turn each, in a criss-cross or diagonal pattern. After each one has been tightened one full turn, return to the first one and tighten them all one-half turn, following the same pattern. Finally, tighten each of them one-quarter turn at a time until each fastener has been tightened to the proper torque. To loosen and remove the fasteners, the procedure would be reversed.

Component disassembly

Component disassembly should be done with care and purpose to help ensure that the parts go back together properly. Always keep track of the sequence in which parts are removed. Make note of special characteristics or marks on parts that can be installed more than one way, such as a grooved thrust washer on a shaft. It is a good idea to lay the disassembled parts out on a clean surface in the order that they were removed. It may also be helpful to make sketches or take instant photos of components before removal.

When removing fasteners from a component, keep track of their locations. Sometimes threading a bolt back in a part, or putting the washers and nut back on a stud, can prevent mix-ups later. If nuts and bolts cannot be returned to their original locations, they should be kept in a compartmented box or a series of small boxes. A cupcake or muffin tin is ideal for this purpose, since each cavity can hold the bolts and nuts from a particular area (i.e. oil pan bolts, valve cover bolts, engine mount bolts, etc.). A pan of this type is especially helpful when working on assemblies with very small parts, such as the carburetor, alternator, valve train or interior dash and trim pieces. The cavities can be marked with paint or tape to identify the contents.

Whenever wiring looms, harnesses or connectors are separated, it is a good idea to identify the two halves with numbered pieces of masking tape so they can be easily reconnected.

Gasket sealing surfaces

Throughout any vehicle, gaskets are used to seal the mating surfaces between two parts and keep lubricants, fluids, vacuum or pressure contained in an assembly.

Many times these gaskets are coated with a liquid or paste-type gasket sealing compound before assembly. Age, heat and pressure can sometimes cause the two parts to stick together so tightly that they are very difficult to separate. Often, the assembly can be loosened by striking it with a soft-face hammer near the mating surfaces. A regular hammer can be used if a block of wood is placed between the hammer and the part. Do not hammer on cast parts or parts that could be easily damaged. With any particularly stubborn part, always recheck to make sure that every fastener has been removed.

Avoid using a screwdriver or bar to pry apart an assembly, as they can easily mar the gasket sealing surfaces of the parts, which must remain smooth. If prying is absolutely necessary, use an old broom handle, but keep in mind that extra clean up will be necessary if the wood splinters.

After the parts are separated, the old gasket must be carefully scraped off and the gasket surfaces cleaned. Stubborn gasket material can be soaked with rust penetrant or treated with a special chemical to soften it so it can be easily scraped off. A scraper can be fashioned from a piece of copper tubing by flattening and sharpening one end. Copper is recommended because it is usually softer than the surfaces to be scraped, which reduces the chance of gouging the part. Some gaskets can be removed with a wire brush, but regardless of the method used, the mating surfaces must be left clean and smooth. If for some reason the gasket surface is gouged, then a gasket sealer thick enough to fill scratches will have to be used during reassembly of the components. For most applications, a non-drying (or semi-drying) gasket sealer should be used.

Hose removal tips

Warning: *If the vehicle is equipped with air conditioning, do not disconnect any of the A/C hoses without first having the system depressurized by a dealer service department or a service station.*

Hose removal precautions closely parallel gasket removal precautions. Avoid scratching or gouging the surface that the hose mates against or the connection may leak. This is especially true for radiator hoses. Because of various chemical reactions, the rubber in hoses can bond itself to the metal spigot that the hose fits over. To remove a hose, first loosen the hose clamps that secure it to the spigot. Then, with slip-joint pliers, grab the hose at the clamp and rotate it around the spigot. Work it back and forth until it is completely free, then pull it off. Silicone or other lubricants will ease removal if they can be applied between the hose and the outside of the spigot. Apply the same lubricant to the inside of the hose and the outside of the spigot to simplify installation.

As a last resort (and if the hose is to be replaced with a new one anyway), the rubber can be slit with a knife and the hose peeled from the spigot. If this must be done, be careful that the metal connection is not damaged.

If a hose clamp is broken or damaged, do not reuse it. Wire-type clamps usually weaken with age, so it is a good idea to replace them with screw-type clamps whenever a hose is removed.

Tools

A selection of good tools is a basic requirement for anyone who plans to maintain and repair his or her own vehicle. For the owner who has few tools, the initial investment might seem high, but when compared to the spiraling costs of professional auto maintenance and repair, it is a wise one.

To help the owner decide which tools are needed to perform the tasks detailed in this manual, the following tool lists are offered: *Maintenance and minor repair, Repair/overhaul* and *Special.*

The newcomer to practical mechanics should start off with the *maintenance and*

Dial caliper

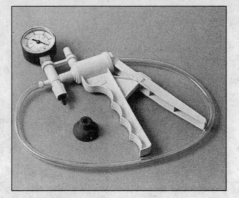

Hand-operated vacuum pump

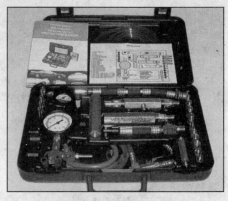

Fuel pressure gauge set

Compression gauge with spark plug hole adapter

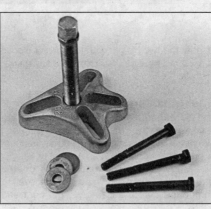

Damper/steering wheel puller

General purpose puller

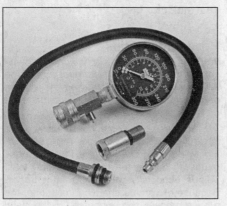

Hydraulic lifter removal tool

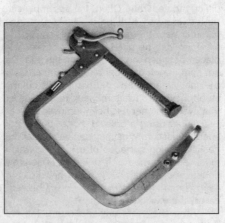

Valve spring compressor

Valve spring compressor

Ridge reamer

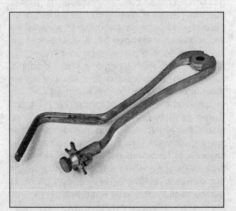

Piston ring groove cleaning tool

Ring removal/installation tool

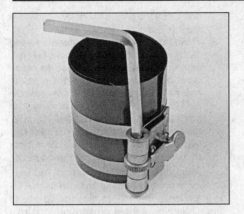

Ring compressor

Cylinder hone

Brake hold-down spring tool

Torque angle gauge

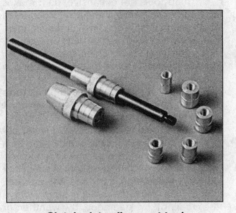

Clutch plate alignment tool

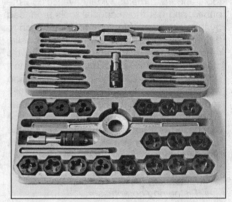

Tap and die set

minor repair tool kit, which is adequate for the simpler jobs performed on a vehicle. Then, as confidence and experience grow, the owner can tackle more difficult tasks, buying additional tools as they are needed. Eventually the basic kit will be expanded into the repair and overhaul tool set. Over a period of time, the experienced do-it-yourselfer will assemble a tool set complete enough for most repair and overhaul procedures and will add tools from the special category when it is felt that the expense is justified by the frequency of use.

Maintenance and minor repair tool kit

The tools in this list should be considered the minimum required for performance of routine maintenance, servicing and minor repair work. We recommend the purchase of combination wrenches (box-end and open-end combined in one wrench). While more expensive than open end wrenches, they offer the advantages of both types of wrench.

Combination wrench set (1/4-inch to 1 inch or 6 mm to 19 mm)
Adjustable wrench, 8 inch
Spark plug wrench with rubber insert
Spark plug gap adjusting tool
Feeler gauge set
Brake bleeder wrench
Standard screwdriver (5/16-inch x 6 inch)

Phillips screwdriver (No. 2 x 6 inch)
Combination pliers - 6 inch
Hacksaw and assortment of blades
Tire pressure gauge
Grease gun
Oil can
Fine emery cloth
Wire brush
Battery post and cable cleaning tool
Oil filter wrench
Funnel (medium size)
Safety goggles
Jackstands (2)
Drain pan

Note: *If basic tune-ups are going to be part of routine maintenance, it will be necessary to purchase a good quality stroboscopic timing light and combination tachometer/dwell meter. Although they are included in the list of special tools, it is mentioned here because they are absolutely necessary for tuning most vehicles properly.*

Repair and overhaul tool set

These tools are essential for anyone who plans to perform major repairs and are in addition to those in the maintenance and minor repair tool kit. Included is a comprehensive set of sockets which, though expensive, are invaluable because of their versatility, especially when various extensions and drives are available. We recommend the 1/2-inch drive over the 3/8-inch drive. Although the larger drive is bulky and more expensive, it has the capacity of accepting a very wide range of large sockets. Ideally, however, the mechanic should have a 3/8-inch drive set and a 1/2-inch drive set.

Socket set(s)
Reversible ratchet
Extension - 10 inch
Universal joint
Torque wrench (same size drive as sockets)
Ball peen hammer - 8 ounce
Soft-face hammer (plastic/rubber)
Standard screwdriver (1/4-inch x 6 inch)
Standard screwdriver (stubby - 5/16-inch)
Phillips screwdriver (No. 3 x 8 inch)
Phillips screwdriver (stubby - No. 2)
Pliers - vise grip
Pliers - lineman's
Pliers - needle nose
Pliers - snap-ring (internal and external)
Cold chisel - 1/2-inch
Scribe
Scraper (made from flattened copper tubing)
Centerpunch
Pin punches (1/16, 1/8, 3/16-inch)
Steel rule/straightedge - 12 inch
Allen wrench set (1/8 to 3/8-inch or 4 mm to 10 mm)
A selection of files
Wire brush (large)
Jackstands (second set)
Jack (scissor or hydraulic type)

Note: *Another tool which is often useful is an electric drill with a chuck capacity of 3/8-inch and a set of good quality drill bits.*

Special tools

The tools in this list include those which are not used regularly, are expensive to buy, or which need to be used in accordance with their manufacturer's instructions. Unless these tools will be used frequently, it is not very economical to purchase many of them. A consideration would be to split the cost and use between yourself and a friend or friends. In addition, most of these tools can be obtained from a tool rental shop on a temporary basis.

This list primarily contains only those tools and instruments widely available to the public, and not those special tools produced by the vehicle manufacturer for distribution to dealer service departments. Occasionally, references to the manufacturer's special tools are included in the text of this manual. Generally, an alternative method of doing the job without the special tool is offered. However, sometimes there is no alternative to their use. Where this is the case, and the tool cannot be purchased or borrowed, the work should be turned over to the dealer service department or an automotive repair shop.

Valve spring compressor
Piston ring groove cleaning tool
Piston ring compressor
Piston ring installation tool
Cylinder compression gauge
Cylinder ridge reamer
Cylinder surfacing hone
Cylinder bore gauge
Micrometers and/or dial calipers
Hydraulic lifter removal tool
Balljoint separator
Universal-type puller
Impact screwdriver
Dial indicator set
Stroboscopic timing light (inductive pick-up)
Hand operated vacuum/pressure pump
Tachometer/dwell meter
Universal electrical multimeter
Cable hoist
Brake spring removal and installation tools
Floor jack

Buying tools

For the do-it-yourselfer who is just starting to get involved in vehicle maintenance and repair, there are a number of options available when purchasing tools. If maintenance and minor repair is the extent of the work to be done, the purchase of individual tools is satisfactory. If, on the other hand, extensive work is planned, it would be a good idea to purchase a modest tool set from one of the large retail chain stores. A set can usually be bought at a substantial savings over the individual tool prices, and they often come with a tool box. As additional tools are

needed, add-on sets, individual tools and a larger tool box can be purchased to expand the tool selection. Building a tool set gradually allows the cost of the tools to be spread over a longer period of time and gives the mechanic the freedom to choose only those tools that will actually be used.

Tool stores will often be the only source of some of the special tools that are needed, but regardless of where tools are bought, try to avoid cheap ones, especially when buying screwdrivers and sockets, because they won't last very long. The expense involved in replacing cheap tools will eventually be greater than the initial cost of quality tools.

Care and maintenance of tools

Good tools are expensive, so it makes sense to treat them with respect. Keep them clean and in usable condition and store them properly when not in use. Always wipe off any dirt, grease or metal chips before putting them away. Never leave tools lying around in the work area. Upon completion of a job, always check closely under the hood for tools that may have been left there so they won't get lost during a test drive.

Some tools, such as screwdrivers, pliers, wrenches and sockets, can be hung on a panel mounted on the garage or workshop wall, while others should be kept in a tool box or tray. Measuring instruments, gauges, meters, etc. must be carefully stored where they cannot be damaged by weather or impact from other tools.

When tools are used with care and stored properly, they will last a very long time. Even with the best of care, though, tools will wear out if used frequently. When a tool is damaged or worn out, replace it. Subsequent jobs will be safer and more enjoyable if you do.

How to repair damaged threads

Sometimes, the internal threads of a nut or bolt hole can become stripped, usually from overtightening. Stripping threads is an all-too-common occurrence, especially when working with aluminum parts, because aluminum is so soft that it easily strips out.

Usually, external or internal threads are only partially stripped. After they've been cleaned up with a tap or die, they'll still work. Sometimes, however, threads are badly damaged. When this happens, you've got three choices:

1) *Drill and tap the hole to the next suitable oversize and install a larger diameter bolt, screw or stud.*
2) *Drill and tap the hole to accept a threaded plug, then drill and tap the plug to the original screw size. You can also buy a plug already threaded to the original size. Then you simply drill a hole to the specified size, then run the threaded plug into the hole with a bolt and jam*

nut. Once the plug is fully seated, remove the jam nut and bolt.
3) *The third method uses a patented thread repair kit like Heli-Coil or Slimsert. These easy-to-use kits are designed to repair damaged threads in straight-through holes and blind holes. Both are available as kits which can handle a variety of sizes and thread patterns. Drill the hole, then tap it with the special included tap. Install the Heli-Coil and the hole is back to its original diameter and thread pitch.*

Regardless of which method you use, be sure to proceed calmly and carefully. A little impatience or carelessness during one of these relatively simple procedures can ruin your whole day's work and cost you a bundle if you wreck an expensive part.

Working facilities

Not to be overlooked when discussing tools is the workshop. If anything more than routine maintenance is to be carried out, some sort of suitable work area is essential.

It is understood, and appreciated, that many home mechanics do not have a good workshop or garage available, and end up removing an engine or doing major repairs outside. It is recommended, however, that the overhaul or repair be completed under the cover of a roof.

A clean, flat workbench or table of comfortable working height is an absolute necessity. The workbench should be equipped with a vise that has a jaw opening of at least four inches.

As mentioned previously, some clean, dry storage space is also required for tools, as well as the lubricants, fluids, cleaning solvents, etc. which soon become necessary.

Sometimes waste oil and fluids, drained from the engine or cooling system during normal maintenance or repairs, present a disposal problem. To avoid pouring them on the ground or into a sewage system, pour the used fluids into large containers, seal them with caps and take them to an authorized disposal site or recycling center. Plastic jugs, such as old antifreeze containers, are ideal for this purpose.

Always keep a supply of old newspapers and clean rags available. Old towels are excellent for mopping up spills. Many mechanics use rolls of paper towels for most work because they are readily available and disposable. To help keep the area under the vehicle clean, a large cardboard box can be cut open and flattened to protect the garage or shop floor.

Whenever working over a painted surface, such as when leaning over a fender to service something under the hood, always cover it with an old blanket or bedspread to protect the finish. Vinyl covered pads, made especially for this purpose, are available at auto parts stores.

Booster battery (jump) starting

Booster battery (jump) starting

Observe these precautions when using a booster battery to start a vehicle:

a) *Before connecting the booster battery, make sure the ignition switch is in the Off position.*

b) *Turn off the lights, heater and other electrical loads.*

c) *Your eyes should be shielded. Safety goggles are a good idea.*

d) *Make sure the booster battery is the same voltage as the dead one in the vehicle.*

e) *The two vehicles MUST NOT TOUCH each other!*

f) *Make sure the transaxle is in Neutral (manual) or Park (automatic).*

g) *If the booster battery is not a maintenance-free type, remove the vent caps and lay a cloth over the vent holes.*

Connect the red jumper cable to the positive (+) terminals of each battery (**see illustration**).

Connect one end of the black jumper cable to the negative (-) terminal of the booster battery. The other end of this cable should be connected to a good ground on the vehicle to be started, such as a bolt or bracket on the body.

Start the engine using the booster battery, then, with the engine running at idle speed, disconnect the jumper cables in the reverse order of connection.

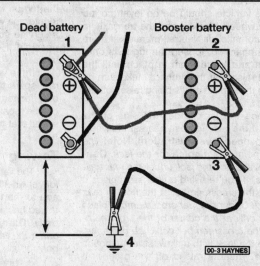

Make the booster battery cable connections in the numerical order shown (note that the negative cable of the booster battery is NOT attached to the negative terminal of the dead battery)

Jacking and towing

Jacking

The jack supplied with the vehicle should be used only for raising the vehicle when changing a tire or placing jackstands under the frame. **Warning**: *Never work under the vehicle or start the engine when this jack is being used as the only means of support.*

The vehicle should be on level ground with the wheels blocked and the transaxle in Park (automatic) or Neutral (manual). If a tire is being changed, loosen the lug nuts one-half turn and leave them in place until the wheel is raised off the ground. Make sure no one is in the vehicle as it's being raised off the ground.

Place the jack under the side of the vehicle at the jacking point nearest the wheel to be changed **(see illustration)**. **Note**: *The jacking point has a notch for the jack.* **Caution**: *Never place the jack under the rear trailing arms.* If you're using a floor jack, place it beneath the crossmember at the front or rear. **Warning**: *Under the rear crossmember, place the jack only at the center of the crossmember, or the crossmember could be damaged.* Operate the jack with a slow, smooth motion until the wheel is raised off the ground. If you're using jackstands, position them beneath the support points along the front or rear side sills. Remove the lug nuts, pull off the wheel, install the spare and thread the lug

nuts back on with the beveled sides facing in. Tighten snugly, but wait until the vehicle is lowered to tighten completely.

Lower the vehicle, remove the jack and tighten the lug nuts (if loosened or removed) in a criss-cross pattern. If possible, tighten them with a torque wrench (see Chapter 1 for the torque figures). If you don't have access to a torque wrench, have the nuts checked by a service station or repair shop as soon as possible. Retighten the lug nuts after 500 miles.

If the vehicle is equipped with a temporary spare tire, remember that it is intended only for temporary use until the regular tire can be repaired. Do not exceed the maximum speed that the tire is rated for.

Towing

The vehicle must be towed with the front (drive) wheels off the ground to prevent damage to the transaxle. If the vehicle must be towed backward, place the front wheels on a dolly. **Caution**: *Don't use the hook loops under the vehicle for towing (they're intended only for use as tie-downs).*

A wheel lift is recommended. A flatbed truck can also be used. In this case, pull the vehicle onto the truck towards the front, using J-hooks at the front suspension control arms with the points turned down.

The jack supplied with the vehicle fits over the rocker panel flange

While towing, the parking brake must be released and the transaxle must be in Neutral. The steering must be unlocked (ignition switch in the OFF position). Don't exceed 50 mph (35 mph on rough roads).

Safety is a major consideration while towing and all applicable state and local laws must be obeyed. A safety chain system must be used at all times. Remember that power steering and power brakes will not work with the engine off.

Automotive chemicals and lubricants

A number of automotive chemicals and lubricants are available for use during vehicle maintenance and repair. They include a wide variety of products ranging from cleaning solvents and degreasers to lubricants and protective sprays for rubber, plastic and vinyl.

Cleaners

Carburetor cleaner and choke cleaner is a strong solvent for gum, varnish and carbon. Most carburetor cleaners leave a dry-type lubricant film which will not harden or gum up. Because of this film it is not recommended for use on electrical components.

Brake system cleaner is used to remove brake dust, grease and brake fluid from the brake system, where clean surfaces are absolutely necessary. It leaves no residue and often eliminates brake squeal caused by contaminants.

Electrical cleaner removes oxidation, corrosion and carbon deposits from electrical contacts, restoring full current flow. It can also be used to clean spark plugs, carburetor jets, voltage regulators and other parts where an oil-free surface is desired.

Demoisturants remove water and moisture from electrical components such as alternators, voltage regulators, electrical connectors and fuse blocks. They are non-conductive and non-corrosive.

Degreasers are heavy-duty solvents used to remove grease from the outside of the engine and from chassis components. They can be sprayed or brushed on and, depending on the type, are rinsed off either with water or solvent.

Lubricants

Motor oil is the lubricant formulated for use in engines. It normally contains a wide variety of additives to prevent corrosion and reduce foaming and wear. Motor oil comes in various weights (viscosity ratings) from 0 to 50. The recommended weight of the oil depends on the season, temperature and the demands on the engine. Light oil is used in cold climates and under light load conditions. Heavy oil is used in hot climates and where high loads are encountered. Multi-viscosity oils are designed to have characteristics of both light and heavy oils and are available in a number of weights from 5W-20 to 20W-50.

Gear oil is designed to be used in differentials, manual transmissions and other areas where high-temperature lubrication is required.

Chassis and wheel bearing grease is a heavy grease used where increased loads and friction are encountered, such as for wheel bearings, balljoints, tie-rod ends and universal joints.

High-temperature wheel bearing grease is designed to withstand the extreme temperatures encountered by wheel bearings in disc brake equipped vehicles. It usually contains molybdenum disulfide (moly), which is a dry-type lubricant.

White grease is a heavy grease for metal-to-metal applications where water is a problem. White grease stays soft under both low and high temperatures (usually from -100 to +190-degrees F), and will not wash off or dilute in the presence of water.

Assembly lube is a special extreme pressure lubricant, usually containing moly, used to lubricate high-load parts (such as main and rod bearings and cam lobes) for initial start-up of a new engine. The assembly lube lubricates the parts without being squeezed out or washed away until the engine oiling system begins to function.

Silicone lubricants are used to protect rubber, plastic, vinyl and nylon parts.

Graphite lubricants are used where oils cannot be used due to contamination problems, such as in locks. The dry graphite will lubricate metal parts while remaining uncontaminated by dirt, water, oil or acids. It is electrically conductive and will not foul electrical contacts in locks such as the ignition switch.

Moly penetrants loosen and lubricate frozen, rusted and corroded fasteners and prevent future rusting or freezing.

Heat-sink grease is a special electrically non-conductive grease that is used for mounting electronic ignition modules where it is essential that heat is transferred away from the module.

Sealants

RTV sealant is one of the most widely used gasket compounds. Made from silicone, RTV is air curing, it seals, bonds, waterproofs, fills surface irregularities, remains flexible, doesn't shrink, is relatively easy to remove, and is used as a supplementary sealer with almost all low and medium temperature gaskets.

Anaerobic sealant is much like RTV in that it can be used either to seal gaskets or to form gaskets by itself. It remains flexible, is solvent resistant and fills surface imperfections. The difference between an anaerobic sealant and an RTV-type sealant is in the curing. RTV cures when exposed to air, while an anaerobic sealant cures only in the absence of air. This means that an anaerobic sealant cures only after the assembly of parts, sealing them together.

Thread and pipe sealant is used for sealing hydraulic and pneumatic fittings and vacuum lines. It is usually made from a Teflon compound, and comes in a spray, a paint-on liquid and as a wrap-around tape.

Chemicals

Anti-seize compound prevents seizing, galling, cold welding, rust and corrosion in fasteners. High-temperature ant-seize, usually made with copper and graphite lubricants, is used for exhaust system and exhaust manifold bolts.

Anaerobic locking compounds are used to keep fasteners from vibrating or working loose and cure only after installation, in the absence of air. Medium strength locking compound is used for small nuts, bolts and screws that may be removed later. High-strength locking compound is for large nuts, bolts and studs which aren't removed on a regular basis.

Oil additives range from viscosity index improvers to chemical treatments that claim to reduce internal engine friction. It should be noted that most oil manufacturers caution against using additives with their oils.

Gas additives perform several functions, depending on their chemical makeup. They usually contain solvents that help dissolve gum and varnish that build up on carburetor, fuel injection and intake parts. They also serve to break down carbon deposits that form on the inside surfaces of the combustion chambers. Some additives contain upper cylinder lubricants for valves and piston rings, and others contain chemicals to remove condensation from the gas tank.

Miscellaneous

Brake fluid is specially formulated hydraulic fluid that can withstand the heat and pressure encountered in brake systems. Care must be taken so this fluid does not come in contact with painted surfaces or plastics. An opened container should always be resealed to prevent contamination by water or dirt.

Weatherstrip adhesive is used to bond weatherstripping around doors, windows and trunk lids. It is sometimes used to attach trim pieces.

Undercoating is a petroleum-based, tar-like substance that is designed to protect metal surfaces on the underside of the vehicle from corrosion. It also acts as a sound-deadening agent by insulating the bottom of the vehicle.

Waxes and polishes are used to help protect painted and plated surfaces from the weather. Different types of paint may require the use of different types of wax and polish. Some polishes utilize a chemical or abrasive cleaner to help remove the top layer of oxidized (dull) paint on older vehicles. In recent years many non-wax polishes that contain a wide variety of chemicals such as polymers and silicones have been introduced. These non-wax polishes are usually easier to apply and last longer than conventional waxes and polishes.

Conversion factors

Length (distance)

Inches (in)	X	25.4	= Millimeters (mm)	X 0.0394	= Inches (in)
Feet (ft)	X	0.305	= Meters (m)	X 3.281	= Feet (ft)
Miles	X	1.609	= Kilometers (km)	X 0.621	= Miles

Volume (capacity)

Cubic inches (cu in; in^3)	X	16.387	= Cubic centimeters (cc; cm^3)	X 0.061	= Cubic inches (cu in; in^3)
Imperial pints (Imp pt)	X	0.568	= Liters (l)	X 1.76	= Imperial pints (Imp pt)
Imperial quarts (Imp qt)	X	1.137	= Liters (l)	X 0.88	= Imperial quarts (Imp qt)
Imperial quarts (Imp qt)	X	1.201	= US quarts (US qt)	X 0.833	= Imperial quarts (Imp qt)
US quarts (US qt)	X	0.946	= Liters (l)	X 1.057	= US quarts (US qt)
Imperial gallons (Imp gal)	X	4.546	= Liters (l)	X 0.22	= Imperial gallons (Imp gal)
Imperial gallons (Imp gal)	X	1.201	= US gallons (US gal)	X 0.833	= Imperial gallons (Imp gal)
US gallons (US gal)	X	3.785	= Liters (l)	X 0.264	= US gallons (US gal)

Mass (weight)

Ounces (oz)	X	28.35	= Grams (g)	X 0.035	= Ounces (oz)
Pounds (lb)	X	0.454	= Kilograms (kg)	X 2.205	= Pounds (lb)

Force

Ounces-force (ozf; oz)	X	0.278	= Newtons (N)	X 3.6	= Ounces-force (ozf; oz)
Pounds-force (lbf; lb)	X	4.448	= Newtons (N)	X 0.225	= Pounds-force (lbf; lb)
Newtons (N)	X	0.1	= Kilograms-force (kgf; kg)	X 9.81	= Newtons (N)

Pressure

Pounds-force per square inch (psi; lbf/in^2; lb/in^2)	X	0.070	= Kilograms-force per square centimeter (kgf/cm^2; kg/cm^2)	X 14.223	= Pounds-force per square inch (psi; lbf/in^2; lb/in^2)
Pounds-force per square inch (psi; lbf/in^2; lb/in^2)	X	0.068	= Atmospheres (atm)	X 14.696	= Pounds-force per square inch (psi; lbf/in^2; lb/in^2)
Pounds-force per square inch (psi; lbf/in^2; lb/in^2)	X	0.069	= Bars	X 14.5	= Pounds-force per square inch (psi; lbf/in^2; lb/in^2)
Pounds-force per square inch (psi; lbf/in^2; lb/in^2)	X	6.895	= Kilopascals (kPa)	X 0.145	= Pounds-force per square inch (psi; lbf/in^2; lb/in^2)
Kilopascals (kPa)	X	0.01	= Kilograms-force per square centimeter (kgf/cm^2; kg/cm^2)	X 98.1	= Kilopascals (kPa)

Torque (moment of force)

Pounds-force inches (lbf in; lb in)	X	1.152	= Kilograms-force centimeter (kgf cm; kg cm)	X 0.868	= Pounds-force inches (lbf in; lb in)
Pounds-force inches (lbf in; lb in)	X	0.113	= Newton meters (Nm)	X 8.85	= Pounds-force inches (lbf in; lb in)
Pounds-force inches (lbf in; lb in)	X	0.083	= Pounds-force feet (lbf ft; lb ft)	X 12	= Pounds-force inches (lbf in; lb in)
Pounds-force feet (lbf ft; lb ft)	X	0.138	= Kilograms-force meters (kgf m; kg m)	X 7.233	= Pounds-force feet (lbf ft; lb ft)
Pounds-force feet (lbf ft; lb ft)	X	1.356	= Newton meters (Nm)	X 0.738	= Pounds-force feet (lbf ft; lb ft)
Newton meters (Nm)	X	0.102	= Kilograms-force meters (kgf m; kg m)	X 9.804	= Newton meters (Nm)

Vacuum

Inches mercury (in. Hg)	X	3.377	= Kilopascals (kPa)	X 0.2961	= Inches mercury
Inches mercury (in. Hg)	X	25.4	= Millimeters mercury (mm Hg)	X 0.0394	= Inches mercury

Power

Horsepower (hp)	X	745.7	= Watts (W)	X 0.0013	= Horsepower (hp)

Velocity (speed)

Miles per hour (miles/hr; mph)	X	1.609	= Kilometers per hour (km/hr; kph)	X 0.621	= Miles per hour (miles/hr; mph)

Fuel consumption*

Miles per gallon, Imperial (mpg)	X	0.354	= Kilometers per liter (km/l)	X 2.825	= Miles per gallon, Imperial (mpg)
Miles per gallon, US (mpg)	X	0.425	= Kilometers per liter (km/l)	X 2.352	= Miles per gallon, US (mpg)

Temperature

Degrees Fahrenheit = (°C x 1.8) + 32   Degrees Celsius (Degrees Centigrade; °C) = (°F - 32) x 0.56

*It is common practice to convert from miles per gallon (mpg) to liters/100 kilometers (l/100km), where mpg (Imperial) x l/100 km = 282 and mpg (US) x l/100 km = 235

DECIMALS to MILLIMETERS

Decimal	mm	Decimal	mm
0.001	0.0254	0.500	12.7000
0.002	0.0508	0.510	12.9540
0.003	0.0762	0.520	13.2080
0.004	0.1016	0.530	13.4620
0.005	0.1270	0.540	13.7160
0.006	0.1524	0.550	13.9700
0.007	0.1778	0.560	14.2240
0.008	0.2032	0.570	14.4780
0.009	0.2286	0.580	14.7320
		0.590	14.9860
0.010	0.2540		
0.020	0.5080		
0.030	0.7620		
0.040	1.0160	0.600	15.2400
0.050	1.2700	0.610	15.4940
0.060	1.5240	0.620	15.7480
0.070	1.7780	0.630	16.0020
0.080	2.0320	0.640	16.2560
0.090	2.2860	0.650	16.5100
		0.660	16.7640
0.100	2.5400	0.670	17.0180
0.110	2.7940	0.680	17.2720
0.120	3.0480	0.690	17.5260
0.130	3.3020		
0.140	3.5560		
0.150	3.8100		
0.160	4.0640	0.700	17.7800
0.170	4.3180	0.710	18.0340
0.180	4.5720	0.720	18.2880
0.190	4.8260	0.730	18.5420
		0.740	18.7960
0.200	5.0800	0.750	19.0500
0.210	5.3340	0.760	19.3040
0.220	5.5880	0.770	19.5580
0.230	5.8420	0.780	19.8120
0.240	6.0960	0.790	20.0660
0.250	6.3500		
0.260	6.6040		
0.270	6.8580	0.800	20.3200
0.280	7.1120	0.810	20.5740
0.290	7.3660	0.820	20.8280
		0.830	21.0820
0.300	7.6200	0.840	21.3360
0.310	7.8740	0.850	21.5900
0.320	8.1280	0.860	21.8440
0.330	8.3820	0.870	22.0980
0.340	8.6360	0.880	22.3520
0.350	8.8900	0.890	22.6060
0.360	9.1440		
0.370	9.3980		
0.380	9.6520		
0.390	9.9060	0.900	22.8600
0.400	10.1600	0.910	23.1140
0.410	10.4140	0.920	23.3680
0.420	10.6680	0.930	23.6220
0.430	10.9220	0.940	23.8760
0.440	11.1760	0.950	24.1300
0.450	11.4300	0.960	24.3840
0.460	11.6840	0.970	24.6380
0.470	11.9380	0.980	24.8920
0.480	12.1920	0.990	25.1460
0.490	12.4460	1.000	25.4000

FRACTIONS to DECIMALS to MILLIMETERS

Fraction	Decimal	mm	Fraction	Decimal	mm
1/64	0.0156	0.3969	33/64	0.5156	13.0969
1/32	0.0312	0.7938	17/32	0.5312	13.4938
3/64	0.0469	1.1906	35/64	0.5469	13.8906
1/16	0.0625	1.5875	9/16	0.5625	14.2875
5/64	0.0781	1.9844	37/64	0.5781	14.6844
3/32	0.0938	2.3812	19/32	0.5938	15.0812
7/64	0.1094	2.7781	39/64	0.6094	15.4781
1/8	0.1250	3.1750	5/8	0.6250	15.8750
9/64	0.1406	3.5719	41/64	0.6406	16.2719
5/32	0.1562	3.9688	21/32	0.6562	16.6688
11/64	0.1719	4.3656	43/64	0.6719	17.0656
3/16	0.1875	4.7625	11/16	0.6875	17.4625
13/64	0.2031	5.1594	45/64	0.7031	17.8594
7/32	0.2188	5.5562	23/32	0.7188	18.2562
15/64	0.2344	5.9531	47/64	0.7344	18.6531
1/4	0.2500	6.3500	3/4	0.7500	19.0500
17/64	0.2656	6.7469	49/64	0.7656	19.4469
9/32	0.2812	7.1438	25/32	0.7812	19.8438
19/64	0.2969	7.5406	51/64	0.7969	20.2406
5/16	0.3125	7.9375	13/16	0.8125	20.6375
21/64	0.3281	8.3344	53/64	0.8281	21.0344
11/32	0.3438	8.7312	27/32	0.8438	21.4312
23/64	0.3594	9.1281	55/64	0.8594	21.8281
3/8	0.3750	9.5250	7/8	0.8750	22.2250
25/64	0.3906	9.9219	57/64	0.8906	22.6219
13/32	0.4062	10.3188	29/32	0.9062	23.0188
27/64	0.4219	10.7156	59/64	0.9219	23.4156
7/16	0.4375	11.1125	15/16	0.9375	23.8125
29/64	0.4531	11.5094	61/64	0.9531	24.2094
15/32	0.4688	11.9062	31/32	0.9688	24.6062
31/64	0.4844	12.3031	63/64	0.9844	25.0031
1/2	0.5000	12.7000	1	1.0000	25.4000

Safety first!

Regardless of how enthusiastic you may be about getting on with the job at hand, take the time to ensure that your safety is not jeopardized. A moment's lack of attention can result in an accident, as can failure to observe certain simple safety precautions. The possibility of an accident will always exist, and the following points should not be considered a comprehensive list of all dangers. Rather, they are intended to make you aware of the risks and to encourage a safety conscious approach to all work you carry out on your vehicle.

Essential DOs and DON'Ts

DON'T rely on a jack when working under the vehicle. Always use approved jackstands to support the weight of the vehicle and place them under the recommended lift or support points.

DON'T attempt to loosen extremely tight fasteners (i.e. wheel lug nuts) while the vehicle is on a jack - it may fall.

DON'T start the engine without first making sure that the transmission is in Neutral (or Park where applicable) and the parking brake is set.

DON'T remove the radiator cap from a hot cooling system - let it cool or cover it with a cloth and release the pressure gradually.

DON'T attempt to drain the engine oil until you are sure it has cooled to the point that it will not burn you.

DON'T touch any part of the engine or exhaust system until it has cooled sufficiently to avoid burns.

DON'T siphon toxic liquids such as gasoline, antifreeze and brake fluid by mouth, or allow them to remain on your skin.

DON'T inhale brake lining dust - it is potentially hazardous (see *Asbestos* below).

DON'T allow spilled oil or grease to remain on the floor - wipe it up before someone slips on it.

DON'T use loose fitting wrenches or other tools which may slip and cause injury.

DON'T push on wrenches when loosening or tightening nuts or bolts. Always try to pull the wrench toward you. If the situation calls for pushing the wrench away, push with an open hand to avoid scraped knuckles if the wrench should slip.

DON'T attempt to lift a heavy component alone - get someone to help you.

DON'T *rush or take unsafe shortcuts to finish a job.*

DON'T allow children or animals in or around the vehicle while you are working on it.

DO wear eye protection when using power tools such as a drill, sander, bench grinder, etc. and when working under a vehicle.

DO keep loose clothing and long hair well out of the way of moving parts.

DO make sure that any hoist used has a safe working load rating adequate for the job.

DO get someone to check on you periodically when working alone on a vehicle.

DO carry out work in a logical sequence and make sure that everything is correctly assembled and tightened.

DO keep chemicals and fluids tightly capped and out of the reach of children and pets.

DO remember that your vehicle's safety affects that of yourself and others. If in doubt on any point, get professional advice.

Steering, suspension and brakes

These systems are essential to driving safety, so make sure you have a qualified shop or individual check your work. Also, compressed suspension springs can cause injury if released suddenly - be sure to use a spring compressor.

Airbags

Airbags are explosive devices that can **CAUSE** injury if they deploy while you're working on the vehicle. Follow the manufacturer's instructions to disable the airbag whenever you're working in the vicinity of airbag components.

Asbestos

Certain friction, insulating, sealing, and other products - such as brake linings, brake bands, clutch linings, torque converters, gaskets, etc. - may contain asbestos or other hazardous friction material. Extreme care must be taken to avoid inhalation of dust from such products, since it is hazardous to health. If in doubt, assume that they do contain asbestos.

Fire

Remember at all times that gasoline is highly flammable. Never smoke or have any kind of open flame around when working on a vehicle. But the risk does not end there. A spark caused by an electrical short circuit, by two metal surfaces contacting each other, or even by static electricity built up in your body under certain conditions, can ignite gasoline vapors, which in a confined space are highly explosive. Do not, under any circumstances, use gasoline for cleaning parts. Use an approved safety solvent.

Always disconnect the battery ground (-) cable at the battery before working on any part of the fuel system or electrical system. Never risk spilling fuel on a hot engine or exhaust component. It is strongly recommended that a fire extinguisher suitable for use on fuel and electrical fires be kept handy in the garage or workshop at all times. Never try to extinguish a fuel or electrical fire with water.

Fumes

Certain fumes are highly toxic and can quickly cause unconsciousness and even death if inhaled to any extent. Gasoline vapor falls into this category, as do the vapors from some cleaning solvents. Any draining or pouring of such volatile fluids should be done in a well ventilated area.

When using cleaning fluids and solvents, read the instructions on the container carefully. Never use materials from unmarked containers.

Never run the engine in an enclosed space, such as a garage. Exhaust fumes contain carbon monoxide, which is extremely poisonous. If you need to run the engine, always do so in the open air, or at least have the rear of the vehicle outside the work area.

The battery

Never create a spark or allow a bare light bulb near a battery. They normally give off a certain amount of hydrogen gas, which is highly explosive.

Always disconnect the battery ground (-) cable at the battery before working on the fuel or electrical systems.

If possible, loosen the filler caps or cover when charging the battery from an external source (this does not apply to sealed or maintenance-free batteries). Do not charge at an excessive rate or the battery may burst.

Take care when adding water to a non maintenance-free battery and when carrying a battery. The electrolyte, even when diluted, is very corrosive and should not be allowed to contact clothing or skin.

Always wear eye protection when cleaning the battery to prevent the caustic deposits from entering your eyes.

Household current

When using an electric power tool, inspection light, etc., which operates on household current, always make sure that the tool is correctly connected to its plug and that, where necessary, it is properly grounded. Do not use such items in damp conditions and, again, do not create a spark or apply excessive heat in the vicinity of fuel or fuel vapor.

Secondary ignition system voltage

A severe electric shock can result from touching certain parts of the ignition system (such as the spark plug wires) when the engine is running or being cranked, particularly if components are damp or the insulation is defective. In the case of an electronic ignition system, the secondary system voltage is much higher and could prove fatal.

Hydrofluoric acid

This extremely corrosive acid is formed when certain types of synthetic rubber, found in some O-rings, oil seals, fuel hoses, etc. are exposed to temperatures above 750-degrees F (400-degrees C). The rubber changes into a charred or sticky substance containing the acid. *Once formed, the acid remains dangerous for years. If it gets onto the skin, it may be necessary to amputate the limb concerned.*

When dealing with a vehicle which has suffered a fire, or with components salvaged from such a vehicle, wear protective gloves and discard them after use.

Troubleshooting

Contents

This section provides an easy reference guide to the more common problems which may occur during the operation of your vehicle. These problems and possible causes are grouped under various components or systems; i.e. Engine, Cooling System, etc., and also refer to the Chapter and/or Section which deals with the problem.

Remember that successful troubleshooting is not a mysterious black art practiced only by professional mechanics. It's simply the result of a bit of knowledge combined with an intelligent, systematic approach to the problem. Always work by a process of elimination, starting with the simplest solution and working through to the most complex - and never overlook the obvious. Anyone can forget to fill the gas tank or leave the lights on overnight, so don't assume that you are above such oversights.

Finally, always get clear in your mind why a problem has occurred and take steps to ensure that it doesn't happen again. If the electrical system fails because of a poor connection, check all other connections in the system to make sure that they don't fail as well. If a particular fuse continues to blow, find out why - don't just go on replacing fuses. Remember, failure of a small component can often be indicative of potential failure or incorrect functioning of a more important component or system.

Engine

1 Engine will not rotate when attempting to start

1   Battery terminal connections loose or corroded. Check the cable terminals at the battery. Tighten the cable or remove corrosion as necessary.
2   Battery discharged or faulty. If the cable connections are clean and tight on the battery posts, turn the key to the On position and switch on the headlights and/or windshield wipers. If they fail to function, the battery is discharged.
3   Automatic transaxle not completely engaged in Park or Neutral or clutch pedal not completely depressed.
4   Broken, loose or disconnected wiring in the starting circuit. Inspect all wiring and connectors at the battery, starter solenoid and ignition switch.
5   Starter motor pinion jammed in flywheel ring gear. If manual transaxle, place transaxle in gear and rock the vehicle to manually turn the engine. Remove starter (Chapter 5) and inspect pinion and flywheel at earliest convenience.
6   Starter solenoid faulty (Chapter 5).
7   Starter motor faulty (Chapter 5).
8   Ignition switch faulty (Chapter 12).

2 Engine rotates but will not start

1   Fuel tank empty.
2   Fault in the fuel injection system (Chapter 4).
3   Battery discharged (engine rotates slowly). Check the operation of electrical components as described in the previous Section.
4   Battery terminal connections loose or corroded (see previous Section).
5   Fuel pump inertia switch disabled (frequently occurs after a collision - even a minor one) or fuel pump faulty (Chapter 4).
6   Excessive moisture on, or damage to, ignition components (see Chapter 5).
7   Worn, faulty or incorrectly gapped spark plugs (Chapter 1).
8   Broken, loose or disconnected wiring in the starting circuit (see previous Section).
9   Broken, loose or disconnected wires at the ignition coil or faulty coil (Chapter 5).

3 Starter motor operates without rotating engine

1   Starter pinion sticking. Remove the starter (Chapter 5) and inspect.

2   Starter pinion or flywheel teeth worn or broken. Remove the flywheel/driveplate access cover and inspect.

4 Engine hard to start when cold

1   Battery discharged or low. Check as described in Section 1.
2   Fault in the fuel or electrical systems (Chapters 4 and 5).

5 Engine hard to start when hot

1   Air filter clogged (Chapter 1).
2   Fault in the fuel or electrical systems (Chapters 4 and 5).
3   Corroded battery connections, especially ground (see Chapter 1).

6 Starter motor noisy or excessively rough in engagement

1   Pinion or flywheel gear teeth worn or broken. Remove the cover at the rear of the engine (if so equipped) and inspect.
2   Starter motor mounting bolts loose or missing.

7 Engine starts but stops immediately

1   Loose or faulty electrical connections at coil or alternator.
2   Low fuel pressure. Check the fuel pump (see Chapter 4).
3   Fault in the ignition system RUN circuit or ignition switch (see Chapter 12).
4   Vacuum leak at the gasket surfaces of the intake manifold. Make sure all mounting bolts/nuts are tightened securely and all vacuum hoses connected to the manifold are positioned properly and in good condition.

8 Engine lopes while idling or idles erratically

1   Vacuum leakage. Check the mounting bolts/nuts at the intake manifold for tightness. Make sure all vacuum hoses are connected and in good condition. Use a stethoscope or a length of fuel hose held against your ear to listen for vacuum leaks while the engine is running. A hissing sound will be heard. A soapy water solution will also detect leaks.
2   Fault in the fuel or electrical systems (Chapters 4 and 5).
3   Leaking EGR valve or plugged PCV valve (see Chapters 1 and 4).
4   Air filter clogged (Chapter 1).
5   Fuel pump not delivering sufficient fuel to the fuel injection system (see Chapter 4).
6   Leaking head gasket. Perform a compression check (Chapter 2).
7   Camshaft lobes worn (see Chapter 2).

9 Engine misses at idle speed

1   Spark plugs worn, fouled, or not gapped properly (Chapter 1).
2   Fault in the fuel or electrical systems (Chapters 4 and 5).
3   Faulty spark plug wires (Chapter 1).

10 Engine misses throughout driving speed range

1   Fuel filter clogged and/or impurities in the fuel system (Chapter 1).
2   Faulty or incorrectly gapped spark plugs (Chapter 1).
3   Fault in the fuel or electrical systems (Chapters 4 and 5).
4   Incorrect ignition timing (Chapter 5).
5   Faulty coil-pack (Chapter 5).
6   Defective spark plug wires (Chapter 1).
7   Faulty emissions system components (Chapter 4).
8   Low or uneven cylinder compression pressures. Perform a compression test (Chapter 2).
9   Weak or faulty ignition system (Chapter 5).
10   Vacuum leaks at the intake manifold or vacuum hoses (see Section 8).

11 Engine stalls

1   Fuel filter clogged and/or water and impurities in the fuel system (Chapter 1).
2   Coil-pack or plug wires damp or damaged (Chapter 5).
3   Fault in the fuel system or sensors (Chapters 4).
4   Faulty emissions system components (Chapter 4).
5   Faulty or incorrectly gapped spark plugs (Chapter 1). Also check the spark plug wires (Chapter 1).
6   Vacuum leak at the intake manifold or vacuum hoses. Check as described in Section 8.

12 Engine lacks power

1   Fault in the fuel or electrical systems (Chapters 4 and 5).
2   Faulty or incorrectly gapped spark plugs (Chapter 1).
3   Faulty coil (Chapter 5).
4   Brakes binding (Chapter 1 and Chapter 9).
5   Automatic transaxle fluid level incorrect (Chapter 1).
6   Clutch slipping (Chapter 6).
7   Fuel filter clogged and/or impurities in the fuel system (Chapter 1).
8   Emissions control system not functioning properly (Chapter 4).
9   Use of substandard fuel. Fill the tank with the proper octane fuel.

10   Low or uneven cylinder compression pressures. Perform a compression test (Chapter 2).

13   Engine backfires

1   Emissions system not functioning properly (Chapter 4).
2   Fault in the fuel or electrical systems (Chapters 4 and 5).
3   Faulty secondary ignition system, faulty plug wires or coil pack (Chapters 1 and 5).
4   Fault in the engine control system (Chapter 4).
5   Vacuum leak at the intake manifold or vacuum hoses. Check as described in Section 8.
6   Valves sticking (Chapter 2)

14   Pinging or knocking engine sounds during acceleration or uphill

1   Incorrect grade of fuel. Fill the tank with fuel of the proper octane rating.
2   Fault in the fuel or electrical systems (Chapters 4 and 5).
3   Improper spark plugs. Check the plug type. Also check the plugs and wires for damage (Chapter 1).
4   Faulty emissions system (Chapter 4).
5   Vacuum leak. Check as described in Section 8.

15   Engine diesels (continues to run) after switching off

1   Fault in the fuel or electrical systems (Chapters 4 and 5).
2   Excessive engine operating temperature. Probable causes of this are a malfunctioning thermostat, clogged radiator, faulty water pump (see Chapter 3).

Engine electrical system

16   Battery will not hold a charge

1   Alternator drivebelt defective or not adjusted properly (Chapter 1).
2   Electrolyte level low or battery discharged (Chapter 1).
3   Battery terminals loose or corroded (Chapter 1).
4   Alternator not charging properly (Chapter 5).
5   Loose, broken or faulty wiring in the charging circuit (Chapter 5).
6   Short in the vehicle wiring causing a continuous drain on battery (refer to Chapter 12 and the Wiring Diagrams).
7   Battery defective internally.

17   Ignition light fails to go out

1   Fault in the alternator or charging circuit (Chapter 5).
2   Alternator drivebelt defective or not properly adjusted (Chapter 1).

18   Ignition light fails to come on when key is turned on

1   Instrument cluster warning light bulb defective (Chapter 12).
2   Alternator faulty (Chapter 5).
3   Fault in the instrument cluster printed circuit, dashboard wiring or bulb holder (Chapter 12).

Fuel system

19   Excessive fuel consumption

1   Dirty or clogged air filter element (Chapter 1).
2   Emissions system not functioning properly (Chapter 4).
3   Fault in the fuel or electrical systems (Chapters 4 and 5).
4   Fault in the engine control system (Chapter 4).
5   Low tire pressure or incorrect tire size (Chapter 1).

20   Fuel leakage and/or fuel odor

1   Leak in a fuel feed or vent line (Chapter 4).
2   Tank overfilled. Fill only to automatic shut-off.
3   Evaporative emissions system canister clogged (Chapter 4).
4   Vapor leaks from system lines (Chapter 4).
5   Fault in the engine control system (Chapter 4).

Cooling system

21   Overheating

1   Insufficient coolant in the system (Chapter 1).
2   Water pump drivebelt defective or not adjusted properly (Chapter 1).
3   Radiator core blocked or radiator grille dirty and restricted (see Chapter 3).
4   Thermostat faulty (Chapter 3).
5   Fan blades broken or cracked (Chapter 3).
6   Fault in electric fan motor or wiring (see Chapter 3).
7   Expansion tank cap not maintaining proper pressure. Have the cap pressure tested by gas station or repair shop.

22   Overcooling

1   Thermostat faulty (Chapter 3).
2   Inaccurate temperature gauge (Chapter 12).

23   External coolant leakage

1   Deteriorated or damaged hoses or loose clamps. Replace hoses and/or tighten the clamps at the hose connections (Chapter 1).
2   Water pump seals defective. If this is the case, water will drip from the weep hole in the water pump body (Chapter 3).
3   Leakage from radiator core or header tank. This will require the radiator to be professionally repaired (see Chapter 3 for removal procedures).
4   Engine drain plug leaking (Chapter 1) or water jacket core plugs leaking (see Chapter 2).

24   Internal coolant leakage

Note: *Internal coolant leaks can usually be detected by examining the oil. Check the dipstick and inside of the cylinder head cover for water deposits and an oil consistency like that of a milkshake.*
1   Leaking cylinder head gasket. Have the cooling system pressure tested.
2   Cracked cylinder bore or cylinder head. Dismantle the engine and inspect (Chapter 2).

25   Coolant loss

1   Too much coolant in the system (Chapter 1).
2   Coolant boiling away due to overheating (see Section 15).
3   External or internal leakage (see Sections 23 and 24).
4   Faulty expansion tank cap. Have the cap pressure tested.

26   Poor coolant circulation

1   Inoperative water pump. A quick test is to pinch the top radiator hose closed with your hand while the engine is idling, then let it loose. You should feel the surge of coolant if the pump is working properly (see Chapter 3).
2   Restriction in the cooling system. Drain, flush and refill the system (Chapter 1). If necessary, remove the radiator (Chapter 3) and have it reverse flushed.
3   Water pump drivebelt defective or not adjusted properly (Chapter 1).
4   Thermostat sticking (Chapter 3).

Clutch

27 Fails to release (pedal pressed to the floor - shift lever does not move freely in and out of Reverse)

1   Leak in the clutch hydraulic system. Check the master cylinder, slave cylinder and lines (see Chapter 6).
2   Clutch plate warped or damaged (Chapter 6).

28 Clutch slips (engine speed increases with no increase in vehicle speed)

1   Clutch plate oil soaked or lining worn. Remove clutch (Chapter 6) and inspect (check for a leaking rear main oil seal or transaxle input shaft seal).
2   Clutch plate not seated. It may take 30 or 40 normal starts for a new one to seat.

29 Grabbing (chattering) as clutch is engaged

1   Oil on clutch plate lining. Remove (Chapter 6) and inspect. Correct any leakage source.
2   Worn or loose engine or transaxle mounts. These units move slightly when the clutch is released. Inspect the mounts and bolts (Chapter 2).
3   Worn splines on clutch plate hub. Remove the clutch components (Chapter 6) and inspect.
4   Warped pressure plate or flywheel. Remove the clutch components and inspect.

30 Squeal or rumble with clutch fully disengaged (pedal depressed)

1   Worn, defective or broken release bearing (Chapter 6).
2   Worn or broken diaphragm fingers (Chapter 6).

31 Clutch pedal stays on floor

1   Linkage or release bearing binding. Inspect the linkage or remove the clutch components as necessary.
2   Make sure proper pedal stop (bumper) is installed.

Manual transaxle

32 Knocking noise at low speeds

1   Worn driveaxle constant velocity (CV) joints (see Chapter 8).
2   Worn side gear shaft counterbore in differential case (see Chapter 7A).

33 Noise most pronounced when turning

Differential gear noise (see Chapter 7A).

34 Clunk on acceleration or deceleration

1   Loose engine or transaxle mounts (see Chapters 2 and 7A).
2   Worn differential pinion shaft in case.
3   Worn side gear shaft counterbore in differential case (see Chapter 7A).
4   Worn or damaged driveaxle inner CV joints (see Chapter 8).

35 Noisy in Neutral with engine running

1   Input shaft bearing worn.
2   Damaged main drive gear bearing.
3   Worn countershaft bearings.
4   Worn or damaged countershaft end play shims.

36 Noisy in all gears

1   Any of the above causes, and/or:
2   Insufficient lubricant (see the checking procedures in Chapter 1).

37 Noisy in one particular gear

1   Worn, damaged or chipped gear teeth for that particular gear.
2   Worn or damaged synchronizer for that particular gear.

38 Slips out of gear

1   Damaged shift linkage.
2   Interference between the floor shift handle and console.
3   Broken or loose engine mounts.
4   Shift mechanism stabilizer bar loose.
5   Improperly installed shifter boot.
6   Damaged or worn transaxle internal components.

39 Difficulty in engaging gears

1   Clutch not releasing completely (see clutch adjustment in Chapter 1).
2   Loose, damaged or out-of-adjustment shift linkage. Make a thorough inspection, replacing parts as necessary (Chapter 7).

40 Leaks lubricant

1   Excessive amount of lubricant in the transaxle (see Chapter 1 for correct checking procedures). Drain lubricant as required.

2   Side cover loose or gasket damaged.
3   Driveaxle oil seal or speedometer oil seal in need of replacement (Chapter 7).

Automatic transaxle

Note: *Due to the complexity of the automatic transaxle, it's difficult for the home mechanic to properly diagnose and service this component. For problems other than the following, the vehicle should be taken to a dealer service department or a transmission shop.*

41 General shift mechanism problems

1   Chapter 7 deals with checking and adjusting the shift linkage on automatic transaxles. Common problems which may be attributed to poorly adjusted linkage are:
   Engine starting in gears other than Park or Neutral.
   Indicator on shifter pointing to a gear other than the one actually being selected.
   Vehicle moves when in Park.
2   Refer to Chapter 7 to adjust the linkage.

42 Transaxle will not downshift with accelerator pedal pressed to the floor

Chapter 7 deals with adjusting the throttle cable to enable the transaxle to downshift properly. This requires special equipment and should be done by professionals.

43 Transaxle slips, shifts roughly, is noisy or has no drive in forward or reverse gears

1   There are many probable causes for the above problems, but the home mechanic should be concerned with only one possibility - fluid level.
2   Before taking the vehicle to a repair shop, check the level and condition of the fluid as described in Chapter 1. Correct fluid level as necessary or change the fluid and filter if needed. If the problem persists, have a professional diagnose the probable cause.

44 Fluid leakage

1   Automatic transaxle fluid is a deep red color when new, but it can darken with age. Fluid leaks should not be confused with engine oil, which can easily be blown by air flow to the transaxle. A good way to tell the difference is to place a drop of transaxle fluid from the dipstick on a clean, lint-free paper towel, then do the same thing with a drop of engine oil. This will enable you to compare the two.
2   To pinpoint a leak, first remove all built-up dirt and grime from around the transaxle. Degreasing agents and/or steam cleaning will achieve this. With the underside clean, drive

the vehicle at low speeds so air flow will not blow the leak far from its source. Raise the vehicle and determine where the leak is coming from. Common areas of leakage are:

a) **Pan:** *Tighten the mounting bolts and/or replace the pan gasket as necessary (see Chapter 7).*
b) **Filler pipe:** *Replace the rubber seal where the pipe enters the transaxle case.*
c) **Transaxle lubricant lines:** *Tighten the connectors where the lines enter the transaxle case and/or replace the lines.*
d) **Vent pipe:** *Transaxle overfilled and/or water in lubricant (see checking procedures, Chapter 1).*
e) **Speedometer connector:** *Replace the O-ring where the speedometer cable enters the transaxle case (Chapter 7).*

45 Transaxle lubricant brown or has a burned smell

Transaxle lubricant burned (see Chapter 1).

Driveaxles

46 Clicking noise in turns

Worn or damaged outer joint. Check for cut or damaged seals. Repair as necessary (Chapter 8).

47 Knock or clunk when accelerating after coasting

Worn or damaged inner joint. Check for cut or damaged seals. Repair as necessary (Chapter 8).

48 Shudder or vibration during acceleration

1 Worn or damaged CV joints. Repair or replace as necessary (see Chapter 8).
2 Sticking CV joint assembly. Correct or replace as necessary (see Chapter 8).

49 Vibration at highway speeds

1 Out-of-balance front wheels or tires (see Chapters 1 and 10).
2 Out-of-round front tires (see Chapters 1 and 10).
3 Worn CV joints (see Chapter 8).

Rear axle

50 Noise

1 Road noise. No corrective procedures available.
2 Tire noise. Inspect tires and check tire pressures (Chapter 1).

3 Rear wheel bearings loose, worn or damaged (Chapter 1).

Brakes

Note: *Before assuming that a brake problem exists, make sure that the tires are in good condition and inflated properly (see Chapter 1), that the front end alignment is correct and that the vehicle is not loaded with weight in an unequal manner.*

51 Vehicle pulls to one side during braking

1 Incorrect tire pressures (see Chapter 1).
2 Front end out of alignment (have the front end aligned).
3 Front or rear tires not matched to one another.
4 Restricted brake lines or hoses (see Chapter 9).
5 Defective, damaged or oil contaminated disc brake pads on one side. Inspect as described in Chapter 9.
6 Excessive wear of brake pad material or disc on one side. Inspect and correct as necessary.
7 Loose or disconnected front suspension components. Inspect and tighten all bolts to the specified torque (Chapter 10).
8 Defective caliper assembly. Remove the caliper and inspect for a stuck piston or other damage (Chapter 9).

52 Noise (high-pitched squeal with the brakes applied)

Disc brake pads worn out. The noise comes from the wear sensor (if equipped) rubbing against the disc or the actual pad backing plate itself if the material is completely worn away. Replace the pads with new ones immediately (Chapter 9). If the pad material has worn completely away, the brake discs should be inspected for damage as described in Chapter 9.

53 Excessive brake pedal travel

1 Partial brake system failure. Inspect the entire system (Chapter 9) and correct as required.
2 Insufficient fluid in the master cylinder. Check (Chapter 1), add fluid and bleed the system if necessary (Chapter 9).
3 Rear brakes not adjusting properly. Make a series of starts and stops while the vehicle is in Reverse. If this does not correct the situation, remove the drums and inspect the self-adjusters (Chapter 9).

54 Brake pedal feels spongy when depressed

1 Air in the hydraulic lines. Bleed the brake

system (Chapter 9).
2 Faulty flexible hoses. Inspect all system hoses and lines. Replace parts as necessary.
3 Master cylinder mounting bolts/nuts loose.
4 Master cylinder defective (Chapter 9).

55 Excessive effort required to stop vehicle

1 Power brake booster not operating properly (Chapter 9).
2 Excessively worn linings or pads. Inspect and replace if necessary (Chapter 9).
3 One or more caliper pistons or wheel cylinders seized or sticking. Inspect and rebuild as required (Chapter 9).
4 Brake linings or pads contaminated with oil or grease. Inspect and replace as required (Chapter 9).
5 New pads or shoes installed and not yet seated. It will take a while for the new material to seat against the drum (or disc).

56 Pedal travels to the floor with little resistance

1 Little or no fluid in the master cylinder reservoir caused by leaking wheel cylinder(s), leaking caliper piston(s), loose, damaged or disconnected brake lines. Inspect the entire system and correct as necessary.
2 Worn master cylinder (see Chapter 9).
3 Loose, damaged or disconnected brake lines (see Chapter 9).

57 Brake pedal pulsates during brake application

1 Disc or drum defective. Remove (Chapter 9) and check for excessive lateral runout and parallelism (disc) or out-of-roundness (drum). Have the disc or drum resurfaced or replace it with a new one.

58 Dragging brakes

1 Incorrect adjustment of brake light switch (see Chapter 9).
2 Master cylinder pistons not returning correctly (see Chapter 9).
3 Restricted brake lines or hoses (see Chapters 1 and 9).
4 Incorrect parking brake adjustment (see Chapter 9).

59 Grabbing or uneven braking action

1 Malfunction of proportioning valve (see Chapter 9).
2 Contaminated brake linings (see Chapter 9).
3 Binding brake pedal mechanism (see Chapter 9).

60   Parking brake does not hold

Parking brake cables improperly adjusted (see Chapters 1 and 9).

Suspension and steering systems

61   Vehicle pulls to one side

1   Tire pressures uneven (Chapter 1).
2   Defective tire (Chapter 1).
3   Excessive wear in suspension or steering components (Chapter 10).
4   Front end in need of alignment.
5   Front brakes dragging. Check the calipers for binding (see Chapter 9).

62   Shimmy, shake or vibration

1   Tire or wheel out-of-balance or out-of-round. Have professionally balanced.
2   Worn wheel bearings (Chapter 10).
3   Strut dampers and/or suspension components worn or damaged (Chapter 10).
4   Excessive wheel runout (see Chapter 10).
5   Blister or bump on tire (see Chapter 10).

63   Excessive pitching and/or rolling around corners or during braking

1   Worn strut dampers (see Chapter 10).
2   Broken or weak springs and/or suspension components. Inspect as described in Chapter 10.
3   Loose stabilizer bar (see Chapter 10).

64   Excessively stiff steering

1   Lack of fluid in power steering fluid reservoir (Chapter 1).
2   Incorrect tire pressures (Chapter 1).
3   Front end out of alignment.

65   Excessive play in steering

1   Wheel bearing(s) worn (see Chapter 10).
2   Tie-rod end loose (see Chapter 10).
3   Rack and pinion loose (see Chapter 10).
4   Worn or loose steering intermediate shaft (see Chapter 10).

66   Lack of power assistance

1   Steering pump drivebelt faulty or not adjusted properly (Chapter 1).
2   Fluid level low (Chapter 1).
3   Hoses or lines restricted. Inspect and replace parts as necessary.

4   Air in power steering system. Bleed the system (Chapter 10).

67   Excessive tire wear (not specific to one area)

1   Incorrect tire pressures (Chapter 1).
2   Tires out-of-balance. Have professionally balanced.
3   Wheels damaged. Inspect and replace as necessary.
4   Suspension or steering components excessively worn (Chapter 10).
5   Overloaded vehicle.
6   Tires not rotated regularly.

68   Excessive tire wear on outside edge

1   Inflation pressures incorrect (Chapter 1).
2   Excessive speed in turns.
3   Front end alignment incorrect (excessive toe-in). Have professionally aligned.
4   Suspension arm bent or twisted (Chapter 10).

69   Excessive tire wear on inside edge

1   Inflation pressures incorrect (Chapter 1).
2   Front end alignment incorrect. Have professionally aligned.
3   Loose or damaged steering components (Chapter 10).

70   Tire tread worn in one place

1   Tires out-of-balance.
2   Damaged or buckled wheel. Inspect and replace if necessary.
3   Defective tire (Chapter 1).

71   Wheel makes a thumping noise

1   Blister or bump on tire (see Chapter 10).
2   Improper strut damper action (see Chapter 10).

72   Steering wheel does not return to the straight-ahead position

1   Lack of lubrication at balljoints and tie-rod ends (see Chapter 10).
2   Binding in balljoints (see Chapter 10).
3   Binding in steering column (see Chapter 10).
4   Lack of lubricant in rack and pinion assembly (see Chapter 10).
5   Front wheel alignment (see Chapter 10).

73   Abnormal noise at the front end

1   Loose wheel nuts (see Chapter 1 for torque specifications).
2   Lack of lubrication at balljoints and tie-rod ends (see Chapters 1 and 10).
3   Damaged strut mounting (see Chapter 10).
4   Worn control arm bushings or tie-rod ends (see Chapter 10).
5   Loose stabilizer bar (see Chapter 10).
6   Loose suspension bolts (see Chapter 10).

74   Wander or poor steering stability

1   Mismatched or uneven tires (see Chapter 10).
2   Wheel alignment (see Chapter 10).
3   Worn strut assemblies (see Chapter 10).
4   Loose stabilizer bar (see Chapter 10).
5   Broken or sagging springs (see Chapter 10).
6   Wheel alignment (see Chapter 10).

75   Erratic steering when braking

1   Wheel bearings worn (see Chapter 10).
2   Broken or sagging springs (see Chapter 10).
3   Leaking caliper (see Chapter 9).
4   Warped discs or drums (see Chapter 9).

76   Suspension bottoms

1   Overloaded vehicle.
2   Worn strut dampers (see Chapter 10).
3   Incorrect, broken or sagging springs (see Chapter 10).

77   Cupped tires

1   Wheels out of alignment (see Chapter 10).
2   Worn strut dampers (see Chapter 10).
3   Worn wheel bearings (see Chapter 1).
4   Excessive tire or wheel runout (see Chapter 10).
5   Worn balljoints (see Chapter 10).

78   Rattling or clicking noise in rack and pinion

1   Insufficient or improper lubricant in rack and pinion assembly (see Chapter 10).
2   Rack and pinion attachment loose (see Chapter 10).

Chapter 1
Tune-up and routine maintenance

Contents

Specifications

Recommended lubricants, fluids and capacities

Note: *Listed here are manufacturer recommendations at the time this manual was written. Manufacturers occasionally upgrade their fluid and lubricant specifications, so check with your local auto parts store for current recommendations.*

Engine oil type	API "certified for gasoline engines"
Viscosity	
Models through 2005	5W-30
2006 and later models	5W-20
Capacity (with filter change)	
2.0L SPI engine	4.0 qts
2.0L Zetec-E , SVT and 2.3L engines	4.5 qts
Brake fluid type	DOT 3 or DOT 4 heavy-duty brake fluid
Power steering fluid type	MERCON automatic transmission fluid

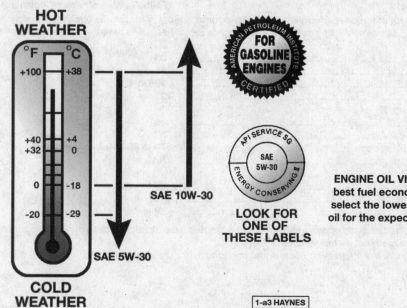

HOT WEATHER

°F °C

+100 +38

+40 +4
+32 0

0 -18

-20 -29

SAE 10W-30

SAE 5W-30

COLD WEATHER

FOR GASOLINE ENGINES — AMERICAN PETROLEUM INSTITUTE CERTIFIED

API SERVICE SG — SAE 5W-30 — ENERGY CONSERVING II

LOOK FOR ONE OF THESE LABELS

ENGINE OIL VISCOSITY CHART For best fuel economy and cold starting, select the lowest SAE viscosity grade oil for the expected temperature range

1-a3 HAYNES

Recommended lubricants, fluids and capacities (continued)

Automatic transaxle fluid
   Type.. MERCON V automatic transmission fluid
   Approximate capacity*
      Drain and refill .... 3.1 qts
      Dry fill (complete transaxle) .... 6.7 to 6.9 qts
Manual transaxle lubricant
   Type
      IB5 transaxle (2.0L SPI engine)................................. Synthetic manual transaxle fluid
      MTX-75 manual transaxle
         Models through 2005 .... MERCON-V automatic transmission fluid
         2006 and later models .... Synthetic manual transaxle fluid
      MT 285 (six-speed)... Synthetic manual transaxle fluid
   Capacity (approximate)
      Models except MT 285 .... 2.1 qts
      MT 285.. 1.8 qts
Coolant
   Type .... 50/50 mixture of ethylene glycol-
                                          based antifreeze and water
   Capacity (approximate)
      2.0L engines
         2000 through 2004 models .... 6.1 quarts
         2005 and later models.. 7.2 quarts
      2.3L engines (all years) .... 7.6 quarts

**Cylinder/coil terminal
locations - 2.0L Zetec models
through 2004**

Drive belt deflection
All engines .... Automatic tensioner

**Cylinder/coil/terminal
locations - 2.0L SPI models
through 2004**

Brakes
Disc brake pad lining thickness (minimum)........................... 1/16 inch
Rear drum brake shoe lining thickness (minimum) .... 1/32 inch

Ignition system
Spark plug type***
   2.0L SPI engine
      2000 .... Motorcraft AGSF-34PP
      2001 and 2002.. Motorcraft AGSF-34EE
      2003 .... Motorcraft AGSF-34EEM
   2.0L Zetec-E engine .... Motorcraft AZFS-32FE
   2.3L engine .... Motorcraft AGSF-22YPC
Spark plug gap
   2.0L SPI engine... 0.054 in
   2.0L Zetec-E, 2.3L and 2005 and later 2.0L engines...................... 0.051 in
Firing order 1-3-4-2

Torque specifications   **Ft-lbs** (unless otherwise indicated)

Note: *One foot-pound (ft-lb) of torque is equivalent to 12 inch-pounds (in-lbs) of torque. Torque values below approximately 15 ft-lbs are expressed in inch-pounds, since most foot-pound torque wrenches are not accurate at these smaller values.*

Wheel lug nuts
   2000 63
   2001 and later... 94
Spark plugs .... 108 in-lbs
Oil pan drain plug 21
Manual transaxle drain plug
   IB5 26
   MTX 75 and MTX 285 33
Manual transaxle speed sensor bolt .... 70 to 89 in-lbs
Automatic transaxle drain plug... NA
Automatic transaxle pan bolts
   Models through 2004 .... 62 in-lbs
   2005 .... 95 in-lbs
   2006 and later models .... 89 in-lbs

Measure the amount drained and add approximately the same amount. Use dipstick to determine the exact amount (see text).

** *A used belt is one that's been run for ten minutes or more.*

*** *If the Vehicle Emission Control Information decal under the hood lists a different specification, use the decal specification.*

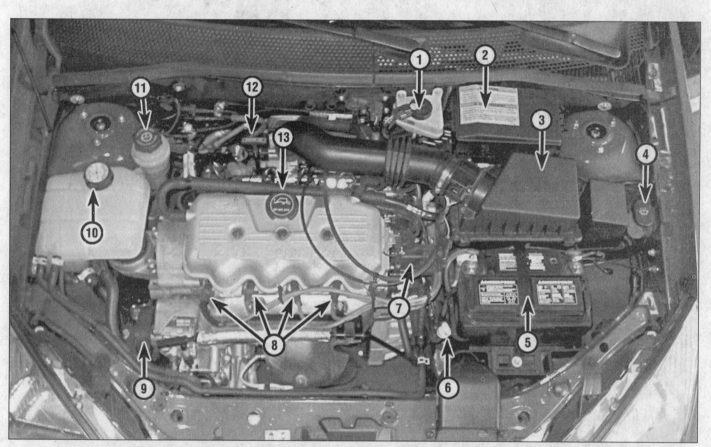

Typical engine compartment components (2.0L SPI engine shown, 2.0L Zetec-E similar)

1	Brake/clutch fluid reservoir	
2	Fuse box	
3	Air filter housing	
4	Windshield washer fluid reservoir	
5	Battery	
6	Transaxle fluid dipstick	
7	Ignition coil pack/spark plug wires	
8	Spark plugs	
9	Drivebelt	
10	Engine coolant expansion tank	
11	Power steering fluid reservoir	
12	Engine oil dipstick	
13	Oil filler cap	

Typical engine compartment underside components

1	Air conditioning compressor	5	Brake hoses	9	Drivebelt
2	Exhaust pipe	6	Disc brake calipers	10	Engine oil drain plug
3	Automatic transaxle fluid pan	7	Balljoints	11	Power steering gear (rack and pinion)
4	Front suspension strut assemblies	8	Outer driveaxle boots		

Typical rear underside components

1	Exhaust system hanger	3	Coil spring
2	Drum brake assembly	4	Fuel tank

1 Maintenance schedule

The following maintenance intervals are based on the assumption that the vehicle owner will be doing the maintenance or service work, as opposed to having a dealer service department do the work. Although the time/mileage intervals are loosely based on factory recommendations, most have been shortened to ensure, for example, that such items as lubricants and fluids are checked/changed at intervals that promote maximum engine/driveline service life. Also, subject to the preference of the individual owner interested in keeping his or her vehicle in peak condition at all times, and with the vehicle's ultimate resale in mind, many of the maintenance procedures may be performed more often than recommended in the following schedule. We encourage such owner initiative.

When the vehicle is new it should be serviced initially by a factory authorized dealer service department to protect the factory warranty. In many cases the initial maintenance check is done at no cost to the owner.

Every 250 miles or weekly, whichever comes first

Check the engine oil level (see Section 4)
Check the engine coolant level (see Section 4)
Check the windshield washer fluid level (see Section 4)
Check the brake fluid level (see Section 4)
Check the tires and tire pressures (see Section 5)

Every 3000 miles or 3 months, whichever comes first

All items listed above plus . . .
Check the power steering fluid level (see Section 6)
Check the automatic transaxle fluid level (see Section 7)
Change the engine oil and oil filter (see Section 8)

Every 6000 miles or 6 months, whichever comes first

All items listed above plus . . .
Check the clutch pedal travel (see Section 9)
Inspect and, if necessary, replace the underhood hoses (see Section 10)
Check/adjust the drivebelts (see Section 11)
Check/service the battery (see Section 12)

Every 12,000 miles or 12 months, whichever comes first

All items listed above plus . . .
Inspect/replace the windshield wiper blades (see Section 13)
Replace the air filter (see Section 14)
Replace the crankcase emission filter (models so equipped) (see Section 15)
Check the PCV valve (see Section 15)
Check the fuel system (see Section 16)
Inspect the cooling system (see Section 17)
Inspect the exhaust system (see Section 18)
Rotate the tires (see Section 19)
Inspect the steering and suspension components (see Section 20)
Inspect the brake system (see Section 21)
Check the parking brake linkage (see Section 21)
Inspect the clutch hydraulic linkage (see Section 22)
Check/replenish the manual transaxle lubricant (see Section 23)

Every 15,000 miles

Replace the cabin air filter (models through 2004) (see Section 24)

Every 30,000 miles or 30 months, whichever comes first

Replace the spark plugs (except models with platinum spark plugs) (see Section 25)
Check/replace the spark plug wires, if equipped, (see Section 26)
Service the cooling system (drain, flush and refill) (see Section 27)
Change the automatic transaxle fluid and filter (see Section 28)

Every 60,000 miles

Inspect and, if necessary, replace the timing belt (see Chapter 2)
Replace the PCV valve (see Section 15)
Replace the spark plugs (models with platinum spark plugs) (see Section 25)
Replace fuel filter

2   Introduction

Warning: *The electric cooling fan on these models can activate at any time, even when the ignition is in the Off position. Disconnect the fan motor or negative battery cable when working in the vicinity of the fan.*

This Chapter is designed to help the home mechanic maintain the Focus with the goals of maximum performance, economy, safety and reliability in mind.

Included is a master maintenance schedule, followed by procedures dealing specifically with each item on the schedule. Visual checks, adjustments, component replacement and other helpful items are included. Refer to the accompanying illustrations of the engine compartment and the underside of the vehicle for the locations of various components.

Servicing your vehicle in accordance with the mileage/time maintenance schedule and the step-by-step procedures will result in a planned maintenance program that should produce a long and reliable service life. Keep in mind that it is a comprehensive plan, so maintaining some items but not others at the specified intervals will not produce the same results.

As you service your vehicle, you will discover that many of the procedures can - and should - be grouped together because of the nature of the particular procedure you're performing or because of the close proximity of two otherwise unrelated components to one another.

For example, if the vehicle is raised for chassis lubrication, you should inspect the exhaust, suspension, steering and fuel systems while you're under the vehicle. When you're rotating the tires, it makes good sense to check the brakes since the wheels are already removed. Finally, let's suppose you have to borrow or rent a torque wrench. Even if you only need it to tighten the spark plugs, you might as well check the torque of as many critical fasteners as time allows.

The first step in this maintenance program is to prepare yourself before the actual work begins. Read through all the procedures you're planning to do, then gather up all the parts and tools needed. If it looks as if you might run into problems during a particular job, seek advice from a mechanic or an experienced do-it-yourselfer.

3   Tune-up general information

The term tune-up is used in this manual to represent a combination of individual operations rather than one specific procedure.

If, from the time the vehicle is new, the routine maintenance schedule is followed closely and frequent checks are made of fluid levels and high wear items, as suggested throughout this manual, the engine will be kept in relatively good running condition and the need for additional work will be minimized.

4.2 The engine oil level is checked with a dipstick

More likely than not, however, there will be times when the engine is running poorly. This is even more likely if a used vehicle, which has not received regular and frequent maintenance checks, is purchased. In such cases, an engine tune-up will be needed outside of the regular routine maintenance intervals.

The first step in any tune-up or diagnostic procedure to help correct a poor running engine is a cylinder compression check. A compression check (see Chapter 2C) will help determine the condition of internal engine components and should be used as a guide for tune-up and repair procedures. If, for instance, a compression check indicates serious internal engine wear, a conventional tune-up will not improve the performance of the engine and would be a waste of time and money. Because of its importance, the compression check should be done by someone with the right equipment and the knowledge to use it properly.

The following procedures are those most often needed to bring a generally poor running engine back into a proper state of tune.

Minor tune-up

Check all engine related fluids (see Section 4)
Check all underhood hoses (see Section 10)
Check and adjust the drivebelts (see Section 11)
Clean, inspect and test the battery (see Section 12)
Check the air filter (see Section 14)
Check the PCV valve (models so equipped) (see Section 15)
Check the crankcase ventilation filter (models so equipped) (see Section 15)
Check the cooling system (see Section 17)
Replace the spark plugs (see Section 25)
Inspect the spark plug and coil wires (see Section 26)

Major tune-up

All items listed under Minor tune-up, plus

Replace the air and crankcase ventilation filters (see Sections 14 and 15)

Replace the spark plug wires (see Section 25)
Check the fuel system (see Chapter 4)
Replace the fuel filter (see Chapter 4)
Check the ignition system (see Chapter 5)
Check the charging system (see Chapter 5)
Check the EGR system (see Chapter 6)

4   Fluid level checks (every 250 miles or weekly)

1   Fluids are an essential part of the lubrication, cooling, brake and windshield washer systems. Because the fluids gradually become depleted and/or contaminated during normal operation of the vehicle, they must be periodically replenished. See *Recommended lubricants, fluids and capacities* at the beginning of this Chapter before adding fluid to any of the following components. **Note:** *The vehicle must be on level ground when fluid levels are checked. Fluid level checking points are shown in the accompanying illustrations and the illustrations near the beginning of this Chapter.*

Engine oil

Refer to illustrations 4.2, 4.4 and 4.6
2   The oil level is checked with a dipstick, which is attached to the engine block **(see illustration)**. The dipstick handle may be near the windshield washer and power steering fluid reservoirs, at the back of the engine or at the timing belt end of the engine. The dipstick extends through a metal tube down into the oil pan.
3   The oil level should be checked before the vehicle has been driven, or about 5 minutes after the engine has been shut off. If the oil is checked immediately after driving the vehicle, some of the oil will remain in the upper part of the engine, resulting in an inaccurate reading on the dipstick.
4   Pull the dipstick from the tube and wipe all the oil from the end with a clean rag or paper towel. Insert the clean dipstick all the way back into the tube and pull it out again. Note the oil at the end of the dipstick. At its highest point, the level should be above the MIN or ADD mark, in the SAFE range **(see illustration)**.
5   It takes one quart of oil to raise the level from the MIN or ADD mark to the MAX or FULL mark. Do not allow the level to drop below the MIN or ADD mark, or oil starvation may cause engine damage. Conversely, overfilling the engine (adding oil above the MAX or FULL mark) may cause oil-fouled spark plugs, oil leaks or oil seal failures.
6   To add oil, remove the filler cap located on the valve cover **(see illustration)**. After adding oil, wait a few minutes to allow the level to stabilize, then pull out the dipstick and check the level again. Add more oil if required. Install the filler cap and tighten it by hand only.
7   Checking the oil level is an important preventive maintenance step. A consistently low oil level indicates oil leakage through damaged seals, defective gaskets or worn

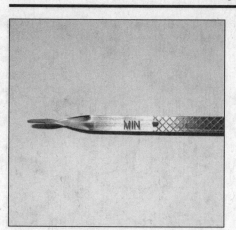

4.4 The oil level should be in the Safe range - if it's below the MIN or ADD mark, add enough oil to bring it up to or near the MAX or FULL mark

4.6 Turn the oil filler cap counterclockwise to remove it - always make sure the area around the opening is clean before unscrewing the cap (to prevent dirt from contaminating the engine)

4.8 The coolant expansion tank is clearly marked with LOW and FULL marks - make sure the level is slightly above the LOW mark when the engine is cold and at or near the FULL mark when the engine is warmed up

rings or valve guides. The condition of the oil should also be checked. If the oil looks milky in color or has water droplets in it, the cylinder head gasket may be blown or the head or block may be cracked. The engine should be checked immediately. Whenever you check the oil level, slide your thumb and index finger up the dipstick before wiping off the oil. If you see small dirt or metal particles clinging to the dipstick, the oil should be changed (see Section 8).

Engine coolant

Refer to illustration 4.8

Warning: *Do not allow antifreeze to come in contact with your skin or painted surfaces of the vehicle. Flush contaminated areas immediately with plenty of water. Do not store new coolant or leave old coolant lying around where it's accessible to children or pets - they are attracted by its sweet smell. Ingestion of even a small amount of coolant can be fatal! Wipe up garage floor and drip pan coolant spills immediately. Keep antifreeze containers covered and repair leaks in your cooling system immediately. Antifreeze is also flammable, so keep it away from open flames and other heat sources. Check with local authorities on disposal of used antifreeze. Many communities have collection centers that will see that antifreeze is disposed of safely.*

Note: *Non-toxic antifreeze is now manufactured and available at auto parts stores, but even this type should be disposed of properly.*

8   All vehicles covered by this manual are equipped with a pressurized coolant expansion tank, located in the right rear corner of the engine compartment, connected by a hose to the radiator and engine **(see illustration)**.

9   The coolant level in the expansion tank should be checked regularly. **Warning:** *Do not remove the pressure cap to check the coolant level when the engine is warm.* The level in the expansion tank varies with the temperature of the engine. When the engine is cold, the coolant level should be at or

slightly above the ADD mark on the tank. Once the engine has warmed up, the level should be at or near the FULL HOT mark. If it isn't, allow the engine to cool, then remove the cap from the tank and add a 50/50 mixture of ethylene glycol based antifreeze and water.

10   Drive the vehicle and recheck the coolant level. Do not use rust inhibitors or additives. If only a small amount of coolant is required to bring the system up to the proper level, water can be used. However, repeated additions of water will dilute the antifreeze and water solution. In order to maintain the proper ratio of antifreeze and water, always top up the coolant level with the correct mixture. An empty plastic milk jug or bleach bottle makes an excellent container for mixing coolant.

11   If the coolant level drops consistently, there may be a leak in the system. Inspect the radiator, hoses, filler cap, drain plugs and water pump (see Section 17). If no leaks are noted, have the expansion tank cap pressure tested by a service station.

12   If you have to remove the expansion tank cap, wait until the engine has cooled completely, then wrap a thick cloth around the cap and unscrew it slowly. If coolant or steam escapes, let the engine cool down longer, then remove the cap.

13   Check the condition of the coolant as well. It should be relatively clear. If it is brown or rust colored, the system should be drained, flushed and refilled. Even if the coolant appears to be normal, the corrosion inhibitors wear out, so it must be replaced at the specified intervals.

Brake/clutch fluid

Refer to illustration 4.15

14   The master cylinder fluid reservoir is mounted on the engine compartment firewall. On manual transaxle models, the same reservoir is used for the brake and clutch hydraulic systems.

15   The fluid level should be between the MAX and MIN lines on the side of the reservoir **(see illustration)**. If the fluid level is low, wipe the top of the reservoir and the cap with a clean rag to prevent contamination of the system as the cap is unscrewed.

16   Add only the specified brake fluid to the reservoir (see *Recommended lubricants, fluids and capacities* at the front of this Chapter or your owner's manual). Mixing different types of brake fluid can damage the system. Fill the reservoir to the MAX line. **Warning:** *Brake fluid can harm your eyes and damage painted surfaces, so use extreme caution when handling or pouring it. Do not use brake fluid that has been standing open or is more than one year old. Brake fluid absorbs moisture from the air. Excess moisture can damage the braking system.*

17   While the reservoir cap is off, check the master cylinder reservoir for contamination. If

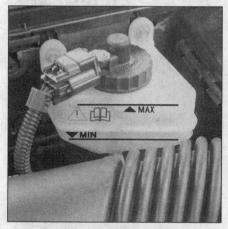

4.15 The brake fluid level should be kept between the MIN and MAX marks on the translucent plastic reservoir - unscrew the cap to add fluid; on manual transaxle models, the same reservoir contains the clutch fluid and is connected to the clutch master cylinder by a hose

rust deposits, dirt particles or water droplets are present, the system should be drained and refilled by a dealer service department or repair shop.

18   After filling the reservoir to the proper level, make sure the cap is seated to prevent fluid leakage and/or contamination.

19   The fluid level in the master cylinder will drop slightly as the brake shoes or pads at each wheel wear down during normal operation. If the brake fluid level drops significantly, check the entire system for leaks immediately. Examine all brake lines, hoses and connections, along with the calipers, wheel cylinders and master cylinder (see Section 21).

20   When checking the fluid level, if you discover one or both reservoirs empty or nearly empty, the brake system should be bled (see Chapter 9).

Windshield washer fluid

Refer to illustration 4.21

21   The windshield washer fluid reservoir is mounted in the engine compartment. On models through 2004, the reservoir is located between the left front fender and the air filter housing **(see illustration)**. On 2005 and later models, the reservoir is located near the right fender.

22   In milder climates, plain water can be used in the reservoir, but it should be kept no more than 2/3 full to allow for expansion if the water freezes. In colder climates, use windshield washer system antifreeze, available at any auto parts store, to lower the freezing

4.21 The windshield washer fluid reservoir is located at the left or right side of the engine compartment

point of the fluid. Mix the antifreeze with water in accordance with the manufacturer's directions on the container. **Caution:** *Do not use cooling system antifreeze - it will damage the vehicle's paint.*

---

5   Tire and tire pressure checks (every 250 miles or weekly)

Refer to illustrations 5.2, 5.3, 5.4a, 5.4b and 5.8

1   Periodic inspection of the tires may spare you the inconvenience of being

5.2 Use a tire tread depth indicator to monitor tire wear - they are available at auto parts stores and service stations and cost very little

stranded with a flat tire. It can also provide you with vital information regarding possible problems in the steering and suspension systems before major damage occurs.

2   The original tires on this vehicle are equipped with 1/2-inch wide bands that will appear when tread depth reaches 1/16-inch, at which point the tires can be considered worn out. Tread wear can be monitored with a simple, inexpensive device known as a tread depth indicator **(see illustration)**.

3   Note any abnormal tread wear **(see illustration)**. Tread pattern irregularities such

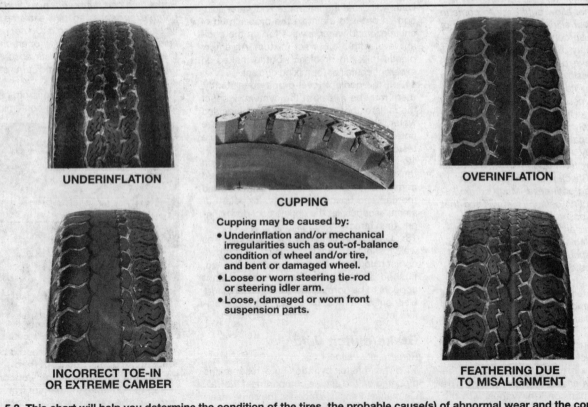

UNDERINFLATION

CUPPING

Cupping may be caused by:
- Underinflation and/or mechanical irregularities such as out-of-balance condition of wheel and/or tire, and bent or damaged wheel.
- Loose or worn steering tie-rod or steering idler arm.
- Loose, damaged or worn front suspension parts.

OVERINFLATION

INCORRECT TOE-IN OR EXTREME CAMBER

FEATHERING DUE TO MISALIGNMENT

5.3 This chart will help you determine the condition of the tires, the probable cause(s) of abnormal wear and the corrective action necessary

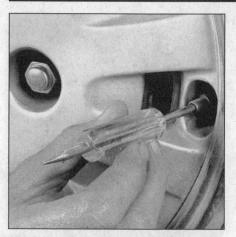

5.4a If a tire loses air on a steady basis, check the valve core first to make sure it's snug (special inexpensive wrenches are commonly available at auto parts stores)

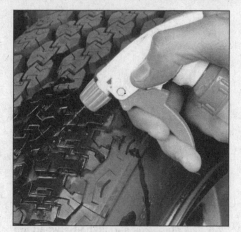

5.4b If the valve core is tight, raise the corner of the vehicle with the low tire and spray a soapy water solution onto the tread as the tire is turned slowly - leaks will cause small bubbles to appear

5.8 To extend the life of the tires, check the air pressure at least once a week with an accurate gauge (don't forget the spare!)

as cupping, flat spots and more wear on one side than the other are indications of front end alignment and/or balance problems. If any of these conditions are noted, take the vehicle to a tire shop or service station to correct the problem.

4   Look closely for cuts, punctures and embedded nails or tacks. Sometimes a tire will hold air pressure for a short time or leak down very slowly after a nail has embedded itself in the tread. If a slow leak persists, check the valve stem core to make sure it is tight **(see illustration)**. Examine the tread for an object that may have embedded itself in the tire or for a "plug" that may have begun to leak (radial tire punctures are repaired with a plug that is installed in the puncture). If a puncture is suspected, it can be easily verified by spraying a solution of soapy water onto the puncture area **(see illustration)**. The soapy solution will bubble if there is a leak. Unless the puncture is unusually large, a tire shop or service station can normally repair the tire.

5   Carefully inspect the inner sidewall of each tire for evidence of brake fluid leakage. If you see any, inspect the brakes immediately.

6   Correct air pressure adds miles to the lifespan of the tires, improves mileage and enhances overall ride quality. Tire pressure cannot be accurately estimated by looking at a tire, especially if it's a radial. A tire pressure gauge is essential. Keep an accurate gauge in the glovebox. The pressure gauges attached to the nozzles of air hoses at gas stations are often inaccurate.

7   Always check tire pressure when the tires are cold. Cold, in this case, means the vehicle has not been driven over a mile in the three hours preceding a tire pressure check. A pressure rise of four to eight pounds is not uncommon once the tires are warm.

8   Unscrew the valve cap protruding from the wheel or hubcap and push the gauge firmly onto the valve stem **(see illustration)**. Note the reading on the gauge and compare

the figure to the recommended tire pressure shown on the tire placard on the tire sidewall or the driver's side door jamb. Be sure to reinstall the valve cap to keep dirt and moisture out of the valve stem mechanism. Check all four tires and, if necessary, add enough air to bring them up to the recommended pressure.

9   Don't forget to keep the spare tire inflated to the specified pressure (see your owner's manual or the tire sidewall). Note that the pressure recommended for the compact spare is higher than for the tires on the vehicle.

6   Power steering fluid level check (every 3000 miles or 3 months)

Refer to illustration 6.2

1   Check the power steering fluid level periodically to avoid steering system problems, such as damage to the pump. **Caution:** *DO NOT hold* the steering *wheel against either stop (extreme left or right turn) for more than five seconds. If you do, the power steering pump could be damaged.*

2   The power steering reservoir is located at the right rear corner of the engine compartment or on top of the power steering pump. The reservoir has LOW and FULL fluid level marks on the side **(see illustration)**. The fluid level can be seen without removing the reservoir cap.

3   Park the vehicle on level ground and apply the parking brake.

4   Run the engine until it has reached normal operating temperature. With the engine at idle, turn the steering wheel back and forth about 10 times to get any air out of the steering system. Shut the engine off with the wheels in the straight-ahead position.

5   Note the fluid level on the side of the reservoir. It should be between the two marks.

6   Add small amounts of fluid until the level is correct. **Caution:** *Do not overfill the reservoir. If too much fluid is added, remove the excess with a clean syringe or suction pump.*

7   Check the power steering hoses and connections for leaks and wear.

8   Check the condition and tension of the power steering pump drivebelt (see Section 11).

7   Automatic transaxle fluid level check (every 3000 miles or 3 months)

Refer to illustrations 7.4 and 7.6

1   The automatic transaxle fluid level should be carefully maintained. Low fluid level can lead to slipping or loss of drive, while overfilling can cause foaming and loss of fluid. Either condition can cause transaxle damage.

2   Since transmission fluid expands as it heats up, the fluid level should only be checked when the transaxle is warm (at normal operating temperature). If the vehicle has just been driven over 20 miles the transaxle can be considered warm. **Caution:** *If the vehicle has just been driven for a long time at*

6.2 The power steering fluid reservoir is located next to the coolant expansion tank - the fluid level must be between the LOW and FULL marks

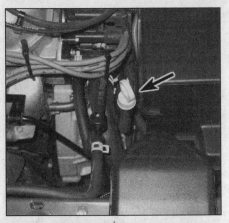

7.4 The automatic transaxle dipstick is located at the front side of the engine, next to the battery

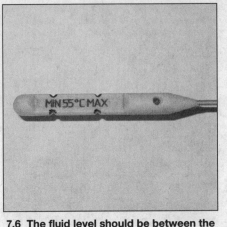

7.6 The fluid level should be between the notches of the high-temperature range; the low-temperature range should be used only for reference

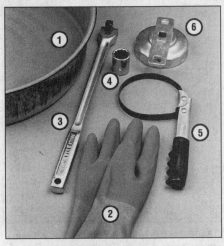

8.2 These tools are required when changing the engine oil and filter

high speed or in city traffic in hot weather, or if it has been pulling a trailer, an accurate fluid level reading cannot be obtained. Allow the transaxle to cool down for about 30 minutes. You can also check the transaxle fluid level when the transaxle is cold. If the vehicle has not been driven for over five hours and the fluid is about room temperature (70 to 95-degrees F), the transaxle is cold. However, the cold temperature scale on the dipstick should be used only for reference; recheck its reading with the transaxle warm as soon as possible.

3   Immediately after driving the vehicle, park it on a level surface, set the parking brake and start the engine. While the engine is idling, depress the brake pedal and move the selector lever through all the gear ranges, beginning and ending in P.

4   Locate the automatic transaxle dipstick in the engine compartment near the battery **(see illustration)**.

5   With the engine still idling, pull the dipstick from the tube, wipe it off with a clean rag, push it all the way back into the tube and withdraw it again, then note the fluid level.

6   The fluid level should be between the low and full notches of the high temperature

scale (hot range) **(see illustration)**. If the level is low, add the specified automatic transmission fluid through the dipstick tube. Use a funnel to prevent spills.

7   Add just enough of the recommended fluid to fill the transaxle to the proper level. It takes about one pint to raise the level from the lower notch to the upper notch when the fluid is hot, so add the fluid a little at a time and keep checking the level until it's correct.

8   The condition of the fluid should also be checked along with the level. If the fluid is black or a dark reddish-brown color, or if it smells burned, it should be changed (see Section 28). If you are in doubt about its condition, purchase some new fluid and compare the two for color and smell.

8   Engine oil and filter change (every 3000 miles or 3 months)

Refer to illustrations 8.2, 8.7, 8.11 and 8.16

1   Frequent oil changes are among the most important preventive maintenance procedures that can be done by the home mechanic. As engine oil ages, it becomes diluted and contaminated, which leads to premature engine wear. Although some sources recommend oil filter changes every other oil change, a new filter should be installed every time the oil is changed.

2   Make sure that you have all the necessary tools before you begin this procedure **(see illustration)**. You should also have plenty of rags or newspapers handy for mopping up oil spills.

3   Access to the oil drain plug and filter will be improved if the vehicle can be lifted on a hoist, driven onto ramps or supported by jackstands. **Warning:** *Do not work under a vehicle that's supported only by a bumper, hydraulic or scissors-type jack - always use jackstands!*

4   If you haven't changed the oil on this vehicle before, get under it and locate the oil drain plug and the oil filter. The exhaust components will be warm as you work, so note

1   **Drain pan** - It should be fairly shallow in depth, but wide to prevent spills
2   **Rubber gloves** - When removing the drain plug and filter, you will get oil on your hands (the gloves will prevent burns)
3   **Breaker bar** - Sometimes the oil drain plug is tight, and a long breaker bar is needed to loosen it
4   **Socket** - To be used with the breaker bar or a ratchet (must be the correct size to fit the drain plug - six-point preferred)
5   **Filter wrench** - This is a metal band-type wrench, which requires clearance around the filter to be effective
6   **Filter wrench** - This type fits on the bottom of the filter and can be turned with a ratchet or breaker bar (different-size wrenches are available for different types of filters)

how they are routed to avoid touching them when you are under the vehicle.

5   Start the engine and allow it to reach normal operating temperature - oil and sludge will flow out more easily when warm. Park on a level surface and shut off the engine when it's warmed up. Remove the oil filler cap.

6   Raise the vehicle and support it on jackstands. Make sure it is safely supported!

7   Being careful not to touch the hot exhaust components, position a drain pan under the plug in the bottom of the engine oil pan **(see illustration)**, then remove the plug. It's a good idea to wear an old glove while unscrewing the plug the final few turns to avoid being scalded by hot oil.

8   It may be necessary to move the drain pan slightly as oil flow slows to a trickle. Inspect the old oil for the presence of metal particles.

9   After all the oil has drained, wipe off the drain plug with a clean rag. Any small metal particles clinging to the plug would immediately contaminate the new oil.

10   Clean the area around the drain plug opening, reinstall the plug and tighten it

8.7 Use a box-end wrench or six-point socket to remove the oil drain plug without rounding it off

securely, being careful not to strip the threads.

11   Move the drain pan into position under the oil filter, located on the rear firewall side of the engine, near the timing belt cover (see illustration).

12   Loosen the oil filter by turning it counterclockwise with a filter wrench. Any standard filter wrench will work.

13   Sometimes the oil filter is screwed on so tightly that it cannot be loosened. If it is, punch a metal bar or long screwdriver directly through it, as close to the engine as possible, and use it as a lever to turn the filter. Be prepared for oil to spurt out of the canister as it is punctured.

14   Once the filter is loose, use your hands to unscrew it from the block. Just as the filter is detached from the block, immediately tilt the open end up to prevent the oil inside the filter from spilling out. Warning: *The engine may still be hot, so be careful.*

15   Using a clean rag, wipe off the mounting surface on the block. Make sure the old gasket does not remain stuck to the mounting surface.

16   Compare the old filter with the new one to make sure they are the same type. Smear some engine oil on the rubber gasket of the new filter and screw it into place (see illustration). Overtightening the filter will damage the gasket, so don't use a filter wrench. Most filter manufacturers recommend tightening the filter by hand only (follow the tightening procedure on the filter canister or packing box).

17   Remove all tools and materials from under the vehicle, being careful not to spill the oil in the drain pan, then lower the vehicle.

18   Add 3-1/2 quarts of new oil to the engine (see Section 4 if necessary). Use a funnel to prevent oil from spilling onto the top of the engine. Wait a few minutes to allow the oil to drain into the pan, then check the level on the dipstick. If the oil level is in the Safe range, install the filler cap.

19   Start the engine and run it for about a minute. While the engine is running, look under the vehicle and check for leaks at the oil pan drain plug and around the oil filter. If either one is leaking, stop the engine and tighten the plug or filter slightly.

20   Stop the engine, wait a few minutes, then recheck the level on the dipstick. Add oil as necessary to bring the level into the SAFE range.

21   During the first few trips after an oil change, make it a point to check frequently for leaks and proper oil level.

22   The old oil drained from the engine cannot be reused in its present state and should be recycled. Check with your local auto parts store, disposal facility or environmental agency to see if they will accept the oil for recycling. After the oil has cooled it can be drained into a container (capped plastic jugs, topped bottles, milk cartons, etc.) for transport to one of these disposal sites. Don't dispose of the oil by pouring it on the ground or down a drain.

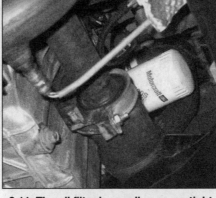

8.11 The oil filter is usually on very tight and will require a special wrench for removal - DO NOT use the wrench to tighten the new filter!

---

9   Clutch pedal freeplay check (every 6000 miles or 6 months)

1   Measure pedal height from the floorboard to the top center of the pedal pad. Depress the clutch pedal by hand until resistance is first felt, then measure the difference between the two measurements.

2   The pedal freeplay should be 10 mm or less. If the freeplay is greater, there may be a problem with the clutch assembly. The clutch pedal itself is not adjustable.

3   Check the clutch fluid level (see Section 4). If the fluid level is correct, Refer to Chapter 6 for analysis of the clutch pressure plate and/or disc.

---

10   Underhood hose check and replacement (every 6000 miles or 6 months)

Warning: *Replacement of air conditioning hoses must be left to a dealer service department or air conditioning shop that has the equipment to depressurize the system safely. Never remove air conditioning components or hoses until the system has been depressurized.*

General

1   High temperatures under the hood can cause the deterioration of the rubber and plastic hoses used for engine, accessory and emission systems operation. Inspect the hoses periodically for cracks, loose clamps, material hardening and leaks.

2   Information specific to the cooling system hoses can be found in Section 17.

3   Most (but not all) hoses are secured to the fittings with clamps. Where clamps are used, check to be sure they haven't lost their tension, allowing the hose to leak. If clamps aren't used, make sure the hose has not

8.16 Lubricate the oil filter gasket with clean engine oil before installing the filter on the engine

expanded and/or hardened where it slips over the fitting, allowing it to leak.

PCV system hose

4   To reduce hydrocarbon emissions, crankcase blow-by gas is vented through the PCV valve in the valve cover to the intake manifold via a rubber hose. The blow-by gases mix with incoming air in the intake manifold before being burned in the combustion chambers.

5   Check the PCV hose for cracks, leaks and other damage. Disconnect it from the cylinder head cover and the intake manifold and check the inside for obstructions. If it's clogged, clean it out with solvent.

Vacuum hoses

6   It is quite common for vacuum hoses, especially those in the emissions system, to be color coded or identified by colored stripes molded into each hose. Various systems require hoses with different wall thicknesses, collapse resistance and temperature resistance. When replacing hoses, be sure the new ones are made of the same material.

7   Often the only effective way to check a hose is to remove it completely from the vehicle. If more than one hose is removed, be sure to label the hoses and fittings to ensure correct installation.

8   When checking vacuum hoses, be sure to include any plastic T-fittings in the check. Inspect the fittings for cracks and the hose where it fits over each fitting for distortion, which could cause leakage.

9   A small piece of vacuum hose (1/4-inch inside diameter) can be used as a stethoscope to detect vacuum leaks. Hold one end of the hose to your ear and probe around vacuum hoses and fittings, listening for the "hissing" sound characteristic of a vacuum leak. Warning: *When probing with the vacuum hose stethoscope, be careful not to allow your body or the hose to come into contact with moving engine components such as drivebelts, the cooling fan, etc.*

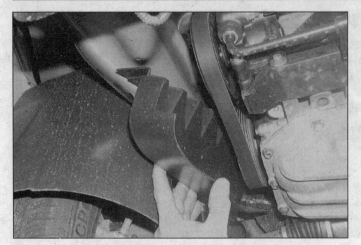

11.4 Removing the drivebelt lower cover

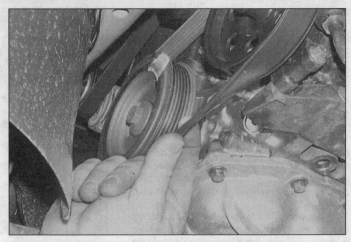

11.5 Twist the drivebelt to check its condition

Fuel hose

Warning: *Gasoline is extremely flammable, so take extra precautions when you work on any part of the fuel system. Don't smoke or allow open flames or bare light bulbs near the work area, and don't work in a garage where a gas-type appliance (such as a water heater or clothes dryer) is present. If you spill any fuel on your skin, rinse it off immediately with soap and water. When you perform any kind of work on the fuel tank, wear safety glasses and have a Class B type fire extinguisher on hand. The fuel system on these vehicles is under pressure. You must relieve this pressure before servicing the fuel lines. Refer to Chapter 4 for the fuel pressure relief procedure.*

10   Check all rubber fuel lines for deterioration and chafing. Check especially for cracks in areas where the hose bends and just before fittings, such as where a hose attaches to the fuel tank, fuel filter or a fuel injection component.

11   If any fuel lines show damage, deterioration or wear, they should be replaced (see Chapter 4). Be sure to use fuel line that is designed for use in fuel injection systems and is an exact duplicate of the original.

12   Spring-type clamps are commonly used on fuel lines. These clamps often lose their tension over a period of time, and can be "sprung" during the removal process. As a result, it is recommended that all spring-type clamps be replaced with screw clamps whenever a hose is replaced.

Metal lines

13   Sections of metal line are often used for fuel line between the fuel pump and fuel injection unit. Check carefully to be sure the line has not been bent and crimped and that cracks have not started in the line, particularly where bends occur.

14   If a section of metal fuel line must be replaced, use original equipment replacement line only, since other types of tubing do not have the strength necessary to withstand vibration caused by the engine. **Warning:** *The fuel system pressure must be relieved before any fuel lines can be replaced* (see Chapter 4).

15   Check the metal brake lines where they enter the master cylinder and brake proportioning unit (if used) for cracks in the lines and loose fittings. Any sign of brake fluid leakage calls for an immediate thorough inspection of the brake system.

---

11 Drivebelt check and replacement (every 6000 miles or 6 months)

Refer to illustrations 11.4, 11.5, 11.6, 11.8a, 11.8b, 11.8c and 11.8d

1   The vehicles covered by this manual use a single serpentine belt. The condition and tension of the drivebelt is critical to the oper-ation of the engine and accessories. Excessive tension causes bearing wear, while insufficient tension produces slippage, noise, component vibration and belt failure. Because of their composition and the high stresses to which they are subjected, drivebelts stretch and deteriorate as they get older. As a result, they must be periodically checked and adjusted.

Check

2   A single auxiliary drivebelt is fitted at the right-hand side of the engine. The length of the drivebelt varies according to whether air conditioning is fitted. An automatic adjuster is used, so checking the drivebelt tension is unnecessary.

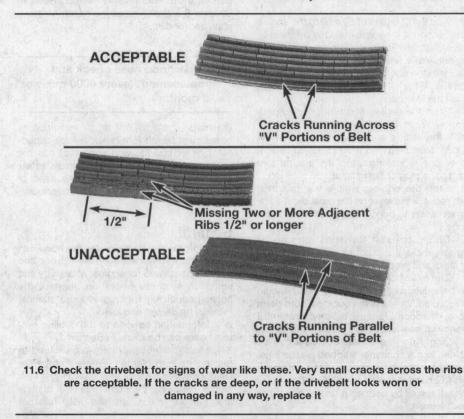

ACCEPTABLE

Cracks Running Across "V" Portions of Belt

1/2"

Missing Two or More Adjacent Ribs 1/2" or longer

UNACCEPTABLE

Cracks Running Parallel to "V" Portions of Belt

11.6 Check the drivebelt for signs of wear like these. Very small cracks across the ribs are acceptable. If the cracks are deep, or if the drivebelt looks worn or damaged in any way, replace it

11.8a To loosen the belt tensioner, insert a 3/8-inch drive ratchet or breaker bar into the tensioner hole and pull the handle toward the front of the vehicle

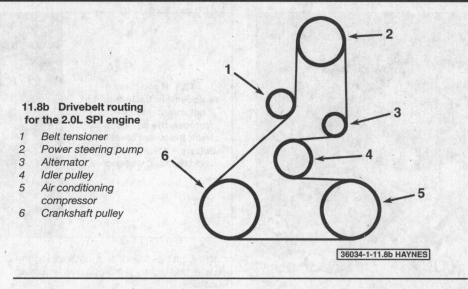

11.8b Drivebelt routing for the 2.0L SPI engine

1   Belt tensioner
2   Power steering pump
3   Alternator
4   Idler pulley
5   Air conditioning compressor
6   Crankshaft pulley

36034-1-11.8b HAYNES

3   Due to their function and material make-up, drivebelts are prone to failure after a long period of time, and should therefore be inspected regularly.

4   Since the drivebelt is located very close to the right-hand side of the engine compartment, it is possible to gain better access by raising the front of the vehicle and removing the right-hand wheel, then unbolting the drivebelt lower cover from the underbody **(see illustration)**.

5   With the engine stopped, inspect the full length of the drivebelt for cracks and separation of the belt plies. It will be necessary to turn the engine (using a wrench or socket and bar on the crankshaft pulley bolt) in order to move the belt from the pulleys so that the belt can be inspected thoroughly. Twist the belt between the pulleys so that both sides can

be viewed **(see illustration)**. Also check for fraying, and glazing which gives the belt a shiny appearance. Check the pulleys for nicks, cracks, distortion and corrosion.

6   Note that it is not unusual for a ribbed belt to exhibit small cracks in the edges of the belt ribs, and unless these are extensive or very deep, belt replacement is not essential **(see illustration)**.

Replacement

7   To remove the drivebelt, first raise the front of the vehicle and support it on jackstands. Remove the drivebelt lower cover, which is secured by two bolts.

8   Using a wrench on the tensioner center bolt, turn the tensioner clockwise to release the drivebelt tension. Note how the drivebelt is routed, then remove the belt from the pulleys **(see illustrations)**.

9   Fit the new drivebelt onto the crankshaft, alternator, power steering pump, and air conditioning compressor pulleys, as applicable, then turn the tensioner counterclockwise and locate the drivebelt on the pulley. Make sure that the drivebelt is correctly seated in all of the pulley grooves, then release the tensioner.

10   Install the drivebelt lower cover and lower the car to the ground.

Tensioner replacement

11   The drivebelt tensioner is attached to the right-hand rear corner of the engine block (right as seen from the driver's seat). Remove the auxiliary drivebelt as described previously in this Section.

12   Access to the three tensioner mounting fasteners is not that easy - it will be a matter of personal preference whether to work from

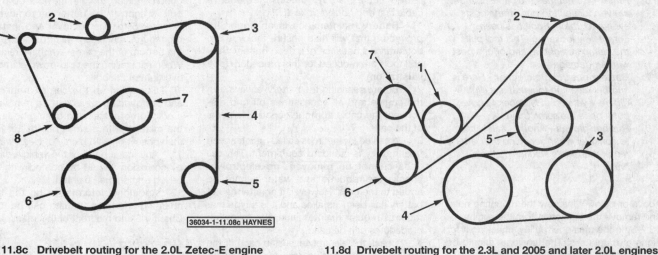

36034-1-11.08c HAYNES

11.8c Drivebelt routing for the 2.0L Zetec-E engine

1	Alternator	5	Air conditioning compressor
2	Idler pulley	6	Crankshaft pulley
3	Power steering pump	7	Water pump pulley
4	Drivebelt	8	Belt tensioner

11.8d Drivebelt routing for the 2.3L and 2005 and later 2.0L engines

1	Idler pulley	5	Water pump pulley
2	Power steering pump pulley	6	Belt tensioner
3	Air conditioning compressor	7	Alternator
4	Crankshaft pulley		

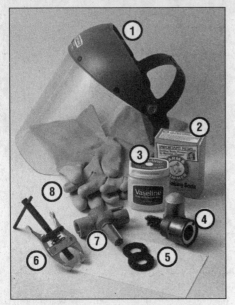

12.1 Tools and materials required for battery maintenance

1   **Face shield/safety goggles** - *When removing corrosion with a brush, the acidic particles can easily fly up into your eyes*

2   **Baking soda** - *A solution of baking soda and water can be used to neutralize corrosion*

3   **Petroleum jelly** - *A layer of this on the battery posts will help prevent corrosion*

4   **Battery post/cable cleaner** - *This wire brush cleaning tool will remove all traces of corrosion from the battery posts and cable clamps*

5   **Treated felt washers** - *Placing one of these on each post, directly under the cable clamps, will help prevent corrosion*

6   **Puller** - *Sometimes the cable clamps are very difficult to pull off the posts, even after the nut/bolt has been completely loosened. This tool pulls the clamp straight up and off the post without damage*

7   **Battery post/cable cleaner** - *Here is another cleaning tool that is a slightly different version of Number 4 above, but it does the same thing*

8   **Rubber gloves** - *Another safety item to consider when servicing the battery; remember that's acid inside the battery!*

above or below. Unscrew the mounting nuts, and remove the tensioner from the engine.

13   Spin the tensioner pulley, checking it for signs of roughness. The tensioner should be capable of providing significant tension when tested - rotate the pulley to load the spring, and check for free movement. Also inspect the tensioner pulley for signs of cracking or other deterioration.

14   The tensioner is not a serviceable com-

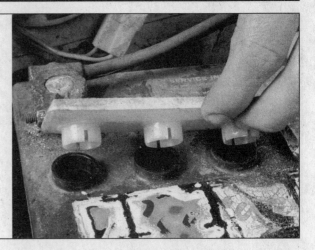

12.4 If you have a replacement battery that is not maintenance-free, remove the cell caps to check the water level in the battery - if the level is low, add distilled water only

ponent - if it has failed, or is not keeping the belt at a satisfactory tension, a new unit must be installed.

15   Installation is a reversal of removal.

---

12   Battery check, maintenance and charging (every 6000 miles or 6 months)

Check and maintenance

Refer to illustrations 12.1, 12.4, 12.8a, 12.8b, 12.8c and 12.8d

Warning: *Certain precautions must be followed when checking and servicing the battery. Hydrogen gas, which is highly flammable, is always present in the battery cells, so keep lighted tobacco and all other flames and sparks away from it. The electrolyte inside the battery is actually diluted sulfuric acid, which will cause injury if splashed on your skin or in your eyes. It will also ruin clothes and painted surfaces. When removing the battery cables, always detach the negative cable first and hook it up last!*

1   Battery maintenance is an important procedure that will help ensure that you are not stranded because of a dead battery. Several tools are required for this procedure **(see illustration)**.

2   Before servicing the battery, always turn the engine and all accessories off and disconnect the cable from the negative terminal of the battery.

3   A sealed (sometimes called maintenance free) battery is standard equipment. The cell caps cannot be removed, no electrolyte checks are required and water cannot be added to the cells. However, if an aftermarket battery has been installed and it is a type that requires regular maintenance, the following procedures can be used.

4   Check the electrolyte level in each of the battery cells **(see illustration)**. It must be above the plates. There's usually a split-ring indicator in each cell to indicate the correct level. If the level is low, add distilled water only, then install the cell caps. **Caution:** *Overfilling the cells may cause electrolyte to spill over*

during periods of heavy charging, causing corrosion and damage to nearby components.

5   If the positive terminal and cable clamp on your vehicle's battery is equipped with a rubber protector, make sure that it's not torn or damaged. It should completely cover the terminal.

6   The external condition of the battery should be checked periodically. Look for damage such as a cracked case.

7   Check the tightness of the battery cable clamps to ensure good electrical connections and inspect the entire length of each cable, looking for cracked or abraded insulation and frayed conductors.

8   If corrosion (visible as white, fluffy deposits) is evident, remove the cables from the terminals, clean them with a battery brush and reinstall them **(see illustrations)**. Corrosion can be kept to a minimum by installing specially treated washers available at auto parts stores or by applying a layer of petroleum jelly or grease to the terminals and cable clamps after they are assembled.

9   Make sure that the battery carrier is in good condition and that the hold-down clamp bolt is tight. If the battery is removed (see Chapter 5 for the removal and installation procedure), make sure that no parts remain in the bottom of the carrier when it's reinstalled. When reinstalling the hold-down clamp, don't overtighten the bolt.

10   Corrosion on the carrier, battery case and surrounding areas can be removed with a solution of water and baking soda. Apply the mixture with a small brush. Let it work, then rinse it off with plenty of clean water.

11   Any metal parts of the vehicle damaged by corrosion should be coated with a zinc-based primer, then painted.

12   Additional information on the battery, charging and jump starting can be found in Chapter 5 and the front of this manual.

Charging

13   Remove all of the cell caps (if equipped) and cover the holes with a clean cloth to prevent spattering electrolyte. Disconnect the negative battery cable and hook the battery charger leads to the battery posts (positive to positive, negative to negative), then plug in

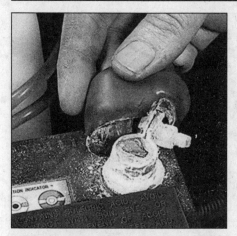

12.8a Battery terminal corrosion usually appears as light, fluffy powder

12.8b Removing the cable from a battery post with a wrench - sometimes special battery pliers are required for this procedure if corrosion has caused deterioration of the nut hex (always remove the ground cable first and hook it up last!)

12.8c Regardless of the type of tool used on the battery posts, a clean, shiny surface should be the result

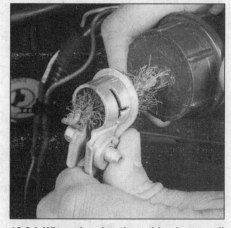

12.8d When cleaning the cable clamps, all corrosion must be removed (the inside of the clamp is tapered to match the taper on the post, so don't remove too much material)

the charger. Make sure it is set at 12 volts if it has a selector switch.

14   If you're using a charger with a rate higher than two amps, check the battery regularly during charging to make sure it doesn't overheat. If you're using a trickle charger, you can safely let the battery charge overnight after you've checked it regularly for the first couple of hours.

15   If the battery has removable cell caps, measure the specific gravity with a hydrometer every hour during the last few hours of the charging cycle. Hydrometers are available inexpensively from auto parts stores - follow the instructions that come with the hydrometer. Consider the battery charged when there's no change in the specific gravity reading for two hours and the electrolyte in the cells is gassing (bubbling) freely. The specific gravity reading from each cell should be very close to the others. If not, the battery probably has a bad cell(s).

16   Some batteries with sealed tops have built-in hydrometers on the top that indicate the state of charge by the color displayed in the hydrometer window. Normally, a bright-colored hydrometer indicates a full charge and a dark hydrometer indicates the battery still needs charging. Check the battery manufacturer's instructions to be sure you know what the colors mean.

17   If the battery has a sealed top and no built-in hydrometer, you can hook up a digital voltmeter across the battery terminals to check the charge. A fully charged battery should read 12.6 volts or higher.

18   Further information on the battery and jump starting can be found in Chapter 5 and at the front of this manual.

13   Windshield wiper blade check and replacement (every 12,000 miles or 12 months)

1   Road film can build up on the wiper blades and affect their efficiency, so they should be washed regularly with a mild detergent solution.

Check

2   The windshield wiper and blade assembly should be inspected periodically for damage, loose components and cracked or worn blade elements. The action of the wiping mechanism can loosen bolts, nuts and fasteners, so they should be checked and tightened, as necessary, at the same time the wiper blades are checked.

3   If the wiper blade elements are cracked, worn or warped, or no longer clean adequately, they should be replaced with new ones.

Replacement

Refer to illustrations 13.5a and 13.5b

4   Park the wiper blades in a convenient position to be worked on. To do this, run the wipers then turn the ignition key to Off when the wiper blades reach the desired position.

5   Push the release pin to release the blade, unhook the wiper arm from the blade

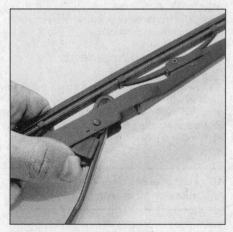

13.5a To release the blade holder, push the release pin . . .

(see illustrations) and take the blade off. Slide the new blade onto the wiper arm until the blade locks. Make sure the spring lock secures the blade to the pin.

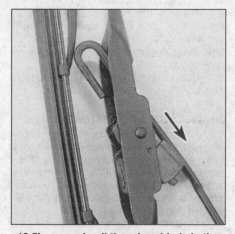

13.5b . . . and pull the wiper blade in the direction of the arrow to separate it from the arm

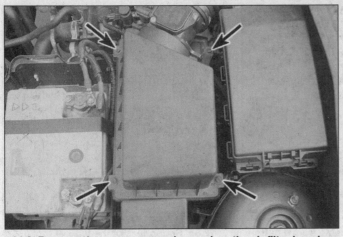

14.2 Remove the cover screws (arrows) on the air filter housing

14.3 Lift the cover and remove the filter element, taking note of which way it was installed

14   Air filter replacement (every 12,000 miles or 12 months)

1   The air filter cannot be cleaned. If it's dirty, replace it. **Note:** *On models through 2002, the air cleaner is in the engine compartment. On 2003 and later 2.3L engines and all 2005 models, the air cleaner is located in the left fenderwell.*

Removal

2.0L models (through 2004)
Refer to illustrations 14.2 and 14.3

2   Remove the screws securing the air filter box lid **(see illustration)**.
3   Raise the filter housing cover and pull out the filter element **(see illustration)**.
4   Installation is the reverse of the removal steps.

2.3L and 2005 and later 2.0L models
5   Refer to Chapter 11 and remove the left fenderwell liner.
6   Disconnect the electrical connector at the MAF sensor.
7   Remove the bolts and loosen the clamp to disconnect the air inlet pipe.
8   Remove the bolts and lower the air cleaner box, open the box and replace the filter. **Note:** *On 2003 and later models with the 2.3L Zetec engine, the filter and housing are replaced as a unit.*
9   Installation is the reverse of the removal steps.

Inspection and installation
10   Inspect the rubber seal on the air cleaner element. Replace the element if the seal is worn or damaged. Also replace the filter if replacement is indicated on the maintenance schedule or if it is so dirty that you can't clearly see the light from a flashlight held against the opposite side.
11   Clean the inner sealing surface between the air cleaner housing and cover.
12   Before installing the new air filter, check it for deformed seals and holes in the paper. If

the filter is marked TOP, be sure the marked side faces up.
13   The remainder of installation is the reverse of the removal steps.

15   PCV valve and filter replacement (every 12,000 miles or 12 months)

1   Most of the covered models have the PCV valve mounted in the crankcase ventilation oil separator, which is mounted low on the engine (follow the PCV hose from the air cleaner housing). On 2.0L SPI engines, the PCV valve is located in the valve cover.
2   Allow the engine to completely cool before removing the PCV valve. On SPI engines, disconnect the PCV hose from the valve, then twist the PCV valve out of the valve cover grommet.
3   On all 2.3L and 2005 2.0L models, raise the front of the vehicle and support it securely on jackstands. Remove the under-engine splash shield.
4   Refer to Chapter 2C and remove the intake manifold for access to the PCV valve.
5   Disconnect the hose from the valve at the oil separator. Push in the two tabs and twist the PCV valve out.
6   On all models, test the valve by shaking it. If it doesn't rattle, replace it.

PCV filter replacement
Refer to illustration 15.8
7   Remove the air cleaner cover (refer to Section 14).
8   Pull the PCV filter out of its pocket in the air cleaner housing **(see illustration)**. Inspect the filter and replace it if it's clogged or damaged.

16   Fuel system check (every 12,000 miles or 12 months)

Warning: *Gasoline is extremely flammable, so take extra precautions when you work on any part of the fuel system. Don't smoke or allow open flames or bare light bulbs near the*

work area, and don't work in a garage where a gas-type appliance (such as a water heater or clothes dryer) is present. If you spill any fuel on your skin, rinse it off immediately with soap and water. When you perform any kind of work on the fuel system, wear safety glasses and have a Class B type fire extinguisher on hand.

1   If you smell gasoline while driving or after the vehicle has been sitting in the sun, inspect the fuel system immediately.
2   Remove the gas filler cap and inspect if for damage and corrosion. The gasket should have an unbroken sealing imprint. If the gasket is damaged or corroded, install a new cap.
3   Inspect the fuel feed and return lines for cracks. Make sure that the connections between the fuel lines and fuel injection system and between the fuel lines and the in-line fuel filter are tight. **Warning:** *You must relieve fuel system pressure before servicing fuel injection system components. The fuel system pressure relief procedure is outlined in Chapter 4.*
4   Since some components of the fuel system - the fuel tank and part of the fuel feed and return lines, for example - are underneath the vehicle, they can be inspected more easily with the vehicle raised on a hoist. If a hoist

15.8 The PCV system air filter (arrow) is located in the air cleaner housing - remove the air filter for access

Check for a chafed area that could fail prematurely.

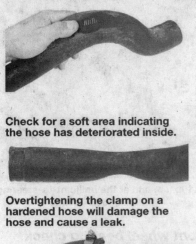

Check for a soft area indicating the hose has deteriorated inside.

Overtightening the clamp on a hardened hose will damage the hose and cause a leak.

Check each hose for swelling and oil-soaked ends. Cracks and breaks can be located by squeezing the hose.

17.4 Hoses, like drivebelts, have a habit of failing at the worst possible time - to prevent the inconvenience of a blown radiator or heater hose, inspect them carefully as shown here

is unavailable, raise the vehicle and support it on jackstands.

5   With the vehicle raised and safely supported, inspect the gas tank and filler neck for punctures, cracks and other damage. The connection between the filler neck and the tank is particularly critical. Sometimes a rubber filler neck will leak because of loose clamps or deteriorated rubber. Inspect all fuel tank mounting brackets and straps to be sure that the tank is securely attached to the vehicle. **Warning:** *Do not, under any circumstances, try to repair a fuel tank (except rubber components). A welding torch or any open flame can easily cause fuel vapors inside the tank to explode.*

6   Carefully check all rubber hoses and metal lines leading away from the fuel tank. Check for loose connections, deteriorated hoses, crimped lines and other damage. Repair or replace damaged sections as necessary (see Chapter 4).

17 Cooling system check (every 12,000 miles or 12 months)

Refer to illustration 17.4

1   Many major engine failures can be attributed to a faulty cooling system. If the vehicle is equipped with an automatic transaxle, the cooling system also plays an important role in prolonging transaxle life because it cools the transmission fluid.

2   The engine should be cold for the cooling system check, so perform the following procedure before the vehicle is driven for the day or after it has been shut off for at least three hours.

3   Remove the cap on the coolant tank and clean it thoroughly, inside and out, with clean water. Also clean the filler neck on the radiator. The presence of rust or corrosion in the filler neck means the coolant should be changed (see Section 27). The coolant inside the tank should be relatively clean and transparent. If it's rust colored, drain the system and refill it with new coolant.

4   Carefully check the radiator hoses and the smaller diameter heater hoses **(see illustrations in Chapter 3)**. Inspect each coolant hose along its entire length, replacing any hose which is cracked, swollen or deteriorated **(see illustration)**. Cracks will show up better if the hose is squeezed. Pay close attention to hose clamps that secure the hoses to cooling system components. Hose clamps can pinch and puncture hoses, resulting in coolant leaks.

5   Make sure that all hose connections are tight. A leak in the cooling system will usually show up as white or rust colored deposits on the area adjoining the leak. If wire-type clamps are used on the hoses, it may be a good idea to replace them with screw-type clamps.

6   Clean the front of the radiator and air conditioning condenser with compressed air, if available, or a soft brush. Remove all bugs, leaves, etc. embedded in the radiator fins. Be extremely careful not to damage the cooling fins or cut your fingers on them.

7   If the coolant level has been dropping consistently and no leaks are detectable, have the expansion tank cap and cooling system pressure checked at a service station.

18 Exhaust system check (every 12,000 miles or 12 months)

1   With the engine cold (at least three hours after the vehicle has been driven), check the complete exhaust system from the engine to the end of the tailpipe. Ideally, the inspection should be done with the vehicle on a hoist to permit unrestricted access. If a hoist is not available, raise the vehicle and support it securely on jackstands.

2   Check the exhaust pipes and connections for evidence of leaks, severe corrosion and damage. Make sure that all brackets and hangers are in good condition and tight.

3   At the same time, inspect the underside

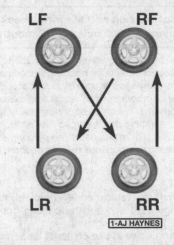

19.2 The recommended rotation pattern for radial tires

of the body for holes, corrosion, open seams, etc. which may allow exhaust gases to enter the passenger compartment. Seal all body openings with silicone sealant or body putty.

4   Rattles and other noises can often be traced to the exhaust system, especially the mounts and hangers. Try to move the pipes, muffler and catalytic converter. If the components can come in contact with the body or suspension parts, secure the exhaust system with new mounts.

5   Check the running condition of the engine by inspecting inside the end of the tailpipe. The exhaust deposits here are an indication of engine state-of-tune. If the pipe is black and sooty or coated with white deposits, the engine is in need of a tune-up, including a thorough fuel system inspection and adjustment. Also, the catalytic converter may be malfunctioning (see Chapter 4).

19 Tire rotation (every 12,000 miles or 12 months)

Refer to illustration 19.2

1   The tires should be rotated at the specified intervals and whenever uneven wear is noticed. Since the vehicle will be raised and the tires removed anyway, check the brakes also (see Section 21).

2   Radial tires must be rotated in a specific pattern **(see illustration)**.

3   Refer to the information in *Jacking and towing* at the front of this manual for the proper procedure to follow when raising the vehicle and changing a tire. If the brakes are to be checked, do not apply the parking brake, as stated.

4   The vehicle must be raised on a hoist or supported on jackstands to get two wheels at a time off the ground. Make sure the vehicle is safely supported!

5   After the rotation procedure is finished, check and adjust the tire pressures as necessary and be sure to check the lug nut tightness.

20   Suspension and steering check (every 12,000 miles or 12 months)

Note: *The steering linkage and suspension components should be checked periodically. Worn or damaged suspension and steering linkage components can result in excessive and abnormal tire wear, poor ride quality and vehicle handling and reduced fuel economy. For detailed illustrations of the steering and suspension components, refer to Chapter 10.*

Strut check

1   Park the vehicle on level ground, turn the engine off and set the parking brake. Check the tire pressures.

2   Push down at one corner of the vehicle, then release it while noting the movement of the body. It should stop moving and come to rest in a level position within one or two bounces.

3   If the vehicle continues to move up and down or if it fails to return to its original position, a worn or weak strut is probably the reason.

4   Repeat the above check at each of the three remaining corners of the vehicle.

5   Raise the vehicle and support it securely on jackstands.

6   Check the shock struts for evidence of fluid leakage. A light film of fluid on the shaft is no cause for concern. Make sure that any fluid noted is from the shocks and not from some other source. If leakage is noted, replace both struts at that end of the vehicle (front or rear).

7   Check the struts to be sure that they are securely mounted and undamaged. Check the upper mounts for damage and wear. If damage or wear is noted, replace both struts on that end of the vehicle.

8   If struts must be replaced, refer to Chapter 10 for the procedure.

20.10a To check the balljoints, try to move the lower edge of each front wheel in and out while watching or feeling for movement at the top of the tire . . .

Front suspension and steering check

Refer to illustration 20.10a, 20.10b and 20.11

9   Visually inspect the steering system components for damage and distortion. Look for leaks and damaged seals, boots and fittings.

10   Wipe off the lower end of the steering knuckle and control arm assembly. Have an assistant grasp the lower edge of the tire and move the wheel in and out while you look for movement at the balljoint-to-steering knuckle joint **(see illustrations)**. If there is any movement, the balljoints must be replaced (see Chapter 10).

11   Grasp each front tire at the front and rear edges, push in at the rear, pull out at the front and feel for play in the steering system components **(see illustration)**. If any freeplay is noted, check the steering gear mounts and the tie-rod ends for looseness. If the steering gear mounts are loose, tighten them. If the tie-rod ends are loose, they will probably need to be replaced (see Chapter 10).

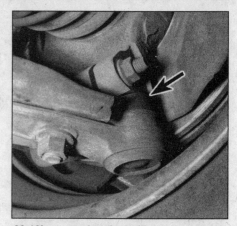

20.10b . . . and at the balljoint-to-steering knuckle joint (arrow)

Front wheel bearing check

Refer to illustration 20.12

Note: *The front wheel bearings are a "cartridge" design and are permanently lubricated and sealed at the factory. They require no scheduled maintenance or adjustment. They can, however, be checked for excessive play. If the following check indicates that either of the front bearings is faulty, replace both bearings.*

12   Grasp each front tire at the front and rear edges, then push in and out on the wheel and feel for play **(see illustration)**. There should be no noticeable movement. Turn the wheel and listen for noise from the bearings. If either of these conditions is noted, refer to Chapter 10 for the bearing replacement procedure.

Driveaxle Constant Velocity (CV) joint boot check

Refer to illustration 20.14

13   If the driveaxle rubber boots are damaged or deteriorated, serious and costly damage can occur to the CV joints.

14   It is very important that the boots be

20.11 To check the steering gear mounts and tie-rod connections for play, grasp each front tire like this and try to move it back and forth - if play is noted, check the steering gear mounts and make sure they're tight; if either tie-rod is worn or bent, replace it

20.12 To check the wheel bearings, try to move the tire in and out - if any play is noted, or if the bearings feel rough or sound noisy when the tire is rotated, the bearings need to be replaced

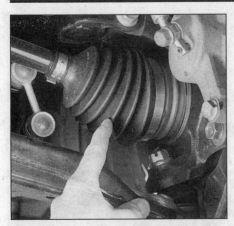

20.14 Flex the driveaxle boots by hand to check for cracks and/or leaking grease

kept clean, so wipe them off before inspection. Check the four boots (two on each driveaxle) for cracks, tears, holes, deteriorated rubber and loose or missing clamps. Also check for grease flung around the CV joint boot area, which also indicates a hole in the boot. Pushing on the boot surface can reveal cracks not ordinarily visible (**see illustration**).
15 If damage or deterioration is evident check the CV joints for damage (see Chapter 8) and replace the boot(s) with new ones.

---

21 Brake check (every 12,000 miles or 12 months)

Note: *In addition to the specified intervals, the brake system should be inspected each time the wheels are removed or a malfunction is indicated. Because of the obvious safety considerations, the following brake system checks are some of the most important maintenance procedures you can perform on your vehicle.*

21.11 The front disc brake pads can be checked easily through the inspection hole in each caliper - position a ruler or tape measure against the pads and measure the lining thickness

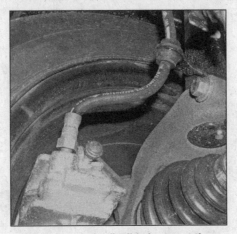

21.7 Check the flexible hoses at the brake calipers

Symptoms of brake system problems

1 If you hear a squealing or scraping noise when the brakes are applied, inspect the pads immediately or expensive damage to the rotors could result.
2 Any of the following symptoms could indicate a brake system defect: the vehicle pulls to one side when the brake pedal is depressed, the brakes make squealing or dragging noises when applied, brake pedal travel is excessive, the pedal pulsates or brake fluid leaks are noted (usually on the inner side of the tire or wheel). If any of these conditions are noted inspect the brake system immediately.

Brake lines and hoses

Refer to illustration 21.7
Note: *Steel tubing is used throughout the brake system, with the exception of flexible, reinforced hoses at the front and rear wheels. Periodic inspection of these hoses and lines is very important.*
3 Park the vehicle on level ground and turn the engine off.
4 Remove the wheel covers. Loosen, but do not remove, the lug nuts.

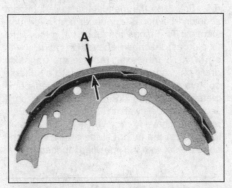

21.15 If the lining is bonded to the brake shoe, measure the lining thickness from the outer surface to the metal shoe, as shown here; if the lining is riveted to the shoe, measure from the lining outer surface to the rivet head

5 Raise the vehicle and support it securely on jackstands.
6 Remove the wheels (see *Jacking and towing* at the front of this manual, or refer to your owner's manual, if necessary).
7 Check all brake hoses and lines for cracks, chafing of the outer cover, leaks, blisters and distortion (**see illustration**). Check all threaded fittings for leaks and make sure the brake hose mounting bolts and clips are secure.
8 If leaks or damage are discovered they must be fixed immediately. Refer to Chapter 9 for detailed information on brake system repair procedures.

Front disc brakes
Refer to illustration 21.11
Note: *All models are equipped with front disc brakes and rear drum brakes.*
9 If it hasn't already been done, raise the front of the vehicle and support it securely on jackstands. Apply the parking brake and remove the front wheels.
10 The disc brake calipers, which contain the pads, are now visible. Each caliper has an outer and an inner pad - all pads should be checked.
11 Note the pad thickness by looking through the inspection hole in the caliper (**see illustration**). If the lining material is less than listed in this Chapter's Specifications, or if it is tapered from end to end, the pads should be replaced (see Chapter 9). Keep in mind that the lining material is riveted or bonded to a metal plate or shoe - the metal portion is not included in this measurement.
12 Check the condition of the brake disc. Look for score marks, deep scratches and overheated areas (they will appear blue or discolored). If damage or wear is noted, the disc can be removed and resurfaced by an automotive machine shop or replaced with a new one. Refer to Chapter 9 for more detailed inspection and repair procedures.

Rear drum brakes
Refer to illustration 21.15
13 Refer to Chapter 9 and remove the rear brake drums.
14 **Warning:** *Brake dust produced by lining wear and deposited on brake components is hazardous to your health. DO NOT blow it out with compressed air and DO NOT inhale it! DO NOT use gasoline or solvents to remove the dust. Brake system cleaner should be used to flush the dust into a drain pan. After the brake components are wiped clean with a damp rag, dispose of the contaminated rag(s) and solvent in a covered and labeled container.*
15 Note the thickness of the lining material on the rear brake shoes (**see illustration**) and look for signs of contamination by brake fluid and grease. If the lining material is within 1/32-inch of the recessed rivets or metal shoes, replace the brake shoes with new ones. The shoes should also be replaced if they are cracked, glazed (shiny lining surfaces) or contaminated with brake fluid or

24.3 Release the clips at the front of the cowl grille panel . . .

24.4 . . . and remove the panel to get at the filter

grease. See Chapter 9 for the replacement procedure.

16   Check the shoe return and hold-down springs and the adjusting mechanism to make sure they are installed correctly and in good condition. Deteriorated or distorted springs, if not replaced, could allow the linings to drag and wear prematurely.

17   Check the wheel cylinders for leakage by carefully peeling back the rubber boots. If brake fluid is noted behind the boots, the wheel cylinders must be replaced (see Chapter 9).

18   Check the drums for cracks, score marks, deep scratches and hard spots, which will appear as small discolored areas. If imperfections cannot be removed with emery cloth, the drums must be resurfaced by an automotive machine shop (see Chapter 9 for more detailed information).

19   Refer to Chapter 9 and install the brake drums.

20   Install the wheels, remove the jackstands, lower the vehicle and tighten the lug nuts.

Parking brake check

21   The parking brake cable and linkage should be periodically checked for damage and for wear caused by rubbing on the vehicle.

22   The easiest, and perhaps most obvious, method of checking the parking brake is to park the vehicle on a steep hill with the parking brake set and the transaxle in Neutral. If the parking brake cannot prevent the vehicle from rolling, refer to Chapter 9 and adjust it.

22   Clutch hydraulic linkage inspection (every 12,000 miles or 12 months)

1   Check the line running from the brake and clutch fluid reservoir to the master cylinder for leaks. Replace the line and bleed the hydraulic system if there's any sign of fluid leakage (see Chapter 8).

2   Pull back the rubber boot from the slave cylinder on the side of the clutch hydraulic line and check for fluid leaks. Slight moisture

inside the boot is acceptable, but if fluid runs out, refer to Chapter 8 and overhaul or replace the slave cylinder.

23   Manual transaxle lubricant level check and change (every 12,000 miles or 12 months)

Lubricant level check

Note: *The transaxle lubricant should not deteriorate under normal driving conditions. However, it is recommended that you check the level occasionally.*

1   Park the vehicle on a level surface. Turn the engine off, apply the parking brake and block the wheels. Open the hood and locate the fill plug on the front side of the transaxle.

2   To protect the transaxle from contamination, wipe off any dirt or grease in the area around the fill plug before removing the plug.

3   Remove the fill plug. The lubricant level should be within 5 to 10 mm of the fill plug hole.

4   Add the proper type of transaxle lubricant, if necessary, and reinstall the plug.

Lubricant change

5   Changing the manual transaxle lubricant shouldn't be necessary under normal circumstances. To change the lubricant, remove the fill plug as described above. On models with an MTX 75 transaxle, remove the transaxle drain plug and drain the fluid into a suitable container. After the fluid has drained completely, install the drain plug and tighten it securely. Models with an iB5 don't have a drain plug; you'll have to remove one of the driveaxles to drain the fluid. Fill the transaxle to the correct level with the specified lubricant.

24   Cabin air filter replacement (every 15,000 miles)

Refer to illustrations 24.3, 24.4 and 24.5

Note 1: *The cabin air filter on left-hand drive cars is located in the passenger's side of the*

24.5 Lift out the cabin air filter, noting the direction it was installed

cowl chamber. The following photos show filter replacement on a right-hand drive model.

Note 2: *2005 and later models do not have a cabin air filter.*

1   Pull the windshield wiper arms away from the windshield until they lock in their vertical position.

2   Open the hood.

3   Using a small screwdriver if necessary, release the three retaining catches at the front of the cowl grille panel **(see illustra-tion)**.

4   Lift out the cowl grille panel **(see illustration)**.

5   Release the clip at either side, and lift up the cabin filter. Pull the filter element from the housing, and discard it **(see illustration)**.

6   Install the new filter using a reversal of the removal procedure, noting the following points:

a) *Make sure that the filter is installed with the TOP/OPEN arrow marking facing upwards.*

b) *Clean the rubber seals on the filter access cover before replacing it.*

c) *Ensure that the filter access cover is properly seated, otherwise the cover seals will leak, allowing water into the car interior.*

25.1a Spark plug wire layout (2.0L Zetec-E engine)

25.1b Spark plug wire layout (2.0L SPI engine)

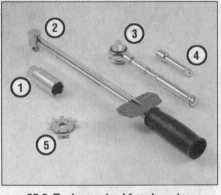

25.2 **Tools required for changing spark plugs**

1   **Spark plug socket** - *This will have special padding inside to protect the spark plug's porcelain insulator*
2   **Torque wrench** - *Although not mandatory, using this tool is the best way to ensure the plugs are tightened properly*
3   **Ratchet** - *Standard hand tool to fit the spark plug socket*
4   **Extension** - *Depending on model and accessories, you may need special extensions and universal joints to reach one or more of the plugs*
5   **Spark plug gap gauge** - *This gauge for checking the gap comes in a variety of styles. Make sure the gap for your engine is included*

25   Spark plug replacement (see the maintenance schedule for service intervals)

Refer to illustrations 25.1a, 25.1b, 25.2, 25.5a, 25.5b, 25.6 and 25.10
Note 1: *Every time a spark plug wire is detached from a spark plug or the coil, silicone dielectric compound (a special grease available at auto parts stores) must be applied to the inside of each spark plug wire boot and*

25.5a **Spark plug manufacturers recommend using a wire-type gauge when checking the gap - if the wire does not slide between the electrodes with a slight drag, adjustment is required**

terminal before reconnection. Use a small standard screwdriver to coat the entire inside surface of each boot with a thin layer of the compound. **Note 2:** *If you are reinstalling the old spark plugs, make sure that each one is placed in its original position.*

1   The spark plugs are located in the center of the cylinder head on 2.0L Zetec engines and on the front (radiator) side of the cylinder head on 2.0L SPI engines **(see illustrations)**. **Note:** *2.3L and 2005 and later 2.0L engines do not have spark plug wires. Small individual ignition coils are mounted over each spark plug. To reach the spark plugs, see Chapter 5B for coil removal.*
2   In most cases, the tools necessary for spark plug replacement include a spark plug socket which fits onto a ratchet (spark plug sockets are padded inside to prevent damage to the porcelain insulators on the new plugs), various extensions and a gap gauge to check and adjust the gaps on the new plugs **(see illustration)**. A special plug wire removal tool is available for separating the

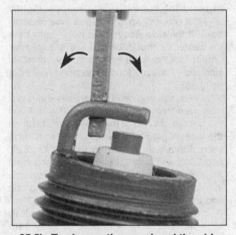

25.5b **To change the gap, bend the side electrode only, as indicated by the arrows, and be very careful not to crack or chip the porcelain insulator surrounding the center electrode**

wire boots from the spark plugs, but it isn't absolutely necessary. A torque wrench should be used to tighten the new plugs.
3   The best approach when replacing the spark plugs is to purchase the new ones in advance, adjust them to the proper gap and replace the plugs one at a time. When buying the new spark plugs, be sure to obtain the correct plug type for your particular engine. This information can be found on the Vehicle Emission Control Information label located under the hood and in this Chapter's Specifications. If differences exist between the plug specified on the emissions label and in the Specifications, assume that the emissions label is correct.
4   Allow the engine to cool completely before attempting to remove any of the plugs. While you are waiting for the engine to cool, check the new plugs for defects and adjust the gaps.
5   The gap is checked by inserting the proper thickness gauge between the electrodes at the tip of the plug **(see illustration)**.

25.6 When removing the spark plug wires, pull only on the boot and twist it back-and-forth

TWIST AND PULL

25.10 A length of snug-fitting rubber hose will save time and prevent damaged threads when installing the spark plugs

The gap between the electrodes should be the same as the one specified on the Vehicle Emissions Control Information label or the Specifications at the front of this Chapter. The wire should just slide between the electrodes with a slight amount of drag. If the gap is incorrect, use the adjuster on the gauge body to bend the curved side electrode slightly until the proper gap is obtained **(see illustration)**. If the side electrode is not exactly over the center electrode, bend it with the adjuster until it is. Check for cracks in the porcelain insulator (if any are found, the plug should not be used).

6   With the engine cool, remove the spark plug wire from one spark plug. Pull only on the boot at the end of the wire - do not pull on the wire. A plug wire removal tool should be used if available **(see illustration)**. On 2.3L and 2005 and later 2.0L engines, disconnect the electrical connector from the spark plug's individual coil, then remove the mounting bolt and the coil for access to the spark plug.

7   If compressed air is available, use it to blow any dirt or foreign material away from the spark plug hole. The idea here is to eliminate the possibility of debris falling into the cylinder as the spark plug is removed.

8   Place the spark plug socket over the plug and remove it from the engine by turning it in a counterclockwise direction.

9   Compare the spark plug to those shown in the photos on the inside back cover to get an indication of the general running condition of the engine.

10   Coat the threads of the new plug with a thin layer of anti-seize compound, being careful not to get it on the electrodes, then thread it into the hole until you can no longer turn it with your fingers, then tighten it with a torque wrench (if available) or the ratchet. It is a good idea to slip a short length of rubber hose over the end of the plug to use as a tool to thread it into place **(see illustration)**. The hose will grip the plug well enough to turn it, but will start to slip if the plug begins to cross-thread in the hole. This will prevent damaged threads and the accompanying repair costs.

11   Before pushing the spark plug wire onto the end of the plug, inspect it following the procedures outlined in Section 26.

12   Attach the plug wire to the new spark plug, again using a twisting motion on the boot until it is seated on the spark plug. On models with coil-on-plug ignition, put a small

dab of dielectric grease inside the boot end of the coil before installation on the spark plug.

13   Repeat the procedure for the remaining spark plugs, replacing them one at a time to prevent mixing up the spark plug wires.

26 Spark plug wire check and replacement (every 30,000 miles or 30 months)

Refer to illustration 26.8
Note: *Every time a spark plug wire is detached from a spark plug or the coil, silicone dielectric compound (a special grease available at auto parts stores) should be applied to the inside of each boot before reconnection. Use a small standard screwdriver to coat the entire inside surface of each boot with a thin layer of the compound.*

1   The spark plug wires should be checked and, if necessary, replaced at the same time the new spark plugs are installed. **Warning:** *Don't touch the spark plug or coil wires with the engine running. The moisture on your skin can conduct high ignition voltage even through good wires, causing serious electrical shocks.*

2   The easiest way to identify bad wires is to make a visual check while the engine is running. In a dark, well-ventilated garage, start the engine and look at each plug wire. Be careful not to come into contact with any moving engine parts. If there is a break in the wire, you will see arcing or a small spark at the damaged area. If arcing is noticed, make a note to obtain new wires.

3   The spark plug wires should be inspected one at a time, beginning with the spark plug for the number one cylinder (the one nearest the right end of the engine), to prevent confusion. Clearly label each original plug wire with a piece of tape marked with the correct number. The plug wires must be reinstalled in the correct order to ensure proper engine operation.

4   Disconnect the plug wire from the first spark plug. A removal tool can be used **(see illustration 25.6)**, or you can grab the wire boot, twist it slightly and pull the wire free. Do not pull on the wire itself, only on the rubber boot.

5   Push the wire and boot back onto the end of the spark plug. It should fit snugly. If it

26.8 Twist the boot side-to-side to release it from the coilpack and check for any corrosion

doesn't, detach the wire and boot once more and use a pair of pliers to carefully crimp the metal connector inside the wire boot until it does.

6   Using a clean rag that's damp with solvent, wipe the entire length of the wire to remove built-up dirt and grease.

7   Once the wire is clean, check for burns, cracks and other damage. Do not bend the wire sharply or you might break the conductor.

8   Squeeze the locking tabs on the plug wire retainer to free the wire from the coil pack **(see illustration)**. **Caution:** *Don't pull on the wire. Inspect the wire, then reinstall it. Be sure the wires are connected to the proper terminals.*

9   Inspect each of the remaining spark plug wires, making sure that each one is securely fastened at the coil pack and spark plug when the check is complete.

10   If new spark plug wires are required, purchase a set for your specific engine model. Pre-cut wire sets with the boots already installed are available. Remove and replace the wires one at a time to avoid mixups in the firing order.

27.4 The radiator drain fitting is located at the lower left corner of the radiator and is accessible from beneath the vehicle - unscrew it to drain the coolant

27   Cooling system servicing (draining, flushing and refilling) (every 30,000 miles or 30 months)

Warning: *Do not allow antifreeze to come in contact with your skin or painted surfaces of the vehicle. Rinse off spills immediately with plenty of water. Antifreeze is highly toxic if ingested. Never leave antifreeze lying around in an open container or in puddles on the floor; children and pets are attracted by it's sweet smell and may drink it. Check with local authorities about disposing of used antifreeze. Many communities have collection centers that will see that antifreeze is disposed of safely.*

1   Periodically, the cooling system should be drained, flushed and refilled to replenish the antifreeze mixture and prevent formation of rust and corrosion, which can impair the performance of the cooling system and cause engine damage. When the cooling system is serviced, all hoses and the radiator cap should be checked and replaced if necessary.

Draining
Refer to illustration 27.4

2   Apply the parking brake and block the wheels. If the vehicle has just been driven, wait several hours to allow the engine to cool down before beginning this procedure.

3   Once the engine is completely cool, remove the radiator cap and recovery tank cap to vent the cooling system.

4   Move a large container under the radiator drain to catch the coolant and open the drain fitting **(see illustration)**.

5   After the coolant stops flowing out of the radiator, remove the container.

6   Check the condition of the radiator hoses, heater hoses and clamps (see Section 17 if necessary).

7   Replace any damaged clamps or hoses.

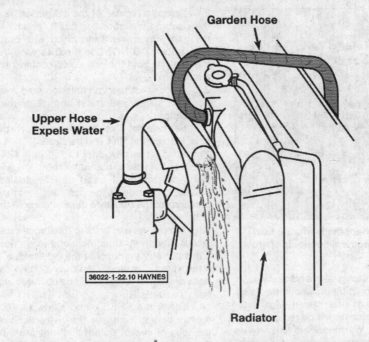

27.10 With the thermostat removed, disconnect the upper radiator hose and flush the radiator and engine block with a garden hose

Flushing
Refer to illustration 27.10

8   Once the system is completely drained, remove the thermostat from the engine (see Chapter 3). Then reinstall the thermostat housing without the thermostat. This will allow the system to be thoroughly flushed.

9   Tighten the radiator drain plug. Turn your heating system controls to Hot, so the heater core will be flushed at the same time as the rest of the cooling system.

10   Disconnect the upper radiator hose from the radiator, then place a garden hose in the upper radiator inlet and flush the system until the water runs clear at the upper radiator hose **(see illustration)**.

11   If the radiator is severely corroded, damaged or leaking, it should be removed (see Chapter 3) and taken to a radiator repair shop.

12   Remove the overflow hose from the coolant expansion tank. Drain the tank and flush it with clean water, then reconnect the hose.

Refilling
13   Close and tighten the radiator drain. Reinstall the thermostat (see Chapter 3).

14   Loosen the clamp and detach the heater hose from the engine. Fill the cooling system with new coolant (a 50/50 mixture of water and antifreeze) through the hose until it begins to flow from the fitting on the engine. Use a funnel inserted in the hose to prevent spills.

15   Connect the heater hose to the fitting on the engine, then fill the expansion tank with the coolant mixture up to the MAX mark.

16   Install the expansion tank cap, then run the engine at a fast idle until it reaches nor-

mal operating temperature (run it until the fans activate twice).

17   Turn the engine off and allow it to cool, then check the coolant level. Add coolant as necessary to bring the level up to the MAX mark. Check the system for leaks.

28   Automatic transaxle fluid and filter change (every 30,000 miles or 30 months)

Refer to illustrations 28.5 and 28.9

1   Before beginning work, purchase the specified transmission fluid (see *Recommended lubricants and fluids* at the beginning of this Chapter) and a new filter. The filter will

28.5 Remove all the pan bolts except the three at the driver's side front corner - after removing the other bolts, loosen the three bolts two turns each

28.9 Disconnect the transaxle fluid temperature electrical connector (arrow)

come with a new pan gasket and seal.

2   The fluid should be drained immediately after the vehicle has been driven. More sediment and contaminants will be removed with the fluid if it's hot. **Warning:** *Fluid temperature can exceed 350-degrees F in a hot transaxle, so wear gloves when draining the fluid.*

3   After the vehicle has been driven to warm up the fluid, raise it and support it on jackstands.

4   Position a drain pan capable of holding six quarts under the transaxle. Be careful not to touch any of the hot exhaust components.

5   There is no transaxle fluid drain plug. Remove all of the pan bolts except for the three at the driver's side **(see illustration)**. Unscrew the three remaining bolts two turns, but leave them in place to support the pan.

6   Using a plastic scraper tool to separate the silicone sealant, separate the pan from the transaxle case and allow the fluid to drain out. Try not to splash fluid as the gasket seal is broken and the pan is detached.

7   Once the fluid has drained, remove the three bolts and detach the pan.

8   Scrape all traces of the old gasket from the pan and the transaxle case, then clean the pan with solvent and dry it with compressed air. DO NOT use a rag to wipe out the pan (lint from the pan could contaminate the transaxle).

9   Disconnect the transmission fluid temperature sensor electrical connector **(see illustration)**.

10   Remove the filter bolts and detach the filter. Discard the filter and the seal.

11   Attach the new seal to the new filter, then bolt the filter to the transaxle.

12   Apply a small bead of RTV sealant around the flange of the pan, then hold the pan against the transaxle case and install the bolts.

13   Tighten the pan bolts to the torque listed in this Chapter's Specifications in a crisscross pattern. Work up to the final torque in three steps. **Caution:** *Don't overtighten the bolts or the pan flange could be distorted and leaks could result.*

14   Lower the vehicle, and allow the RTV sealant time to cure (see the instructions on the tube of sealant). With the engine off, fill the transaxle with fluid (see Section 7 if necessary). Use a funnel to prevent spills. It is best to add a little fluid at a time, continually checking the level with the dipstick. Allow the fluid time to drain into the pan.

15   Start the engine and shift the selector into all positions from Park through Low, then shift into Park and apply the parking brake.

16   With the engine idling, check the fluid level. Lower the vehicle, drive it for several miles, then recheck the fluid level and look for leaks at the transaxle pan.

29   Fuel filter replacement (every 60,000 miles or 48 months)

Warning: *Gasoline is extremely flammable, so take extra precautions when you work on any part of the fuel system. Don't smoke or allow open flames or bare light bulbs near the work area, and don't work in a garage where a gas-type appliance (such as a water heater or clothes dryer) is present. Since gasoline is carcinogenic, wear latex gloves when there's a possibility of being exposed to fuel, and, if you spill fuel on your skin, rinse it off immediately with soap and water. Mop up any spills immediately and do not store fuel-soaked rags where they could ignite. When you perform any kind of work on the fuel system, wear safety glasses and have a Class B type fire extinguisher on hand.*

1   The fuel filter is mounted under the vehicle in front of the fuel tank.

2   Inspect the hose fittings at both ends of the filter to see if they're clean. If more than a light coating of dust is present, clean the fittings before proceeding.

3   Relieve the fuel pressure (see Chapter 4), then disconnect the cable from the negative terminal of the battery. There are two different kinds of quick-connect fittings used on the fuel filter: a "squeeze" type and a "push clip" type. To disengage the "squeeze" type, press the locking tangs together. To disengage the "push clip" type, pull the locking tang out and push the clip through the coupling.

4   Grasp the fuel hoses, one at a time, and pull them straight off the filter. Be prepared for fuel spillage.

5   Use a screwdriver to loosen the clamp, while noting the direction the fuel filter is installed.

6   Remove the filter from the bracket and install the new filter in the same direction.

7   Carefully push each hose onto the filter until it's seated against the collar on the fittings and clicks into place. Make sure the hose fittings are locked into place by trying to pull the fittings off from the filter - if they come off during operation, a fire could result.

8   Reconnect the negative battery cable, then turn the ignition key to the On position and check for fuel leaks.

Chapter 2 Part A
2.0L SPI engine

Contents

Specifications

General

Type	Inline four-cylinder, SOHC
Engine VIN code	P
Displacement	2.0 liters (121 cubic inches)
Bore	3.34 inches
Stroke	3.46 inches
Firing order	1-3-4-2

Cylinder/coil/terminal
locations - 2.0L SPI

Cylinder head and valve train

Rocker arm ratio	1.65:1
Valve lifters	
Diameter (standard)	0.8740 to 0.8745 inch
Clearance in bore	
Standard	0.0009 to 0.0026 inch
Service limit	0.005 inch
Roundness	0.0005 inch
Collapsed lifter gap	0 to 0.177 inch
Lifter bore diameter	0.8766 +/- 0.0006 inch

Camshaft

Camshaft journal diameter	1.8020 to 1.8030 inch
Lobe lift	0.245 inch
Allowable lobe lift loss	0.005 inch
Theoretical valve lift (measured at valve end of rocker arm)	0.405 inch
Endplay	
Standard	0.0008 to 0.0078 inch
Service limit	0.0078 inch
Journal-to-bearing (oil) clearance	0.0013 to 0.0033 inch
Runout limit	0.005 inch (runout of center bearing relative to No. 1 and No. 5)
Out-of-round limit	0.003 inch
Assembled gear face runout	
Crankshaft	0.026 inch
Camshaft	0.011 inch

Torque specifications

Ft-lbs (unless otherwise indicated)

Note: *One foot-pound (ft-lb) of torque is equivalent to 12 inch-pounds (in-lbs) of torque. Torque values below approximately 15 ft-lbs are expressed in inch-pounds, since most foot-pound torque wrenches are not accurate at these smaller values.*

Camshaft sprocket bolt	77
Camshaft position sensor	180 in-lbs
Camshaft thrust plate-to-head bolts...	89 in-lbs
Crankshaft damper bolt	88
Cylinder head bolts* (in sequence - see illustration 12.15)	
Step 1	37
Step 2	Loosen 1/2 turn
Step 3	37
Step 4	Tighten 1/4 turn from Step 3
Step 5	Tighten 1/4 turn from Step 4
Exhaust manifold nuts..	20
Flywheel/driveplate bolts..	60
Intake manifold nuts	
Step 1	120 in-lbs
Step 2	Tighten 1/4 turn
Oil pan drain plug	See Chapter 1
Oil pan baffle bolts	18
Oil pan-to-block bolts	18
Oil pump-to-block bolts	120 in-lbs
Oil screen bolts...	89 in-lbs
Rocker arm bolt...	18
Valve cover bolts	80 in-lbs
Timing belt tensioner attaching bolt..	18

Cylinder head bolts are torque-to-yield design. Always replace them with new ones whenever they are removed.

1   General information

This Part of Chapter 2 is devoted to in-vehicle repair procedures for the 2.0L SPI SOHC engine used in Focus models through 2004. All information concerning engine removal and installation and engine block and cylinder head overhaul can be found in Chapter 2C.

The following repair procedures are based on the assumption that the engine is installed in the vehicle. If the engine has been removed from the vehicle and mounted on a stand, many of the steps outlined in this Part of Chapter 2 will not apply.

The Specifications included in this Part of Chapter 2 apply only to the procedures contained in this Part. Chapter 2C contains the Specifications necessary for cylinder head and engine block rebuilding.

2   Repair operations possible with the engine in the vehicle

Many major repair operations can be accomplished without removing the engine from the vehicle.

Clean the engine compartment and the exterior of the engine with some type of degreaser before any work is done. It will make the job easier and help keep dirt out of the internal areas of the engine.

Depending on the components involved, it may be helpful to remove the hood to improve access to the engine as repairs are performed (see Chapter 11 if necessary). Cover the fenders to prevent damage to the paint. Special pads are available, but an old bedspread or blanket will also work.

If vacuum, exhaust, oil or coolant leaks develop, indicating a need for gasket or seal replacement, the repairs can generally be made with the engine in the vehicle. The intake and exhaust manifold gaskets, timing cover gasket, oil pan gasket, crankshaft oil seals and cylinder head gasket are all accessible with the engine in place.

Exterior engine components, such as the intake and exhaust manifolds, the oil pan, the water pump, the starter motor, the alternator, and the fuel system components can be removed for repair with the engine in place.

Since the cylinder head can be removed without pulling the engine, valve component servicing can also be accomplished with the engine in the vehicle. Replacement of the timing belt is also possible with the engine in the vehicle.

In extreme cases caused by a lack of necessary equipment, repair or replacement of piston rings, pistons, connecting rods and rod bearings is possible with the engine in the vehicle. However, this practice is not recommended because of the cleaning and preparation work that must be done to the components involved.

3   Top Dead Center (TDC) for number one piston - locating

Refer to illustration 3.5

1   Top Dead Center (TDC) is the highest point in the cylinder that each piston reaches as it travels up-and-down when the crankshaft turns. Each piston reaches TDC on the compression stroke and again on the exhaust stroke, but TDC generally refers to piston position on the compression stroke.

2   Positioning the piston(s) at TDC is an essential part of many procedures such as rocker arm removal, camshaft and timing belt removal.

3   Before beginning this procedure, be sure to place the transaxle in Neutral and apply the parking brake or block the rear wheels. Also, disable the ignition system by disconnecting all four spark plug wires from the plugs and grounding them on the engine using jumper wires with alligator clips. Remove the spark plugs (see Chapter 1).

4   In order to bring any piston to TDC, the crankshaft must be turned using one of the methods outlined below. When looking at the drivebelt end of the engine, normal crankshaft rotation is clockwise.

a)   *The preferred method is to turn the crankshaft with a socket and ratchet attached to the bolt threaded into the front of the crankshaft.*

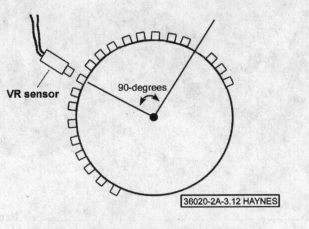

3.5 Align the ninth tooth from the missing tooth with the VR sensor

5.2 The drivebelt tensioner is secured by a single mounting bolt and comes off as an assembly

b) *A remote starter switch, which may save some time, can also be used. Follow the instructions included with the switch. Once the piston is close to TDC, use a socket and ratchet as described in the previous paragraph.*

c) *If an assistant is available to turn the ignition switch to the Start position in short bursts, you can get the piston close to TDC without a remote starter switch. Make sure your assistant is out of the vehicle, away from the ignition switch, then use a socket and ratchet as described above to complete the procedure.*

Note: *The 2.0L SPI engine is not equipped with a distributor. Piston position must be determined by feeling for compression at the number one spark plug hole, then aligning the crankshaft wheel and VR sensor as described in the next Step.*

5   The crankshaft pulley has 35 teeth, evenly spaced every 10-degrees around the pulley, and a gap where a 36th tooth would be. The gap is located at 90-degrees before top dead center (BTDC). Turn the crankshaft (see Step 4) until you feel compression at the number one spark plug hole, then turn it slowly until the ninth tooth from the missing tooth on the crankshaft wheel is aligned with the variable reluctance (VR) sensor **(see illustration)**. **Note:** *If the valve cover is removed, you can verify the number one piston is at TDC by checking the number one cylinder rocker arms - they should feel slightly loose and not be putting any pressure on the valves (the valve springs should not be compressed).*

6   After the number one piston has been positioned at TDC on the compression stroke, TDC for any of the remaining pistons can be located by turning the crankshaft and following the firing order. Make a mark 180-degrees (18 teeth on the crankshaft pulley) from the TDC position. Rotate the crankshaft 180-degrees to set the next cylinder in the firing order (1-3-4-2) at TDC. For example, rotating the crankshaft 180-degrees clockwise from

the number one TDC position will set the number three piston at TDC. Rotating the crankshaft another 180-degrees clockwise (back to where it was for number one) will set the number four piston at TDC, etc.

---

4   Valve lifter clearance - checking

Caution: *Be sure to perform this procedure after a valve job or whenever the camshaft, rocker arms or rocker arm supports (fulcrums) are replaced. Insufficient clearance can cause the valves to remain open all the time, resulting in rough running and expensive engine damage. Also, excessive clearance (usually caused by worn components) can result in noise in the valve cover area (clattering) and reduced engine performance.*

1   The valve stem-to-rocker arm clearance must be within specification with the valve lifter completely collapsed. A special tool is available to compress the lifters. Check with an auto parts store or dealer service department.

2   To check the clearance, crank the engine with the ignition off until the number one cylinder is at Top Dead Center (TDC) on the compression stoke. With the spark plug removed and your finger over the hole, the compression can be felt.

3   Mark the crankshaft pulley with chalk or white paint at TDC and 180 degrees opposite (see Section 3).

4   The hydraulic lifter should be slowly bled down until it is completely collapsed. If the clearance is insufficient, check with an auto-motive machine shop to determine the best way to solve the problem (usually, resurfacing the valve stem(s) and/or replacing the valve(s) and/or valve seat(s) are the options available). If the clearance is excessive, check the follow-ing components for wear:

a) *Rocker arms*
b) *Rocker arm supports (fulcrums)*
c) *Hydraulic lifters*

d) *Valve tips*
e) *Camshaft lobes*

5   With the number one piston at TDC on the compression stroke, check the following valves:

No. 1 intake, No. 1 exhaust
No. 2 intake

6   Rotate the crankshaft clockwise 180-degrees and check the following valves:

No. 3 intake, No. 3 exhaust

7   Rotate the pulley clockwise 180-degrees (back to the original position) and check the following valves:

No. 4 intake, No. 4 exhaust
No. 2 exhaust

---

5   Timing belt - removal, inspection and installation

Refer to illustrations 5.2, 5.4a, 5.4b, 5.5a through 5.5c, 5.6, 5.9, 5.11a and 5.11b

Removal and inspection

**** CAUTION ****
The timing system is complex. Severe engine damage will occur if you make any mistakes. Do not attempt this procedure unless you are highly experienced with this type of repair. If you are at all unsure of your abilities, consult an expert. Double-check all your work and be sure everything is correct before you attempt to start the engine.

1   Disconnect the cable from the negative terminal of the battery. Raise the vehicle and support it securely on jackstands. Remove the right front wheel.

2   Remove the accessory drivebelt (see Chapter 1). Remove the drivebelt tensioner center bolt and remove the tensioner **(see illustration)**.

5.4a Remove the upper nuts and bolts . . .

5.4b . . . and the lower nuts and bolts

3   Remove the power steering pump reservoir and set it aside (see Chapter 10). Unbolt the coolant expansion tank and set it aside with the hoses still connected (see Chapter 3).
4   Remove the timing belt cover **(see illustrations)**. **Note:** *It may be necessary to remove the engine mount to get the cover out. If so, support the engine under the oil pan with a jack and block of wood and refer to Section 18 for engine mount details.*
5   Use a socket and breaker bar on the crankshaft damper bolt **(see illustration)** and rotate the engine clockwise until the timing mark on the camshaft pulley is aligned with the one on the cylinder head and the crankshaft pulley mark is aligned with the TDC mark on the oil pump housing **(see illustrations)**.
6   Loosen the belt tensioner bolt, pry the tensioner to one side and retighten the bolt to hold the tensioner in position **(see illustration)**.
7   Remove the spark plugs (see Chapter 1).
8   Securely block the rear wheels so the vehicle can't roll. Jack up the front end and place it securely on jackstands, then remove the splash shield from the passenger's side of the vehicle.

5.5a Turn the crankshaft with a socket and breaker bar on the pulley bolt

5.5b Align the mark on the crankshaft sprocket with the notch in the oil pump housing . . .

9   Hold the crankshaft from turning with a chain wrench or strap wrench. Remove the crankshaft damper bolt **(see illustration)**, then remove the damper.
10   Remove the timing belt.
11   If you're installing a new belt, be sure it's the correct type. Belts with squared or rounded teeth are used in production **(see illustration)**. The two types are not interchangeable. Inspect the belt's condition **(see illustration)**. Also, check the water pump (see Chapter 3) and replace it, if necessary.

5.5c . . . and the mark on the camshaft sprocket with the mark on the cylinder head

5.6 Pry the tensioner to the left with an 8mm Allen wrench (left arrow), then slip a 1/8-inch drill bit into the hole (right arrow) to lock the tensioner in the released position

5.9 Hold the crankshaft damper with a chain wrench or strap wrench and unscrew the bolt (if a chain wrench is used, wrap a section of old drivebelt around the damper to protect it)

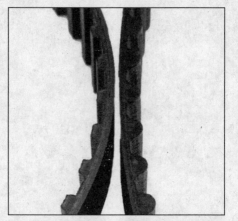

5.11a The timing belt may have squared or rounded teeth - if you replace the belt, be sure to use the same type that's on the engine

17   Tighten the tensioner attaching bolt to the torque listed in this Chapter's Specifications.

18   The remainder of installation is the reverse of the removal steps.

6   Valve cover - removal and installation

Refer to illustration 6.3

1   Disconnect the PCV hose from the valve cover.

2   Detach both spark plug wire looms from the valve cover and position them out of the way.

3   Remove the valve cover bolts, then lift off the cover and gasket **(see illustration)**. If the cover is stuck, bump it lightly with a rubber mallet to break the gasket seal.

4   Installation is the reverse of the removal steps. Make sure the gasket surfaces on the cylinder head and valve cover are perfectly clean (wiping them with a rag soaked in lacquer thinner or acetone may help). Press the new gasket firmly into the groove in the valve cover (don't use any sealant on the gasket). Tighten the cover bolts evenly to the torque listed in this Chapter's Specifications.

Installation

> **∗∗ CAUTION ∗∗**
>
> Before starting the engine, carefully rotate the crankshaft by hand through at least two full revolutions (use a socket and breaker bar on the crankshaft pulley center bolt). If you feel any resistance, STOP! There is something wrong - most likely, valves are contacting the pistons. You must find the problem before proceeding. Check your work and see if any updated repair information is available.

12   Check to make sure the timing marks on the camshaft and crankshaft sprockets are still properly aligned.

13   Starting at the crankshaft, install a new belt in a counterclockwise direction over the pulleys. Be sure to keep the belt span from the crankshaft to the camshaft tight while installing it over the remaining pulleys.

14   Loosen the belt tensioner attaching bolt so the tensioner snaps into place against the belt.

15   Install the crankshaft damper and bolt and tighten it to the torque listed in this Chapter's Specifications.

16   Rotate the crankshaft two complete revolutions clockwise and stop on the second revolution at the point where the crankshaft sprocket returns to the TDC position **(see illustration 5.5b)**. Verify that the camshaft sprocket is also at TDC **(see illustration 5.5c)**. If it isn't, the belt has jumped a tooth and the installation procedure will have to be repeated.

7   Camshaft oil seal - replacement

Refer to illustration 7.6

1   Disconnect the negative cable from the battery.

2   Remove the accessory drivebelt (see Chapter 1).

3   Remove the engine timing belt (see Section 5).

4   Insert a suitable bar through the camshaft pulley to lock it, remove the retaining bolt and withdraw the sprocket.

5   Using a suitable hooked tool, pry the seal out.

6   Apply a light coat of clean engine oil to the lip of the new seal. Place the seal in place and draw it into position, using a long bolt the same thread size as the pulley bolt and a suit-

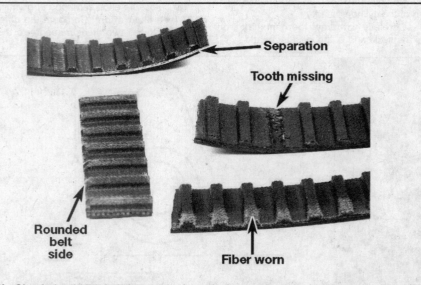

5.11b Check the timing belt for cracked or missing teeth. If the belt is cracked or worn, check the pulleys for nicks and burrs. Wear on one side of the belt indicates pulley misalignment problems

6.3 Three bolts (arrows) secure the valve cover

7.6 Installing the camshaft oil seal - if the special tool (shown here, available at most auto parts stores) is not available, try using a large socket

8.5a The rocker arms are mounted diagonally, in parallel rows

able driver piece such as a large socket **(see illustration)**.

7   Reinstall the sprocket and tighten the bolt to the torque listed in this Chapter's Specifications.

8   The remainder of installation is the reverse of the removal steps.

---

8   Camshaft(s), lifters and rocker arms - removal, inspection and installation

Refer to illustrations 8.5a and 8.5b

Removal

1   Disconnect the negative cable from the battery.

2   Remove the air cleaner intake duct (see Chapter 4).

3   Remove the valve cover (see Section 6).

4   Remove the drivebelt (see Chapter 1).

5   Remove the flange bolts and remove the fulcrums, rocker arms, lifter guide retainer, lifter guides and lifters **(see illustrations)**. Keep the components in their originally installed sequence by marking them with a piece of numbered tape or by using a suitable sub-divided box (such as an egg carton). If the lifters are not marked with color codes, be sure to mark each lifter so you know which end faces the front of the engine, since you must reinstall the lifters so they rotate in the same direction they originally did.

6   Remove the ignition coil pack (see Chapter 5).

7   Remove the timing belt (see Section 5).

8   Pass a rod or large screwdriver through one of the holes in the camshaft pulley to lock it and unscrew the sprocket bolt. Remove the sprocket.

9   Remove the two bolts and pull out the camshaft thrust plate.

10   Remove the cup plug from the transaxle end of the cylinder head.

11   Carefully withdraw the camshaft from the transaxle end of the cylinder head.

Inspection

Refer to illustrations 8.15, 8.17a, 8.17b and 8.17c

12   Check each lifter for wear on the camshaft contact surface and cylinder head contact surface. Replace worn lifters.

13   Inspect the camshaft for wear, particularly on the lobes. Look for places where the hardened surface of the lobe is flaking off, scored or showing excessive wear. Replace the camshaft if any of these conditions exist. Pitting isn't cause for replacement unless it occurs at the toe (the highest point of the cam lobe).

14   Using a micrometer, measure the camshaft bearing journals (the raised round areas). Compare your measurements with this Chapter's Specifications. If the measurements are out of specification, replace the camshaft.

15   Measure each cam lobe at points A and B **(see illustration)**. Compare the difference between the two measurements to the lobe

8.5b Remove the bolt (arrow), then lift out the fulcrum and rocker arm

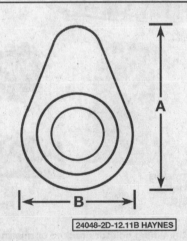

24048-2D-12.11B HAYNES

8.15 Subtract the base circle measurement (B) from the lobe height (A) to get the camshaft lobe lift

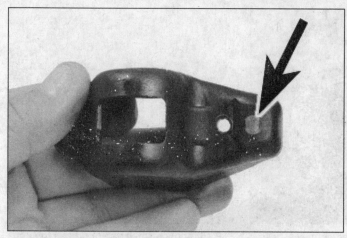

8.17a Check the rocker arm surfaces that contact the valve stem and lifter . . .

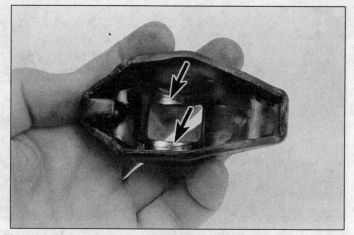

8.17b . . . the fulcrum seats in the rocker arms . . .

lift listed in this Chapter's Specifications. If it's not within specification, replace the camshaft.

16 Measure the camshaft bearing bore diameter in the cylinder head and compare with that listed in this Chapter's Specifications. If it's excessive, have the bearing bores machined to accept an oversized camshaft.

17 Inspect each rocker arm for wear at the points where it rides on the lifter, fulcrum and valve stem **(see illustrations)**. Replace any rocker arms or fulcrums that show excessive wear. Replace rocker arms and fulcrums as pairs. Do not replace just a fulcrum or rocker arm.

Installation

18 Installing the camshaft, lifters and rocker arms is the reverse of removal, but observe the following points.

19 Lubricate the camshaft bearings and lobes with engine assembly lube before inserting the camshaft into the cylinder head. Rotate the camshaft as it's inserted and be careful not to nick or gouge the bearing surfaces.

20 A new oil seal should always be installed after the camshaft has been installed (see Section 7). Apply thread locking compound to the pulley bolt threads. Reinstall the pulley and tighten the bolt to the torque listed in this Chapter's Specifications.

21 Install and adjust the timing belt as described in Section 5.

22 Lubricate the hydraulic lifters with engine oil before inserting them into their original bores. Position the lifters with their guide flats parallel to the centerline of the camshaft and the color code dots opposite the oil feed holes. Install the guides, retainers, rocker arms and fulcrums in their original positions, then install the bolts and tighten them to the torque listed in this Chapter's Specifications.

23 If any components are being replaced, check the collapsed tappet clearance, as described in Section 4.

9 Valve springs, retainers and seals - replacement

Refer to illustrations 9.4, 9.8a, 9.8b and 9.15

Note: *Broken valve springs and defective valve stem seals can be replaced without removing the cylinder head. Special tools and a compressed air source are normally required to perform this operation, so read through this Section carefully and rent or buy the tools before beginning the job.*

1 Refer to Section 6 and remove the valve cover from the cylinder head.

2 Remove the spark plug from the cylinder that has the defective component. If all of the valve stem seals are being replaced, all of the spark plugs should be removed.

3 Turn the crankshaft until the piston in the affected cylinder is at top dead center on the compression stroke (see Section 3 for instructions). If you're replacing all of the valve stem seals, begin with cylinder number one and work on the valves for one cylinder at a time. Move from cylinder-to-cylinder following the firing order sequence (see this Chapter's Specifications).

4 Thread an adapter into the spark plug hole **(see illustration)** and connect an air hose from a compressed air source to it. Most auto parts stores can supply the air hose adapter. **Note:** *Many cylinder compression gauges utilize a screw-in fitting that may work with your air hose quick-disconnect fitting.*

5 Apply compressed air to the cylinder. **Warning:** *The piston may be forced down by compressed air, causing the crankshaft to turn suddenly. If the wrench used when positioning the number one piston at TDC is still attached to the bolt in the crankshaft nose, it could cause damage or injury when the crankshaft moves.* **Caution:** *Expensive engine damage may occur if the crankshaft is turned separately from the camshaft. If the timing belt is not installed, be careful not to let air pressure turn the crankshaft.*

6 The valves should be held in place by air pressure. If they aren't, the valves and faces are in such poor condition that the cylinder head should be removed so they can be inspected.

7 Remove the bolt, fulcrum and rocker arm for the valve with the defective part. If all

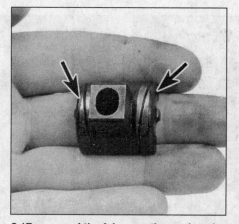

8.17c . . . and the fulcrums themselves for wear and galling

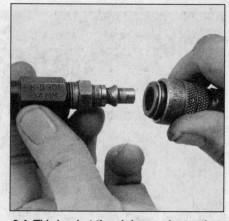

9.4 This is what the air hose adapter that threads into the spark plug hole looks like - they're commonly available from auto parts stores

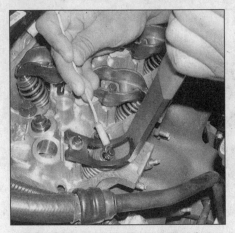

9.8a The recommended valve spring compressor is a lever type that pivots on the rocker arm fulcrum nut or bolt head

9.8b Use a valve spring compressor to compress the springs, then remove the keepers from the valve stem with a magnet or small needle-nose pliers

9.15 Apply a small dab of grease to each keeper as shown here before installation - it'll hold them in place on the valve stem as the spring is released

of the valve stem seals are being replaced, all of the rocker arms should be removed (see Section 8).

8   Compress the valve spring with a lever-type compressor, pivoting on the fulcrum nut or bolt head **(see illustration)**. Remove the keepers **(see illustration)**, spring retainer and valve spring, then remove the guide seal. **Note:** *If air pressure fails to hold the valve in the closed position during this operation, the valve face or seat is probably damaged. If so, the cylinder head will have to be removed for additional repair operations.*

9   Wrap a rubber band or tape around the top of the valve stem so the valve won't fall into the combustion chamber, then release the air pressure.

10   Inspect the valve stem for damage. Rotate the valve in the guide and check the end for eccentric movement, which would indicate that the valve is bent.

11   Move the valve up-and-down in the guide and make sure it doesn't bind. If the valve stem binds, either the valve is bent or

the guide is damaged. In either case, the head will have to be removed for repair.

12   Reapply air pressure to the cylinder to retain the valve in the closed position, then remove the tape or rubber band from the valve stem.

13   Lubricate the valve stem with engine oil and install a new guide seal. Use the installation tool provided with the new seal to prevent damage to the seal.

14   Install the lower seat and valve spring in position over the valve.

15   Install the valve spring retainer. Compress the valve spring and carefully position the keepers in the groove. Apply a small dab of grease to the inside of each keeper to hold it in place **(see illustration)**.

16   Remove the pressure from the spring tool and make sure the keepers are seated.

17   The remainder of installation is the reverse of the removal steps.

18   Start and run the engine, then check for oil leaks and unusual sounds coming from the valve cover area.

10   Intake manifold - removal and installation

Refer to illustrations 10.7 and 10.10
Warning: *Wait until the engine is completely cool before beginning this procedure.*
Note: *This engine is equipped with IMRC, or Intake Manifold Runner Control, which changes the intake tract for better torque at lower speeds. It is mounted between the intake manifold and the cylinder head, using the same studs.*

1   Relieve the fuel system pressure (see Chapter 4).

2   Clamp-off the coolant hose to the intake manifold, then detach the hose from its fitting on the manifold.

3   Disconnect the negative cable from the battery.

4   Remove the air cleaner intake tube (see Chapter 4).

5   Disconnect the electrical connectors for the crankshaft position sensor and camshaft position sensor (see Chapter 5) and the fuel

10.7 Detach the accelerator cable from the throttle cam - on automatic transaxle models, disconnect the kickdown cable as well

10.10 Unbolt the intake manifold brace

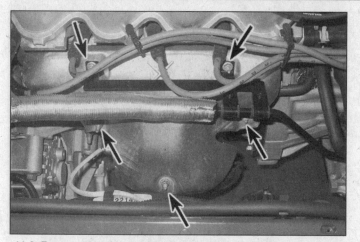

11.3 Remove the exhaust manifold heat shield nuts (arrows) and remove the shield

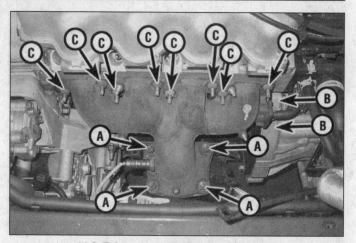

11.6 Exhaust manifold mounting details

injector harness (located at the passenger's side strut tower). If the IMRC is being removed, disconnect the IMRC electrical connector, located at the left end of the IMRC.

6   Disconnect the fuel lines (see Chapter 4).

7   Detach the accelerator cable (and kickdown cable on automatic transaxle models) from the throttle lever **(see illustration)**. Remove the cable bracket from the intake manifold.

8   Disconnect the vacuum hoses from the fuel pressure regulator, intake manifold, brake booster, EVAP solenoid valve and the pressure feedback sensor.

9   Unscrew the EGR tube from the EGR valve at the fitting below the valve, and remove the engine oil dipstick tube from the engine. Disconnect the electrical connectors at the TPS and IAC valve.

10   Remove the intake manifold brace **(see illustration)** and the bolts/nuts that secure the manifold. Slide the manifold off the studs and remove the gasket. The IMRC can remain in place on the intake studs.

11   Using a scraper, clean all traces of old gasket and sealant from the mating surfaces of the intake manifold and cylinder head. **Caution:** *The cylinder head and manifold are made of aluminum, which can easily be scratched or gouged. Be very careful when using the scraper. Aerosol gasket removal solvents are commonly available from auto parts stores and may prove helpful.*

12   Clean the intake manifold studs, then apply a light coat of clean engine oil to the threads. It's best to replace the IMRC-to-cylinder head gasket at this time. Pull the IMRC off the studs, install the IMRC gasket, then slide the IMRC back onto the studs.

13   Slip a new intake manifold gasket over the studs. Install the manifold and tighten the nuts evenly to the torque listed in this Chapter's Specifications.

14   The remainder of installation is the reverse of the removal steps.

15   Check the coolant level and add some, as necessary, to bring it to the appropriate level (see Chapter 1).

11   Exhaust manifold - removal and installation

Refer to illustrations 11.3 and 11.6

Note: *Because of the heating and cooling cycles exhaust components (particularly exhaust manifolds) are subjected to, fasteners frequently become frozen and are difficult to remove. Apply penetrating oil to the threads and allow it to soak in before removal. Tapping lightly on the fastener head may help the oil penetrate. When installing the exhaust manifold, apply anti-seize compound to the fasteners so they'll be easier to remove next time.*

1   Disconnect the negative cable from the battery.

2   Disconnect the electrical connector from the heated oxygen sensor.

3   Remove the nuts securing the exhaust manifold heat shield **(see illustration)**. It will help to apply a little penetrating oil to the studs before beginning.

4   Remove the cooling fan and shroud (see Chapter 3).

5   Disconnect the catalytic converter intake pipe from the exhaust manifold. Remove the nuts and studs that secure the EGR tube to the exhaust manifold.

6   Remove the exhaust manifold attaching nuts and slip the manifold off the studs **(see illustration)**. Remove the gasket.

7   Using a scraper, clean all traces of old gasket and carbon from the manifold and its mounting surface on the cylinder head. **Caution:** *The cylinder head is made of aluminum, which can easily be scratched or gouged. Be very careful when using the scraper. Aerosol gasket removal solvents are commonly available from auto parts stores and may prove helpful.*

8   Position a new gasket on the studs. Install the manifold and tighten its mounting nuts evenly to the torque listed in this Chapter's Specifications.

9   Install the heat shield and tighten its nuts to the torque listed in this Chapter's Specifications.

10   The remainder of installation is the reverse of the removal steps.

12   Cylinder head - removal and installation

Refer to illustrations 12.15, 12.19 and 12.20

Caution: *The engine must be completely cool before beginning this procedure.*

Note: *The following procedure describes removing the cylinder head with the intake and exhaust manifolds attached, which may be easier if all you need to do is replace the head gasket. However, if you're planning to do any cylinder head servicing (such as a valve job), it will probably be easier to first disconnect the intake and exhaust manifolds from the cylinder head, tying them out of the way so the head can be removed separately (see Sections 10 and 11).*

Removal

1   Place the No. 1 piston at top dead center (TDC) (see Section 3).

2   Relieve the fuel system pressure and disconnect the fuel supply line at the fuel rail (see Chapter 4).

3   Remove the battery (see Chapter 5).

4   Drain the cooling system (see Chapter 1).

5   Remove the air cleaner and its outlet tube (see Chapter 4).

6   Label and disconnect the vacuum hoses from the fitting on the intake manifold, and at the fuel pressure regulator, EGR valve, PCV valve and idle air control valve. Refer to Section 10 and remove the intake manifold brace.

7   Label and disconnect all electrical connectors attaching the cylinder head to the engine and vehicle. Disconnect the two large PCM connectors located near the power steering fluid reservoir.

8   Disconnect the throttle cable (and cruise control cable if equipped) from the throttle lever. Detach the cable bracket from the manifold.

9   Disconnect the heated oxygen sensor electrical connector at the cooling fan shroud.

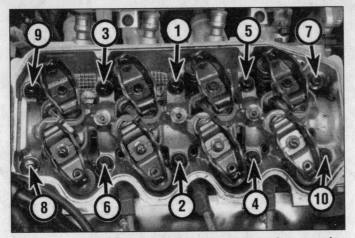

12.15 Cylinder head bolt TIGHTENING sequence - when removing the head, loosen in the reverse order

12.19 Remove the cylinder head locating dowels from the block

10   Remove the engine oil dipstick tube from the engine.

11   Remove the accessory drivebelt, alternator and air conditioning compressor (see Chapters 1, 5 and 3). Loosen the single nut and four lower bolts that secure the accessory bracket to the engine by four turns each. Remove the bracket's front uppermost bolt.

12   Detach the exhaust manifold from the catalytic converter (see Chapter 4). While in the exhaust manifold area, disconnect the electrical connectors at the block for the knock sensor and engine oil pressure switch.

13   Remove the timing belt and valve cover (see Sections 5 and 6).

14   Disconnect the coolant hoses from the thermostat housing and throttle body (see Chapter 3).

15   Loosen the cylinder head bolts in the opposite order of the tightening sequence **(see illustration)**. Loosen in several stages.

16   Remove and discard the cylinder head bolts. The bolts are a stretch type that must be replaced with new ones whenever they're removed.

17   Remove the cylinder head with the intake and exhaust manifolds attached.

18   Remove the old gasket.

19   Note the locations of the cylinder head dowels, then remove them **(see illustration)**.

20   Remove all traces of old gasket material from the head and cylinder block mating surfaces **(see illustration)**. Clean the surfaces with a rag soaked in lacquer thinner or acetone. **Caution:** *The cylinder head is made of aluminum and can easily be scratched or gouged, so scrape carefully. Gasket removal solvents are commonly available at auto parts stores and may prove helpful.* **Note:** *It's a good idea to check the cylinder head gasket surface for warpage while the head is off the vehicle. This procedure, as well as other information on cylinder head servicing, is in Chapter 2C.*

Installation

21   Place a new head gasket on the cylinder block and then locate the cylinder head on the dowels. **Caution:** *If you've replaced any*

12.20 Stuff rags into the cylinder bores to keep debris from falling down where you can't retrieve it, then carefully scrape all old gasket material from the mating surface on the block (clean the cylinder head surface as well)

dowels, make sure they're completely seated in the block. Also make sure they don't protrude as high as the combined height of the head gasket and the recess in the cylinder head. If the dowels protrude too far, the head will not seat properly against the gasket.

22   Apply a thin coat of clean engine oil to the threads of new cylinder head bolts. Install the bolts and tighten them in the stages listed in this Chapter's Specifications, following the proper tightening sequence **(see illustration 12.15)**.

23   The remainder of installation is the reverse of the removal steps.

24   Run the engine and check for leaks.

13 Oil pan - removal and installation

Refer to illustration 13.5

1   Disconnect the negative cable from the battery.

2   Securely block the rear wheels so the

13.5 Remove the coolant tube bolt (arrow)

vehicle won't roll, then jack up the front and place it securely on jackstands. DO NOT get under a vehicle that's supported only by a jack!

3   Drain the engine oil (see Chapter 1).

4   Remove the catalytic converter (see Chapter 4). Note that the bracket that supports the rear end of the converter outlet pipe bolts to the oil pan. Remove this bracket.

5   Remove the bolts securing the axleshaft bracket to the engine, and the bolt securing the coolant tube to the oil pan **(see illustration)**.

6   Unbolt the oil pan from the engine and lower it clear. If it's stuck, bump it gently with a rubber mallet. Don't pry between the pan and engine block or the mating surfaces may be damaged. Also, don't lose the oil pan-to-transaxle spacers.

7   Remove the gasket from the oil pan.

8   Unbolt the oil strainer from the oil pump, if necessary (see Section 14).

9   Using a plastic scraper, clean all traces of old gasket from the mating surfaces of the oil pan and engine block. Be extremely careful not to scratch or gouge the delicate aluminum gasket surfaces on the oil pan. Gasket

removal solvents are available at auto parts stores and may prove helpful. Wipe the gasket surfaces clean with a rag soaked in lacquer thinner or acetone. Thoroughly clean the threads of the oil pan bolts.

10   Install the oil strainer, using a new gasket. Tighten the bolts securely.

11   Install a new oil pan gasket in the pan. Be sure the tabs are pressed all the way into the gasket channel in the pan.

12   Apply a 1/8-inch bead of silicone sealant to the corners of the block and to the points where the oil pump meets the crankshaft rear seal retainer. **Note:** *The oil pan must be installed within 10 minutes after the sealant is applied.*

13   Position the oil pan on the engine. Install the pan-to-engine bolts and tighten them to the torque listed in this Chapter's Specifications, working in a criss-cross pattern.

14   .Retighten the oil pan-to-transaxle bolts to the torque listed in this Chapter's Specifications.

15   The remainder of installation is the reverse of the removal steps.

16   Check oil level on the dipstick (see Chapter 1). Run the engine and check for leaks.

14   Oil pump - removal and installation

1   Disconnect the negative cable from the battery.

2   Place the number one cylinder at top dead center (TDC) on the compression stroke (see Section 3).

3   Remove the drivebelt (see Chapter 1). Remove the drivebelt tensioner.

4   Place a jack beneath the engine to support it. Use a block of wood between the jack and oil pan to protect the pan.

5   Remove the damper from the right engine mount. Unbolt the mount from the bracket, loosen the mount through-bolt and pivot the mount away from the engine.

6   Remove the timing belt cover (see Section 5).

7   Pivot the engine mount back into position and reattach it to the engine. Remove the jack from beneath the engine.

8   Loosen the timing belt tensioner bolt, pry the tensioner toward the rear of the engine and tighten the bolt to hold the tensioner in this position.

9   Securely block the rear wheels so the vehicle won't roll, then jack up the front and place it securely on jackstands. DO NOT get under a vehicle that's supported only by a jack!

10   Remove the splash shield from the passenger's side of the vehicle.

11   Remove the catalytic converter (see Chapter 4).

12   Remove the oil pan (see Section 13).

13   Remove the oil filter (see Chapter 1).

14   Remove the crankshaft damper and timing belt (see Section 5). Remove the timing belt pulley and guide from the crankshaft.

15   Remove the crankshaft position sensor (see Chapter 5).

16   Unbolt the oil pump from the engine. Take off the oil pump and gasket.

17   Unbolt the screen and cover assembly from the pump.

18   Remove and discard the crankshaft front oil seal from the pump.

19   Using a gasket scraper, carefully clean all traces of old gasket from the pump, screen and engine. Be very careful not to scratch or gouge the gasket mating surfaces. Gasket removal solvents are available from auto parts stores and may prove helpful. Wipe the mating surfaces clean with a rag soaked in lacquer thinner or acetone.

20   Lubricate the outer edge of a new crankshaft seal with light engine oil, then install the seal. Lubricate the seal lip with light engine oil. To install the seal, place the oil pump on wood blocks, and drive the new seal into place with a hammer and socket that's slightly smaller in diameter than the outer edge of the seal.

21   Place the oil pump gasket on the pump. Pour oil into the pump and rotate its shaft to prime it, then position the pump on the engine. Use a small screwdriver, inserted through the oil pick-up hole, to guide the pump drive gear onto the crankshaft and make sure the pump seats securely against the block. Don't install the oil strainer until the pump is correctly installed on the engine.

22   Install the oil pump mounting bolts and tighten them evenly to the torque listed in this Chapter's Specifications. Make sure the oil pump gasket doesn't extend below the sealing surface on the cylinder block.

23   Install the oil screen, using a new gasket, then tighten its bolts to the torque listed in this Chapter's Specifications.

24   Install the timing belt guide on the crankshaft with its flanged side away from the timing belt.

25   The remainder of installation is the reverse of the removal steps. Be sure to follow the timing belt installation and alignment mark checking procedures in Section 5.

26   Fill the engine with oil and check its level (see Chapter 1). Run the engine and check for oil leaks.

15   Flywheel/driveplate - removal and installation

1   Raise the vehicle and support it securely on jackstands, then refer to Chapter 7 and remove the transaxle. If it's leaking, now would be a very good time to replace the transaxle input shaft seal or torque converter-to-transaxle seal.

2   Remove the pressure plate and clutch disc (see Chapter 8) (manual transaxle equipped vehicles). Now is a good time to check/replace the clutch components.

3   Use a center-punch to make alignment marks on the flywheel/driveplate and crank-

shaft to ensure correct alignment during reinstallation.

4   Remove the bolts that secure the flywheel/driveplate to the crankshaft. If the crankshaft turns, wedge a screwdriver through the starter opening to jam the flywheel.

5   Remove the flywheel/driveplate from the crankshaft. Since the flywheel is fairly heavy, be sure to support it while removing the last bolt.

6   Clean the flywheel to remove grease and oil. Inspect the surface for cracks, rivet grooves, burned areas and score marks. Light scoring can be removed with emery cloth. Check for cracked and broken ring gear teeth. Lay the flywheel on a flat surface and use a straightedge to check for warpage.

7   Clean and inspect the mating surfaces of the flywheel/driveplate and the crankshaft. If the crankshaft rear seal is leaking, replace it before reinstalling the flywheel/driveplate.

8   Position the flywheel/driveplate against the crankshaft. Be sure to align the marks made during removal. Note that some engines have an alignment dowel or staggered bolt holes to ensure correct installation. Before installing the bolts, apply thread locking compound to the threads.

9   Wedge a screwdriver through the starter motor opening to keep the flywheel/driveplate from turning as you tighten the bolts in a criss-cross pattern to the torque listed in this Chapter's Specifications.

10   The remainder of installation is the reverse of the removal procedure.

16   Crankshaft front oil seal - replacement

1   Disconnect the negative cable from the battery.

2   Remove the drivebelt (see Chapter 1).

3   Securely block the rear wheels so the vehicle won't roll, then jack up the front and place it securely on jackstands. DO NOT get under a vehicle that's supported only by a jack!

4   Remove the splash shield from the passenger's side of the vehicle.

5   Remove the crankshaft damper and timing belt (see Section 5).

6   Remove the timing belt pulley and guide from the crankshaft (see Section 5).

7   Using a suitable hooked tool, pry out the oil seal from the oil pump housing.

8   Apply a coat of light engine oil to the lip of the new seal and press it into position using a seal replacer tool, if available. If not, tap the seal into position with a socket with an outside diameter slightly smaller than the outside diameter of the seal.

9   The remainder of installation is the reverse of the removal steps. Be sure to follow the timing belt installation procedures in Section 5.

18.3 Support the engine with a jack and block of wood whenever you remove the mount fasteners

18.9a The front engine mount mounting bolts (arrows)

17 Crankshaft rear oil seal - replacement

1   Disconnect the battery negative cable.
2   Remove the transaxle (see Chapter 7).
3   On automatic transaxle models, remove the driveplate (see Section 15).
4   On manual transaxle models, remove the flywheel (see Section 15).
5   Pry the old seal out of the seal retainer using a seal removal tool (if available) or a screwdriver with its tip protected by a rag.
6   On all models, coat the lip of the new seal with clean engine oil.
7   Press the new seal into position. If the seal retainer is removed from the engine, use a block of wood and a hammer. If the retainer is still on the engine, use a special tool, available at most auto parts stores.
8   The remainder of installation is the reverse of the removal steps.
9   Run the engine and check for oil leaks.

18 Engine mounts - check and replacement

Refer to illustrations 18.3, 18.9a, 18.9b and 18.9c

1   Engine mounts seldom require attention, but broken or deteriorated mounts should be replaced immediately or the added strain placed on the driveline components may cause damage or wear.

Check

2   During the check, the engine must be raised slightly to remove the weight from the mounts.
3   Raise the vehicle and support it securely on jackstands, then position a jack under the engine oil pan **(see illustration)**. Place a large block of wood between the jack head and the oil pan, then carefully raise the engine just enough to take the weight off the mounts. **Warning:** *DO NOT place any part of your body under the engine when it's supported only by a jack!*

4   Check the mounts to see if the rubber is cracked, hardened or separated from the metal.
5   Check for relative movement between the mount and the engine or frame. Use a large screwdriver or prybar to attempt to move the mounts. If movement is noted, lower the engine and tighten the mount fasteners.
6   Rubber preservative should be applied to the mounts to slow deterioration.

Replacement

7   Disconnect the negative battery cable from the battery.
8   Support the engine with a jack **(see illustration 19.3)**.
9   Remove the fasteners and detach the mount from the engine and chassis **(see illustrations)**.
10   Installation is the reverse of the removal procedures with the following additions.
11   Use thread locking compound on the mount bolts and tighten the bolts securely.

18.9b Mounting bolts for the rear engine mount (arrows)

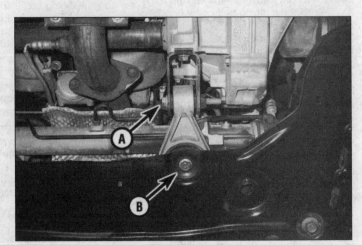

18.9c Remove the through-bolt (A) and the frame bolt (B) to remove the transaxle mount

Chapter 2 Part B
2.0L Zetec-E engine

Contents

Specifications

General

Engine type	Four-cylinder, in-line, DOHC
Engine VIN code	
Zetec-E engine	3
Duratec (SVT) engine	5
Displacement	1989 cc (121 cubic inches)
Bore	3.341 inches
Stroke	3.467 inches
Firing order	1-3-4-2

36034-1-00.A HAYNES

Cylinder location and coil terminal arrangement

Camshafts

Camshaft bearing journal diameter	1.022 to 1.024 inches
Camshaft bearing journal-to-cylinder head running clearance	0.0007 to 0.0027 inch
Camshaft endplay	0.003 to 0.009 inch

Valves

Valve clearances (cold)	
Intake	0.004 to 0.007 inch
Exhaust	0.011 to 0.013 inch

Cylinder head

Maximum permissible gasket surface distortion	0.004 inch

Lubrication

Engine oil capacity	See Chapter 1
Oil pressure (engine at operating temperature)	
At idle (800 to 850 rpm)	19 to 36 psi
At 4000 rpm	53 to 81 psi

Torque specifications   Ft-lbs (unless otherwise indicated)

Note: *One foot-pound (ft-lb) of torque is equivalent to 12 inch-pounds (in-lbs) of torque. Torque values below approximately 15 ft-lbs are expressed in inch-pounds, since most foot-pound torque wrenches are not accurate at these smaller values.*

Camshaft bearing cap bolts	
Zetec-E engines	
Stage 1	89 in-lbs
Stage 2	168 in-lbs
Duratec (SVT) engines	
Stage 1	89 in-lbs
Stage 2	132 in-lbs

Torque specifications (continued)

Ft-lbs (unless otherwise indicated)

Note: *One foot-pound (ft-lb) of torque is equivalent to 12 inch-pounds (in-lbs) of torque. Torque values below approximately 15 ft-lbs are expressed in inch-pounds, since most foot-pound torque wrenches are not accurate at these smaller values.*

Camshaft sprocket bolts	50
Crankshaft pulley bolt	85
Crankshaft rear oil seal carrier bolts	15
Cylinder head bolts **(in sequence - see illustration 12.42)**	
Stage 1	132 in-lbs
Stage 2	30
Stage 3	Angle-tighten a further 90°
Valve cover bolts	60 in-lbs
Exhaust manifold heat shield bolts	89 in-lbs
Exhaust manifold nuts and bolts	144 in-lbs
Flywheel bolts	83
Intake manifold nuts and bolts	156 in-lbs
Lower crankcase to cylinder block	
Zetec-E engine	16
Duratec (SVT) engine	22
Oil pick-up pipe bolts	84 in-lbs
Oil pump-to-cylinder block bolts	88 in-lbs
Oil pan to lower crankcase	
Stage 1	53 in-lbs
Stage 2	89 in-lbs
Spark plug cover bolts (Duratec SVT)	88 in-lbs
Timing belt covers	
Lower cover bolts	60 in-lbs
Middle cover bolts	37
Upper cover bolts	89 in-lbs
Timing belt guide pulley bolt	17
Timing belt tensioner bolt	18
Transaxle-to-engine bolts	35
Variable camshaft timing assembly (Duratec SVT)	
Bolt to camshaft	89

1   General information

How to use this Chapter

This Part of Chapter 2 is devoted to repair procedures possible while the engine is still installed in the vehicle. Since these procedures are based on the assumption that the engine is installed in the vehicle, if the engine has been removed from the vehicle and mounted on a stand, some of the preliminary dismantling steps outlined will not apply.

Information concerning engine/transmission removal and replacement and engine overhaul, can be found in Part C of this Chapter.

Engine description

The Zetec-E engine is of sixteen-valve, double overhead camshaft (DOHC), four-cylinder, in-line type, mounted transversely at the front of the vehicle, with the transmission on its left-hand end. Apart from the plastic timing belt covers, fiberglass intake manifold and the cast-iron cylinder block/crankcase, all major engine castings are of aluminum alloy. The engine differs from previous generations of the Zetec in that it has a cast aluminum alloy lower crankcase that is bolted to the underside of the cylinder block/crankcase, with a pressed-steel oil pan bolted under that. This arrangement offers greater rigidity than the normal oil pan arrangement, and helps to reduce engine vibration.

The crankshaft runs in five main bearings, the center main bearing's upper half incorporating thrustwashers to control crankshaft endplay. The connecting rods rotate on horizontally-split bearing shells at their big-ends. The pistons are attached to the connecting rods by wrist pins that are an interference fit in the connecting rod small-end eyes. The aluminum alloy pistons are fitted with three piston rings: two compression rings and an oil control ring. After manufacture, the cylinder bores and piston skirts are measured and classified into three grades, which must be carefully matched together to ensure the correct piston/cylinder clearance; no oversizes are available to permit reboring.

The intake and exhaust valves are each closed by coil springs; they operate in guides that are shrink-fitted into the cylinder head, as are the valve seat inserts.

The two camshafts are driven by the same toothed timing belt, each operating eight valves via conventional cam followers with shims. Each camshaft rotates in five bearings that are line-bored directly in the cylinder head and the (bolted-on) bearing caps; this means that the bearing caps are not available separately from the cylinder head, and must not be interchanged with caps from another engine.

The water pump is bolted to the right-hand end of the cylinder block, inboard of the timing belt, and is driven with the steering pump and alternator by a multi-ribbed auxiliary drivebelt from the crankshaft pulley.

When working on this engine, note that Torx-type (both male and female heads) and hexagon socket (Allen head) fasteners are widely used; a good selection of sockets, with the necessary adapters, will be required, so that these can be unscrewed without damage and, on reassembly, tightened to the torque wrench settings specified.

The Duratec engine is a high-performance version of the Zetec four-cylinder, installed only in the SVT models. Many of the components have been redesigned for increased performance, but repair procedures are very similar to those for the Zetec-E. One significant difference is that the intake camshaft of the Duratec engine has a Variable Camshaft Timing assembly and the intake manifold is of a two-piece design with variable-length runners.

Lubrication system

Lubrication is by means of an eccentric-rotor trochoidal pump, which is mounted on the crankshaft right-hand end, and draws oil through a strainer located in the oil pan. The pump forces oil through an externally-mounted full-flow cartridge-type filter. From the filter, the oil is pumped into a main gallery in the cylinder block/crankcase, from where it is distributed to the crankshaft (main bearings) and cylinder head.

The connecting rod bearings are supplied with oil via internal drillings in the crankshaft. Each piston crown is cooled by a spray of oil directed at its underside by a jet. These jets are fed by passages off the crankshaft oil supply galleries, with spring-loaded valves to ensure that the jets open only when there is sufficient pressure to guarantee a good oil supply to the rest of the engine components; where the jets are not fitted, separate blanking plugs are provided so that the passages are sealed, but can be cleaned at overhaul.

The cylinder head is provided with two oil galleries, one on the intake side and one on the exhaust, to ensure constant oil supply to the camshaft bearings and cam followers. A retaining valve (inserted into the cylinder head's top surface, in the middle, on the intake side) prevents these galleries from being drained when the engine is switched off. The valve incorporates a ventilation hole in its upper end, to allow air bubbles to escape from the system when the engine is restarted.

While the crankshaft and camshaft bearings receive a pressurized supply, the camshaft lobes and valves are lubricated by splash, as are all other engine components.

Repair operations possible with the engine in the vehicle

The following major repair operations can be accomplished without removing the engine from the vehicle. However, owners should note that any operation involving the removal of the oil pan requires careful forethought, depending on the level of skill and the tools and facilities available; refer to the relevant text for details.

a) Compression pressure - testing.
b) Valve cover - removal and installation.
c) Timing belt covers - removal and installation.
d) Timing belt - replacement.
e) Timing belt tensioner and sprockets - removal and installation.
f) Camshaft oil seals - replacement.
g) Camshafts and cam followers - removal and installation.
h) Cylinder head - removal, overhaul and installation.
i) Cylinder head and pistons - Decarbonizing.
j) Oil pan - removal and installation.
k) Crankshaft oil seals - replacement.
l) Oil pump - removal and installation.
m) Piston/connecting rod assemblies - removal and installation (but see note below).

n) Flywheel - removal and installation.
o) Engine/transmission mounts - removal and installation.

Note: It is possible to remove the pistons and connecting rods (after removing the cylinder head and oil pan) without removing the engine. However, this is not recommended; work of this nature is more easily and thoroughly completed with the engine removed from the vehicle, as described in Chapter 2D.

Clean the engine compartment and the exterior of the engine with some type of degreaser before any work is done (and/or clean the engine using a steam cleaner). It will make the job easier and will help to keep dirt out of the internal areas of the engine.

Depending on the components involved, it may be helpful to remove the hood, to improve access to the engine as repairs are performed (refer to Chapter 11 if necessary). Cover the fenders to prevent damage to the paint; special covers are available, but an old bedspread or blanket will also work.

2 Compression test - description and interpretation

1 When engine performance is down, or if misfiring occurs which cannot be attributed to the ignition or fuel systems, a compression test can provide diagnostic clues as to the engine's condition. If the test is performed regularly, it can give warning of trouble before any other symptoms become apparent.

2 The engine must be fully warmed-up to normal operating temperature, the oil level must be correct, the battery must be fully charged and the spark plugs must be removed. The aid of an assistant will also be required.

3 Disable the ignition system by disconnecting the ignition coil's electrical connector.

4 Referring to Chapter 12, identify and remove the fuel pump fuse from the fusebox. Now start the engine and allow it to run until it stalls. If the engine will not start, at least keep it cranking for about 10 seconds. The fuel system should now be depressurized, preventing unburned fuel from soaking the catalytic converter as the engine is turned over during the test.

5 Install a compression tester to the Number 1 cylinder spark plug hole - the type of tester which screws into the plug thread is to be preferred.

6 Have an assistant hold the throttle wide open and crank the engine on the starter motor; after one or two revolutions, the compression pressure should build up to a maximum figure and then stabilize. Record the highest reading obtained.

7 The compression will build up fairly quickly in a healthy engine. Low compression on the first stroke, followed by gradually-increasing pressure on successive strokes, indicates worn piston rings. A low compression on the first stroke which does not rise on successive strokes, indicates leaking valves or a blown head gasket (a cracked cylinder

head could also be the cause). Deposits on the underside of the valve heads can also cause low compression. Record the highest gauge reading obtained, then repeat the procedure for the remaining cylinders.

8 Due to the variety of testers available, and the fluctuation in starter motor speed when cranking the engine, different readings are often obtained when carrying out the compression test. For this reason, specific compression pressure figures are not quoted by the manufacturer. However, the most important factor is that the compression pressures are uniform in all cylinders, and that is what this test is mainly concerned with.

9 If the pressure in any cylinder is considerably lower than the others, add a teaspoonful of clean oil into that cylinder through its spark plug hole and repeat the test.

10 If the addition of oil temporarily improves the compression pressure, this indicates that bore or piston ring wear is responsible for the pressure loss. No improvement suggests that leaking or burnt valves, or a blown head gasket, may be to blame.

11 A low reading from two adjacent cylinders is almost certainly due to the head gasket having blown between them; the presence of coolant in the engine oil will confirm this.

12 If one cylinder is about 20 percent lower than the others and the engine has a slightly rough idle, a worn camshaft lobe or faulty cam follower/shim could be the cause.

13 If the compression is unusually high, the combustion chambers are probably coated with carbon deposits. If this is the case, the cylinder head should be removed and decarbonized.

14 On completion of the test, install the spark plugs, then reconnect the ignition system coil and install the fuel pump fuse.

3 Top Dead Center (TDC) for Number 1 piston - locating

Refer to illustrations 3.5a, 35.b, 3.6, 3.7a, 3.7b and 3.7c

1 Top dead center (TDC) is the highest point of the cylinder that each piston reaches as the crankshaft turns. Each piston reaches its TDC position at the end of its compression stroke, and then again at the end of its exhaust stroke. For the purpose of engine timing, TDC on the compression stroke for the Number 1 piston is used. The Number 1 cylinder is at the timing belt end of the engine. Proceed as follows.

2 Disconnect the battery negative cable (see Chapter 1).

3 Remove all the spark plugs as described in Chapter 1, then remove the valve cover as described in Section 4.

4 Using a wrench or socket on the crankshaft pulley bolt (remove the panel in the fenderwell liner for access), rotate the crankshaft clockwise until the intake valves for the Number 1 cylinder have opened and just closed again.

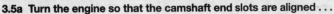

3.5a Turn the engine so that the camshaft end slots are aligned . . .

3.5b . . . then insert the metal strip into the slots to locate and set the shafts to TDC

5   The camshafts each have a machined slot at the transmission end of the engine; both slots will be completely horizontal, and at the same height as the cylinder head machined surface, when the engine is at TDC on the Number 1 cylinder. Service tool 303-376 is used to check this position, and to positively locate the camshafts in position. Fortunately, a substitute tool can be made from a strip of metal 5 mm thick (while the strip's thickness is critical, its length and width are not, but should be approximately 180 to 230 mm long by 20 to 30 mm wide) **(see illustrations).**

6   A TDC timing hole is provided on the front of the cylinder block to permit the crankshaft to be located more accurately at TDC. The blanking plug is located behind the catalytic converter, and access is not easy - also, take care against burning if the engine is still warm **(see illustration).**

7   Unscrew the timing pin blanking plug and screw in the timing pin (service tool 303-620); this tool is obtainable from a dealer or a tool supplier. An alternative pin can be made from an M10 diameter bolt, cut down so that the length from the underside of the bolt head to the tip is exactly 63.4 mm **(see illustra-**

tions). It may be necessary to slightly turn the crankshaft either way (remove the tool from the camshafts first) to be able to fully insert the timing pin.

8   Turn the engine forwards slowly until the crankshaft comes into contact with the timing pin - in this position, the engine is set to TDC on the Number 1 cylinder.

9   Before rotating the crankshaft again, make sure that the timing pin is removed. When operations are complete, do not forget to install the blanking plug.

10   If the timing pin is not available, insert a length of wooden dowel (about 150 mm/ 6 in long) or similar into the Number 1 spark plug hole until it rests on the piston crown. Turn the engine back from its TDC position, then forward (taking care not to allow the dowel to be trapped in the cylinder) until the dowel stops rising - the piston is now at the top of its compression stroke and the dowel can be removed.

11   There is a 'dead' area around TDC (as the piston stops rising, pauses and then begins to descend) which makes it difficult to find the exact location of TDC by this method; if accuracy is required, either carefully establish the exact mid-point of the dead area (per-

haps by using a dial gauge and probe), or refer to Step 5.

12   Once the Number 1 cylinder has been positioned at TDC on the compression stroke, TDC for any of the other cylinders can then be located by rotating the crankshaft clockwise 180° at a time and following the firing order (see Specifications).

3.6 Remove the timing hole blanking plug - catalytic converter removed for clarity

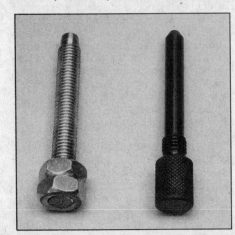

3.7a Home-made (left) and genuine (right) timing pins

3.7b Insert the timing pin in the hole . . .

3.7c . . . and screw it fully into position

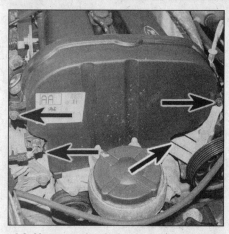

4.3 Unscrew the timing belt upper cover bolts (arrows)

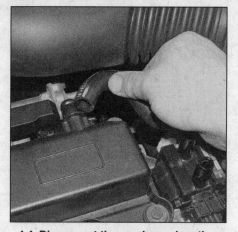

4.4 Disconnect the crankcase breather hose from the cover

4.5 Twist the spark plug wire boots, then remove the plug wires from the spark plugs

4   Valve cover - removal and installation

Refer to illustrations 4.3, 4.4, 4.5, 4.6a and 4.6b

Removal

1   Disconnect the battery negative cable (see Chapter 5).
2   Where applicable, disconnect the ground cable and power steering pipe support bracket from the cylinder head rear support plate/engine lifting eye. Move the pipe to one side.
3   Unscrew the four bolts securing the plastic timing belt upper cover to the cylinder head **(see illustration)**. It will not be possible to completely remove the cover, as the engine/transmission right-hand mounting restricts this; however, once unbolted, the cover can be moved to one side to permit the removal of the valve cover.
4   Disconnect the crankcase breather hose from the valve cover fitting **(see illustration)**. On SVT models, disconnect the electrical connector from the VCT solenoid, at the engine side of the upper timing cover.
5   Unplug the spark plug wires from the spark plugs and withdraw them, unclipping the leads from the cover **(see illustration)**. On SVT models, first remove the screws and the spark plug wire cover. On models with coil-on-plug ignition, disconnect the electrical connectors at the coils, then unbolt and remove the individual coils.
6   Working progressively, unscrew the valve cover retaining bolts, noting the (captive) spacer sleeve and rubber seal at each, then withdraw the cover **(see illustrations)**.
7   Discard the cover gasket; this must be replaced whenever it is disturbed. Check that the sealing faces are undamaged and that the rubber seal at each bolt hole is serviceable; replace any worn or damaged seals.

Installation

8   On installation, clean the cover and cylinder head gasket faces carefully, then fit a new gasket to the cover, ensuring that it is located correctly by the rubber seals and spacer sleeves.
9   Install the cover to the cylinder head, ensuring as the cover is tightened that the gasket remains seated.
10   Working in a diagonal sequence from the center outwards, first tighten the cover bolts by hand only. Once all the bolts are hand-tight, go around once more in sequence, and tighten the bolts to the specified torque wrench setting.
11   Install the spark plug wires, clipping them into place so that they are correctly routed; each is numbered and can also be identified by the numbering on its respective coil terminal. On SVT models, replace the spark plug wire cover. On models with coil-on-plug ignition, reinstall the coils, using a small amount of dielectric grease inside the boot end, then connect the electrical connectors to each coil.
12   Reconnect the crankcase breather hose and install the timing belt upper cover bolts. Reconnect the VCT solenoid connector on SVT models.
13   Reconnect the ground cable and power steering pipe to the engine lifting eye, and reconnect the battery. On completion, run the engine and check for signs of oil leakage.

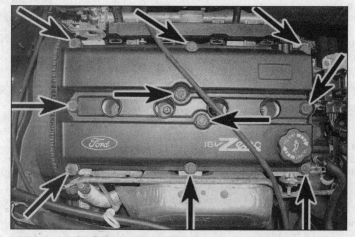

4.6a Remove the retaining bolts (arrows) . . .

4.6b . . . and lift off the valve cover

5.3 Check the valve clearances with a feeler gauge of the specified thickness

6.4a Unscrew and remove the pulley bolt . . .

6.4b . . . and remove the crankshaft pulley

5   Valve clearances - checking and adjustment

Note: *For DIY purposes, note that while checking the valve clearances is an easy operation, changing the shims requires the use of a manufacturers special tool - owners may prefer to have this work carried out by a dealer.*

Checking

Refer to illustration 5.3

1   Remove the valve cover as described in Section 4.

2   Set the Number 1 cylinder to TDC on the compression stroke as described in Section 3. The intake and exhaust cam lobes of the Number 1 cylinder will be pointing upwards (though not vertical) and the valve clearances can be checked.

3   Working on each valve in turn, measure the clearance between the base of the cam lobe and the shim using feeler gauges **(see illustration)**. Record the thickness of the blade required to give a firm sliding fit on all four valves of the Number 1 cylinder.

4   Now turn the crankshaft clockwise through 180° so that the valves of cylinder Number 3 are pointing upwards. Measure and record the valve clearances for cylinder Number 3. The clearances for cylinders 4 and 2 can be measured after turning the crankshaft through 180° each time. Any measured valve clearances that do not fall in the specified range (see Specifications) must be adjusted.

Adjustment

Note: *Use of the manufacturer special tool is highly recommended, as the design of the camshafts and cylinder head and the lack of space mean that it would not be possible to use a screwdriver or similar tool to depress the cam follower without serious risk of damage to the cylinder head. The only alternative is to measure the clearances very carefully (measure each several times, record the clear-*ances *measured, and take the average as determining the true value. Access can then be gained to the shims by removing the camshafts (see Section 11) so that all relevant shims can be changed without the need for special tools. This approach requires very careful, methodical work if the camshafts are not to be removed and replaced several times.*

5   If adjustment is required, the shim thicknesses must be changed by depressing the cam follower and removing the old shim, then fitting a new one.

6   Before changing a shim, the piston for the relevant cylinder needs to be lowered from its TDC position by turning the crankshaft approximately 90° clockwise. If this is not done, the piston will be too close to the valve to allow the cam follower to be depressed, and there is a risk of the valve being bent.

7   Dealer technicians use service tool 303-563A, which is bolted onto the cylinder head above each camshaft in turn using two of the camshaft bearing cap bolt locations - a spacer 8 x 12 mm (or equivalent thickness of 8 mm washers) may be required to allow the tool to be bolted onto the head. Locate the operating end of the tool onto the cam follower and operate the handle to depress the cam follower.

8   Take great care not to scratch or otherwise damage the cam follower and its housing. Remove the shim with a small screwdriver or magnetic probe, taking care not to scratch or damage the cam follower, then slowly release the pressure applied to the tool. Do not rotate the camshaft while a shim is removed - the risk of damage to the cam lobe and/or cam follower is too great.

9   Record the thickness of the shim (in mm) which is engraved on the side facing away from the camshaft. If the marking is missing or illegible, a micrometer will be needed to establish shim thickness.

10   If the valve clearance was too small, a thinner shim must be installed. If the clearance was too large, a thicker shim must be installed. When the shim thickness and the valve clearance are known, the required thickness of the new shim can be calculated as follows:

Sample calculation - clearance too small
   Desired clearance (A) = 0.15 mm
   Measured clearance (B) = 0.09 mm
   Shim thickness found (C) = 2.55 mm
   Thickness required (D) =
   $C + B - A = 2.49 mm$

Sample calculation - clearance too large
   Desired clearance (A) = 0.30 mm
   Measured clearance (B) = 0.36 mm
   Shim thickness found (C) = 2.19 mm
   Thickness required (D) =
   $C + B - A = 2.25 mm$

11   Depress the cam follower again, and press the correct shim into the recess in the cam follower with the thickness marking facing downwards. Ensure that the shim is properly located in the cam follower, and apply a smear of clean oil to it.

12   When all the clearances of the first cylinder's valves have been set, rotate the crankshaft through two full turns clockwise to settle the shims. Return the cylinder to TDC on the compression stroke and recheck the valve clearances. Repeat the procedure from step 10 onwards if any are still incorrect.

13   Repeat the process for the remaining cylinders, turning the crankshaft to bring each in turn first to the TDC position and then 90° after TDC, as described above.

14   It will be helpful for future adjustment if a record is kept of the thickness of shim fitted at each position. The shims required can be purchased in advance once the clearances and the existing shim thicknesses are known. It is permissible to interchange shims between cam followers to achieve the correct clearances, but it is not advisable to turn the camshaft with any shims removed, since there is a risk that the cam lobe will jam in the empty cam follower.

15   When all the clearances are correct, remove the tool, then install the valve cover as described in Section 4.

7.1a Unscrew the expansion tank mount bolt (arrow) . . .

7.1b . . . and unclip the tank at the rear

7.2 Lift out the power steering fluid reservoir

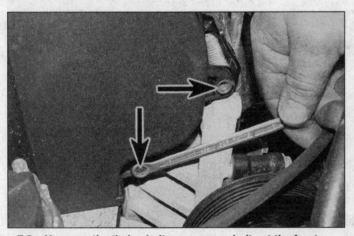

7.3a Unscrew the timing belt upper cover bolts at the front . . .

7.3b . . . and at the rear (arrows)

6 Crankshaft pulley - removal and installation

Removal

Refer to illustrations 6.4a and 6.4b

1   Remove the auxiliary drivebelt - either remove the drivebelt completely, or just secure it clear of the crankshaft pulley, depending on the work to be carried out (see Chapter 1).

2   If the pulley is being removed as part of another procedure (such as timing belt replacement) it will be easier to set the engine to TDC now (as described in Section 3) before removing the crankshaft pulley bolt.

3   The crankshaft must now be held or locked to prevent its rotation while the pulley bolt is unscrewed. Two holes are provided in the front face of the pulley, for use with a forked holding tool (with a bolt at each end of the forks, to locate in the holes). Such a tool can easily be fabricated from metal strips, but if preferred, proceed as follows:

a) If the engine/transaxle is still installed in the vehicle, select high gear and have an assistant apply the brakes hard.

b) If the engine/transaxle has been removed but not yet separated, remove the starter motor (see Chapter 5) and lock the flywheel ring gear by jamming it with a screwdriver against the bellhousing.

c) If the engine/transaxle has been removed and separated, use the method shown in Section 17, for removing the flywheel.

Note: *NEVER use the timing pin as a means of locking the crankshaft - it is not strong enough for this, and will shear off. Always ensure that the timing pin is removed before the crankshaft pulley bolt (or similar fasteners) is slackened or tightened.*

4   Unscrew the pulley bolt and remove the pulley, noting which way round it is fitted **(see illustrations)**.

Installation

5   The manufacturer does not require that a new pulley bolt be installed; however, note that it is tightened to a very high torque. Given its important role, it would be worth replacing the bolt when installing the pulley, especially if it is known to have been loosened previously.

6   Installation is the reverse of the removal procedure; ensure that the pulley's keyway is aligned with the crankshaft's locating key.

Tighten the pulley bolt to the specified torque setting, locking the crankshaft using the same method as for loosening.

7 Timing belt covers - removal and installation

Upper cover

Removal

Refer to illustrations 7.1a, 7.1b, 7.2, 7.3a, 7.3b, 7.4, 7.5a, 7.5b, 7.5c, 7.6, 7.7a and 7.7b

1   To improve access to the cover, remove the coolant expansion tank mounting bolt, unclip it at the rear, and move the tank to one side without disconnecting the hoses **(see illustrations)**. Remove the drivebelt and drivebelt idler pulley (see Chapter 1).

2   Unclip the power steering fluid reservoir from its location, and move it aside, again without disturbing the hoses **(see illustration)**.

3   Unscrew the four bolts and withdraw the upper cover as far as possible **(see illustrations)**. To remove the upper cover completely, the engine must be supported, as the right-hand engine mount must be removed.

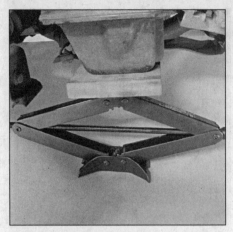

7.4 Jack and block of wood supporting the engine

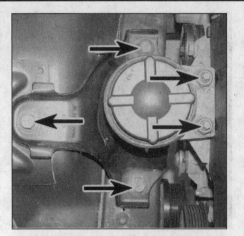

7.5a Engine right-hand mount nuts/bolts (arrows)

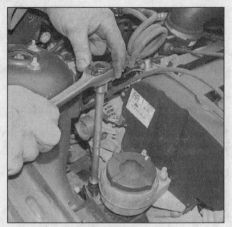

7.5b Loosen the nuts and bolts . . .

4　Position a jack at the timing belt end of the oil pan, with a large block of wood between the oil pan and the jack head, and raise the jack so that the weight of the engine is supported **(see illustration)**.

5　Mark the fitted position of the engine mounting on the inner fender before removing it. Progressively loosen and remove the nuts/bolts, then lift off the right-hand mounting **(see illustrations)**.

6　To completely remove the cover, the engine right-hand mounting studs must be unscrewed - these have Torx end fittings, so they can be unscrewed using a suitable socket **(see illustration)**.

7　Unclip the cylinder head temperature sensor wiring plug attached to the rear of the cover, then lift off the upper cover and remove it **(see illustrations)**.

Installation

8　Installation is the reverse of the removal procedure. Tighten the mounting studs securely, align the engine mounting with the marks made before removal, and tighten all bolts to the specified torque setting.

Middle cover

Removal

Refer to illustrations 7.15a, 7.15b and 7.16

9　Unbolt the coolant expansion tank,

7.5c . . . and take off the engine mount

unclip it from the fender, and position it to one side without disconnecting the hoses.

10　Unclip the power steering fluid reservoir from its location, and move it aside, again without disturbing the hoses.

11　Support the engine using a floor jack and large block of wood beneath the oil pan. Unbolt the engine right-hand mount.

12　Loosen the water pump pulley bolts.

7.6 Unscrew and remove the engine mount studs

13　Remove the auxiliary drivebelt (see Chapter 1).

14　Remove the timing belt upper cover as described previously in this Section.

15　Unbolt the water pump pulley, and also the auxiliary drivebelt idler pulley **(see illustrations)**.

16　Unscrew the four middle cover bolts (one of which is a Torx type - note its location) and withdraw the cover **(see illustration)**.

7.7a Unclip the wiring plug at the rear of the cover . . .

7.7b . . . then lift off the cover

7.15a Unbolt and remove the water pump pulley . . .

7.15b . . . and the auxiliary drivebelt idler pulley

7.16 Remove the timing belt middle cover

7.19a Unscrew the bolts (arrows) . . .

7.19b . . . and remove the timing belt lower cover

7.22 Remove the inner shield (cylinder head removed for clarity)

Installation

17   Installation is the reverse of the removal procedure. Ensure the cover edges engage correctly with each other, and note the torque settings specified for the various fasteners.

Lower cover

Removal

Refer to illustrations 7.19a and 7.19b

18   Remove the crankshaft pulley (see Section 6).

19   Unscrew the cover's securing bolts and withdraw it **(see illustrations)**.

Installation

20   Installation is the reverse of the removal procedure. Ensure the cover edges engage correctly with each other, and note the torque settings specified for the various fasteners.

Inner shield/cover

Removal

Refer to illustration 7.22

21   Remove the timing belt, its tensioner components and the camshaft sprockets (see Sections 8 and 9).

22   The shield is secured to the cylinder head by two bolts at the top; unscrew these and withdraw the shield **(see illustration)**.

Installation

23   Installation is the reverse of the removal procedure; note the torque settings specified for the various fasteners.

---

8   Timing belt - removal, installation and tensioning

Note: *To carry out this operation, a new timing belt (where applicable), a new valve cover gasket and some special tools (see text) will be required.*

Removal

> **** CAUTION ****
> The timing system is complex. Severe engine damage will occur if you make any mistakes. Do not attempt this procedure unless you are highly experienced with this type of repair. If you are at all unsure of your abilities, consult an expert. Double-check all your work and be sure everything is correct before you attempt to start the engine.

Refer to illustrations 8.3, 8.11a, 8.11b and 8.12
1   Disconnect the negative battery cable (see Chapter 5).

2   Apply the parking brake, then jack up the right-hand front wheel, and support the vehicle on an axle stand (see *Jacking and Towing*).
3   Remove the fasteners securing the right-hand front fenderwell liner in position, and withdraw the liner for access to the auxiliary drivebelt and crankshaft pulley **(see illustration)**. Also unbolt and remove the auxiliary drivebelt lower cover.

8.3 Remove the right-hand front fenderwell liner

4   Loosen the three water pump pulley bolts while the drivebelt is still installed.

5   Remove the crankshaft pulley as described in Section 6, then unbolt and remove the timing belt lower cover, referring to Section 7 if necessary. Also unbolt and remove the water pump pulley. Once this has been done, the car can be lowered if preferred.

6   Remove the timing belt upper and middle covers as described in Section 7.

7   Remove the valve cover as described in Section 4.

8   Set the engine to TDC on the Number 1 cylinder, as described in Section 3. For this operation, the timing pin described must be used to ensure accuracy. Once the spark plugs have been removed, cover their holes with clean rags, to prevent dirt from dropping in.

9   Before removing the timing belt, note that manufacturer service tool 303-376 will be needed, to set the camshafts to their TDC position. Fortunately, a substitute tool can be made from a strip of metal 5 mm thick (while the strip's thickness is critical, its length and width are not, but should be approximately 180 to 230 mm long by 20 to 30 mm wide) **(see illustration 3.5b)**.

10   If the timing belt is to be re-used (and this is not recommended), mark it with paint to indicate its direction of rotation (clockwise, viewed from the timing belt end of the engine).

11   Loosen the timing belt tensioner bolt, and turn the tensioner clockwise, using an Allen key in the hole provided. Now unscrew the bolt and unhook the tensioner from the inner shield **(see illustrations)**.

12   Ensuring that the sprockets are turned as little as possible, slide the timing belt off the sprockets and pulleys, and remove it **(see illustration)**.

13   If the timing belt is not being installed right now (or if the belt is being removed as part of another procedure, such as cylinder head removal), temporarily install the engine right-hand mount and tighten the bolts securely.

14   If the old belt is likely to be reinstalled, check it carefully for any signs of uneven wear, splitting, cracks (especially at the roots

8.11a Unscrew the bolt . . .

8.11b . . . then unhook and remove the timing belt tensioner

of the belt teeth).

15   Even if a new belt is to be installed, check the old one for signs of oil or coolant. If evident, trace the source of the leak and rectify it, then clean the engine timing belt area and related components to remove all traces of oil or coolant. Do not simply install a new belt in this instance, or its service life will be greatly reduced, increasing the risk of engine damage if it fails in service.

16   Always replace the belt if there is the slightest doubt about its condition. As a precaution against engine damage, the belt must be replaced as a matter of course at the intervals given in Chapter 1; if the car's history is unknown, the belt should be replaced irrespective of its apparent condition whenever the engine is overhauled.

17   Similarly check the belt tensioner, replacing it if there is any doubt about its condition. Check also the sprockets and pulleys for signs of wear or damage (and particularly cracking), and ensure that the tensioner and guide pulleys rotate smoothly on their bearings; replace any worn or damaged components. **Note:** *It is considered good practice by many professional mechanics to replace tensioner and guide pulley assemblies as a matter of course, whenever the timing belt is replaced.*

Installation

> **** CAUTION ****
> Before starting the engine, carefully rotate the crankshaft by hand through at least two full revolutions (use a socket and breaker bar on the crankshaft pulley center bolt). If you feel any resistance, STOP! There is something wrong - most likely, valves are contacting the pistons. You must find the problem before proceeding. Check your work and see if any updated repair information is available.

Refer to illustrations 8.19, 8.25a, 8.25b and 8.26

18   Without turning the crankshaft more than a few degrees, check that the engine is still set to TDC on the Number 1 cylinder - i.e., that the timing pin is still inserted.

19   The TDC position of the camshafts must now be set, and for this, the camshaft sprocket bolts must be loosened. A holding tool will be required to prevent the camshaft sprockets from rotating while their bolts are slackened and retightened; either obtain manufacturer service tool 205-072, or fabricate a substitute

8.12 When removing the timing belt, ensure the sprockets do not turn

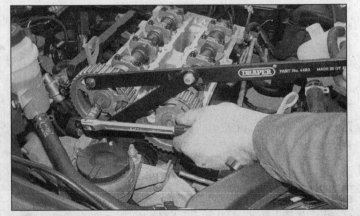

8.19 Use a sprocket holding tool while loosening the camshaft sprocket bolts

8.25a Use an Allen key to set the tensioner pointer in the center of the square window . . .

8.25b . . . then hold it while the tensioner bolt is tightened to the specified torque

as follows. Find two lengths of steel strip, one approximately two feet long and the other about eight inches long, and three bolts with nuts and washers; one nut and bolt forming the pivot of a forked tool, with the remaining nuts and bolts at the tips of the 'forks', to engage with the sprocket spokes (see illustration). Note 1: *Do not use the camshaft setting tool (whether manufacturer or not) to prevent rotation while the camshaft sprocket bolts are loosened or tightened; the risk of damage to the camshaft concerned and to the cylinder head is far too great. Use only a forked holding tool applied directly to the sprockets, as described.* Note 2: *As an alternative, the camshaft can be held with a large open-end wrench on the hex portion of the camshaft while loosening the sprocket bolts.*

20 Loosen the camshaft sprocket bolts, ensuring that the camshafts are turned as little as possible as this is done. The bolts should be loose enough that the sprockets are free to turn on the shafts. It is essential that the bolts are left loose until the timing belt has been installed and tensioned, otherwise the valve timing will not be accurate.

21 The tool described in Step 9 is now required. Rest the tool on the cylinder head mating surface, and slide it into the slot in the left-hand end of both camshafts. The tool should slip snugly into both slots while resting on the cylinder head mating surface. if one camshaft is only slightly out of alignment, rotate the camshaft gently and carefully until the tool will fit. Once the camshafts are set at TDC, the positions of the sprockets are less important - they can move independently of the camshafts, to allow the timing belt to be accurately installed and tensioned.

22 When installing the belt, note that the tensioner must not be installed until after the belt is fully positioned around the sprockets and pulley(s).

23 Install the timing belt; if the original is being reinstalled, ensure that the marks and notes made on removal are followed, so that the belt is installed to run in the same direction. Starting at the crankshaft sprocket, work counterclockwise around the guide pulley(s) and camshaft sprockets. Ensure that the belt teeth engage correctly with those on the sprockets.

24 Any slack in the belt should be kept on the tensioner side - the 'front' run must be kept taut, without altering the position of the crankshaft or the camshafts. If necessary, the camshaft sprockets can be turned slightly in relation to the camshafts (which remain fixed by the aligning tool).

25 When the belt is a good fit on the sprockets and guide pulley(s), the belt tensioner can be installed. Hook the tensioner into the timing belt inner shield, and insert the bolt loosely. Using the Allen key, turn the tensioner counterclockwise until the arrow is aligned with the mark or square hole on the bracket, then tighten the tensioner bolt to its specified torque (see illustrations). Note: *The timing belt tensioner automatically adjusts the tension by internal spring forces - checking the tension once set, for instance, by depressing or twisting the timing belt, will not give a meaningful result.*

26 Tighten both camshaft sprocket bolts to the specified torque, holding the sprockets stationary using the tool described in Step 19 (see illustration).

27 Remove the camshaft aligning tool and the timing pin. Temporarily install the crankshaft pulley, and rotate the crankshaft through two full turns clockwise to settle and tension the timing belt, returning to the position described in Section 3. Check that the timing pin can be fully installed, then install the camshaft aligning tool; it should slip into place as described in Step 21. If all is well, proceed to Step 30.

28 If one camshaft is only just out of line, attach the forked holding tool to its sprocket, adjust its position as required, and check that any slack created in the belt has been taken up by the tensioner; rotate the crankshaft two turns clockwise and install the camshaft aligning tool to check that it now fits as it should. If all is well, proceed to Step 29.

29 If either camshaft is significantly out of line, use the holding tool described in Step 19 above to prevent its sprocket from rotating while its retaining bolt is loosened - the camshaft can then be rotated carefully until the camshaft aligning tool will slip into place; take care not to disturb the relationship of the

sprocket to the timing belt. Without disturbing the sprocket's new position on the camshaft, tighten the sprocket bolt to its specified torque setting. Remove the camshaft aligning tool and timing pin, and rotate the crankshaft two more turns clockwise, and install the tool to check that it now fits as it should.

30 The remainder of the reassembly procedure is the reverse of removal, noting the following points:

a) Make sure that the timing pin and camshaft aligning tool are removed.

b) When replacement the engine right-hand mount, remember to install the timing belt upper cover.

c) Tighten all fasteners to the specified torque settings.

9 Timing belt tensioner and sprockets - removal and installation

Tensioner

1 Removing the tensioner should only be attempted as part of the timing belt replacement procedure, described in Section 8. While it is possible to reach the tensioner when only the timing belt upper and middle covers have been removed (see Section 7),

8.26 Tighten the camshaft sprocket bolts to the specified torque

9.5a Unscrew and remove the retaining bolt from each . . .

9.5b . . . and remove the camshaft sprockets

9.6a Crankshaft sprocket FRONT marking

the whole timing belt procedure must be followed, to ensure that the valve timing is correctly reset once the belt's tension has been disturbed.

2 Remove and check the tensioner as described in Section 8. **Note:** *It is considered good practice by many professional mechanics to replace tensioner assemblies as a matter of course, whenever the timing belt is replaced.*

3 Once the old tensioner has been removed as described, the new tensioner can be installed in its place during the belt replacement procedure - there are no special procedures involved in setting the new tensioner.

Camshaft and crankshaft sprockets

Removal

Refer to illustrations 9.5a, 9.5b, 9.6a, 9.6b and 9.6c

Note: *On SVT models, the intake camshaft sprocket incorporates the hydraulic VCT actuator.*

4 As with the tensioner, removing any of the sprockets involves releasing the timing belt tension, so the whole timing belt procedure (Section 8) must be followed. While it may be possible to remove the sprockets once their respective covers have been removed (Section 7), the complete timing belt removal/ replacement procedure must be followed, to ensure that the valve timing is correctly reset once the belt's tension has been disturbed.

5 With the timing belt removed, the camshaft sprockets can be detached once their retaining bolts have been loosened as described in Section 8; although not essential, it is good working practice to mark the sprockets for position **(see illustrations)**.

6 The crankshaft sprocket can be pulled off the end of the crankshaft once the crankshaft (grooved) pulley and the timing belt have been removed. Note the FRONT marking identifying the sprocket's outboard face

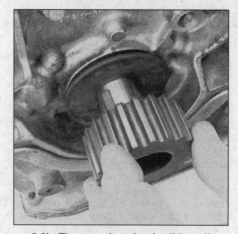

9.6b The sprocket simply slides off the crankshaft

and the thrustwasher behind it; note which way the thrustwasher is installed **(see illustrations)**. Note the sprocket-locating Woodruff key; if this is loose, it should be removed for safe storage with the sprocket.

7 Check the sprockets as described in Section 8.

Installation

8 Installation is the reverse of the removal procedure. Install and tension the timing belt as described in Section 8.

Timing belt guide pulley(s)

Removal

Refer to illustration 9.11

9 To remove the upper guide pulley, remove the timing belt upper and middle covers as described in Section 7.

10 To remove the lower guide pulley (early models only), remove the timing belt lower cover as described in Section 7.

11 Loosen the guide pulley bolt, and withdraw the pulley from the belt **(see illustration)**. Care must be taken as the pulley is removed, so that the timing belt does not come off the sprockets. On early models, if

both pulleys are to be changed, it may be advisable to only remove one at a time, if possible.

12 Check the condition of the pulley(s) as described in Section 8. **Note:** *It is considered good practice by many professional mechanics to replace guide pulley assemblies as a matter of course, whenever the timing belt is replaced.*

9.6c Remove the thrustwasher if necessary

9.11 Remove the timing belt guide pulley (timing belt already removed)

10.6a Fit the seal, lips inwards, using your fingers . . .

10.6b . . . then tap it home using a large socket

11.3 The Number 2 camshaft bearing marking

Installation

13   Installation is the reverse of the removal procedure; tighten the pulley bolts to the specified torque setting.

10 Camshaft oil seals - replacement

Refer to illustrations 10.6a and 10.6b

1   Remove the timing belt as described in Section 8, and take off the camshaft sprocket(s) as required, as described in Section 9. Even if only one seal is leaking, it is prudent to replace both at the same time.

2   Try prying the seal out first, but take care not to damage the head, bearing cap, or camshaft, as this will result in further leaks, even with a new seal. An alternative is to drill a small hole in the seal, thread in a small self-tapping screw, and use pliers on the screw head to pull the seal out.

3   If the seal proves difficult to remove, unbolt the camshaft right-hand bearing cap and withdraw the defective oil seal; note that the cap is fitted using sealant, which must be cleaned off, and fresh sealant applied when replaced. On SVT models, there is one large bearing cap that fits over both camshafts,

and also contains the oil passageway and solenoid for the VCT assembly.

4   Clean the seal housing and polish off any burrs or raised edges, which may have caused the seal to fail in the first place. Where applicable, install the bearing cap, using sealant and tightening the cap bolts as described in Section 11. On SVT models, whenever the front bearing cap is removed, replace the oil seal surrounding the oil feed passage to the VCT.

5   To fit a new seal, the manufacturer recommend the use of their service tool 303-039, with a bolt (10 mm thread size, 70 mm long) and a washer, to draw the seal into place when the camshaft bearing cap is bolted down; a substitute is to use a suitable socket.

6   Grease the seal lips to ease installation, then fit it over the end of the camshaft using your fingers. Draw or tap the seal into place until it is flush with the housing/bearing cap outer edge **(see illustrations)**.

7   Install the sprocket to the camshaft, tightening the retaining bolt loosely.

8   The remainder of the reassembly procedure, including checking the camshaft alignment (valve timing) and setting the timing belt tension, is as described in Section 8.

11 Camshafts and cam followers - removal, inspection and installation

Removal

Refer to illustrations 11.3, 11.4a, 11.4b, 11.5a and 11.5b

1   Remove the timing belt as described in Section 8.

2   Remove the camshaft sprockets as described in Section 9; while both are the same and could be interchanged, it is good working practice to mark them so that each is replaced only to its original location.

3   All the camshaft bearing caps have a single-digit identifying number etched on them. The exhaust camshaft's bearing caps are numbered in sequence 0 (right-hand cap) to 4 (left-hand cap), the intake's 5 (right-hand cap) to 9 (left-hand cap). Each cap is to be fitted so that its numbered side faces outwards, to the front (exhaust) or to the rear (intake) **(see illustration)**. If no marks are present, or they are hard to see, make your own - the bearing caps must be replaced in their original positions.

4   Working in the sequence shown, loosen the camshaft bearing cap bolts progressively by half a turn at a time **(see illustration)**.

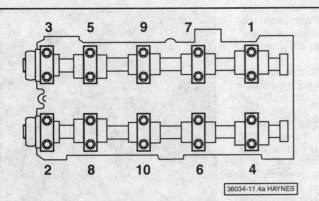

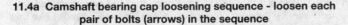

11.4a Camshaft bearing cap loosening sequence - loosen each pair of bolts (arrows) in the sequence

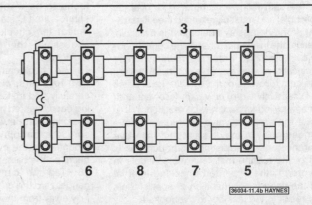

11.4b Camshaft bearing cap loosening sequence on SVT models - loosen each pair of bolts in the sequence

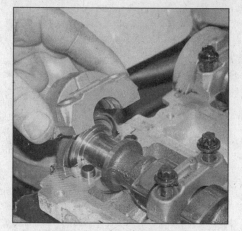

11.5a Remove the bearing caps . . .

11.5b . . . then lift out the camshafts

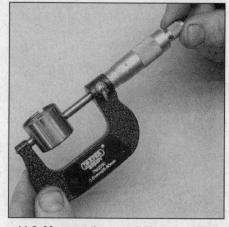

11.8 Measure the cam follower outside diameter at several points

Work only as described, to release gradually and evenly the pressure of the valve springs on the caps.

5   Withdraw the caps, noting their markings and the presence of the locating dowels, then remove the camshafts and withdraw their oil seals **(see illustrations)**. The intake camshaft can be identified by the reference lobe for the camshaft position sensor; therefore, there is no need to mark the camshafts.

6   Obtain sixteen small, clean containers, and number them 1 to 16. Using a rubber suction tool (such as a valve-lapping tool), withdraw each cam follower in turn and place them in the containers. Do not interchange the cam followers, or the rate of wear will be much increased. Make sure the shims remain with their corresponding cam followers, to ensure correct replacement.

Inspection
Refer to illustrations 11.8 and 11.11

7   With the camshafts and cam followers removed, check each for signs of obvious wear (scoring, pitting, etc) and for roundness and replace if necessary.

8   Measure the outside diameter of each cam follower - take measurements at the top and bottom of each cam follower, then a second set at right-angles to the first; if any measurement is significantly different from the others, the cam follower is tapered or oval (as applicable) and must be replaced **(see illustration)**. If the necessary equipment is available, measure the inside diameter of the corresponding cylinder head bore. No manufacturer's specifications were available at time of writing; if the cam followers or the cylinder head bores are excessively worn, new cam followers and/or a new cylinder head may be required.

9   If the engine's valve components have sounded noisy, it may be just that the valve clearances need adjusting. Although this is part of the routine maintenance schedule in Chapter 1, the extended checking interval and the need for dismantling or special tools may result in the task being overlooked.

10   Visually examine the camshaft lobes for score marks, pitting, galling (wear due to rubbing) and evidence of overheating (blue, discolored areas). Look for flaking away of the hardened surface layer of each lobe. If any such signs are evident, replace the component concerned.

11   Examine the camshaft bearing journals and the cylinder head bearing surfaces for signs of obvious wear or pitting. If any such signs are evident, consult an automotive machine shop for advice. Also check that the bearing oilways in the cylinder head are clear **(see illustration)**.

12   Using a micrometer, measure the diameter of each journal at several points. If the diameter of any one journal is less than the specified value, replace the camshaft.

13   To check the bearing journal running clearance, remove the cam followers, use a suitable solvent and a clean lint-free rag to clean carefully all bearing surfaces, then install the camshafts and bearing caps with a strand of Plastigage across each journal. Tighten the bearing cap bolts in the given sequence (see *Installation*) to the specified torque setting (do not rotate the camshafts), then remove the bearing caps and use the scale provided to measure the width of the compressed strands. Scrape off the Plastigage with your fingernail or the edge of a credit card - don't scratch or nick the journals or bearing caps.

14   If the running clearance of any bearing is found to be worn to beyond the specified service limits, install a new camshaft and repeat the check; if the clearance is still excessive, the cylinder head must be replaced.

15   To check camshaft endplay, remove the cam followers, clean the bearing surfaces carefully and install the camshafts and bearing caps. Tighten the bearing cap bolts to the specified torque wrench setting, then measure the endplay using a dial indicator mounted on the cylinder head so that its tip bears on the camshaft right-hand end.

16   Tap the camshaft fully towards the gauge, zero the gauge, then tap the camshaft fully away from the gauge and note the gauge reading. If the endplay measured is found to be at or beyond the specified service limit, install a new camshaft and repeat the check;

if the clearance is still excessive, the cylinder head must be replaced.

Installation
Refer to illustrations 11.20a, 11.20b, 11.20c, 11.21, 11.22a, 11.22b, 11.23a, 11.23b, 11.27, 11.29a and 11.29b

17   As a precaution against the valves hitting the pistons when the camshafts are replaced, remove the timing pin and turn the engine approximately 90° back from the TDC position - this should move all the pistons an equal distance down the bores. This is only a precaution - if the engine is known to be at TDC on the Number 1 cylinder, and the camshafts are replaced as described below, valve-to-piston contact should not occur.

18   On reassembly, liberally oil the cylinder head cam follower bores and the cam followers. Carefully install the cam followers to the cylinder head, ensuring that each cam follower is replaced to its original bore, and is the correct way up. Some care will be required to enter the cam followers squarely into their bores. Make sure that the shims are installed in their previously-noted positions.

19   It is highly recommended that new camshaft oil seals are installed, as a precaution against later failure - it would seem a false economy to install old seals, especially since

11.11 Check that the camshaft bearing oilways are not blocked with dirt like this one (arrow)

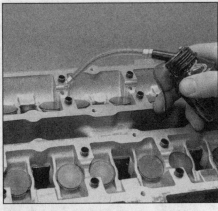

11.20a Lubricate the camshaft bearing surfaces . . .

11.20b . . . then install the camshafts . . .

11.20c . . . ensuring that the slot at the transmission end is approximately horizontal

11.21 Apply sealant to each of the bearing caps at the timing belt end

11.22a Apply a little oil to the camshaft surface . . .

11.22b . . . then install the camshaft bearing caps

they may not seal, having been disturbed. The new seals are installed after the caps are tightened - see Section 10.

20 Liberally oil the camshaft bearings (not the caps) and lobes. Ensuring that each camshaft is in its original location, install the camshafts, locating each so that the slot in its left-hand end is approximately parallel to, and just above, the cylinder head mating surface **(see illustrations)**. Check that, as each camshaft is laid in position, the metal strip TDC setting tool will fit into the slot.

21 Ensure that the locating dowels are pressed firmly into their recesses and check that all mating surfaces are completely clean, unmarked and free from oil. Apply a thin film of suitable sealant (the manufacturer recommends a sealant to specification WSK-M4G348-A5) to the mating surfaces of each camshaft's right-hand bearing cap **(see illustration)**.

22 Apply a little oil to the camshaft as shown, then install each of the camshaft bearing caps to its previously-noted position,

so that its numbered side faces outwards, to the front (exhaust) or to the rear (intake) **(see illustrations)**.

23 Ensuring that each cap is kept square to the cylinder head as it is tightened down and working in the sequence shown, tighten the camshaft bearing cap bolts slowly and by one turn at a time, until each cap touches the cylinder head **(see illustration)**.

24 Next, go round again in the same sequence, tightening the bolts to the specified Stage 1 torque setting.

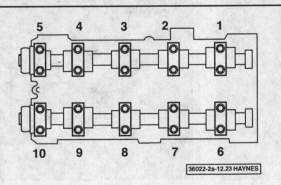

36022-2a-12.23 HAYNES

11.23a Camshaft bearing cap tightening sequence

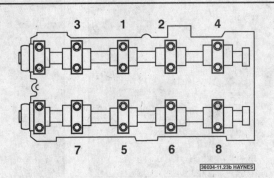

36034-11.23b HAYNES

11.23b Camshaft bearing cap tightening sequence - SVT models

11.27 Set the camshafts to TDC using the metal strip in the slotted ends

11.29a Install the camshaft sprockets . . .

11.29b . . . and secure with the retaining bolts, tightened only loosely at this stage

25   With all the bolts tightened to the Stage 1 torque, go round in sequence once more, tightening them to the Stage 2 torque setting.

26   Wipe off all surplus sealant, so that none is left to find its way into any oilways. Follow the sealant manufacturer's instructions as to the time needed for curing; usually, at least an hour must be allowed between application of the sealant and starting the engine (including turning the engine for further reassembly work).

27   Once the caps are fully tightened, it makes sense to check the valve clearances before proceeding - assuming that the tool described in Section 5 is not available, the camshafts have to be removed to allow any of the shims to be changed. Turning the camshafts with the timing belt removed carries a risk of the valves hitting the pistons, so (if not already done) remove the timing pin and turn the crankshaft 90° counterclockwise first. Set the camshafts to TDC on the Number 1 cylinder using the setting tool (see Section 8) to establish a starting point, then proceed as described in Section 5 **(see illustration)**. When all the clearances have been checked, bring the crankshaft back to TDC, and install the timing pin.

28   Install new camshaft oil seals as described in Section 10.

29   Using the marks and notes made on dismantling to ensure that each is replaced to its original camshaft, install the sprockets to the camshafts, tightening the retaining bolts loosely **(see illustrations)**. **Caution:** *On SVT models, the VCT actuator/sprocket must go on the* intake *camshaft.*

30   The remainder of the reassembly procedure, including replacement of the timing belt and setting the valve timing, is as described in Section 8. On completion (if not already done), check and adjust the valve clearances as described in Section 5.

12   Cylinder head - removal and installation

Note: *The procedure below describes removing the cylinder head without the intake manifold, which was found to be the easiest option in practice - the intake manifold can be unbolted from the head, and moved rearwards to allow the head to be withdrawn. If preferred, however, the intake manifold may be removed completely as described in Chapter 4.*

12.7 Disconnect the camshaft position sensor wiring plug

Removal

Refer to illustrations 12.7, 12.8a, 12.8b, 12.8c, 12.10a, 12.10b, 12.10c, 12.11a, 12.11b, 12.12a, 12.12b, 12.15a, 12.15b, 12.16, 12.17, 12.18, 12.19a, 12.19b, 12.23 and 12.24

1   Referring to Chapter 12, identify and remove the fuel pump fuse from the fusebox. Now start the engine and allow it to run until it stalls. If the engine will not start, at least keep

12.8a Use a screwdriver to pry out the wire clips . . .

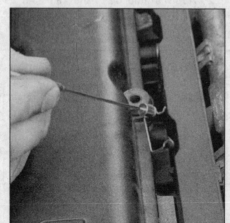

12.8b . . . recover the clips using a magnetic tool . . .

12.8c . . . then lift off the injector wiring busbar

12.10a The intake manifold is located on studs (arrow indicates one) . . .

12.10b . . . which must be unscrewed and removed . . .

it cranking for about 10 seconds. The fuel system should now be depressurized.

2   Disconnect the negative battery terminal (see Chapter 5).

3   Drain the cooling system as described in Chapter 1. It is preferable when removing the cylinder head for the front wheels to remain on the ground as much as possible, as this makes working on the top of the engine easier. Also, once the right-hand engine mount has been removed (for removing the timing belt), the engine must be further supported if the front of the car is raised.

4   Remove the timing belt as described in Section 8, and the camshafts as described in Section 11.

5   Temporarily install the engine right-hand mount, tightening the bolts securely. Also install the valve cover, to protect the top of the engine until the cylinder head bolts are removed.

6   Remove the air cleaner intake duct, and disconnect the accelerator cable, using the information in Chapter 4A. On 2003 and later non-SVT models, disconnect the EGR pipe and remove the EGR valve (see Chapter 4).

7   Disconnect the wiring plug from the camshaft position sensor, located at the rear of the head, at the transmission end (see illustration). On SVT engines, remove the

engine-lifting bracket at the intake manifold.

8   Using a small screwdriver, pry up and remove the four wire clips (one on each injector) securing the injector wiring busbar - use a magnetic holding tool to prevent the wire clips falling down the back of the engine as they are removed. Lift off the wiring busbar, and move it to the rear (see illustrations).

9   The intake manifold is secured by seven bolts, and a stud and nut at either end. Note that the right-hand nut also secures a wiring support bracket - unclip the wiring before removing the bracket. Loosen and remove the manifold nuts and bolts. On SVT models, disconnect the IMRC (intake manifold runner control) cable and the knock sensor connector.

10   The manifold cannot easily be removed from the end studs, so the studs themselves must be unscrewed from the cylinder head - Torx end fittings are provided to make unscrewing the studs easier. Remove the studs, and move the manifold fully to the rear, clear of the head (see illustrations). Note that a set of four new intake manifold gaskets should be obtained for replacement. Note: *On SVT models, the intake manifold is a two-piece design. Separate the outer manifold to gain access to the mounting bolts/studs for the inner manifold.*

12.10c . . . before moving the manifold assembly rearwards away from the head

11   Remove the alternator as described in Chapter 5. This is necessary, since the alternator mounting bracket is attached to the head, and one of the bracket bolts can only be taken out with the alternator removed. To improve access, disconnect the large injection harness multi-plug and the cylinder head temperature wiring plug above the alternator (see illustrations).

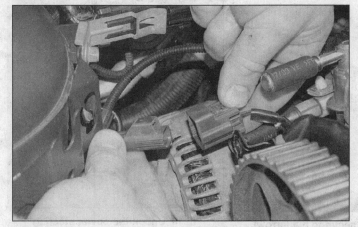

12.11a Disconnect the cylinder head temperature wiring plug . . .

12.11b . . . then unclip and separate the injection harness multi-plug

12.12a Unbolt the ground wire from the engine lifting eye

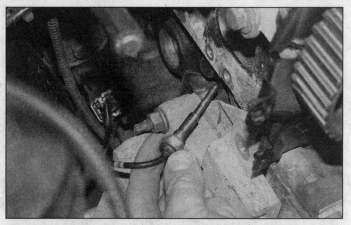

12.12b Unscrew and remove the cylinder head temperature sensor

12.15a Unscrew the three bolts (arrows) . . .

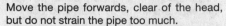

12.15b . . . and remove the thermostat housing from the head

12 Disconnect the ground wire attached to the engine rear lifting eye. To avoid damaging it, unscrew and remove the cylinder head temperature sensor **(see illustrations)**.

13 Unbolt and remove the alternator mounting bracket, which is secured by three bolts and one nut. Alternatively, remove just the single bolt securing the bracket to the head, leaving the bracket in place.

14 Remove the ignition coil as described in Chapter 5.

15 There are two options regarding the thermostat housing - either disconnect the hoses from it (noting their positions), or unscrew the three bolts and detach the housing from the head **(see illustrations)**. If the latter option is chosen, the hoses can remain in place, but a new housing O-ring seal must be obtained for replacement.

16 At the front of the head, unbolt and separate the power steering fluid pipe support brackets at either end **(see illustration)**.

Move the pipe forwards, clear of the head, but do not strain the pipe too much.

17 Remove the nut securing the upper end of the dipstick tube, and move the tube away from the head **(see illustration)**.

18 Remove the power steering pump as described in Chapter 10 (the fluid pipes need not be disconnected, providing the pump is supported, clear of the engine). Unbolt the power steering pump mounting bracket, which is secured by three bolts and one nut,

12.16 Unbolt one of the power steering fluid pipe brackets

12.17 Dipstick tube securing nut (arrow)

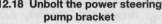

12.18 Unbolt the power steering pump bracket

12.19a Unscrew the four bolts (arrows) . . .

12.19b . . . and remove the heat shield

12.23 Remove the cylinder head bolts

12.24 Lift off the cylinder head

and remove the bracket from the head (see illustration).

19 Unscrew the bolts securing the exhaust manifold heat shield, and lift the shield off (see illustrations). It is quite likely that diffi-culty will be experienced removing the bolts, as corrosion may have effectively rounded-off the bolt heads - be sure to use a close-fitting socket or box-end wrench. If the bolts cannot be removed, as a last resort, the heat shield will have to be destroyed to remove it - take care, however, that the wiring for the oxygen sensor (located just below the heat shield) is not damaged during this operation.

20 The front section of the exhaust (which includes the catalytic converter) must now be removed as described in Chapter 4, leaving the exhaust manifold attached to the head.

21 Before loosening the cylinder head bolts, check around the head to ensure that there is nothing still attached to it, nor anything else that would interfere with the head being lifted off. Move any wiring or hoses aside as neces-sary.

22 Although it is unlikely to be relevant in the case of the DIY mechanic, it should be noted that, according to the manufacturer, the cylinder head should not be removed until it has cooled to ambient temperature.

23 Using a Torx key or socket (TX 55 size), loosen the ten cylinder head bolts progres-sively and by half a turn at a time, working in the reverse order of the sequence shown for tightening (see illustration 12.42). Remove the bolts, and store them carefully if they are to be re-used (see illustration). The manu-facturer states that the bolts may be re-used twice only - if there is any doubt about this, it is preferable to obtain a complete set of new bolts for replacement.

24 Lift the cylinder head away; use assis-tance if possible, as it is a heavy assembly (see illustration).

25 If the head is stuck, be careful how you choose to free it. Remember that the cylinder head is made of aluminum alloy, which is eas-ily damaged. Striking the head with tools car-ries the risk of damage, and the head is located on two dowels, so its movement will

be limited. Do not, under any circumstances, lever the head between the mating surfaces, as this will certainly damage the sealing sur-faces for the gasket, leading to leaks. Try rocking the head free, to break the seal, tak-ing care not to damage any of the surround-ing components.

26 Once the head has been removed, recover the gasket from the two dowels, and discard it.

Inspection

Note: *For dismantling the cylinder head, and other procedures relating to the valves, refer to Chapter 2D.*

27 The mating faces of the cylinder head and cylinder block must be perfectly clean before replacement the head. Use a hard plastic or wood scraper to remove all traces of gasket and carbon; also clean the piston crowns.

28 Take particular care during the cleaning operations, as aluminum alloy is easily dam-aged. Also, make sure that the carbon is not allowed to enter the oil and water passages - this is particularly important for the lubrica-tion system, as carbon could block the oil supply to the engine's components. Using adhesive tape and paper, seal the water, oil and bolt holes in the cylinder block.

29 To prevent carbon entering the gap between the pistons and bores, smear a little grease in the gap. After cleaning each piston, use a small brush to remove all traces of grease and carbon from the gap, then wipe away the remainder with a clean rag.

30 Check the mating surfaces of the cylin-der block and the cylinder head for nicks, deep scratches and other damage. If slight, they may be removed carefully with a file, but if excessive, replacement is necessary as it is not permissible to machine the surfaces.

31 If warpage of the cylinder head gasket surface is suspected, use a straight-edge to check it for distortion. Refer to Part C of this Chapter if necessary.

32 The factory states that the cylinder head bolts can be re-used twice, but they should be checked carefully before doing so. Exam-

ine the threads in particular for any signs of damage. If any of the thread inside the cylin-der head holes has been removed with the bolts, seek expert advice before proceeding. Lay the bolts out next to each other, and com-pare their length - if any one has stretched, so that it is longer than the rest, it should not be re-used, and it is probably advisable to replace all the bolts as a set. If there is any doubt as to the condition of the bolts, install new ones - the cost of a set of bolts is nothing compared to the problems which may be caused if a bolt shears or strips when being tightened.

33 If the cylinder head bolts are re-used, paint or scribe the top of each bolt with a single dot or line, as a reminder if the head has to be removed at a later date.

Installation

Refer to illustrations 12.37a, 12.37b, 12.40, 12.41, 12.42, 12.43 and 12.44

34 Wipe clean the mating surfaces of the cylinder head and cylinder block. Check that the two locating dowels are in position in the cylinder block.

35 The cylinder head bolt holes must be free from oil or water. This is most important, because a hydraulic lock in a cylinder head bolt hole can cause a fracture of the block casting when the bolt is tightened.

12.37a Lay the new head gasket in position over the dowels . . .

12.37b . . . head gasket 'teeth' should be at the front of the block

36   The new head gasket is selected according to a number cast on the front face of the cylinder block, in front of the Number 1 cylinder. Consult a dealer or your parts supplier for details - if in doubt, compare the new gasket with the old one.

37   Position a new gasket over the dowels on the cylinder block surface, so that the TOP/OBEN mark is uppermost; where applicable, the 'tooth' (or teeth, according to engine size) should protrude towards the front of the vehicle (see illustrations).

38   Temporarily install the crankshaft pulley and rotate the crankshaft counterclockwise so that the Number 1 cylinder's piston is lowered to approximately 20 mm before TDC, thus avoiding any risk of valve/piston contact and damage during reassembly.

39   As the cylinder head is such a heavy and awkward assembly to install, it is helpful to make up a pair of guide studs from two 10 mm (thread size) studs approximately 90 mm long, with a screwdriver slot cut in one end - two old cylinder head bolts (if available) with their heads cut off would make a good starting point. Screw these guide studs, screwdriver slot upwards to permit removal, into the bolt holes at diagonally-opposite corners of the cylinder block surface (or into those where the locating dowels are fitted); ensure that approximately 70 mm of stud protrudes

12.40 Cylinder head locating dowels (arrows)

12.41 Apply a light coating of oil to the cylinder head bolt threads

above the gasket.

40   Install the cylinder head, sliding it down the guide studs (if used) and locating it on the dowels (see illustration). Unscrew the guide studs (if used) when the head is in place.

41   The manufacturer does not state whether or not the cylinder head bolts should be oiled when replaced, but experience suggests that coating the threads with a little light oil is useful - do not apply more than a light film of oil, however (see illustration). Fit

the cylinder head bolts carefully, and screw them in by hand only until finger-tight.

42   Working progressively and in the sequence shown, first tighten all the bolts to the specified Stage 1 torque setting (see illustration).

43   With all the bolts tightened to Stage 1, tighten them further in sequence to the Stage 2 torque setting (see illustration).

44   Stage 3 involves tightening the bolts through an angle, rather than to a torque.

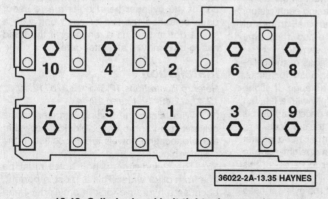

36022-2A-13.35 HAYNES

12.42 Cylinder head bolt tightening sequence

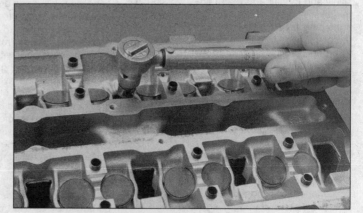

12.43 Tightening the bolts to the Stage 2 torque . . .

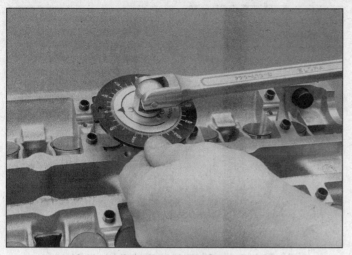

12.44 . . . then through the Stage 3 angle, here using an angle gauge

13.7 Studs in place, ready for oil pan installation (seen with engine removed)

Each bolt in sequence must be rotated through the specified angle - special angle gauges are available from tool outlets, but a 90° angle is equivalent to a quarter-turn, and this is easily judged by assessing the start and end positions of the socket handle or torque wrench **(see illustration)**.

45 Once all the bolts have been tightened to Stage 3, no subsequent tightening is necessary.

46 Before proceeding with replacement, turn the crankshaft forwards to TDC, and check that the setting tools described in Section 3 can be inserted. Do not turn the engine more than necessary while the timing belt is removed, or the valves may hit the pistons - for instance, if the engine is accidentally turned past the TDC position, turn it back slightly and try again - do not bring the engine round a full turn.

47 Replacement of the other components removed is a reversal of removal, noting the following points:

a) *Install the catalytic converter with reference to Chapter 4 if necessary, using new gaskets.*

b) *Install the camshafts as described in Section 11, and the timing belt as described in Section 8.*

c) *Tighten all fasteners to the specified torque, where given, and use new gaskets.*

d) *Ensure that all hoses and wiring are correctly routed, and that hose clips and wiring connectors are securely installed.*

e) *Refill the cooling system as described in Chapter 1.*

f) *Check all disturbed joints for signs of oil or coolant leakage once the engine has been restarted and warmed-up to normal operating temperature.*

13 Oil pan - removal and installation

Removal

Note: *The full procedure outlined below must be followed so that the mating surfaces can be cleaned and prepared to achieve an oil-tight joint on reassembly.*

1 Apply the parking brake, then jack up the front of the vehicle and support it on axle stands (see *Jacking and Towing*).

2 Referring to Chapter 1 if necessary, drain the engine oil, then clean and install the engine oil drain plug, tightening it to the specified torque wrench setting. Although not

strictly necessary as part of the dismantling procedure, owners are advised to remove and discard the oil filter, so that it can be replaced with the oil. On 2002 and later models, remove the catalytic converter (see Chapter 4A).

3 A conventional oil pan gasket is not used, and sealant is used instead.

4 Progressively unscrew the oil pan retaining bolts. Break the joint by striking the oil pan with the palm of the hand, then lower the oil pan away, turning it as necessary to clear the exhaust system.

5 Unfortunately, the use of sealant can make removal of the oil pan more difficult. Take care when levering between the mating faces, otherwise they will be damaged, resulting in leaks when finished. With care, a putty knife can be used to cut through the sealant.

Installation

Refer to illustrations 13.7, 13.8, 13.9 and 13.12

6 On reassembly, thoroughly clean and degrease the mating surfaces of the cylinder block/crankcase and oil pan, removing all traces of sealant, then use a clean rag to wipe out the oil pan and the engine's interior.

7 The manufacturer recommends that ten M6x20 mm studs are used when replacing the oil pan, to ensure that it is aligned correctly. If this is not done, some of the sealant may enter the blind holes for the oil pan bolts, preventing the bolts from being fully screwed in. Obtain ten suitable studs, and cut a slot across the end of each, so that they can be unscrewed; install them to the locations indicated **(see illustrations)**.

8 Apply a 1/8-inch wide bead of sealant to the oil pan flange so that the bead is approximately 3/16-inch from the outside edge of the flange. Make sure the bead is around the inside edge of the bolt holes **(see illustration)**. **Note:** *The oil pan must be installed within 10 minutes of applying the sealant.*

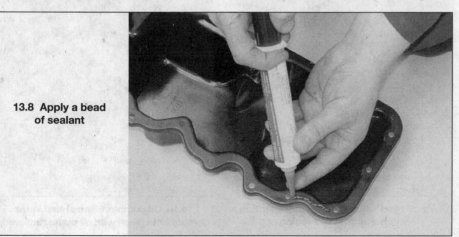

13.8 Apply a bead of sealant

13.9 Install the oil pan over the studs

13.12 Tighten the oil pan bolts to the Stage 2 torque

9   Install the oil pan over the studs, and insert six of the oil pan bolts into the available holes, tightening them by hand only at this stage **(see illustration)**.
10   Unscrew the studs, then install the rest of the oil pan bolts.
11   Tighten all the bolts to the specified Stage 1 torque, in a criss-cross pattern.
12   When all the oil pan bolts have been tightened to Stage 1, go round again in sequence, and tighten the bolts to the Stage 2 setting **(see illustration)**.
13   Lower the car to the ground. Wait at least 1 hour for the sealant to cure (or whatever time is indicated by the sealant manufacturer) before refilling the engine with oil. Trim off the excess sealant with a sharp knife. If removed, fit a new oil filter with reference to Chapter 1.

14   Oil pump - removal, inspection and installation

Removal

Note: *While this task is theoretically possible when the engine is in place in the vehicle, in practice, it requires so much preliminary dismantling and is so difficult to carry out due to* the restricted access, that owners are advised to remove the engine from the vehicle first. Note, however, that the oil pump pressure relief valve can be removed with the engine in place - see Step 9.
1   Remove the timing belt (see Section 8). On 2003 and later models, refer to Chapter 3 and unbolt and set aside the air conditioning compressor, without disconnect the lines, then remove the compressor mounting bracket from the engine.
2   Withdraw the crankshaft sprocket and the thrustwasher behind it, noting which way the thrustwasher is fitted (see Section 9).
3   Remove the oil pan (see Section 13). On 2003 and later models, remove the drivebelt tensioner.
4   Unscrew the two bolts securing the oil pump pick-up/strainer pipe to the base of the lower crankcase, and withdraw it. Discard the gasket.
5   Progressively unscrew and remove the ten bolts securing the lower crankcase to the base of the engine. Remove the lower crankcase, and recover any spacer washers, noting where they are installed, as these must be used on replacement. Recover the gasket, and remove any traces of sealant at the joint with the oil pump.

6   Unbolt the pump from the cylinder block/crankcase. Withdraw and discard the gasket, then remove the crankshaft right-hand oil seal. Thoroughly clean and degrease all components, particularly the mating surfaces of the pump, the oil pan and the cylinder block/crankcase.

Inspection

Refer to illustrations 14.7a, 14.7b, 14.10, 14.11, 14.12a and 14.12b
7   Unscrew the Torx screws and remove the pump cover plate; noting any identification marks on the rotors, withdraw the rotors **(see illustrations)**.
8   Inspect the rotors for obvious signs of wear or damage, and replace if necessary; if either rotor, the pump body, or its cover plate are scored or damaged, the complete oil pump assembly must be replaced.
9   The oil pressure relief valve can be disassembled, if required, without disturbing the pump. With the vehicle parked on firm level ground, apply the parking brake securely and raise its front end, supporting it securely on axle stands. Remove the front right-hand wheel and auxiliary drivebelt cover (see Chapter 1) to provide access to the valve.
10   Unscrew the threaded plug and recover

14.7a Remove the oil pump cover . . .

14.7b . . . and withdraw the rotors, noting which way they are facing

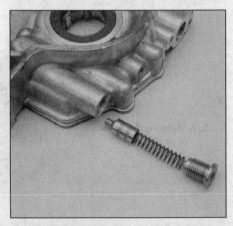

14.10 Oil pump pressure relief valve components (seen with oil pump removed)

14.11 Tighten the relief valve cover plug securely

14.12a Oil the housing and rotors as they are installed

14.12b Tighten the oil pump cover bolts securely

the valve spring and plunger **(see illustration)**.

11 Reassembly is the reverse of the disassembly procedure; ensure the spring and valve are reinstalled the correct way and tighten the threaded plug securely **(see illustration)**.

12 When reassembling the oil pump, oil the housing and components as they are installed; tighten the oil pump cover bolts securely **(see illustrations)**.

Installation

Refer to illustrations 14.14a, 14.14b, 14.15, 14.19a, 14.19b, 14.20, 14.21, 14.22a, 14.22b and 14.22c

13 The oil pump must be primed on installation, by pouring clean engine oil into it and rotating its inner rotor a few turns.

14 Rotate the pump's inner rotor to align with the flats on the crankshaft, then install the pump (and new gasket) and insert the bolts, tightening them lightly at first **(see illustrations)**.

15 Using a suitable straight-edge and feeler gauges, check that the pump is both centered exactly around the crankshaft and aligned squarely so that its (oil pan) mating surface is exactly the same amount - between 0.015 and 0.031-inch - below that of the cyl-

14.14a Place the new gasket into position . . .

14.14b . . . then install the oil pump, and tighten the bolts loosely

inder block/crankcase on each side of the crankshaft **(see illustration)**. Being careful not to disturb the gasket, move the pump into the correct position and tighten its bolts to the specified torque setting.

16 Check that the pump is correctly located; if necessary, unbolt it again and repeat the full procedure to ensure that the pump is correctly aligned.

17 Install a new oil pump housing oil seal

(see Section 16).

18 Apply a little RTV sealant to the joints between the oil pump and cylinder block. **Note:** *Once this sealant has been applied, the lower crankcase must be installed and the bolts fully tightened within 10 minutes.*

19 Install the new gasket in place, then raise the lower crankcase into position and loosely secure with the bolts **(see illustrations)**.

14.15 Check the alignment of the oil pump with the crankcase

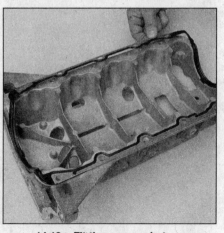

14.19a Fit the new gasket . . .

14.19b . . . then install the lower crankcase

14.20 Check the alignment of the lower crankcase and engine block

14.21 Tighten the lower crankcase bolts to the specified torque

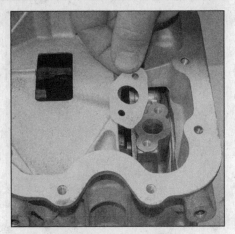

14.22a Using a new gasket . . .

20   The lower crankcase must now be aligned with the cylinder block before the bolts are tightened. Using a straight-edge and feeler gauges, check the alignment of the end faces **(see illustration)**.

21   Tighten the lower crankcase bolts to the specified torque, ensuring that the alignment with the cylinder block is not lost **(see illustration)**.

22   Using grease to stick the gasket in place on the pump, install the pickup/strainer pipe, tightening the retaining bolts to the specified torque **(see illustrations)**.

23   The remainder of reassembly is the reverse of the removal procedure; refer to the relevant text for details where required.

14.22b . . . install the oil pump pickup/ strainer pipe . . .

14.22c . . . and tighten the bolts to the specified torque

15   Oil pressure warning light switch - removal and installation

Removal

Refer to illustrations 15.4a and 15.4b

1   The switch is screwed into the rear of the cylinder block, next to the oil filter.

2   With the vehicle parked on firm level ground, open the hood and disconnect the negative battery cable (see Chapter 5).

3   Raise the front of the vehicle and support it securely on axle stands.

4   Unplug the wiring from the switch and unscrew it; be prepared for some oil loss **(see illustrations)**.

Installation

5   Installation is the reverse of the removal procedure; apply a thin smear of suitable sealant to the switch threads, and tighten it securely. Check the engine oil level and top-off as necessary (see Chapter 1). Check for correct warning light operation, and for signs of oil leaks once the engine has been restarted and warmed-up to normal operating temperature.

16   Crankshaft oil seals - replacement

Note: *Don't try to pry these seals out without removing the oil pump or seal carrier - the seals are too soft, and the amount of space available is too small, for this to be possible without considerable risk of damage to the seal housing and/or the crankshaft journal. Follow exactly the procedure given below.*

Oil pump housing oil seal

Refer to illustrations 16.2 and 16.7

1   Remove the oil pump (see Section 14).

2   Drive the oil seal out of the pump from

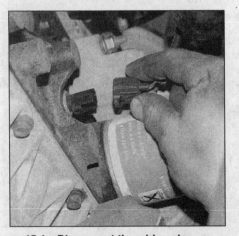

15.4a Disconnect the wiring plug . . .

15.4b . . . then unscrew and remove the oil pressure warning light switch

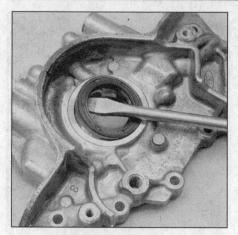

16.2 Pry out the oil seal from the oil pump housing

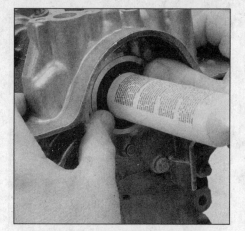

16.7 The oil seal can be pressed in by hand in most cases

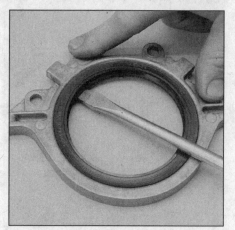

16.13 Pry out the crankshaft rear oil seal

behind; if care is taken, the seal can be pried out with a screwdriver **(see illustration)**.

3   Clean the seal housing and crankshaft, polishing off any burrs or raised edges, which may have caused the seal to fail in the first place.

4   Install the oil pump (see Section 14). Grease the lips and periphery of the new seal to ease installation.

5   To fit a new seal, the manufactuer recommends the use of their service tool 21-093A, with the crankshaft pulley bolt, to draw the seal into place.

6   One of the problems with installing the new seal is that the seal lips may catch on the edge of the crankshaft, which will ruin the seal. A plastic tube or bottle of the right size can be used to overcome this problem, by slipping the plastic over the crankshaft, sliding the seal in place, then pulling the plastic tube out.

7   As long as the seal is kept square, it can usually be seated using hand pressure only, but if preferred, a socket of suitable size could be used to tap the seal home **(see illustration)**.

8   The remainder of reassembly is the reverse of the removal procedure; refer to the relevant text for details where required. Check for signs of oil leakage when the engine is restarted.

Flywheel end oil seal

Refer to illustrations 16.13, 16.15a, 16.15b, 16.16a, 16.16b, 16.18a and 16.18b

9   Remove the transmission as described in Chapter 7, and the clutch assembly as described in Chapter 8.

10   Unbolt the flywheel (see Section 17).

11   Remove the oil pan (see Section 13).

12   Unbolt the oil seal carrier; remove and discard its gasket.

13   Supporting the carrier evenly on wooden blocks, drive the oil seal out of the carrier from behind; if care is taken, the seal can be pried out with a screwdriver **(see illustration)**.

14   Clean the seal housing and crankshaft, polishing off any burrs or raised edges, which may have caused the seal to fail in the first place. Clean also the mating surfaces of the

16.15a Using a new gasket . . .

cylinder block/crankcase and carrier, using a scraper to remove all traces of the old gasket - be careful not to scratch or damage the material of either - then use a suitable solvent to degrease them.

15   Position the carrier, complete with the new gasket **(see illustrations)**.

16   Using a suitable straight-edge and feeler gauges, check that the carrier is both centered exactly around the crankshaft and aligned squarely so that its (oil pan) mating

16.16a Check the alignment of the oil seal carrier using feeler gauges . . .

16.15b . . . position the oil seal carrier, and tighten the bolts loosely

surface is exactly the same amount - between 0.015 and 0.013-inch - below that of the cylinder block/crankcase on each side of the crankshaft. Being careful not to disturb the gasket, move the carrier into the correct position and tighten its bolts to the specified torque setting **(see illustrations)**.

17   Check that the carrier is correctly located; if necessary, unbolt it again and repeat the full procedure to ensure that the

16.16b . . . then tighten the bolts to the specified torque

16.18a Slide the oil seal on using a plastic bottle . . .

16.18b . . . or a plastic strip wrapped around the crankshaft

17.4 One method of jamming the flywheel ring gear to prevent rotation

carrier is correctly aligned.

18 The manufacturer's recommended method of seal installation is to use service tool 303-291, with two flywheel bolts to draw the seal into place. If this is not available, make up a guide from a thin sheet of plastic (perhaps cut from a plastic bottle) **(see illustrations)**. Lubricate the lips of the new seal and the crankshaft shoulder with grease, then offer up the seal, with the guide feeding the seal's lips over the crankshaft shoulder. Press the seal evenly into its housing by hand only and use a soft-faced mallet gently to tap it into place until it is flush with the surrounding housing.

19 Wipe off any surplus oil or grease; the remainder of the reassembly procedure is the reverse of dismantling, referring to the relevant text for details where required. Check for signs of oil leakage when the engine is restarted.

17 Flywheel - removal, inspection and installation

Removal

Refer to illustration 17.4

1 Remove the transaxle as described in Chapter 7A. Now is a good time to check components such as oil seals and replace them if necessary.

2 Remove the clutch as described in Chapter 6. Now is a good time to check or replace the clutch components and release bearing.

3 Use a center-punch or paint to make alignment marks on the flywheel and crankshaft to make replacement easier - the bolt holes are slightly offset, and will only line up one way, but making a mark eliminates the guesswork (and the flywheel is heavy).

4 Hold the flywheel stationary using one of the following methods:

a) *If an assistant is available, insert one of the transaxle mounting bolts into the cylinder block, and have the assistant engage a wide-bladed screwdriver with the starter ring gear teeth while the bolts are loosened.*

b) *Alternatively, a piece of angle-iron can be engaged with the ring gear, and located against the transaxle mounting bolt.*

c) *A further method is to fabricate a piece of flat metal bar with a pointed end to engage the ring gear - fit the tool to the transaxle bolt, and use washers and packing to align it with the ring gear, then tighten the bolt to hold it in position* **(see illustration)**.

5 Loosen and remove each bolt in turn and ensure that new replacements are obtained for reassembly; these bolts are subjected to severe stresses and so must be replaced, regardless of their apparent condition, whenever they are disturbed.

6 Withdraw the flywheel, remembering that it is very heavy - do not drop it.

Inspection

7 Clean the flywheel to remove grease and oil. Inspect the surface for cracks, rivet grooves, burned areas and score marks. Light scoring can be removed with emery cloth. Check for cracked and broken ring gear teeth. Lay the flywheel on a flat surface and use a straight-edge to check for warpage.

8 Clean and inspect the mating surfaces of the flywheel and the crankshaft. If the oil

seal is leaking, replace it (see Section 16) before replacing the flywheel. If the engine has covered a high mileage, it may be worth installing a new seal as a matter if course, given the amount of work needed to access it.

9 While the flywheel is removed, carefully clean its inboard (right-hand) face, particularly the recesses that serve as the reference points for the crankshaft speed/position sensor. Clean the sensor's tip and check that the sensor is securely fastened.

Installation

Refer to illustrations 17.10a, 17.10b and 17.11

10 On installation, ensure that the engine/transaxle adapter plate is in place (where necessary), then install the flywheel on the crankshaft so that all bolt holes align - it will fit only one way - check this using the marks made on removal. Install the new bolts, tightening them by hand **(see illustrations)**.

11 Lock the flywheel by the method used on dismantling. Working in a diagonal sequence to tighten them evenly and increasing to the final amount in two or three stages,

17.10a Place the flywheel into position . . .

17.10b . . . and secure with the new bolts

17.11 Tighten the flywheel bolts to the specified torque

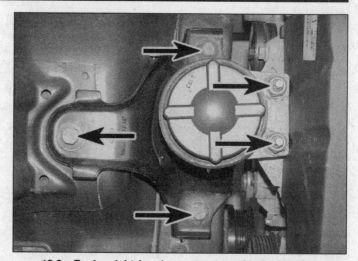

18.9a Engine right-hand mount nuts and bolts (arrows)

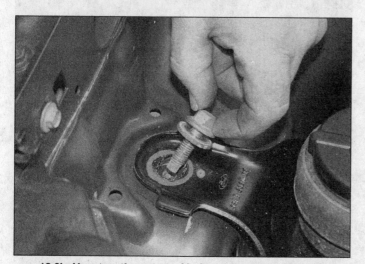

18.9b Unscrew the nuts and bolts, and remove them . . .

18.9c . . . then take off the mount completely

tighten the new bolts to the specified torque setting (see illustration).

12 The remainder of reassembly is the reverse of the removal procedure; refer to the relevant text for details where required.

18 Engine/transaxle mounts - inspection and replacement

Inspection

1 The engine/transaxle mounts seldom require attention, but broken or deteriorated mounts should be replaced immediately, or the added strain placed on the driveline components may cause damage or wear.

2 During the check, the engine/transaxle must be raised slightly, to remove its weight from the mounts.

3 Apply the parking brake, then jack up the front of the vehicle and support it on axle stands (see *Jacking and Towing*). Remove the engine under shield, if equipped. Position a

jack under the oil pan, with a large block of wood between the jack head and the oil pan, then carefully raise the engine/transaxle just enough to take the weight off the mounts.

4 Check the mounts to see if the rubber is cracked, hardened or separated from the metal components. Sometimes, the rubber will split right down the center.

5 Check for relative movement between each mount's brackets and the engine/transaxle or body (use a large screwdriver or lever to attempt to move the mountings). If movement is noted, lower the engine and check the mount nuts and bolts for tightness.

Replacement

Refer to illustrations 18.9a, 18.9b, 18.9c, 18.10a, 18.10b, 18.10c, 18.10d, 18.11a and 18.11b

6 The engine mounts can be removed if the weight of the engine/transaxle is supported by one of the following alternative methods.

7 Either support the weight of the assem-

bly from underneath using a jack and a suitable piece of wood between the jack and the oil pan (to prevent damage), or from above by attaching a hoist to the engine. A third method is to use a suitable engine support fixture (these can be rented) with end pieces that will engage in the water channel on each side of the hood opening. Using an adjustable hook and chain connected to the engine, the weight of the engine and transaxle can then be taken from the mounts.

8 Once the weight of the engine and transaxle is suitably supported, any of the mounts can be unbolted and removed.

9 To remove the engine right-hand mount, first mark the positions of the three bolts relative to the mount plate. Unscrew the three bolts securing the mount to the inner fender, and the two nuts securing it to the engine. Lift off the mount completely (see illustrations).

10 To remove the left-hand mount, first remove the battery and battery tray as described in Chapter 5, then loosen the clips and remove the air intake duct. Unscrew the five mount nuts (noting that the center one is

18.10a Engine left-hand mount nuts (arrows)

18.10b Unscrew the nuts and lift off the upper section . . .

18.10c . . . then unscrew a further three nuts (arrows) . . .

18.10d . . . and remove the lower section from the transaxle

larger than the rest) from the engine left-hand mount, then lift off the upper bracket (see illustrations). Unscrew the three nuts and remove the lower half of the mount from the transaxle (see illustrations).

11   To remove the engine rear mount/link, apply the parking brake, then jack up the front of the vehicle and support it on axle stands (see *Jacking and towing*). Unscrew the through-bolts and remove the engine rear mount link from the bracket on the transaxle and from the bracket on the underbody (see illustrations). Hold the engine stationary while the bolts are being removed, since the link will be under tension. **Note:** *The two through-bolts are of different lengths - if the bolts are replaced in the wrong positions, the rearmost bolt will interfere with the steering rack.*

12   Replacement of all mounts is a reversal of the removal procedure. Do not fully tighten the mount nuts/bolts until all of the mounts are in position. Check that the mount rubbers do not twist or distort as the mount bolts and nuts are tightened. The final tightening should be done when the full weight of the engine/transaxle is on the mounts.

18.11a Engine rear mount through-bolts (arrows)

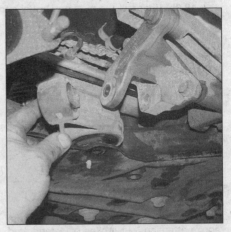

18.11b Remove the engine rear mount

Chapter 2 Part C
2.3L and 2005 and later 2.0L engines

Contents

Specifications

General

Engine type	Four-cylinder, in-line, DOHC
Engine code	
2.0L	N
2.3L	Z
Displacement	
2.0L	1989 cc (121 cubic inches)
2.3L	2300 cc (140 cubic inches)
Bore, 2.0L and 2.3L	3.445 inches
Stroke	
2.0L	3.274 inches
2.3L	3.703 inches
Firing order	1-3-4-2 (No 1 cylinder at timing chain end)
Direction of crankshaft rotation	Clockwise (seen from right-hand side of vehicle)

Camshafts

Camshaft bearing journal diameter	0.982 to 0.983 inch
Camshaft bearing journal-to-cylinder head running clearance	0.001 to 0.003 inch
Camshaft endplay	0.003 to 0.009 inch

Valves

Valve clearances (cold)	
Intake	0.008 to 0.0011 inch
Exhaust	0.010 to 0.013 inch

Cylinder head

Maximum permissible gasket surface distortion	0.004 inch

Lubrication

Engine oil capacity	See Chapter 1
Oil pressure, engine at operating temperature, 2000 rpm	29 to 39 psi

Torque Specifications

Ft-lbs (unless otherwise indicated)

Note: *One foot-pound (ft-lb) of torque is equivalent to 12 inch-pounds (in-lbs) of torque. Torque values below approximately 15 ft-lbs are expressed in inch-pounds, since most foot-pound torque wrenches are not accurate at these smaller values.*

Air conditioning compressor mounting bolts	18
Alternator mounting bolts	18
Auxiliary drivebelt idler pulley	18
Camshaft bearing cap bolts	
Step 1	hand-tight
Step 2	62 in-lbs
Step 3	144 in-lbs
Camshaft sprocket bolts	
Models through 2006	48
2007 and later models	53
Catalytic converter heat shield bolts	89 in-lbs
Catalytic converter nuts/bolts	35
Catalytic converter-to-head nuts	41
Water pump pulley bolts	180 in-lbs
Water pump mounting bolts	89 in-lbs
Crankshaft pulley bolt (new)	
Step 1	74
Step 2	Rotate an additional 90 degrees
Crankshaft rear oil seal carrier bolts	89 in-lbs
Cylinder head bolts	
Step 1	44 in-lbs
Step 2	132 in-lbs
Step 3	33
Step 4	Angle-tighten a further 90°
Step 5	Angle-tighten a further 90°
Valve cover bolts	89 in-lbs
Engine mounts:	
Left-hand mounting (transmission)	
Lower section	59
Upper section	
Center nut	98
Four outer nuts	35
Right-hand mounting lower bracket	41
Right-hand mounting upper section	
To body	35
To engine	
2005 and earlier models	59
2006 and later models	66
Transaxle roll restrictor	35
Flywheel bolts	
Step 1	37
Step 2	50
Step 3	83
Intake manifold nuts and bolts	156 in-lbs
Oil pick-up pipe bolts	84 in-lbs
Oil pressure switch	132 in-lbs
Power steering pump bracket bolts	17
Spark plugs	
Models through 2006	132 in-lbs
2007 and later models	108 in-lbs
Starter motor mounting bolts	18
Oil pan drain plug	21
Oil pan-to-lower crankcase	
Front bolts	89 in-lbs
Pan-to-crankcase bolts	18
Oil pan-to-bellhousing bolts	35
Thermostat housing	89 in-lbs
Timing chain cover	
8mm bolts	89 in-lbs
13mm bolts	35
Timing chain tensioner bolts	89 in-lbs
Transmission-to-engine bolts	35

1 General information

How to use this Chapter

This Part of Chapter 2 is devoted to repair procedures possible while the engine is still installed in the vehicle. Since these procedures are based on the assumption that the engine is installed in the vehicle, if the engine has been removed from the vehicle and mounted on a stand, some of the preliminary disassembly steps outlined will not apply.

Information concerning engine/transmission removal and replacement and engine overhaul, can be found in Part C of this Chapter.

Engine description

The engines covered by this Chapter are both of sixteen-valve, double overhead camshaft (DOHC), four-cylinder, in-line design, mounted transversely at the front of the vehicle, with the transmission on its left-hand end.

The engine is designed for lighter weight, lower emissions and increased durability over the previous engines. New features include the plastic timing belt covers and a fiberglass intake manifold. All major engine castings are of aluminum alloy, including the block and crankcase. The intake manifold is located at the radiator side of the engine and the exhaust to the firewall side, the opposite of the manifolding on other Focus four-cylinder engines.

The crankshaft runs in five main bearings, the center main bearing's upper half incorporating thrustwashers to control crankshaft endplay. The connecting rods rotate on horizontally-split bearing shells at their big-ends. The pistons are attached to the connecting rods by wrist pins that are an interference fit in the connecting rod small-end eyes. The aluminum alloy pistons are fitted with three piston rings: two compression rings and an oil control ring.

Due to the precision fitting of the engine's rotating and reciprocating internal components, the manufacturer does not supply any components for rebuilding or repairing the short-block. After its service life, the engine block and its components must be replaced as a unit only.

The intake and exhaust valves are each closed by coil springs; they operate in guides that are shrink-fitted into the cylinder head, as are the valve seat inserts.

The two camshafts are driven by the same toothed timing chain, each operating eight valves via conventional cam followers with shims. Previous engines used timing belts. Each camshaft rotates in five bearings that are line-bored directly in the cylinder head and the (bolted-on) bearing caps; this means that the bearing caps are not available separately from the cylinder head, and must not be interchanged with caps from another engine.

The water pump is bolted to the right-hand end of the cylinder block, inboard of the timing belt, and is driven with the steering pump and alternator by a multi-ribbed auxiliary drivebelt from the crankshaft pulley.

When working on this engine, note that Torx-type (both male and female heads) and hexagon socket (Allen head) fasteners are widely used; a good selection of sockets, with the necessary adapters, will be required, so that these can be unscrewed without damage and, on reassembly, tightened to the torque wrench settings specified.

Lubrication system

Lubrication is by means of an eccentric-rotor pump, which is mounted on the bottom of the block and driven by a dedicated chain from the crankshaft sprocket. The pump draws oil through a strainer located in the oil pan, and forces it through an externally-mounted full-flow cartridge-type filter. From the filter, the oil is pumped into a main gallery in the cylinder block/crankcase, from where it is distributed to the crankshaft (main bearings) and cylinder head.

The big-end bearings are supplied with oil via internal drillings in the crankshaft. Each piston crown is cooled by a spray of oil directed at its underside by a jet. These jets are fed by passages off the crankshaft oil supply galleries, with spring-loaded valves to ensure that the jets open only when there is sufficient pressure to guarantee a good oil supply to the rest of the engine components; where the jets are not fitted, separate blanking plugs are provided so that the passages are sealed, but can be cleaned at overhaul.

The cylinder head is provided with two oil galleries, one on the intake side and one on the exhaust, to ensure constant oil supply to the camshaft bearings and cam followers. A retaining valve (inserted into the cylinder head's top surface, in the middle, on the intake side) prevents these galleries from being drained when the engine is switched off. The valve incorporates a ventilation hole in its upper end, to allow air bubbles to escape from the system when the engine is restarted.

While the crankshaft and camshaft bearings receive a pressurized supply, the camshaft lobes and valves are lubricated by splash, as are all other engine components.

2 Repair operations possible with the engine in the car

The following major repair operations can be accomplished without removing the engine from the vehicle. However, owners should note that any operation involving the removal of the oil pan requires careful forethought, depending on the level of skill and the tools and facilities available; refer to the relevant text for details.

a) Compression pressure - testing.
b) Valve cover - removal and replacement.

c) Timing chain covers - removal and replacement.
d) Timing chain - replacement.
e) Timing chain tensioner and sprockets - removal and replacement.
f) Camshaft oil seals - replacement.
g) Camshafts and cam followers - removal and replacement.
h) Cylinder head - removal, overhaul and replacement.
i) Cylinder head and pistons - decarbonising.
j) Oil pan - removal and replacement.
k) Crankshaft oil seals - replacement.
l) Oil pump - removal and replacement.
m) Flywheel - removal and replacement.
n) Engine/transmission mountings - removal and replacement.

Clean the engine compartment and the exterior of the engine with some type of degreaser before any work is done (and/or clean the engine using a steam cleaner). It will make the job easier and will help to keep dirt out of the internal areas of the engine.

Depending on the components involved, it may be helpful to remove the hood, to improve access to the engine as repairs are performed (refer to Chapter 11 if necessary). Cover the fenders to prevent damage to the paint; special covers are available, but an old bedspread or blanket will also work.

3 Compression test - description and interpretation

1 When engine performance is down, or if misfiring occurs which cannot be attributed to the ignition or fuel systems, a compression test can provide diagnostic clues as to the engine's condition. If the test is performed regularly, it can give warning of trouble before any other symptoms become apparent.

2 The engine must be fully warmed-up to normal operating temperature, the oil level must be correct, the battery must be fully charged and the spark plugs must be removed. The aid of an assistant will also be required.

3 Disable the ignition system by disconnecting the ignition coil's electrical connector.

4 Referring to Chapter 12, identify and remove the fuel pump fuse from the fusebox. Now start the engine and allow it to run until it stalls. If the engine will not start, at least keep it cranking for about 10 seconds. The fuel system should now be depressurized, preventing unburned fuel from soaking the catalytic converter as the engine is turned over during the test.

5 Fit a compression tester to the No 1 cylinder spark plug hole - the type of tester which screws into the plug thread is preferred.

6 Have the assistant hold the throttle wide open and crank the engine on the starter motor; after one or two revolutions, the compression pressure should build up to a maxi-

4.5 Slide the tool/metal bar into the slots in the ends of the camshafts

4.6 Remove the timing hole plug . . .

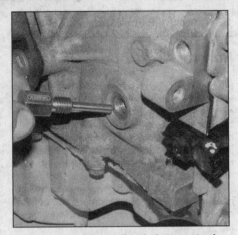

4.7 . . . and insert the timing peg tool

mum figure and then stabilize. Record the highest reading obtained.

7   The compression will build up fairly quickly in a healthy engine. Low compression on the first stroke, followed by gradually-increasing pressure on successive strokes, indicates worn piston rings. A low compression on the first stroke which does not rise on successive strokes, indicates leaking valves or a blown head gasket (a cracked cylinder head could also be the cause). Deposits on the underside of the valve heads can also cause low compression. Record the highest gauge reading obtained, then repeat the procedure for the remaining cylinders.

8   Due to the variety of testers available, and the fluctuation in starter motor speed when cranking the engine, different readings are often obtained when carrying out the compression test. For this reason, specific compression pressure figures are not quoted by Ford. However, the most important factor is that the compression pressures are uniform in all cylinders, and that is what this test is mainly concerned with.

9   If the pressure in any cylinder is considerably lower than the others, introduce a teaspoonful of clean oil into that cylinder through its spark plug hole and repeat the test.

10   If the addition of oil temporarily improves the compression pressure, this indicates that bore or piston wear is responsible for the pressure loss. No improvement suggests that leaking or burnt valves, or a blown head gasket, may be to blame.

11   A low reading from two adjacent cylinders is almost certainly due to the head gasket having blown between them; the presence of coolant in the engine oil will confirm this.

12   If one cylinder is about 20 percent lower than the others and the engine has a slightly rough idle, a worn camshaft lobe or faulty cam follower/shim could be the cause.

13   If the compression is unusually high, the combustion chambers are probably coated with carbon deposits. If this is the case, the cylinder head should be removed and decarbonized.

14   On completion of the test, install the spark plugs, then reconnect the ignition system coil and install the fuel pump fuse.

4   Top Dead Center (TDC) for No 1 piston - locating

Refer to illustrations 4.5, 4.6, and 4.7

1   Top dead center (TDC) is the highest point of the cylinder that each piston reaches as the crankshaft turns. Each piston reaches its TDC position at the end of its compression stroke, and then again at the end of its exhaust stroke. For the purpose of engine timing, TDC on the compression stroke for No 1 piston is used. No 1 cylinder is at the timing belt end of the engine. Proceed as follows.

2   Disconnect the battery negative cable (see Chapter 1).

3   Remove all the spark plugs as described in Chapter 1, then remove the valve cover as described in Section 4.

4   Using a wrench or socket on the crankshaft pulley bolt (remove the panel in the fenderwell liner for access), rotate the crankshaft clockwise until the intake valves for No 1 cylinder have opened and just closed again.

5   The camshafts each have a machined slot at the transmission end of the engine; both slots will be completely horizontal, and at the same height as the cylinder head machined surface, when the engine is at TDC on No 1 cylinder. Ford service tool 303-465 is used to check this position, and to positively locate the camshafts in position. Fortunately, a substitute tool can be made from a strip of metal 5 mm thick (while the strip's thickness is critical, its length and width are not, but should be approximately 180 to 230 mm long by 20 to 30 mm wide) **(see illustration). Caution:** *Never use the camshaft alignment tool as a means to stop the engine from rotating or engine damage can result - use only the timing pin tool for this purpose.*

6   A TDC timing hole is provided on the front of the cylinder block to permit the crank-

shaft to be located more accurately at TDC. The blanking plug is located behind the catalytic converter, and access is not easy - also, take care against burning if the engine is still warm **(see illustration).**

7   Unscrew the timing pin blanking plug and screw in the timing pin (Ford service tool 305-507); this tool is obtainable from Ford dealers or a tool supplier **(see illustration).** An alternative pin can be made from an M10 diameter bolt, cut down so that the length from the underside of the bolt head to the tip is exactly 63.4 mm. It may be necessary to slightly turn the crankshaft either way (remove the tool from the camshafts first) to be able to fully insert the timing pin.

8   Turn the engine forwards slowly until the crankshaft comes into contact with the timing pin - in this position, the engine is set to TDC on No 1 cylinder.

9   Before rotating the crankshaft again, make sure that the timing pin is removed. When operations are complete, do not forget to install the blanking plug.

10   If the timing pin is not available, insert a length of wooden dowel (about 150 mm/6 in long) or similar into the No 1 spark plug hole until it rests on the piston crown. Turn the engine back from its TDC position, then forward (taking care not to allow the dowel to be trapped in the cylinder) until the dowel stops rising - the piston is now at the top of its compression stroke and the dowel can be removed.

11   There is a 'dead' area around TDC (as the piston stops rising, pauses and then begins to descend) which makes it difficult to locate the exact location of TDC by this method; if accuracy is required, either carefully establish the exact mid-point of the dead area (perhaps by using a dial gauge and probe), or refer to paragraph 5.

12   Once No 1 cylinder has been positioned at TDC on the compression stroke, TDC for any of the other cylinders can then be located by rotating the crankshaft clockwise 180° at a time and following the firing order (see Specifications).

5.2 Disconnect the electrical connector from the camshaft position sensor

5.3 Unclip the wiring harness from the camshaft cover

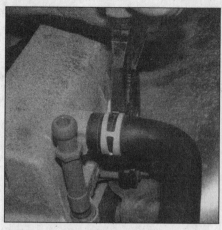
5.4 Use a pair of pliers to squeeze the clamp and remove the PCV hose from the valve cover

5.8 Check the rubber seal on each valve cover bolt for damage

5.10 Insert the bolts through the cover and gasket, making sure the gasket is fully located in its groove

5 Camshaft cover - removal and installation

Removal

Refer to illustrations 5.2, 5.3, 5.4 and 5.8

1   Disconnect the negative battery cable (see Chapter 1).
2   Disconnect the electrical connector from the camshaft position sensor **(see illustration)**. Pull up the boot on the coolant temperature sensor electrical connector.
3   Detach the wiring harness from the camshaft cover **(see illustration)**.
4   Disconnect the positive crankcase ventilation (PCV) hose from the camshaft cover **(see illustration)**. On models with secondary air injection, disconnect the oxygen sensor electrical connector.
5   Unscrew the three engine upper plastic cover retaining pegs from the camshaft cover retaining studs. Note the position of the retaining studs.
6   Carefully unbolt and remove the individual coils from the spark plugs and withdraw them, unclipping the leads from the cover.
7   Working progressively, unscrew the cylinder head cover retaining bolts and withdraw the cover.

8   Discard the cover gasket; this must be replaced whenever it is disturbed. Check that the sealing faces are undamaged, and that the rubber seal at each retaining bolt is serviceable **(see illustration)**; renew any worn or damaged seals.

Installation

Refer to illustrations 5.10 and 5.11

9   On installation, clean the cover and cylinder head gasket faces carefully, then fit a new gasket to the cover, ensuring that it locates correctly in the cover grooves.
10   Insert the retaining bolts, complete with rubber seals and spacer at each bolt location, then replace the cover to the cylinder head **(see illustration)**. Start all bolts finger-tight, ensuring that the gasket remains seated in its groove.
11   Working in the sequence shown **(see illustration)**, tighten the cover bolts to the specified torque.

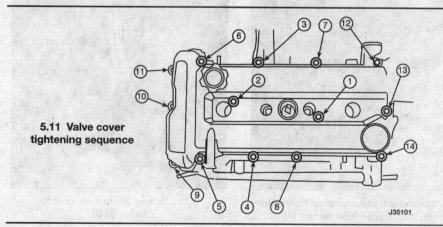
5.11 Valve cover tightening sequence

J35101

6.4 Intake manifold lower mounting bolt

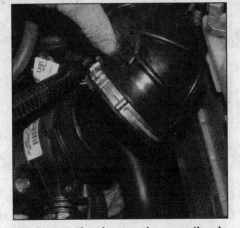

6.5 Loosen the clamp and remove the air intake pipe

6.6 Twist the outer cable to release it from the mounting bracket

6   Intake manifold - removal and installation

Warning: *Gasoline is extremely flammable, so take extra precautions when disconnecting any part of the fuel system. Don't smoke, or allow naked flames or bare light bulbs in or near the work area. Don't work in a garage where a gas appliance (such as a clothes dryer or water heater) is installed. If you spill gasoline on your skin, rinse it off immediately. Have a fire extinguisher rated for gasoline fires handy, and know how to use it.*

Removal
Refer to illustrations 6.4, 6.5, 6.6, 6.7a, 6.7b and 6.10

1   Park the vehicle on firm, level ground, apply the handbrake, then jack up the front of the vehicle and support it on axle stands (see *Jacking and vehicle support*).
2   Disconnect the battery negative cable (see Chapter 1).
3   Refer to Chapter 3 and remove the engine cooling fans and shroud.
4   From underneath the vehicle, remove the lower oil level dipstick tube retaining bolt, and the intake manifold lower retaining bolt **(see illustration)**.

5   Release the securing clamp and detach the air intake pipe from the throttle body **(see illustration).**
6   On models so equipped, remove the snow shield over the throttle body. Unclip the accelerator inner cable from the throttle linkage, then twist the outer cable to release it from the bracket **(see illustration).**
7   Unplug the two electrical connectors from the throttle position (TP) sensor and the idle air control (IAC) valve **(see illustrations).**
8   Carefully pull the vacuum hoses (for the brakes, the fuel pulse damper and the purge valve) to release them from the intake manifold.
9   Detach the wiring harness from across the top of the intake manifold (releasing it from any relevant connectors and retaining clips, marking or labeling them as they are unplugged), then move the wiring loom to one side of the engine bay.
10   Remove the upper retaining bolt **(see illustration)** and withdraw the oil level dipstick tube out from the engine. Replace the O-ring at the bottom of the dipstick tube on reassembly.
11   Unscrew the seven bolts securing the intake manifold to the cylinder head and with-

draw it enough to disconnect the PCV hose behind it and the electrical connector from the knock sensor on the block. **Note:** *There are three sizes of bolts. Make note of their locations on disassembly.* Take care not to damage vulnerable components such as the EGR pipe and valve as the manifold assembly is drawn out of the engine compartment.

Installation
Refer to illustration 6.12
12   Installation is the reverse of the removal procedure, noting the following points:

a) *When using a scraper and solvent to remove all traces of old gasket material and sealant from the manifold and cylinder head, be careful to ensure that you do not scratch or damage the material of either; the cylinder head is made of aluminum alloy, while the manifold is a plastic molding - any solvents used must be suitable for this application. If the gasket was leaking, have the mating surfaces checked for warpage at an automotive machine shop. While it may be possible to have the cylinder head gasket surface skimmed if necessary, to remove any dis-*

6.7a Disconnect the electrical connectors from the throttle position sensor (TPS) . . .

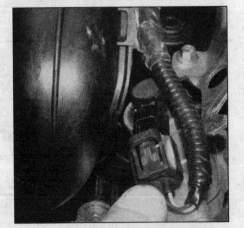

6.7b . . . and the idle air control valve (IAC)

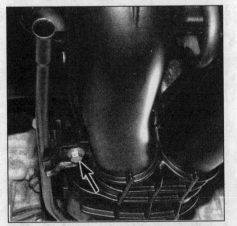

6.10 Remove the oil level dipstick tube upper retaining bolt

6.12 Install the new EGR gasket

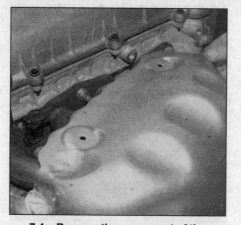

7.4a Remove the upper part of the exhaust manifold heat shield . . .

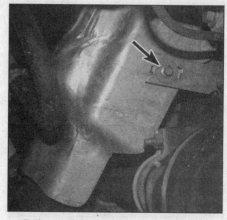

7.4b . . . then remove the lower heat shield bolts (one side shown here)

tortion, the manifold must be replaced if it is found to be warped, cracked - check with special care around the mounting points for components such as the idle speed control valve and EGR pipe - or otherwise faulty.

b) Provided the relevant mating surfaces are clean and flat, a new gasket will be sufficient to ensure the joint is gas-tight. Do not use any kind of silicone-based sealant on any part of the fuel system or intake manifold.

c) Fit new gaskets to the four intake ports and one to the EGR port in the manifold **(see illustration)**, then locate the manifold on the head and install the retaining bolts.

d) Tighten the bolts evenly to the torque listed in the Specifications at the beginning of this Chapter. Work from the center outwards, to avoid warping the manifold.

e) Replace the remaining parts in the reverse order of removal - tighten all fasteners to the torque wrench settings specified and fit a new O-ring seal to the bottom of the dipstick tube.

f) Make sure the wiring loom is routed correctly and the connections fitted as labeled upon removal.

g) Before starting the engine, check the accelerator cable for correct adjustment and the throttle linkage for smooth operation.

h) When the engine is fully warmed-up, check for signs of fuel, intake and/or vacuum leaks.

i) Road test the vehicle, and check for proper operation of all disturbed components.

---

7 Exhaust manifold - removal, inspection and installation

Warning: *The engine must be completely cool before beginning this procedure.*

Removal

Refer to illustrations 7.4a, 7.4b, 7.5, 7.6 and 7.7

1 Park the vehicle on firm, level ground, apply the handbrake, then jack up the front of the vehicle and support it on axle stands (see *Jacking and vehicle support*).

2 Disconnect the negative battery cable (see Chapter 1).

3 Disconnect and remove the oxygen sen-

sor (see Chapter 4A).

4 Undo the bolts and withdraw the upper part of the heat shield, then undo the two lower retaining bolts and remove the lower part from the exhaust manifold **(see illustrations)**.

5 From under the vehicle, unscrew the two retaining nuts to disconnect the exhaust system front down-pipe from the manifold **(see illustration)**.

6 Undo the bolts and remove the exhaust manifold lower retaining bracket **(see illustration)**.

7 Remove the nuts and detach the exhaust manifold and gasket. Take care not to damage vulnerable components as the manifold assembly is maneuvered out of the engine compartment. When removing the manifold with the engine in the vehicle, additional clearance can be obtained by unscrewing the studs from the cylinder head; a female Torx-type socket will be required **(see illustration)**. **Note:** *On models with the PZEV 2.0L engine, the catalytic converter is part of the exhaust manifold. On these vehicles, you must unbolt and set aside the power steering pump and several other components at the rear of the engine in order to remove the exhaust manifold/converter from the top instead of the bottom.*

7.5 Remove the two bolts from the front exhaust pipe

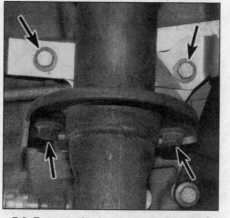

7.6 Remove the four bolts at the lower manifold support bracket

7.7 The exhaust studs can be removed for more manifold-removal clearance using a Torx socket

8.3 Use a flywheel locking tool to hold the flywheel

8.6 Always use a new bolt when installing the crankshaft pulley

9.3 Loosen the three water pump bolts

Inspection

8   When using a scraper to remove all traces of old gasket material and carbon deposits from the manifold and cylinder head mating surfaces, be careful to ensure that you do not scratch or damage the material of either component - any solvents used must be suitable for this application. If the gasket was leaking, check the manifold and cylinder head for warpage, this may need to be done at an automotive machine shop, resurface if necessary. **Caution:** *When scraping, be very careful not to gouge or scratch the delicate aluminum alloy cylinder head.*

9   Provided both mating surfaces are clean and flat, a new gasket will be sufficient to ensure the joint is gas-tight. Do not use any kind of exhaust sealant upstream of the catalytic converter.

Installation

10   Installation is the reverse of the removal procedure, noting the following points:

a) Fit a new manifold gasket over the cylinder head studs.

b) Install the manifold, and tighten the nuts to the torque listed in the Specifications at the beginning of this Chapter.

c) Fit a new gasket to the front pipe (where fitted).

d) Where a catalytic converter was unbolted, use new nuts on installation.

e) Run the engine, and check for exhaust leaks.

8   Crankshaft pulley - removal and replacement

Note 1: *Only turn the engine in the normal direction of rotation - clockwise from the right-hand side of the vehicle.*

Note 2: *The crankshaft pulley retaining bolt is very tight and Ford uses a special tool (T78P-4851-A) to lock the pulley to prevent it from turning. A two-pin spanner may also work to keep the crankshaft from moving while remov-*

ing the pulley bolt. A new pulley retaining bolt will be required on installation.

Caution: *The pulley and crankshaft timing gear are not on a keyway, they are held in place by the crankshaft retaining bolt. Make sure the engine is set at TDC (see Section 4) before the pulley is removed.*

Removal

Refer to illustration 8.3

1   Remove the auxiliary drivebelt - either remove the drivebelt completely, or just secure it clear of the crankshaft pulley, depending on the work to be carried out (see Chapter 1).

2   Set the engine to TDC (see Section 4).

3   The crankshaft must now be locked to prevent its rotation while the pulley bolt is unscrewed. If the special tool is not available proceed as follows:

a) *Remove the rubber plug from the transmission bellhousing or, on automatics, unbolt the small metal cover plate from the oil pan, and use a large screwdriver or similar to lock the flywheel/driveplate ring gear teeth while an assistant loosens the pulley bolt; take care not to damage the teeth or the surrounding castings when using this method.*

b) *If the engine/transmission has been removed and separated, lock the flywheel/driveplate using a locking tool* **(see illustration)**.

4   Unscrew the pulley bolt and remove the pulley.

Installation

Refer to illustration 8.6

5   Ensure that the engine is still set to TDC as in Section 4, then lightly oil the seal area of the crankshaft and install the pulley.

6   Ensure that a new retaining bolt is used **(see illustration)**, and tighten it only hand-tight.

7   Insert a one-inch-long 6mm bolt through the hole, which should be at the bottom when the pulley is in its TDC position, and thread it into the timing cover. This locates the pulley

exactly in its TDC position. **Warning:** *The pulley is not keyed to the crankshaft, this procedure is the only way to establish the proper relationship between the crankshaft pulley and the engine.*

8   Have an assistant use a two-pin spanner to securely hold the pulley while you tighten the pulley center-bolt to Specifications.

9   Remove the 6mm locating bolt from the pulley. The remainder of the installation is the reverse of the removal procedure.

9   Timing chain cover - removal and installation

Note: *Only turn the engine in the normal direction of rotation - clockwise from the right-hand side of the vehicle.*

Removal

Refer to illustrations 9.3, 9.7, 9.9, 9.10 and 9.11

1   Remove the camshaft cover as described in Section 5.

2   Apply the handbrake, then jack up the front of the vehicle and support it on axle stands (see *Jacking and vehicle support*). Remove the right-hand front wheel and remove the splash apron from under the right-hand front wheelwell.

3   Loosen the water pump pulley retaining bolts by approximately three turns **(see illustration)**.

4   Remove the auxiliary drivebelt (see Chapter 1A).

5   Remove the power steering pump as described in Chapter 10.

6   Remove the crankshaft pulley (see Section 8).

7   Disconnect the crankshaft position (CKP) sensor wiring connector **(see illustration)**.

8   Unscrew the retaining bolts and remove the water pump pulley.

9   Undo the retaining bolts and move the coolant expansion tank to one side, discon-

9.7 Disconnect the electrical connector from the crankshaft position sensor (CKP)

9.9 Unbolt and set aside the coolant expansion tank

9.10 With the engine supported, remove the engine mount

nect the lower coolant hose if required **(see illustration)**.

10   Support the engine using a floorjack and block of wood beneath the oil pan, then unscrew the nuts/bolts securing the engine/transmission right hand mounting bracket and remove the mounting from the engine **(see illustration)**.

11   Unbolt and remove the auxiliary drive-belt idler pulley **(see illustration)**.

12   Unscrew the timing chain cover retaining bolts (noting their positions for installation) and withdraw the cover from the engine.

Installation

Refer to illustrations 9.13a and 9.13b

13   Installation is the reverse of the removal procedure (using the relevant Sections); note the following points:

  a) *Clean the sealant from the timing cover, cylinder block and cylinder head mating surfaces. When using a scraper and solvent to remove all traces of old gasket/sealant from the mating surfaces, be careful to ensure that you do not scratch or damage the material of either component - any solvents used must be suitable for this application. If the gasket was leaking, have the mating surfaces checked for warpage - this may need to be done at an automotive machine shop.*

  b) *Provided the relevant mating surfaces are clean and flat, apply a (3.0mm) bead of silicone sealant around the timing chain cover and the inner bolt holes* **(see illustration)**. **Note:** *The cover must be fitted within 10 minutes of applying the sealant.*

  c) *Tighten the timing chain cover bolts to the specified torque settings at the beginning of this Chapter, following the sequence shown* **(see illustration)**.

  d) *Retime the engine to TDC and align the crankshaft pulley as described in Sections 4 and 8.*

  e) *Use a new O-ring on the power steering pressure hose.*

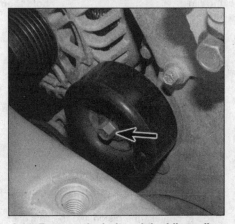

9.11 Remove the bolt and the idler pulley

9.13a Apply a 3mm bead of sealant around the timing chain cover, including around the inner bolt holes

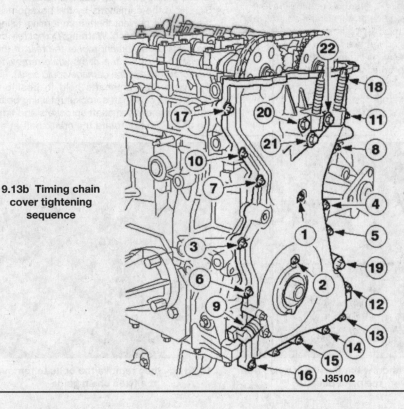

9.13b Timing chain cover tightening sequence

10.4 Push against the timing chain guide to depress the tensioner, then insert a 1.5mm locking pin

10.6 Use a large wrench on the hex portion of the camshafts to hold them while removing the sprocket bolts

10   Timing chain, tensioner and guides - removal, inspection and installation

Note 1: *Only turn the engine in the normal direction of rotation - clockwise (as seen from the right-hand side of the vehicle).*

Note 2: *The following procedure is made easier by supporting the engine (with a floor-jack from below or an engine support fixture from above) and loosening or removing the motor mounts to allow the engine to be lowered somewhat for better access.*

Removal

** CAUTION **

The timing system is complex. Severe engine damage will occur if you make any mistakes. Do not attempt this procedure unless you are highly experienced with this type of repair. If you are at all unsure of your abilities, consult an expert. Double-check all your work and be sure everything is correct before you attempt to start the engine.

Refer to illustrations 10.4, 10.6, 10.7a, 10.7b and 10.8

1   Remove the camshaft cover as described in Section 5. Refer to Chapter 3 and remove the coolant recovery bottle, then remove the battery and battery tray (see Chapter 5A).

2   Set the engine to TDC as described in Section 4.

3   Remove the timing chain cover as described in Section 9.

4   Loosen the timing chain tensioner by inserting a small screwdriver into the access hole in the tensioner and releasing the pawl mechanism. Press against the timing chain guide to depress the piston into the tensioner housing - when fully depressed, insert a locking pin (approximately 1.5 mm) to lock the piston in its compressed position **(see illustration)**.

5   Hold the camshafts by the hexagon on the shafts to prevent them from turning, using an open-end wrench. **Warning:** *Do not rely on the camshaft alignment tool at the rear of the camshafts to hold the cams while removing the sprockets. Engine damage could result.*

6   With the camshafts held in position, remove the camshaft sprocket retaining bolts and remove the camshaft sprockets and timing chain. Do not rotate the crankshaft at all

until the final timing chain installation **(see illustration)**.

7   If required, unbolt the fixed timing chain guide and withdraw the tensioner timing chain guide from its pivot pin on the cylinder head **(see illustrations)**.

8   To remove the tensioner, undo the two retaining bolts and remove the timing chain tensioner from the cylinder block, taking care not to remove the locking pin **(see illustration)**.

9   To remove the timing chain sprocket from the crankshaft, the oil pump drive chain will need to be removed as described in Section 15. Note which way it is installed, then mark the sprocket to ensure correct installation.

Inspection

Note: *Keep all components identified for position to ensure correct installation.*

10   Clean all components thoroughly and wipe dry.

11   Examine the chain tensioner and tensioner guide for excessive wear or other damage. Check the guides for deep grooves made by the timing chain.

12   Examine the timing chain for excessive wear. Hold it horizontally and check how

10.7a Withdraw the tensioner guide from the pivot pin . . .

10.7b . . . then remove the bolts to remove the fixed chain guide

10.8 With the locking pin (drill bit) in place, remove the bolts and the tensioner

much movement exists in the chain links. If there is any doubt, compare it to a new chain. Renew as necessary.

13   Examine the teeth of the camshaft and crankshaft sprockets for excessive wear and damage.

14   Before installation the timing chain tensioner, the piston must be compressed and locked until installation (if not already done on removal). To do this, insert a small screwdriver into the access hole in the tensioner and release the pawl mechanism. Now lightly clamp the tensioner in a soft-jawed vice and slowly compress the piston. Do not apply excessive force and make sure that the piston remains aligned with its cylinder. When completely compressed, insert a locking pin/1.5 mm diameter wire rod into the special hole to lock the piston in its compressed position.

Installation

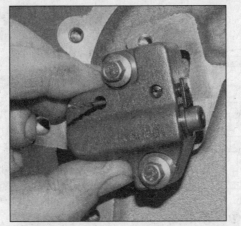

10.16 Install the timing chain tensioner (still in the locked position) to the block

10.17 Install the timing chain guides to the block

> ** CAUTION **
> Before starting the engine, carefully rotate the crankshaft by hand through at least two full revolutions (use a socket and breaker bar on the crankshaft pulley center bolt). If you feel any resistance, STOP! There is something wrong - most likely, valves are contacting the pistons. You must find the problem before proceeding. Check your work and see if any updated repair information is available.

Refer to illustrations 10.16, 10.17, 10.19, 10.20 and 10.22

15   If not already fitted, slide the crankshaft drive sprocket (and washer, where fitted) onto the crankshaft. Ensure it is installed the same way round as noted on removal (see Section 15, for further information on instal-ling the oil pump drive chain).

16   Replace the tensioner to the cylinder block and tighten the retaining bolts to the specified torque setting. Take care not to remove the locking pin **(see illustration)**.

17   Replace the fixed timing chain guide and

tighten the two retaining bolts, then slide the tensioner timing chain guide back into place on the upper pivot pin **(see illustration)**.

18   Replace the intake camshaft sprocket onto the camshaft, DO NOT tighten the retaining bolt at this stage.

19   With the timing chain around the exhaust camshaft sprocket replace the timing chain and sprocket, feeding the timing chain around the crankshaft drive sprocket and intake camshaft sprocket **(see illustration)**.

20   With the timing chain in place, hold pressure against the tensioner guide and withdraw the tensioner locking pin. This will then tension the timing chain **(see illustration)**.

21   Check that the engine is still set to TDC (as described in Section 4).

22   Tighten both camshaft retaining bolts, to the torque setting specified in the Specifications at the beginning of this Chapter. **Note:** *Use an open-end wrench on the hexagon on the camshafts to stop them from turning* **(see illustration)**.

23   Replace the timing chain cover as described in Section 9, and the crankshaft pulley as described in Section 8.

24   Remove the camshaft locking plate and crankshaft timing peg and turn the engine (in

10.19 Install the camshaft sprockets with the chain in position

the direction of engine rotation) two full turns. Replace the camshaft locking plate and crankshaft timing peg to make sure the engine is still set at TDC (see Section 4 for further information).

25   Replace the camshaft cover as described in Section 5.

10.20 While holding pressure against the tensioner with the guide, remove the tensioner locking pin

10.22 Use an large wrench on the hex portion to hold the camshaft while installing the sprocket bolt

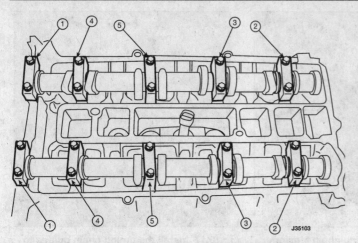

11.4 Camshaft bearing cap bolt LOOSENING sequence

11.5a Note the identification marks on each of the camshaft bearing caps . . .

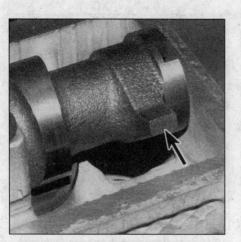

11.5b . . . and the reference lobe for the CMP on the intake camshaft

11.6a Use a rubber suction cup (like a valve-lapping tool) to remove the tappets

11.6b Write down the thickness number under each tappet - different sizes are available

11 Camshafts and tappets - removal, inspection and installation

Note: *Only turn the engine in the normal direction of rotation - clockwise from the right-hand side of the vehicle.*

Removal

Refer to illustrations 11.4, 11.5a, 11.5b, 11.6a and 11.6b

1   Remove the camshaft cover as described in Section 5.

2   Remove the timing hole plug and insert a timing peg to position the crankshaft at TDC (obtainable from Ford dealers (303-507) or a tool supplier). For further information on setting the engine to TDC, see Section 4.

3   Remove the timing chain and camshaft sprockets as described in Section 10.

4   Working in the sequence shown **(see illustration)**, loosen the camshaft bearing cap bolts progressively by half a turn at a time. Work only as described, to release gradually and evenly the pressure of the valve springs on the caps.

5   Withdraw the camshaft bearing caps, noting their markings, then remove the camshafts. The intake camshaft can be identified by the reference lobe for the camshaft position sensor; therefore, there is no need to mark the camshafts **(see illustrations)**.

6   Obtain sixteen small, clean containers, and number them 1 to 16. Using a rubber suction cup, withdraw each bucket tappet in turn and place them in the containers. Do not interchange the bucket tappets as they are of different sizes; the shim is part of the bucket tappet **(see illustrations)**. Different sizes of bucket tappets are available in the event of wear on the valves or repair on the cylinder head assembly.

Inspection

Refer to illustrations 11.8, 11.9, 11.11, 11.12a and 11.12b

7   With the camshafts and tappets removed, check each for signs of obvious wear (scoring, pitting, etc) and for roundness, and replace if necessary.

8   Measure the outside diameter of each tappet **(see illustration)** - take measurements at the top and bottom of each tappet, then a

second set at right-angles to the first; if any measurement is significantly different from the others, the tappet is tapered or oval (as applicable) and must be replaced. If the necessary equipment is available, measure the inside diameter of the corresponding cylinder head bore. If the tappets or the cylinder head bores

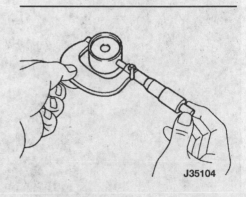

11.8 Use a micrometer to measure the tappet diameters

11.9 Check the camshaft lobes for pitting, wear and score marks - if scoring is excessive as shown here, replace the camshaft

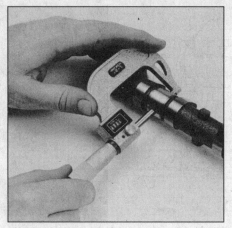

11.11 Measure each camshaft journal with a micrometer

11.12a Lay a strip of Plastigage on each camshaft journal

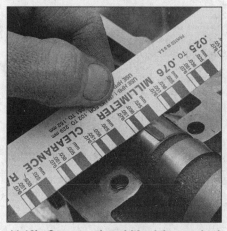

11.12b Compare the width of the crushed Plastigage to the scale on the envelope to determine the running clearance

are excessively worn, new tappets and/or a new cylinder head will be required.

9   Visually examine the camshaft lobes for score marks, pitting, galling (wear due to rubbing) and evidence of overheating (blue, discolored areas). Look for flaking away of the hardened surface layer of each lobe **(see illustration)**. If any such signs are evident, replace the component concerned.

10   Examine the camshaft bearing journals and the cylinder head bearing surfaces for signs of obvious wear or pitting. If any such signs are evident, renew the component concerned.

11   Using a micrometer, measure the diameter of each journal at several points **(see illustration)**. If any measurement is significantly different from the others, renew the camshaft.

12   To check the bearing journal running clearance, remove the tappets, use a suitable solvent and a clean lint-free rag to clean carefully all bearing surfaces, then replace the camshafts and bearing caps with a strand of Plastigage across each journal **(see illustration)**. Tighten the bearing cap bolts to the specified torque wrench setting (do not rotate the camshafts), then remove the bearing caps and use the scale provided to measure the width of the compressed strands **(see illustration)**. Scrape off the Plastigage with your fingernail or the edge of a credit card - don't scratch or nick the journals or bearing caps.

13   If the running clearance of any bearing is found to be worn to beyond the specified service limits, install a new camshaft and repeat the check; if the clearance is still excessive, the cylinder head must be replaced.

14   To check camshaft endplay, remove the tappets, clean the bearing surfaces carefully, and replace the camshafts and bearing caps. Tighten the bearing cap bolts to the specified torque wrench setting, then measure the endplay using a DTI (Dial Test Indicator, or dial gauge) mounted on the cylinder head so that its tip bears on the camshaft right-hand end.

15   Tap the camshaft fully towards the gauge, zero the gauge, then tap the camshaft fully away from the gauge, and note the gauge reading. If the endplay measured is found to be at or beyond the specified service limit, fit a new camshaft and repeat the check; if the clearance is still excessive, the cylinder head must be replaced.

Installation
Refer to illustrations 11.16, 11.18, 11.20 and 11.21

16   On reassembly, liberally oil the cylinder head tappet bores and the tappets **(see illustration)**. Carefully replace the tappets to the cylinder head, ensuring that each tappet is returned its original bore. Some care will be required to enter the tappets squarely into their bores.

17   Turn the engine back approximately 45° so that there are no pistons at the top of the cylinders.

18   Liberally oil the camshaft bearings and lobes **(see illustration)**. Ensuring that each camshaft is in its original location, replace the camshafts, locating each so that the slot in its left-hand end is approximately parallel to, and just above, the cylinder head mating surface.

19   All camshaft bearing caps have an identifying number and letter etched on them. The exhaust camshaft's bearing caps are numbered in sequence E1 to E5 and the inlet camshaft's bearing caps I1 to I5 **(see illustration 11.5a)**.

11.16 Oil the tappets liberally during installation

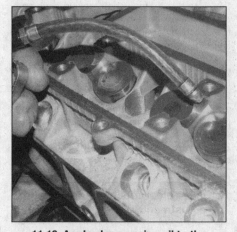

11.18 Apply clean engine oil to the camshaft lobes and journals before installation

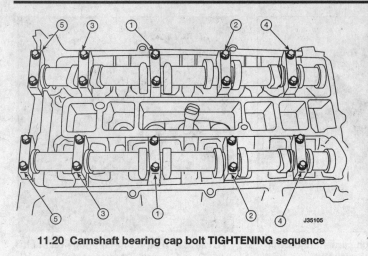

11.20 Camshaft bearing cap bolt TIGHTENING sequence

11.21 Fit the camshaft tool to ensure the camshafts are in the TDC position

20   Ensuring that each cap is kept square to the cylinder head as it is tightened down, and working in the sequence shown **(see illustration)**, tighten the camshaft bearing cap bolts slowly and by one turn at a time, until each cap touches the cylinder head. Next, go around again in the same sequence, tightening the bolts to the first stage torque setting specified, then once more, tightening them to the second stage setting. Work only as described, to impose gradually and evenly the pressure of the valve springs on the caps.

21   Fit the camshaft aligning tool; it should slip into place as described in Section 4, paragraph 12 **(see illustration)**.

22   Replace the camshaft sprockets, complete with timing chain, to the ends of the camshafts. DO NOT tighten the camshaft sprocket retaining bolts at this stage.

23   Turn the engine (in the direction of rotation) approximately 45° back to TDC. For further information on setting the engine to TDC, see Section 4.

24   With the camshafts held in position (by using an open-ended spanner on the hexagon on the shaft), tighten the camshaft sprocket retaining bolts to the specified torque.

25   Remove the camshaft locking plate and crankshaft timing peg and turn the engine (in the direction of engine rotation) two full turns. Replace the camshaft locking plate and crankshaft timing peg to make sure the engine is still set at TDC (see Section 4 for further information).

26   Replace the timing chain cover upper and lower blanking plugs, coat the blanking plug threads with a suitable sealant to prevent leaks.

27   Replace the camshaft cover as described in Section 5.

12   Valve clearances - checking and adjustment

Note: *Only turn the engine in the normal direction of rotation - clockwise from the right-hand side of the vehicle.*

Checking

Refer to illustration 12.3

1   Remove the camshaft cover as described in Section 5.

2   Set the engine to TDC on cylinder No 1 as described in Section 4. The inlet and exhaust cam lobes of No 1 cylinder will be pointing upwards (though not vertical) and the valve clearances can be checked.

3   Working on each valve, measure the clearance between the base of the cam lobe and the bucket tappet using feeler blades **(see illustration)**. Record the thickness of the blade required to give a firm sliding fit on all the valves of No 1 cylinder. The desired clearances are given in the Specifications. Note that the clearances for intake and exhaust valves are different. The intake camshaft is at the front of the engine and the exhaust camshaft at the rear. Record all four clearances.

4   Now turn the crankshaft clockwise through 180° so that the valves of cylinder No 3 are pointing upwards. Check and record the four valve clearances for cylinder No 3. The clearances for cylinders 4 and 2 can be checked after turning the crankshaft through 180° each time.

12.3 Measure the clearance between the base of the camshaft lobe and the bucket using feeler gauges

Adjustment

Refer to illustration 12.6

5   If adjustment is required, the bucket tappets must be changed by removing the camshafts as described in Section 11.

6   If the valve clearance was too small, a thinner bucket tappet must be fitted. If the clearance was too large, a thicker bucket tappet must be fitted. The bucket tappet has a number engraved on the inside **(see illustration)**, if the marking is missing or illegible, a micrometer will be needed to establish bucket tappet thickness.

7   When the bucket tappet thickness and the valve clearance are known, the required thickness of the new bucket tappet can be calculated as follows:

Sample calculation - clearance too small
Desired clearance (A) = 0.25 mm
Measured clearance (B) = 0.20 mm
Tappet thickness found (C) = 2.55 mm
Thickness required (D) = C + B - A = 2.50 mm

Sample calculation - clearance too large
Desired clearance (A) = 0.30 mm
Measured clearance (B) = 0.36 mm
Tappet thickness found (C) = 2.19 mm
Thickness required (D) = C + B - A = 2.25 mm

8   With the correct thickness bucket tap-

12.6 Each tappet has a number engraved inside

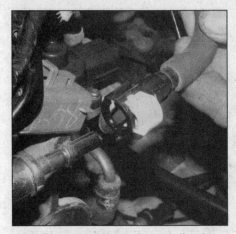

13.9 Disconnect the fuel supply line from the fuel rail

13.10 Disconnect the hoses from the coolant housing

13.11 Remove the upper alternator bracket bolt

pets installed in the cylinder head, replace the camshafts as described in Section 11.

9 Check that the valve clearances are now correct, as described in Steps 2 to 4. If any clearances are still not within specification then carry out the adjustment procedure again.

10 It will be helpful for future adjustment if a record is kept of the thickness of bucket fitted at each position. The buckets required can be purchased in advance once the clearances and the existing bucket thicknesses are known.

11 When all the clearances are correct, replace the camshaft cover as described in Section 5.

13 Cylinder head - removal and installation

Note 1: *The following text assumes that the cylinder head will be removed with both intake and exhaust manifolds attached; this simplifies the procedure, but makes it a bulky and heavy assembly to handle - an engine hoist will be required, to prevent the risk of injury, and to prevent damage to any delicate components as the assembly is removed and*

installed. If it is wished to remove the manifolds first, proceed as described in Sections 6 and 7 of this Chapter; amend the following procedure accordingly.

Note 2: *Only turn the engine in the normal direction of rotation - clockwise from the right-hand side of the vehicle.*

Removal

Refer to illustrations 13.9, 13.10, 13.11, 13.12 and 13.14

1 With the vehicle parked on firm level ground, open the hood and disconnect the negative battery cable (see Chapter 1).

2 Whenever you disconnect any vacuum lines, coolant and emissions hoses, wiring loom connectors, ground straps and fuel lines as part of the following procedure, always label them clearly, so that they can be correctly reassembled.

3 Drain the cooling system as described in Chapter 1.

4 Remove the intake manifold as described in Section 6.

5 Remove the exhaust manifold and heat shields as described in Section 7.

6 Remove the camshaft cover as described in Section 5.

7 Remove the timing chain and sprockets

as described in Section 10.

8 Release the pressure in the fuel system by removing the fuel pump fuse - see wiring diagrams in Chapter 12. Start the engine and allow it to run until the engine stalls. Crank the engine for approximately 5 seconds to make sure the manifold pressure has been released. The fuel pump fuse can now be installed.

9 Release the fuel feed pipe from the fuel injector rail **(see illustration),** see Chapter 4A for more information. Plug or cap all open fittings, to prevent any ingress of dirt etc.

10 Disconnect the coolant hoses from the coolant housing on the left-hand end of the cylinder head **(see illustration).**

11 Slacken and remove the upper retaining bolt from the alternator assembly **(see illustration).**

12 Undo the securing bolt and disconnect the ground lead from the cylinder head above the alternator assembly **(see illustration).**

13 Remove the camshafts and tappets as described in Section 11.

14 Working in the sequence shown **(see illustration),** loosen the ten cylinder head bolts progressively and by one turn at a time. Remove each bolt in turn, and ensure that new ones are obtained for reassembly; these bolts are subjected to severe stresses and so

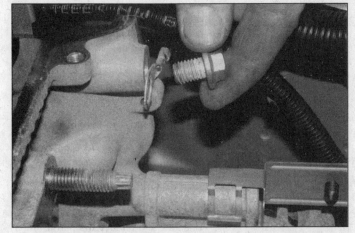

13.12 Disconnect the ground wire at the cylinder head

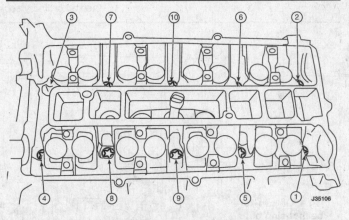

13.14 Cylinder head bolt LOOSENING sequence

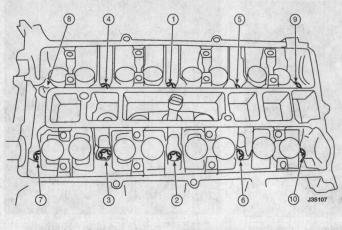

13.23a Cylinder head bolt TIGHTENING sequence

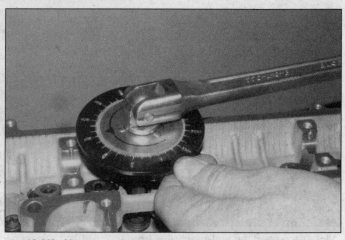

13.23b Use an angle-gauge for the final stages of cylinder head tightening

must be replaced, regardless of their apparent condition, whenever they are removed.

15   Lift the cylinder head away; get assistance if possible, as it is a heavy assembly. Remove the gasket and discard it, note the position of the dowels and any directional markings on the gasket. If resistance is felt, do not pry between the head and the block as damage to the mating surfaces may result. Use a large prybar inserted into one of the exhaust or intake ports to rock the head, breaking the gasket seal.

Installation

Refer to illustrations 13.23a and 13.23b

16   The mating faces of the cylinder head and cylinder block must be perfectly clean before installing the head. Use a hard plastic or wood scraper to remove all traces of gasket and carbon; also clean the piston crowns. Take particular care, as the soft aluminum alloy is easily damaged. Also, make sure that the carbon is not allowed to enter the oil and water passages - this is particularly important for the lubrication system, as carbon could block the oil supply to any of the engine's components. Using adhesive tape and paper, seal the water, oil and bolt holes in the cylinder block. Clean all the pistons in the same way.

17   Check the mating surfaces of the cylinder block and the cylinder head for nicks, deep scratches and other damage. If excessive, machining may be the only alternative to replacement.

18   If warpage of the cylinder head gasket surface is suspected, use a straight-edge to check it for distortion. Refer to Part D of this Chapter, if necessary.

19   Wipe clean the mating surfaces of the cylinder head and cylinder block. Check that the locating dowels are in position in the cylinder block, and that all cylinder head bolt holes are free from oil. Apply a small dab of RTV sealant to the top of the block at the timing chain end of the engine.

20   Position a new gasket over the dowels on the cylinder block surface, making sure it is fitted the correct way up.

21   Rotate the crankshaft counter-clockwise so that No 1 cylinder's piston is lowered to approximately 20 mm before TDC, thus avoiding any risk of valve/piston contact and damage during reassembly.

22   Replace the cylinder head, locating it on the dowels. Fit the **new** cylinder head bolts; carefully enter each into its hole and screw it in, by hand only, until finger-tight.

23   Working progressively and in the sequence shown, use first a torque wrench, then an ordinary socket extension bar and an

angle gauge to tighten the cylinder head bolts **(see illustrations)**. This is completed in stages given in the Specifications Section at the beginning of this Chapter. **Note:** *Once tightened correctly following this procedure, the cylinder head bolts do not require check-tightening, and must not be retorqued.*

24   Reinstall the tappets, the camshafts, and the timing chain as described in Sections 10 and 11.

25   The remainder of reassembly is the reverse of the removal procedure, noting the following points:

a) *See the installation procedures in the relevant Sections and tighten all nuts and bolts to the torque specified.*

b) *Refill the cooling system, and top-up the engine oil.*

c) *Check all disturbed connections for signs of oil or coolant leakage, once the engine has been restarted and warmed-up to normal operating temperature.*

14   Oil pan - removal and installation

Removal

Refer to illustrations 14.4 and 14.5

1   Apply the handbrake, then jack up the front of the vehicle and support it on axle stands (see *Jacking and vehicle support*).

2   Drain the engine oil, then clean and replace the engine oil drain plug, tightening it to the specified torque wrench setting. **Note:** *If the drain plug seal is damaged, a new drain plug will be required.* Although not strictly necessary as part of the disassembly procedure, owners are advised to remove and discard the oil filter, so that it can be replaced with the oil (see Chapter 1). Refer to Section 7 and remove the oil dipstick tube mounting bolts and the dipstick tube.

3   Remove the timing chain cover-to-oil pan bolts and studs, including the nut securing the wiring harness there.

4   Unscrew and remove the pan-to-transmission bolts **(see illustration)**.

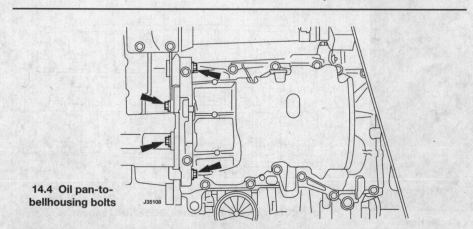

14.4 Oil pan-to-bellhousing bolts

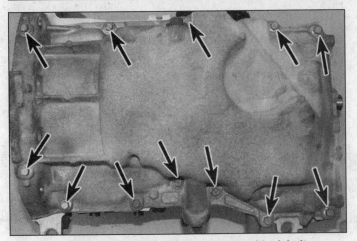

14.5 Remove all the perimeter oil pan-to-block bolts

14.7 Apply a 3 mm bead of RTV sealant all around the oil pan flange

5   Progressively unscrew the oil pan retaining bolts **(see illustration)**. Use a scraper to break the sealant around the oil pan, taking care not to damage the mating surfaces of the oil pan and cylinder block. Lower the oil pan and withdraw it with the engine/transmission.

Installation

Refer to illustrations 14.7 and 14.9

6   On reassembly, thoroughly clean and degrease the mating surfaces of the cylinder block/crankcase and oil pan, then use a clean rag to wipe out the pan.

7   Apply a 3.0 mm bead of sealant to the oil pan flange so that the bead is around the inside edge of the bolt holes **(see illustration)**. **Note:** *The oil pan must be installed within 4 minutes of applying the sealant.*

8   Lift the oil pan and insert the retaining bolts, do not tighten them at this stage.

9   Install the oil pan bolts, starting with those at the transaxle end, then the timing cover bolts/studs, and then the perimeter bolts to the block. Tighten all bolts in the indicated sequence to the torque listed in this Chapter's Specifications **(see illustration)**.

10   Inspect the O-ring on the end of the oil dipstick tube, and replace if necessary before reinstalling the tube to the engine.

11   Lower the car to the ground and refill the engine with oil (and install a new oil filter).

12   Check for signs of oil leaks once the engine has been restarted and warmed-up to normal operating temperature.

15 Oil pump - removal, inspection and installation

Note 1: *While this task is theoretically possible when the engine is in place in the vehicle, in practice, it requires so much preliminary disassembly, and is so difficult to carry out due to the restricted access, that owners are advised to remove the engine from the vehicle first. All the illustrations used in this Section are with the engine out of the vehicle and the engine upside down on a work bench.*

Note 2: *In addition to the new pump gasket and other replacement parts required, read through Section 14, and ensure that the necessary tools and facilities are available.*

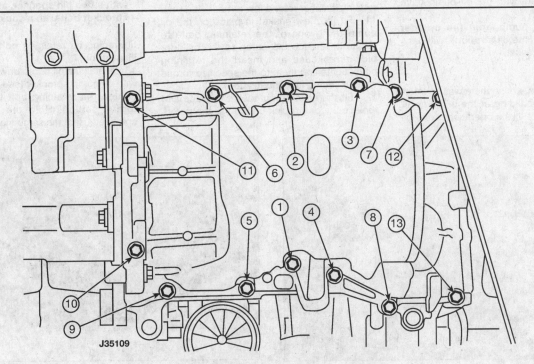

J35109

14.9 Oil pan fastener TIGHTENING sequence

15.3 Remove the two bolts securing the oil pump pickup pipe to the oil pump

15.4 Remove the chain guide mounting bolts, the chain guide and the tensioner

Removal

Refer to illustrations 15.3, 15.4, 15.5 and 15.7

1 Remove the timing chain as described in Section 10.

2 Remove the oil pan as described in Section 14.

3 Undo the two bolts securing the oil pump pick-up pipe to the pump **(see illustration)**. Discard the O-ring/gasket.

4 Undo the two retaining bolts and remove the oil pump chain guide, then undo the retaining bolt and remove the oil pump chain tensioner **(see illustration)**.

5 Hold the oil pump drive sprocket to prevent it from turning and slacken the sprocket retaining bolt **(see illustration).**

6 Undo the bolt and remove the oil pump sprocket complete with the oil pump drive chain.

7 Unbolt the pump from the cylinder block/crankcase **(see illustration)**. Withdraw and discard the gasket.

Inspection

8 At the time of writing there was no information on the rebuilding of the oil pump. If there is any doubt in the operation of the oil

pump, then the complete pump assembly should be replaced.

Installation

Refer to illustrations 15.11, 15.12, 15.13 and 15.14

9 Thoroughly clean and degrease all components, particularly the mating surfaces of the pump, the oil pan, and the cylinder block/crankcase. When using a scraper and solvent to remove all traces of old gasket/sealant from the mating surfaces, be careful to ensure that you do not scratch or damage the material of either component - any solvents used must be suitable for this application.

10 The oil pump must be primed on installation, by pouring clean engine oil into it, and rotating its inner rotor a few turns.

11 Fit the new gasket in place on the oil pump using one of the retaining bolts to locate it, replace the pump to the cylinder block/crankcase and insert the retaining bolts, tightening them to the specified torque wrench setting **(see illustration)**.

12 Fit the new O-ring/gasket in place and replace the pump pick-up pipe to the pump,

15.5 Hold the oil pump drive sprocket with a two pin spanner, and remove the sprocket bolt with a socket and ratchet

tightening its retaining bolts securely **(see illustration)**.

13 Install the oil pump drive chain complete with oil pump sprocket **(see illustration)** and tighten the retaining bolt to the specified torque setting. Hold the oil pump drive sprocket (using the same method as removal)

15.7 Remove the four mounting bolts and the oil pump assembly

15.11 Use one of the retaining bolts to locate the new gasket in place on the oil pump

15.12 Fit a new O-ring to the oil pump pick-up pipe

15.13 Align the flats on the oil pump driveshaft and oil pump sprocket when installing

to prevent it from turning when tightening the sprocket retaining bolt.

14   Install the oil pump chain tensioner to the cylinder block, making sure the spring is located correctly (see illustration). Tighten the retaining bolt to its specified torque setting.

15   Install the oil pump chain guide to the cylinder block, tightening the two retaining bolts to their specified torque setting.

16   Install the timing chain as described in Section 10.

17   Install the oil pan as described in Section 14.

16   Oil filter housing - removal and installation

Refer to illustrations 16.3 and 16.5
Note: The oil filter has coolant passing through its housing to help cool the engine oil.

1   Disconnect the negative battery cable (see Chapter 1).

2   Disconnect the wiring connector from the oil pressure switch on the filter housing.

3   Unscrew the four retaining bolts from

the filter housing and withdraw the housing from the cylinder block (see illustration), and be prepared for some oil spillage. Discard the gasket.

4   On reassembly, thoroughly clean any gasket or sealant from the mating surfaces of the cylinder block and oil filter housing.

5   Installation is the reverse of the removal procedure, using a new gasket between the housing and the block (see illustration). Check for signs of oil or coolant leaks once the engine has been restarted and warmed-up to normal operating temperature.

17   Oil pressure warning light switch - removal and installation

Removal

Refer to illustration 17.1

1   The switch is screwed into the oil filter housing on the front of the cylinder block (see illustration).

2   Disconnect the negative battery cable (see Chapter 1).

3   If required, raise the front of the vehicle,

15.14 Make sure the spring on the tensioner is hooked behind the bolt during installation

and support it securely on axle stands - this will give better access to the switch.

4   Disconnect the wiring connector from the switch, and unscrew it; be prepared for some oil loss.

16.3 Remove the four mounting bolts and pull the filter housing from the block

16.5 Use one of the mounting bolts to locate the new gasket on the housing before installation

17.1 The oil pressure sending unit is screwed into the oil filter housing

Installation

5   Installation is the reverse of the removal procedure; apply a thin smear of suitable sealant to the switch threads, and tighten it to the specified torque wrench setting. Check the engine oil level, and top-up as necessary. Check for signs of oil leaks once the engine has been restarted and warmed-up to normal operating temperature.

18   Crankshaft oil seals - replacement

Timing chain end oil seal

Refer to illustration 18.4

1   Remove the crankshaft pulley as described in Section 8 of this Chapter.
2   Using a screwdriver, pry the old oil seal from the timing cover. Take care not to damage the surface of the timing cover and crankshaft. If the oil seal is tight, carefully drill two holes diagonally opposite each other in the oil seal, then insert self-tapping screws and use a pair of pliers to pull out the oil seal.
3   Wipe clean the seating in the timing cover and the nose of the crankshaft.
4   Smear clean engine oil on the outer periphery and sealing lips of the new oil seal, then start it into the timing cover by pressing it in squarely. Using a large socket or metal tubing, drive in the oil seal until flush with the outer surface of the timing cover. Make sure the oil seal remains square as it is being inserted. Wipe off any excess oil **(see illustration)**.
5   Replace the crankshaft pulley as described in Section 8 of this Chapter.

Transaxle end oil seal

Refer to illustration 18.13

Note: *The manufacturer recommends removing the oil pan first, to install a new rear seal and retainer. If you perform this replacement*

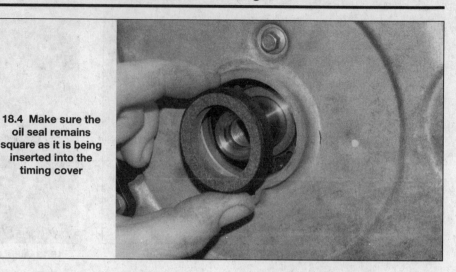

18.4 Make sure the oil seal remains square as it is being inserted into the timing cover

without removing the oil pan, make sure to use RTV sealant at the seal retainer-to-pan mating surface or you may have oil leaks later.
6   Remove the transmission (see the relevant Part of Chapter 7).
7   On manual transaxle models, remove the clutch assembly (see Chapter 6).
8   Unbolt the flywheel/driveplate (see Section 19).
9   Remove the oil pan (see Section 14).
10   Undo the six retaining bolts and remove the oil seal carrier from the cylinder block. Where applicable, remove and discard its gasket. **Note:** *The seal and its retainer plate are replaced as a unit - the seal is not available separately.*
11   Clean the seal housing and crankshaft, polishing off any burrs or raised edges, which may have caused the seal to fail in the first place. Where applicable, clean also the mating surfaces of the cylinder block/crankcase, using a scraper to remove all traces of the old gasket/sealant - be careful not to scratch or damage the material of either - then use a suitable solvent to degrease them.

12   Use a special sleeve to slide the seal over the crankshaft, if this is not available, make up a guide from a thin sheet of plastic or similar, lubricate the lips of the new seal and the crankshaft shoulder with oil, then offer up the oil seal carrier, with the guide feeding the seal's lips over the crankshaft shoulder.
13   Being careful not to damage the oil seal, move the carrier into the correct position, and tighten its bolts in the correct sequence to the specified torque wrench setting **(see illustration)**.
14   Wipe off any surplus oil or grease; the remainder of the reassembly procedure is the reverse of disassembly, referring to the relevant text for details where required. Check for signs of oil leakage when the engine is restarted.

19   Flywheel/driveplate - removal, inspection and installation

Removal

Refer to illustration 19.4

1   Remove the transmission (see the relevant Part of Chapter 7). Now is a good time to check components such as oil seals and renew them if necessary.
2   Where appropriate, remove the clutch (see Chapter 6). Now is a good time to check or renew the clutch components.
3   Use a center-punch or paint to make alignment marks on the flywheel/driveplate and crankshaft, to ensure correct alignment during installation.
4   Prevent the flywheel/driveplate from turning by locking the ring gear teeth, or by bolting a strap between the flywheel/driveplate and the cylinder block/crankcase **(see illustration)**. Slacken the bolts evenly until all are free.
5   Remove each bolt in turn, and ensure that new ones are obtained for reassembly; these bolts are subjected to severe stresses, and so must be replaced, regardless of their apparent condition, whenever they are disturbed.

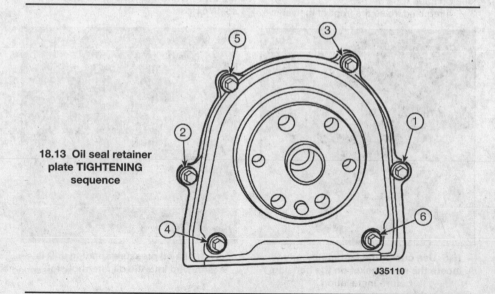

18.13 Oil seal retainer plate TIGHTENING sequence

J35110

19.4 Lock the flywheel/driveplate while the flywheel mounting bolts are removed

19.10 Apply thread-locking liquid to the new flywheel bolts during installation

6   Withdraw the flywheel/driveplate from the end of the crankshaft. **Note:** *Take care when removing the flywheel/driveplate as it is a very heavy component. Wear gloves, as the edges of the starter ring gear can be sharp.*

Inspection

7   Clean the flywheel/driveplate to remove grease and oil. Inspect the surface for cracks, rivet grooves, burned areas and score marks. Light scoring can be removed with emery cloth. Check for cracked and broken ring gear teeth. Lay the flywheel/driveplate on a flat surface, and use a straight-edge to check for warpage.

8   Clean and inspect the mating surfaces of the flywheel/driveplate and the crankshaft. If the crankshaft left-hand oil seal is leaking, replace it (see Section 18) before installing the flywheel/driveplate.

9   While the flywheel/driveplate is removed, clean carefully its inboard (right-hand) face. Thoroughly clean the threaded bolt holes in the crankshaft - this is important, since if old sealer remains in the threads, the bolts will settle over a period and will not retain their correct torque wrench settings.

Installation

Refer to illustrations 19.10 and 19.11

10   On installation, fit the flywheel/driveplate to the crankshaft so that all bolt holes align - it will fit only one way - check this using the marks made on removal. Apply suitable sealer to the threads of the new bolts then insert them **(see illustration).**

11   Lock the flywheel/driveplate by the method used on disassembly. Working in a diagonal sequence to tighten them evenly, and increasing to the final amount in three stages, tighten the new bolts to the specified torque **(see illustration).**

12   The remainder of reassembly is the reverse of the removal procedure.

20   Engine/transmission mounts - inspection and replacement

General

1   The engine/transmission mounts seldom require attention, but broken or deteriorated mounts should be replaced immediately, or the added strain placed on the driveline components may cause damage or wear.

2   While separate mounts may be removed and installed individually, if more than one is disturbed at a time - such as if the engine/transmission unit is removed from its mounts - they must be reassembled and their fasteners tightened in the position marked on removal.

3   On reassembly, the complete weight of the engine/transmission unit must not be taken by the mounts until all are correctly aligned with the marks made on removal. Tighten the engine/transmission mounting fasteners to their specified torque.

Inspection

4   During the check, the engine/transmission unit must be raised slightly, to remove its weight from the mounts.

5   Raise the front of the vehicle, and support it securely on axle stands. Position a jack under the oil pan, with a large block of wood between the jack head and the oil pan, then carefully raise the engine/transmission just enough to take the weight off the mountings. **Warning:** *DO NOT place any part of your body under the engine when it is supported only by a jack.*

6   Check the mounts to see if the rubber is cracked, hardened or separated from the metal components. Sometimes the rubber will split right down the center.

7   Check for relative movement between each mount's brackets and the engine/transmission or body (use a large screwdriver or lever to attempt to move the mounts). If movement is noted, lower the engine and check-tighten the mounting fasteners.

Replacement

Note: *The following paragraphs assume the engine is supported beneath the oil pan as described earlier.*

Right-hand mount

Refer to illustrations 20.10a and 20.10b

8   Remove the coolant expansion bottle from the right-hand inner fender, as described in Chapter 3.

19.11 Tighten the new bolts using the flywheel-locking method used during removal to secure the flywheel/driveplate

20.10a Remove the two lock-nuts and the three bolts . . .

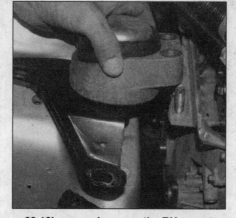

20.10b . . . and remove the RH mount from the vehicle

20.12 Loosen the hose clamp and remove the air intake tube

9   Mark the position of the mounting on the vehicle, right-hand inner fender panel.

10   With the engine/transmission supported, unscrew the two locking nuts from the engine casing, then undo the three retaining bolts to the vehicle inner fender panel and withdraw the mounting from the vehicle **(see illustrations)**.

11   On installation, tighten all fasteners to the torque wrench settings specified. Tighten the two locking nuts to the engine casing first, then release the hoist or jack to allow the mounting bracket to rest on the vehicle inner fender panel. Re-align the marks made on removal, then tighten the three mounting bracket-to-inner fender retaining bolts.

Left-hand mount

Refer to illustrations 20.12, 20.13 and 20.14

Note: *The mount securing nuts are self-locking, and must therefore be replaced whenever they have been removed.*

12   Undo the retaining clip from the air intake hose **(see illustration),** then lift the complete air cleaner assembly and remove it from the vehicle (see Chapter 4A).

13   With the transmission supported, note the position of the mount then unscrew the center retaining nut to release the mount from

20.13 Unscrew the center nut in the LH mount

the transmission **(see illustration)**.

14   Unscrew the four outer retaining nuts to dismantle the mount from the mounting bracket **(see illustration)**. To remove the mounting bracket, undo the retaining bolts and remove the bracket from the left-hand inner fender panel.

15   On installation, use new self-locking nuts. Re-align the mount in the position noted

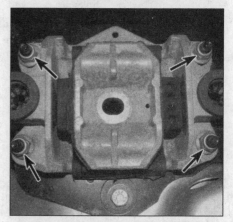

20.14 Remove the four outer bolts from the LH mount

on removal, then tighten all fasteners to the specified torque.

Rear mount (roll restrictor)

Refer to illustrations 20.16a and 20.16b

16   Unbolt the mount from the subframe and the transmission by unscrewing the mount's center bolts **(see illustrations)**.

17   On installation, ensure that the bolts are securely tightened to the specified torque.

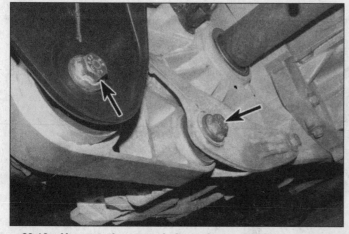

20.16a Unscrew the center bolts at the rear engine mount . . .

20.16b . . . and remove the roll-restrictor mount from the subframe and transmission

Chapter 2 Part D
General engine overhaul procedures

Contents

Specifications

2.0L engines through 2004

Valves

Valve play in guide	
2.0L Zetec-E and Duratec SVT engines...	0.0007 to 0.0025 inch
2.0L SPI engine	
Intake...	0.0008 to 0.0027 inch
Exhaust...	0.0018 to 0.0037 inch

Cylinder head

Maximum permissible gasket surface distortion...................................	0.004 inch

Cylinder block

Cylinder bore diameter	
Class 1..	3.3411 to 3.3415 inches
Class 2..	3.3415 to 3.3419 inches
Class 3..	3.3419 to 3.3423 inches

Pistons and piston rings

Piston diameter	
Class 1..	3.3399 to 3.3403 inches
Class 2..	3.3403 to 3.3407 inches
Class 3..	3.3407 to 3.3411 inches
Piston-to-cylinder bore clearance	
2.0L Zetec-E and Duratec SVT engines...	0.00039 to 0.00118 inch
2.0L SPI engine...	0.00078 to 0.00158 inch
Piston ring end gaps - installed	
Top and second compression rings	
2.0L Zetec-E and Duratec SVT engines.....................................	0.0118 to 0.0197 inch
2.0L SPI engine...	0.0100 to 0.0300 inch
Oil control ring	
2.0 Zetec-E and Duratec SVT engines...................................	0.016 to 0.055 inch
2.0L SPI engine...	0.016 to 0.066 inch
Ring gap spacing...	120°

Crankshaft

Crankshaft endplay
    2.0L Zetec-E and Duratec SVT engines.. 0.0035 to 0.0102 inch
    2.0L SPI engine... 0.0040 to 0.0120 inch
Main bearing journal diameter (all) .... 2.2844 to 2.2852 inches
Main bearing running clearance
    2.0L Zetec-E and Duratec SVT engines.. 0.0004 to 0.0022 inch
    2.0L SPI engine... 0.0008 to 0.0026 inch

Torque specifications

Connecting rod bearing cap nuts
    2.0L SPI engine... 28
    2.0 Zetec-E and Duratec SVT engines
        Stage 1 26
        Stage 2 .... Tighten an additional 90-degrees
Main bearing cap bolts
    2.0L SPI engine... 73
    2.0 Zetec-E and Duratec SVT engines
        Stage 1 18
        Stage 2 .... Tighten an additional 60-degrees
For additional torque specifications, refer to Chapters 2A or 2B.

2.3L and 2005 and later 2.0L engines

Valves

Stem-to-guide clearance
    Intake .... 0.0009 inch
    Exhaust .... 0.0011 inch

Cylinder head

Maximum permissible gasket surface distortion.. 0.0003 inch

Cylinder block

Cylinder bore diameter... 3.444 to 3.446 inches

Pistons and piston rings

Piston diameter
    Class 1 .... 3.4440 to 3.4450 inches
    Class 2 .... 3.4452 to 3.4456 inches
    Class 3 .... 3.4440 to 3.4460 inches
Piston-to-cylinder bore clearance .... 0.0009 to 0.0017 inch
Piston ring end gaps - installed
    Top compression ring.. 0.06 to 0.012 inch
    2nd compression ring .... 0.012 to 0.0017 inch
    Oil control ring.. 0.007 to 0.027 inch

Crankshaft

Crankshaft endplay .... 0.008 to 0.016 inch
Main bearing journal diameter... 2.046 to 2.47 inches
Main bearing running clearance .... 0.0007 to 0.0013 inch

Torque specifications

Connecting rod bearing cap nuts.. NA
Main bearing cap bolts... NA
For additional torque specifications, refer to Chapter 2C.

1   General information and precautions

How to use this Chapter

This Part of Chapter 2 is devoted to engine/transaxle removal and installation, to those repair procedures requiring the removal of the engine/transaxle from the vehicle, and to the overhaul of engine components. It includes only the Specifications relevant to those procedures. Refer to Parts A, B or C for additional Specifications, and for all torque wrench settings.

General information

The information ranges from advice concerning preparation for an overhaul and the purchase of replacement parts, to detailed step-by-step procedures covering removal and installation of internal engine components and the inspection of parts.

The following Sections have been written based on the assumption that the engine has been removed from the vehicle. For information concerning in-vehicle engine repair, as well as removal and installation of the external components necessary for the overhaul, see Parts A , B or C of this Chapter.

When overhauling the engine, it is essential to establish first exactly what replacement parts are available.

2   Engine overhaul - general information

It's not always easy to determine when, or if, an engine should be completely overhauled, as a number of factors must be considered.

High mileage is not necessarily an indication that an overhaul is needed, while low

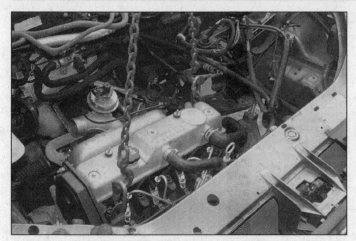

3.4a Make sure the lifting chains are secure . . .

3.4b . . . and lower the engine/transaxle to the ground

mileage doesn't preclude the need for an overhaul. Frequency of servicing is probably the most important consideration. An engine that's had regular and frequent oil and filter changes, as well as other required maintenance, will most likely give many thousands of miles of reliable service. Conversely, a neglected engine may require an overhaul very early in its life.

Excessive oil consumption is an indication that piston rings, valve seals and/or valve guides are in need of attention. Make sure that oil leaks aren't responsible before deciding that the rings and/or guides are worn. Perform a cylinder compression or leakdown check (Part A or B of this Chapter) to determine the extent of the work required.

Loss of power, rough running, knocking or metallic engine noises, excessive valve train noise and high fuel consumption rates may also point to the need for an overhaul, especially if they're all present at the same time. If a full service doesn't remedy the situation, major mechanical work is the only solution.

An engine overhaul involves restoring all internal parts to the specification of a new engine. **Note:** *Always check first what replacement parts are available before planning any overhaul operation. Ford dealers, or a good engine reconditioning specialist/automotive parts supplier, may be able to suggest alternatives that will enable you to find aftermarket replacement parts.*

During an overhaul, it is usual to replace the piston rings, and to rebore and/or hone the cylinder bores; where the rebore is done by an automotive machine shop, new oversize pistons and rings will also be installed - all these operations, of course, assume the availability of suitable replacement parts. The main and connecting rod bearings are generally replaced and, if necessary, the crankshaft may be reground to restore the journals.

Generally, the valves are serviced as well during an overhaul, since they're usually in less-than-perfect condition at this point. While the engine is being overhauled, other components, such as the starter and alterna-

tor, can be replaced as well, or rebuilt, if the necessary parts can be found. The end result should be an as-new engine that will give many trouble-free miles. **Note:** *Critical cooling system components such as the hoses, drivebelt, thermostat and water pump MUST be replaced with new parts when an engine is overhauled. The radiator should be checked carefully, to ensure that it isn't clogged or leaking (see Chapter 3). Also, as a general rule, the oil pump should be replaced when an engine is rebuilt.*

Before beginning the engine overhaul, read through the entire procedure to familiarize yourself with the scope and requirements of the job. Overhauling an engine isn't difficult, but it is time-consuming. Plan on the vehicle being off the road for a minimum of two weeks, especially if parts must be taken to an automotive machine shop for repair or reconditioning. Check on availability of parts, and make sure that any necessary special tools and equipment are obtained in advance. Most work can be done with typical hand tools, although a number of precision measuring tools are required for inspecting parts to determine if they must be replaced. Often, an automotive machine shop will handle the inspection of parts, and will offer advice concerning reconditioning and replacement. **Note:** *Always wait until the engine has been completely disassembled, and all components, especially the cylinder block/crankcase, have been inspected, before deciding what service and repair operations must be performed by an automotive machine shop. Since the block's condition will be the major factor to consider when determining whether to overhaul the original engine or buy a rebuilt one, never purchase parts or have machine work done on other components until the cylinder block/crankcase has been thoroughly inspected.* As a general rule, time is the primary cost of an overhaul, so it doesn't pay to install worn or sub-standard parts.

As a final note, to ensure maximum life and minimum trouble from a rebuilt engine, everything must be assembled with care, in a spotlessly-clean environment. **Note:** *On the*

2.3L and all 2005 engines, because of the fine tolerances in the bearing shells, no service operations are permitted on the cylinder block/crank assembly. In the event of any failure, the complete cylinder block, pistons and crank assembly must be replaced as a unit.

3 Engine/transaxle removal - methods and precautions

Refer to illustrations 3.4a and 3.4b

If you've decided that an engine must be removed for overhaul or major repair work, several preliminary steps should be taken.

Locating a suitable place to work is extremely important. Adequate work space, along with storage space for the vehicle, will be needed. If a workshop or garage isn't available, at the very least, a flat, level, clean work surface made of concrete or asphalt is required.

Cleaning the engine compartment and engine/transaxle before beginning the removal procedure will help keep tools clean and organized.

The engine can be withdrawn by removing it complete with the transaxle; the vehicle's body must be raised and supported securely, sufficiently high that the engine/transaxle can be unbolted as a single unit and lowered to the ground; the engine/transaxle unit can then be withdrawn from under the vehicle and separated. This method is only recommended if the vehicle can be raised on a frame-contact type hoist. Alternatively, the transaxle can be removed first (as described in Chapter 7) and the engine can then be removed from above. In either case, an engine hoist or A-frame will therefore be necessary. Make sure the equipment is rated in excess of the combined weight of the engine and transaxle. Safety is of primary importance, considering the potential hazards involved in removing the engine/transaxle from the vehicle **(see illustrations).**

If this is the first time you have removed an engine, an assistant should ideally be

4.8a Disconnect the camshaft position sensor (see Chapter 2A or 2B)

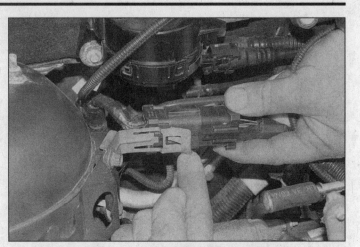

4.8b Unclip the injection wiring connection . . .

available. Advice and aid from someone more experienced would also be useful. There are many instances when one person cannot simultaneously perform all of the operations required when removing the engine/ transaxle from the vehicle.

Plan the operation ahead of time. Arrange for, or obtain, all of the tools and equipment you'll need prior to beginning the job. Some of the equipment necessary to perform engine/transaxle removal and installation safely and with relative ease, and which may have to be hired or borrowed, includes (in addition to the engine hoist) a heavy-duty floor jack, a strong pair of axle stands, some wooden blocks, and an engine dolly (a low, wheeled platform capable of taking the weight of the engine/transaxle, so that it can be moved easily when on the ground). A complete set of wrenches and sockets (as described in the beginning of this manual) will obviously be needed, together with plenty of rags and cleaning solvent for mopping-up spilled oil, coolant and fuel. If the hoist is to be rented, make sure that you arrange for it in advance, and perform all of the operations possible without it beforehand. This will save you money and time.

Plan for the vehicle to be out of use for quite a while. A machine shop will be required to perform some of the work that the do-it-yourselfer can't accomplish without special equipment. These establishments often have a busy schedule, so it would be a good idea to consult them before removing the engine, to accurately estimate the amount of time required to rebuild or repair components that may need work.

Always be extremely careful when removing and installing the engine/transaxle. Serious injury can result from careless actions. By planning ahead and taking your time, the job (although a major task) can be accomplished successfully.

4.8c . . . then disconnect it

4 Engine/transaxle - removal, separation and installation

Note: *Read through the entire Section, as well as reading the advice in the preceding Section, before beginning this procedure. In this procedure, the engine and transaxle are removed as a unit, lowered to the ground and removed from underneath, then separated outside the vehicle. Following this procedure will require*

the use of a frame-contact type vehicle hoist. However, if preferred, the transaxle can be removed from the engine first (as described in Chapter 7A or 7B) - this leaves the engine free to be lifted out from above (eliminating the need for a vehicle hoist).

Removal

Refer to illustrations 4.8a, 4.8b, 4.8c, 4.9a, 4.9b, 4.10, 4.11a, 4.11b, 4.15, 4.16, 4.31a, 4.31b, 4.31c, 4.34a, 4.34b, 4.41a and 4.41b

1   Park the vehicle on firm, level ground, apply the parking brake firmly, and loosen the nuts securing both front wheels.

2   Depressurize the fuel system as described in Chapter 4A.

3   Drain the cooling system as described in Chapter 1.

4   Working on each side in turn, unscrew the front suspension strut center nuts exactly five turns each while holding the shock absorber center rods with an Allen key. On 2005 and later models, loosen the three nuts on the left-hand strut/spring bracket by four turns. **Note:** *It is important not to over-loosen the nuts - make sure there is still sufficient thread engaged with the nut.*

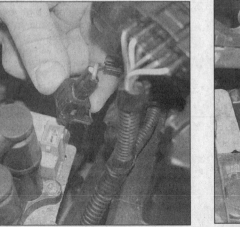

4.9a Disconnect the condenser wiring plug . . .

4.9b . . . and the coil main wiring plug

4.10 Cut the cable-tie securing the shift cables to the transaxle - disconnect the wiring plug (arrow)

4.11a Disconnect the intake manifold vacuum hoses

4.11b Note the location of the two charcoal canister hoses

5   Remove the battery and battery tray as described in Chapter 5A.

6   Remove the air cleaner and intake ducting as described in Chapter 4A. Unbolt and remove the air intake duct below the air cleaner, leading to the engine compartment front panel. Where applicable, also disconnect the ground cable located below the air cleaner.

7   Disconnect the accelerator cable from the throttle body, using the information in Chapter 4A.

8   Disconnect the camshaft position sensor wiring plug at the rear of the cylinder head, then unclip and disconnect the injection wiring harness connector behind the power steering fluid reservoir **(see illustrations)**.

9   Disconnect the wiring plugs at the ignition coil **(see illustrations)**.

10   On manual transaxle models, unclip the shift cables from the location on top of the transaxle, and disconnect the wiring plug next to it **(see illustration)**.

11   At the intake manifold, disconnect the vacuum hoses from the fuel pressure regulator and for the brake booster. Also disconnect the charcoal canister hoses, if applicable **(see illustrations)**.

12   Disconnect the knock sensor wiring plug next to the engine oil dipstick tube (see Chapter 2A or 2B).

13   Referring to Chapter 5A if necessary, disconnect the wiring from the alternator.

14   On models without air conditioning, disconnect the small wiring connector from the power steering pump.

15   Unscrew the bolt securing the coolant expansion tank to the inner fender, unclip the tank at the rear, and move the tank aside without disconnecting the hoses **(see illustration)**.

16   Unclip the power steering fluid reservoir from its location, and lay it to one side without disconnecting the hoses - try to ensure that it stays upright **(see illustration)**.

17   Disconnect the radiator, heater and expansion tank hoses from the thermostat housing. On automatic transaxle models,

separate the heater hose at the connection above the transaxle.

18   Disconnect the radiator bottom hose and heater hose from the connections at the water pump.

19   Remove the radiator fan assembly using the information in Chapter 3.

20   Referring to Chapter 6, disconnect the fluid supply pipe for the clutch master cylinder at the connection on the transaxle. Be prepared for some fluid spillage, and plug the end of the pipe to prevent further fluid loss. Tie the pipe up out of the way, and wash off any spilled fluid. **Warning:** *Brake fluid is poisonous, flammable, and will attack paintwork and plastics.*

21   Raise the vehicle on the hoist.

22   Remove the auxiliary drivebelt as described in Chapter 1.

23   Trace the fluid pipes from the power steering pump under the car, and detach the pipe retaining bracket from the engine/transaxle or subframe.

24   Unbolt the power steering pump using the information in Chapter 10, and tie it up without disturbing the pipe connections.

25   On models with air conditioning, unbolt

the air conditioning compressor using the information in Chapter 3, and tie it up out of the way. **Warning:** *The air conditioning system is under high pressure - don't disconnect the refrigerant lines.*

26   On manual transaxle models, referring to Chapter 7A if necessary, disconnect the shift cables from the transaxle levers. On models with the MTX 75 transaxle, disconnect the shift cables from the brackets on top of the transaxle.

27   On automatic transaxle models, unbolt the support bracket for the transaxle fluid dipstick, and release the dipstick from its location.

28   Referring to Chapter 5A, remove the starter motor.

29   Remove both driveaxles from the transaxle, as described in Chapter 8.

30   Support the engine from below, close to the engine rear mounting. Loosen the engine rear mounting bolts, and remove the mounting. Note that it is only necessary to support the engine as the bolts are loosened and removed - once the mounting has been taken off, the support can be carefully removed.

31   Disconnect the wiring plugs from the following:

4.15 Unclip the coolant expansion tank at the rear, then move it aside

4.16 Lift the power steering fluid reservoir out of its location

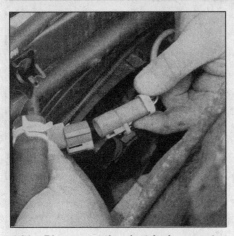

4.31a Disconnect the electrical connector for the oxygen sensor . . .

4.31b . . . the oil pressure warning light switch . . .

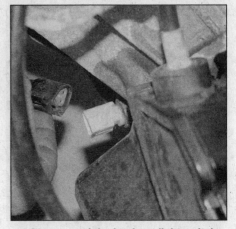

4.31c . . . and the back-up light switch

a) *Exhaust gas oxygen sensor (trace the wiring back from the sensor to the plug)* **(see illustration)**.
b) *Oil pressure warning light switch* **(see illustration)**.
c) *Crankshaft position sensor (on the front of the engine, at the transaxle end)*.
d) *Vehicle speed sensor (on top of the transaxle)*.
e) *Reverse light switch (at the front of the transaxle)* **(see illustration)**.

32 Remove the exhaust manifold as described in Chapter 4A. Ensure that the flexible section of the exhaust front pipe is not bent excessively as the manifold is removed.
33 Remove the exhaust front section as described in Chapter 4A.
34 Taking precautions against fuel spillage, disconnect the fuel lines at the connections into the engine compartment, prying out the colored locking clip with a small screwdriver. Note that the fuel supply pipe connection is colored white, with the return connection being red **(see illustrations)**. Where applicable, disconnect the ground cable below the fuel line connections. **Warning:** *Refer to 'Safety first!' and the warnings in Chapter 4A when disconnecting fuel lines - extreme fire risk.*
35 Disconnect the hoses from the charcoal canister, located behind the power steering fluid reservoir; note the positions of the hoses, for use when installing **(see illustration 4.11b)**. **Note:** *On most models the evaporative canister is mounted at the rear of the vehicle, near the fuel tank.*
36 Connect a hoist and raise it so that the weight of the engine and transaxle are just supported. Arrange the hoist and sling so that the engine and transaxle are kept level when they are being withdrawn from the vehicle. Remove the lower engine-to-transaxle fasteners now, since they will be more difficult to access when the powertrain is on the floor.
37 Unscrew and remove the right- and left-hand engine/transaxle mounts, referring to the relevant Part of Chapter 2 as necessary.
38 Check around the engine and transaxle assembly from above and below, to ensure that all associated attachments are discon-

nected and positioned out of the way. Engage the services of an assistant to help in guiding the assembly clear of surrounding components.
39 Consider how the engine will be removed from under the car, before lowering it. If a wheeled trolley is available, this makes the task of moving the engine much easier. If the engine is lowered onto a piece of carpet or a sheet of wood, this can be used to drag the engine out from under the car, without damage.
40 Carefully lower the engine/transaxle assembly clear of the mounts, guiding the assembly past any obstructions, and taking care that surrounding components are not damaged **(see illustrations)**.
41 Raise the vehicle on the hoist and remove the engine/transaxle assembly out from underneath.
42 Once the engine/transaxle assembly is clear of the vehicle, move it to an area where it can be cleaned and worked on.

Separation

43 Rest the engine and transaxle assembly on a firm, flat surface, and use wooden blocks as wedges to keep the unit steady.
44 Note the routing and location of any wir-

4.34a Pry out the colored locking clip . . .

ing on the engine/transaxle assembly, then methodically disconnect it.

Manual transaxle models
45 Refer to the information in Chapter 7A, Section 8.

Automatic transaxle models
46 Refer to the information in Chapter 7B, Section 9.

Reconnection
47 To reconnect the transaxle and engine, reverse the operations used to separate them. Above all, do not use excessive force during these operations - if the two will not mate together easily, forcing them will only lead to damage. *Do not tighten the bellhousing bolts to force the engine and transaxle together.* Ensure that the bellhousing and cylinder block mating faces will butt together evenly without obstruction, before tightening the bolts fully. Reconnect any wiring on the engine/transaxle assembly, routing it as noted on removal.

Installation
48 Maneuver the engine/transaxle under the car.
49 Slowly lower the vehicle on the hoist,

4.34b . . . and disconnect the fuel lines at the firewall

4.40a Lower the engine clear of the mounts . . .

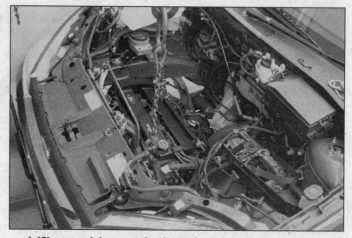

4.40b . . . and down so that it can be removed from the front

making sure the engine/transaxle assembly is positioned so that it doesn't contact any components in the engine compartment as the vehicle is lowered.

50   Attach the engine hoist, and lift the unit into position until the right- and left-hand mounts can be reassembled. Initially, tighten the mounting nuts and bolts only lightly.

51   Install the engine rear mount, and tighten the bolts by hand.

52   Rock the engine/transaxle gently to settle it on its mounts, then tighten all the mounting nuts and bolts to the specified torques. Once the engine/transaxle is fully supported by its mounts, the hoist can be removed.

53   The remainder of the installation procedure is the direct reverse of the removal procedure, noting the following points:

a) *Tighten all fasteners to the specified torque settings, where applicable.*

b) *Ensure that all sections of the wiring harness follow their original routing; use new cable-ties to secure the harness in position, keeping it away from sources of heat and abrasion.*

c) *Ensure that all hoses are correctly routed and are secured with the correct hose clamps, where applicable. If the hose clamps cannot be used again, worm-drive clamps should be installed in their place.*

d) *On vehicles with manual transaxle, check and if necessary adjust the shift cables with reference to Chapter 7A.*

e) *Refill the cooling system as described in Chapter 1.*

f) *Refill the engine with appropriate grade and quantity of oil, where necessary (Chapter 1).*

g) *Refill or top-off the transaxle oil or fluid (see Chapter 1).*

h) *Check and if necessary adjust the accelerator cable with reference to Chapter 4A.*

i) *When the engine is started for the first time, check for air, coolant, lubricant and fuel leaks from manifolds, hoses, etc. If the engine has been overhauled, read the notes in Section 19 before attempting to start it.*

5   Engine overhaul - disassembly sequence

1   It is much easier to disassemble and work on the engine if it is mounted on a portable engine stand. These stands can often be rented from a tool shop. Before the engine is mounted on a stand, the flywheel/driveplate should be removed (Part A or B of this Chapter) so that the stand bolts can be tightened into the end of the cylinder block/crankcase.

2   If a stand is not available, it is possible to disassemble the engine with it mounted on blocks, on a sturdy workbench or on the floor. Be extra-careful not to tip or drop the engine when working without a stand.

3   If you are going to obtain a reconditioned engine, all external components must be removed first, to be transferred to the replacement engine (just as they will if you are doing a complete engine overhaul yourself). **Note:** *When removing the external components from the engine, pay close attention to details that may be helpful or important during installation. Note the installed position of gaskets, seals, spacers, pins, washers, bolts and other small items.* These external components include the following:

a) *Alternator and mounting bracket (Chapter 5A).*

b) *Power steering pump and air conditioning compressor mounting brackets.*

c) *Spark plug wires and spark plugs (Chapter 1).*

d) *Fuel injection and emission control system components (Chapter 4A or 4B).*

e) *Thermostat and housing (Chapter 3).*

f) *Dipstick tube.*

g) *All electrical switches and sensors.*

h) *Intake and exhaust manifolds (Chapter 4A).*

i) *Oil filter (Chapter 1).*

j) *Engine/transaxle mounting brackets (Chapter 2A or 2B).*

k) *Flywheel/driveplate (Chapter 2A or 2B).*

4   If you are obtaining a 'short-block' engine (which consists of the engine cylinder

block/crankcase, crankshaft, pistons and connecting rods all assembled), then the cylinder head, oil pan, lower crankcase (where applicable), oil pump and timing belt will have to be removed also.

5   If you are planning a complete overhaul, the engine can be disassembled and the internal components removed in the following order.

a) *Alternator and mounting bracket (Chapter 5A).*

b) *Intake and exhaust manifolds (Chapter 4A).*

c) *Timing belt and toothed pulleys (Chapter 2A or 2B).*

d) *Cylinder head (Chapter 2A or 2B).*

e) *Power steering pump and air conditioning compressor mounting brackets.*

f) *Flywheel/driveplate (Chapter 2A or 2B).*

g) *Oil pan (Chapter 2A or 2B).*

h) *Oil pump - and, where applicable, lower crankcase (Chapter 2A or 2B).*

i) *Piston/connecting rod assemblies (Section 9).*

j) *Crankshaft (Section 10).*

6   Before beginning the disassembly and overhaul procedures, make sure that you have all of the correct tools necessary.

6   Cylinder head - disassembly

Refer to illustrations 6.3, 6.7a, 6.7b, 6.8a and 6.8b

Note: *New and reconditioned cylinder heads are available from the manufacturers, and from engine overhaul specialists. Due to the fact that some specialist tools are required for the disassembly and inspection procedures, and new components may not be readily available (refer to Section 1), it may be more practical and economical for the home mechanic to purchase a reconditioned head, rather than to disassemble, inspect and recondition the original head.*

1   Remove the camshaft(s) and cam followers (Chapter 2A or 2B).

2   Remove the cylinder head (Chapter 2A, 2B or 2C).

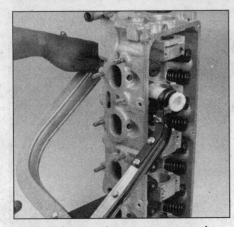

6.3 Using a spring compressor and a plastic deep-well adapter, compress the spring to expose the keepers

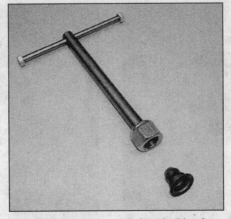

6.7a Make a seal removal tool with a bar, drill it for a cross-handle at the top, pin a large nut (whose threads just "bite" into the seal) on the bar so that the nut will turn with the bar

6.7b Using the homemade tool to remove the valve stem oil seals

3   Using a valve spring compressor, compress each valve spring in turn until the keepers can be removed. A special valve spring compressor will be required, to reach into the deep wells in the cylinder head without risk of damaging the cam follower bores; such compressors are now widely available from most good auto parts stores. Release the compressor, and lift off the retainer and spring **(see illustration)**.

4   If, when the valve spring compressor is screwed down, the retainer refuses to free and expose the valve keepers, gently tap the top of the tool, directly over the retainer, with a light hammer. This will free the seat.

5   Withdraw the valve through the combustion chamber. If it binds in the guide (won't pull through), push it back in, and de-burr the area around the groove with a fine file or whetstone; take care not to mark the cam follower bores.

6   Recover the valve stem oil seals from their locations in the cylinder head. As the seals are removed, note whether they are of different colors for the intake and exhaust valves - compare with the new parts, and note this for installation. As a guide, the intake valve seals are green, and the exhaust seals are red.

7   On Zetec-E engines, the valve stem seals are integral with the valve spring lower seat, and are thus an unusual design; removing the seals can be extremely tricky, due to limited access and the shape of the seal 'assembly'. The manufacturer recommends the use of their service tool 303-374 to extract the seals; while this is almost indispensable if the seals are to be removed without risk of (extremely expensive) damage to the cylinder head, we found that a serviceable substitute can be made using a nut of suitable size, a bar and a rollpin. Screw on the tool so that it bites into the seal, then draw the seal off the valve guide **(see illustrations)**.

8   It is essential that the valves are kept together with their keepers, spring seats and springs, and in their correct sequence (unless they are so badly worn that they are to be replaced). If they are going to be kept and used again, place them in a labeled plastic bag or similar small container **(see illustrations)**. Note that the Number 1 valve is nearest to the timing belt end of the engine; the intake and exhaust valve positions can be deduced from the installed positions of the intake and exhaust manifolds.

7   Cylinder head and valve components - cleaning and inspection

1   Thorough cleaning of the cylinder head and valve components, followed by a detailed inspection, will enable you to decide how much valve service work must be carried out during the engine overhaul. **Note:** *If the engine has been severely overheated, it is best to assume that the cylinder head is warped, and to check carefully for signs of this.*

Cleaning

2   Scrape away all traces of old gasket material and sealing compound from the cylinder head.

3   Scrape away the carbon from the combustion chambers and ports, then wash the cylinder head thoroughly with a suitable solvent.

4   Scrape off any heavy carbon deposits that may have formed on the valves, then use a power-operated wire brush to remove deposits from the valve heads and stems.

Inspection

Note: *Be sure to perform all the following*

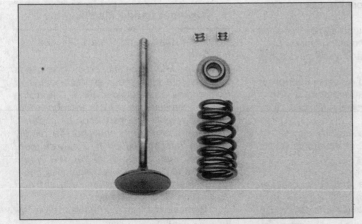

6.8a Valve, keepers, retainer and valve spring

6.8b Use a labeled plastic bag to store and identify valve components

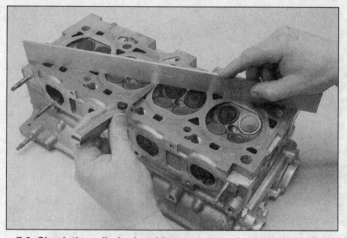

7.6 Check the cylinder head for warpage using a straightedge and feeler gauges

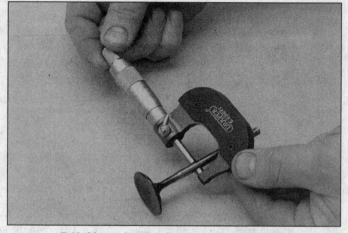

7.12 Measuring the diameter of a valve stem

inspection procedures before concluding that the services of a machine shop or engine overhaul specialist are required. Make a list of all items that require attention.

Cylinder head
Refer to illustration 7.6

5 Inspect the head very carefully for cracks, evidence of coolant leakage, and other damage. If cracks are found, a new cylinder head should be obtained.

6 If warpage of the cylinder head gasket surface is suspected, use a straight-edge to check it for distortion **(see illustration)**. If feeler gauges are used, the degree of distortion can be assessed more accurately, and compared with the value specified. Check for distortion along the length and across the width of the head, and along both diagonals. If the head is warped, it may be possible to have it machined flat at an automotive machine shop.

7 Examine the valve seats in each of the combustion chambers. If they are severely pitted, cracked or burned, then they will need to be replaced or re-cut by an engine overhaul specialist. If they are only slightly pitted, this can be removed by grinding-in the valve heads and seats with fine valve-grinding compound, as described below.

8 If the valve guides are worn, indicated by a side-to-side motion of the valve, new guides must be installed. Measure the diameter of the existing valve stems (see below) and the bore of the guides, then calculate the clearance, and compare the result with the specified value; if the clearance is excessive, replace the valves or guides as necessary.

9 The replacement of valve guides is best carried out by an engine overhaul specialist.

10 If the valve seats are to be re-cut, this must be done only after the guides have been replaced.

Valves
Refer to illustrations 7.12 and 7.15

11 Examine the head of each valve for pitting, burning, cracks and general wear, and check the valve stem for scoring and wear

ridges. Rotate the valve, and check for any obvious indication that it is bent. Look for pits and excessive wear on the tip of each valve stem. Replace any valve that shows any such signs of wear or damage.

12 If the valve appears satisfactory at this stage, measure the valve stem diameter at several points, using a micrometer **(see illustration)**. Any significant difference in the readings obtained indicates wear of the valve stem. Should any of these conditions be apparent, the valve(s) must be replaced.

13 If the valves are in satisfactory condition, they should be ground (lapped) into their respective seats, to ensure a smooth gas-tight seal. If the seat is only lightly pitted, or if it has been re-cut, fine grinding compound only should be used to produce the required finish. Coarse valve-grinding compound should not be used unless a seat is badly burned or deeply pitted; if this is the case, the cylinder head and valves should be inspected by an expert, to decide whether seat re-cutting, or even the replacement of the valve or seat insert, is required.

14 Valve grinding is carried out as follows. Place the cylinder head upside-down on a bench, with a block of wood at each end to give clearance for the valve stems.

15 Smear a trace of (the appropriate grade) valve-grinding compound on the seat face,

and press a suction grinding tool onto the valve head. With a semi-rotary action, grind the valve head to its seat, lifting the valve occasionally to redistribute the grinding compound **(see illustration)**. A light spring placed under the valve head will greatly ease this operation. If coarse grinding compound is being used, work only until a dull, matte even surface is produced on both the valve seat and the valve, then wipe off the used compound, and repeat the process with fine compound.

16 When a smooth unbroken ring of light grey matte finish is produced on both the valve and seat, the grinding operation is complete. Do not grind in the valves any further than absolutely necessary, or the seat will be prematurely sunk into the cylinder head.

17 When all the valves have been ground-in, carefully wash off all traces of grinding compound, using a suitable solvent, before reassembly of the cylinder head.

Valve components
Refer to illustration 7.18

18 Examine the valve springs for signs of damage and discoloration, and also measure their free length (where no length is specified, compare each of the existing springs with new components) **(see illustration)**.

7.15 Grinding-in a valve seat

7.18 Measure the valve spring free length

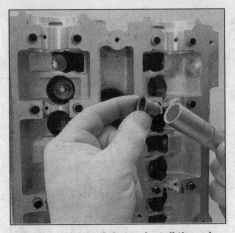

8.2 Use a deep socket to install the valve stem seals

8.3 Lubricate the valve stem, then install the valve in the head

8.4a Install the valve spring . . .

8.4b . . . and the retainer

19   Stand each spring on a flat surface, and check it for squareness. If any of the springs are damaged, distorted, or have lost their tension, obtain a complete set of new springs.

20   Check the retainers and keepers for obvious wear and cracks. Any questionable parts should be replaced, as extensive damage will occur if they fail during engine operation. Any damaged or excessively-worn parts must be replaced; the valve spring lower seat/stem oil seals must be replaced as a matter of course whenever they are disturbed.

21   Check the cam followers as described in Chapter 2A or 2B.

8   Cylinder head - reassembly

Refer to illustrations 8.2, 8.3, 8.4a, 8.4b, 8.5a and 8.5b

1   Regardless of whether or not the head was sent away for repair work of any sort, make sure that it is clean before beginning reassembly. Be sure to remove any metal particles and abrasive grit that may still be present from operations such as valve grinding or head resurfacing. Use compressed air, if available, to blow out all the oil holes and passages. **Caution:** *Wear safety goggles when using compressed air.*

2   Lubricate the new valve stem oil seals, then install them to the cylinder head, pressing them in squarely using a deep socket of suitable diameter **(see illustration)**. Note that the intake and exhaust seals are usually different colors - green for the intake valves, red for the exhaust valves.

3   Beginning at one end of the head, lubricate and install the first valve. Apply moly-based grease or clean engine oil to the valve stem, and install the valve **(see illustration)**. Where the original valves are being re-used, ensure that each is installed in its original guide. If new valves are being installed, insert them into the locations to which they have been ground.

4   Install the valve spring and retainer **(see illustrations)**.

5   Compress the spring with a valve spring compressor, and carefully install the keepers in the stem groove. Apply a small dab of grease to each keeper to hold it in place if necessary; grease is also useful for sticking each half of the keepers to a screwdriver, or similar tool, for installation **(see illustrations)**. Slowly release the compressor, and make sure the keepers seat properly.

6   When the valve is installed, place the cylinder head flat on the bench and, using a hammer and block of wood, tap the end of the valve stem gently, to settle the components.

7   Repeat the procedure for the remaining valves. Be sure to return the components to their original locations - don't mix them up!

8   Install the cam followers and camshaft(s) (Chapter 2A or 2B).

9   Piston/connecting rod assemblies - removal

Refer to illustrations 9.2a, 9.2b, 9.4, 9.5. 9.7a and 9.7b

Note: *While this task is theoretically possible when the engine is in place in the vehicle, in practice, it requires so much preliminary dismantling, and is so difficult to carry out due to the restricted access, that owners are advised to remove the engine from the vehicle first. The following paragraphs assume the engine is removed from the car.*

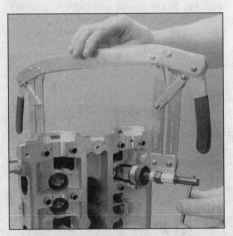

8.5a Position the valve spring compressor, and compress the valve spring . . .

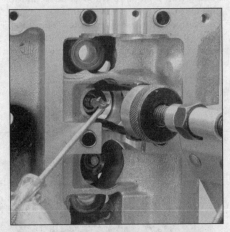

8.5b . . . then fit the keepers to the groove, holding them in with grease and a screwdriver

9.2a Unbolt the oil pickup pipe/filter and return pipe . . .

9.2b . . . then unbolt the lower crankcase and remove it

9.4 Each connecting rod and cap can be marked on the flat, machined surfaces

1   Remove the cylinder head and oil pan with reference to Chapter 2A or 2B.
2   Unbolt the oil pump pick-up tube/filter and return pipe, from the lower crankcase. On Zetec-E engines, unbolt and remove the lower crankcase; recover the rubber gasket - a new one must be used when reassembling **(see illustrations)**.
3   The connecting rods and caps are of 'cracked' design. During production, the connecting rod and cap are forged as one piece, then the cap is broken apart from the rod using a special technique. Because of this design, the mating surfaces of each cap and rod are unique and, therefore, nearly impossible to mix up.
4   There should be markings on the connecting rod caps, with corresponding marks on the connecting rods **(see illustration)**. Make sure these marks are visible before removing the caps, and if not, make your own using a center-punch. This is so that you can be certain of installing each piston/connecting rod assembly the right way, to its correct (original) bore, with the cap also installed the right way.
5   Each piston has an arrow stamped into its crown, pointing towards the timing belt

end of the engine **(see illustration)**.
6   Use your fingernail to feel if a ridge has formed at the upper limit of ring travel (about 6 mm down from the top of each cylinder). If carbon deposits or cylinder wear have produced ridges, they must be completely removed with a special tool called a ridge reamer. Follow the manufacturer's instructions provided with the tool. **Caution:** *Failure to remove the ridges before attempting to remove the piston/connecting rod assemblies may result in piston and/or ring breakage.*
7   Loosen each of the connecting rod bearing cap bolts half a turn at a time, until they can be removed by hand. Remove the Number 1 cap and bearing **(see illustrations)**. Don't drop the bearing out of the cap.
8   Remove the upper bearing shell, and push the connecting rod/piston assembly out through the top of the engine. Use a wooden hammer handle to push on the connecting rod's bearing recess. If resistance is felt, double-check that all of the ridge was removed from the cylinder (see Step 6).
9   Repeat the procedure for the remaining cylinders.
10   After removal, reassemble the connecting rod bearing caps and bearings on their

respective connecting rods, and install the bolts finger-tight. Leaving the old bearings in place until reassembly will help prevent the bearing recesses from being accidentally nicked or gouged. New bearings should be used on reassembly.
11   Don't attempt to separate the pistons from the connecting rods. This is a job for a machine shop with the proper equipment.

10 Crankshaft - removal

Refer to illustrations 10.2 and 10.4
Note 1: *On the 2.3L and all 2005 engines, because of the fine tolerances in the bearing shells, no service operations are permitted on the cylinder block/crank assembly. In the event of any failure, the complete cylinder block, pistons and crank assembly must be replaced as a unit. The following procedures are for the earlier 2.0L engines.*
Note 2: *The crankshaft can be removed only after the engine/transaxle has been removed from the vehicle. It is assumed that the transaxle and flywheel/driveplate, timing belt, lower crankcase, cylinder head, oil pan, oil*

9.5 Arrow stamped on the top of the piston points to the timing belt end of the engine

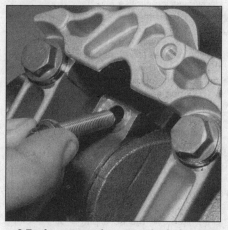

9.7a Loosen and remove the bolts . . .

9.7b . . . then take off the connecting rod cap

10.2 Checking the crankshaft endplay with a dial indicator

10.4 Main bearing caps are marked with cylinder number and arrowhead

11.2 Marker pens can be used as shown to identify bearings without damaging them

pump pick-up/strainer pipe and oil baffle, oil pump, and piston/connecting rod assemblies, have already been removed. The crankshaft rear main oil seal carrier must be unbolted from the cylinder block/crankcase before proceeding with crankshaft removal.

1   Before the crankshaft is removed, check the endplay. Mount a dial indicator with the probe in line with the crankshaft and touching the end of the crankshaft.

2   Push the crankshaft fully away from the gauge, and zero it. Next, lever the crankshaft towards the gauge as far as possible, and check the reading obtained **(see illustration)**. The distance that the crankshaft moved is its endplay; if it is greater than specified, check the crankshaft thrust surfaces for wear. If no wear is evident, new thrustwashers should correct the endplay. On some engines, the thrustwasher/thrust control bearing is part of the Number 3 (center) main bearing.

3   If a dial gauge is not available, feeler gauges can be used. Gently lever or push the crankshaft all the way towards the right-hand end of the engine. Slip feeler gauges between the crankshaft and the right-hand face of the Number 3 (center) main bearing to determine the clearance.

4   Check the main bearing caps, to see if they are marked to indicate their locations. They should be numbered consecutively from the timing belt end of the engine - if not, mark them with number-stamping dies or a center-punch. The caps will also have an embossed arrow pointing to the timing belt end of the engine **(see illustration)**. Noting, where applicable, the different fasteners (for the oil baffle nuts) used on caps 2 and 4, loosen the cap bolts a quarter-turn at a time each, starting with the left- and right-hand end caps and working toward the center, until they can be removed by hand.

5   Gently tap the caps with a soft-faced hammer, then separate them from the cylinder block/crankcase. If necessary, use the bolts as levers to remove the caps. Try not to drop the bearing shells if they come out with the caps.

6   Carefully lift the crankshaft out of the engine. It may be a good idea to have an

assistant available, since the crankshaft is quite heavy. With the bearings in place in the cylinder block/crankcase and main bearing caps, return the caps to their respective locations on the block, or install the lower crankcase, and tighten the bolts finger-tight. Leaving the old bearings in place until reassembly will help prevent the bearing recesses from being accidentally nicked or gouged. New bearings should be used on reassembly.

11 Cylinder block/crankcase - cleaning and inspection

Cleaning

Refer to illustrations 11.2, 11.5, 11.8 and 11.9

1   For complete cleaning, remove the water pump, all external components, and all electrical switches/sensors. Unbolt the piston-cooling oil jets or blanking plugs (as applicable). Note that Ford states that the piston-cooling oil jets (where fitted) must be replaced whenever the engine is disassembled for full overhaul.

2   Remove the main bearing caps or lower crankcase, and separate the bearings from the caps/lower crankcase and the cylinder block. Mark or label the bearings, indicating which bearing throw they were removed from, and whether they were in the cap or the block, then set them aside **(see illustration)**. Wipe clean the block and cap bearing recesses, and inspect them for nicks, gouges and scratches.

3   Unbolt and remove the oil/water pumps from the timing belt end of the engine, if not already removed.

4   Scrape all traces of gasket from the cylinder block/lower crankcase, taking care not to damage the sealing surfaces.

5   Remove all oil gallery plugs (if present). The plugs are usually very tight - they may have to be drilled out and the holes re-tapped. Use new plugs when the engine is reassembled. Remove the core plugs by knocking them sideways in their bores with a hammer and a punch, then grasping them with large pliers and pulling them back through their

holes **(see illustration)**.

6   If any of the castings are extremely dirty, they should be taken to an automotive machine shop for cleaning. After the castings are returned, clean all oil holes and oil galleries one more time. Flush all internal passages with warm water until the water runs clear, then dry thoroughly, and apply a light film of oil to all machined surfaces, to prevent rusting. If you have access to compressed air, use it to speed the drying process, and to blow out all the oil holes and galleries (always take safety precautions when using compressed air).

7   If the castings are not very dirty, you can do an adequate cleaning job with hot soapy water (as hot as you can stand!) and a stiff brush. Take plenty of time, and do a thorough job. Regardless of the cleaning method used, be sure to clean all oil holes and galleries very thoroughly, and to dry all components completely; protect the machined surfaces as described above, to prevent rusting.

8   All threaded holes must be clean and dry, to ensure accurate torque readings during reassembly; now is also a good time to clean and check the threads of all principal

11.5 The core plugs can be removed by tapping in one edge until the plug turns sideways, then pulling them out with pliers

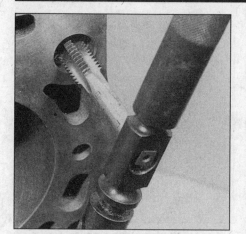

11.8 All bolt holes in the block should be cleaned and restored with a tap

11.9 A large socket on an extension can be used to drive the new core plugs into their bores

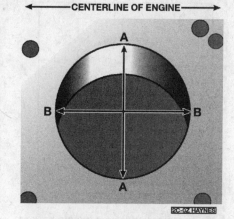

11.14 Measure the diameter of each cylinder at a right angle to the engine centerline (A), and parallel to engine centerline (B) - out-of-round is the difference between A and B, taper is the difference between A and B at the top of the cylinder and A and B at the bottom of the cylinder

bolts - however, note that some, such as the cylinder head and flywheel/driveplate bolts, must be replaced as a matter of course whenever they are disturbed. Run the proper-size tap into each of the holes, to remove rust, corrosion, thread sealant or sludge, and to restore damaged threads **(see illustration)**. If possible, use compressed air to clear the holes of debris produced by this operation. **Caution:** *Wear safety goggles when using compressed air.*

9 When all inspection and repair procedures are complete (see below) and the block is ready for reassembly, apply suitable sealant to the new oil gallery plugs, and insert them into the holes in the block. Tighten them securely. After coating the sealing surfaces of the new core plugs with suitable sealant, install them in the cylinder block/crankcase. Make sure they are driven in straight and seated properly, or leakage could result. Special tools are available for this purpose, but a large socket with an outside diameter that will just slip into the core plug, used with an extension and hammer, will work just as well **(see illustration)**.

10 Install the oil gallery plugs or (new) piston cooling oil jets (as applicable), tightening their retaining bolts securely. Also install all other external components removed, referring to the relevant Chapter of this manual for further details where required. Where applicable, install the main bearing caps and tighten the bolts finger-tight.

11 If the engine is not going to be reassembled right away, cover it with a large plastic bag to keep it clean. Apply a thin coat of engine oil to all machined surfaces to prevent rust.

Inspection

Refer to illustrations 11.14, 11.15 and 11.23

12 Visually check the castings for cracks and corrosion. Look for stripped threads in the threaded holes. If there has been any history of internal coolant leakage, it may be worthwhile having an engine overhaul specialist check the cylinder block/crankcase for cracks with special equipment. If defects are found, have them repaired, if possible, or

replace the assembly.

13 Check each cylinder bore for scuffing and scoring.

14 **Note:** *The cylinder bores must be measured with all the crankshaft main bearing caps bolted in place (without the crankshaft or bearings) to the specified torque settings.* Measure the diameter of each cylinder at the top (just under the ridge area), center and bottom of the cylinder bore, parallel to the crankshaft axis. Next, measure each cylinder's diameter at the same three locations across the crankshaft axis **(see illustration)**. Note the measurements obtained.

15 Measure the piston diameter at right-angles to the wrist pin axis, just above the bottom of the skirt; again, note the results **(see illustration)**.

16 To obtain the piston-to-bore clearance, measure the bore and piston skirt as described above, and subtract the skirt diameter from the bore measurement. If the precision measuring tools shown are not available, the condition of the pistons and bores can be assessed, though not quite as accurately, by using feeler gauges as follows:

a) *Select a feeler gauge of thickness equal to the specified piston-to-bore clearance (where given), and slip it into the cylinder along with the matching piston. The piston must be positioned in the correct orientation. The feeler gauge must be between the piston and cylinder on one of the thrust faces (at right-angles to the wrist pin bore).*

b) *The piston should slip down the cylinder (with the feeler gauge in place) with moderate pressure; if it falls through or slides through easily, the clearance is excessive, and a new piston will be required. If the piston binds at the lower end of the cylinder, and is loose toward the top, the cylinder is tapered. If tight spots are encountered as the piston/feeler gauge is rotated in the cylinder, the cylinder is out-of-round (oval).*

17 Repeat these procedures for the remaining pistons and cylinder bores.

18 Compare the results with the Specifications at the beginning of this Chapter; if any measurement is beyond the dimensions specified for that class (check the piston crown marking to establish the class or size of piston fitted), or if any bore measurement is significantly different from the others (indicating that the bore is tapered or out-of-round), the piston or bore is excessively-worn.

19 Worn pistons must be replaced - check for availability with a Ford dealer or engine reconditioning specialist.

20 If any of the cylinder bores are badly scuffed or scored, or if they are excessively-worn, out-of-round or tapered, the usual course of action would be to have the cylinder block/crankcase rebored, and to install new, oversized, pistons on reassembly. See a Ford dealer or engine reconditioning specialist for advice.

21 If the bores are in reasonably good condition and not excessively worn, then it may

11.15 Measure the piston skirt diameter at right-angles to the piston-pin axis, just above the base of the skirt

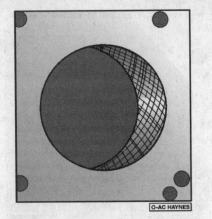

11.23 Typical cylinder bore honing pattern

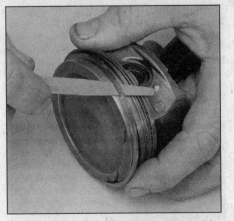

12.2 Use feeler gauges to ease the old rings from the pistons if a ring removal tool is not available

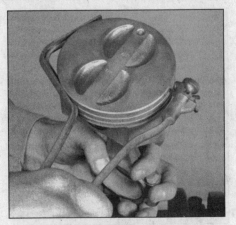

12.4a The piston ring grooves can be cleaned with a special tool, as shown here . . .

12.4b . . . or a section of broken ring, if available

only be necessary to replace the piston rings.

22   If this is the case, the bores should be honed, to allow the new rings to bed-in correctly and provide the best possible seal. Before honing the bores, install the main bearing caps without the bearing shells, and tighten the bolts to the specified torque wrench setting. **Note:** *If you don't have the tools, or don't want to tackle the honing operation, most engine reconditioning specialists will do it for a reasonable fee.*

23   Two types of cylinder hones are commonly available - the flex hone or 'bottle-brush' type, and the more traditional surfacing hone with spring-loaded stones. Both will do the job and are used with a power drill, but for the less-experienced mechanic, the 'bottle-brush' hone will probably be easier to use. You will also need some honing oil, and rags. Proceed as follows:

a) *Mount the hone in the drill, compress the stones, and slip it into the first bore. Be sure to wear safety goggles or a face shield.*

b) *Lubricate the bore with plenty of honing oil, switch on the drill, and move the hone up and down the bore, at a pace that will produce a fine cross-hatch pattern on the cylinder walls. Ideally, the cross-hatch lines should intersect at approximately a 60° angle (see illustration). Be sure to use plenty of lubricant, and don't take off any more material than is absolutely necessary to produce the desired finish. **Note:** Piston ring manufacturers may specify a different cross-hatch angle - read and follow any instructions included with the new rings.*

c) *Don't withdraw the hone from the bore while it's running. Instead, switch off the drill, and continue moving the hone up and down the bore until it comes to a complete stop, then compress the stones and withdraw the hone. If you're using a 'bottle-brush' hone, switch off the drill, then turn the chuck in the normal direction of rotation while withdrawing the hone from the bore.*

d) *Wipe the oil out of the bore, and repeat the procedure for the remaining cylinders.*

e) *When all the cylinder bores are honed, chamfer the top edges of the bores with a small file, so the rings won't catch when the pistons are installed. Be very careful not to nick the cylinder walls with the end of the file.*

f) *The entire cylinder block/crankcase must be washed very thoroughly with warm, soapy water, to remove all traces of the abrasive grit produced during the honing operation. **Note:** The bores can be considered clean when a lint-free white cloth - dampened with clean engine oil - used to wipe them out doesn't pick up any more honing residue, which will show up as grey areas on the cloth. Be sure to run a brush through all oil holes and galleries, and flush them with running water.*

g) *When the cylinder block/crankcase is completely clean, rinse it thoroughly and dry it, then lightly oil all exposed machined surfaces, to prevent rusting.*

24   The cylinder block/crankcase should now be completely clean and dry, with all components checked for wear or damage, and repaired or overhauled as necessary. Install as many ancillary components as possible, for safekeeping. If reassembly is not to start immediately, cover the block with a large plastic bag to keep it clean, and protect the machined surfaces as described above to prevent rusting.

12 Piston/connecting rod assemblies - inspection

Refer to illustrations 12.2, 12.4a and 12.4b

1   Before the inspection process can be carried out, the piston/connecting rod assemblies must be cleaned, and the original piston rings removed from the pistons.

2   Using a piston ring removal tool, carefully remove the rings from the pistons. Be careful not to nick or gouge the pistons in the process, and mark or label each ring as it is removed, so that its original top surface can be identified on reassembly, and so that it

can be returned to its original groove. Take care also with your hands - piston rings are sharp. If a piston ring removal tool is not available, the rings can be removed by hand, expanding them over the top of the pistons **(see illustration)**.

3   Scrape all traces of carbon from the top of the piston. A hand-held wire brush or a piece of fine emery cloth can be used, once the majority of the deposits have been scraped away. Do not, under any circumstances, use a wire brush mounted in a drill motor to remove deposits from the pistons - the piston material is soft, and may be eroded away by the wire brush.

4   Use a piston ring groove-cleaning tool to remove carbon deposits from the ring grooves. If a tool isn't available, but replacement rings have been found, a piece broken off the old ring will do the job **(see illustrations)**. Be very careful to remove only the carbon deposits - don't remove any metal, and do not nick or scratch the sides of the ring grooves. Protect your fingers - piston rings are sharp.

5   Once the deposits have been removed, clean the piston/rod assemblies with solvent, and dry them with compressed air (if available). Make sure the oil return holes in the back sides of the ring grooves, and the oil

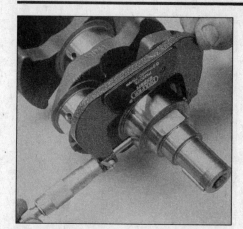

13.5 Measure the diameter of each crankshaft journal at several points, to detect taper and out-of-round conditions

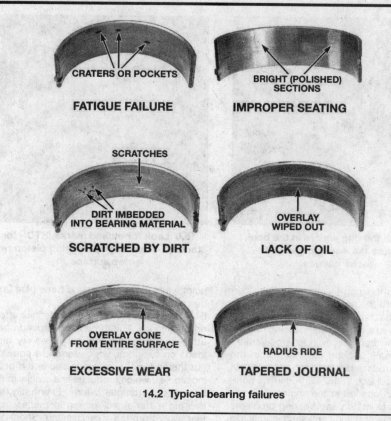

14.2 Typical bearing failures

hole in the lower end of each rod, are clear.

6   If the pistons and cylinder walls aren't damaged or worn excessively and if the cylinder block/crankcase is not rebored, new pistons won't be necessary. Normal piston wear appears as even vertical wear on the piston thrust surfaces, and slight looseness of the top ring in its groove.

7   Carefully inspect each piston for cracks around the skirt, at the pin bosses, and at the ring lands (between the ring grooves).

8   Look for scoring and scuffing on the thrust faces of the skirt, holes in the piston, and burned areas at the edge of the crown. If the skirt is scored or scuffed, the engine may have been suffering from overheating and/or abnormal combustion, which caused excessively-high operating temperatures. The cooling and lubrication systems should be checked thoroughly. A hole in the piston is an indication that abnormal combustion (pre-ignition) was occurring. Burned areas at the edge of the piston crown are usually evidence of spark knock (detonation). If any of the above problems exist, the causes must be corrected, or the damage will occur again. The causes may include faulty injectors, intake air leaks, incorrect fuel/air mixture, incorrect ignition timing, or EGR system malfunctions.

9   Corrosion of the piston, in the form of small pits, indicates that coolant is leaking into the combustion chamber and/or the crankcase. Again, the cause must be corrected, or the problem may persist in the rebuilt engine.

10   Check the piston-to-rod clearance by twisting the piston and rod in opposite directions. Any noticeable play indicates excessive wear, which must be corrected. The piston/connecting rod assemblies should be taken to an engine reconditioning specialist to have the pistons, wrist pins and rods checked, and new components installed as required.

11   Don't attempt to separate the pistons from the connecting rods. This is a task for an engine reconditioning specialist, due to the special heating equipment, press, mandrels and supports required to do the job. If the piston/connecting rod assemblies do require

this sort of work, have the connecting rods checked for bend and twist, since only such engine repair specialists will have the facilities for this purpose.

12   Check the connecting rods for cracks and other damage. Temporarily remove the connecting rod bearing caps and the old bearing shells, wipe clean the rod and cap bearing recesses, and inspect them for nicks, gouges and scratches. After checking the rods, replace the old bearings, slip the caps into place, and tighten the bolts finger-tight.

13   Crankshaft - inspection

Refer to illustration 13.5

1   Clean the crankshaft, and dry it with compressed air if available. Be sure to clean the oil holes with a pipe cleaner or oil gallery brush. **Warning:** *Wear eye protection when using compressed air.*

2   Check the main and crankpin (connecting rod) bearing journals for uneven wear, scoring, pitting and cracking.

3   Run a fingernail across each journal several times. If the journal feels too rough, it should be reground.

4   Remove all burrs from the crankshaft oil holes with a stone, file or scraper.

5   Using a micrometer, measure the diameter of the main bearing and crankpin (connecting rod) journals, and compare the results with the Specifications at the beginning of this Chapter **(see illustration)**.

6   By measuring the diameter at a number of points around each journal's circumference, you will be able to determine whether or not

the journal is out-of-round. Take the measurement at each end of the journal, near the webs, to determine if the journal is tapered.

7   If the crankshaft journals are damaged, tapered, out-of-round, or worn beyond the limits specified in this Chapter, the crankshaft must be taken to an engine overhaul specialist, who will regrind it, and who can supply the necessary undersize bearings, where available.

8   Check the oil seal journals at each end of the crankshaft for wear and damage. If either seal has worn an excessive groove in its journal, consult an engine overhaul specialist, who will be able to advise whether a repair is possible, or whether a new crankshaft is necessary.

Note: *Steel aftermarket repair sleeves are available for many engines that can be used to repair the front seal area of the crankshaft, saving the expense of a new crankshaft. Check with your auto parts store.*

14   Main and connecting rod bearings - inspection

Refer to illustration 14.2

1   Even though the main and connecting rod bearing shells should be replaced during the engine overhaul (where possible), the old shells should be retained for close examination, as they may reveal valuable information about the condition of the engine.

2   Bearing failure occurs because of lack of lubrication, the presence of dirt or other foreign particles, overloading the engine, and corrosion **(see illustration)**. Regardless of

16.3 With the ring square in the bore, measure the ring end gap with feeler gauges

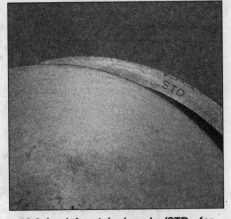

16.6 Look for etched marks (STD - for standard-sized ring) identifying piston ring top surface

16.7a Installing the spacer/expander in the oil control ring groove

16.7b Do NOT use a piston ring installation tool when installing the oil ring side rails

the cause of bearing failure, it must be corrected before the engine is reassembled, to prevent it from happening again.

3   When examining the bearing shells, remove them from the cylinder block/crankcase and main bearing caps and from the connecting rods and caps, then lay them out on a clean surface in the same general position as their location in the engine. This will enable you to match any bearing problems with the corresponding crankshaft journal. Do not touch any shell's bearing surface with your fingers while checking it, or the delicate surface may be scratched.

4   Dirt or other foreign matter gets into the engine in a variety of ways. It may be left in the engine during assembly, or it may pass through filters or the crankcase ventilation system. It may get into the oil, and from there into the bearings. Metal chips from machining operations and normal engine wear are often present. Abrasives are sometimes left in engine components after reconditioning, especially when parts are not thoroughly cleaned using the proper cleaning methods. Whatever the source, these foreign objects often end up embedded in the soft bearing material, and are easily recognized. Large particles will not embed in the material, and will score or gouge the shell and journal. The best prevention for this cause of bearing failure is to clean all parts thoroughly, and to keep everything spotlessly-clean during engine assembly. Frequent and regular engine oil and filter changes are also recommended.

5   Lack of lubrication (or lubrication breakdown) has a number of inter-related causes. Excessive heat (which thins the oil), overloading (which squeezes the oil from the bearing face) and oil leakage (from excessive bearing clearances, worn oil pump or high engine speeds) all contribute to lubrication breakdown. Blocked oil passages, which usually are the result of misaligned oil holes in a bearing shell, will also starve a bearing of oil, and destroy it. When lack of lubrication is the cause of bearing failure, the bearing material is wiped or extruded from the shell's steel backing. Temperatures may increase to the

point where the steel backing turns blue from overheating.

6   Driving habits can have a definite effect on bearing life. Full-throttle, low-speed operation (laboring the engine) puts very high loads on bearings, which tends to squeeze out the oil film. These loads cause the bearings to flex, which produces fine cracks in the bearing face (fatigue failure). Eventually, the bearing material will loosen in pieces, and tear away from the steel backing. Short-distance driving leads to corrosion of bearings, because insufficient engine heat is produced to drive off condensed water and corrosive gases. These products collect in the engine oil, forming acid and sludge. As the oil is carried to the engine bearings, the acid attacks and corrodes the bearing material.

7   Incorrect bearing installation during engine assembly will lead to bearing failure as well. Tight-fitting shells leave insufficient bearing running clearance, and will result in oil starvation. Dirt or foreign particles trapped behind a bearing result in high spots, which lead to failure. Do not touch any bearing's surface with your fingers during reassembly; there is a risk of scratching the delicate surface, or of depositing particles of dirt on it.

15 Engine overhaul - reassembly sequence

1   Before reassembly begins, ensure that all new parts have been obtained, and that all necessary tools are available. Read through the entire procedure, to familiarize yourself with the work involved, and to ensure that all items necessary for reassembly of the engine are at hand.

2   In addition to all normal tools and materials, suitable sealant will be required for certain seal surfaces. The various sealants recommended by the manufacturer appear in the relevant procedures in Chapter 2A, 2B or 2C. In all other cases, provided the relevant mating surfaces are clean and flat, new gaskets will be sufficient to ensure joints are oil-tight. *Do not* use any kind of silicone-based sealant

on any part of the fuel system or intake manifold, and *never* use exhaust sealants upstream of the catalytic converter (between the engine and the converter). **Caution:** *Certain types of high-volatility RTV sealant can foul the oxygen sensor and cause it to fail. Be sure that any RTV used is a low-volatility type and meets manufacturer specifications for use on engines equipped with an oxygen sensor.*

3   In order to save time and avoid problems, engine reassembly can be carried out in the following order:

a) *Crankshaft (Section 17).*
b) *Piston/connecting rod assemblies (Section 18).*
c) *Oil pump (Chapter 2A, 2B or 2C).*
d) *Oil pan (Chapter 2A, 2B or 2C).*
e) *Flywheel/driveplate (Chapter 2A or 2B).*
f) *Cylinder head (Chapter 2A, 2B or 2C).*
g) *Timing belt and toothed pulleys (Chapter 2A, 2B or 2C).*
h) *Engine external components.*

4   At this stage, all engine components should be absolutely clean and dry, with all faults repaired. All components should be neatly arranged on a completely clean work surface or in individual containers.

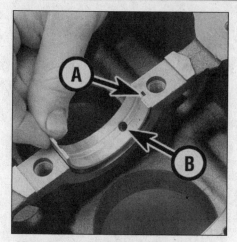

17.4a Ensure that the tab (A) and oil hole (B) are correctly aligned when installing the bearings

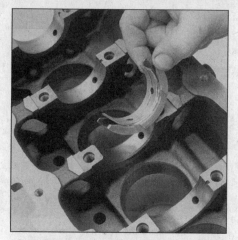

17.4b Note the thrustwashers fitted to the number 3 main bearing insert

17.6 Lay the Plastigage strips on the main bearing journals, parallel to the crankshaft centerline

16 Piston rings - installation

Refer to illustrations 16.3, 16.6, 16.7a and 16.7b

1   Before installing new piston rings, check the end gaps. Lay out each piston set with a piston/connecting rod assembly, and keep them together as a matched set from now on.

2   Insert the top compression ring into the first cylinder, and square it up with the cylinder walls by pushing it in with the top of the piston. The ring should be near the bottom of the cylinder, at the lower limit of ring travel.

3   To measure the end gap, slip feeler gauges between the ends of the ring, until a gauge equal to the gap width is found **(see illustration)**. The feeler gauge should slide between the ring ends with a slight amount of drag. Compare the measurement to the value given in the Specifications Section of this Chapter; if the gap is larger or smaller than specified, double-check to make sure you have the correct rings before proceeding. If you are assessing the condition of used rings, have the cylinder bores checked and measured by an engine reconditioning specialist, so that you can be sure of exactly which component is worn, and seek advice as to the best course of action to take.

4   If the end gap is still too small, it must be opened up by careful filing of the ring ends using a fine file. If it is too large, very careful checking is required of the dimensions of all components, as well as of the new parts.

5   Repeat the procedure for each ring that will be installed in the first cylinder, and for each ring in the remaining cylinders. Remember to keep rings, pistons and cylinders matched up.

6   Install the piston rings as follows. Where the original rings are being installed, use the marks or notes made on removal, to ensure that each ring is installed to its original groove and the same way up. New rings generally have their top surfaces identified by markings

(often an indication of size, such as STD, or the word TOP) - the rings must be installed with such markings facing up **(see illustration)**. **Note:** *Always follow the instructions printed on the ring package or box - different manufacturers may require different approaches. Do not mix up the top and second compression rings, as they usually have different cross-sections.*

7   The oil control ring (lowest one on the piston) should be installed first. It is composed of three separate elements. Slip the spacer/expander into the groove. Next, install the lower side rail. Don't use a piston ring installation tool on the oil ring side rails, as they may be damaged. Instead, place one end of the side rail into the groove between the spacer/expander and the ring land, hold it firmly in place, and slide a finger around the piston while pushing the rail into the groove. Next, install the upper side rail in the same manner **(see illustrations)**.

8   After the three oil ring components have been installed, check that both the upper and lower side rails can be turned smoothly in the ring groove.

9   The second compression (middle) ring is installed next, followed by the top compression ring - ensure their marks are facing up. Don't expand either ring any more than necessary to slide it over the top of the piston.

10   With all the rings in position, space the ring gaps (including the elements of the oil control ring) uniformly around the piston at 120° intervals. Repeat the procedure for the remaining pistons and rings.

17 Crankshaft - installation and main bearing clearance check

1   Crankshaft installation is the first major step in engine reassembly. It is assumed at this point that the cylinder block/crankcase and crankshaft have been cleaned, inspected and repaired or reconditioned as necessary. Position the engine upside-down.

2   Remove the main bearing cap bolts, and lift out the caps. Lay the caps out in the proper order, to ensure correct installation.

3   If they're still in place, remove the old bearing shells from the block and the main bearing caps. Wipe the bearing recesses with a clean, lint-free cloth. They must be kept spotlessly clean.

Main bearing running clearance check

Refer to illustrations 17.4a, 17.4b, 17.6, 17.7 and 17.10

4   Clean the backs of the new main bearing shells. Fit the shells with an oil groove in each main bearing location in the block. Note the thrustwashers integral with the Number 3 (center) upper main bearing shell, or the thrustwasher halves installed on either side of the Number 3 upper main bearing location. Install the other shell from each bearing set in the corresponding main bearing cap. Make sure the tab on each bearing fits into the notch in the block or cap/lower crankcase. Also, the oil holes in the block must line up with the oil holes in the bearing **(see illustrations)**. Don't hammer the bearings into place, and don't nick or gouge the bearing faces. No lubrication should be used at this time.

5   Clean the bearing surfaces in the block and the crankshaft main bearing journals with a clean, lint-free cloth. Check or clean the oil holes in the crankshaft, as any dirt here will go straight through the new bearings.

6   Once you're certain the crankshaft is clean, carefully lay it in position in the main bearings. Trim several pieces of the appropriate-size Plastigage (they must be slightly shorter than the width of the main bearings), and place one piece on each crankshaft main bearing journal, parallel with the crankshaft centerline **(see illustration)**.

7   Clean the bearing surfaces of the caps and bearings, then fit the bearings to the main

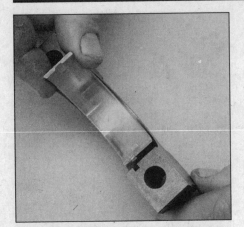

17.7 Make sure the tab on the cap bearing half engages the cap properly

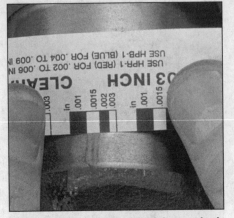

17.10 Compare the width of the crushed Plastigage to the scale on the envelope to determine the main bearing oil clearance - there are metric and standard scales on the envelope, so make sure you read the correct one

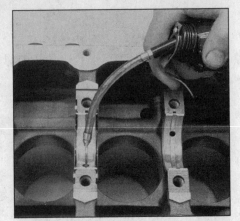

17.13 Oil the bearing inserts before final crankshaft installation

bearing caps **(see illustration)**. Install the caps in their respective positions (don't mix them up) with the arrows pointing to the timing belt end of the engine. Don't disturb the Plastigage.

8   Working on one cap at a time, from the center main bearing outwards (and ensuring that each cap is tightened down squarely and evenly onto the block), tighten the main bearing cap bolts to the specified torque wrench setting.

9   Remove the bolts, and carefully lift off the main bearing caps. Don't disturb the Plastigage or rotate the crankshaft. If any of the main bearing caps are difficult to remove, tap them gently from side-to-side with a soft-faced mallet to loosen them.

10   Compare the width of the crushed Plastigage on each journal with the scale printed on the Plastigage envelope to obtain the main bearing running clearance **(see illustration)**. Check the Specifications to make sure that the clearance is correct.

11   If the clearance is not as specified, seek the advice of an engine reconditioning specialist - if the crankshaft journals are in good condition, it may be possible simply to replace the bearings to achieve the correct clearance. If this is not possible, the crankshaft must be reground by a specialist who can supply the necessary undersized bearings. First though, make sure that no dirt or oil was between the bearings and the caps or block when the clearance was measured. If the Plastigage is noticeably wider at one end than the other, the journal may be tapered.

12   Carefully scrape all traces of the Plastigage material off the main bearing journals and the bearing surfaces. Be very careful not to scratch the bearing - use your fingernail or the edge of a credit card.

Final installation
Refer to illustrations 17.13, 17.15 and 17.16

13   Carefully lift the crankshaft out of the engine. Clean the bearing surfaces of the bearings in the block, then apply a thin, uni-

form layer of clean moly-based grease, engine assembly lubricant, or clean engine oil to each surface **(see illustration)**. Coat the thrustwasher surfaces as well.

14   Lubricate the crankshaft oil seal journals with moly-based grease, engine assembly lubricant, or clean engine oil.

15   Make sure the crankshaft journals are clean, then lay the crankshaft back in place in the block **(see illustration)**.

16   Install and tighten the main bearing caps as follows:

   a) *Clean the surfaces of the bearings in the caps, then lubricate them. Install the caps in their respective positions, with the arrows pointing to the timing belt end of the engine.*

   b) *Working on one cap at a time, from the center main bearing outwards (and ensuring that each cap is tightened down squarely and evenly onto the block), tighten the main bearing cap bolts to the specified torque setting* **(see illustration)**.

17.15 Install the crankshaft

17   Rotate the crankshaft a number of times by hand, to check for any obvious binding.

18   Check the crankshaft endplay (see Section 13). It should be correct if the crankshaft thrustwashers/thrust control bearing(s) aren't worn or damaged, or have been replaced.

19   Install the crankshaft rear main oil seal carrier and install a new seal (Chapter 2A or 2B).

18   Piston/connecting rod assemblies - installation and bearing clearance check

1   Before installing the piston/connecting rod assemblies, the cylinder bores must be perfectly clean, the top edge of each cylinder must be chamfered, and the crankshaft must be in place.

2   Remove the bearing cap from the Number 1 cylinder connecting rod (refer to the marks noted or made on removal). Remove the original bearing shells, and wipe the bearing recesses of the connecting rod and cap with a clean, lint-free cloth. They must be kept spotlessly clean.

17.16 Tighten the main bearing caps, starting with the center cap then working out towards the ends

18.3 The locating tab on each connecting rod bearing must engage with the notch in the connecting rod or cap

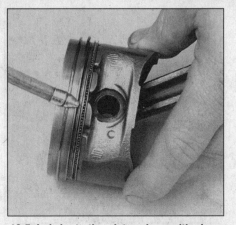

18.5 Lubricate the piston rings with clean oil before installing the ring compressor

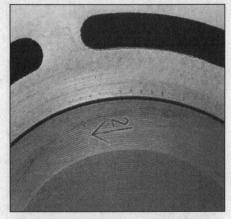

18.7 Make sure the arrow on the piston crown is facing the timing belt end of the engine

Connecting rod bearing oil clearance check

Refer to illustrations 18.3, 18.5, 18.7, 18.9, 18.12a and 18.12b

3   Clean the back of the new upper bearing, install it on the connecting rod, then install the other half of the bearing set to the bearing cap. Make sure the tab on each shell fits into the notch in the rod or cap recess **(see illustration)**. Don't lubricate the bearing at this time. **Caution:** *Don't hammer the shells into place, and don't nick or gouge the bearing face.*

4   It's critically important that all mating surfaces of the bearing components are perfectly clean and oil-free when they're assembled.

5   Position the piston ring gaps as described in Section 16, lubricate the piston and rings with clean engine oil, and attach a piston ring compressor to the piston **(see illustration)**. Leave the skirt protruding about a quarter-inch, to guide the piston into the cylinder bore. The rings must be compressed until they're flush with the piston.

6   Rotate the crankshaft until the Number 1 crankpin journal is at BDC (Bottom Dead

Center), and apply a coat of engine oil to the cylinder walls.

7   Arrange the Number 1 piston/connecting rod assembly so that the arrow on the piston crown points to the timing belt end of the engine **(see illustration)**. Gently insert the assembly into the Number 1 cylinder bore, and rest the bottom edge of the ring compressor on the engine block.

8   Tap the top edge of the ring compressor to make sure it's contacting the block around its entire circumference.

9   Gently tap on the top of the piston with the end of a wooden hammer handle, while guiding the connecting rod onto the crankpin **(see illustration)**. The piston rings may try to pop out of the ring compressor just before entering the cylinder bore, so keep some pressure on the ring compressor. Work slowly, and if any resistance is felt as the piston enters the cylinder, stop immediately. Find out what's binding, and fix it before proceeding. Do not, for any reason, force the piston into the cylinder - you might break a ring and/or the piston.

10   To check the bearing running clearance, cut a piece of the appropriate-size Plastigage slightly shorter than the width of the connecting rod bearing, and lay it in place on the

Number 1 crankpin journal, parallel with the crankshaft centerline.

11   Clean the connecting rod-to-cap mating surfaces, and install the connecting rod bearing cap. Make sure the etched number on the cap is on the same side as that on the rod.

12   Tighten each pair of cap bolts first to the specified Stage 1 torque, then through the Stage 2 angle - 90° is the equivalent of a quarter-turn or right-angle, which can easily be judged by assessing the start and end positions of the socket handle or torque wrench used; for accuracy, however, use an angle gauge **(see illustrations)**.

13   Unscrew the bolts and detach the cap, being very careful not to disturb the Plastigage.

14   Compare the width of the crushed Plastigage to the scale printed on the Plastigage envelope, to obtain the running clearance. Compare it to the Specifications to make sure the clearance is correct.

15   If the clearance is not as specified, seek the advice of an engine reconditioning specialist - if the crankshaft journals are in good condition, it may be possible simply to replace the bearings to achieve the correct clearance. If this is not possible, the crank-

18.9 With the ring compressor in place, use the handle of a hammer to gently drive the piston into the cylinder

18.12a Tighten the bearing cap bolts to the specified torque . . .

18.12b . . . then through the specified angle - note the use of an angle-torque gauge

18.22a Lay the gasket into position . . .

18.22b . . . then install the lower crankcase

18.23 Check the alignment of the lower crankcase (except SPI engines)

shaft must be reground by a specialist, who can also supply the necessary undersized bearings. First though, make sure that no dirt or oil was trapped between the bearings and the connecting rod or cap when the clearance was measured. Also, recheck the crankpin journal diameter. If the Plastigage was wider at one end than the other, the crankpin journal may be tapered.

16   Carefully scrape all traces of the Plastigage material off the journal and the bearing surface. Be very careful not to scratch the bearing - use your fingernail or the edge of a credit card.

Final piston/connecting rod installation

Refer to illustrations 18.22a, 18.22b, 18.23 and 18.24

17   Make sure the bearing surfaces are perfectly clean, then apply a uniform layer of clean moly-based grease, engine assembly lubricant, or clean engine oil, to both of them. You'll have to push the piston into the cylinder to expose the bearing surface of the shell in the connecting rod.

18   Slide the connecting rod back into place on the crankpin journal, install the bearing cap, and then tighten the bolts in the stages described above.

19   Repeat the entire procedure for the remaining piston/connecting rod assemblies.

20   The important points to remember are:

a) *Keep the backs of the bearings and the recesses of the connecting rods and caps perfectly clean when assembling them.*

b) *Make sure you have the correct piston/ rod assembly for each cylinder - use the etched cylinder numbers to identify the front-facing side of both the rod and its cap.*

c) *The arrow on the piston crown must face the timing belt end of the engine.*

d) *Lubricate the cylinder bores with clean engine oil.*

e) *Lubricate the bearing surfaces when installing the bearing caps after the running clearance has been checked.*

21   After all the piston/connecting rod assemblies have been properly installed, rotate the crankshaft a number of times by hand to check for any obvious binding.

22   Use a little grease to stick the new gasket in place, then position the lower crankcase (all engines except SPI) and loosely secure with the bolts **(see illustrations)**.

23   On all engines except SPI, the lower crank-case must now be aligned with the cylinder block before the bolts are tightened. Using a straight-edge and feeler gauges, check the protrusion or gap all around **(see illustration)**. Spacer shims are available in various thicknesses to correct the alignment - unless new components have been installed, use the same spacers found on removal.

24   Tighten the lower crankcase bolts to the specified torque, ensuring that the alignment with the cylinder block is not lost **(see illustration)**.

19   Engine - initial start-up after overhaul

Warning: *Have a fire extinguisher handy when starting the engine for the first time.*

1   With the engine installed in the vehicle, double-check the engine oil and coolant levels. Make a final check that everything has been reconnected, and that there are no tools or rags left in the engine compartment.

2   Remove the spark plugs and disable the ignition system by unplugging the ignition coil wiring connectors.

3   Remove fuse Number 12 (in the engine compartment fusebox) to disable the fuel pump; this is necessary to prevent flooding the catalytic converter with unburned fuel.

4   Crank the engine with the starter until the oil pressure warning light goes out.

5   As applicable, reconnect all wiring, and install fuse Number 12 and the spark plugs. Switch on the ignition and listen for the fuel pump; it will run for a little longer than usual, due to the lack of pressure in the system, but wait until the pump stops running.

6   Start the engine. It may take a few

moments for the fuel system to build up pressure, but the engine should start without much effort.

7   After the engine starts, allow it to warm up to normal operating temperature. While the engine is warming up, thoroughly check for fuel, oil and coolant leaks.

8   Shut the engine off and recheck the engine oil and coolant levels.

9   Drive the vehicle to an area with no traffic, accelerate from 30 to 50 mph, then allow the vehicle to slow to 30 mph with the throttle closed. Repeat the procedure 10 or 12 times. This will load the piston rings and cause them to seat properly against the cylinder walls. Check again for oil and coolant leaks.

10   Drive the vehicle gently for the first 500 miles (no sustained high speeds) and frequently check the oil level. It is not unusual for an engine to use oil during the break-in period.

11   After approximately 500 to 600 miles, change the oil and filter.

12   For the next few hundred miles, drive the vehicle normally. Do not pamper it or abuse it.

13   After 2000 miles, change the oil and filter again and consider the engine broken in.

18.24 Tighten the lower crankcase bolts to the specified torque (except SPI engines)

Chapter 3
Cooling, heating & air conditioning systems

Contents

Specifications

Coolant
Mixture type..	See *Lubricants and fluids*
Cooling system capacity	See Chapter 1

System pressure
Pressure test	18 psi - see cap for actual value (should hold this pressure for 2 minutes)

Thermostat
Starts to open	
2.0L SPI engine...	190-degrees
2.0L Zetec-E engine...	197-degrees
2.3L and 2005 and later 2.0L engines......................	194-degrees
Fully open	
2.0L SPI engine...	215-degrees
2.0L Zetec-E engine...	222-degrees
2.3L and 2005 and later 2.0L engines......................	223-degrees

Air conditioning system
Refrigerant...	R134a
Refrigerant oil capacity when refilling............................	200 cc

Torque Specifications
Ft-lbs (unless otherwise indicated)

Note: *One foot-pound (ft-lb) of torque is equivalent to 12 inch-pounds (in-lbs) of torque. Torque values below approximately 15 ft-lbs are expressed in inch-pounds, since most foot-pound torque wrenches are not accurate at these smaller values.*

Air conditioning accumulator/drier-to-subframe bolts	62 in-lbs
Air conditioning compressor mounting bolts	18
Air conditioning condenser mounting bolts	96 in-lbs
Air conditioning high pressure cut-off switch...................................	84 in-lbs
Compressor center pulley bolt	120 in-lbs
Radiator mounting bracket-to-subframe bolts..................................	18
Refrigerant line to condenser	72 in-lbs
Refrigerant line to compressor	15
Refrigerant line connection	72 in-lbs
Thermostat housing-to-cylinder head bolts	
2.0L SPI engine...	132 in-lbs
2.0L Zetec-E engine..	15
2.3L and 2005 and later 2.0L engines..	89 in-lbs
Thermostat cover/water outlet-to-thermostat housing bolts	89 in-lbs
Timing belt idler pulley	18
Water pump bolts	
2.0L SPI engine...	18
2.0L Zetec-E engine..	156 in-lbs
2.3L and 2005 and later 2.0L engines..	89 in-lbs
Water pump housing to cylinder block..	156 in-lbs
Water pump pulley bolts	18

1   General information

Warning 1: *DO NOT attempt to remove the expansion tank cap, or to disturb any part of the cooling system, while it or the engine is hot, as there is a very great risk of scalding. If the expansion tank cap must be removed before the engine and radiator have fully cooled down (even though this is not recommended) the pressure in the cooling system must first be released. Cover the cap with a thick layer of cloth, to avoid scalding, and slowly unscrew the filler cap until a hissing sound can be heard. When the hissing has stopped, showing that pressure is released, slowly unscrew the filler cap further until it can be removed; if more hissing sounds are heard, wait until they have stopped before unscrewing the cap completely. At all times, keep well away from the filler opening.*

Warning 2: *Do not allow coolant to come in contact with your skin, or with the painted surfaces of the vehicle. Rinse off spills immediately with plenty of water. Never leave coolant lying around in an open container, or in a puddle in the driveway or on the garage floor. Children and pets are attracted by its sweet smell, but coolant is fatal if ingested. Check with local authorities about disposing of used antifreeze. Many communities have collection centers that will see that antifreeze is disposed of safely.*

Warning 3: *If the engine is hot, the electric cooling fan may start rotating even if the engine is not running, so be careful to keep hands, hair and loose clothing well clear when working in the engine compartment.*

Warning 4: *The models covered by this manual have Supplemental Restraint Systems (SRS), known as airbags. To avoid accidental deployment of the airbag and possible injury, always disconnect the battery ground (negative) cable, then the positive battery cable and wait two minutes before working near any of the airbag system components (see Chapter 12). Do not use electrical test equipment on any of the airbag system wires or tamper with them in any way.*

Engine cooling system

All vehicles covered by this manual employ a pressurized engine cooling system with thermostatically-controlled coolant circulation. The coolant is circulated by an impeller-type pump, bolted to the right-hand end of the cylinder block, inboard of the timing belt. On all models the pump is driven by the crankshaft pulley via the auxiliary drivebelt. The coolant flows through the cylinder block around each cylinder; in the cylinder head, cast-in coolant passages direct coolant around the intake and exhaust ports, near the spark plug areas and close to the exhaust valve areas.

A wax-pellet type thermostat is located in a housing attached to the engine. During warm-up, the closed thermostat prevents coolant from circulating through the radiator. Instead, it returns through the coolant pipe running across the front of the engine to the radiator or expansion tank. The supply to the heater is made from the rear of the thermostat housing. As the engine nears normal operating temperature, the thermostat opens and allows hot coolant to travel through the radiator, where it is cooled before returning to the engine.

The radiator is of aluminum construction, and has plastic end tanks. On models with automatic transmission, the fluid cooler is located across the front of the radiator.

The cooling system is sealed by a pressure-type filler cap in the expansion tank. The pressure in the system raises the boiling point of the coolant, and increases the cooling efficiency of the radiator. When the engine is at normal operating temperature, the coolant expands, and the surplus is displaced into the expansion tank. When the system cools, the surplus coolant is automatically drawn back from the tank into the radiator.

The temperature gauge and cooling fan(s) are controlled by the cylinder head temperature (CHT) sensor that transmits a signal to the powertrain control module (PCM) to operate them.

Fail-Safe cooling system mode (Zetec-E engines only)

The cooling system on Zetec-E engines is equipped with a fail-safe mode, which comes into operation in stages when the operating temperature of the engine is too high.

Stage 1

The CHT sensor transmits a signal to the engine PCM, which then moves the gauge into the red zone.

If the engine is not switched off and the temperature continues to rise the multi-function warning light will come on.

Stage 2

The engine PCM will control the engine by starting to cut out two cylinders and restricting the engine to below 3000 rpm. When this occurs the engine warning light will also illuminate. **Note:** *If the temperature should drop to normal, the ignition will have to be switched off and then on again, to revert back to four cylinders. The warning light can only be turned off with a scan tool (see Chapter 4B).*

Stage 3

If the engine temperature continues to rise, the engine will be totally disabled before major engine damage occurs. The engine warning light will begin to flash, indicating to the driver that the engine will be switched off after 30 seconds.

Heating/ventilation system

The heating system consists of a blower fan and heater core located in the heater unit, with hoses connecting the heater core to the engine cooling system. Hot engine coolant is circulated through the heater core. When the heater temperature control on the instrument panel is operated, a flap door opens to expose the heater box to the passenger compartment. When the blower control is operated, the blower fan forces air through the unit according to the setting selected. The heater controls are linked to the flap doors by cables.

Incoming fresh air for the ventilation system passes through a cabin air filter mounted below the windshield cowl panel (see Chapter 1) - this ensures that most particles will be removed before the air enters the cabin. However, it is vital that the cabin filter is changed regularly, since a blocked filter will significantly reduce airflow to the cabin, leading to ineffective defrosting.

The ventilation system air distribution is controlled by cable-operated flap doors on the heater housing. All the vehicles have a recirculated air function, with the flap being controlled by a servo motor.

Air conditioning system

See Section 11.

2   Engine coolant (antifreeze) - general information

Warning: *Engine coolant (anti-freeze) contains ethylene glycol and other constituents, which are toxic if taken internally. They can also be absorbed into the skin after prolonged contact. Do not allow coolant to come in contact with your skin, or with the painted surfaces of the vehicle. Rinse off spills immediately with plenty of water. Never leave coolant lying around in an open container, or in a puddle in the driveway or on the garage floor. Children and pets are attracted by its sweet smell, but coolant is fatal if ingested. Check with local authorities about disposing of used antifreeze. Many communities have collection centers that will see that antifreeze is disposed of safely*

Note: *Refer to the relevant part of Chapter 1 for further information on coolant replacement.*

The cooling system should be filled with a water/ethylene glycol-based coolant solution, of a strength which will prevent freezing down to at least -20-degrees F, or lower if the local climate requires it. Coolant also provides protection against corrosion, and increases the boiling point.

The cooling system should be maintained according to the schedule described in the relevant part of Chapter 1. If the engine coolant used is old or contaminated it is likely to cause damage, and encourage the formation of corrosion and scale in the system. Use coolant that is to the manufacturers specification and to the correct concentration.

Before adding the coolant, check all hoses and hose connections, because coolant tends to leak through very small openings. Engines don't normally consume coolant, so if the level goes down, find the cause and correct it.

3.3 Removing the coolant hose

4.6 Pull the thermostat cover back to remove the thermostat

4.7 Arrow shows the position of the air bleed valve

The engine coolant concentration should be between 40% and 55%. If the concentration drops below 40% there will be insufficient protection. Hydrometers are available at most automotive accessory shops to test the coolant concentration.

3 Cooling system hoses - disconnection and replacement

Refer to illustration 3.3
Note: *Refer to the warnings given in Section 1 of this Chapter before starting work.*
1   If the checks described in the relevant part of Chapter 1 reveal a faulty hose, it must be replaced as follows.
2   First drain the cooling system (see Chapter 1); if the coolant is not due for replacement, the drained coolant may be re-used, if it is collected in a clean container.
3   To disconnect any hose, use a pair of pliers to release the spring clamps (or a screwdriver to loosen screw-type clamps), then move them along the hose clear of the union. Carefully work the hose off its fittings **(see illustration)**. The hoses can be removed with relative ease when new - on an older car, they may have stuck.
4   If a hose proves stubborn, try to release it by rotating it on its fittings before attempting to work it off. Gently pry the end of the hose with a blunt instrument (such as a flat-bladed screwdriver), but do not apply too much force, and take care not to damage the pipe fittings or hoses. Note in particular that the radiator hose fittings are fragile; do not use excessive force when attempting to remove the hoses. If all else fails, cut the hose with a sharp knife, then slit it so that it can be peeled off in two pieces. While expensive, this is preferable to buying a new radiator. Check first, however, that a new hose is readily available.
5   When installing a hose, first slide the clamps onto the hose, then work the hose onto its unions. If the hose is stiff, use soap as a lubricant, or soften it by soaking it in boiling water, but take care to prevent scalding.

6   Work each hose end fully onto its fitting, then check that the hose is settled correctly and is properly routed. Slide each clip along the hose until it is behind the flared end of the fitting, before tightening it securely.
7   Refill the system with coolant (see Chapter 1).
8   Check carefully for leaks as soon as possible after disturbing any part of the cooling system.

4 Thermostat - removal, testing and installation

Note: *Refer to the warnings given in Section 1 of this Chapter before starting work.*

Removal
Refer to illustrations 4.6, 4.7 and 4.8
1   Disconnect the battery negative cable (see Chapter 1).
2   Drain the cooling system (see Chapter 1). If the coolant is relatively new or in good condition, drain it into a clean container and re-use it.
3   On 2.3L and 2005 2.0L engines, remove the accessory drivebelt (see Chapter 2C). Unbolt the power steering hose bracket, then unbolt and set aside the compressor, without disconnecting the hoses (see Section 12). Remove the cooling fan and shroud (see Section 5).
4   On Duratec-SVT models, remove the ignition coil cover for access to the thermostat cover bolts.
5   Release the hose clamps, then twist the radiator hoses to remove them from the thermostat cover or housing.
6   Loosen and remove the bolts from the thermostat cover and withdraw from the thermostat housing **(see illustration)**.
7   Withdraw the thermostat, noting the position of the air bleed valve **(see illustration)**, and how the thermostat is installed (i.e., which end is facing outwards). **Note:** *On 2.3L and 2005 and later 2.0L engines, the thermostat and thermostat housing are replaced as a unit only.*

4.8 Remove the thermostat rubber seal

8   Remove the thermostat rubber seal **(see illustration)**. Install a new seal on installation.

Testing
General
9   Before assuming the thermostat is to blame for a cooling system problem, check the coolant level (see Chapter 1), the auxiliary drivebelt tension and condition, and the temperature gauge operation.
10   If the engine seems to be taking a long time to warm up (based on heater output or temperature gauge operation), the thermostat is probably stuck open. Replace the thermostat.
11   Equally, a lengthy warm-up period might suggest that the thermostat is missing - it may have been removed or inadvertently omitted by a previous owner or mechanic. Don't drive the vehicle without a thermostat - the engine management system's PCM will stay in warm-up mode for longer than necessary, causing emissions and fuel economy to suffer.
12   If the engine runs hot, use your hand to check the temperature of the radiator top hose. If the hose isn't hot, but the engine is, the thermostat is probably stuck closed, preventing the coolant inside the engine from escaping to the radiator - replace the thermostat.

5.1 Undo the retaining screw and lift out the resistor

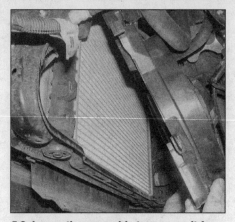

5.8 Lower the assembly to remove it from below the vehicle

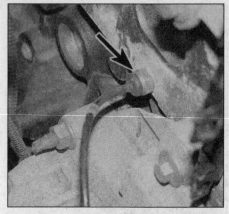

6.4 Remove the CHT sensor (arrow) - 2.0L Zetec-E engines

13 If the radiator top hose is hot, it means that the coolant is flowing and the thermostat is open. Consult the *Troubleshooting* Section at the front of this manual to assist in tracing possible cooling system faults.

Thermostat test

14 If the thermostat remains in the open position at room temperature, it is faulty, and must be replaced.

15 To test it fully, suspend the thermostat on a length of string in a container of cold water, with a thermometer beside it; ensure that neither touches the side of the container.

16 Heat the water, and check the temperature at which the thermostat begins to open; compare this value with that specified. Checking the fully-open temperature may not be possible in an open container, if it is higher than the boiling point of water at atmospheric pressure. Remove the thermostat and allow it to cool down; check that it closes fully.

17 If the thermostat does not open and close as described, if it sticks in either position, or if it does not open at the specified temperature, it must be replaced.

Installation

18 Installation is the reverse of the removal procedure, noting the following points:

a) *Clean the mating surfaces carefully, and replace the thermostat's sealing ring.*

b) *Fit the thermostat in the same position as noted on removal.*

c) *Tighten the thermostat cover/housing bolts to the specified torque setting.*

d) *Reconnect all the coolant hoses, then refill the cooling system as described in Chapter 1.*

e) *Start the engine and allow it to reach normal operating temperature, then check for leaks and proper thermostat operation.*

---

5   Radiator electric cooling fan(s) - testing, removal and installation

---

Note: *Refer to the warnings given in Section 1 of this Chapter before starting work.*

Testing
Refer to illustration 5.1

1   The radiator cooling fan is controlled by the engine management system's PCM, acting on the information received from the cylinder head temperature sensor. Where twin fans or two-speed fans are installed, control is through a resistor assembly, secured to the top of the fan shroud - this can be replaced separately if faulty **(see illustration)**.

2   First, check the relevant fuses and relays (see Chapter 12).

3   To test the fan motor, unplug the electrical connector, and use fused jumper wires to connect the fan directly to the battery. If the fan still does not work, replace the motor.

4   If the motor proved sound, the fault lies in the cylinder head temperature sensor (see Section 6), in the wiring loom (see Chapter 12 for testing details) or in the engine management system (see Chapter 4).

Removal
Refer to illustration 5.8

5   Disconnect the negative battery cable (see Chapter 5).

6   Unplug the cooling fan electrical connector(s), and release the wiring loom from the fan shroud.

7   Unclip the shroud from its upper radiator mountings, then lift the assembly to disengage it from its lower mountings.

8   Withdraw the fan(s) and shroud as an assembly from underneath the vehicle **(see illustration)**.

9   The fan motor can be removed from the fan assembly by cutting off the plastic cable ties, then removing the three mounting nuts. **Note:** *On some models, the fan and shroud must be replaced as a unit only.*

Installation

10   Installation is the reverse of the removal procedure, noting the following points:

a) *When installing the fan to the motor, make sure it has located correctly before installing the retaining clip.*

b) *Ensure that the shroud is settled correctly at all four mounting points before finally clipping into position.*

---

6   Cylinder head temperature (CHT) sensor - removal and installation

---

Note: *Refer to the warnings given in Section 1 of this Chapter before starting work.*

1   All engines except the 2.0L SPI have a cylinder head temperature (CHT) sensor that does not read coolant temperature, versus the 2.0L SPI engine which has a conventional engine coolant temperature sensor (ECT).

Removal
2.0L Zetec-E engines
Refer to illustration 6.4

2   Remove the alternator as described in Chapter 5.

3   Disconnect the wiring connector from the sensor. **Note:** *On 2.3L and 2005 and later 2.0L engines, the CHT sensor is on top of the engine, between two of the spark plugs. On all other (non-SPI) engines, the CHT sensor is on the side of the cylinder head.*

4   Loosen and remove the sensor from the cylinder head **(see illustration)**.

2.0L SPI engines
Refer to illustration 6.7

5   Remove the ignition coilpack (see Chapter 5).

6   Drain the cooling system (see Chapter 1).

7   Loosen and remove the sensor from the cylinder head **(see illustration)**.

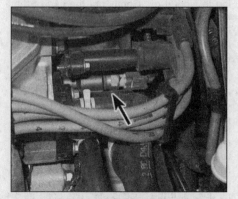

6.7 Location of ECT sensor (arrow) on 2.0L SPI engines

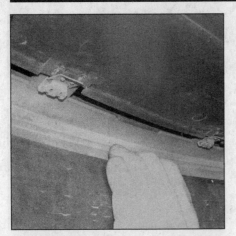

7.2 Unclip the lower radiator cover from the rear of the front bumper - on some models it is retained by plastic pushpins

7.4a Use a cable tie (arrow), to support the condenser and . . .

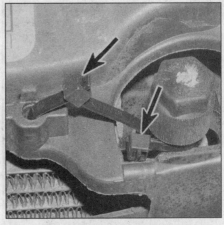

7.4b . . . two cable ties (arrows) to support the other side

Installation

8   Installation is the reverse of the removal procedure, noting the following points:

a) *Screw in the sensor, tighten it securely and reconnect its electrical connector.*

b) *Install any hoses and components removed for access.*

c) *On 2.0L SPI engines, refill the cooling system (see Chapter 1).*

7   Radiator and expansion tank - removal, inspection and installation

Refer to illustrations 7.2, 7.4a, 7.4b, 7.5a, 7.5b, 7.6a and 7.6b

Note: *Refer to the warnings given in Section 1 of this Chapter before starting work.*

Radiator
Removal

Note: *If leakage is the reason for removing the radiator, bear in mind that minor leaks can often be cured using a radiator sealant added to the coolant with the radiator in place.*

Warning: *The air conditioning system is under high pressure. Do not loosen any fittings or remove any components until the system has been discharged. Air conditioning refrigerant should be properly discharged into an EPA-approved container at a dealer service department or an automotive air conditioning repair facility. Always wear eye protection when disconnecting air conditioning system fittings.*

1   Remove the radiator fan and shroud assembly as described in Section 5. On 2005 and later models, remove the pushpins securing the lower part of the radiator.

2   To provide greater clearance for the radiator to be lowered and removed, ensure that the parking brake is firmly applied, then raise and support the front of the car on axle stands (see *Jacking and Towing*). Remove the radiator lower cover **(see illustration)**.

3   Drain the cooling system (see Chapter 1).

7.5a Unscrew the four bolts from the mounting bracket (arrows indicate two) . . .

Disconnect all the hoses from the radiator. On models with an automatic transaxle, separate the transmission fluid cooler from the left and right mounting brackets and set it aside, supporting it by mechanic's wire or cable-ties.

4   On vehicles with air conditioning, support the condenser from the front top crossmember to keep it in position **(see illustrations)**.

5   Remove the two bolts (each side) from the mounting bracket below the radiator **(see**

7.6a Move the radiator in the direction of the arrow to unclip it from the condenser

7.5b . . . and remove the bottom mounting rubbers

illustration) (disconnect the electrical connector on the horn if required); retrieve the bottom mounting rubbers **(see illustration)**, noting which way up they are installed, and store them carefully.

6   Carefully unclip the radiator from the air conditioning condenser (where applicable) and withdraw it from the vehicle, leaving the air conditioning condenser in place **(see illustrations)**.

7.6b Air conditioning condenser supported by cable ties

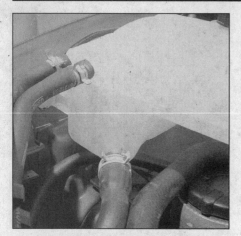

7.11 Disconnect the three hoses from the expansion tank

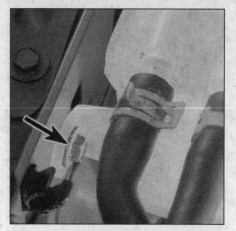

7.12a Remove the mounting bolt (arrow) . . .

7.12b . . . and lift off the locating clip (arrow)

Inspection

7   With the radiator removed, it can be inspected for leaks and damage. If it needs repair, have a radiator specialist or dealer service department perform the work, as special techniques are required.

8   Insects and dirt can be removed from the radiator with a garden hose or a soft brush. Take care not to damage the cooling fins as this is being done.

Installation

9   Installation is the reverse of the removal procedure, noting the following points:

a) *Be sure the mounting rubbers are seated properly at the base of the radiator.*

b) *After installation, refill the cooling system with the recommended coolant (see Chapter 1).*

c) *Start the engine, and check for leaks. Allow the engine to reach normal operating temperature, indicated by the radiator top hose becoming hot. Once the engine has cooled (ideally, leave overnight), recheck the coolant level, and add more if required.*

Expansion tank

Refer to illustrations 7.11, 7.12a and 7.12b

10   With the engine completely cool, remove the expansion tank filler cap to release any pressure, then install the cap.

11   Disconnect the hoses from the tank **(see illustration)**, upper hose first. As each hose is disconnected, drain the tank's contents into a clean container. If the coolant is not due for replacement, the drained coolant may be re-used, if it is kept clean.

12   Unscrew the tank's mounting bolt and lift out from the inner strut panel **(see illustrations)**.

13   Wash out the tank, and inspect it for cracks and chafing - replace it if damaged.

14   Installation is the reverse of the removal procedure. Refill the cooling system with the recommended coolant (see Chapter 1), then start the engine and allow it to reach normal operating temperature, indicated by the radi-

ator top hose becoming hot. Recheck the coolant level and add more if required, then check for leaks.

---

8   Water pump - check, removal and installation

Note: *Refer to the warnings given in Section 1 of this Chapter before starting work.*

Check

1   A failure in the water pump can cause serious engine damage due to overheating.

2   There are three ways to check the operation of the water pump while it's installed on the engine. If the pump is defective, it should be replaced with a new or rebuilt unit.

3   With the engine running at normal operating temperature, squeeze the radiator top hose. If the water pump is working properly, a pressure surge should be felt as the hose is released. **Warning:** *Keep your hands away from the radiator electric cooling fan blades.*

4   Water pumps are equipped with weep or vent holes. If a failure occurs in the pump seal, coolant will leak from the hole. In most cases you'll need a flashlight to find the hole on the water pump from underneath to check for leaks.

5   The water pump is at the timing belt end of the engine - to check for a leak, it may be helpful to remove the timing belt covers, as described in Chapter 2A or 2B.

6   If the water pump shaft bearings fail, there may be a howling sound at the drivebelt end of the engine while it's running. Shaft wear can be felt if the water pump pulley is rocked up and down.

7   Don't mistake drivebelt slippage, which causes a squealing sound, for water pump bearing failure.

Removal

Refer to illustrations 8.12, 8.14 and 8.15

8   Disconnect the negative battery cable (see Chapter 5).

9   Drain the cooling system (see Chapter 1).

10   Loosen the water pump pulley bolts. **Note:** *You may need a strap wrench to hold the pulley while loosening the bolts.*

11   Remove the auxiliary drivebelt as described in Chapter 1.

12   Unscrew the bolts and remove the water pump pulley **(see illustration)**.

13   On SPI engines, remove the timing belt as described in Chapter 2A or 2B. If the belt is fouled with coolant, it must be replaced as a matter of course, also if the belt is approaching its scheduled replacement (see Chapter 1). On all non-SPI engines, the water pump can be removed without removing the timing belt. If the water pump housing needs to be replaced on Zetec-E engines, then the timing belt will have to be removed to access the housing bolts.

14   Disconnect the coolant hose from the water pump housing, and unbolt the timing belt idler pulley. Remove the water pump mounting bolts **(see illustration)**.

15   If the water pump housing must be removed, remove the retaining bolts and maneuver the housing out of the engine compartment **(see illustration)**. Recover the sealing ring or gasket. **Note:** *To access the water pump on 2.3L and 2005 2.0L engines, remove the engine cooling fan (see Section 5) and*

8.12 Remove the water pump pulley

8.14 Remove the water pump bolts (Zetec-E shown, other models have three bolts)

8.15 Coolant pump housing (Zetec-E shown)

9.2 Unscrew these three screws (arrows) to remove the footwell trim

unbolt and set aside the air-conditioning compressor without disconnecting the hoses (see Section 12).

Installation

16   Clean the pump mating surfaces carefully; the gasket must be replaced whenever it is disturbed. Install the pump and tighten the bolts to the specified torque setting. On water pumps with an O-ring seal, replace the O-ring and lubricate it with clean coolant.

17   The remainder of the installation procedure is the reverse of removal, noting the following points:

a)   *Tighten all fittings to the specified torque settings (where given).*

b)   *Where applicable, check the timing belt for contamination and replace if required, as described in Chapter 2.*

c)   *On completion, refill the cooling system as described in Chapter 1.*

9   Heater/ventilation components - removal and installation

Note: *Refer to the warnings given in Section 1 of this Chapter before starting work.*

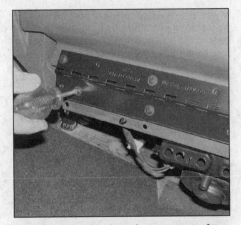

9.3a Remove the three lower screws from the glovebox hinge . . .

9.3b . . . then push both sides of the glovebox in to remove

Heater blower motor

Removal

Refer to illustrations 9.2, 9.3a, 9.3b, 9.4a, 9.4b, 9.5a, 9.5b and 9.6

1   Disconnect the negative battery cable (see Chapter 5).

2   Remove the three screws securing the lower passenger side footwell trim **(see illus-**

tration), then withdraw the panel from the vehicle.

3   Remove the three screws from the glovebox hinge, and remove the glovebox, pushing in at both sides to release from the fascia **(see illustrations)**.

4   Remove the securing screw, and detach the ventilation hose from the motor assembly **(see illustrations)**.

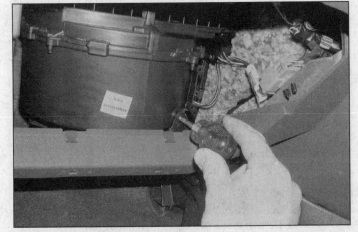

9.4a Remove the screw from the air vent . . .

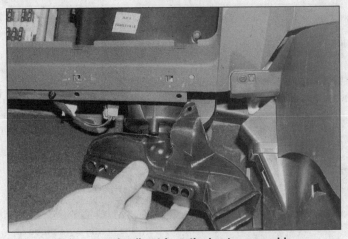

9.4b . . . and pull out from the heater assembly

9.5a Disconnect the wiring connector and remove the screws . . .

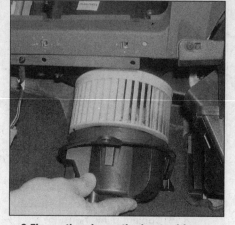

9.5b . . . then lower the heater blower motor from the housing

9.6 The resistor is to the right of the heater blower motor

5   Unplug the motor's electrical connector, and undo the three screws securing the motor in place. Remove the motor from the housing **(see illustrations)**.

6   The motor's control resistor can be removed by removing the screw at one end of the resistor, then pulling the resistor out of the heater housing **(see illustration)**.

Installation

7   Installation is the reverse of the removal procedure.

Heater core

Warning: *The models covered by this manual have Supplemental Restraint Systems (SRS), known as airbags. To avoid accidental deployment of the airbag and possible injury, always disconnect the battery ground (negative) cable, then the positive battery cable and wait two minutes before working near any of the impact sensors, steering column, or instrument panel (see Chapter 12). Do not use any electrical test equipment on any of the airbag system wires or tamper with them in any way.*
Note: *This is a difficult procedure for the home mechanic. On models through 2001, it involves removal of the instrument panel,*

which entails disconnecting many electrical connectors and finding difficult-to-access fasteners. If you attempt the procedure, make sure to tag all connections before disassembly, and keep that various fasteners in marked plastic bags. On later models, the heater core can be removed more easily, although the instrument panel will need to be removed if the heater core housing requires replacement.

Removal

Models through 2001

Refer to illustrations 9.10, 9.12, 9.14, 9.15a, 9.15b, 9.15c, 9.16, 9.17 and 9.18

8   Disconnect the negative battery cable (see Chapter 5).

9   Apply the parking brake, then raise and support the front of the car on axle stands. Drain the cooling system (see Chapter 1).

10   Disconnect the coolant hoses from the heater core pipes protruding through the engine compartment firewall **(see illustration)**.

11   Working inside the passenger compartment, remove the instrument panel as described in Chapter 11.

12   Unclip the five ventilation hoses from the

crash pad crossmember, and detach them from the heater housing **(see illustration)**.

13   Working your way around the crash pad crossmember, unclip the wiring harness and remove the securing bolts for any ground connections.

14   Remove the two securing bolts from the fusebox **(see illustration)**.

15   Remove the securing bolts from the ends of the crash pad crossmember bracket, including the one inside the right-hand pillar. Unscrew the center securing bolts, then remove the crossmember from the firewall **(see illustrations)**.

16   Remove the retaining screws and unclip the bottom sections from the heater unit **(see illustration)**.

17   Detach the securing clips from the heater unit casing, and remove the screws to release the heater core lower casing **(see illustration)**.

18   Remove the screw to release the retaining bracket from the heater core inside the casing (take care not to damage the heater core on removal) **(see illustration)**.

2002 and later models

19   Drain the cooling system and disconnect the hoses at the firewall.

9.10 Detach the two heater hoses from the heater core pipes at the firewall

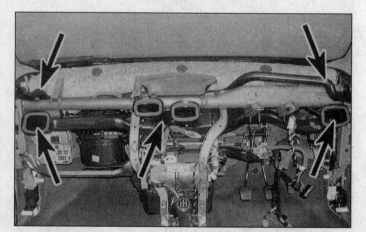

9.12 Detach these five ventilation hoses (arrows)

9.14 Remove the two screws (arrows) from the fusebox

9.15a Undo the three bolts (arrows) at each end of the crossmember . . .

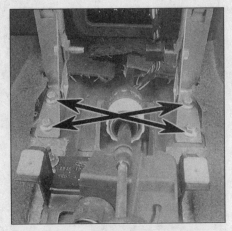

9.15b . . . four bolts (arrows) at the center . . .

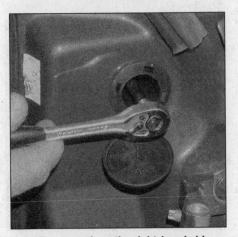

9.15c . . . and, on the right-hand side, unclip the cap from the front pillar and remove the securing bolt

9.16 Remove both parts of the lower heater casing

9.17 Heater core comes out with the casing

20 Refer to Chapter 11 and remove the floor console and the rear air ducts in the console.
21 Remove the panel below the glove box and remove the curved center panel that connects the dash to the floor console.
22 Unbolt the floor air duct on the passen-

ger side, and the vent hose.
23 Unbolt the accelerator pedal and disconnect the throttle cable or electrical connector at the pedal.
24 Remove the two triangular steel braces that connect the cross-cowl support tube to the floor at the center of the dash.
25 Use a small screwdriver to pry off the

lower half of the heater housing. On 2005 and later models, the cover is one-piece and is secured by clips and one screw.
26 Lower the housing, with rags on the floor to collect any spilled coolant, and remove the heater core from the housing.

Installation

27 Installation is the reverse of the removal procedure. Additional metal clips may be required to secure the heater unit's bottom casing to the heater unit, as the plastic ones may break on removal.
28 Refill the cooling system with the recommended coolant (see Chapter 1). Start the engine and allow it to reach normal operating temperature, indicated by the radiator top hose becoming hot. Recheck the coolant level and add more if required, then check for leaks. Check the operation of the heater.

Cabin air filter

29 Refer to the relevant part of Chapter 1.

Instrument panel vents

Refer to illustrations 9.30 and 9.31
30 Using a flat-bladed tool and a pad to protect the dash, pry out the vents from the dash (see illustration).

9.18 Remove the foam seal and the screw (arrow)

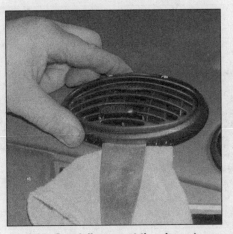

9.30 Carefully pry out the air vents

9.31 Vent can be pushed out from the rear of the dash

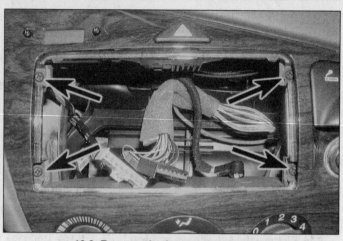

10.3 Remove the four screws (arrows)

31 It may be necessary to remove the glovebox (see Chapter 11) to aid the removal of the passenger air vent **(see illustration)**; the radio/cassette (Chapter 12) to aid the removal of the center air vents; and the main light switch (Chapter 12) to aid the removal of the driver's air vent.

32 Installation is a reversal of removal.

10 Heater/air conditioning controls - removal and installation

Note: *Refer to the warnings given in Section 1 of this Chapter before starting work.*

Heater control panel

Refer to illustrations 10.3 and 10.4

1 Disconnect the negative battery cable (see Chapter 5).

2 Remove the radio/cassette player as described in Chapter 12. Pull out and remove the ashtray.

3 Remove the four screws from inside the radio/cassette player opening **(see illustration)**, then carefully unclip the heater control panel from the dash.

4 Taking careful note of all their locations, disconnect the various wiring connectors from the rear of the panel and unclip the heater operating cables from the temperature and direction controls **(see illustration)**.

5 Make sure that nothing remains attached to the panel, then withdraw it from the dash.

Blower, direction and temperature controls

Refer to illustrations 10.7a and 10.7b

6 Remove the heater control panel as described in Steps 1 through 5.

7 Remove the four securing screws at the back of the control panel and withdraw the control switch assembly. If not already done, pull off the control knobs, then remove the retaining screw from the back of the switch, twist them to release from the switch assembly **(see illustrations)**.

8 Installation is the reverse of the removal procedure. Check the operation of the controls on completion.

Air conditioning switch

Refer to illustration 10.10

9 Remove the heater control panel as

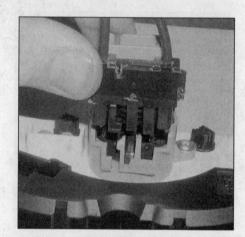

10.4 Use a thin screwdriver to release the heater cable unit

described above.

10 Remove the screws from the back of the control panel to release the switch assembly (the air conditioning, air recirculation, heated rear window and heated windshield switches are a single complete assembly) **(see illustration)**.

10.7a Pull the control knob off the switch . . .

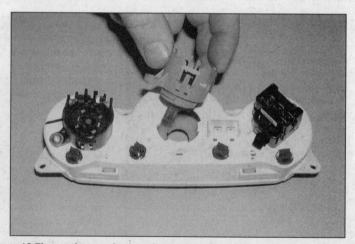

10.7b . . . then undo the screw and remove the switch from its bayonet fitting

10.10 The switches come as a complete assembly

11   Installation is the reverse of the removal procedure. Check the operation of the switches on completion.

11   Air conditioning system - general information and precautions

General information

The air conditioning system consists of a condenser mounted in front of the radiator, an evaporator mounted adjacent to the heater core, a compressor driven by an auxiliary drivebelt, an accumulator/drier, and the plumbing connecting all of the above components - this contains a choke (or 'venturi') mounted in the inlet to the evaporator, which creates the drop in pressure required to produce the cooling effect.

A blower fan forces the warmer air of the passenger compartment through the evaporator core (rather like a radiator in reverse), transferring the heat from the air to the refrigerant. The liquid refrigerant boils off into low-pressure vapor, taking the heat with it when it leaves the evaporator.

Precautions

Warning: *The air conditioning system is under high pressure. Do not loosen any fittings or remove any components until after the system has been discharged. Air conditioning refrigerant should be properly discharged and recovered at a dealer service department, or an automotive air conditioning repair facility capable of handling R134a refrigerant. Always wear eye protection when disconnecting air conditioning system fittings.*

When a vehicle is equipped with an air conditioning system, it is necessary to observe the following special precautions whenever dealing with any part of the system, its associated components, and any items that necessitate disconnection of the system:

a) *While the refrigerant used - R134a - is less damaging to the environment than the previously-used R12, it is still a very dangerous substance. It must not be allowed into contact with the skin or eyes, or there is a risk of frostbite. It must also not be discharged in an enclosed space - while it is not toxic, there is a risk of suffocation. The refrigerant is heavier than air, and so must never be discharged over a pit.*

b) *The refrigerant must not be allowed to come in contact with a flame, otherwise a poisonous gas will be created - under certain circumstances, this can form an explosive mixture with air. For similar reasons, smoking in the presence of refrigerant is highly dangerous, particularly if the vapor is inhaled through a lighted cigarette.*

c) *Never discharge the system to the atmosphere - R134a is not an ozone-depleting ChloroFluoroCarbon (CFC) like R12, but is instead a hydrofluorocarbon, which causes environmental damage by contributing to the 'greenhouse effect' if released into the atmosphere.*

d) *R134a refrigerant must not be mixed with R12; the system uses different seals (now green-colored, previously black) and has different fittings requiring different tools, so that there is no chance of the two types of refrigerant becoming mixed accidentally.*

e) *If for any reason the system must be disconnected, entrust this task to a dealer or an air conditioning shop.*

f) *It is essential that the system be professionally discharged prior to using any form of heat - welding, soldering, brazing, etc - in the vicinity of the system, before having the vehicle oven-dried at a temperature exceeding 160-degrees F after repainting, and before disconnecting any part of the system.*

12   Air conditioning system components - removal and installation

Warning: *The air conditioning system is under high pressure. Do not loosen any fittings or remove any components until after the system has been discharged. Air conditioning refrigerant should be recovered and properly discharged into an approved type of container at a dealer service department or an automotive air conditioning repair facility capable of handling R134a refrigerant. Cap or plug the pipe lines as soon as they are disconnected, to prevent the entry of moisture. Always wear eye protection when disconnecting air conditioning system fittings.*

Note: *This Section refers to the components of the air conditioning system itself - refer to Sections 9 and 10 for details of components common to the heating/ventilation system.*

Note 2: *Refer to the warnings given in Section 1 of this Chapter before starting work.*

Condenser

1   Have the refrigerant discharged and recovered at a dealer service department or an automotive air conditioning repair facility.

2   Disconnect the negative battery cable (see Chapter 5).

3   Apply the parking brake, then raise the front of the vehicle and support on axle stands.

4   Unclip the radiator undershield and remove.

5   Unbolt the refrigerant lines from the condenser. Immediately cap the open fittings, to prevent the entry of dirt and moisture.

6   Remove the two bolts from each side of the radiator support bracket (note that the condenser is also mounted on the brackets in front of the radiator), have a jack or pair of axle stands ready to support the weight.

7   Disengage the condenser upper mountings, then unclip it from the radiator and remove it from below. Store it upright, to prevent fluid loss. Take care not to damage the condenser fins.

8   Installation is the reverse of removal. Replace the O-rings and lubricate with refrigerant oil. If a new condenser is being installed, add 30 ml of new refrigerant oil to the condenser.

9   Have the system evacuated, charged and leak-tested by the specialist who discharged it.

Evaporator

10   The evaporator is mounted inside the heater housing with the heater core. Apart from the need to have the refrigerant discharged, the procedure is as described in Section 9 of this Chapter. Unlike the heater core, the evaporator requires removal of the instrument panel to remove the heater core/evaporator housing (see Chapter 11).

11   Unbolt the heater unit assembly from the firewall to remove the evaporator. Installation is the reverse of removal. If a new evaporator is being installed, add 90 ml of new refrigerant oil to the evaporator. **Note:** *The evaporator and its housing must only be replaced as a unit.*

12   Have the system evacuated, charged and leak-tested by the specialist who discharged it.

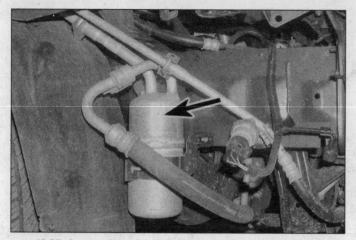

12.25 Accumulator (arrow) situated under the right-hand front fender

12.35 Arrow shows the location of the high pressure switch

Compressor

13   Have the refrigerant discharged and recovered at a dealer service department or an automotive air conditioning repair facility.

14   Disconnect the negative battery cable (see Chapter 1).

15   Apply the parking brake, then raise the front of the vehicle and support on axle stands.

16   Remove the undershield and then loosen the auxiliary drivebelt as described in Chapter 1.

17   Unscrew the clamping bolt to disconnect the refrigerant lines from the compressor. Plug the line connections to prevent entry of any dirt or moisture.

18   Unbolt the compressor from the cylinder block/crankcase, unplug its electrical connector, then withdraw the compressor from the vehicle. **Note:** *Keep the compressor level during handling and storage. If the compressor has seized, or if you find metal particles in the refrigerant lines, the system must be flushed out by an air conditioning technician, and the accumulator/drier must be replaced.*

19   Prior to installation, turn the compressor clutch center six times, to disperse any oil that has collected in the head.

20   Install the compressor in the reverse order of removal; replace all seals disturbed.

21   If you are installing a new compressor, drain the old oil from the old compressor into a graduated container, then put that same amount of new oil in the new compressor.

22   Have the system evacuated, charged and leak-tested by the specialist that discharged it.

Accumulator/drier

Refer to illustration 12.25

23   Have the refrigerant discharged and recovered at a dealer service department or an automotive air conditioning repair facility.

24   Disconnect the negative battery cable (see Chapter 5).

25   The accumulator/drier, which acts as a

reservoir and filter for the refrigerant, is located under the right-hand front fender **(see illustration)**. Using a plastic clamp-type tool (available at auto parts stores just for air conditioning connections) disconnect the refrigerant line next to the accumulator/drier from the compressor. Immediately cap the open fittings, to prevent the entry of dirt and moisture, then unplug the pressure cycling switch electrical connector.

26   Apply the parking brake, then raise the front of the vehicle and support on axle stands.

27   Remove the right-hand front wheel. Unscrew the inner fenderwell liner and remove from the vehicle.

28   Using the release tool, disconnect the refrigerant line from the accumulator/drier. Remove the refrigerant line screw-on cap. Immediately cap the open fittings, to prevent the entry of dirt and moisture.

29   Unbolt the accumulator/drier from the front suspension subframe.

30   Withdraw the accumulator/drier.

31   Install the accumulator/drier in the reverse order of removal; replace all seals disturbed.

32   If you are installing a new accumulator/drier, top-up with new oil to the volume removed, plus 90 ml of extra refrigerant oil.

33   Have the system evacuated, charged and leak-tested by the specialist that discharged it.

High pressure cut-off switch

Refer to illustration 12.35

34   Have the refrigerant discharged at a dealer service department or an automotive air conditioning repair facility.

35   Unplug the switch electrical connector, and unscrew the switch **(see illustration)**.

36   Installation is the reverse of the removal procedure. Replace the O-rings and lubricate with refrigerant oil.

37   Have the system evacuated, charged and leak-tested by the specialist that dis-

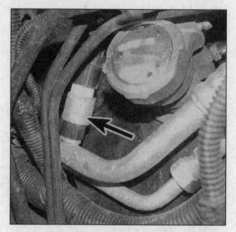

12.42 Low pressure cycling switch (arrow) in air conditioning pipe by the brake booster

charged it. Check the operation of the air conditioning system.

Low pressure cycling switch

Refer to illustration 12.42

Warning: *Ensure that the air conditioning system has been filled; otherwise the system could be damaged.*

38   Unscrew the carbon canister purge valve (if equipped), from the firewall and move to one side.

39   Pull off the low pressure switch electrical connector. Bridge the connector contacts for the air conditioning low pressure switch.

40   Start the engine and switch on the air conditioning.

41   Let the engine idle for 30 seconds, then switch off the engine.

42   Unscrew the low pressure switch **(see illustration)**.

43   Installation is the reverse of the removal procedure.

44   Check the operation of the air conditioning system.

Chapter 4 Part A
Fuel and exhaust systems

Contents

Specifications

General

System type	Sequential Electronic Fuel injection (SEFI)
Fuel octane requirement	87 unleaded
Idle speed	700 ± 30 rpm (regulated by engine management system - no adjustment possible)
CO content at idle	Less than 0.3%

Fuel system data

Note: *The resistance values quoted below are typical, but may be used for guidance. Generally, a faulty component will be indicated by a zero or infinity reading, rather than a slight deviation from the values given. Always have your findings verified before buying a new component (if possible, perform the same test on a new component, and compare the results).*

Fuel pressure, key on, engine off	35 to 65 psi
Fuel injectors, resistance	13.7 to 15.2 ohms
Idle speed control valve, resistance	6 to 14 ohms
Idle increase solenoid valve, resistance	50 to 120 ohms
Crankshaft speed/position sensor, resistance	200 to 450 ohms
Camshaft position sensor, resistance	200 to 900 ohms
Intake air temperature sensor, resistance:	
At -40°F	860 to 900 k ohms
At 68°F	35 to 40 k ohms
At 212°F	1.9 to 2.5 k ohms
At 248°F	1.0 to 1.3 k ohms
Throttle potentiometer, resistance - see text	400 to 6000 ohms

Torque specifications

Ft-lbs (unless otherwise indicated)

Note: *One foot-pound (ft-lb) of torque is equivalent to 12 inch-pounds (in-lbs) of torque. Torque values below approximately 15 ft-lbs are expressed in inch-pounds, since most foot-pound torque wrenches are not accurate at these smaller values.*

Camshaft position sensor	15
Catalytic converter	
Front support bracket bolts	16
Lower support bracket bolts	35
To-manifold nuts (replace)	35
Catalytic converter bolts to cylinder head (2.3L and 2005 and later 2.0L engines)	41
Crankshaft position sensor	
Models through 2004	84 in-lbs
2005 models	15
2006 and later models	62 in-lbs
Cylinder head temperature sensor (replace)	
Models through 2004	84 in-lbs
2005 and later models	108 in-lbs
EGR valve	84 in-lbs
Exhaust flange nuts/bolts, clamp nuts	35
Exhaust heat shield fasteners	84 in-lbs
Exhaust manifold	132 in-lbs
Fuel pressure regulator mounting bolts	48 in-lbs

Torque specifications (continued)   **Ft-lbs** (unless otherwise indicated)

Fuel rail bolts	84 in-lbs
Fuel rail supply pipe retaining plate bolts	
Models through 2004	80 in-lbs
2005 and later models	35 in-lbs
Idle speed control valve	84 in-lbs
Intake manifold	156 in-lbs
Knock sensor	15
Power steering pressure switch	15

1   General information and precautions

General information

The fuel system consists of a fuel tank (mounted under the body, beneath the rear seats), fuel hoses, an electric fuel pump mounted in the fuel tank, and a sequential electronic fuel injection system controlled by an EEC-V engine management control module (also called the PCM, or Electronic Control Unit).

The electric fuel pump supplies fuel under pressure to the fuel rail, which distributes fuel to the injectors. A pressure regulator controls the system pressure in relation to intake tract depression. From the fuel rail, fuel is injected into the intake ports, just above the intake valves, by four fuel injectors. The aluminum alloy fuel rail is mounted to the intake manifold.

The amount of fuel supplied by the injectors is precisely controlled by the PCM. The module uses the signals from the crankshaft position sensor, and the camshaft position sensor, to trigger each injector separately in cylinder firing order (sequential injection), with benefits in terms of better fuel economy and leaner exhaust emissions.

The PCM is the heart of the entire engine management system, controlling the fuel injection, ignition and emissions control systems. The module receives information from various sensors which is then computed and compared with pre-set values stored in its memory, to determine the required period of injection.

Information on crankshaft position and engine speed is generated by a crankshaft position sensor. The inductive head of the sensor runs just above the engine flywheel and scans a series of 36 protrusions on the flywheel periphery. As the crankshaft rotates, the sensor transmits a pulse to the system's ignition module every time a protrusion passes it. There is one missing protrusion in the flywheel periphery at a point corresponding to 90° BTDC. The ignition module recognizes the absence of a pulse from the crankshaft position sensor at this point to establish a reference mark for crankshaft position. Similarly, the time interval between absent pulses is used to determine engine speed. This information is then fed to the PCM for further processing.

The camshaft position sensor is located in the cylinder head so that it registers with a lobe on the camshaft. The camshaft position sensor functions in the same way as the crankshaft position sensor, producing a series of pulses; this gives the PCM a reference point, to enable it to determine the firing order, and operate the injectors in the appropriate sequence.

The mass airflow sensor is based on a 'hot-wire' system, sending the PCM a constantly-varying (analog) voltage signal corresponding to the mass of air passing into the engine. Since air mass varies with temperature (cold air being denser than warm), measuring air mass provides the module with a very accurate means of determining the correct amount of fuel required to achieve the ideal air/fuel mixture ratio.

The 2.0L SPI engine uses a traditional coolant temperature sensor, while all other engines have a cylinder head temperature sensor. The latter sensor is seated in a blind hole in the cylinder head, and measures the temperature of the metal directly. This component is an NTC (Negative Temperature Coefficient) thermistor - that is, a semi-conductor whose electrical resistance decreases as its temperature increases. It provides the PCM with a constantly-varying (analog) voltage signal, corresponding to the temperature of the engine. This is used to refine the calculations made by the module, when determining the correct amount of fuel required to achieve the ideal air/fuel mixture ratio.

Intake air temperature information is supplied by the intake air temperature sensor built into the airflow sensor. This component is also an NTC thermistor - see the previous paragraph - providing the module with a signal corresponding to the temperature of air passing into the engine. This is used to refine the calculations made by the module, when determining the correct amount of fuel required to achieve the ideal air/fuel mixture ratio.

A throttle position sensor is mounted on the end of the throttle valve spindle, to provide the PCM with a constantly-varying (analog) voltage signal corresponding to the throttle opening. This allows the module to register the driver's input when determining the amount of fuel required by the engine.

Road speed is monitored by the vehicle speed sensor. This component is a Hall-effect generator, mounted on the transmission's speedometer drive. It supplies the module with a series of pulses corresponding to the vehicle's road speed, enabling the module to control features such as the fuel shut-off on overrun.

The clutch pedal position is monitored by a switch fitted to the pedal bracket. This sends a signal to the PCM.

Where power steering is installed, a pressure-operated switch is screwed into the power steering system's high-pressure pipe. The switch sends a signal to the PCM to increase engine speed to maintain idle speed when the power steering pump loads up the engine (typically, during parking maneuvers).

The oxygen sensor in the exhaust system provides the module with constant feedback - 'closed-loop' control - which enables it to adjust the mixture to provide the best possible operating conditions for the catalytic converter.

The air intake side of the system consists of an air cleaner housing, the mass airflow sensor, an intake hose and duct, and a throttle housing.

The throttle valve inside the throttle housing is controlled by the driver, through the accelerator pedal. As the valve opens, the amount of air that can pass through the system increases. As the throttle valve opens further, the mass airflow sensor signal alters, and the PCM opens each injector for a longer duration, to increase the amount of fuel delivered to the intake ports.

Both the idle speed and mixture are under the control of the PCM, and cannot be adjusted.

Precautions

Warning: *Gasoline is extremely flammable, so take extra precautions when you work on any part of the fuel system. Don't smoke or allow open flames or bare light bulbs near the work area, and don't work in a garage where a gas-type appliance (such as a water heater or a clothes dryer) is present. Since gasoline is carcinogenic, wear fuel-resistant gloves when there's a possibility of being exposed to fuel, and, if you spill any fuel on your skin, rinse it off immediately with soap and water. Mop up any spills immediately and do not store fuel-soaked rags where they could ignite. The fuel system is under constant pressure, so, if any fuel lines are to be disconnected, the fuel pressure in the system must be relieved first (see Section 2). When you perform any kind of work on the fuel system, wear safety glasses and have a Class B type fire extinguisher on hand.*

2   Fuel system - depressurization

Refer to illustrations 2.3 and 2.4
Warning 1: *Refer to the* **Warning** *in Section 1 before proceeding.*

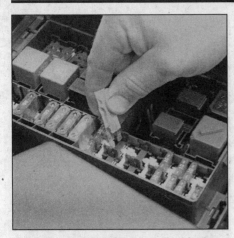

2.3 Remove fuse No 12 to disable the fuel pump

2.4 Schrader valve cap on fuel rail

4.3a Pry out the colored insert with a small screwdriver . . .

Warning 2: *The following procedure will merely relieve the pressure in the fuel system - remember that fuel will still be present in the system components, and take precautions accordingly before disconnecting any of them.*

1   The fuel system referred to in this Chapter is defined as the fuel tank and tank-mounted fuel pump/fuel gauge sender unit, the fuel filter, the fuel injector, fuel pressure regulator, and the metal pipes and flexible hoses of the fuel lines between these components. All these contain fuel, which will be under pressure while the engine is running and/or while the ignition is switched on.

2   The pressure will remain for some time after the ignition has been switched off, and must be relieved before any of these components is disturbed for servicing work.

3   The simplest depressurization method is to disconnect the fuel pump electrical supply by removing the fuel pump fuse or relay (in the engine compartment fusebox) and starting the engine **(see illustration)**. If the engine does not start, crank it on the starter for a few seconds, otherwise, allow the engine to idle until it dies through lack of fuel. Turn the engine over once or twice on the starter to ensure that all pressure is released, then switch off the ignition; do not forget to install the fuse when work is complete.

4   If an adapter is available to fit the Schrader-type valve on the fuel rail pressure test/release fitting (identifiable by its blue plastic cap, and located on the fuel rail), this may be used to release the fuel pressure **(see illustration)**. The adapter (tool number 23-033 or equivalent) operates similar to a drain tap - turning the tap clockwise releases the pressure. If the adapter is not available, place cloth rags around the valve, then remove the cap and allow the fuel pressure to dissipate. Install the cap on completion.

5   Note that, once the fuel system has been depressurized and drained (even partially), it will take significantly longer to restart the engine - perhaps several seconds of cranking - before the system is refilled and pressure restored.

3   Unleaded gasoline - general information and usage

The fuel recommended by the manufacturer is given in the Specifications section of this Chapter.

All gasoline models are designed to run on fuel with a minimum octane rating of 87 (RON). All models have a catalytic converter, and so must be run on unleaded fuel only. Under no circumstances should leaded or lead-replacement fuel be used, as this will damage the catalytic converter.

Super unleaded gasoline can also be used in all models if desired, though there is no advantage in doing so.

4   Fuel lines and fittings - general information

Warning: *Refer to the* **Warning** *in Section 1 before proceeding.*

Disconnecting and connecting couplings

Refer to illustrations 4.3a and 4.3b

1   Special snap-together couplings are employed at many of the unions in the fuel feed and return lines.

2   Before disconnecting any fuel system component, relieve the residual pressure in the system (see Section 2), and equalize tank pressure by removing the fuel filler cap.

Warning: *This procedure will merely relieve the increased pressure necessary for the engine to run - remember that fuel will still be present in the system components, and take precautions accordingly before disconnecting any of them.*

3   Release the union by prying out the colored insert with a small screwdriver and carefully pulling the coupling apart **(see illustrations)**. Use rags to soak up any spilled fuel. Where the unions are color-coded, the pipes cannot be confused. Where both unions are the same color, note carefully which pipe is connected where, and ensure that they are correctly reconnected on reinstallation. Other

4.3b . . . then separate the coupling

quick-connect fittings used on these vehicles include: connectors with two tabs, squeeze the two tabs together and pull the connection apart; connectors with a collar which can be pulled back when two tangs are pressed in; and connectors that use spring-lock couplings, separated by using a plastic tool (sold in inexpensive sets in auto parts stores) which clamps over the connection and releases the spring so the connection can be separated.

4   To reconnect one of these couplings, press the pipe fully into place, then press in the insert until it snaps into place. Switch the ignition on and off five times to pressurize the system, and check for any sign of fuel leakage around the disturbed coupling before attempting to start the engine.

Check

5   Checking procedures for the fuel lines are included in Chapter 1.

Component replacement

6   If any damaged sections are to be replaced, use original-equipment replacement hoses or pipes, constructed from exactly the same material as the section being replaced. Do not install substitutes constructed from inferior or inappropriate material; this could cause a fuel leak or a fire. Any replacement

5.1 Loosen the clip on the air intake duct

5.2 Disconnect the wiring from the airflow sensor

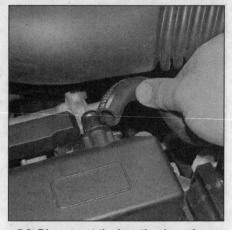

5.3 Disconnect the breather hose from the valve cover

5.4 Remove the air cleaner cover screws

5.6 Remove the air cleaner base

5.9 Remove the air intake duct

hoses must be specifically marked for use with high-pressure fuel injection systems.

7   Before detaching or disconnecting any part of the fuel system, note the routing of all hoses and pipes, and the orientation of all clamps and clips. Replacement sections must be installed in exactly the same manner.

8   Before disconnecting any part of the fuel system, be sure to relieve the fuel system pressure (see Section 2), and equalize tank pressure by removing the fuel filler cap. Also disconnect the negative battery cable (see Chapter 1). Cover the fitting being disconnected with a rag, to absorb any fuel that may spray out.

5   Air cleaner assembly and air intake components - removal and installation

Air cleaner assembly

Refer to illustrations 5.1, 5.2, 5.3, 5.4 and 5.6
Note 1: *The air filter cannot be cleaned. If it's dirty, replace it. On models through 2002, the air cleaner is in the engine compartment. On 2003 and 2004 2.3L engines and all 2005 and later models, the air cleaner is located in the*

left fenderwell. Also see Chapter 1 for air cleaner housing details.
Note 2: *On some models, the air filter and housing are replaced as a unit.*
1   Loosen the clip and disconnect the air intake duct from the mass airflow sensor on the air cleaner **(see illustration)**.
2   Disconnect the wiring from the airflow sensor **(see illustration)**.
3   Disconnect the breather hose leading to

the valve cover **(see illustration)**.
4   Remove the four screws securing the cover to the air cleaner housing **(see illustration)**.
5   Withdraw the cover and remove the filter element.
6   Lift the air cleaner base to release it from the rubber grommets **(see illustration)**.
7   Check the rubber grommets for deterioration and replace them if necessary.

5.11a Pry out the two plastic clips at the front . . .

5.11b . . . then unclip at the rear, and remove the front air intake duct complete

6.2 Unhook the accelerator cable from the pedal

6.4a Extract the securing clip . . .

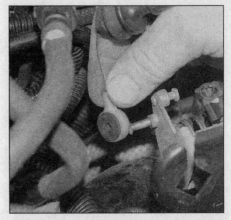

6.4b . . . then pry off the accelerator cable end fitting

8   Installation is the reverse of the removal procedure. Ensure that the base pegs seat fully in their rubber grommets, and that the mass airflow sensor is correctly located.

Air intake components
Refer to illustrations 5.9, 5.11a and 5.11b

9   To remove the air intake duct between the mass airflow sensor and throttle housing, loosen the retaining clips at either end, and carefully ease off the duct **(see illustration)**.

10   To remove the air intake duct attached to the air cleaner base, first remove the air cleaner assembly as described in Steps 1 through 6.

11   Pry up the two clips securing the duct to the engine compartment front panel, then separate the two halves of the duct at the sleeve joint next to the battery. The rear half of the duct is clipped into the engine left-hand mounting bracket. The duct can, however, be removed complete, with some maneuvering **(see illustrations)**. **Note:** *2.3L and 2005 2.0L models with the air cleaner mounted in the fenderwell have a large air resonator housing in the engine compartment, behind the right headlight.*

12   Replacement is a reversal of removal.

---

6   Accelerator cable - removal, installation and adjustment

Removal
Refer to illustrations 6.2, 6.4a, 6.4b and 6.5

1   Remove five screws and take out the trim panel above the driver's footwell to gain access to the accelerator pedal; unclip the diagnostic connector plug from the panel as it is removed.

2   Disconnect the inner cable from the top of the pedal by pulling the end of the cable out, and unhooking the inner cable through the slot at the top of the pedal **(see illustration)**.

3   Pry the rubber grommet from the firewall, and remove the cable and end fitting through into the engine compartment.

4   Disconnect the inner cable from the quadrant on the throttle housing by extracting the retaining clip, then prying the end fit-

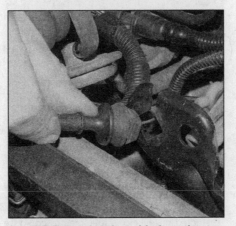

6.5 Removing the cable from the support bracket

ting off sideways **(see illustrations)**.

5   Release the cable from the supports in the engine compartment, noting how it is routed **(see illustration)**.

Installation
6   Installation is a reversal of removal. The rubber grommet must be fitted to the firewall first, and the cable end fitting pushed through it. When the cable is reconnected at each end, check its operation as follows.

Adjustment
7   The cable is self-adjusting. Check that the throttle quadrant moves smoothly and easily from the fully-closed to the fully-open position and back again as an assistant depresses and releases the accelerator pedal.

---

7   Accelerator pedal - removal and installation

Removal
Refer to illustration 7.2

1   Remove five screws and take out the trim panel above the driver's footwell to gain access to the accelerator pedal; unclip the diagnostic connector plug from the panel as it is removed.

7.2 Accelerator pedal, showing cable attachment and mounting nuts

2   Detach the accelerator cable from the pedal (see Section 6), then unscrew the three nuts and remove the accelerator pedal assembly **(see illustration)**.

Installation
3   Install in the reverse order of removal. On completion, check the action of the pedal and the cable to ensure that the throttle has full unrestricted movement, and fully returns when released.

---

8   Fuel pump/fuel pressure - checking

Warning: *Refer to the* **Warning** *in Section 1 before proceeding.*

Fuel pump operation check
1   Switch on the ignition, and listen for the fuel pump (the sound of an electric motor running, audible from beneath the rear seats). Assuming there is sufficient fuel in the tank, the pump should start and run for approximately one or two seconds, then stop, each time the ignition is switched on. **Note:** *If the pump runs continuously all the time the ignition is switched on, the electronic control system is running in the backup (or 'limp-home'*

9.7 Exhaust heat shield and 'flat nut' fastener (arrow)

9.8a Using a special tool to disconnect the exhaust front mounting rubbers

9.8b Exhaust rear mounting rubber (arrow)

mode referred to by the manufacturer as 'Limited Operation Strategy' (LOS). This almost certainly indicates a fault in the EEC-V module itself, and the vehicle should therefore be taken for diagnostic testing (see Section 14) - do not waste time or risk damaging the components by trying to test the system without the proper facilities.

2   On models with a 2.0L Zetec-E engine, listen for fuel return noises from the fuel pressure regulator. It should be possible to feel the fuel pulsing in the regulator and in the feed hose from the fuel filter.

3   If the pump does not run at all, check the fuse, relay and wiring (see Chapter 12). Check also that the fuel cut-off switch (located in the lower trim panel on the right-hand side of the driver's footwell) has not been activated; if it has, reset it as described below:

a) Turn off the ignition.
b) If the switch has been triggered, the switch tab will be in the raised position. Press the switch in to reset it.
c) Turn the ignition switch to position II (so that the instrument panel warning lights come on), then return it to position I. The engine can then be started as normal.

Note: The switch must not be reset immediately after an accident if there is a risk of fuel spillage.

Fuel pressure check

4   A fuel pressure gauge will be required for this check, and should be connected in the fuel line between the fuel filter and the fuel rail, in accordance with the gauge maker's instructions. A pressure gauge equipped with an adapter to suit the Schrader-type valve on the fuel rail pressure test/release fitting (identifiable by its blue plastic cap, and located on the end of the fuel rail - refer to illustration 2.4) will be required. If the special tool 29-033 is available, the tool can be attached to the valve, and a conventional-type pressure gauge attached to the tool.

5   If using the service tool, ensure that its tap is turned fully counterclockwise, then attach it to the valve. Connect the pressure gauge to the service tool. If using a fuel pres-

sure gauge with its own adapter, connect it in accordance with its maker's instructions.

2.0L SPI engines through 2003 and all 2004 and later models

Note: On these models, the fuel pressure regulator is located in the fuel tank and is integrated with the fuel pump/sending unit assembly.

6   Turn all the accessories Off and switch the ignition key On (engine not running). The fuel pump should run for approximately two seconds. Note the reading on the gauge. If the fuel pressure is higher than specified, replace the fuel pressure regulator. If the fuel pressure is too low, the fuel filter or in-tank strainer could be clogged, the lines could be restricted or leaking, a fuel injector could be leaking, or the fuel pressure regulator and/or fuel pump could be defective.

7   Start the engine and let it idle at normal operating temperature. The pressure should remain within the range listed in this Chapter's Specifications. If the pressure is lower than specified, check the items listed in Step 6.

Note: If no obvious problems are found, most likely the fuel pressure regulator and/or the fuel pump is defective. In this situation, it is recommended that both the fuel pressure regulator and fuel pump are replaced to prevent any future fuel pressure problems (see Section 10).

2.0L Zetec-E engines through 2003

8   Turn all the accessories Off and switch the ignition key On (engine not running). The fuel pump should run for approximately two seconds. Note the reading on the gauge - it should fall within the range given in this Chapter's Specifications.

9   Now start the engine and allow it to idle - the fuel pressure should be 5 to 10 psi below the pressure recorded in Step 8.

10   If the fuel pressure is lower than specified, pinch off the fuel return line. **Caution:** Use special pliers designed specifically for pinching a rubber fuel line (available at most auto parts stores). Use of any other type pliers may damage the fuel line. **Caution:** Do not allow the fuel pressure to rise above 65 psi or damage to the fuel pressure regulator

may occur. If the fuel pressure rises, replace the fuel pressure regulator (see Section 15). If the fuel pressure is still lower than specified, check the fuel lines and the fuel filter for restrictions. If no restriction is found, remove the fuel pump assembly (see Section 10) and check the strainer for restrictions. If no problems are found, replace the fuel pump.

11   If the fuel pressure recorded in Step 8 is higher than specified, check the fuel return line for restrictions. If no restrictions are found, replace the fuel pressure regulator (see Section 15).

12   Reconnect the vacuum hose to the pressure regulator - the pressure should immediately decrease by about 50 to 10 psi. If it doesn't, verify that there is 12 to 14 in-Hg of vacuum present at the hose. If vacuum is not present at the hose, check the hose for a restriction or a break. If vacuum is present, replace the fuel pressure regulator.

All models

13   Turn the engine off and check the gauge - the fuel pressure should hold steady. After five minutes, it should not drop below the minimum listed in this Chapter's Specifications. If it does drop, the fuel pump or fuel pressure regulator could be defective, or a fuel injector could be leaking.

14   After the testing is done, relieve the fuel pressure (see Section 2) and remove the fuel pressure gauge.

---

9   Fuel tank - removal, inspection and installation

Warning: Refer to the **Warning** in Section 1 before proceeding.

Removal

Refer to illustrations 9.7, 9.8a, 9.8b, 9.9, 9.10a, 9.10b, 9.11, 9.12, 9.15a, 9.15b, 9.16a and 9.16b

1   Run the fuel level as low as possible prior to removing the tank.

2   Relieve the residual pressure in the fuel system (see Section 2), and equalize tank

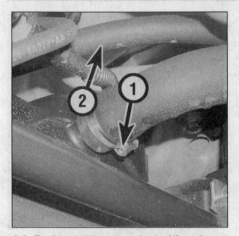

9.9 Fuel tank filler pipe clamp (1) and vent hose (2)

9.10a Charcoal canister (arrow) at the rear of the tank

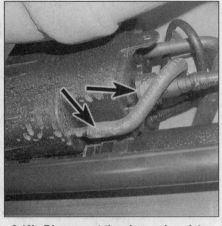

9.10b Disconnect the charcoal canister hoses (arrows)

pressure by removing the fuel filler cap.

3   Disconnect the negative battery cable (see Chapter 5).

4   Using a siphoning kit (available at most auto parts stores), siphon the fuel into an approved gasoline container. **Warning:** *Do not start the siphoning action by mouth!*

5   Chock the front wheels, loosen the rear wheel nuts, then jack up the rear of the car and support it on axle stands (see *Jacking and Towing*). Remove the rear wheels.

6   Unscrew and remove the nuts at the exhaust flange behind the flexible section of pipe at the front, and separate the joint. Have an axle stand or similar support ready, on which the front part of the exhaust can be supported.

7   Unscrew and remove the fasteners securing the exhaust heat shield at the rear **(see illustration)**; remove the heat shield, noting how it is installed.

8   Unhook the exhaust system mounting rubbers at the front and rear **(see illustrations)**, and allow the exhaust system to rest on the rear suspension crossmember, and at the front, on an axle stand or similar. There is no need to remove the exhaust from under the car (although this will greatly improve working room) - maneuver the exhaust under

the car in order to clear the fuel tank. **Note:** *To remove the rear portion of the exhaust, which is one-piece, the pipe must be cut. Putting it back together again will require welding at an exhaust shop.*

9   Loosen the clamps and disconnect the filler pipe and vent hose from the fuel tank **(see illustration)**. Note the exact fitted positions of the clips, for use when replacing. Do not use any sharp tools to pry the pipes from the tank fittings, or the pipes may be damaged, leading to leakage on completion.

10   At the charcoal canister at the rear of the tank, pull off the vapor hose at the base, and release the fitting from the hose at the side **(see illustrations)**. Note the respective positions of the hoses carefully for replacement.

11   Depress the metal clip used to locate the charcoal canister, then lift the canister upwards to free it from the clip, and remove it from under the car **(see illustration)**.

12   Position a container beneath the fuel filter **(see illustration)**, then disconnect the fuel supply hose from the filter intake by prying out the insert to release the fitting. Be prepared for some loss of fuel.

13   Disconnect the fuel return line at the connector next to the fuel filter. Note that the return pipe is identified by a red color band. On 2005

9.11 Removing the charcoal canister from behind the fuel tank

and later models, the system is "returnless" and does not have a return fuel line.

14   Remove the bolts securing the heat shield, if equipped, to the fuel tank straps. Support the fuel tank using a floor jack and block of wood.

15   Unscrew and remove the tank strap bolt **(see illustrations)** and unhook the straps, noting how they are installed.

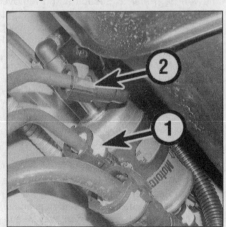

9.12 Fuel supply (1) and return (2) connections

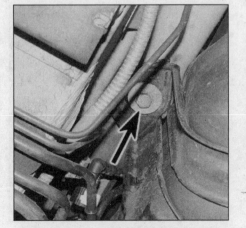

9.15a Tank strap bolt (arrow) at the front of the tank

9.15b Unscrew the tank strap bolt

9.16a Lower the fuel tank . . .

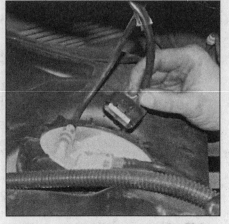

9.16b . . . then disconnect the remaining fuel lines and wiring

10.2a Release the fitting lugs with a small screwdriver . . .

16   Taking care that the wiring and fuel lines are not strained, partially lower the fuel tank **(see illustration)**. Release the fuel lines from the attachments on the tank as necessary. When the tank has been sufficiently lowered, disconnect the fuel pump/gauge sender wiring plug from the top of the tank **(see illustration)**.

17   Lower the fuel tank and withdraw it from under the vehicle. If necessary, disconnect the supply hose from the fuel pump. The filter may also be removed at this time.

Inspection

18   While removed, the fuel tank can be inspected for damage or deterioration. Removal of the fuel pump/fuel gauge sender unit (see Section 10) will allow a partial inspection of the interior. If the tank is contaminated with sediment or water, rinse it out with clean fuel. Do not under any circumstances undertake any repairs on a leaking or damaged fuel tank; this work must be carried out by a professional who has experience in this critical and potentially-dangerous work.

19   While the fuel tank is removed from the vehicle, it should be placed in a safe area where sparks or open flames cannot ignite the fumes coming out of the tank. Be espe-

cially careful inside garages where a gas type appliance is located, because it could cause an explosion.

20   Check the condition of the filler pipe and replace it if necessary.

Installation

21   If a new tank is being installed, transfer the roll-over valves, vent hose and filler pipe to the new tank.

22   Installation is a reversal of the removal procedure. Ensure that all connections are securely fitted. When replacing the quick-release couplings, press them together and secure with the colored insert. If evidence of contamination was found, do not return any previously-drained fuel to the tank unless it is carefully filtered first.

---

10   Fuel pump/fuel gauge sender unit - removal and installation

---

Warning: *Refer to the* **Warning** *in Section 1 before proceeding.*

Note: *Dealer technicians use a special wrench to unscrew the pump/sender unit retaining ring, but ordinary tools can be used successfully (see text).*

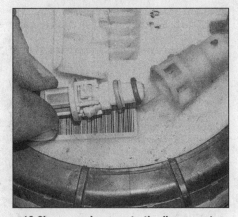

10.2b . . . and separate the lines - note the O-rings

Removal

Refer to illustrations 10.2a, 10.2b, 10.3a, 10.3b, 10.4, 10.5a, 10.5b, 10.7a, 10.7b and 10.8

1   A combined fuel pump and fuel gauge sender unit is located in the top face of the fuel tank. The combined unit can only be detached and withdrawn from the tank after the tank is released and lowered from under the vehicle. Refer to Section 9 and remove the fuel tank, then proceed as follows.

2   With the fuel tank removed, disconnect the fuel supply and return lines (if still attached to the tank) from their respective stubs by releasing the lugs using a small screwdriver. Note that the fuel supply line connector is identified by a white band, and the return line connector by a red band. Make sure that both O-rings are recovered from each line as they are disconnected **(see illustrations)**.

3   Unscrew and remove the special retaining ring. The manufacturer specifies the use of their service tool 310-069 (a large socket/ wrench with projecting teeth to engage the fuel pump/sender unit retaining ring's slots) for this task. A large pair of slip-joint pliers, or an oil filter removal strap wrench, may be sufficient for this task, but we used a tool made from two long bolts and two strips of metal **(see illustrations)**.

10.3a Using a home-made tool to unscrew . . .

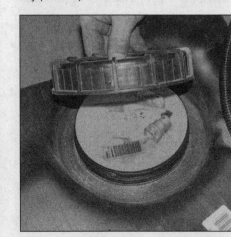

10.3b . . . and remove the retaining ring

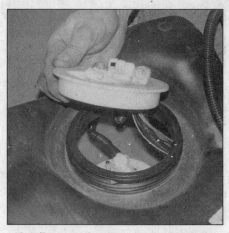

10.4 Remove the top cover as far as the wiring allows

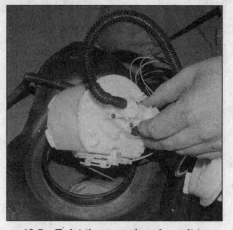

10.5a Twist the pump/sender unit to release the retaining lugs at the base . . .

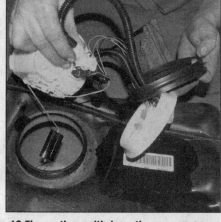

10.5b . . . then withdraw the cover, pump and rubber seal, without damaging the float arm

4   With the retaining ring removed, the pump/sender top cover can be withdrawn. Feed the wiring out through the opening, noting that the cover cannot be completely removed until the pump/sender unit is also removed from the tank **(see illustration)**.

5   Turn the pump/sender unit counterclockwise inside the tank (this is quite stiff to turn), then carefully withdraw the unit, taking care not to damage the sender unit float or its arm **(see illustrations)**.

6   If not already done, remove the rubber seal from the periphery of the pump. The seal must be replaced whenever the pump/sender unit is removed from the tank.

7   If required, the sender unit can be separated from the pump by squeezing together the lugs below its mounting at the side **(see illustrations)**. Check the availability of a new sender separately, before removing the sender.

Installation

8   Installation is a reversal of removal, noting the following points:

a) Ensure that the pump/sender unit seats fully and squarely in the tank before twisting it clockwise to secure it. Check that the unit is firmly located before proceeding.

b) Turn the pump/sender top cover so that the arrows on the tank and unit are aligned **(see illustration)**.

c) Install a new rubber seal and tighten the retaining ring securely.

d) Install the fuel tank as described in Section 9.

11 Fuel tank roll-over valves - removal and installation

Warning: Refer to the **Warning** in Section 1 before proceeding.

Removal

1   The roll-over valves are located in rubber grommets in the top of the fuel tank, with hoses leading rearwards to the carbon canister. Their purpose is to prevent fuel loss if the vehicle becomes inverted in a crash.

2   Remove the fuel tank as described in Section 9.

3   Release the vent hose from the clip on the top of the tank.

4   Carefully pry the roll-over valve from the rubber grommet and remove it together with the hose.

5   Check the condition of the rubber grommet and replace it if necessary.

Installation

6   Installation is a reversal of removal, but apply a light smear of clean engine oil to the rubber grommet, to ease Installation.

12 Fuel tank filler pipe - removal and installation

Warning: Refer to the **Warning** in Section 1 before proceeding.

Removal

Refer to illustrations 12.4a, 12.4b, 12.4c, 12.5a, 12.5b, 12.6a, 12.6b and 12.6c

1   Disconnect the negative battery cable (see Chapter 5).

2   Equalize tank pressure by removing the fuel filler cap.

3   Chock the front wheels, loosen the right-hand rear wheel nuts, then jack up the rear of the car and support it on axle stands (see Jacking and Towing). Remove the right-hand rear wheel - this is not absolutely essential, but will make the job easier.

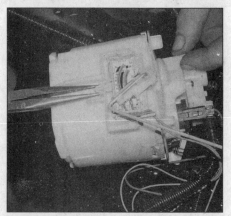

10.7a Squeeze the lugs at the side . . .

10.7b . . . and remove the sender unit

10.8 Top cover and tank alignment arrows

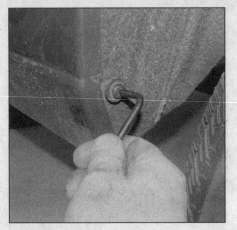

12.4a The rear fenderwell liner is secured by a combination of screws . . .

12.4b . . . and clips, which can be pried out . . .

12.4c . . . before removing the liner completely

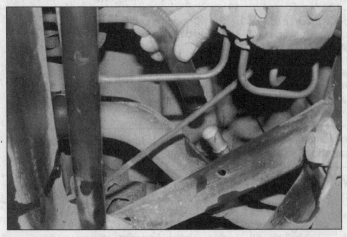

12.5a Disconnect the vent hose . . .

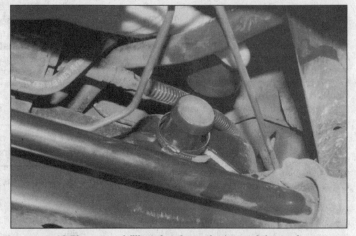

12.5b . . . and filler pipe from the rear of the tank

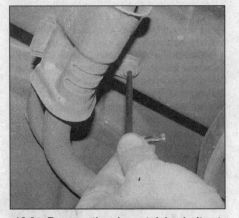

12.6a Remove the pipe retaining bolts at the top . . .

12.6b . . . and at the bottom . . .

12.6c . . . then maneuver the filler pipe out from under the fenderwell

4   Release and remove the various fasteners used to secure the right-hand rear fenderwell liner, then maneuver the liner out from the fenderwell **(see illustrations)**.

5   Loosen the clamp and disconnect the filler pipe and vent hose from the fuel tank **(see illustrations)**. Note the exact positions of the clips, for use when replacing. Do not use any sharp tools to pry the pipes from the tank fittings, or the pipes may be damaged, leading to leakage on completion.

6   The filler pipe is secured by two bolts (one top and bottom) - remove the bolts to release the pipe. It is now possible to remove the pipe from under the fenderwell **(see illustrations)**.

7   Check the condition of the filler pipe and hose and replace if necessary.

Installation

8   Installation is a reversal of removal. Tighten the rear crossmember bolts to the specified torque (refer to Chapter 10 Specifications). **Note:** *The filler pipe assembly must be replaced as a unit - the rubber hose portion can not be replaced separately.*

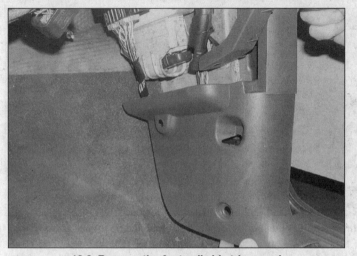

13.3 Remove the footwell side trim panel

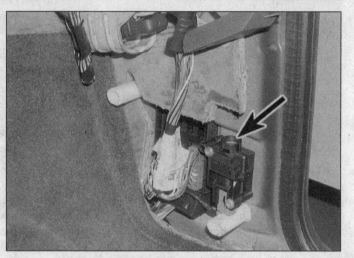

13.4 Fuel cut-off switch location

13 Fuel cut-off switch - removal and installation

Note: *To reset the switch after it has been triggered, first check that there are no signs that fuel is escaping. Turn off the ignition. If the switch has been triggered, the switch tab will be in the raised position. Press the switch down to reset it. Turn the ignition switch to position II (so that the instrument panel warning lights come on), then return it to position I. The engine can then be started as normal.*

Removal

Refer to illustrations 13.3 and 13.4

1   The fuel cut-off (or inertia) switch is located behind the driver's footwell side trim panel. First disconnect the negative battery cable (see Chapter 5).

2   Pull up the weatherstrip from the driver's door opening, and release it from the side trim.

3   Pry out the two screwhead covers, then unscrew and remove the two screws securing the trim panel. Remove the trim panel for access to the cut-off switch **(see illustration)**.

4   Unscrew and remove the two switch securing screws **(see illustration)**, then disconnect the wiring plug and remove the switch.

Installation

5   Installation is a reversal of removal, but make sure that the switch is reset. Start the engine to prove this.

14 Fuel injection system - check

Refer to illustration 14.2

Warning: *Refer to the* **Warning** *in Section 1 before proceeding.*

1   If a fault appears in the fuel injection system, first ensure that all the system wiring connectors are securely connected and free

of corrosion - also refer to Steps 6 through 9 below. Then ensure that the fault is not due to poor maintenance; i.e., check that the air cleaner filter element is clean, the spark plugs are in good condition and correctly gapped, the valve clearances are correct, the cylinder compression pressures are correct, the ignition system wiring is in good condition and securely connected, and the engine breather hoses are clear and undamaged, referring to Chapter 1, Chapter 2A or 2B and Chapter 5B.

2   A diagnostic connector is incorporated in the engine management system wiring harness, into which dedicated electronic test equipment can be plugged (the connector is located behind a small panel in the driver's side lower dash - unclip and remove the panel for access) **(see illustration)**. The test equipment is capable of 'interrogating' the engine management system PCM electronically and accessing its internal fault log (reading trouble codes).

3   Trouble codes can only be extracted from the PCM using a dedicated trouble code reader. See Chapter 4B for trouble code information.

4   Experienced home mechanics equipped with an accurate tachometer and a carefully-calibrated exhaust gas analyzer may be able to check the exhaust gas CO content and the engine idle speed; if these are found to be out of specification, then the vehicle must be taken to a suitably-equipped dealer service department or other repair shop for assessment. Neither the air/fuel mixture (exhaust gas CO content) nor the engine idle speed are manually adjustable; incorrect test results indicate the need for maintenance (possibly, injector cleaning) or a fault within the fuel injection system.

Limited Operation Strategy - precaution

5   Certain faults, such as failure of one of the engine management system sensors, will

cause the system will revert to a backup (or 'limp-home') mode, referred to by the manufactuer as 'Limited Operation Strategy' (LOS). This is intended to be a 'get-you-home' facility only - the engine management warning light will come on when this mode is in operation.

6   In this mode, the signal from the defective sensor is substituted with a fixed value (it would normally vary), which may lead to loss of power, poor idling, and generally-poor running, especially when the engine is cold.

7   However, the engine may in fact run quite well in this situation, and the only clue (other than the warning light) would be that the exhaust CO emissions (for example) will be higher than they should be.

8   Bear in mind that, even if the defective sensor is correctly identified and renewed, the engine will not return to normal running until the trouble code is erased, taking the system out of LOS. This also applies even if the cause of the fault was a loose connection or damaged piece of wire - until the trouble code is erased, the system will continue in LOS.

14.2 Diagnostic connector location in driver's lower dash panel

15.5a Throttle body housing bolts (arrows)

15.5b Remove the throttle body housing

15.6 Install a new throttle body housing gasket

15.11a Use a screwdriver to pry out the wire clips . . .

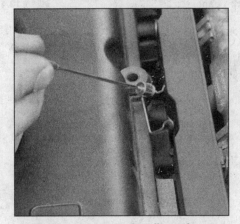

15.11b . . . recover the clips using a magnetic tool . . .

15.11c . . . then lift off the injector wiring busbar

15 Fuel injection system components - removal and installation

Warning: *Refer to the* **Warning** *in Section 1 before proceeding.*

Throttle body housing

Refer to illustrations 15.5a, 15.5b and 15.6

1   The housing is located on the left-hand side of the intake manifold. First disconnect the negative battery cable (see Chapter 5).

2   Remove the air intake duct as described in Section 5.

3   Disconnect the accelerator cable (and cruise control cable, if equipped) from the throttle body housing, using the information in Section 6. **Note:** *Some models will have a plastic "snow" shield that must be removed for access to the linkage.*

4   Disconnect the throttle position sensor multi-plug.

5   Unscrew and remove the four mounting bolts and withdraw the throttle housing from the intake manifold **(see illustrations)**. Discard the rubber gasket and obtain a new one. **Note:** *Take care when cleaning the inside of the housing, as it is treated with a special coating during manufacture, which could be removed by over-enthusiastic cleaning, or by*

use of powerful solvents. On 2005 and later models, The throttle body should not be cleaned at all.

6   Installation is a reversal of removal, but clean the mating faces and install a new gasket, and tighten the mounting bolts securely **(see illustration)**.

Fuel rail and injectors

Refer to illustrations 15.11a, 15.11b, 15.11c, 15.12, 15.14, 15.15 and 15.16

7   Relieve the residual pressure in the fuel system (see Section 2), and equalize tank pressure by removing the fuel filler cap.
Warning: *This procedure will merely relieve the increased pressure necessary for the engine to run - remember that fuel will still be present in the system components, and take precautions accordingly before disconnecting any of them.*

8   Disconnect the negative battery cable (see Chapter 5).

9   Loosen the retaining clips at either end, and remove the air intake duct.

10   Disconnect the accelerator cable (and cruise control cable, if equipped) from the throttle body housing, using the information in Section 6.

11   On models through 2004, using a small screwdriver, pry up and remove the four clips

(one on each injector) securing the injector wiring busbar - use a magnetic holding tool to prevent the wire clips falling down the back of the engine as they are removed. Lift off the wiring busbar, and move it to the rear **(see illustrations)**.

12   On models with a 2.0L Zetec-E engine, disconnect the vacuum hose from the fuel pressure regulator and fuel pulse damper **(see illustration)**. Both are on the fuel rail. On

15.12 Disconnect the fuel pressure regulator vacuum hose (2.0L Zetec-E engines only)

15.14 Remove the fuel rail

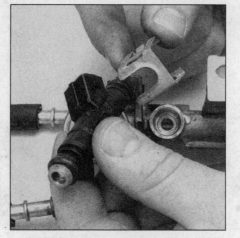

15.15 Pry out the securing clips and remove the injectors

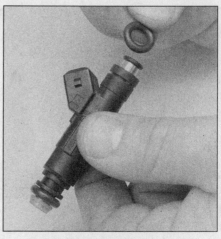

15.16 Remove the injector O-rings

models with a 2.0L SPI engine, unplug the electrical connector from the fuel pressure sensor on the fuel rail.

13 Disconnect the fuel supply and return lines, noting their positions. The supply line is color-coded white, and the return line is color-coded red. On 2.3L and 2005 and later 2.0L engines, disconnect the electrical connectors from the individual ignition coils over the spark plugs.

14 Unscrew and remove the two bolts securing the fuel rail. Pulling the fuel rail equally at both ends, remove it squarely from the intake manifold **(see illustration)**.

15 If required, remove the clips and carefully pull the injectors from the fuel rail **(see illustration)**.

16 Using a screwdriver if necessary, pry the O-rings from the grooves at each end of the injectors. Discard the O-rings and obtain new ones **(see illustration)**.

17 Installation is the reverse of the removal procedure, noting the following points:

a) *Lubricate the new O-rings with clean engine oil to aid installation.*

b) *Ensure that the hoses and wiring are routed correctly, and secured on reconnection by any clips or ties provided.*

c) *Install the accelerator cable as described in Section 6.*

d) *On completion, switch the ignition on to activate the fuel pump and pressurize the system, without cranking the engine. Check for signs of fuel leaks around all disturbed unions and joints before attempting to start the engine.*

Fuel pressure regulator

Refer to illustrations 15.22 and 15.23

Note: *Except for Zetec-E engines, all models are a "returnless" fuel system; an electronic pressure sensor mounted on the fuel rail transmits a signal to the PCM, which controls the speed of the fuel pump in order to supply the fuel rail with the required amount of pressure.*

18 Relieve the residual pressure in the fuel system (see Section 2), and equalize tank pressure by removing the fuel filler cap.

Warning: *This procedure will merely relieve the increased pressure necessary for the engine to run - remember that fuel will still be present in the system components, and take precautions accordingly before disconnecting any of them.*

19 Disconnect the negative battery cable (see Chapter 5).

20 Disconnect the fuel supply and return lines, noting their positions. The supply line is color-coded white, and the return line is color-coded red.

21 Disconnect the vacuum hose from the fuel pressure regulator.

22 Undo the two bolts and remove the fuel pressure regulator from the fuel rail **(see illustration)**.

23 Using a screwdriver if necessary, pry the O-ring from the groove in the fuel pressure regulator **(see illustration)**. Discard the O-ring, and obtain a new one.

24 Installation is a reversal of removal, but lubricate the new O-ring with clean engine oil to aid installation. Tighten the mounting bolts to the specified torque.

Idle speed control valve

Refer to illustrations 15.25 and 15.27

25 The valve is located on the intake manifold, next to the throttle housing. The valve is on the inside of the intake manifold, making access especially difficult **(see illustration)**.

26 Loosen the retaining clips at either end, and remove the air cleaner intake duct.

15.22 Fuel pressure regulator mounting bolts (arrows)

15.23 Always install a new O-ring (arrow)

15.25 Idle air control valve - seen with intake manifold removed

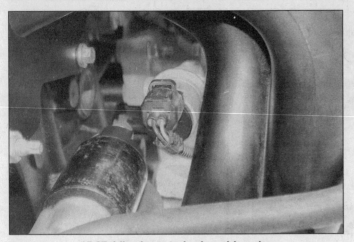

15.27 Idle air control valve wiring plug

15.32 Disconnect the airflow sensor wiring plug

27 Disconnect the wiring plug from the valve **(see illustration)**.
28 Unscrew the mounting bolts and remove the valve from the intake manifold. Remove the alternator as described in Chapter 5A, or ultimately, if suitable tools are not available, it may be simpler to remove the intake manifold (Section 16) for access.
29 Recover the rubber seal from the valve, and discard it. Obtain a new seal for replacement.
30 Installation is a reversal of removal, but note the following points.

   a) Clean the mating surfaces, and install a new seal.
   b) Tighten the valve bolts to the specified torque.
   c) Once the wiring and battery are reconnected, start the engine and allow it to idle. When it has reached normal operating temperature, check that the idle speed is stable, and that no induction (air) leaks are evident. Switch on all electrical loads (headlights, heated rear window, etc), and check that the idle speed is still satisfactory.

Mass airflow sensor

Refer to illustration 15.32
31 Loosen the clip and disconnect the air intake duct from the mass airflow sensor on the air cleaner cover. If necessary, remove the air cleaner cover for improved access. On 2.3L and 2005 2.0L engines, remove the left fenderwell liner for better access to the MAF sensor.
32 Disconnect the wiring from the sensor **(see illustration)**.
33 Unscrew the crosshead mounting screws and remove the sensor from the air cleaner cover.
34 Installation is a reversal of removal. **Caution:** *If the MAF housing is removed for any reason, make sure the screen does not fall out, and is in place at the front of the MAF housing when reinstalled.*

Intake air temperature sensor

35 The sensor is an integral part of the mass airflow sensor, and cannot be replaced separately.

Powertrain control module (PCM)

Refer to illustration 15.39
Note: *The module is fragile. Take care not to drop it, or subject it to any other kind of impact. Do not subject it to extremes of temperature, or allow it to get wet. The module wiring plug must never be disconnected while the ignition is switched on.*
36 The powertrain control module is located behind the dash, on the right-hand side. First disconnect the negative battery cable (see Chapter 5).
37 Remove the glovebox as described in Chapter 11.
38 Remove the four screws securing the passenger's side lower trim panel. Remove the panel from the dash.
39 Remove the two screws securing the central locking module, and lower the module out of position; there is no need to disconnect the wiring **(see illustration)**.
40 Release the spring clips securing the module bracket in position, and remove the module downward into the footwell.
41 The PCM wiring connector is protected by a tamperproof shield, secured by a shear-bolt and welded nut, which must be drilled to remove the bolt. Great care must be taken not to damage the wiring harness during drilling.
42 First drill a 1/8-inch pilot hole in the nut, then enlarge the hole using a 5/16-inch drill until the shear-bolt can be removed.
43 With the shear-bolt removed, slide off the tamperproof shield **(see illustration)**.
44 Remove the wiring connector securing screw, then disconnect the plug from the

15.39 Remove the central locking module for access to the PCM

15.46 Crankshaft position sensor (arrow) - SPI engine

15.48a Unscrew the mounting bolt . . .

15.48b . . . and withdraw the sensor

PCM, and remove the module from the car.

45 Installation is a reversal of removal. Use a new shear-bolt, and tighten it until the head shears off.

Crankshaft position sensor

Refer to illustrations 15.46, 15.48a and 15.48b

Note: *On 2005 and later engines, the CKP cannot be reused if it is removed from the engine. Make sure that yours tests as bad before replacing it. The new sensor will come with an installation tool.*

46 The sensor is located on the front left-hand side of the engine on 2.0L Zetec-E engines, and at the timing belt end of the engine on all other engines (see illustration). For improved access, apply the parking brake then jack up the front of the vehicle and support it on axle stands (see *Jacking and Towing*).

47 If equipped, unclip the cover from the crankshaft position sensor on the front of the engine, then disconnect the wiring plug.

48 Unscrew the mounting bolt and with-draw the sensor (see illustrations). If a spacer is present between the sensor and engine, it is vital that this is replaced when replacing the sensor, or the sensor head will hit the rotor teeth.

49 Installation is a reversal of removal. Tighten the sensor retaining bolt to the specified torque. **Caution:** *On 2.3L and 2005 2.0L engines, the CKP sensor must be aligned precisely. Refer to Chapter 2C for the procedure to set the engine at TDC. With the timing pin installed, align the CKP sensor with the alignment tool provided with the new sensor.*

Camshaft position sensor

Refer to illustrations 15.52a and 15.52b

50 The camshaft position sensor is located at the rear of the cylinder head - on the left-hand side (as seen from the driver's seat).

51 Loosen the retaining clips at either end, and remove the air intake duct. Disconnect the breather hose from the valve cover.

52 Disconnect the wiring connector from the sensor, then unscrew the sensor retaining bolt and withdraw the sensor from the cylinder head (see illustrations).

53 Installation is a reversal of removal. Tighten the sensor retaining bolt to the specified torque.

Cylinder head temperature sensor (Zetec-E engines only)

Refer to illustrations 15.56 and 15.57

54 The sensor is located on the right-hand end of the cylinder head on Zetec-E engines. On 2.3L and 2005 and later 2.0L engines, the sensor is located on top of the cylinder head, between the middle two spark plugs. There is no need to drain the coolant, as the sensor measures the temperature of the metal directly. 2.0L SPI engines have a conventional CTS Coolant Temperature Sensor (see Chapter 3).

55 On Zetec-E and Duratec (SVT) engines only, remove the alternator as described in Chapter 5A.

56 Disconnect the wiring from the temperature sensor (see illustration).

15.52a Disconnect the wiring plug . . .

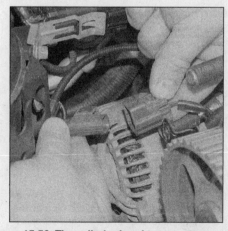

15.52b . . . then remove the sensor from the cylinder head

15.56 The cylinder head temperature sensor wiring plug is clipped to the timing belt upper cover (Zetec-E and Duratec SVT shown)

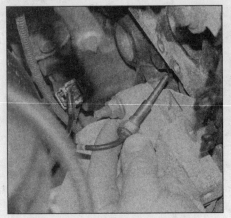

15.57 Removing the cylinder head temperature sensor

15.59 Disconnect the plug from the throttle position sensor

15.65 Remove the clutch pedal switch

57   Unscrew and remove the sensor **(see illustration)**.
58   Installation is a reversal of removal. Clean the sensor mounting hole, then install the sensor and tighten it to the specified torque.

Throttle position sensor
Refer to illustration 15.59
59   The sensor is located on the side of the throttle body housing. First disconnect the sensor wiring plug **(see illustration)**.
60   Remove the retaining screws, and withdraw the unit from the throttle housing. *Do not* force the sensor's center to rotate past its normal operating sweep; the unit will be seriously damaged.
61   Installation is a reversal of removal, but ensure that the sensor is correctly orientated, by locating its center on the D-shaped throttle shaft (throttle closed), and aligning the sensor body so that the screws pass easily into the throttle housing.

Vehicle speed sensor
62   Refer to Chapter 7A.

Output shaft speed sensor
63   Refer to Chapter 7B, Section 5.

Clutch pedal position switch
Refer to illustration 15.65
64   Remove five screws and take out the trim panel above the driver's footwell to gain access to the clutch pedal; unclip the diagnostic connector plug from the panel as it is removed.
65   Reach up and disconnect the wiring from the clutch switch at the top of the pedal, then twist the switch counterclockwise and remove it from the pedal bracket **(see illustration)**.
66   Installation is a reversal of removal.

Power steering pressure switch
Refer to illustration 15.67
67   The switch is screwed into the power steering system's high-pressure pipe at the front right-hand side of the engine compartment **(see illustration)**. On some models, access is improved by removing the radiator grille as described in Chapter 11.
68   Releasing its clip, unplug the switch's electrical connector, then unscrew the switch

from the power steering high pressure pipe. Place a wad of rag underneath, to catch any spilled fluid. If a sealing washer is installed, replace it if it is worn or damaged.
69   Installation is the reverse of the removal procedure, noting the following points:
a) *Tighten the switch to the specified torque.*
b) *Top-up the fluid reservoir (see 'Weekly checks') to replace any fluid lost from the system.*
c) *If a significant amount of fluid was lost, bleed the power steering system as described in Chapter 10.*

Oxygen sensor
70   Refer to Chapter 4B.

---

16   Manifolds - removal and installation

Note: *Refer to the warning note in Section 1 before proceeding.*

Intake manifold
Removal
Refer to illustrations 16.3, 16.4, 16.5a, 16.5b, 16.5c, 16.6 and 16.7
1   Depressurize the fuel system as described in Section 2, then disconnect the

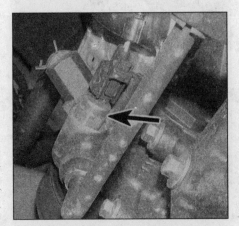

15.67 Power steering pressure switch (arrow)

negative battery cable (see Chapter 5).
2   Remove the air cleaner and inlet duct as described in Section 5, and disconnect the accelerator cable using the information in Section 6. To provide working room on 2.3L and 2005 and later 2.0L models, remove the engine cooling fan and shroud (see Chapter 3). **Note:** *Some models have a "snow" shield over the throttle linkage.*
3   Disconnect the brake booster vacuum hose from the base of the manifold - squeeze the end fitting and pull to release it **(see illustration)**. Remove the engine oil dipstick and its tube.
4   Trace the injection wiring harness back to the large multi-plug located behind the power steering fluid reservoir, and disconnect the plug **(see illustration)**. Also disconnect the wiring plug from the camshaft position sensor, located at the rear of the cylinder head, at the transmission end. Tag and disconnect all electrical connectors from the throttle body.
5   On models through 2004, disconnect the fuel supply and return lines from the fuel rail, noting their installed positions. The supply line is color-coded white, and the return line is color-coded red **(see illustrations)**. On earlier models, the manifold is removed complete with the fuel rail. On later models, the fuel rail is attached to the cylinder head, not the intake manifold. **Note:** *Protect the alternator from fuel*

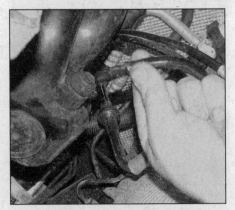

16.3 Disconnect the brake booster vacuum hose from the intake manifold - seen from below

16.4 Disconnect the injection harness wiring plug

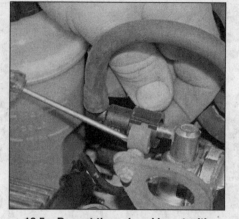

16.5a Pry out the colored insert with a screwdriver . . .

16.5b . . . then disconnect the return line from the fuel rail

spillage with rags or a plastic bag. On models so equipped, disconnect the intake manifold runner control (IMRC) cable.

6 Unscrew and remove the manifold support bracket (SPI engines) and manifold retaining bolts, and the nut at either end, noting that some of them are not easily accessible - it may be necessary to jack up the front of the car and support it securely on jackstands and gain access from below. Note that the right-hand nut also secures a wiring support bracket - unclip the wiring before removing the bracket. Once the two nuts have been removed, unscrew their studs from the cylinder head - the studs have Torx-end fittings to make removal easier **(see illustration)**.

7 Check that there is nothing else attached to the manifold which would prevent its removal. Withdraw the manifold from the engine, keeping it as level as possible, to reduce fuel spillage from the fuel rail. Recover the four gaskets, and discard them - new ones must be used on installation **(see illustration)**. **Note:** Duratec (SVT) engines have a two-piece intake manifold. Separate the clamp and remove the outer manifold to access the bolts securing the inner manifold to the engine.

Installation

8 Installation is a reversal of removal, but note the following additional points:

a) Clean the mating faces of the intake manifold and cylinder head, and use new gaskets.
b) Tighten the nuts/bolts to the specified torque.
c) When the engine is fully warmed-up, check for signs of fuel, intake and/or vacuum leaks.
d) Road test the vehicle and check for proper operation of all disturbed components.

Exhaust manifold

Warning: The engine (and exhaust) must be completely cold before starting this procedure. Ideally, the vehicle should have been left to cool overnight.

Note: On models through 2004, the exhaust manifold is a separate component, while on later models it is integrated with the catalytic converter.

Removal

Refer to illustrations 16.11, 16.12a, 16.12b, 16.13a, 16.13b, 16.13c, 16.14a, 16.14b, 16.14c, 16.15, 16.16a, 16.16b, 16.17a, 16.17b and 16.17c

9 Disconnect the battery negative (ground) lead.

10 Apply the parking brake, then jack up

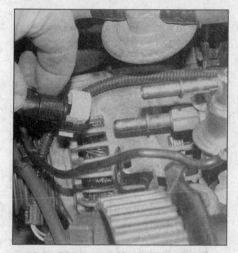

16.5c Disconnect the fuel supply line

the front of the car and support it on axle stands.

11 Disconnect the wiring plug from the oxygen sensor in the exhaust front pipe; the wiring plug is located above the radiator, and is bright green **(see illustration)**.

12 Unscrew the four bolts securing the exhaust manifold heat shield, and lift the

16.6 Removing one of the intake manifold studs

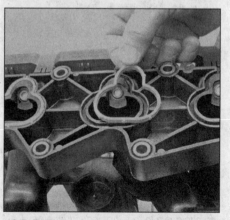

16.7 Replace the intake manifold gaskets

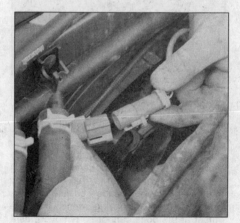

16.11 Disconnect the oxygen sensor wiring plug

16.12a Remove the four bolts (arrows) . . .

16.12b . . . and lift off the exhaust manifold heat shield

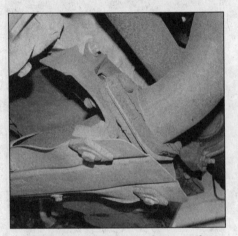

16.13a View of the rear clamp, at the exhaust front joint . . .

16.13b . . . and the two clamp bolts to be unscrewed (arrows)

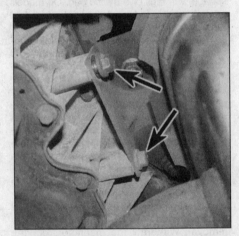

16.13c Catalytic converter clamp-to-cylinder block bolts (arrows) - seen from below

16.14a Unscrew the two nuts . . .

16.14b . . . and separate the exhaust front joint

16.14c Recover the joint gasket

shield off (see illustrations). It is quite likely that difficulty will be experienced removing the bolts, as corrosion may have effectively rounded-off the bolt heads - be sure to use a close-fitting socket or ring wrench from the outset. If the bolts cannot be removed, as a last resort, the heat shield will have to be destroyed to remove it - take care, however,

that the wiring for the oxygen sensor (installed just below the heat shield) is not damaged during this operation. **Note:** *On most models, the catalytic converter is mounted directly to the manifold. On Duratec (SVT) models, the manifold is a long set of individual pipes leading down to the converter, which is under the engine. On 2.3L and 2005 2.0L engines, the*

exhaust manifold is at the rear of the engine, not the radiator side.

13   Under the car, unscrew and remove the bolts securing the exhaust front pipe/catalytic converter support brackets - one bracket in front of the catalytic converter-to-center section joint, and one securing the catalytic converter clamp to the cylinder block (see illustrations).

16.15 Remove one of the power steering
pipe brackets

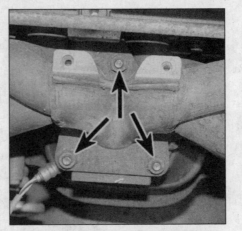

16.16a Loosen the three manifold-to-
catalytic converter nuts (arrows) . . .

16.16b . . . then carefully lower the
converter assembly

16.17a Remove the manifold from the studs . . .

16.17b . . . then recover the plastic sleeves . . .

14   Remove the nuts and separate the catalytic converter-to-center section joint; recover the gasket (see illustrations). Position a jack underneath the front pipe, to support it when the manifold-to-catalytic converter joint is separated.

15   Returning to the engine compartment, remove the two power steering pipe mounting brackets at either side of the manifold (see illustration).

16   Check that the jack under the front pipe is supporting its weight, then slowly loosen and remove the three nuts securing the catalytic converter to the manifold (new nuts must be used when installed). Use the jack to lower the front section of exhaust until the three studs are clear of the manifold, then recover the ring gasket and discard it. Lower the catalytic converter completely, and remove it from under the car (see illustrations). Treat the converter assembly with care - if handled roughly, the ceramic element inside may be fractured.

17   Unscrew and remove the six bolts and three nuts securing the manifold to the cylinder head. Withdraw the manifold from the studs; recover the metal gasket and the two

16.17c . . . and the metal gasket

plastic sleeves from the outer studs (see illustrations).

18 · Before lifting the converter into position, loosen the two bolts at the base of the front support bracket so that the rear half of the bracket is free to slide - once the converter is fully installed, these bolts can be tightened.

16.19 Install a new ring gasket to the
manifold joint

Installation

Refer to illustration 16.19

19   Installation is a reversal of removal, but fit new gaskets and tighten all nuts and bolts to the specified torque (see illustration).

17   Exhaust system - general information, removal and installation

General information

1   On models through 2004, the catalytic converter is mounted vertically, below the manifold. A short intermediate pipe, containing a flexible section, connects the converter to the factory-installed one-piece rear section, which contains the center and rear mufflers. To replace either muffler, the original rear section must be cut through mid-way between the center and rear mufflers.

2   Before making any cut, examine the replacement exhaust section for comparison, and if necessary, adjust the cutting points as required. Bear in mind that there must be some 'overlap' allowance, as the original and replacement sections are sleeved together.

3   The system is suspended throughout its entire length by rubber mountings. A rigid two-part clamp arrangement supports the catalytic converter.

4   To remove a part of the system, first jack up the front or rear of the car, and support it on axle stands (see *Jacking and Towing*). Alternatively, position the car over an inspection pit, or on car ramps.

5   The manufacturer recommends that all nuts (such as flange joint nuts, clamp joint nuts, or converter-to-manifold nuts) are replaced on reassembly - given that they may be in less-than-perfect condition as a result of corrosion, this seems a good idea, especially as it will make subsequent removal easier.

Catalytic converter

Removal

6   Refer to Section 16, Steps 11 to 18.

7   Before installing the converter, loosen the two bolts at the base of the front support bracket so that the rear half of the bracket is free to slide - once the converter is fully installed, these bolts can be tightened.

Installation

Refer to illustration 17.8

8   Installation is a reversal of removal. Clean up any sleeve joints before mating them together. Use new gaskets, nuts and bolts as necessary, and tighten all fasteners to the specified torque **(see illustration)**. **Note:** *Exhaust sealant paste should not be used on any part of the exhaust system upstream of the catalytic converter (between the engine and the converter) - even if the sealant does not contain additives harmful to the converter, pieces of it may break off and foul the element, causing local overheating.*

Intermediate pipe

Removal

9   To prevent possible damage to the flexible section of pipe in front of the second flange joint, dealer technicians cable-tie two

17.8 Install a new exhaust front joint gasket

strips of thick metal on either side, down the length of the flexible section.

10   Loosen and remove the nuts at the flange joints at either end of the pipe (new nuts should be used for reinstallation). When both ends are free, separate the joints.

11   Taking care not to bend or strain the flexible section excessively, lower the rear end of the pipe and withdraw it over the subframe and out from under the car. Recover the gasket at either end of the pipe, and discard them - new ones must be used when installing.

Installation

12   Installation is a reversal of removal. Use new gaskets and nuts, and tighten the flange joint nuts to the specified torque.

Center muffler

Removal

13   If the original rear section is still intact, it must be cut at a point between the center and rear mufflers. The cutting point is 80 inches back from the face of the flange joint in front of the center muffler; take care to cut the pipe at right-angles to the pipe (and to **only** cut the pipe); clean up any rough edges.

14   If a new rear muffler has been installed, there will be a clamped sleeve joint at the rear of the center muffler. Loosen the clamp nuts, but do not try to separate the sleeve joint at this stage.

15   Loosen and remove the nuts, and separate the exhaust at the flange joint in front of the center muffler (use new nuts on installation). Recover the gasket, and discard it - a new one must be used on installation.

16   Unhook the center muffler from its rubber mountings. If a sleeve joint is used at the rear, twist and pull the pipes to separate the joint. Remove the center muffler from under the car.

Installation - all models

17   Installation is a reversal of removal. Clean up any sleeve joints before mating them together. Use new gaskets and nuts, and tighten all fasteners to the specified torque.

Rear muffler

Removal

18   If the original exhaust rear section is still installed, it will be necessary to cut the pipe between the center and rear mufflers to install the service replacement section. The cutting point is 80 inches behind the face of the flange in front of the center muffler.

19   Bear in mind the advice in Step 3 before making any cut; take care to cut the pipe at right-angles to the pipe (and to **only** cut the pipe); clean up any rough edges.

20   Unhook the rear muffler from its mounting rubber(s).

21   If the rear muffler has been replaced previously, loosen the clamp nuts until the joint is free, then twist and pull the pipes relative to each other, to free and separate the sleeve joint.

22   Remove the rear muffler from under the car.

Installation

23   Installation is a reversal of removal. Clean up any sleeve joints before mating them together. Use new nuts (or a new clamp), and tighten the nuts to the specified torque.

Heat shield(s)

24   The heat shields are secured to the underside of the body by special nuts, or by bolts. A shield is installed below the catalytic converter, to reduce the risk of fire when parking over dry grass or leaves, for example - otherwise, the shields are installed above the exhaust, to reduce radiated heat affecting the cabin or fuel tank.

25   Each shield can be removed separately, but note that some overlap each other, making it necessary to loosen another section first. If a shield is being removed to gain access to a component located behind it, it may prove sufficient in some cases to remove the retaining nuts and/or bolts, and simply lower the shield, without disturbing the exhaust system. Otherwise, remove the exhaust section as described earlier.

Chapter 4 Part B
Emissions and engine control systems

Contents

Specifications

Torque specifications   Ft-lbs (unless otherwise indicated)

Note: *One foot-pound (ft-lb) of torque is equivalent to 12 inch-pounds (in-lbs) of torque. Torque values below approximately 15 ft-lbs are expressed in inch-pounds, since most foot-pound torque wrenches are not accurate at these smaller values.*

EGR clamp nut	84 in-lbs
EGR cooler mounting bolts	17
EGR pipe flange bolts	15
EGR pipe union nuts	30
EGR valve mounting bolts	15
Oxygen sensor	35

1   General information

Emission control systems

All models covered by this manual are designed to use unleaded gasoline, and are controlled by the EEC-V engine management system to give the best compromise between driveability, fuel consumption and exhaust emission production. In addition, a number of systems are installed that help to minimize other harmful emissions. A crankcase emission control system is installed, which reduces the release of pollutants from the engine's lubrication system, and a catalytic converter is installed which reduces exhaust gas pollutants. An evaporative loss emission control system is installed which reduces the release of gaseous hydrocarbons from the fuel tank. An Exhaust Gas Recirculation (EGR) system returns a portion of the exhaust gasses back to the combustion chamber, which reduces the combustion chamber temperature, and thus lowers the oxides of nitrogen (NOx) in the exhaust. On 2005 and later 2.0L engines, there is a Secondary Air Injection system to further reduce exhaust emissions.

Crankcase emission control

To reduce the emission of unburned hydrocarbons from the crankcase into the atmosphere, the engine is sealed and the blow-by gases and oil vapor are drawn from inside the crankcase, through a wire-mesh oil separator, into the intake tract to be burned by the engine during normal combustion.

Under all conditions, the gases are forced out of the crankcase by the (relatively) higher crankcase pressure.

Exhaust emission control

To minimize the amount of pollutants that escape into the atmosphere, all gasoline models are equipped with a three-way catalytic converter in the exhaust system. The fuel injection system is of the closed-loop type, in which an oxygen sensor in the exhaust system provides the engine management system PCM with constant feedback, enabling the PCM to adjust the air/fuel mixture to optimize combustion. Removal of the catalytic converter is covered in Chapter 4A.

The oxygen sensor has a built-in heating element, controlled by the PCM through the oxygen sensor relay, to quickly bring the sensor's tip to its optimum operating temperature. The sensor's tip is sensitive to oxygen, and sends a voltage signal to the PCM that varies according on the amount of oxygen in the exhaust gas. If the intake air/fuel mixture is too rich, the exhaust gases are low in oxygen so the sensor sends a low-voltage signal, the voltage rising as the mixture weakens and the amount of oxygen rises in the exhaust gases. Peak conversion efficiency of all major pollutants occurs if the intake air/fuel mixture is maintained at the chemically-correct ratio for the complete combustion of gasoline of 14.7 parts (by weight) of air to 1 part of fuel (the stoichiometric ratio). The sensor output voltage alters in a large step at this point, the PCM using the signal change as a reference point and correcting the intake air/fuel mixture accordingly by altering the fuel injector pulse width.

Models covered by this manual are equipped with two sensors, one before and one after the converter. This allows a more accurate monitoring of the exhaust gas, and a faster reaction time from the PCM; the efficiency of the converter can also be monitored.

An Exhaust Gas Recirculation (EGR) system is also used. This reduces the level of nitrogen oxides produced during combustion by introducing a proportion of the exhaust gas back into the intake manifold, under certain engine operating conditions, via a plunger valve. The system is controlled electronically by the engine management PCM.

Evaporative emission control

To minimize the escape of unburned hydrocarbons into the atmosphere, an evaporative loss emission control system is employed. The fuel tank filler cap is sealed and a charcoal canister is mounted behind the fuel tank to collect the gasoline vapors released from the fuel contained in the fuel tank. It stores them until they can be drawn from the canister (under the control of the fuel injection/ignition system PCM) via the purge valve(s) into the intake tract, where they are then burned by the engine during normal combustion.

2.2 Charcoal canister (arrow) at the rear of the fuel tank

2.3 Canister purge valve in the engine compartment

To ensure that the engine runs correctly when it is cold and/or idling and to protect the catalytic converter from the effects of an over-rich mixture, the purge control valve(s) are not opened by the PCM until the engine has warmed-up, and the engine is under load; the valve solenoid is then modulated on and off to allow the stored vapor to pass into the intake tract.

2   Evaporative loss emission control system - component replacement

Refer to illustrations 2.2 and 2.3

1   The evaporative loss emission control system consists of the purge valve, the activated charcoal filter canister and a series of connecting vacuum hoses. Little is possible by way of routine maintenance, except to check that the vacuum hoses are clear and undamaged. Careless servicing work may lead to the hoses becoming crushed - always take care to

route these and other hoses correctly.
2   The canister is located behind the fuel tank, under the car **(see illustration)**. Removal of the components is described as part of the fuel tank removal procedure, in Chapter 4A.
3   The purge valve is located at the right-hand rear of the engine compartment (right as seen from the driver's seat) **(see illustration)**. Disconnect the hoses (noting their positions) and wiring plug from the valve, then release it from its mounting bracket. Installation is a reversal of removal. **Note:** *On 2005 and later models, there is a heat shield over the purge valve. Remove the shield for access to the valve.*

3   Crankcase emission system - component replacement

1   The crankcase emission control (or positive crankcase ventilation - PCV) system consists of hoses connecting the crankcase to the

air cleaner or intake manifold. Oil separator units are used on some engines, usually at the left-hand end or on the front of the engine.
2   The system requires no attention other than to check at regular intervals that the hoses, valve and oil separator are free of blockages and in good condition.

PCV valve

Note: *Also refer to Chapter 1, Section 15 for more information about PCV valve replacement.*

3   To remove the PCV valve installed at the left-hand side of the engine (left as seen from the driver's seat), proceed as follows.
4   Access to the PCV valve is not easy. The valve is located behind the catalytic converter, and below the thermostat housing, in a raised section of the engine block at the far left-hand end of the engine, adjacent to the transmission. Trace the ventilation hose to the valve, and disconnect it.
5   The valve can be removed from its location by pulling it out.

3.11a Unscrew the three retaining bolts (arrows) . . .

3.11b . . . and remove the oil separator

3.13 When installing the oil separator, use a new gasket

4.3 EGR solenoid valve location on engine compartment firewall

6   If the hose connecting the PCV valve to the intake manifold is damaged, the thermostat housing must be removed for access, as described in Chapter 3.

7   Wash the valve in suitable solvent (such as engine degreaser), and ensure that all passages are clear. Check the hoses for signs of damage, especially at the hose ends. Where an O-ring is used to seal the valve into its location, check the condition of the O-ring before installation.

8   Installation is a reversal of removal. Make sure that the hoses are securely and correctly installed, and that the hoses are routed as before.

Oil separator

Refer to illustrations 3.11a, 3.11b and 3.13

9   The oil separator is located on the front of the engine block, behind the exhaust manifold and catalytic converter. To gain access, the exhaust manifold and catalytic converter will almost certainly have to be removed, as described in Chapter 4A.

10   Either disconnect the hose leading to the separator, or pull out the PCV valve.

11   The separator is secured by three bolts. Unscrew the bolts and remove the separator, recovering the gasket **(see illustrations)**.

12   If not already done, remove the PCV valve from the separator. Wash out the oil separator using a suitable solvent (such as engine degreaser), and ensure that its passages are clear.

13   Installation is a reversal of removal, reconnecting any electrical connectors disconnected. Use a new gasket, and tighten the retaining bolts securely **(see illustration)**.

4   Exhaust Gas Recirculation (EGR) system - component replacement

1   The EGR system consists of the EGR valve, the modulator (solenoid) valve and a series of connecting vacuum hoses. All models

have a differential pressure feedback sensor.

2   The EGR valve is mounted on a flange joint at the exhaust manifold, and is connected to a second flange joint at the throttle housing by a metal pipe.

EGR solenoid

Refer to illustration 4.3

3   The EGR solenoid is mounted centrally at the rear of the engine compartment, on the firewall **(see illustration)**.

4   Disconnect the vacuum hoses from the valve, noting their locations - the top hose leads to a connection at the air cleaner, while the two smaller hoses connect to the EGR valve itself and into the brake booster vacuum hose. Disconnect the wiring plug from the unit, then unscrew the two mounting bolts and remove it from the firewall.

5   Installation is a reversal of removal.

EGR valve

6   Remove the air cleaner outlet tube for room to access the EGR valve. On 2.3L and 2005 and later 2.0L engines, drain the cooling system (see Chapter 1) and disconnect the coolant hose from the EGR valve.

7   Disconnect the vacuum hose from the top of the valve, then loosen the clamp nut on the metal pipe at the base of the valve, and release the pipe connection (it may not be possible to fully separate the joint until the valve is removed).

8   Unscrew and remove the two valve mounting bolts, and withdraw the valve from its location. Recover the gasket, and discard it - a new one must be used when installing.

9   Installation is a reversal of removal, noting the following points:

a)   *Place the valve into position, using a new gasket, and tighten the mounting bolts hand-tight.*

b)   *Tighten the pipe union nut to the specified torque, then tighten the mounting bolts to the specified torque.*

EGR differential pressure sensor

10   The differential pressure sensor (where installed) is located on the engine compartment firewall, next to the EGR solenoid.

11   Note the positions of the vacuum hoses for installation (they are of different diameter), then disconnect them from the ports on the sensor.

12   Disconnect the sensor wiring plug, then unscrew the sensor mounting bolts and remove the sensor from its location.

13   Installation is a reversal of removal, making sure that the hoses are correctly installed.

EGR pipework

Exhaust manifold-to-EGR valve pipe

14   Loosen the pipe union nuts at either end of the pipe, and disconnect the vacuum hoses from the feed pipe connections halfway along the main pipe.

15   Withdraw the pipe from the rear of the engine.

16   Installation is a reversal of removal. Tighten the union nuts to the specified torque.

EGR valve supply pipe

17   Remove the EGR valve as described previously in this Section.

18   Unscrew and remove the two bolts securing the pipe flange below the EGR valve location, and separate the joint.

19   Unbolt and remove the engine lifting eye installed next to the ignition coil, then loosen the EGR pipe clamp bolt also located next to the coil.

20   Disconnect the wiring plugs from the ignition coil, and from the throttle position sensor. Also release the brake booster vacuum pipe connection at the front of the throttle housing by depressing the locking collar.

21   Unscrew and remove the two bolts securing the pipe flange at the throttle housing, and separate the joint. Recover the O-ring seal, and discard it - a new one must be used when installing.

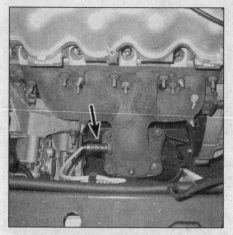

5.3 Heated oxygen sensor (arrow)

22 Withdraw the pipe from the engine, feeding it carefully past any obstructions, and noting how the various pipes and hoses are routed around it, for use when installing.
23 Installation is a reversal of removal. Use a new O-ring seal at the front flange joint, and tighten all bolts to the specified torque.

5   Oxygen sensors - removal and installation

Note: *There are two oxygen sensors, one before and one after the catalytic converter. The one before the converter is of the heated type. This enables more efficient monitoring of the exhaust gas, allowing a faster response time. The overall efficiency of the converter itself can also be checked.*

Removal

Refer to illustration 5.3

1 Remove the four bolts securing the heat shield to the exhaust manifold, and lift away the heat shield for access to the sensor (see Chapter 4A). **Note:** *It may be easier to remove the sensor if the engine has been warmed up first, but take care working around hot exhaust components.*
2 Trace the wiring from the sensor body back to its wiring plug, and disconnect it. On models with two sensors, the second sensor is located in the exhaust pipe, under the oil pan. Note how the wiring is routed, as it must not come into contact with hot exhaust components.
3 Unscrew the sensor from its location, and remove it **(see illustration)**. Once removed, take great care that the sensor is not dropped or damaged. Keep the sensor tip clean while it is removed. **Note:** *It is helpful to use a special socket, available at auto parts stores, to remove/replace an oxygen sensor.*

Installation

4 It may be beneficial to clean the sensor before installing it, especially if the sensor tip appears to be contaminated. However, great

care must be exercised, as the tip will be damaged by any abrasives, and by certain solvents. Seek the advice of a dealer before cleaning the sensor.
5 Installation is a reversal of removal, noting the following points:
a) Apply a little anti-seize compound to the sensor threads, taking care not to allow any on the sensor tip, and tighten the sensor to the specified torque.
b) Reconnect the wiring, ensuring that it is routed clear of any hot exhaust components.
c) If required, proof that the sensor is working can be gained by having the exhaust emissions checked, and compared with the figure quoted in Chapter 4A. Remember that a faulty sensor will have generated a fault code - if this code is still logged in the PCM electronic memory, the engine management system may still be in LOS (refer to Chapter 4A, Section 14).

6   Catalytic converter - general information, removal and installation

General information

1 The catalytic converter reduces harmful exhaust emissions by chemically converting the more poisonous gases to ones which (in theory at least) are less harmful. The chemical reaction is known as an 'oxidizing' reaction, or one where oxygen is 'added'.
2 Inside the converter is a honeycomb structure, made of ceramic material and coated with the precious metals palladium, platinum and rhodium (the 'catalyst' which promotes the chemical reaction). The chemical reaction generates heat, which itself promotes the reaction - therefore, once the car has been driven several miles, the body of the converter will be very hot.
3 The ceramic structure contained within the converter is understandably fragile, and will not withstand rough treatment. Since the converter runs at a high temperature, driving through deep water (in flood conditions, for example) is to be avoided, since the thermal stresses imposed when plunging the hot converter into cold water may well cause the ceramic internals to fracture, resulting in a 'blocked' converter - a common cause of failure. A converter which has been damaged in this way can be checked by shaking it (do not strike it) - if a rattling noise is heard, this indicates probable failure.

Precautions

4 The catalytic converter is a reliable and simple device which needs no maintenance in itself, but there are some facts of which an owner should be aware if the converter is to function properly for its full service life:

a) DO NOT use leaded gasoline (or lead-replacement gasoline) in a car equipped with a catalytic converter - the lead (or other additives) will coat the precious metals, reducing their converting efficiency and will eventually destroy the converter.
b) Always keep the ignition and fuel systems well-maintained in accordance with the routine maintenance schedule (see Chapter 1).
c) If the engine develops a misfire, do not drive the car at all (or at least as little as possible) until the fault is cured.
d) DO NOT push- or tow-start the car - this will soak the catalytic converter in unburned fuel, causing it to overheat when the engine does start.
e) DO NOT switch off the ignition at high engine speeds - i.e., do not 'blip' the throttle immediately before switching off the engine.
f) DO NOT use fuel or engine oil additives - these may contain substances harmful to the catalytic converter.
g) DO NOT continue to use the car if the engine burns oil to the extent of leaving a visible trail of blue smoke.
h) Remember that the catalytic converter operates at very high temperatures. DO NOT, therefore, park the car in dry undergrowth, over long grass or piles of dead leaves after a long run.
i) As mentioned above, driving through deep water should be avoided if possible. The sudden cooling effect may fracture the ceramic honeycomb, damaging it beyond repair.
j) Remember that the catalytic converter is FRAGILE - do not strike it with tools during servicing work, and take care handling it when removing it from the car for any reason.
k) In some cases, a sulphurous smell (like that of rotten eggs) may be noticed from the exhaust. This is common to many catalytic converter-equipped cars, and has more to do with the sulfur content of the brand of fuel being used than the converter itself.
l) If a substantial loss of power is experienced, remember that this could be due to the converter being blocked. This can occur simply as a result of high mileage, but may be due to the ceramic element having fractured and collapsed internally (see Step 3). A new converter is the only cure in this instance.
m) The catalytic converter, used on a well-maintained and well-driven car, should last for between 50,000 and 100,000 miles - if the converter is no longer effective, it must be replaced.

Removal and installation

5 The catalytic converter is part of the exhaust system - refer to the relevant Section of Chapter 4A.

7   Secondary Air Injection system

General information

1   The secondary air injection system reduces hydrocarbons (HC) and carbon monoxide (CO) during cold starts, when the catalytic converter has not yet reached operating temperature, and helps warm up the catalyst more quickly by pumping air into the hot exhaust stream, which raises the temperature of the exhaust gasses. When the hot exhaust gasses are combined with more air, oxygen in that air helps to burn up any HC and CO not already consumed during combustion.

2   The system consists of the air pump, air pump solenoid, shutoff valve, several check valves, pipes and hoses connecting the pump, a shutoff valve and relay (located in the engine compartment fuse and relay box) and the Powertrain Control Module (PCM).

3   The air pump is an electrically-driven device, and its circuit is controlled by the PCM. With information from the Intake Air Temperature sensor and other sensors, the PCM determines when to energize the relay, which sends voltage to the pump.

4   The air pump solenoid controls vacuum to the shutoff valve. When the PCM turns on the relay, intake manifold vacuum is admitted to the shutoff valve.

5   Because the secondary air injection system seldom operates for more than a minute at a time, the system should prove to be reliable and trouble-free. If you have a Check Engine light, use a code reader to determine if there is a trouble code related to the system. If you have a code related to one of the system components, the following procedures will tell you how to replace it.

Component replacement

Secondary Air system check valve

6   Locate the vacuum check valve in the vacuum line between the throttle body and the pump solenoid valve.

7   To remove the check valve, simply disconnect the vacuum lines from both ends of the valve. Remove the two mounting bolts.

8   Installation is the reverse of removal. Make sure the side that is labeled "VAC" is facing towards the vacuum source (the throttle body). The other hose goes to the pump.

Secondary Air system pump

9   Remove the right-hand headlight assembly (see Chapter 12). The pump is located under the right side of the right frame rail.

10   Mark the hose locations, then unclip the hoses and disconnect them.

11   Disconnect the vacuum hose to the pump.

12   Disconnect the electrical connector.

13   Remove the mounting bolts for the pump assembly at the frame rail and lift up the pump to remove it.

14   Installation is the reverse of removal.

8   On-Board Diagnostic system (OBD-II) and diagnostic trouble codes

OBD-II system general description

The U.S. Environmental Protection Agency (EPA) and the California Air Resources Board (CARB) are the government agencies primarily responsible for the second generation of onboard diagnostic systems, known as OBD-II. Auto manufacturers started to introduce OBD-II systems on some 1994 models, and they became standard on 1996 and later vehicles. OBD-II systems differ from earlier onboard diagnostic systems in the following major ways:

a)   *Specific programmed self-tests, called "system monitors," that let the PCM test the operation of subsystems and components.*

b)   *A standard list of basic system operating data, called system "parameters," transmitted by the PCM to a diagnostic scan tool.*

c)   *A standardized library of diagnostic trouble codes (DTC) used by all carmakers.*

d)   *A standardized diagnostic connector, called a data link connector (DLC), used by all auto manufacturers.*

Onboard diagnostic systems before OBD-II had a wide variety of test capabilities, operating parameter information (or lack of it), and trouble code displays. No two auto manufacturers provided exactly the same kind of information. OBD-II is an attempt to standardize diagnostic capabilities worldwide and to ensure that all vehicles provide minimum basic information to promote more accurate repairs and more reliable emission control. Although all auto manufacturers must meet the basic requirements of OBD-II, they also are free to provide enhanced diagnostic capabilities of their own design for their vehicle electronic systems. OBD-II is not an electronic control system, nor is it separate from any vehicle's engine management system. Rather, OBD-II is a set of diagnostic requirements that each auto manufacturer must incorporate into its particular electronic control system.

OBD-II System Monitors

The OBD-II system "monitors" are self-tests programmed into the EEC-V PCM. An OBD-II system can perform up to 11 emission system monitor tests. Three of these monitors run continuously whenever the vehicle is being operated. They are: misfire detection, fuel system monitoring, and comprehensive component monitoring. The PCM performs other monitors, known as noncontinuous monitors, once per trip. These are: catalytic converter, evaporative emissions, secondary air, oxygen sensor, oxygen sensor heater, and EGR system monitors. The PCM also may have a monitor test for the air conditioning system to detect refrigerant leakage.

Monitor tests occur during a key-on, engine-run, key-off cycle when certain operating conditions, or enabling criteria, are met. Test criteria include information such as elapsed time since startup, engine speed, throttle position, engine coolant temperature, and vehicle speed. Any driving cycle that includes an emission monitor test is called a trip. Clearing DTC memory following repairs also clears monitor results from memory.

The PCM starts, directs, processes, and communicates the results of monitor tests using a software program called the "diagnostic executive," or simply the "executive." The diagnostic executive performs the emission monitor tests on each vehicle trip. Specific driving requirements must be met to start and finish each monitor. Often, the executive must delay completion of a monitor because not all criteria are met. The executive can delay a monitor for several reasons. Delays fall into three categories: (1) suspended, (2) pending, and (3) conflicting.

A test can be suspended when another test with a higher priority takes precedence. All of the emission self-tests are prioritized, and the executive may suspend a low-priority monitor so that one with higher priority can run. The executive only runs some secondary tests after the system passes certain primary tests. When the secondary tests are delayed, awaiting primary test results, they are pending. Conflicts also can occur as different monitors use the same circuits or components. In such cases, the executive requires each test to finish before allowing another to begin.

The diagnostic executive conducts three types of tests: (1) passive, (2) active, and (3) intrusive. A passive test monitors a system or component without affecting its operation. If a passive test fails, an active test will start. During an active test, the PCM sends a test signal on the suspect circuit so that it can evaluate the response. Active testing does not disable the component or suspend control system operation. Intrusive tests do affect engine performance and emissions, and the executive performs these tests only after the passive and active tests both fail.

When a monitor test ends, a pass or fail report is recorded in PCM memory by the diagnostic executive. Most monitor failures do not set a DTC and light the MIL unless failure occurs during two consecutive trips. When checking monitor test status with a scan tool, the scan tool display can read complete or not complete, supported or not supported.

Misfire monitor

Poor cylinder combustion that causes engine misfire also causes an increase of HC emissions in the exhaust. The excess HC that results from a misfire also can overload the catalytic converters and accelerate their deterioration. The OBD-II system checks for, and alerts the driver, of an engine misfire that could damage the converter or raise emissions above standards.

Whenever a cylinder misfires, combustion pressure drops momentarily and slows down the piston. Because this retarded piston movement also slows the crankshaft, the CKP sensor can detect engine misfire. The CKP signal of a running engine produces a predictable waveform with evenly spaced peaks. When a misfire slows the crankshaft, it interrupts the even spacing of the waveform cycles. By comparing the CKP and CMP sensor signals, the PCM also can determine which cylinder misfired.

To prevent a false DTC from occurring from conditions that mimic a misfire, such as excessive driveline vibration caused by rough roads, the monitor maintains a misfire counter for each cylinder, which records the number of misfires that occurred during the past 200 and 1000 crankshaft revolutions. Whenever the monitor reports a misfire, the diagnostic executive program checks all of the cylinder misfire counters. A DTC sets only if one or more of the counters has significantly more misfire counts than the others.

OBD-II has two categories of misfire: those that can damage the catalytic converter, and those that can cause exhaust emissions to exceed federal standards by more than 50 percent. The executive sets a DTC immediately and flashes the MIL if the monitor detects misfire in more than 15 percent of the cylinder firings during 200 crankshaft revolutions. This is a type A misfire. A less serious type B misfire, is one in which two percent of the cylinder firing opportunities misfire during 1000 crankshaft revolutions. The executive sets a DTC and lights the MIL if a type B misfire occurs during two consecutive trips.

Fuel system monitor

The EEC-V system uses two fuel control parameters: short-term fuel trim (STFT) and long-term fuel trim (LTFT). The OBD-II diagnostic executive monitors how well the PCM is regulating the air/fuel mixture. The fuel-trim values indicate how much fuel is being added to, or removed from, the mixture to keep the engine running at peak efficiency. Fuel-trim factors are a PCM response based on feedback from the HO2S and other system inputs. Short-term fuel trim responds immediately to a change in operating conditions; long-term fuel trim reacts more slowly in response to general trends.

The fuel system monitor will detect when fuel trim is operating at the limits and can no longer compensate for operating conditions that lead to an overly rich or lean air/fuel mixtures. The OBD-II fuel system monitor measures fuel trim as a percentage. A fuel system monitor failure must occur on two consecutive trips before a DTC sets and the MIL lights.

Comprehensive component monitor

The comprehensive component monitor checks PCM input and output signals for malfunctions affecting any component or circuit not evaluated by another monitor. Typically, the PCM looks for open or short circuits and

for out-of-range values. Additionally, "rationality" test check input signals, and "functionality" tests check output circuits to compare signals from one device with those of another.

Catalytic converter monitor

The PCM uses signals from two heated oxygen sensors (HO2S), one upstream and the other downstream from each catalytic converter, to evaluate converter operation. By comparing voltage signals of the downstream HO2S and the upstream HO2S, the PCM calculates how much oxygen each catalyst retains. With a good catalyst, a voltage signal from the downstream HO2S will have little switching activity, while the voltage signal from the upstream HO2S crosses the midpoint of the operating range vigorously. The more that downstream HO2S activity matches that of the upstream HO2S, the greater the degree of converter deterioration.

Oxygen sensor monitor

This monitor runs several tests by evaluating data from the heater circuit reference signals from each sensor. The upstream (precatalyst) HO2S monitor checks for high and low threshold voltage and switching frequency. Switching frequency, or crosscounts, is the number of times the signal voltage crosses the midpoint of the sensor signal range during a specific time. An HO2S monitor also evaluates sensor response by measuring the time required to perform a lean-to-rich and a rich-to-lean transition. The PCM compares test results to previously stored values. Because downstream (post-catalyst) O2S voltage fluctuations are slight and the signal seldom crosses the midpoint of the range, the monitor samples voltage level under lean and rich operation. During rich-running conditions, the monitor looks for a fixed, low-voltage signal from the downstream sensor. During lean conditions, the monitor looks for downstream HO2S voltage to stay high and steady. The diagnostic executive lights the MIL to alert the driver of a malfunction, if an HO2S monitor fails on two consecutive trips.

Evaporative emission system monitor

The OBD-II evaporative emission system monitor checks for canister purge volume and leakage. Most systems use a solenoid-operated purge valve to vent vapors from the charcoal canister to the intake manifold during cruising. Typically, the PCM closes the system to atmospheric pressure and opens the purge valve to begin an evaporative monitor test. A pressure sensor on the fuel tank sends information to the PCM on how fast vacuum increases in the system. The PCM uses this pressure sensor feedback to calculate purge flow rate. To perform a vapor leak test, the PCM closes the purge valve to create a sealed system. Any leakage in the system will cause pressure to drop, and this pressure change is reported to the PCM by the pressure sensor. An evaporative failure

8.26 The Data Link Connector (DLC) is located under the driver's side of the dash

must occur on two consecutive trips before a DTC sets and the MIL lights.

EGR system monitor

The EGR monitor tests EGR flow and determines if the system is operating efficiently. To do this, the PCM opens and closes the EGR valve while monitoring the amount of change in the EGR sensor voltage signal. The monitor then calculates EGR system efficiency by comparing these live samples to values in the lookup tables that correspond to exhaust gas flow. If the EGR efficiency level does not meet the programmed standard in two consecutive trips, the MIL lights and a DTC sets.

Freeze frame

Freeze frame is an OBD-II PCM feature that records all related sensor and actuator activity on the PCM data stream whenever an emission fault is detected and a DTC is set. After it is created, the freeze frame is stored in PCM memory where it can be retrieved for later analysis on a scan tool. This ability to look at the circuit conditions and values when a fault occurs is a valuable tool when troubleshooting an intermittent problem.

Drive Cycles

For a complete test of the system, the engine must be running at normal operating temperature; but some initial tests can be done on a cold engine. For some procedures, such as troubleshooting a no-start problem, you must start with a cold engine. Other examples include problems that only occur when the engine is cold or operating in open loop. Often, you can check engine operation immediately after a cold start and then monitor engine performance as it goes into closed loop.

Before it will allow an emissions certification test, the PCM must receive a pass from all of the onboard monitors. These monitors test the integrity of emission system components at various speeds, loads, and temperatures during normal driving conditions. With an onboard monitor test suspended, pending, or conflicting, the vehicle must be driven through a specific drive cycle to perform all of the emission control monitor checks. The system must complete and pass all of the monitors.

These warm-up conditioning procedures are an important part of troubleshooting. You can view data parameter values on a scan tool during the drive cycle, and a DTC will set if a fault occurs. Look for unusual circuit activity, such as high or low signals, voltage dropouts, and a lack of switching. When you spot a problem on one circuit, also look for unusual activity on related circuits. After all repairs are made, retest to verify that the problem is gone and then clear the DTC memory. Code clearing is a scan tool function that resets all monitors.

Malfunction indicator lamp

Although it may still be labeled CHECK ENGINE, the warning lamp on the instrument panel is called the malfunction indicator lamp (MIL) in an OBD-II system. The PCM lights the MIL when an emission control malfunction occurs or when a system or component fails one of the OBD-II self-test monitors as described previously. Other EEC-V system problems also may light the MIL, but not all diagnostic trouble codes (DTC) cause the MIL to light. That is, you may find a DTC stored in the PCM memory with no indication on the MIL.

Unlike the CHECK ENGINE lamp on older vehicles, the MIL on an OBD-II system will not always turn off when an intermittent problem goes away. If the PCM detects an emission control problem on two consecutive trips and lights the MIL, it will stay lit until the problem is fixed, the system passes the related self-test monitor, and the MIL is turned off by a scan tool. Additionally, DTC's cannot be made to flash on the MIL as was possible with some diagnostic systems on older vehicles.

Data link connector

Refer to illustration 8.26

Another standardized component required by OBD-II is the 16-pin data link connector (DLC) located under the driver's side of the instrument panel **(see illustration)**. This DLC replaces the variety of diagnostic connectors used by auto manufacturers before OBD-II. Diagnostic information can be obtained through the DLC only by using a scan tool that is compatible with OBD-II.

Diagnostic equipment

Refer to illustrations 8.28 and 8.29

Some diagnostic equipment for engine and emission control systems costs several thousands of dollars and is not practical for the home mechanic. Several equipment companies, however, are building more and more electronic test equipment that is intended for the do-it-yourself mechanic and is available at economical prices.

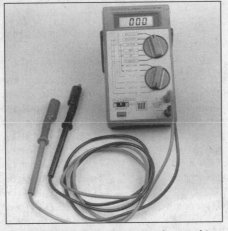

8.28 Digital multimeters can be used to test all types of circuits. Because of their high impedance, they are more accurate than analog meters for measuring voltage in low-voltage circuits

Digital multimeter

A digital volt-ohm-ammeter, or multimeter, is necessary instead of an analog meter for several reasons. An analog meter cannot display voltage, ohms, or amperage measurements in increments of hundredths and thousandths of a unit. When working with electronic systems, which are usually very low-voltage circuits, this kind of precise reading is most important. Another good reason for the digital multimeter is its high input impedance. The digital multimeter has high-resistance internal circuitry of 10 million ohms or more. Because a voltmeter is connected in parallel with the circuit when testing, none of the voltage being measured should drop across the parallel path of the meter. If you are measuring a low-voltage circuit, such as the HO2S signal voltage, a fraction of a volt is a significant amount when diagnosing a problem **(see illustration)**.

Scan tool

A hand-held scan tool, or scanner, is a small test computer that communicates with the vehicle PCM. Scanners originally were intended for professional driveability technicians and cost several thousand dollars. Today, several equipment companies are building more economical scanners for the home mechanic. Many of these relatively economical scan tools are compatible with OBD-II systems **(see illustration)**.

An OBD-II scan tool communicates with the vehicle PCM and reads DTC's, as well as system operating parameters. Basic OBD-II diagnostic capabilities consist of reading standard DTC's and the basic list of operating parameters. These are called "generic OBD-II tests" and usually are available from any scan tool compatible with OBD-II. Some scan tools also include advanced OBD-II tests for specific carmakers' systems. If you are considering the purchase of a scanner, be

8.29 Scanners like the Actron Scantool and the AutoXray XP240 are powerful diagnostic aids - programmed with comprehensive diagnostic information, they can tell you just about anything you want to know about your engine management system

sure that it has at least the generic OBD-II capabilities. Then consider whether it has advanced OBD-II capabilities for your vehicle and decide if the price justifies its usefulness. Many scanners can be revised, or updated, with interchangeable cartridges. Others can be reprogrammed easily and economically by the tool distributor.

Diagnostic trouble codes (DTC)

This OBD-II system uses the same library of standardized DTC's used in other manufacturers OBD-II systems, worldwide. The OBD-II DTC's are five-digit, alphanumeric codes. Each DTC begins with a letter, such as P for powertrain. The second digit is either a 0 if the code is a generic, or universal code, used by all auto manufacturers or a 1 if it is unique manufacturer's code. The last three digits indicate the subsystem and circuit or component where the fault has been detected.

OBD-II DTC's can only be read from the PCM memory through the DLC, using a scan tool that is compatible with OBD-II. The DTC's cannot be flashed on the MIL or displayed in any way other than through an OBD-II scan tool.

Clearing codes

To clear a DTC from the PCM memory, connect an OBD-II scan tool to the DLC and follow the tool manufacturer's instructions. Remember that the MIL cannot be turned off for an emission-related DTC until the system passes the appropriate OBD-II self-test monitor.

Do not disconnect the battery to clear the DTC's. It won't work, but it will erase stored operating parameters from the PCM memory and cause the engine to run roughly for some time while the PCM relearns the information.

OBD-II Trouble Codes

Code	Probable cause
P0053	HO2S sensor 1, heater resistance
P0054	HO2S sensor 2, heater resistance
P0102	Mass Airflow (MAF) sensor circuit low input
P0103	Mass Airflow (MAF) sensor circuit high input
P0106	Barometric Pressure sensor circuit performance
P0107	Barometric Pressure sensor circuit low voltage
P0108	Barometric Pressure sensor circuit high voltage
P0109	Barometric Pressure sensor circuit intermittent
P0112	Intake Air Temperature (IAT) sensor circuit low input
P0113	Intake Air Temperature (IAT) sensor circuit high input
P0116	ECT sensor, circuit performance
P0117	Electronic Coolant Temperature (ECT) sensor circuit low input
P0118	Electronic Coolant Temperature (ECT) sensor circuit high input
P0121	In range Throttle Position Sensor (TPS) fault
P0122	Throttle Position Sensor (TPS) circuit low input
P0123	Throttle Position Sensor (TPS) circuit high input
P0125	Insufficient coolant temperature
P0127	Intake Air temperature sensor "A" circuit
P0131	Upstream heated O2 sensor circuit low voltage (Bank 1)
P0133	Upstream heated O2 sensor circuit slow response (Bank 1)
P0135	Upstream heated O2 sensor heater circuit fault (Bank 1)
P0136	Downstream heated O2 sensor fault (Bank 1)
P0141	Downstream heated O2 sensor heater circuit fault (Bank 1)
P0151	Upstream heated O2 sensor circuit low voltage (Bank 2)
P0153	Upstream heated O2 sensor circuit slow response (Bank 2)
P0155	Upstream heated O2 sensor heater circuit fault (Bank 2)
P0156	Downstream heated O2 sensor fault (Bank 2)
P0161	Downstream heated O2 sensor heater circuit fault (Bank 2)
P0171	System Adaptive fuel too lean (Bank 1)
P0172	System Adaptive fuel too rich (Bank 1)
P0174	System Adaptive fuel too lean (Bank 2)
P0175	System Adaptive fuel too rich (Bank 2)
P0176	Flexible Fuel sensor "A" circuit
P0181	Engine Fuel Temperature sensor "A" circuit range
P0182	Engine Fuel Temperature sensor "A" circuit low input
P0183	Engine Fuel Temperature sensor "A" circuit high input
P0186	Engine Fuel Temperature sensor "B" circuit range
P0187	Engine Fuel Temperature sensor "B" circuit low input
P0188	Engine Fuel Temperature sensor "B" circuit high input
P0190	Fuel Rail Pressure sensor circuit performance
P0191	Injector Pressure sensor system performance
P0192	Injector Pressure sensor circuit low input
P0193	Injector Pressure sensor circuit high input
P0300	Random misfire
P0301	Cylinder no. 1 misfire detected
P0302	Cylinder no. 2 misfire detected
P0303	Cylinder no. 3 misfire detected
P0304	Cylinder no. 4 misfire detected
P0320	Ignition Engine Speed input circuit performance
P0324	Knock sensor, module performance
P0325	Knock sensor circuit fault

Code	Probable cause
P0326	Knock sensor circuit performance
P0328	Knock sensor, circuit, high voltage
P0330	Knock sensor 2 circuit malfunction
P0331	Knock sensor 2 range
P0340	Camshaft Position sensor circuit malfunction
P0350	Ignition coil primary/secondary circuit malfunction
P0351	Ignition coil no. 1 primary circuit fault
P0352	Ignition coil no. 2 primary circuit fault
P0353	Ignition coil no. 3 primary circuit fault
P0354	Ignition coil no. 4 primary circuit fault
P0355	Ignition coil E, control circuit
P0400	EGR flow fault
P0401	EGR insufficient flow detected
P0402	EGR excessive flow detected
P0411	Secondary Air Injection system upstream flow
P0412	Secondary Air Injection system circuit malfunction
P0418	Secondary Air Injection system, pump control circuit
P0420	Catalyst system efficiency below threshold (Bank 1)
P0421	Catalyst system efficiency below threshold (Bank 1)
P0430	Catalyst system efficiency below threshold (Bank 2)
P0431	Catalyst system efficiency below threshold (Bank 2)
P0442	EVAP small leak detected
P0443	EVAP VMV circuit fault
P0451	FTP sensor circuit noisy
P0452	EVAP fuel tank pressure sensor low input
P0453	EVAP fuel tank pressure sensor high input
P0455	EVAP Control system leak detected, very small leak
P0457	EVAP Control system leak detected, fuel filler cap loose/off
P0460	Fuel Level sensor circuit malfunction
P0500	VSS malfunction
P0501	VSS range
P0502	VSS intermittent
P0505	IAC valve system fault
P0552	Power Steering Pressure sensor circuit malfunction
P0553	Power Steering Pressure sensor circuit malfunction
P0567	Cruise control system, Resume switch circuit
P0568	Cruise control system, Set switch circuit
P0602	Control Module programming error
P0603	PCM Keep Alive Memory test error
P0605	PCM Read Only Memory test error
P0615	Starter relay, control circuit
P0700	Transmission Control Module, request for MIL light
P0703	Brake switch circuit input malfunction
P0716	Transmission input speed sensor, circuit performance
P0717	Transmission input speed sensor, circuit low voltage
P0720	Output Shaft Speed sensor, insufficient input
P0806	Clutch Pedal Position sensor, circuit performance
P0807	Clutch Pedal Position sensor, circuit low voltage
P0808	Clutch Pedal Position sensor, circuit high voltage
P0851	Park/Neutral position switch, circuit low voltage
P0852	Park/Neutral position switch, circuit high voltage
P0961	Transmission line pressure control solenoid, system performance

Chapter 5 Part A
Starting and charging systems

Contents

Specifications

General
Battery voltage
Engine off .... 12.0 to 12.6 volts
Engine running .... 13.5 to 14.7

Torque specifications   Ft-lbs
Alternator mounting fasteners 33
Starter motor mounting bolts
2.0L engines through 2004 26
2.3L and 2005 2.0L engines 18
All 2006 and later models 26

---

1 General information, precautions and battery disconnection

General information

The engine electrical systems include all ignition, charging and starting components. Because of their engine-related functions, these components are discussed separately from body electrical devices such as the lights, the instruments, etc (which are included in Chapter 12).

Precautions

Always observe the following precautions when working on the electrical system:

a) Be extremely careful when servicing engine electrical components. They are easily damaged if handled, connected or checked improperly.

b) Never leave the ignition switched on for long periods of time when the engine is not running.

c) Do not disconnect the battery leads while the engine is running.

d) Maintain correct polarity when connecting a battery lead from another vehicle during jump starting - see the 'Jump starting' Section at the front of this manual.

e) Always disconnect the negative cable first, and reconnect it last, or the battery may be shorted by the tool being used to loosen the cable clamps.

It's also a good idea to review the safety-related information regarding the engine electrical systems located in the 'Safety first!' section at the front of this manual, before beginning any operation included in this Chapter.

Battery disconnection

Several systems on the vehicle require battery power to be available at all times, either to ensure their continued operation (such as the clock) or to maintain control unit memories (such as that in the engine management system's PCM) which would be wiped if the battery were to be disconnected. Whenever the battery is to be disconnected, first note the following, to ensure that there are no unforeseen consequences of this action:

a) First, on any vehicle with central locking, it is a wise precaution to remove the key from the ignition, and to keep it with you, so that it does not get locked in if the central locking should engage accidentally when the battery is reconnected.

b) The engine management system's PCM will lose the information stored in its memory - referred to by the manufacturer as the 'KAM' (Keep-Alive Memory) - when the battery is disconnected. This includes idling and operating values, and any fault codes detected - in the case of the fault codes, if it is thought likely that the system has developed a fault for which the corresponding code has been logged, the vehicle must be taken to a dealer for the codes to be read, using the special diagnostic equipment necessary for this (see Chapter 4A, Section 14). Whenever the battery is disconnected, the information relating to idle speed control and other operating values will have to be re-programmed into the unit's memory. The PCM does this by itself, but until then, there may be surging, hesitation, erratic idle and a generally inferior level of performance. To allow the PCM to relearn these values, start the engine and run it as close to idle speed as possible until it reaches its normal operating temperature, then run it for approximately two minutes at 1200 rpm. Next, drive the vehicle as far as necessary - approximately 5 miles of varied driving conditions is usually sufficient - to complete the relearning process.

2.3 Battery retaining bolt (arrow)

c) If the battery is disconnected while the alarm system is armed or activated, the alarm will remain in the same state when the battery is reconnected. The same applies to the engine immobilizer system (if equipped).

d) If a trip computer is in use, any information stored in memory will be lost.

e) If a dealer Keycode audio unit is installed, and the unit and/or the battery is disconnected, the unit will not function again on reconnection until the correct security code is entered. Details of this procedure, which varies according to the unit and model year, are given in the Audio Systems Operating Guide supplied with the vehicle when new, with the code itself being given in a Radio Passport and/or a Keycode Label at the same time. Ensure you have the correct code before you disconnect the battery. For obvious security reasons, the procedure is not given in this manual. If you do not have the code or details of the correct procedure, but can supply proof of ownership and a legitimate reason for wanting this information, the vehicle's selling dealer may be able to help.

Devices known as 'memory-savers' (or 'code-savers') can be used to avoid some of the above problems. Precise details vary according to the device used. Typically, it is plugged into the cigarette lighter, and is connected by its own wires to a spare battery; the vehicle's own battery is then disconnected from the electrical system, leaving the 'memory-saver' to pass sufficient current to maintain audio unit security codes and PCM memory values, and also to run permanently-live circuits such as the clock, all the while isolating the battery in the event of a short-circuit occurring while work is carried out.

Warning 1: *Some of these devices allow a considerable amount of current to pass, which can mean that many of the vehicle's systems are still operational when the main battery is disconnected. If a 'memory-saver' is used, ensure that the circuit concerned is actually 'dead' before carrying out any work on it.*

Warning 2: *Do NOT use a memory-saver device when working on or near airbag system components.*

2   Battery - removal, installation, testing and charging

Removal

Refer to illustration 2.3

1   Unclip the battery cover, if equipped, and remove.

2   Disconnect the battery cables, negative cable first - see Section 1.

3   Remove the battery hold-down strap **(see illustration)**. Some models have a hold-down clamp securing it to the bottom of the tray. Remove the bolt and the clamp. On 2006 and later models, the battery clamp is on top of the battery.

4   Lift out the battery. **Caution:** *The battery is heavy.*

5   While the battery is out, inspect and clean the battery tray. If there are any white corrosion deposits on the tray, clean it with a solution of baking soda and water, then wipe dry.

6   If you are replacing the battery, make sure that you get one that's identical, with the same dimensions, amperage rating, cold cranking rating, etc. Dispose of the old battery in a responsible fashion. Most communities have facilities for the collection and disposal of such items - batteries contain sulfuric acid and lead, and must not be simply thrown out with the household garbage.

Installation

7   Installation is the reverse of the removal procedure. **Note:** *After the battery has been disconnected, the engine management system requires approximately 5 miles of driving to relearn its optimum settings. During this period, the engine may not perform normally.*

Testing
Standard and low maintenance battery

8   If the vehicle covers a small annual mileage it is worthwhile checking the specific gravity of the electrolyte every three months to determine the state of charge of the battery. Use a hydrometer to make the check and compare the results with the accompanying table.

9   If the battery condition is suspect, first check the specific gravity of electrolyte in each cell. A variation of 0.040 or more between any cells indicates loss of electrolyte or deterioration of the internal plates.

10   If the specific gravity variation is 0.040 or more, the battery should be replaced. If the cell variation is satisfactory but the battery is discharged, it should be charged, as described later in this Section.

Maintenance-free battery

11   In cases where a 'sealed for life' maintenance-free battery is installed, topping-off and testing of the electrolyte in each cell is not possible. The condition of the battery can therefore only be tested using a battery condition indicator or a voltmeter.

12   Certain models may be equipped with a maintenance-free battery, with a built-in charge condition indicator. The indicator is located in the top of the battery casing, and indicates the condition of the battery from its color. On factory batteries, if the indicator shows green, then the battery is in a good state of charge. If the indicator shows red, then the battery requires charging, as described later in this Section. Other battery manufacturers use different color-coding - refer to their information.

All battery types

13   If testing the battery using a voltmeter, connect the voltmeter across the battery. The test is only accurate if the battery has not been subjected to any kind of charge for the previous six hours. If this is not the case, switch on the headlights for 30 seconds, then wait four to five minutes before testing the battery after switching off the headlights. All other electrical circuits must be switched off, so check that the doors and trunk/liftgate are fully shut when making the test.

14   If the voltage reading is less than 12 volts, then the battery is discharged, while a reading of 12 to 12.4 volts indicates a partially discharged condition.

Ambient temperature:	above 77°F	below 77°F
Fully charged	1.210 to 1.230	1.270 to 1.290
70% charged	1.170 to 1.190	1.230 to 1.250
Discharged	1.050 to 1.070	1.110 to 1.130

Note that the specific gravity readings assume an electrolyte temperature of 80°F for every 10°F below 80°F subtract 0.004. For every 10°F above 80°F add 0.004.

15 If the battery is to be charged, remove it from the vehicle and charge it as described below.

Charging

Note: *The following is intended as a guide only. Always refer to the manufacturer's recommendations (often printed on a label attached to the battery) before charging a battery.*

Standard and low maintenance battery

16 Charge the battery at a rate equivalent to 10% of the battery capacity (e.g., for a 45Ah battery, charge at 4.5A) and continue to charge the battery at this rate until no further rise in specific gravity is noted over a four hour period.

17 Alternatively, a trickle charger charging at the rate of 1.5 amps can safely be used overnight.

18 Specially rapid 'boost' charges that are claimed to restore the power of the battery in 1 to 2 hours are not recommended, as they can cause serious damage to the battery plates through overheating.

19 While charging the battery, note that the temperature of the electrolyte should never exceed 100°F.

Maintenance-free battery

20 This battery type takes considerably longer to fully recharge than the standard type, the time taken being dependent on the extent of discharge, but it can take up to three days.

21 A constant voltage type charger is required, to be set, when connected, to 13.9 to 14.9 volts with a charger current below 25 amps. Using this method, the battery should be re-usable within three hours, giving a voltage reading of 12.5 volts, but this is for a partially discharged battery and, as mentioned, full charging can take considerably longer.

22 If the battery is to be charged from a fully discharged state (condition reading less than 12.2 volts), have it recharged by your dealer or local automotive electrician, as the charge rate is higher and constant supervision during charging is necessary.

3 Charging system - general information and precautions

General information

The charging system includes the alternator, an internal voltage regulator, a no-charge (or 'ignition') warning light, the battery, and the wiring between all the components. The charging system supplies electrical power for the ignition system, the lights, the radio, etc. The alternator is driven by the auxiliary drivebelt at the front of the engine.

The purpose of the voltage regulator is to limit the alternator's voltage to a pre-set value. This prevents power surges, circuit overloads, etc, during peak voltage output.

The charging system doesn't ordinarily require periodic maintenance. However, the drivebelt, battery, wires and connections should be inspected at the intervals outlined in Chapter 1.

The dashboard warning light should come on when the ignition key is turned to positions II or III, then should go off immediately when the engine starts. If it remains on, or if it comes on while the engine is running, there is a malfunction in the charging system. If the light does not come on when the ignition key is turned, and the bulb is in working condition, there is a fault in the alternator.

Precautions

Be very careful when making electrical circuit connections to a vehicle equipped with an alternator, and note the following:

a) *When reconnecting wires to the alternator from the battery, be sure to note the polarity.*

b) *Before using arc-welding equipment to repair any part of the vehicle, disconnect the wires from the alternator and the battery terminals.*

c) *Never start the engine with a battery charger connected.*

d) *Always disconnect both battery cables before using a battery charger.*

e) *The alternator is driven by an engine drivebelt that could cause serious injury if your hand, hair or clothes become entangled in it with the engine running.*

f) *Because the alternator is connected directly to the battery, it could arc or cause a fire if overloaded or shorted-out.*

g) *If steam-cleaning or pressure-washing the engine, wrap a plastic bag over the alternator or any other electrical component and secure them with rubber bands (Do not forget to remove, before restarting the engine).*

h) *Never disconnect the alternator terminals or battery cables while the engine is running.*

4 Charging system - testing

1 If a malfunction occurs in the charging circuit, don't automatically assume that the alternator is causing the problem. First check the following items:

a) *Check the tension and condition of the auxiliary drivebelt - replace it if it is worn or deteriorated (see the relevant part of Chapter 1).*

b) *Ensure the alternator mounting bolts and nuts are tight.*

c) *Inspect the alternator wiring harness and the electrical connections at the alternator; they must be in good condition, and tight.*

d) *Check the large main fuses in the engine compartment (see Chapter 12). If any are blown, determine the cause, repair the circuit and replace the fuse (the vehicle won't start and/or the accessories won't work if the fuse is blown).*

e) *Start the engine and check the alternator for abnormal noises - for example, a shrieking or squealing sound may indicate a badly-worn bearing or brush.*

f) *Make sure that the battery is fully charged - one bad cell in a battery can cause overcharging by the alternator.*

g) *Disconnect the battery cables (negative first, then positive). Inspect the battery posts and the lead clamps for corrosion. Clean them thoroughly if necessary (see Chapter 1). Reconnect the leads.*

2 Using a voltmeter, check the battery voltage with the engine off. It should be approximately 12 volts.

3 Start the engine and check the battery voltage again. Increase engine speed until the voltmeter reading remains steady; it should now be approximately 13.5 to 14.6 volts.

4 Switch on as many electrical accessories as possible (e.g., the headlights, heated rear window and heater blower), and check that the alternator maintains the regulated voltage at around 13 to 14 volts. The voltage may drop and then come back up; it may also be necessary to increase engine speed slightly, even if the charging system is working properly.

5 If the voltage reading is greater than the specified charging voltage, replace the voltage regulator.

6 If the voltmeter reading is less than that specified, the fault may be due to worn brushes, weak brush springs, a faulty voltage regulator, a faulty diode, a severed phase winding, or worn or damaged slip rings. The brushes and slip rings may be checked, but if the fault persists, the alternator should be replaced or taken to an auto-electrician for testing and repair.

5 Alternator - removal and installation

Removal

1 Disconnect the cable from the negative terminal of the battery (see Section 1).

2.0L Zetec-E engines

Refer to illustrations 5.2, 5.3a, 5.3b, 5.4a, 5.4b, 5.5, 5.7a, 5.7b and 5.8

2 Remove the securing bolt from the coolant expansion tank, lift out from securing clip and move to one side (see Chapter 3, Section 7). Remove the drivebelt (see Chapter 1). Lift the power steering reservoir from its retaining bracket and move to one side **(see illustration)**.

3 Unscrew the securing bolt from the wiring loom bracket, and move the wiring to one side (disconnect the multi-plug) **(see illustrations)**.

4 Remove the bolt from the power steering reservoir bracket to release the ground cable (to aid the removal of the alternator, carefully bend the ground bracket down) **(see illustrations)**. On 2003 and 2004 Zetec-E and Duratec (SVT) engines, remove the three bolts from the front engine mount and with a

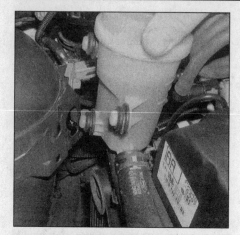

5.2 Lift reservoir from the retaining bracket

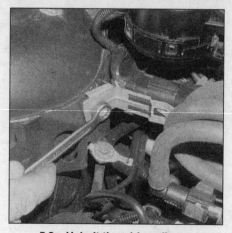

5.3a Unbolt the wiring clip . . .

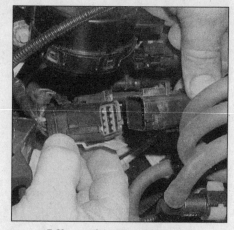

5.3b . . . then disconnect the block connector

wood 2x4 pry the engine forward (toward the radiator) and reinsert one bolt behind the mount to keep the engine from going back to its normal position.

5   Remove the two retaining bolts from the canister purge valve and move to one side **(see illustration)**.

6   Remove the plastic cover, unscrew the nut and disconnect the wiring from the back of the alternator. Disconnect the cylinder head temperature sensor electrical connector.

7   Unscrew and remove the alternator mounting bolt nearest the engine **(see illustration)**. Unscrew the other retaining bolt until it has fully disengaged from the bracket (it will not be possible to remove the bolt from the alternator at this stage) **(see illustration)**.

8   Carefully lift the alternator from the engine, turning it with the pulley facing upwards. Take care not to damage the surrounding components on removal, as there is little room to maneuver the alternator **(see illustration)**.

2.0L SPI engines

9   Remove the bolts holding the power steering pipe brackets to the exhaust manifold and set the pipe aside.

10   Remove the exhaust manifold heat shield (see Chapter 4A).

11   Remove the drivebelt (see Chapter 1).

12   Remove the plastic cover, unscrew the nut and disconnect the wiring from the alternator.

13   Unscrew the alternator mounting bolts and carefully lift the alternator from the engine.

2.3L and 2005 and later 2.0L engines

14   From above, remove the nut securing the top of the alternator's heat shield.

15   From below, remove the lower engine splash shield, then remove the drivebelt (see Chapter 1) and the alternator heat shield lower nut.

16   Remove the air intake tube (see Chapter 4A).

17   Remove the lower alternator-mounting nut.

18   Remove the upper alternator mounting nut.

19   Remove the bolt at the roll-restricting engine mount and, with a helper prying the engine forward, remove the alternator.

20   Installation is the reverse of the removal procedure.

All models

21   If you are replacing the alternator, take the old one with you when purchasing a replacement unit. Your old unit may be needed by the store as a core. Make sure that the new or rebuilt unit is identical to the old alternator. Look at the terminals - they should be the same in number, size and location as the terminals on the old alternator. Finally, look at the identification markings - they will be stamped in the housing, or printed on a tag or plaque affixed to the housing. Make sure that these numbers are the same on both alternators.

22   Many new/rebuilt alternators do not have a pulley installed, so you may have to switch the pulley from the old unit to the new/rebuilt one. When buying an alternator, ask about the installation of pulleys - some auto parts stores will perform this service free of charge when you buy an alternator.

Installation

Note: *One of the mounting bolts on the 2.0L Zetec-E engine will need to be put in place before installing the alternator (see Step 7).*

23   Installation is the reverse of the removal procedure, referring where necessary to the relevant Chapters of this manual. Tighten all nuts and bolts to the specified torque setting.

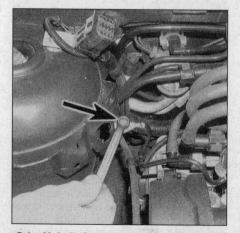

5.4a Unbolt the ground cable (arrow) . . .

5.4b . . . then carefully bend the bracket down (arrow)

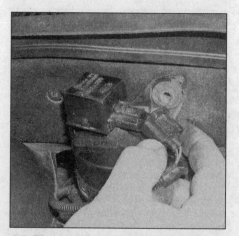

5.5 Disconnect the wiring connector, and move the canister to one side

5.7a Remove the bolt (arrow) . . .

5.7b . . . and remove the lower bolt as far the inner fender

5.8 Turn and lift the alternator out with the pulley facing upwards

6 Alternator brushes and voltage regulator - replacement

Refer to illustrations 6.2, 6.3, 6.4 and 6.5

Note 1: *The following procedure is for the Magneti Marelli unit installed on the project vehicles - the procedure is essentially the same for any other alternators that may be installed on other models.*

Note 2: *The manufacturer does not recommend rebuilding the alternator yourself. Make sure that new brushes and regulator are available before dismantling the alternator.*

1   Remove the alternator from the vehicle (see Section 5) and place it on a clean workbench.

2   Remove the four securing nuts, and withdraw the plastic end cover from the alternator **(see illustration)**.

3   Unclip the plastic cover at the center from the brushes **(see illustration)**.

4   Remove the voltage regulator/brush holder mounting screws and nuts **(see illustration)**.

5   Remove the regulator/brush holder from the rear of the alternator housing **(see illustration)**.

6   Measure the exposed length of each brush. If less than 3/16-inch (5 mm), replace the assembly.

7   Make sure that each brush moves smoothly in the brush holder.

8   Check that the slip rings - the ring of copper on which each brush bears - are clean. Wipe them with a solvent-moistened cloth; if either appears scored or blackened, take the alternator to a repair specialist for advice.

9   Installation is the reverse of the removal procedure.

10   Install the voltage regulator/brush holder, ensuring that the brushes bear correctly on the slip rings, and that they compress into their holders. Tighten the screws securely.

11   Install the rear cover, and tighten the screws securely.

12   Install the alternator as described in Section 5.

7 Starting system - general information and precautions

General information

The starting system consists of a gear reduced starter motor, battery, ignition switch, relay and the wires connecting them. The solenoid is mounted directly on the starter motor.

The solenoid/starter motor assembly is installed in line with the engine, bolting onto the transaxle bellhousing. The relay for the starter circuit is in the fusebox inside the vehicle (relay No 17).

When the ignition key is turned to position III, the starter relay is actuated, providing

6.2 Remove the end cover from the alternator

6.3 Lift off the center cover

6.4 Remove the screws and nuts (arrows)

6.5 Lift the regulator assembly from the alternator

voltage to the starter motor solenoid. The starter motor solenoid engages the drive pinion with the ring gear on the flywheel. The solenoid then switches the battery current to the starter motor, to turn the engine. The starter motor remains engaged until the ignition switch is released.

The starter motor on a vehicle equipped with automatic transmission can be operated only when the selector lever is in Park or Neutral (P or N). On manual transaxle models, the starter can only be engaged when the clutch pedal is depressed.

If the alarm system is armed or activated, the starter motor cannot be operated. The same applies with the engine immobilizer system (if equipped).

Precautions

Always observe the following precautions when working on the starting system:

a) *Excessive cranking of the starter motor can overheat it, and cause serious damage. Never operate the starter motor for more than 15 seconds at a time without pausing to allow it to cool for at least two minutes. Excessive starter operation will also risk unburned fuel collecting in the catalytic converter's element, causing it to overheat when the engine does start.*

b) *The starter is connected by a cable directly from the battery, and could arc or cause a fire if mishandled, overloaded or short-circuited.*

c) *Always detach the cable from the negative terminal of the battery before working on the starting system (see Section 1).*

8   Starting system - testing

Note: *Before diagnosing starter problems, make sure that the battery is fully charged, and ensure that the alarm/engine immobilizer system is not activated.*

1   If the starter motor does not turn at all when the switch is operated, make sure that, on automatic transaxle models, the selector lever is in Park or Neutral (P or N).

2   Make sure that the battery is fully charged, and that all leads, both at the battery and starter solenoid terminals, are clean and secure.

3   If the starter motor spins but the engine is not cranking, the overrunning clutch or (when applicable) the reduction gears in the starter motor may be slipping, in which case the starter motor must be overhauled or replaced. (Other possibilities are that the starter motor mounting bolts are very loose, or that teeth are missing from the flywheel/driveplate ring gear.)

4   If, when the switch is actuated, the starter motor does not operate at all but the solenoid clicks, then the problem lies with either the battery, the main solenoid contacts, or the starter motor itself (or the engine is seized).

5   If the solenoid plunger cannot be heard

9.3 Withdraw the starter from the transmission housing

to click when the switch is actuated, the battery is faulty, there is a fault in the circuit, or the solenoid itself is defective.

6   To check the solenoid, connect a fused jumper lead between the battery (+) and the ignition switch terminal (the small terminal) on the solenoid. If the starter motor now operates, the solenoid is OK, and the problem is in the ignition switch, selector lever position sensor (automatic transmission) or in the wiring.

7   If the starter motor still does not operate, remove it. The brushes and commutator may be checked, but if the fault persists, the motor should be replaced or taken to an auto-electrician for testing and repair.

8   If the starter motor cranks the engine at an abnormally-slow speed, first make sure that the battery is charged, and that all terminal connections are tight. If the engine is partially seized, or has the wrong viscosity oil in it, it will crank slowly.

9   Run the engine until normal operating temperature is reached, then switch off and disable the ignition system by unplugging the ignition coil's electrical connector; remove fuse 12 to disconnect the fuel pump.

10   Connect a voltmeter positive lead to the battery positive terminal, and connect the negative lead to the negative terminal.

11   Crank the engine, and take the voltmeter readings as soon as a steady figure is indicated. Do not allow the starter motor to turn for more than 15 seconds at a time. A reading of 10.5 volts or more, with the starter motor turning at normal cranking speed, is normal. If the reading is 10.5 volts or more but the cranking speed is slow, the solenoid contacts are burned, the motor is faulty, or there is a bad connection. If the reading is less than 10.5 volts and the cranking speed is slow, the starter motor is faulty or there is a problem with the battery.

9   Starter motor - removal and installation

1   Disconnect the negative battery cable - see Section 1.

9.4 Disconnect the wiring from the starter motor

Removal

Refer to illustrations 9.3 and 9.4

2   Apply the parking brake, then jack up the front of the vehicle and support it on axle stands (see *Jacking and Towing*). On 2.0L SPI engines, remove the air cleaner outlet tube from the throttle body for more access to the starter.

3   On Zetec-E engines, remove the MAF sensor, PCV pipe and the upper bolts. Raise the vehicle, disconnect the electrical connectors and remove the lower bolts.

4   On 2.3L and 2005 and later 2.0L models, unbolt and set aside the power steering pump, without disconnecting the lines. Remove the oil pressure sending unit and protect the opening from dirt during starter removal.

5   On Duratec (SVT) engines, remove the intake manifold (See Chapter 2C).

6   Unscrew the mounting bolts from the starter motor, then release the starter motor from the dowels on the transaxle housing and withdraw from the engine **(see illustration)**. The starter is in close quarters, you may have to angle it to withdraw it.

7   Unscrew the nuts and disconnect the wiring from the starter motor as the starter is being withdrawn **(see illustration)**.

Installation

8   Installation is a reversal of removal. Tighten the bolts to the specified torque settings.

10   Starter motor - testing and overhaul

If the starter motor is thought to be suspect, it should be removed from the vehicle and taken to an auto-electrician for testing. Most auto-electricians will be able to supply and install brushes at a reasonable cost. However, check on the cost of repairs before proceeding as it may prove more economical to obtain a new or exchange starter.

Chapter 5 Part B
Ignition system

Contents

Specifications

General

System type	Electronic distributorless ignition system (DIS) with ignition module controlled by EEC-V engine management module (PCM)
Firing order	1-3-4-2
Location of Number 1 cylinder	Timing belt end

Ignition system data

Ignition timing	Controlled by the PCM
Ignition coil resistances (typical):	
Primary windings	0.4 to 0.6 ohms
Secondary windings	10,500 to 16,500 ohms

Torque wrench settings
Ft-lbs (unless otherwise indicated)

Note: *One foot-pound (ft-lb) of torque is equivalent to 12 inch-pounds (in-lbs) of torque. Torque values below approximately 15 ft-lbs are expressed in inch-pounds, since most foot-pound torque wrenches are not accurate at these smaller values.*

Ignition coil mounting bolts	
All except 2.3L and 2005 and later 2.0L	48 in-lbs
2.3L and 2005 and later 2.0L	89 in-lbs
Knock sensor mounting bolt	15

1 General information and precautions

General information

The ignition system is integrated with the fuel injection system to form a combined engine management system under the control of the EEC-V engine management module or Powertrain Control Module (PCM) - see Chapter 4A for further information. The main ignition system components include the ignition switch, the battery, the crankshaft speed/position sensor, knock sensor, the ignition coil, and the spark plugs and spark plug wires.

These engines are equipped with a Distributorless Ignition System (DIS), where the main functions of the conventional distributor are replaced by a computerized module within the PCM. The coil unit operates on the 'waste spark' principle. The coil unit in fact contains two separate coils - one for cylinders 1 and 4, the other for cylinders 2 and 3. Each of the two coils produces HT voltage at both outputs every time its primary coil voltage is interrupted - i.e., cylinders 1 and 4 always 'fire' together, then 2 and 3 'fire' together. When this happens, one of the two cylinders concerned will be on the compression stroke (and will ignite the fuel/air mixture), while the other one is on the exhaust stroke - because the spark on the exhaust stroke has no effect, it is effectively 'wasted', hence the term 'waste spark'.

On 2.3L and 2005 and later 2.0L engines, there is an individual ignition coil for each spark plug, a system referred to as "coil-on-plug." The small coils are bolted to the valve cover right over the plugs, so there are no secondary spark plug wires.

Because there is no distributor to adjust, the ignition timing cannot be altered by conventional means, and the advance and retard functions are carried out by the PCM.

The basic operation is as follows: the PCM supplies a voltage to the input stage of the ignition coil, which causes the primary windings in the coil to be energized. The supply voltage is periodically interrupted by the PCM and this results in the collapse of primary magnetic field, which then induces a much larger voltage in the secondary coil, called the HT voltage. This voltage is directed (via the spark plug wires) to the spark plug in the cylinder. The spark plug electrodes form a gap small enough for the HT voltage to arc across, and the resulting spark ignites the fuel/air mixture in the cylinder. The timing of this sequence of events is critical, and is regulated solely by the PCM.

The PCM calculates and controls the ignition timing primarily according to engine speed, crankshaft position, camshaft position, and intake airflow rate information, received from sensors mounted on and around the engine. Other parameters that affect ignition timing are throttle position and rate of opening, intake air temperature, engine temperature and engine knock, all monitored via sensors mounted on the engine. Note that most of these sensors have a dual role, in that the information they provide is equally useful in determining the fuel requirements as in deciding the optimum ignition or firing point - therefore, removal of some of the sensors mentioned below is described in Chapter 4A.

The PCM computes engine speed and crankshaft position from a toothed impulse rotor attached to the engine flywheel, with an engine speed sensor whose inductive head runs just above rotor. As the crankshaft (and flywheel) rotate, the rotor 'teeth' pass the engine speed sensor, which transmits a pulse to the PCM every time a tooth passes it. At the top dead center (TDC) position, there is one missing tooth in the rotor periphery, which results in a longer pause between signals from the sensor. The PCM recognizes the absence of a pulse from the engine speed sensor at this point, and uses it to establish the TDC position for Number 1 piston. The time interval between pulses, and the location of the missing pulse, allow the PCM to accurately determine the position of the crankshaft and its speed. The camshaft position sensor enhances this information by detecting whether a particular piston is on an intake or an exhaust cycle.

Information on engine load is supplied to the PCM via the air mass meter, and from the throttle position sensor. The engine load is determined by computation based on the quantity of air being drawn into the engine. Further engine load information is sent to the PCM from the knock sensor. The sensor is sensitive to vibration, and detect the knocking which occurs when the engine starts to 'ping' (pre-ignite). If pre-ignition occurs, the PCM retards the ignition timing of the cylinder that is pre-igniting in steps until the pre-ignition ceases. The PCM then advances the ignition timing of that cylinder in steps until it is restored to normal, or until pre-ignition occurs again.

Sensors monitoring engine temperature, throttle position, vehicle road speed, automatic transmission gear position (where applicable) and air conditioning system operation, provide additional input signals to the PCM on vehicle operating conditions. From all this constantly-changing data, the PCM selects, and if necessary modifies, a particular ignition advance setting from a map of ignition characteristics stored in its memory.

In the event of a fault in the system due to loss of a signal from one of the sensors, the PCM reverts to an emergency ('limp-home') program. This will allow the car to be driven, although engine operation and performance will be limited - the ignition timing, for instance, will be set to a fixed value. A warning light on the instrument panel will illuminate if the fault is likely to cause an increase in harmful exhaust emissions.

It should be noted that comprehensive fault diagnosis of all the engine management systems described in this Chapter is only possible with dedicated electronic test equipment. In the event of a sensor failing or other fault occurring, a trouble code will be stored in the PCM's DTC (Diagnostic Trouble Code) log, which can only be extracted from the PCM using a dedicated trouble code scan tool. Refer to Chapter 4B for scan tool and trouble code information. Once the fault has been identified, the removal/installation sequences detailed in the following Sections will then allow the appropriate component(s) to be replaced as required.

Precautions

The following precautions must be observed, to prevent damage to the ignition system components and to reduce risk of personal injury.

a) *Do not keep the ignition on for more than 10 seconds if the engine will not start.*
b) *Ensure that the ignition is switched off before disconnecting any of the ignition wiring.*
c) *Ensure that the ignition is switched off before connecting or disconnecting any ignition test equipment, such as a timing light.*
d) *Do not ground the coil primary or secondary circuits.*

Warning: *Voltages produced by an electronic ignition system are considerably higher than those produced by conventional ignition systems. Extreme care must be taken when working on the system with the ignition switched on. Persons with surgically-implanted cardiac pacemaker devices should keep well clear of the ignition circuits, components and test equipment.*

2   Ignition system - testing

General

1   The components of the ignition system are normally very reliable; most faults are far more likely to be due to loose or dirty connections, or to 'tracking' of HT voltage due to dirt, dampness or damaged insulation, than to the failure of any of the system's components. **Always** check all wiring thoroughly before condemning an electrical component, and work methodically to eliminate all other possibilities before deciding that a particular component is faulty.

2   The old practice of checking for a spark by holding the live end of a spark plug wire a short distance away from the engine is not recommended; not only is there a high risk of a powerful electric shock, but the PCM, HT coil, or power stage may be damaged. Similarly, never try to 'diagnose' misfires by pulling off one spark plug wire at a time. For testing, use a spark tester (available inexpensively in auto parts stores) inserted into a plug lead and grounded with its attached lead. A strong blue spark when the engine is turned over indicates a healthy ignition system.

3   The following tests should be carried out when an obvious fault such as non-starting or a clearly detectable misfire exists. Some faults, however, are more obscure and are often disguised by the fact that the PCM will adopt an emergency program ('limp-home') mode to maintain as much driveability as possible. Faults of this nature usually appear in the form of excessive fuel consumption, poor idling characteristics, lack of performance, knocking or 'pinging' noises from the engine under certain conditions, or a combination of these conditions. Where problems such as this are experienced, the best course is to refer the car to a suitably-equipped garage for diagnostic testing using dedicated test equipment.

Engine will not start
Refer to illustration 2.8

Note: *Remember that a fault with the anti-theft alarm or immobilizer will give rise to apparent starting problems. Make sure that the alarm or immobilizer has been deactivated, referring to the vehicle handbook for details.*

4   If the engine either will not turn over at all, or only turns very slowly, check the battery and starter motor. Connect a voltmeter across the battery terminals (meter positive probe to battery positive terminal) then note the voltage reading obtained while turning the engine over on the starter for (no more than) ten seconds. If the reading obtained is less than approximately 9.5 volts, first check the battery, starter motor and charging system as described in Part A of this Chapter.

5   If the engine turns over at normal speed but will not start, check the HT circuit.

2.8 Diagnostic connector socket location on driver's lower dash panel

3.6 Check all engine compartment ground points for corrosion

6   Connect a timing light (following its manufacturer's instructions) and turning the engine over on the starter motor; if the light flashes, voltage is reaching the spark plugs, so these should be checked first. If the light does not flash, check the spark plug wires themselves using the information given in Chapter 1. If there is a spark, continue with the checks described in Section 3 of this Chapter.

7   If there is still no spark, check the condition of the coil(s), if possible by substitution with a known good unit, or by checking the primary and secondary resistances. If the fault persists, the problem lies elsewhere; if the fault is now cleared, a new coil is the obvious cure. However, check carefully the condition of the HT connections themselves before obtaining a new coil, to ensure that the fault is not due to dirty or poorly-fastened connectors.

8   If the coil is in good condition, the fault is probably within the power stage (built into the PCM), one of the system sensors, or related components (as applicable). In this case, a trouble code should be logged in the diagnostic unit, which could be read using a scan tool **(see illustration)**.

9   Trouble codes can only be extracted from the PCM using a dedicated diagnostic scan tool. Refer to Chapter 4B for scan tool and trouble code information.

Engine misfires

10   An irregular misfire is probably due to a loose connection to one of the ignition coils or system sensors.

11   With the ignition switched off, check carefully through the system, ensuring that all connections are clean and securely fastened.

12   Check the condition of the spark plug wires. Ensure that the leads are routed and clipped so that they come into contact with fewest possible metal surfaces, as this may encourage the HT voltage to 'leak', via poor or damaged insulation. If there is any sign of damage to the insulation, replace the leads as a set.

13   Unless the spark plug wires are known to have been recently replaced, it is considered good practice to eliminate the spark plug wires from fault diagnosis in cases of misfiring by installing a new set as a matter of course.

14   When installing new leads, remove one lead at a time, so that confusion over their installed positions does not arise. If the old leads were damaged, take steps to ensure that the new leads do not become similarly damaged.

15   If the spark plug wires are sound, regular misfiring indicates a problem with the ignition coil or spark plugs. Install new plugs as described in Chapter 1, or test the coil(s) as described in Section 4. A dirty or faulty crankshaft sensor could also be to blame - see Chapter 4A.

16   Any further checking of the system components should be carried out after first checking the PCM for trouble codes - see Chapter 4B.

3   Troubleshooting - general information and preliminary checks

Note: *Both the ignition and fuel systems must ideally be treated as one inter-related engine management system. Although the contents of this section are mainly concerned with the ignition side of the system, many of the components perform dual functions, and some of the following procedures of necessity relate to the fuel system.*

General information

1   The fuel and ignition systems on all engines covered by this manual incorporate an on-board diagnostic system to facilitate fault finding and system testing. Should a fault occur, the PCM stores a series of signals (or trouble codes) for subsequent read-out via the diagnostic connector (see the Section on checking the fuel injection system in Chapter 4A, and the trouble code information in Chapter 4B).

2   If driveability problems have been experienced and engine performance is suspect, the on-board diagnostic system can be used to pinpoint any problem areas, but this requires special test equipment. Once this has been done, further tests may often be necessary to determine the exact nature of the fault; i.e., whether a component itself has failed, or whether it is a wiring or other inter-related problem.

3   Apart from visually checking the wiring and connections, any testing will require the use of a trouble code scanner at least. Refer to Chapter 4B for scan tool and trouble code information.

Preliminary checks

Refer to illustration 3.6

Note: *When carrying out these checks to trace a problem, remember that if the fault has appeared only a short time after any part of the vehicle has been serviced or overhauled, the first place to check is where that work was carried out, however unrelated it may appear, to ensure that no carelessly installed components are causing the problem.*

4   If you are tracing the cause of a 'partial' engine fault, such as lack of performance, in addition to the checks outlined below, check the compression pressures. Check also that the fuel filter and air cleaner element have been replaced at the recommended intervals. Refer to Chapter 1 and Chapter 2C for details of these procedures.

5   Remember that any trouble codes that have been logged will have to be cleared from the PCM memory using a scan tool (see Step 3) before you can be certain the cause of the fault has been fixed.

6   Open the hood and check the condition of the battery connections - remake the connections or replace the cables if a fault is found. Use the same techniques to ensure that all ground points in the engine compartment provide good electrical contact through clean, metal-to-metal joints, and that all are securely fastened **(see illustration)**.

7   Next work methodically around the engine compartment, checking all visible wiring, and the connections between sections of the wiring loom. What you are looking for at this stage is wiring that is obviously damaged by chafing against sharp edges, or against moving suspension/transaxle components and/or the auxiliary drivebelt, by being trapped or crushed between carelessly installed components, or melted by being forced into contact with hot engine castings, coolant pipes, etc. In almost all cases, damage of this sort is caused in the first instance by incorrect routing on reassembly after previous work has been carried out (see the note at the beginning of this sub-Section).

8   Obviously, wires can break or short together inside the insulation so that there is no visible evidence of the fault, but this usually only occurs where the wiring harness has been incorrectly routed so that it is stretched taut or kinked sharply; either of these conditions should be obvious on even a casual inspection. If this is thought to have happened and the fault proves elusive, the suspect section of wiring should be checked very carefully during the more detailed checks that follow.

9   Depending on the extent of the problem, damaged wiring may be repaired by rejoining the break or splicing-in a new length of wire, using solder to ensure a good connection, and covering the insulation with electrician's tape or heat-shrink tubing, as desired. If the damage is extensive, given the implications for the vehicle's future reliability, the best long-term answer may well be to replace that entire section of the harness, however expensive this may appear.

10   When the actual damage has been repaired, ensure that the wiring harness is re-routed correctly, so that it is clear of other components, is not stretched or kinked, and is secured out of harm's way using the plastic clips, guides and ties provided.

11   Check all electrical connectors, ensuring that they are clean, securely fastened, and that each is locked by its plastic tabs or wire clip, as appropriate. If any connector shows external signs of corrosion (accumulations of white or green deposits, or streaks of 'rust'), or if any is thought to be dirty, it must be unplugged and cleaned using electrical contact cleaner. If the connector pins are severely corroded, the connector must be replaced; note that this may mean the replacement of that entire section of the harness.

12   If the cleaner completely removes the corrosion to leave the connector in a satisfactory condition, it would be wise to pack the connector with a non-conductive grease which will exclude dirt and moisture and prevent the corrosion from occurring again.

13   All models have an inductive sensor that determines crankshaft speed and TDC position. On an older engine, it is possible that the tip of the sensor may become contaminated with oil and/or dirt, interfering with its operation and causing a misfire. Refer to

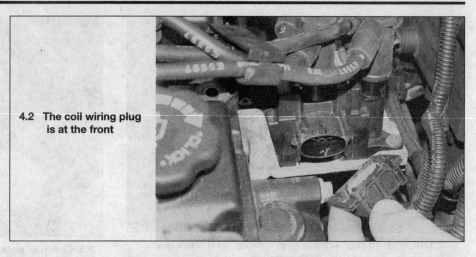

4.2   The coil wiring plug is at the front

Chapter 4A, Section 15, for sensor removal and replacement information.

14   Working methodically around the engine compartment, check carefully that all vacuum hoses and pipes are securely fastened and correctly routed, with no signs of cracks, splits or deterioration to cause air leaks, or of hoses that are trapped, kinked, or bent sharply enough to restrict airflow. Check with particular care at all connections and sharp bends, and replace any damaged or deformed lengths of hose.

15   Check the crankcase breather hoses for splits, poor connections or blockages. Details of the breather system vary according to which engine is installed, but all models have at least one hose running from the top of the engine connected to the air intake duct or intake manifold. The breather hoses run from the engine block (or from the oil filler tube) and carry oil fumes into the engine, to be burned with the fuel/air mixture. A variety of poor-running problems (especially unstable idling) can result from blocked or damaged breather hoses.

16   Working from the fuel tank, via the filter, to the fuel rail (and including the feed and return), check the fuel lines, and replace any that are found to be leaking, trapped or kinked. Check particularly the ends of the hoses - these can crack and deteriorate sufficiently to allow leakage.

17   Check that the accelerator cable is correctly secured and adjusted, and that it is routed with as few sharp turns as possible. Replace the cable if there is any doubt about its condition, or if it appears to be stiff or jerky in operation. Refer to Chapter 4A for further information, if required.

18   Remove the air cleaner cover as described in Chapter 1, and check that the air filter is not clogged or soaked. A clogged air filter will obstruct the intake airflow, causing a noticeable effect on engine performance. Replace the filter if necessary.

19   Start the engine and allow it to idle.
Caution: *Working in the engine compartment while the engine is running requires great care to avoid personal injury; among the dangers are burns from contact with hot components, or contact with moving components such as*

the radiator cooling fan or the auxiliary drivebelt. Refer to 'Safety first!' at the front of this manual before starting, and ensure that your hands, and any long hair or loose clothing, are kept well clear of hot or moving components at all times.

20   Working from the air intake, via the air cleaner assembly and the airflow sensor (or air mass meter) to the throttle housing and intake manifold (and including the various vacuum hoses and pipes connected to these), check for air leaks. Usually, these will be revealed by sucking or hissing noises, but minor leaks may be traced by spraying a solution of soapy water onto the suspect joint; if a leak exists, it will be shown by the change in engine note and the accompanying air bubbles (or sucking-in of the liquid, depending on the pressure difference at that point). If a leak is found at any point, tighten the fastening clamp and/or replace the faulty components, as applicable.

21   Similarly, work from the cylinder head, via the manifold to the tailpipe, to check that the exhaust system is free from leaks. The simplest way of doing this, if the vehicle can be raised and supported safely and with complete security while the check is made, is to temporarily block the tailpipe while listening for the sound of escaping exhaust gases; any leak should be evident. If a leak is found at any point, tighten the fastening clamp bolts and/or nuts, replace the gasket, and/or replace the faulty section of the system, as necessary, to seal the leak.

22   It is possible to make a further check of the electrical connections by wiggling each electrical connector of the system in turn as the engine is idling; a faulty connector will be immediately evident from the engine's response as contact is broken and remade. A faulty connector should be replaced to ensure that the future reliability of the system; note that this may mean the replacement of that entire section of the loom.

23   If the preliminary checks have failed to reveal the fault, the car must be taken to a dealer or suitably-equipped garage for diagnostic testing using electronic test equipment.

4.3 Carefully unplug the spark plug wires from the coil

4.5a Disconnect the radio suppressor wiring plug . . .

4 Ignition coils - removal, testing and installation

Removal

Refer to illustrations 4.2, 4.3, 4.5a, 4.5b and 4.5c

1   The ignition coilpack is bolted to the left-hand end of the cylinder head; on 2.0L SPI engines, the coil is mounted with the secondary towers pointing to the left fender, while on 2.0L Zetec-E and Duratec-SVT engines, the towers point straight up. On Duratec-SVT engines, the coils have a cover that must be removed to access the coils. On 2.3L and 2005 and later 2.0L engines, the individual coils are bolted to the valve cover over each spark plug.

2   Make sure the ignition is switched off, then disconnect the wiring plug from the coil **(see illustration)**. On 2.3L and 2005 2.0L engines, disconnect the electrical connector at each coil, remove the mounting bolt and

pull straight up to remove the coil from the spark plug.

3   Check the coil terminals to see whether they are marked for cylinder numbering - if not, make your own marks to ensure that the spark plug wires are correctly installed. Identify the spark plug wires for position if necessary, then carefully pull them from the coil terminals **(see illustration)**.

4   Unscrew the mounting bolts and remove the ignition coil from the engine compartment.

5   To remove the coilpack with its mounting bracket, disconnect the radio suppression connector, remove the screws and remove the coilpack with its bracket attached **(see illustrations)**.

Testing

6   Using an ohmmeter, measure the resistances of the ignition coil's primary and secondary windings and compare with the information given in the Specifications. Replace the coil if necessary.

Installation

7   Installation is a reversal of removal. Take great care that the spark plug wires are correctly installed, and tighten the coil mounting bolts to the specified torque.

5 Ignition system sensors - removal and installation

Knock sensor

Removal

1   A knock sensor is installed on both 2.0L SPI engines and 2.0L Zetec-E engines. On Zetec-E engines, it's bolted to the firewall-side of the cylinder block, just ahead of the starter motor. On SPI engines, it is located on the front side of the block, just below the exhaust manifold. On 2.3L and 2005 and later 2.0L engines, it is located on the block, behind the intake manifold.

4.5b . . . unscrew the three Torx bolts (two above, one below) . . .

4.5c . . . and remove the coil and mounting bracket

2   The knock sensor wiring plug is clipped to a bracket next to the engine oil dipstick. Slide the wiring plug downward to remove it from the clip, then separate the two halves of the wiring plug.

3   Trace the wiring down to the knock sensor, then unscrew the center bolt and remove the sensor from the engine. On 2.3L and 2005 2.0L engines, the intake manifold must be removed first (see Chapter 4A).

Installation

4   Installation is a reversal of removal, noting the following points:

  a) *Clean the sensor and its location on the engine.*

  b) *The sensor must be positioned so that it does not contact the cylinder head, or the crankcase ventilation system oil separator housing (where applicable).*

  c) *The sensor bolt must be tightened to the specified torque, as this is critical to the sensor's correct operation.*

Crankshaft position sensor

5   Refer to Chapter 4A, Section 15.

---

6   Ignition timing - checking and adjustment

Due to the nature of the ignition system, the ignition timing is constantly being monitored and adjusted by the engine management PCM, and nominal values cannot be given. Therefore, it is not possible for the home mechanic to check the ignition timing.

The only way in which the ignition timing can be checked is using special electronic test equipment, connected to the engine management system diagnostic connector (refer to Chapter 4A). No adjustment of the ignition timing is possible. Should the ignition timing be incorrect, then a fault must be present in the engine management system.

Chapter 6 Clutch

Contents

Specifications

General

Brake/clutch fluid type	See Chapter 1
Transaxle type	
2.0L SPI engine...	iB5
All other models	MTX 75

Note: *Throughout this Chapter, it is often necessary (and more convenient) to refer to the clutch components by the type of transaxle installed in the vehicle.*

Clutch

Lining thickness (wear limit)	0.275 inches
Pedal stroke (not adjustable)...	5.25 inches

Torque specifications   **Ft-lbs** (unless otherwise indicated)

Note: *One foot-pound (ft-lb) of torque is equivalent to 12 inch-pounds (in-lbs) of torque. Torque values below approximately 15 ft-lbs are expressed in inch-pounds, since most foot-pound torque wrenches are not accurate at these smaller values.*

Clutch cover/pressure plate to flywheel*...............................	21
Clutch master/slave cylinder mounting nuts/bolts.................................	80 in-lbs
Clutch release lever clamp bolt..	18

Use new bolts on models with MTX 75 transaxle.

1 General information

All manual transaxle models are equipped with a single dry-plate diaphragm spring clutch assembly. The cover assembly consists of a steel cover (doweled and bolted to the flywheel face), the pressure plate, and a diaphragm spring.

The friction disc is free to slide along the splines of the transaxle input shaft, and is held in position between the flywheel and the pressure plate by the pressure of the dia-phragm spring. Friction lining material is riv-eted to the friction disc (driven plate), which has a spring-cushioned hub.

The clutch release bearing contacts the fingers of the diaphragm spring. Depressing the clutch pedal pushes the release bearing against the diaphragm fingers, moving the center of the diaphragm spring inwards. As the center of the spring is pushed inwards, the outside of the spring pivots outwards, moving the pressure plate backwards and disengaging its grip on the friction disc.

When the pedal is released, the diaphragm spring forces the pressure plate back into contact with the friction linings on the friction disc. The disc is now firmly held between the pressure plate and the flywheel, thus transmitting engine power to the transaxle.

All Focus models have a hydraulically-operated clutch. A master cylinder is mounted below the clutch pedal, and takes its hydraulic fluid supply from a separate chamber in the brake fluid reservoir. Depressing the clutch pedal operates the master cylinder pushrod, and the fluid pressure is transferred along the fluid lines to a slave cylinder mounted inside the bellhousing. The slave cylinder is incorporated into the release bearing - when the slave cylinder operates, the release bearing moves against the diaphragm spring fingers and disengages the clutch.

The hydraulic clutch offers several advantages over a cable-operated clutch - it is completely self-adjusting, requires less pedal effort, and is less subject to wear problems.

Since many of the procedures covered in this Chapter involve working under the vehicle, make sure that it is securely supported on axle stands placed on a firm, level floor (see *Jacking and Towing*). **Note:** *Throughout this Chapter, it is often necessary (and more convenient) to refer to the clutch components by the type of transmission installed - refer to the Specifications at the start of this Chapter.* **Warning:** *The hydraulic fluid used in the system is brake fluid, which is poisonous. Brake fluid can harm your eyes and damage painted surfaces, so use extreme caution when handling or pouring it. Do not use brake fluid which is more than one year old. Brake fluid absorbs moisture from the air. Excess moisture can cause a dangerous loss of braking effectiveness.*

2 Clutch - checking

1   The following checks may be performed to diagnose a clutch problem:

a) *Check the fluid lines from the clutch master cylinder into the bellhousing for damage, signs of leakage, or for kinks or dents which might restrict fluid flow.*

b) *To check 'clutch spin-down time', run the engine at normal idle speed with the transaxle in neutral (clutch pedal up). Disengage the clutch (pedal down), wait several seconds, then engage reverse. No grinding noise should be heard. A grinding noise would most likely indicate a problem in the pressure plate or the friction disc. Remember, however, that the MTX 75 transaxle reverse gear is equipped with a synchromesh, so the*

probable symptom of a clutch fault would be a slight rearwards movement (or attempted movement) of the vehicle. If the check is made on level ground with the parking brake released, the movement would be more noticeable.

c) *To check for complete clutch release, run the engine at idle, and hold the clutch pedal approximately half an inch from the floor. Shift between 1st gear and reverse several times. If the shift is not smooth, or if the vehicle attempts to move forwards or backwards, component failure is indicated.*

d) *Slow or poor operation may be due to air being present in the fluid. This is most likely after servicing work has been carried out, as the system is self-bleeding in normal use. If the system has not been disturbed, air in the system may well be the result of a leak. The system can be bled of air as described in Section 7.*

e) *Check the clutch pedal for excessive wear of the bushings, and for any obstructions which may restrict the pedal movement.*

f) *If clutch failure is apparent after prolonged driving in very wet weather or (particularly) flooding, the clutch friction disc may have corroded to the input shaft, and will therefore not release even when the clutch is depressed. Before attempting to free it, consult a dealer or garage - starting the engine in gear with the clutch depressed may lead to component damage. The likelihood of this problem arising can be reduced by always greasing the input shaft splines when installing clutch components.*

Pedal stroke - checking

2   Turn the steering wheel (from the straight-ahead position) to the left by about 30 degrees.

3   Using tape or a cable-tie, attach the end lip of a measuring tape to the clutch pedal rubber. Alternatively, have an assistant hold the measuring tape in place - either way, make sure that the end of the tape does not move from one measurement to the next.

4   Without touching the pedal, read off and record the distance measured from the pedal to the front of the steering wheel rim (dimension A).

5   Now press the pedal down to its stop, and record the new distance (dimension B). Make sure that the pedal action is not hindered by the carpets or floor mats, or by incorrect installation of the master cylinder.

6   The pedal stroke C is obtained by subtracting dimension A from dimension B:

   C (stroke) = B (depressed dimension) minus A (released dimension)

7   Check that the dimension is within the tolerance given in the Specifications. No adjustment of the pedal stroke is possible - providing the clutch is working satisfactorily, even a dimension outside the tolerance is arguably acceptable. An incorrect pedal

stroke combined with poor clutch operation points to a component failure - check the pedal and master cylinder first.

3 Clutch master cylinder - removal and installation

Warning: *Refer to the* **Warning** *in Section 1 concerning the dangers of hydraulic fluid before proceeding.*

Removal

Refer to illustrations 3.9 and 3.10

1   Disconnect the negative battery cable (see Chapter 5).

2   Working inside the vehicle, move the driver's seat fully to the rear, to allow maximum working area. Remove the fasteners securing the driver's side lower dash trim panel, and remove the panel from the car, unclipping the diagnostic connector plug as the panel is removed.

3   Although not essential, removing the clutch pedal as described in Section 4 will make removing the master cylinder considerably easier.

4   Before proceeding, anticipate some spillage of hydraulic (brake) fluid. If sufficient fluid comes into contact with the carpet, it may be discolored or worse. Place a good quantity of clean rags below the clutch pedal, and have a container ready in the engine compartment.

5   On later models, the underhood electrical junction block may have to be unbolted and set aside to access the fluid connections at the firewall. Use a suction device to remove as much fluid as possible from the reservoir. Remove the brake fluid reservoir cap, and then tighten it back down over a piece of cellophane or cling film, to obtain an airtight seal. This may help to reduce the spillage of fluid when the lines are disconnected.

6   To gain access to the fluid connections where they pass through the engine compartment firewall, jack up the front of the car, and support it on axle stands (see *Jacking and Towing*).

7   Working in the engine compartment, or from below, pull out the securing clip from the top of the fluid supply connection (the larger-diameter pipe). Pull the pipe fitting from the master cylinder; anticipate some fluid loss, and plug or clamp the hose end if possible.

8   To remove the (smaller) fluid pressure pipe, first release it from the support bracket adjacent to the firewall. Pull out the securing clip from above, then pull the pipe fitting out of the base of the cylinder. Again, plug or tape over the pipe end, to avoid losing fluid, and to prevent dirt entry.

9   Returning to the driver's footwell, first unscrew the nut (or pull off the metal clip) which secures the pipe flange to the firewall **(see illustration)**.

10   Remove the two bolts that secure the master cylinder body to the pedal bracket **(see illustration)**. On 2005 and later models,

3.9 Remove the pipe flange clip

3.10 Master cylinder-to-pedal bracket bolts (arrows)

it is suggested that the entire clutch/brake pedal assembly be removed from the vehicle.
11   Unclip the master cylinder sideways from the pedal bracket, then carefully pry off the piston rod from the top of the clutch pedal. Taking care not to tilt the master cylinder (to avoid further fluid spillage), remove it from the footwell.

Installation

12   Installation is a reversal of removal, noting the following points:

a) Tighten the mounting bolts to the specified torque.

b) If necessary, install new clips when reconnecting the fluid pipes.

c) Install the clutch pedal (if removed) as described in Section 4.

d) Remove the cellophane from under the fluid reservoir cap, and top-up the fluid level (see Chapter 1).

e) Refer to Section 7 and bleed the clutch hydraulic system.

f) If the fluid level in the reservoir fell sufficiently, it may be necessary to bleed the brake system also - refer to Chapter 9.

g) On completion, operate the clutch a few times without starting the engine, then check for signs of fluid leakage at the firewall connections in the engine compartment.

h) Start the engine, and check for correct clutch operation.

---

4   Clutch pedal - removal and installation

Removal

Refer to illustrations 4.3, 4.4 and 4.6

1   Disconnect the battery negative cable, and position the cable away from the terminal.

2   Working inside the vehicle, move the driver's seat fully to the rear, to allow maximum working area. Remove the fasteners securing the driver's side lower dash trim panel, and take out the panel, unclipping the diagnostic connector plug as the panel is removed.

3   Unscrew the nut from the end of the pedal pivot shaft, and withdraw the pedal pivot shaft sufficiently through the mounting bracket **(see illustration)**. Unless the brake pedal is also to be removed, the shaft need only be partially withdrawn.

4   Carefully pry off the master cylinder piston rod from the top of the clutch pedal, then unhook and remove the clutch pedal return spring **(see illustration)**. Disconnect the following switches at the pedal assembly: brake light switch; cruise control (if equipped); starter safety switch; and clutch pedal position switch.

5   Remove the clutch pedal; recover the clutch pedal metal sleeve, and the plastic bushings if they are loose.

6   With the pedal removed, inspect and replace the components as necessary **(see**

4.3 Unscrew the pivot shaft nut

4.4 Remove the master cylinder piston rod

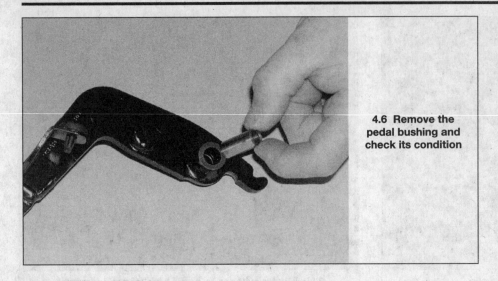

4.6 Remove the pedal bushing and check its condition

illustration). Also check the rubber pad which contacts the clutch pedal switch.

Installation

7　Prior to installing the pedal, apply a little grease to the pivot shaft, sleeve and pedal bushings.

8　Installation is a reversal of the removal procedure, making sure that the bushings and sleeve are correctly located.

9　Check the clutch operation and the pedal stroke, as described in Section 2.

5　Clutch components - removal, inspection and installation

Warning: *Dust created by clutch wear and deposited on the clutch components is a health hazard. DO NOT blow it out with compressed air, and do not inhale any of it. DO NOT use gasoline or petroleum-based solvents to clean off the dust. Brake system*

cleaner should be used to flush the dust into a suitable receptacle. After the clutch components are wiped clean with rags, dispose of the contaminated rags and cleaner in a sealed, marked container.

Removal

Refer to illustrations 5.3 and 5.4

1　Access to the clutch may be gained in one of two ways. The engine/transaxle unit can be removed, as described in Chapter 2C, and the transaxle separated from the engine on the bench. Alternatively, the engine may be left in the vehicle and the transaxle removed independently, as described in Chapter 7A.

2　Having separated the transaxle from the engine, check if there are any marks identifying the relation of the clutch cover to the flywheel. If not, make your own marks using a dab of paint or a marker. These marks will be used if the original cover is reinstalled, and will help to maintain the balance of the unit. A new cover may be installed in any position

allowed by the locating dowels.

3　Unscrew the six clutch cover retaining bolts, working in a diagonal sequence, and loosening the bolts only a turn at a time **(see illustration)**. If necessary, the flywheel may be held stationary using a wide-bladed screwdriver, inserted in the teeth of the starter ring gear and resting against part of the cylinder block. The manufacturer states that on all models new cover bolts must be used during installation.

4　Ease the clutch cover off its locating dowels. Be prepared to catch the clutch friction disc, which will drop out as the cover is removed **(see illustration)**. Note which way the friction disc is installed.

Inspection

5　The most common problem that occurs in the clutch is wear of the clutch friction disc (driven plate). However, all the clutch components should be inspected at this time, particularly if the engine has high mileage. Unless the clutch components are known to be virtually new, it is worth replacing them all as a set (disc, pressure plate and release bearing). Replacing a worn friction disc by itself is not always satisfactory, especially if the old disc was slipping and causing the pressure plate to overheat.

6　Examine the linings of the friction disc for wear and loose rivets, and the disc hub and rim for distortion, cracks, broken torsion springs, and worn splines. The surface of the friction linings may be highly glazed, but as long as the friction material pattern can be clearly seen, and the rivet heads are at least 3/64-inch (1 mm) below the lining surface, this is satisfactory. The disc must be replaced if the lining thickness has worn down to, or just above, the level of the rivet heads.

7　If there is any sign of oil contamination, indicated by shiny black discoloration, the disc must be replaced, and the source of the contamination traced and rectified. This will

5.3 Loosen the clutch cover (pressure plate) retaining bolts

5.4 Remove the clutch cover, and take out the friction disc

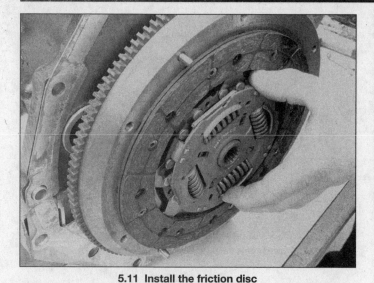

5.11 Install the friction disc

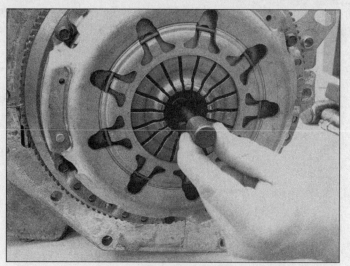

5.14 Use a clutch alignment tool to center the friction disc

be a leaking crankshaft oil seal or transaxle input shaft oil seal. The replacement procedure for the former is given in the relevant Part of Chapter 2. Replacement of the transaxle input shaft oil seal should be entrusted to a dealer service department or transmission specialist, as it involves dismantling the transaxle, and (where applicable) the replacement of the clutch release bearing guide tube, using a press.

8   Check the machined faces of the flywheel and pressure plate. If either is grooved, or heavily scored, replacement is necessary. The pressure plate must also be replaced if any cracks are apparent, or if the diaphragm spring is damaged or its pressure suspect. Pay particular attention to the tips of the spring fingers, where the release bearing acts upon them.

9   With the transaxle removed, it is also advisable to check the condition of the release bearing, as described in Section 6. Having got this far, it is almost certainly worth replacing it. Note that the release bearing is integral with the slave cylinder - the two must

be replaced together; however, given that access to the slave cylinder is only possible with the transaxle removed, not to replace it at this time is probably a false economy.

Installation

Refer to illustrations 5.11, 5.14 and 5.15

10   It is important that no oil or grease is allowed to come into contact with the friction material of the friction disc or the pressure plate and flywheel faces. To ensure this, it is advisable to install the clutch assembly with clean hands, and to wipe down the pressure plate and flywheel faces with a clean dry rag before assembly begins.

11   Place the friction disc against the flywheel, ensuring that it is facing the right way **(see illustration)**. The disc may be marked FLYWHEEL SIDE, but if not, position it so that the raised hub with the cushion springs is facing away from the flywheel.

12   Place the clutch cover over the dowels. Install the retaining bolts (install new ones on MTX 75 transmission models), and tighten

them finger-tight so that the friction disc is gripped lightly, but can still be moved.

13   The friction disc must now be centralized so that, when the engine and transmission are mated, the splines of the gearbox input shaft will pass through the splines in the center of the friction disc hub.

14   Insert a clutch alignment tool through the splined hub of the clutch disc and into the recess in the crankshaft. Move the tool sideways or up-and-down, to move the friction disc in whichever direction is necessary to achieve centralization.

15   Once the clutch is centralized, progressively tighten the cover bolts in a diagonal sequence to the torque setting given in the Specifications **(see illustration)**.

16   Ensure that the input shaft splines and friction disc splines are clean. Apply a thin film of high temperature grease to the input shaft splines - do not apply excessively, however, or it may end up on the friction disc, causing the new clutch to slip.

17   Install the transaxle to the engine.

5.15 Tighten the clutch cover bolts

6   Clutch release bearing (and slave cylinder) - removal, inspection and installation

Removal

Refer to illustrations 6.4a and 6.4b

1   Separate the engine and transaxle as described in the previous Section.

2   The release bearing and slave cylinder are combined into one unit, and cannot be separated.

3   On models with the MTX 75 transaxle, remove the cylinder bleed screw dust cap, and pry out the sealing grommet from the bellhousing as the cylinder is removed - a new grommet (and suitable sealant) must be obtained for installation.

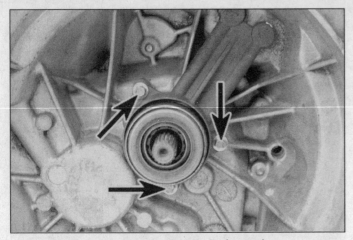

6.4a Unscrew the three bolts (arrows) . . .

6.4b . . . and remove the slave cylinder/release bearing

4   Remove the three mounting bolts, and withdraw the slave cylinder and release bearing from the transaxle bellhousing (see illustrations).

Inspection

5   Check the bearing for smoothness of operation, and replace it if there is any sign of harshness or roughness as the bearing is spun. Do not attempt to disassemble, clean or lubricate the bearing.

6   It is worth replacing the release bearing as a matter of course, unless it is known to be in perfect condition. The manufacturer specifically says not to re-use the slave cylinder (and therefore, the release bearing) on MTX 75 transaxle models.

7   Check the condition of all O-ring seals, and replace if necessary. Considering the difficulty in gaining access to some of the seals if they fail, it would be wise to replace these as a precaution.

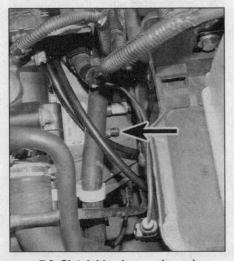

7.3 Clutch bleed screw (arrow)

Installation

8   Installation of the clutch release bearing is a reversal of the removal procedure, noting the following points:

a) *Tighten the mounting bolts to the specified torque.*
b) *On models with the MTX 75 transaxle, install a new sealing grommet to the bellhousing, and seal/secure it in position using a suitable sealant.*
c) *On completion, bleed the system and check for leaks from the slave cylinder fluid connection.*

7   Clutch hydraulic system - bleeding

Refer to illustration 7.3

1   The clutch hydraulic system will not normally require bleeding, and this task should only be necessary when the system has been opened for repair work. However, as with the brake pedal, if the clutch pedal feels at all soggy or unresponsive in operation, this may indicate the need for bleeding.

2   Air in the clutch system could be the result of a leak. Do not overlook the possibility of a leak in the system, for the following reasons:

a) *Leaking fluid will damage paint and/or carpets.*
b) *The clutch system shares its fluid with the braking system, so a clutch system leak could result in brake failure from low fluid level.*
c) *Equally, fluid loss affecting the clutch system could be the result of a braking system fluid leak.*

3   The system bleed screw is located on top of the transaxle bellhousing, next to the fluid pressure pipe (see illustration).

4   Remove the air cleaner and intake duct as described in the Chapter 4A, and the battery and battery tray, as described in Chapter 5A.

5   Move the pipework and wiring harness to one side as necessary to reach the bleed screw.

6   Remove the bleed screw cap.

7   Dealer technicians use a special tool that enables them to use a 'reverse' bleeding technique. This tool is also available through auto parts stores and automotive tool suppliers. For information, this technique is described below. However, the manufacturer also says that conventional brake bleeding techniques can be used, so if this special tool is not available, proceed as described in Step 10.

8   The tool is a pressurized container of brake fluid, which is held at a level below the bleed screw. The fluid reservoir is first drained to the MIN level, then the tool is used to force brake fluid **in** via a tube connected to the bleed screw, until the fluid level in the reservoir reaches the MAX mark.

9   Before bleeding the clutch system, it is recommended that the braking system be bled first, as described in Chapter 9.

10   Bleeding the clutch is much the same as bleeding the brakes - refer to Chapter 9 for the various methods which may be used. Ensure that the level in the brake fluid reservoir is maintained well above the MIN mark at all times, otherwise the clutch and brake hydraulic systems will both need bleeding.

11   On completion, tighten the bleed screw securely, and top-off the brake fluid level to the MAX mark. If possible, test the operation of the clutch before installing all the components removed for access.

12   Failure to bleed correctly may point to a leak in the system, or to a worn master or slave cylinder. At the time of writing, it appears that the master and slave cylinders are only available as complete assemblies - overhaul is not possible.

Chapter 7 Part A
Manual transaxle

Contents

Specifications

General

Transaxle type	Five forward speeds, one reverse. Synchromesh on all forward gears (and reverse gear, on MTX 75 transaxle). Shift linkage operated by twin cables

Transaxle code	
2.0L SPI engine models	iB5
2.0L Zetec-E engine models	MTX 75
Transaxle oil type	See Chapter 1
Transaxle oil capacity	See Chapter 1

Gear ratios

iB5 transaxle

1st	3.154:1
2nd	1.926:1
3rd	1.281:1
4th	0.951:1
5th	0.756:1
Reverse	3.615:1

MTX 75 transaxle

1st	3.667:1
2nd	2.136:1
3rd	1.448:1*
4th	1.028:1
5th	0.767:1
Reverse	3.462:1

MTX 285 transaxle

1st gear	4.44:1*
2nd gear	2.67:1*
3rd gear	1.33:1
4th gear	1.08:1
5th gear	1.33:1
6th gear	1.08:1*
Reverse	2.82:1

Each shaft has a different final ratio, those gears with asterisk have 2.88:1 final drive, the other gears have a 4.25:1 final drive.

Final drive ratios

2.0L SPI engine models	3.610:1
2.0 Zetec-E engine models	3.820:1
2.0L Duratec SVT models	
Upper shaft (1st, 2nd and 6th gears)	2.88
Lower shaft (4th, 5th and Reverse gears)	4.25

Torque specifications   Ft-lbs (unless otherwise indicated)

Note: *One foot-pound (ft-lb) of torque is equivalent to 12 inch-pounds (in-lbs) of torque. Torque values below approximately 15 ft-lbs are expressed in inch-pounds, since most foot-pound torque wrenches are not accurate at these smaller values.*

iB5 transaxle

Engine/transaxle left-hand mounting lower section................................	59
Engine/transaxle left-hand mounting upper section	
Center nut	98
Four outer nuts..	35
Engine/transaxle rear mounting through-bolts..	35
Fluid filler/level plug...	26
Shift cable bracket bolts	15
Shift cable bushing...	84 in-lbs
Shift mechanism to floor	84 in-lbs
Back-up light switch...	156 in-lbs
Shift lever securing bolt	18
Transaxle to engine	35

MTX 75 transaxle

Back-up light switch...	84 in-lbs
Engine/transaxle left-hand mounting lower section................................	59
Engine/transaxle left-hand mounting upper section	
Center nut	98
Four outer nuts..	35
Engine/transaxle rear mount through-bolts...	35
Fluid drain plug..	33
Fluid filler/level plug...	33
Selector mechanism to transaxle...	17
Starter motor mounting bolts	See Chapter 5A
Transaxle to engine	35

MT285 Transaxle

Back-up light switch...	84 in-lbs
Coolant pipe to transaxle	22
Engine/transaxle rear mount	
Center nut	98
Four outer nuts..	35
Bracket to transaxle	59
Fluid drain plug..	33
Fluid filler/level plug...	33
Selector mechanism to transaxle...	17
Starter motor mounting bolts	25
Transaxle to engine	35

1   General information

The vehicles covered by this manual are equipped with either a 5-speed manual, 6-speed manual or a 4-speed automatic transaxle. This Part of Chapter 7 contains information on the manual transaxle. Service procedures for the automatic transaxle are contained in Part B.

The transaxle is contained in a cast-aluminum alloy casing bolted to the engine's left-hand end, and consists of the gearbox and final drive differential - often called a transaxle. The transaxle unit type is stamped on a plate attached to the transaxle. The 5-speed manual transaxles used in the Focus are the iB5, MT285 and MTX 75 types - refer to the Specifications for application details.

Drive is transmitted from the crankshaft via the clutch to the input shaft, which has a splined extension to accept the clutch friction disc. From the input shaft, drive is transmitted to the output shaft, from where the drive is transmitted to the differential ring gear, which rotates with the differential and planetary gears, thus driving the sun gears and driveaxles. The rotation of the planetary gears on their shaft allows the inner wheel to rotate at a slower speed than the outer wheel when the car is cornering.

The input and output shafts are arranged side-by-side, parallel to the crankshaft and driveaxles, so that their gear pinion teeth are in constant mesh. In the neutral position, the output shaft gear pinions rotate freely, so that drive cannot be transmitted to the ring gear. Gear selection is via a floor-mounted lever and shift cable mechanism.

The transaxle selector mechanism causes the appropriate selector fork to move its respective synchro-sleeve along the output shaft, to lock the gear pinion to the syn-

2.5 Remove the cover from the selector mechanism

chro-hub. Since the synchro-hubs are splined to the output shaft, this locks the pinion to the shaft, so that drive can be transmitted. To ensure that gear changing can be made quickly and quietly, all forward gears are equipped with a synchromesh system consisting of synchro rings and spring-loaded fingers, as well as the gear pinions and synchro-hubs. The synchromesh cones are formed on the mating faces of the synchro rings and gear pinions. The MTX 75 and MT285 have synchromesh on reverse gear, and dual synchromesh on 1st, 2nd and 3rd gears, for even smoother gear changing.

Transaxle overhaul

Because of the complexity of the assembly, possible unavailability of replacement parts and special tools necessary, internal repair procedures for the transaxle are not recommended for the home mechanic. The bulk of the information in this Chapter is devoted to removal and replacement procedures.

2 Shift cables - adjustment

iB5 transaxle

Refer to illustration 2.5
Note: *A 1/8-inch drill bit will be required for this adjustment.*

1 Inside the car, move the shift lever to neutral.
2 Carefully unclip the surround panel at the base of the shift lever boot, and move the panel aside for access to the base of the shift lever, disconnecting the switch wiring if necessary.
3 Insert a 1/8-inch drill bit into the shift lever base mechanism, making sure that it is fully inserted.
4 Apply the parking brake, then jack up the front of the car, supporting it on axle stands (see *Jacking and Towing*). Where applicable, remove the engine undershield.
5 At the front face of the transaxle hous-

ing, remove the selector mechanism cover by working around the edge, releasing a total of seven clips **(see illustration)**.
6 Only the selector cable is to be adjusted during this procedure - this is the cable which comes to the lowest point on the front of the transaxle, with its end fitting nearest the engine.
7 Unlock the selector cable by pressing the colored insert towards the engine, and move the transaxle selector lever (not the shift lever inside the car) to its center position by moving it up or down as necessary.
8 Now move the transaxle selector lever fully to its left- and right-hand stop positions, and release it. Lock the selector cable in the final position by moving the colored insert away from the engine.
9 Install the selector mechanism cover, ensuring that the clips engage correctly, and lower the car to the ground.
10 Inside the car, remove the drill bit from the shift lever base mechanism, and install the surround panel.
11 Start the engine, keeping the clutch pedal depressed, and check for correct gear selection.

MTX75 and MT285 transaxles

Note 1: *A special tool will be required in order to carry out the following adjustment. This tool locks the shift lever in the neutral position during adjustment. If the tool is not available, adjustment is still possible by proceeding on a trial-and-error basis, preferably with the help of an assistant to hold the shift lever in the neutral position.*
Note 2: *On some models with the MTX 75 transaxle, access to the shift cables (at the rear of the transaxle) is far from easy, and may in fact only be at all possible from above. If this is found to be the case, removing the air cleaner and the auxiliary fusebox will improve working room.*

12 Apply the parking brake, then jack up the front of the car, supporting it on axle stands (see *Jacking and Towing*). Where applicable, remove the engine undershield and left-hand fenderwell liner.

13 Move the shift lever to Neutral (2005 and earlier models) or 4th gear (2006 and later models).
14 Under the car, the shift and selector levers on the transaxle should be vertical when neutral is selected. On some models, it may only be possible to view the cables from above, and even then, not easily.
15 If adjustment is required, release the adjusters on the cables by depressing the tabs on the sides of the red plastic locking sliders on the selector cable.
16 If using the special tool, inside the car, pry out the shift lever boot frame and pull the boot up onto the shift knob. Lock the shift lever in neutral.
17 If the special tool is not available, have an assistant place the shift lever in the approximate neutral position, and hold it there.
18 With the levers on the transaxle in neutral, lock the red plastic locking sliders by pressing them in.
19 Where applicable, remove the special tool, and install the boot to the shift lever.
20 Lower the car to the ground. Start the engine, keeping the clutch pedal depressed, and check for correct gear selection.

3 Shift cables and gear lever - removal and installation

Note: *On some models with the MTX 75 and MT285 transaxles, access to the shift cables (at the rear of the transaxle) is far from easy, and may in fact only be at all possible from above. If this is found to be the case, removing the air cleaner and the auxiliary fusebox will improve working room.*

Removal

Refer to illustrations 3.7a, 3.7b, 3.8, 3.10a, 3.10b, 3.10c, 3.10d and 3.15

1 Disconnect the negative battery cable (see Chapter 5).
2 Inside the car, place the gear lever in neutral.
3 Apply the parking brake, then loosen the front wheel nuts. Jack up the front of the vehicle and support it on axle stands (see *Jacking and Towing*). Remove both wheels.
4 Remove the engine undershield (where applicable) and the left-hand fenderwell liner.
5 Remove the front section of the exhaust pipe, referring to Chapter 4A. Note particularly that the flexible section of the exhaust must not be bent too far during removal.
6 Remove the washer-type fasteners, and lower the exhaust heat shield from the vehicle underside.
7 At the transaxle, unclip the cover (if equipped) from the selector mechanism. Remove the cables from the support brackets by twisting the spring-loaded knurled collars clockwise (iB5) or counterclockwise (MTX75/MT285). Release the colored plastic clips that secure the cable adjuster(s), and remove the cables from the transaxle levers -

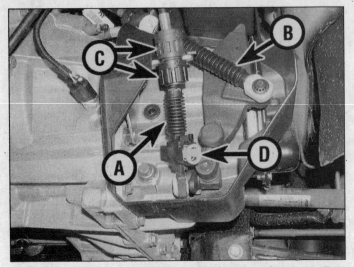

3.7a Selector (A) and shift (B) cables, with support bracket collars (C) and cable adjuster securing clip (D) - iB5 transaxle

3.7b Remove the selector cable - MTX75/MT285 type transaxle shown

note their installed locations **(see illustrations)**. Withdraw the cables downwards from the engine compartment.

8   Unclip and remove the shift lever trim panel, then lift it upwards and disconnect the switch wiring **(see illustration)**.

9   Remove the center console as described in Chapter 11. On 2005 and later models, remove the lower heater case cover and duct (see Chapter 3).

10   Disconnect the shift (white) and selector (black) inner cables from the gear lever by prying off the end fittings. Disconnect the cable casings from the floor brackets by twisting the collars clockwise (iB5) or counterclockwise against each other (MTX 75) **(see illustrations)**.

11   Remove the fasteners securing the heater air duct to the floor, and remove the duct.

12   Unscrew the fasteners securing the side cover panels between the center section of the dash panel and the floor, and remove the panels. Behind these panels, release the clips and remove the screws securing the heater side panels, and remove the panels.

13   Fold back the carpet and insulation material under the center part of the dash for access to the selector cable floor grommet. Remove the two screws and release the grommet from the floor.

14   Pass the cables down through the vehicle floor, and remove them from under the car.

15   If required, the shift lever can be removed by unscrewing the mounting bolts, or the complete shift mechanism can be removed by unscrewing the four nuts **(see illustration)**.

Installation

16   Installation is a reversal of removal. Use new clips when reconnecting the shift cables, and adjust the cables as described in Section 2.

4   Vehicle speed sensor - removal and installation

1   The Focus has an electronic speedometer, rather than the older, cable-driven mechanical type. An electronic sensor is installed in the transaxle (in place of the older speedometer drive pinion), and the speed signal from this sensor is passed to the instrument panel via the engine management PCM. Besides driving

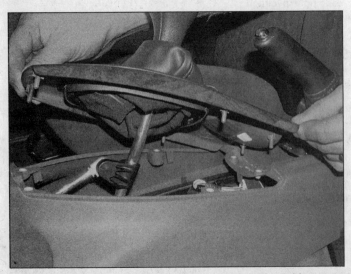

3.8 Unclip the shift lever trim for access to the cables

3.10a Shift lever and cables with center console removed

3.10b Pry the inner cable end fittings with a screwdriver . . .

3.10c . . . and disconnect them from the lever

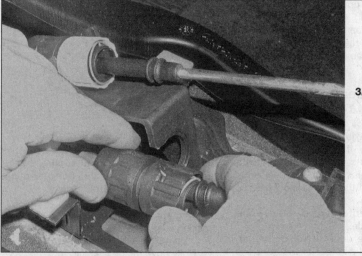

3.10d Release the cable casings from the floor brackets by twisting the knurled collars

the speedometer, the speed sensor signal is used by the PCM as one of the parameters for fuel system-related calculations.

Removal

Refer to illustration 4.3

2   Access to the speed sensor is easiest from below. Apply the parking brake, then loosen the left-hand front wheel nuts. Jack up the front of the car and support it on axle stands (see *Jacking and Towing*).

3   Remove the left-hand front wheel and the fenderwell liner - the sensor is located next to the right-hand driveaxle, at the rear of the transaxle **(see illustration)**.

4   Disconnect the wiring plug from the top of the sensor.

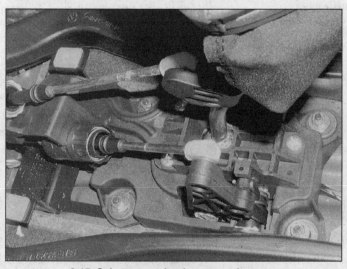

3.15 Selector mechanism mounting nuts

4.3 Vehicle speed sensor (arrow) - seen from below (iB5 model shown)

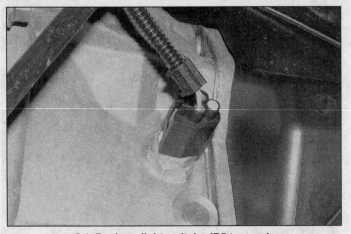

5.1 Back-up light switch - iB5 transaxle

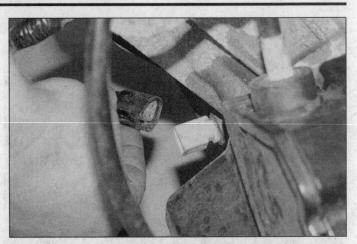

5.2 Disconnect the back-up light switch wiring plug

5   Using needle-nose pliers, pull out the retaining pin at the base of the sensor, noting how it is installed.

6   Pull the sensor out of its location in the transaxle - be prepared for a little oil spillage. Recover the O-ring seal - install a new seal if the old one is in poor condition.

Installation

7   Installation is a reversal of the removal procedure, but lightly oil the O-ring before inserting the assembly in the transaxle casing.

---

5   Back-up light switch - removal and installation

iB5 transaxle

Refer to illustrations 5.1 and 5.2

1   The switch is located on the front of the transaxle, next to the selector cable front cover **(see illustration)**. To improve access, jack up the front left-hand side of the car (see *Jacking and Towing*).

2   Disconnect the wiring plug from the switch **(see illustration)**.

3   Unscrew and remove the switch from the front of the transaxle - anticipate a little oil spillage as this is done.

4   Installation is a reversal of removal. Tighten the switch to the specified torque.

MTX75 and MT285 transaxles

Refer to illustration 5.6

5   The switch is located on top of the transmission. Remove the air cleaner as described in Chapter 4, and the battery and battery tray, as described in Chapter 5A.

6   Disconnect the wiring leading to the back-up light switch on the top of the transaxle **(see illustration)**.

7   Unscrew the mounting bolts and remove the back-up light switch from the cover housing on the transaxle.

8   Installation is a reversal of the removal procedure.

---

6   Oil seals - replacement

1   Oil leaks frequently occur due to wear or deterioration of the driveaxle oil seals, vehicle speed sensor O-ring, or the selector shaft oil seal (iB5). Replacement of these seals is relatively easy, since the repairs can be performed without removing the transaxle from the vehicle.

Driveaxle oil seals

Refer to illustrations 6.4 and 6.7

2   The driveaxle oil seals are located at the sides of the transaxle, where the driveaxles enter the transaxle. If leakage at the seal is suspected, raise the vehicle and support it securely on axle stands. If the seal is leaking, oil will be found on the side of the transaxle below the driveaxle.

3   Refer to Chapter 8 and remove the appropriate driveaxle.

4   Using a large screwdriver or prybar, carefully pry the oil seal out of the transaxle casing, taking care not to damage the transaxle casing **(see illustration)**.

5   Wipe clean the oil seal seat in the transaxle casing.

6   Dip the new oil seal in clean oil, then

5.6 Disconnect the multi-plug, then unscrew the two retaining bolts (arrows) - MTX 75 transaxle

press it a little way into the casing by hand, making sure that it is square to its seat.

7   Using a seal driver or a large socket, carefully drive the oil seal fully into the casing until it contacts the seating **(see illustration)**.

8   When replacing the left-hand driveaxle on the iB5 transaxle, use the protective sleeve which should be provided with factory parts. The sleeve is inserted into the seal, and the

6.4 Pry out the oil seal with a suitable lever

6.7 Drive in the oil seal using a socket

8.3a Pry up the locking clip . . .

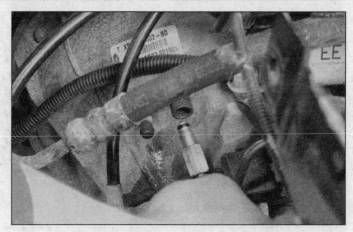

8.3b . . . then pull the clutch hydraulic line out

driveaxle is then inserted through it - the sleeve is then withdrawn.

9   Install the driveaxle (see Chapter 8).

Vehicle speed sensor oil seal

10   The procedure is covered in Section 4.

Selector shaft oil seal (iB5)

11   Apply the parking brake, then jack up the front of the car, supporting it on axle stands.

12   At the front face of the transaxle housing, remove the selector mechanism cover by working around the edge, releasing a total of seven clips.

13   Pry off the retaining clips, then pull the shift and selector cables from the transaxle levers, and detach them from the cable support brackets by turning the knurled collars clockwise.

14   Unscrew and remove the four bolts securing the selector mechanism rear cover to the transaxle housing.

15   Remove the transaxle shift lever by prying off the protective cap and extracting the retaining clip.

16   With the shift lever removed, unscrew the securing bolt and take off the selector lever and dust cover.

17   The selector shaft oil seal can now be pried out of its location. If using a screwdriver or similar sharp tool, take great care not to mark or gouge the selector shaft or the seal housing as this is done, or the new seal will also leak.

18   Before installing the new oil seal, carefully clean the visible part of the selector shaft, and the oil seal housing. Wrap a little tape around the end of the shaft, to protect the seal lips as they pass over it.

19   Smear the new oil seal with a little oil, then carefully guide it over the end of the selector shaft, lips facing inwards (towards the transaxle).

20   Making sure that the seal stays square to the shaft, press it fully along the shaft (if available, a 16 mm box-end wrench is ideal for this).

21   Press the seal fully into its housing, again using the box-end wrench or perhaps a

deep socket. Remove the tape from the end of the shaft.

22   The remainder of installation is a reversal of removal. Tighten the selector lever securing bolt to the specified torque, and use new clips when reconnecting the shift cables.

23   On completion, check and if necessary adjust the cables as described in Section 2.

---

7   Transaxle oil - draining and refilling

Note: *Although not included in the maintenance schedule by the manufacturer, it is a good idea to drain and replace the manual transaxle oil on a regular basis. The frequency with which this needs to be carried out can be left to the individual, but it is certainly advisable on a vehicle that has covered a high mileage.*

iB5 transaxle

1   The iB5 transaxle has no drain plug; the most effective way to drain the oil is to remove one or both driveshafts, as described in Chapter 8.

2   When refilling the transaxle, remember that the vehicle must be level for the oil level to be correct. Refill the transaxle using the information in Chapter 1 - refer to *Recommended lubricants and fluids* in the Chapter 1 Specifications for the type of oil to be used.

MTX75 and MT285 transaxles

3   The drain plug is located in the base of the differential housing - like the oil filler/level plug, a special hexagonal socket (or large Allen key) will be required for removal.

4   The oil is best drained when the transaxle is hot, but bear in mind the risk of burning yourself on hot exhaust components, etc. Apply the parking brake, then jack up the front of the car, and support it on axle stands (see *Jacking and towing*).

5   Where applicable, remove the engine undershield. Position a suitable container under the transaxle drain plug, then unscrew and remove it, and allow the oil to drain.

6   When the flow of oil stops, clean and install the drain plug, and tighten it to the

specified torque.

7   When refilling the transaxle, remember that the vehicle must be level for the oil level to be correct. Refill the transaxle using the information in Chapter 1 - refer to *Recommended lubricants and fluids* in the Chapter 1 Specifications for the type of oil to be used.

---

8   Transaxle - removal and installation

Warning: *The hydraulic fluid used in the system is brake fluid, which is poisonous. Brake fluid can harm your eyes and damage painted surfaces, so use extreme caution when handling or pouring it. Do not use brake fluid which is more than one year old. Brake fluid absorbs moisture from the air. Excess moisture can cause a dangerous loss of braking effectiveness.*

Note: *Read through this procedure before starting work to see what is involved, particularly in terms of lifting equipment. Depending on the facilities available, the home mechanic may prefer to remove the engine and transaxle together, then separate them on the bench, as described in Chapter 2C. The help of an assistant is highly recommended if the transaxle is to be removed (and later installed) on its own.*

Removal - iB5 transaxle

Refer to illustrations 8.3a, 8.3b, 8.4, 8.9, 8.12a, 8.12b, 8.12c, 8.14, 8.18, 8.19, 8.20a, 8.20b and 8.26

1   Remove the air cleaner and intake duct as described in Chapter 4A.

2   Remove the battery and battery tray as described in Chapter 5A, and the ignition coil, as described in Chapter 5B.

3   Make sure that the shift lever is in neutral. Taking adequate precautions against brake fluid spillage (refer to the *Warning* at the start of this Section), pull out the securing clip, then pull the line fitting out of the clutch slave cylinder at the top of the transaxle **(see illustrations)**. Plug or tape over the end of the line, to avoid losing fluid, and to prevent dirt entry.

8.4 Unclip the hydraulic line from the bracket on top of the transaxle

8.9 Unclip and remove the plastic cover from the front of the transaxle

8.12a Unscrew the starter motor mounting bolts . . .

4   Unclip the slave cylinder fluid line from the support bracket, and move it clear of the transaxle **(see illustration)**.

5   On models through 2002, remove the plastic cap from the top of each front suspension strut, at the inner fender mounting in the engine compartment. Holding the piston rod against rotation using an Allen key, loosen each strut's center nut by five full turns using a large box wrench. On 2003 and later models, do not loosen the center nut, but instead loosen the three mounting nuts 5 turns, on the left-hand strut *only*. On 2004 and 2005 models, only loosen the nuts four turns. Remove the plastic cap from the top of each front suspension strut, at the inner fender mounting in the engine compartment. Holding the piston rod against rotation using an Allen key, loosen each strut's center nut by five full turns using a box-end wrench.

6   Before jacking up the front of the car, loosen the front wheel nuts, and if possible, the driveshaft retaining nuts.

7   Apply the parking brake, and chock the rear wheels. Jack up the front of the car, and support it on axle stands (see *Jacking and Towing*). There must be sufficient clearance below the car for the transaxle to be lowered and withdrawn. Remove the front wheels and, where applicable, the engine undershield.

8   Disconnect the wiring plugs from the back-up light switch, and from the vehicle speed sensor, referring to Sections 4 and 5 if necessary.

9   At the front of the transaxle, unclip the cover from the selector mechanism **(see illustration)**. Remove the cables from the support brackets by twisting the spring-loaded knurled collars clockwise. Release the colored plastic clip securing the selector cable adjuster, and remove the cables from the transaxle levers - note their locations. Release the cables from the clips on top of the transaxle, and move the cables clear.

10   Working from below, remove the two fasteners securing the auxiliary drivebelt lower cover, and remove the cover from the engine.

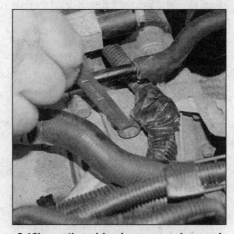

8.12b . . . the wiring harness and ground point is attached to this bolt . . .

11   Remove both driveshafts from the transaxle as described in Chapter 8.

12   Remove the starter motor as described in Chapter 5A. Note that a ground cable is attached to the upper mounting bolt, and the transaxle cable support bracket is secured to the rear bolt **(see illustrations)**. As far as possible, pull the wiring harness through and to one side of the transaxle.

13   Unscrew and remove the two nuts/bolts, and separate the exhaust front pipe at the first flange joint under the car. Unhook the exhaust pipe from the rubber mountings.

14   Unscrew the two through-bolts and remove the engine/transaxle rear mount from the subframe **(see illustration)**.

15   The engine/transaxle must now be supported, as the left-hand mounting must be disassembled and removed. Dealer technicians use a support bar that locates in the tops of the inner fenders - proprietary engine support bars are available from tool rental outlets.

16   If a support bar is not available, an engine hoist should be used. With an engine hoist, the engine/transaxle can be maneuvered more easily and safely. In the workshop, we found the best solution was to move the engine to the required position, and sup-

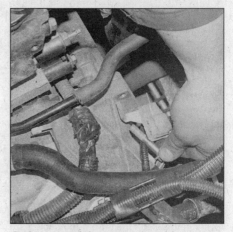

8.12c . . . and the transaxle cable support bracket is attached to this one

port it from below - using the hoist on the transaxle then gave excellent maneuverability, and total control for lowering out.

17   Supporting both the engine and transaxle from below should be considered a last resort, and should only be done if a heavy-duty hydraulic floor jack is used, with a large, flat piece of wood on the jack head to spread the load and avoid damage to the oil

8.14 Remove the engine/transaxle rear mount

8.18 Lift off the top section of the left-hand mount

8.19 Unscrew the two bolts (arrows) securing the mounting brace

8.20a Unscrew the three nuts (arrows) . . .

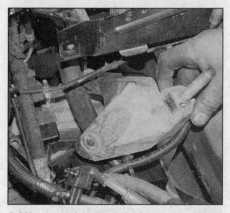

8.20b . . . and remove the lower section of the left-hand mount

pan. Another jack will be needed to lower the transaxle out (if you're not using the hoist method described in Step 16), preferably one made for this purpose, equipped with safety chains (these can be obtained at most equipment rental yards). **Note:** *Always take care when using a hydraulic jack, as it is possible for this type to collapse under load.*

18 With the engine securely supported, progressively unscrew and remove the nuts securing the top section of the engine left-hand mount, and lift it off **(see illustration).**

19 Remove the bolts securing the engine left-hand mounting brace, and remove the brace from the engine mount **(see illustration).**

20 Remove three further nuts, and remove the lower section of the engine left-hand mount - note that one of the nuts secures the clutch hydraulic pipe support bracket **(see illustrations).**

21 Unscrew and remove the uppermost transaxle-to-engine flange bolts - do not remove all the flange bolts at this stage.

22 Taking care that nothing which is still attached to the engine is placed under strain, lower the transaxle as far as possible.

23 Remove the transaxle-to-engine lower flange bolts, noting that, on some models, one of the bolts also retains the power steering pipe support bracket. The flange bolts are of different lengths, so note their positions carefully for replacement.

24 Check that, apart from the remaining flange bolts, there is nothing preventing the transaxle from being lowered and removed. Make sure that any wiring or hoses lying on top of the transaxle are not going to get caught up and stretched as the transaxle is lowered.

25 Unscrew the remaining flange bolts. If the transaxle does not separate on its own, it must be rocked from side-to-side, to free it from the locating dowels. As the transaxle is withdrawn from the engine, make sure its weight is supported at all times - the transaxle input shaft (or the clutch) may otherwise be damaged as it is withdrawn through the clutch assembly bolted to the engine flywheel. Recover the adapter plates installed between

the engine and transaxle, as they may fall out when the two are separated.

26 Keeping the transaxle steady, carefully lower it down and remove it from under the car **(see illustration).** The transaxle will have to be moved forwards to clear the subframe as it is lowered - if the transaxle is being supported from below, take care that it is kept steady.

27 The clutch components can now be inspected with reference to Chapter 6, and replaced if necessary. Unless they are virtually new, it is worth replacing the clutch components as a matter of course, even if the transaxle has been removed for some other reason.

Removal - MTX 75 transaxle

28 Remove the air cleaner and intake duct as described in Chapter 4A. Also remove the air intake from the front panel, and the resonator and air intake tube.

29 Remove the battery and battery tray as described in Chapter 5A, and the ignition coil (models through 2004) as described in Chapter 5B.

30 Unscrew the bolt and disconnect the main ground lead next to the windshield washer reservoir filler neck.

31 If available, attach the special tool to the shift lever as described in Section 3.

32 Make sure that the shift lever is in neutral. Pry off the retaining clips, and pull the shift and selector cable end fittings from the transaxle levers. Release the colored locking sliders by pressing them in. Disconnect the cable casings from the support brackets by turning the knurled collars counterclockwise. Move the cables clear of the transaxle.

33 Taking adequate precautions against brake fluid spillage (refer to the *Warning* at the start of this Section), pull out the securing clip, then pull the fitting out of the clutch slave cylinder at the top of the transaxle. Plug or tape over the end of the fitting, to avoid losing fluid, and to prevent dirt entry.

34 Move the slave cylinder fluid line clear of the transaxle.

35 On models through 2002, remove the

plastic cap from the top of each front suspension strut, at the inner fender mounting in the engine compartment. Holding the piston rod against rotation using an Allen key, loosen each strut's center nut by five full turns using a large box wrench. On 2003 and later models, do not loosen the center nut, but instead loosen the three mounting nuts 5 turns, on the left-hand strut *only*. On 2004 and later models, only loosen the nuts four turns.

36 Before jacking up the front of the car, loosen the front wheel nuts and the driveaxle retaining nuts.

8.26 Lowering out the transaxle

37   Apply the parking brake, and chock the rear wheels. Jack up the front of the car, and support it on axle stands (see *Jacking and Towing*). There must be sufficient clearance below the car for the transaxle to be lowered and withdrawn. Remove the front wheels and where applicable, the engine undershield.

38   Disconnect the wiring plugs from the back-up light switch, and from the vehicle speed sensor, referring to Sections 4 and 5 if necessary.

39   Working from below, remove the two fasteners securing the auxiliary drivebelt lower cover, and remove the cover from the engine.

40   Remove both driveaxles from the transaxle as described in Chapter 8.

41   Remove the starter motor as described in Chapter 5A.

42   Unscrew the flange nuts/bolts at either end, and remove the flexible section of exhaust pipe from under the car. Refer to Chapter 4A and remove the catalytic converter.

43   Unscrew the two through-bolts and remove the engine/transaxle rear mount from the subframe.

44   The engine/transaxle must now be supported, as the left-hand mounting must be disassembled and removed. Dealer technicians use a support bar that locates in the tops of the inner fenders - proprietary engine support bars are available from tool rental outlets.

45   If a support bar is not available, an engine hoist should be used. With an engine hoist, the engine/transaxle can be maneuvered more easily and safely. In the workshop, we found the best solution was to move the engine to the required position, and support it from below - using the hoist on the transaxle then gave excellent maneuverability, and total control for lowering out.

46   Supporting both the engine and transaxle from below should be considered a last resort, and should only be done if a heavy-duty hydraulic floor jack is used, with a large, flat piece of wood on the jack head to spread the load and avoid damage to the oil pan. Another jack will be needed to lower the transaxle out (if you're not using the hoist method described in Step 16), preferably one made for this purpose, equipped with safety chains (these can be obtained at most equipment rental yards). **Note:** *Always take care when using a hydraulic jack, as it is possible for this type to collapse under load.*

47   With the engine securely supported, progressively unscrew and remove the nuts securing the top section of the engine left-hand mount, and lift it off.

48   Remove three further nuts/bolts, and remove the lower section of the engine left-hand mount.

49   Unscrew and remove the two uppermost transaxle-to-engine flange bolts - do not remove all the flange bolts at this stage. The flange bolts are of different lengths, so note their positions carefully for replacement.

50   Swing the transaxle forwards, and wedge it in position with a stout piece of wood, about 13-inches long, between the engine and the subframe.

51   Check that, apart from the remaining flange bolts, there is nothing preventing the transaxle from being lowered and removed. Make sure that any wiring or hoses lying on top of the transaxle are not going to get caught up and stretched as the transaxle is lowered.

52   Unscrew the remaining flange bolts. If the transaxle does not separate on its own, it must be rocked from side-to-side, to free it from the locating dowels. As the transaxle is withdrawn from the engine, make sure its weight is supported at all times - the transaxle input shaft (or the clutch) may otherwise be damaged as it is withdrawn through the clutch assembly bolted to the engine flywheel. Recover the adapter plates installed between the engine and transaxle, as they may fall out when the two are separated.

53   Keeping the transaxle steady, carefully lower it down and remove it from under the car.

54   The clutch components can now be inspected with reference to Chapter 6, and replaced if necessary. Unless they are virtually new, it is worth replacing the clutch components as a matter of course, even if the transaxle has been removed for some other reason.

Installation

55   If removed, install the clutch components (see Chapter 6). Also ensure that the engine-to-transaxle adapter plates are in position on the engine.

56   Where a block of wood was used to wedge the engine forwards for transaxle removal, make sure that it is in place for installation.

57   With the transaxle secured to the hoist/floor jack as on removal, raise it into position, and then carefully slide it onto the engine, at the same time engaging the input shaft with the clutch friction disc splines. If marks were made between the transaxle and engine on removal, these can be used as a guide to correct alignment.

58   Do not use excessive force to install the transaxle - if the input shaft does not slide into place easily, readjust the angle of the transaxle so that it is level, and/or turn the input shaft so that the splines engage properly with the disc. If problems are still experienced, check that the clutch friction disc is correctly centered (Chapter 6).

59   Once the transaxle is successfully mated to the engine, insert as many of the flange bolts as possible, and tighten them progressively, to draw the transaxle fully onto the locating dowels.

60   Install the lower section of the engine left-hand mounting, and tighten the nuts to the specified torque. On the iB5 transaxle, install the mounting brace/pipe support bracket, and tighten the mounting bolts.

61   Where applicable, remove the wedge placed between the engine and subframe.

Raise the transaxle into position, then install the upper section of the engine left-hand mount. Tighten the nuts to the specified torque, noting that the center nut is tightened considerably more than the four outer ones.

62   Install the remaining transaxle-to-engine bolts, and tighten all of them to the specified torque.

63   Install the engine/transaxle rear mount to the subframe, and tighten the through-bolts to the specified torque.

64   Once the engine/transaxle mounts have been replaced, the support bar, engine hoist or supporting jack can be removed.

65   The remainder of installation is a reversal of removal, noting the following points:

   a) *Install the starter motor as described in Chapter 5A.*
   b) *Install the driveshafts as described in Chapter 8.*
   c) *On completion, adjust the gear cables as described in Section 2.*
   d) *Tighten the suspension strut center nuts to the torque listed in the Chapter 10 Specifications.*

9   Transaxle overhaul - general information

The overhaul of a manual transaxle is a complex (and often expensive) engineering task for the DIY home mechanic to undertake, which requires access to specialized equipment. It involves dismantling and reassembly of many small components, measuring clearances precisely and if necessary, adjusting them by the selection shims and spacers. Internal transaxle components are also often difficult to obtain and in many instances, extremely expensive. Because of this, if the transaxle develops a fault or becomes noisy, the best course of action is to have the unit overhauled by a specialist or to obtain an exchange reconditioned unit.

Nevertheless, it is not impossible for the more experienced mechanic to overhaul the transaxle if the special tools are available and the job is carried out in a deliberate step-by-step manner, to ensure that nothing is overlooked.

The tools necessary for an overhaul include internal and external snap-ring pliers, bearing pullers, a slide hammer, a set of pin punches, a dial test indicator, and possibly a hydraulic press. In addition, a large, sturdy workbench and a vise will be required.

During dismantling of the transaxle, make careful notes of how each component is installed to make reassembly easier and accurate.

Before dismantling the transaxle, it will help if you have some idea of where the problem lies. Certain problems can be closely related to specific areas in the transaxle that can make component examination and replacement easier. Refer to *Troubleshooting* at the front of this manual for more information.

Chapter 7 Part B
Automatic transaxle

Contents

Specifications

General

Transaxle type	Electronically-controlled automatic, four forward speeds (one overdrive) and reverse. Selectable overdrive function, torque converter lock-up in 3rd and 4th gears
Transaxle code	4F27E

Gear ratios (typical)

1st	2.816:1
2nd	1.498:1
3rd	1.000:1
4th	0.726:1
Reverse	2.649:1

Torque specifications

Ft-lbs (unless otherwise indicated)

Note: *One foot-pound (ft-lb) of torque is equivalent to 12 inch-pounds (in-lbs) of torque. Torque values below approximately 15 ft-lbs are expressed in inch-pounds, since most foot-pound torque wrenches are not accurate at these smaller values.*

Engine/transaxle left-hand mounting lower section	59
Engine/transaxle left-hand mounting upper section	
Center nut	98
Four outer nuts	35
Engine/transaxle rear mounting nuts	35
Rear engine mount bracket bolts	59
Fluid pan bolts	See Chapter 1
Wheel nuts	See Chapter 1
Torque converter to driveplate (use new nuts)	27
Transaxle lever bolt	84 in-lbs
Transaxle range sensor bolts	84 in-lbs
Transaxle to engine	35

1 General information

The 4F27E automatic transaxle is controlled electronically by the engine management Powertrain Control Module (PCM). This is an all-new four-speed unit, featuring an overdrive top gear and a lock-up torque converter. This unit, which was developed by Mazda and is built in the USA, has been designed specifically for front-wheel-drive applications, and is particularly light and compact.

The transaxle control system is known as ESSC (electronic synchronous shift control) contained within a specially-modified EEC-V engine management system module, only used on Focus automatic models. The electronic control system has a fail-safe mode, which gives the transaxle limited operation in order to drive the vehicle home or to a repair garage. A warning light on the instrument panel tells the driver when this occurs. The EEC-V module uses all the information available from the various transaxle and engine management-related sensors (also see Chapters 4A and 5B) to determine the optimum gearshift points for smoothness, performance and economy. Depending on throttle position and vehicle speed, the module can 'lock-up' the torque converter in 3rd and 4th gear, eliminating torque converter 'slip' and improving fuel consumption.

The transaxle features a selectable overdrive top gear. When this is enabled (using a pushbutton on the underside of the selector lever), a fourth, extra-high ratio can be selected automatically; otherwise, the transaxle will only use three forward speeds. An O/D OFF warning light is illuminated when the overdrive function is disabled.

The unit has been designed to have a low maintenance requirement, the fluid level being checked periodically (see Chapter 1). The fluid is intended to last the life of the transaxle, and is cooled by a separate cooler located next to the radiator.

There is no kickdown switch, as kickdown is controlled by the throttle position sensor in the engine management system.

The gear selector includes the normal P, R, N, D, 2, and 1 positions.

As is normally the case with automatic transaxles, a starter inhibitor relay is used, which prevents the engine from being started (by interrupting the supply to the starter solenoid) when the selector is in any position other than P or N. The intention is to prevent the car moving, which might otherwise happen if the engine were started in position D, for example. The inhibitor system is controlled by the EEC-V module, based on signals received from the engine and transaxle sensors. For more details on relay locations, see Chapter 12.

As a further safety measure, the ignition key can only be removed from the ignition switch when the selector is in P; it is also necessary for the ignition to be on, and for the brake pedal and selector lever locking button (on the side of the lever) to be depressed in order to move the selector from position P. If the vehicle battery is discharged, the selector lever release solenoid will not function. If it is required to move the vehicle in this state, insert a pen or a similar small instrument into the aperture on the left-hand side of the center console. Push the locking lever downwards and move the selector lever to the required position.

2   Troubleshooting - general

In the event of a fault occurring on the transaxle, first check that the fluid level is correct (see Chapter 1). If there has been a loss of fluid, check the oil seals as described in Section 6. Also check the hoses to the fluid cooler in the radiator for leaks. The only other tasks possible for the home mechanic are the replacement of the various transaxle sensors (Section 5); however, it is not advisable to go ahead and replace any sensor until the fault has been positively identified by reading the transaxle DTC (Diagnostic Trouble Code) codes.

Any serious fault that occurs will result in the transaxle entering the fail-safe mode, and a trouble code (or several codes) will be logged in the control module. These codes can only be read using an electronic scan tool. See Chapter 4B for scan tool and trouble code information (but keep in mind that most generic scan tools do not have the capability to retrieve transaxle-related trouble codes).

If the fault persists, it is necessary to determine whether it is of an electrical, mechanical or hydraulic nature; to do this, special test equipment is required. It is therefore essential to have the work carried out by an automatic transaxle specialist or dealer if a transaxle fault is suspected.

Do not remove the transaxle from the vehicle for possible repair before professional troubleshooting has been carried out, since most tests require the transaxle to be in the vehicle.

3   Selector cable - removal, installation and adjustment

Removal

1   Loosen the left-hand front wheel nuts. Apply the parking brake, jack up the front of the vehicle and support it on axle stands. Remove the left-hand front wheel.

2   Remove the front section of the exhaust pipe, referring to Chapter 4A as necessary. Note particularly that the flexible section of the exhaust must not be bent too far during removal.

3   Remove the 'flat nut' fasteners, and lower the exhaust heat shield from the vehicle underside.

4   Locate the end of the selector cable, which is on the front of the transaxle.

5   Disconnect the cable end fitting by prying it off the transaxle selector lever.

6   Unclip the cable casing from the bracket on the transaxle - the cable is secured by a locking collar that must be turned through 90 degrees counterclockwise to remove.

7   Trace the cable back from the selector lever, releasing it from the various clips attaching it to the transaxle and underside of the car. Remove the heat shield, then pry out the grommet from the vehicle floor where the cable passes into the car.

8   Remove the center console as described in Chapter 11.

9   Move the selector lever to P. Working through the front of the selector housing, disconnect the cable inner from the lever by prying the end fitting sideways, then unclip the cable outer from the floor bracket by pulling upwards.

10   Remove the fasteners securing the heater air duct to the floor, and remove the duct.

11   Unscrew the fasteners securing the side cover panels between the center section of the dash panel and the floor, and remove the panels. Behind these panels, release the clips and remove the screw(s) securing the heater lower case and remove the cover.

12   Fold back the carpet and insulation material under the center part of the dash, for access to the selector cable floor grommet. Remove the two screws and release the grommet from the floor.

13   Attach a length of mechanic's wire to the cable as it is withdrawn. Pass the cable up through the vehicle floor, and remove it from inside the car.

Installation

14   Installation is the reverse of removal, using the wire to pull the new cable through the floor, noting the following points:

a)   *Once the cable has been reconnected to the selector lever, shift the lever to position D before reconnecting the cable end fitting at the transaxle lever.*

b)   *Before securing the cable to the transaxle bracket or transaxle lever, check the cable adjustment as described below.*

Adjustment

15   Inside the vehicle, move the selector lever to position D.

16   With the inner cable disconnected from the lever on the transaxle, check that the transaxle lever is in the D position. To do this, it will be necessary to move the lever slightly up and down until it is positioned correctly. A further check can be made by observing that the D mark on the selector lever position sensor is correctly aligned with the mark on the transaxle lever.

17   Check that the cable locking collar beneath the vehicle is still unlocked (i.e., turned counterclockwise by 90 degrees).

18   With both the selector levers inside the vehicle and on the side of the transaxle in position D, install the cable end fitting to the transaxle lever, then turn the locking collar 90 degrees clockwise to lock it. The arrowhead markings on the collar should line up when the collar is locked. On 2005 and later models, the adjuster mechanism is at the attachment point of the cable end, at the arm on the transmission. Flip up the locking cover from the adjuster, position the transmission shifter in Drive, then snap the locking cover back down.

19   Install the left-hand front wheel, then lower the vehicle to the ground. Tighten the wheel nuts to the specified torque.

20   Road test the vehicle to check the operation of the transaxle.

4   Selector components - removal and installation

Selector assembly

Removal

1   Remove the center console as described in Chapter 11.

2   Working through the front of the selector housing, disconnect the cable inner from the lever as described in Section 3.

3   Disconnect the multi-plug wiring connectors at the rear of the assembly, noting their positions, and move the wiring harness clear.

4   Unscrew the four mounting nuts, and withdraw the selector lever assembly.

5   If required, the assembly can be further disassembled (after removing the selector lever knob, as described below) by unclipping the top cover and removing the illumination bulb and inner cover.

Installation

6   Installation is a reversal of the removal

procedure, but adjust the selector cable as described in Section 3.

Selector lever knob

Removal

7   Remove the center console as described in Chapter 11.

8   Disconnect the multi-plug connector for the overdrive switch, at the base of the selector lever.

9   Remove the set screw at the side of the knob, below the overdrive button, then pull the knob upwards off the lever.

Installation

10   Installation is a reversal of removal.

---

5   Transaxle sensors - removal and installation

Vehicle/output shaft speed sensor

1   The Focus has an electronic speedometer, rather than the older, cable-driven mechanical type. An electronic sensor is installed in the transaxle (in place of the older speedometer drive pinion), and the speed signal from this sensor is passed to the instrument panel via the engine management PCM. Besides driving the speedometer, the speed sensor signal is used by the PCM as one of the parameters for fuel system-related calculations, and for determining transaxle gearshift points.

Removal

2   Access to the speed sensor is easiest from below. Apply the parking brake, then loosen the left-hand front wheel nuts. Jack up the front of the car and support it on axle stands (see Jacking and Towing).

3   Remove the left-hand front wheel and the fenderwell liner - the sensor is located at the rear of the transaxle, behind the driveaxles.

4   Disconnect the wiring plug from the sensor, then position a suitable container below the sensor, to catch any transaxle fluid that may be spilled as the sensor is removed.

5   Unscrew the sensor securing bolt, and slowly withdraw the sensor from its location.

6   Check the condition of the O-ring seal on the sensor body - install a new seal if the old one is in poor condition.

Installation

7   Installation is a reversal of the removal procedure, but clean the sensor location and lightly oil the O-ring before inserting the assembly in the transaxle casing. Check the transaxle fluid level as described in Chapter 1 on completion.

Transaxle range sensor

8   The transaxle range sensor is effectively a selector position sensor, the signal from which is used by the EEC-V module to modify

the operation of the transaxle, dependent on which 'gear' is selected. For example, besides controlling gearshift points, depending on the signal received, the module may actuate the starter inhibitor relay, the reversing lights, or the ignition key lock.

Removal

Note: To set the range sensor in its working position, special tool 307415 is required. If this tool is not available, the sensor position must be carefully marked before removal.

9   Access to the range sensor is easiest from below - the sensor is at the front of the transaxle, near the transaxle selector lever. Apply the parking brake, then jack up the front of the car and support it on axle stands (see Jacking and Towing).

10   Pry the selector cable end fitting off the transaxle lever, and disconnect the wiring plug from the sensor.

11   Hold the transaxle lever against rotation, then unscrew the lever retaining bolt, and remove the lever from the sensor.

Caution: If the lever is not held as its bolt is undone, the force required to loosen the bolt will be transmitted to the sensor itself, which may well lead to the sensor being damaged. The same applies when retightening the bolt on completion.

12   Before removing the sensor, make a couple of alignment marks between the sensor and the transaxle, for use when replacing.

13   Take precautions against the possible spillage of transaxle fluid. Unscrew the two sensor retaining bolts, and withdraw the sensor from the transaxle.

Installation

14   Clean the sensor location in the transaxle, and the sensor itself. If a new sensor is being installed, transfer the alignment marks from the old unit to the new one - this will provide an approximate setting, which should allow the car to be driven.

15   Install the sensor, and secure it loosely in position with the two bolts, tightened by hand only at this stage.

16   Special tool 307415 must now be used to set the sensor in its working position. If the tool is not available, realign the marks made prior to removal. When correctly aligned, tighten the two sensor retaining bolts to the specified torque.

17   Install the transaxle lever. Tighten the lever retaining bolt to the specified torque, holding the lever against rotation as the bolt is tightened (refer to the Caution earlier in this Section).

18   Reconnect the selector cable to the transaxle lever, and check the cable adjustment as described in Section 3.

19   On completion, lower the car to the ground.

Turbine (input) shaft speed sensor

20   The turbine shaft speed sensor is

located on top of the transaxle, and is an inductive pick-up sensor that senses the speed of rotation of the input shaft. This information is used by the PCM to control gearchanging and the torque converter lock-up clutch. Removal and installation details are similar to the output shaft speed sensor described earlier in this Section.

Brake pedal position switch

21   The signal from the switch is used by the PCM to disengage the torque converter lock-up, and to allow the selector lever to be moved from the P position when starting the engine. Removal and installation details for the switch will be the same as for the stoplight switch, in Chapter 9.

Brake pedal shift interlock actuator

22   This unit is part of the system used to lock the selector lever in P when the ignition key is removed, and is incorporated in the selector lever itself. Note: The interlock cannot be replaced separately on 2005 and later models. The shift assembly must be replaced.

23   Remove the selector knob as described in Section 4. With the knob removed, the actuator pushrod can be pulled out and removed.

24   Installation is a reversal of removal. Check the operation of the system on completion.

Selector lever shift interlock solenoid

25   The main solenoid controlling the shift interlock system (used to lock the selector lever in P when the ignition key is removed) is located at the base of the selector lever. For access to the solenoid, remove the center console as described in Chapter 11.

Transaxle fluid temperature sensor

26   The fluid temperature sensor signal is used by the PCM to determine whether to allow the operation the torque converter lock-up clutch, and the selection of the overdrive 4th gear. The sensor is located among the transaxle solenoid valves inside the fluid pan - no replacement procedure is suggested by the manufacturer, so any suspected problems should be referred to a dealer.

---

6   Oil seals - replacement

Driveaxle oil seals

The procedure is the same as that for the manual transaxle (refer to Chapter 7A).

Vehicle/output shaft speed sensor oil seal

The procedure is covered in Section 5.

7 Fluid pan - removal and installation

Note: *This procedure is provided principally to cure any leak developing from the fluid pan joint. It is not advisable for the DIY mechanic to remove the fluid pan for any other reason, except recommended changes of fluid and filter (see Chapter 1) since it gives access to internal transaxle components, servicing of which is considered beyond the scope of this Manual.*

Removal

1   Apply the parking brake, then jack up the front of the car and support it on axle stands.
2   Place a suitable container below the pan, as most of the contents of the transaxle will drain when the pan is removed.
3   Progressively unscrew and remove the fluid pan bolts.
4   The fluid pan is 'stuck' to the base of the transaxle by a bead of sealant, so it is unlikely that the pan will fall off once the bolts are removed. Care must now be taken to break the sealant without damaging the mating surfaces. Do not pry the pan down, as this may bend it, or damage the sealing surfaces. The most successful method found is to run a sharp knife around the joint - this should cut through sufficiently to make removal possible without excess effort.

Installation

5   With the fluid pan removed, clean off all traces of sealant from the pan and the mating face on the transaxle. Again, take care not to mark either mating surface.
6   Apply a 1/16-inch thick bead of RTV sealant to the fluid pan mating face, running the bead on the inside of the bolt holes. Do not apply excess sealant, or a bead much thicker than suggested, since the excess could end up inside the pan, and contaminate the internal components.
7   Raise the pan up into position, and insert a few of the bolts to locate it. Install all the remaining bolts, and tighten them progressively to the specified torque.
8   Give the sealant time to cure, then trim off any excess with a knife. Refill the transaxle via the dipstick tube, with reference to Chapter 1.
9   On completion, take the car for a run of several miles to get the fluid up to operating temperature, then re-check the fluid level, and check for signs of leakage.

8 Fluid cooler - removal and installation

Warning: *On models with air conditioning, the condenser in front of the radiator must be removed to allow removal of the fluid cooler. Since this entails disconnecting the refrigerant lines from the condenser, this part of the procedure must be entrusted to an air condi-*

tioning specialist - do not attempt to disconnect the refrigerant lines yourself (refer to the warnings in Chapter 3).
Note: *If a leak is discovered at the fluid cooler connections to the transaxle, do not try to cure it by overtightening the unions, as damage will almost certainly result.*

Removal

1   This procedure should only be attempted when the engine and transaxle are completely cool, otherwise there is a great risk of scalding. The fluid cooler is mounted in front of the radiator.
2   Using cable-ties or string, tie either end of the radiator to the front crossmember, using the holes provided - this is to support the radiator later on, when its lower support bracket is removed.
3   Apply the parking brake, then jack up the front of the car and support it on axle stands (see *Jacking and Towing*).
4   Remove the three screws securing the radiator lower splash shield, and remove the shield from under the car.
5   On models with air conditioning, disconnect the wiring plug from the horn unit (at the left-hand side of the radiator). Unclip the compressor wiring from the radiator support bracket.
6   Ensure that the radiator is supported as described in Step 2, then unscrew the bolts at either side, and remove the radiator lower support bracket.
7   Place a container below the fluid cooler connections, to catch the escaping fluid; also note that, if the engine is still warm, the fluid may be extremely hot. Note the positions of the hose connections, then loosen the hose clamps and detach the hoses from the cooler. Tie the hoses up out of the way, and plug the hose ends to prevent the ingress of dirt.
8   On models with air conditioning, the condenser must now be removed as described in Chapter 3.
9   Remove the self-locking nuts from the fluid cooler mounting brackets (two brackets on the right, and one on the left-hand side), then lift the cooler upwards and out. Try to keep the fluid connections end uppermost, to reduce further fluid loss.
10   If required, the fluid cooler hoses can be removed by unscrewing the union nuts at the transaxle fittings. Trace the hoses around the engine compartment, unclipping them as necessary and noting how the hoses are routed for replacement.

Replacement

11   Clean the fluid cooler fins of any debris as necessary, using a small brush - do not use any other tools, as the fins can easily be damaged.
12   Replacement is a reversal of removal, noting the following points:

a)   *If the fluid hoses were removed, tighten the union nuts at the transaxle to the specified torque.*

b)   *Use new self-locking nuts when replacing the cooler to the mounting brackets.*
c)   *Where applicable, the air conditioning system must be recharged by a specialist once the condenser has been installed.*
d)   *Top-off the transaxle fluid level using the information in Chapter 1.*
e)   *Start the engine and check for signs of fluid leakage from the disturbed connections.*

9 Automatic transaxle - removal and replacement

Removal

1   Remove the air cleaner and intake duct as described in Chapter 4A. Also remove the air intake from the front panel, and the resonator and air intake tube.
2   Remove the battery and battery tray as described in Chapter 5A.
3   Disconnect the vacuum hose from the EGR valve (at the transaxle end of the engine - refer to Chapter 4 for more details).
4   On models through 2002, remove the plastic cap from the top of each front suspension strut, at the inner fender mounting in the engine compartment. Holding the piston rod against rotation using an Allen key, loosen each strut's center nut by five full turns using a large box wrench. On 2003 and later models, do not loosen the center nut, but instead loosen the three mounting nuts 5 turns, on the left-hand strut *only*. On 2004 and later models, only loosen the nuts four turns.
5   Remove the three bolts securing the selector cable/fluid filler tube support bracket to the front of the transaxle. Move the bracket to one side, clear of the transaxle.
6   Before jacking up the front of the car, loosen the front wheel nuts and the driveaxle/hub nuts.
7   Apply the parking brake, and chock the rear wheels. Jack up the front of the car, and support it on axle stands (see *Jacking and Towing*). There must be sufficient clearance below the car for the transaxle to be lowered and withdrawn. Remove the front wheels.
8   Disconnect the selector cable end fitting from the transaxle lever as described in Section 3.
9   Disconnect the wiring plugs from the vehicle/output shaft speed sensor, turbine shaft speed sensor and transaxle range sensor, as described in Section 5.
10   Remove the front section of the exhaust pipe, referring to Chapter 4A as necessary. Note particularly that the flexible section of the exhaust must not be bent too far during removal.
11   Remove both driveaxles from the transaxle as described in Chapter 8.
12   Wipe clean around the fluid supply and return pipes on the front of the transaxle. It is essential that no dirt is introduced into the transaxle.
13   Noting their respective positions, unscrew the union nuts and disconnect the

fluid pipes from the transaxle. Be prepared for loss of fluid, and cover the pipe ends and transaxle pipe fittings, to prevent further loss or dirt entry.

14 Remove the starter motor as described in Chapter 5A. Note that one of the mounting bolts also secures the transaxle ground strap.

15 Working from below, unscrew the through-bolts and remove the engine/transaxle rear mount.

16 The engine/transaxle must now be supported, as the left-hand mount must be disassembled and removed. Dealer technicians use a support bar that locates in the tops of the inner fenders - proprietary engine support bars are available from tool rental outlets.

17 Supporting both the engine and transaxle from below should be considered a last resort, and should only be done if a heavy-duty hydraulic floor jack is used, with a large, flat piece of wood on the jack head to spread the load and avoid damage to the oil pan. Another jack will be needed to lower the transaxle out (if you're not using the hoist method described in Step 16), preferably one made for this purpose, equipped with safety chains (these can be obtained at most equipment rental yards). **Note:** *Always take care when using a hydraulic jack, as it is possible for this type to collapse under load.*

18 With the engine securely supported, progressively unscrew and remove the nuts securing the top section of the engine/transaxle left-hand mount, and lift it off.

19 Remove three further nuts/bolts, and remove the lower section of the engine left-hand mount.

20 Locate the transaxle fluid filler tube, and remove the screw at its base where it enters the transaxle. Pull the tube out of its location, and remove it.

21 Remove the cover (if equipped) from the base of the transaxle bellhousing, for access to the four large torque converter nuts. It will be necessary to turn the engine clockwise only (using a wrench or socket on the crankshaft pulley bolt) in order to bring each of the nuts into view. It may also prove necessary to jam the driveplate ring gear with a suitable tool, to prevent the engine turning as the nuts are unscrewed. Before removing the last nut, paint an alignment mark between the converter stud and driveplate. New nuts must be obtained for replacement.

22 Swing the transaxle forwards, and wedge it in position with a stout piece of wood, about a foot long, between the engine and the subframe.

23 Support the transaxle from below, ideally using a transaxle jack (if one is not available, a sturdy jack with a large, flat piece of

wood on top of the jack head will suffice). Have an assistant ready, to help steady the transaxle as the flange bolts are removed - attempting to remove the transaxle single-handed is not recommended, as it is a heavy assembly which can be awkward to handle.

24 Check that, apart from the remaining flange bolts, there is nothing preventing the transaxle from being lowered and removed. Make sure that any wiring or hoses lying on top of the transaxle are not going to get caught up and stretched as the transaxle is lowered.

25 Unscrew and remove the flange bolts - there are three inserted from the transaxle side, and six from the engine side. Note the bolt locations carefully, as they are of different lengths. If the transaxle does not separate on its own, it must be rocked from side-to-side, to free it from the locating dowels. As the transaxle is withdrawn from the engine, make sure its weight is supported at all times - care must be taken that the torque converter (which is a large, heavy, circular component) does not fall out.

26 Keeping the transaxle steady on the jack head, and maintaining a supporting hand on the torque converter, carefully lower it and remove it from under the car.

27 Once the transaxle has been fully lowered and steadied, bolt a strip of wood or metal across the bellhousing face, with suitable packing, to secure the torque converter firmly in position. The converter hub should be 1-inch below the bellhousing face - this can be determined by placing a straight-edge across the bellhousing, and measuring between it and the center of the converter.

Installation

28 Prior to installation, clean the contact surfaces of the driveplate and torque converter.

29 Check that the torque converter is fully seated in the transaxle, as described in Step 27. **Caution:** *This procedure is important, to ensure that the torque converter is engaged with the fluid pump. If it is not fully engaged, serious damage will occur.*

30 As for removal, use a block of wood to wedge the engine forwards for replacement.

31 With the help of an assistant, raise the transaxle, and locate it on the rear of the driveplate. The torque converter must remain in full engagement during the installation procedure. Use the markings made prior to removal to help align the transaxle.

32 Install the transaxle-to-engine flange bolts to the locations noted on removal, and tighten them progressively, to draw the transaxle fully onto the locating dowels.

33 Align the mark made on removal

between the torque converter and driveplate. Install and tighten the torque converter-to-driveplate nuts to the specified torque - new nuts must be used. Rotate the engine as necessary to bring each nut into view, and lock the ring gear to prevent it turning as the nuts are tightened.

34 Install the lower section of the engine left-hand mounting, and tighten the nuts to the specified torque.

35 Remove the wedge between the engine and subframe. Raise the transaxle into position, then install the upper section of the engine left-hand mount. Tighten the nuts to the specified torque, noting that the center nut is tightened considerably more than the four outer ones.

36 Working from below, install the through-bolts to the engine/transaxle rear mount, and tighten them to the specified torque.

37 Once the engine/transaxle mounts have been installed, the support bar, engine hoist or supporting jack can be removed.

38 Further replacement procedures are a reversal of removal, noting the following points:

a) *Install the starter motor as described in Chapter 5A.*

b) *Install the driveshafts as described in Chapter 8.*

c) *Tighten all fasteners to the specified torque (where given).*

d) *On completion, adjust the selector cable as described in Section 3, and top-off the fluid level as described in Chapter 1A.*

e) *Re-check the transaxle fluid level once the car has been driven.*

f) *Note that, since the battery has been disconnected, the PCM will take time to 're-learn' various settings that will have an adverse effect on how the transaxle performs. After the car has completed a few miles of varied driving, however, the PCM's adaptive values should have been re-established.*

10 Automatic transaxle overhaul - general information

Overhaul of the automatic transaxle should be left to an automatic transaxle specialist or a dealer. Refer to the information given in Section 2 before removing the unit.

Note that, if the vehicle is still within the warranty period, in the event of a fault it is important to take it to a dealer, who will carry out a comprehensive diagnosis procedure using specialist equipment. Failure to do this will invalidate the warranty.

Notes

Chapter 8   Driveaxles

Contents

Specifications

Driveaxle CV joint grease*

Outer joint	
New boot	2.1 ounces
New joint	3.5 ounces
Inner joint	
iB5 manual transaxle	3.5 ounces
MTX75/MT285 manual transaxles	4.4 ounces
Automatic transaxle	4.4 ounces

* **Note:** *Only use grease designed specifically for use in CV joints.*

Torque specifications   Ft-lbs

Driveaxle/hub nut	
Models through 2001	173
2002 through 2004 models	233
2005 and later models	199
Lower arm balljoint clamp bolt	See Chapter 10
Right-hand intermediate shaft bearing	18
Wheel nuts	See Chapter 1
Suspension strut upper mounting nut	35

1   General information

Drive is transmitted from the transaxle differential to the front wheels by means of two driveaxles. The right-hand driveaxle is in two sections, and incorporates a support bearing. The inner driveaxle boots are made of rubber, and the outer driveaxle boots are made of thermoplastic. This gives the outer boot a good resistance to external effects, like road debris and permanent loading when the steering is being turned.

Each driveaxle consists of three main components: the sliding (tripod type) inner joint, the driveaxle itself, and the outer CV (constant velocity) joint. The inner end of the left-hand tripod joint is secured in the differential side gear by the engagement of a snap-ring. The inner tripod of the right-hand driveaxle is located in the intermediate shaft tripod housing. The intermediate shaft is held in the transaxle by the support bearing, which in turn is supported by a bracket bolted to the rear of the cylinder block. The outer CV joint on both driveaxles is of ball-bearing type, and is secured in the front hub by the driveaxle nut.

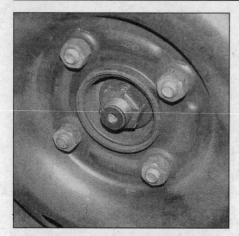

2.1 Loosen the driveaxle nut, before jacking up the vehicle

2.5a Remove the lower balljoint bolt . . .

2.5b . . . then pry the lower arm down using a suitable bar . . .

2   Driveaxles - removal and installation

Removal

Refer to illustrations 2.1, 2.5a, 2.5b, 2.5c and 2.7

1   Remove the wheel cover (or center cover) from the wheel, apply the parking brake, and engage 1st gear or P. Loosen the driveaxle nut about half a turn **(see illustration)**. This nut is very tight - use only high-quality, close-fitting tools, and take adequate precautions against personal injury when loosening it.

2   On models through 2002, remove the plastic cap from the top of each front suspension strut, at the inner fender mounting in the engine compartment. Holding the piston rod against rotation using an Allen key, loosen each strut's center nut by five full turns using a large box wrench. On 2003 and later models, do not loosen the center nut, but instead loosen the three mounting nuts 5 turns, on the left-hand strut *only*. On 2004 and later models, only loosen the nuts four turns.

3   To avoid spillage when the driveaxles are separated from the MTX 75 transaxle, drain the transaxle fluid, as described in Chapter 7A. On models with no draining facilities, use a suitable container to catch the oil/fluid when the driveaxle has been removed.

4   Loosen the front wheel retaining nuts. Apply the parking brake, jack up the front of the vehicle and support it on axle stands. Remove the wheel.

5   Note which way the lower arm balljoint clamp bolt is fitted, then unscrew it from the hub carrier. Pry the balljoint down from the hub carrier; if it is tight, carefully pry the clamp open using a large flat-bladed tool **(see illustrations)**. Take care not to damage the balljoint seal during the separation procedure.

6   Completely unscrew the driveaxle nut. **Note:** *The nut is of special laminated design, and should only be re-used a maximum of 4 times. (It is a good idea to file a small notch in the nut every time it is removed.) We suggest you use a new nut whenever you perform this procedure.*

7   Press the driveaxle through the front hub and hub carrier by pulling the hub carrier outward **(see illustration)**. When the driveaxle is free, support it on an axle stand, making sure that the inner tripod joint is not turned through more than 18 degrees (dam-

2.5c . . . and disengage the balljoint from the hub

age may occur if the joint is turned through too great an angle). **Note:** *On some models, a hub puller is required to push the axle stub through the hub.*

Left-hand side

Refer to illustration 2.8

8   Insert a lever or slide hammer between the inner driveaxle joint and the transaxle case **(see illustration)**. Pry free the inner joint

2.7 Pull the hub/strut assembly outward, to disengage the driveaxle

2.8 Disengage the driveaxle using a slide hammer

2.15a Unscrew the two retaining nuts (arrows)

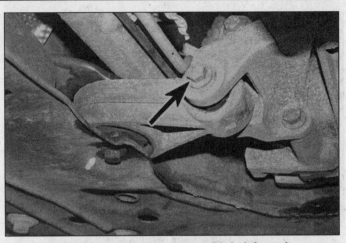

2.15b On automatics, remove this bolt (arrow)

from the differential, taking care not to damage the casing.

9   Take care not to damage the adjacent components and, in particular, make sure that the driveaxle oil seal in the differential is not damaged. If the transaxle was not drained, be prepared for oil spillage.

10   On manual transaxles only, note that if the right-hand driveaxle has already been removed, it is possible to release the left-hand driveaxle by inserting a forked drift from the right-hand side. However, care must be taken to prevent damage to the differential gears, particularly if the special tool is not used.

11   Withdraw the driveaxle from under the vehicle.

12   Extract the snap-ring from the groove on the inner end of the driveaxle, and obtain a new one. Proceed to Step 17.

Right-hand side

Refer to illustrations 2.15a, 2.15b and 2.16

13   The right-hand driveaxle may either be removed complete with the intermediate shaft from the transaxle, or it may be disconnected from the outer end of the intermediate shaft.

14   If the latter course of action is taken, remove the retaining clip from around the larger end of the inner boot, and withdraw the inner tripod joint from the intermediate shaft.

15   If the complete driveaxle is to be removed, proceed as follows. Unscrew the nuts securing the driveaxle support bearing bracket to the rear of the cylinder block **(see illustration)**. On automatic models, it may be necessary to remove the bolt from the rear engine/transaxle mount **(see illustration)**, and lever the engine forwards slightly.

16   Withdraw the complete driveaxle from the transaxle and from the bearing bracket, and remove it from under the vehicle **(see illustration)**. If the transaxle was not drained, be prepared for oil spillage.

Both sides

17   Check the condition of the differential oil seals, and if necessary replace them as described in Chapter 7A (manual transaxle) or Chapter 7B (automatic transaxle). Check

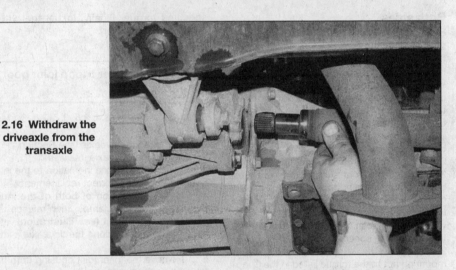

2.16 Withdraw the driveaxle from the transaxle

the support bearing, and if necessary replace it as described in Section 5.

Installation

Right-hand side

18   If the intermediate shaft has not been removed, proceed to Step 21. Otherwise, proceed as follows.

19   Carefully install the complete driveaxle in the support bearing and into the transaxle, taking care not to damage the oil seal. Turn the driveaxle until it engages the splines on the differential gears.

20   Using a new bracket and new nuts, tighten the bolts securing the support bearing to the bracket on the cylinder block to the specified torque. Proceed to Step 26.

21   Locate the inner tripod joint of the driveaxle into the intermediate shaft.

22   After packing the joint with new grease (see Specifications at the beginning of this Chapter), install the boot and tighten retaining clip. Proceed to Step 26.

Left-hand side

Refer to illustration 2.23

23   Locate the new snap-ring in the groove on the inner end of the driveaxle **(see illustration)**.

24   Use a special sleeve to protect the differential oil seal as the driveaxle is inserted. If the sleeve is not used, take great care to avoid damaging the seal (installation sleeves are supplied with new oil seals, where required.)

25   Insert the driveaxle into the transaxle, making sure that the snap-ring is fully engaged.

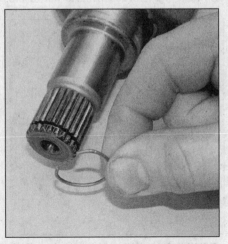

2.23 Fit a new retaining clip to the end of the shaft

2.28 Replace the balljoint shield

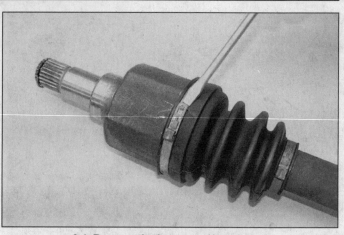

3.4 Remove the boot securing clamps

Both sides

Refer to illustration 2.28

26   Pull the hub carrier outwards, and insert the outer end of the driveaxle through the hub. Turn the driveaxle to engage the splines in the hub, and fully push on the hub. A special tool is available to draw the driveaxle into the hub, but it is unlikely that the splines will be tight. However, if they are, it will be necessary to obtain the tool, or to use a similar home-made tool.

27   Screw on the driveaxle nut finger-tight.

28   Locate the front suspension lower arm balljoint stub in the bottom of the hub carrier, making sure balljoint shield is in place **(see illustration)**. Insert the clamp bolt in the previously-noted position, screw on the nut, and tighten it to the specified torque.

29   Tighten the suspension strut upper mounting nut to the torque listed in the Chapter 10 Specifications.

30   Fill the transaxle with oil or fluid, and check the level as described in the relevant part of Chapter 1.

31   Install the wheel, and lower the vehicle to the ground. Tighten the wheel retaining nuts to the torque listed in the Chapter 1 Specifications.

32   Fully tighten the driveaxle nut to the specified torque. Finally, install the wheel cover (or center cover).

---

3   Driveaxle inner tripod joint boot - replacement

Refer to illustrations 3.4, 3.5, 3.7, 3.8, 3.11, 3.12 and 3.16

1   Remove the driveaxle (see Section 2).

2   Mount the driveaxle in a vise.

3   Mark the driveaxle in relation to the joint housing, to ensure correct replacement.

4   Note the location of both of the inner joint boot retaining clamps, then release the clamps from the boot **(see illustration)**, and slide the boot back along the driveaxle a little way.

5   Remove the inner joint housing from the tripod **(see illustration)**.

6   Check that the inner end of the driveaxle is marked in relation to the splined tripod hub. If not, carefully center-punch the two items, to ensure correct reassembly. Alternatively, use dabs of paint on the driveaxle and one end of the tripod.

7   Extract the snap-ring retaining the tripod on the driveaxle **(see illustration)**.

8   Using a puller, remove the tripod from the end of the driveaxle **(see illustration)**, and slide off the boot.

9   If the outer boot is also to be replaced, remove it with reference to Section 4.

10   Clean the driveaxle, and obtain a new joint retaining snap-ring. The boot retaining clamps must also be replaced.

11   Slide the new boot on the driveaxle, together with new clamps **(see illustration)**.

12   Install the tripod on the driveaxle splines, if necessary using a soft-faced mallet and a suitable socket to drive it fully onto the splines. It must be installed with the chamfered edge leading (towards the driveaxle), and with the previously-made marks aligned **(see illustration)**. Secure it in position using a new snap-ring. Ensure that the snap-ring is fully engaged in its groove.

13   Scoop out all of the old grease from the joint housing, then pack the joint with new grease (see *Specifications* at the beginning of this Chapter). Guide the joint housing onto the tripod joint, making sure that the previously-made marks are aligned.

14   Slide the boot along the driveaxle, and locate it on the tripod joint housing. The small-diameter end of the boot must be located in the groove on the driveaxle.

3.5 Withdraw the joint housing from the tripod joint

3.7 Use snap-ring pliers to remove the snap-ring from the shaft

3.8 Use a puller to remove the tripod

3.11 Slide the boot and the clamps onto the shaft

3.12 Align the marks when reassembling the tripod

3.16 Use boot clamp/pliers to tighten the clamps

15   Ensure that the boot is not twisted or distorted, then insert a small screwdriver under the lip of the boot at the housing end. This will allow trapped air to escape during the next step.

16   Push the housing fully on the tripod, then pull it out by 13/16-inch (20 mm). Remove the screwdriver, then install the retaining clamps and tighten them **(see illustration)**.

17   Install the driveaxle (see Section 2).

4   Driveaxle outer CV joint boot - replacement

Refer to illustrations 4.5, 4.6 and 4.12

1   The outer CV joint boot can be replaced by removing the inner boot first as described in Section 3, or after removing the driveaxle complete as described in Section 2. If the driveaxle is removed, then the inner boot need not necessarily be removed.

2   If required, mount the driveaxle in a vise.

3   Mark the driveaxle in relation to the CV joint housing, to ensure correct replacement.

4   Note the installed location of both of the outer joint boot retaining clamps, then release the clamps from the boot, and slide the boot

4.5 Use a copper hammer to remove the outer CV joint

back along the driveaxle a little way.

5   Using a brass drift or a copper hammer, carefully drive the outer CV joint hub from the splines on the driveaxle **(see illustration)**. Initial resistance will be felt until the internal circlips are released. Take care not to damage the bearing cage.

6   Extract the snap-ring from the end of the driveaxle **(see illustration)**.

7   Slide the boot, and remove it from the driveaxle together with the clamps.

8   Clean the driveaxle, and obtain a new joint retaining snap-ring. The boot retaining clamps must also be replaced.

9   Slide the new boot (together with new clamps) onto the driveaxle.

10   Install a new snap-ring to the groove in the end of the driveaxle.

11   Scoop out all of the old grease, then pack the joint with new grease (see Specifications at the beginning of this Chapter). Take care that the fresh grease does not become contaminated with dirt or grit as it is being applied.

12   Locate the CV joint on the driveaxle so that the splines are aligned, then push the joint until the internal snap-ring is fully engaged **(see illustration)**.

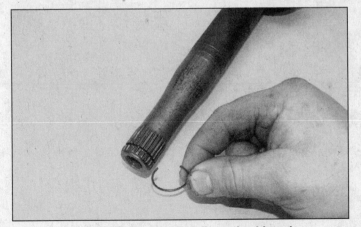

4.6 Replace the retaining clip on the driveaxle

4.12 Make sure the clip (arrow) engages fully when CV joint is reassembled

13 Move the boot along the driveaxle, and locate it over the joint and onto the outer CV joint housing. The small-diameter end of the boot must be located in the groove on the driveaxle.

14 Ensure that the boot is not twisted or distorted, then insert a small screwdriver under the lip of the boot at the housing end, to allow any trapped air to escape.

15 Remove the screwdriver, install the retaining clamps in their previously-noted positions, and tighten them **(see illustration 3.16)**.

5 Driveaxles - inspection and joint replacement

1 If any of the checks described in the relevant part of Chapter 1 reveal apparent excessive wear or play in any driveaxle joint, first remove the wheel cover (or center cover), and check that the driveaxle nut is tightened to the specified torque. Repeat this check on the other side of the vehicle.

2 Road test the vehicle, and listen for a metallic clicking from the front as the vehicle is driven slowly in a circle on full-lock. If a clicking noise is heard, this indicates wear in the outer constant velocity joint, which means that the joint must be replaced; reconditioning is not possible.

3 To replace an outer CV joint, remove the driveaxle as described in Section 2, then separate the joint from the driveaxle with reference to Section 4.

4 If vibration, consistent with road speed, is felt through the car when accelerating, there is a possibility of wear in the inner tripod joints.

5 To replace an inner tripod joint, remove the driveaxle as described in Section 2, then separate the joint from the driveaxle with reference to Section 3.

6 Continual noise from the right-hand driveaxle, increasing with road speed, may indicate wear in the support bearing. To replace this bearing, the driveaxle and intermediate shaft must be removed, and the bearing extracted using a puller.

7 Remove the bearing dust cover, and obtain a new one.

8 Drive or press on the new bearing, applying the pressure to the inner race only. Similarly drive or press on the new dust cover.

Chapter 9 Brakes

Contents

Specifications

Front brakes
Type	Ventilated disc, with single sliding piston caliper
Disc diameter	
Models through 2004	10.16 inches
2005 and later models	10.94 inches
Disc thickness	
Models through 2004	
New	0.87 inch
Minimum	0.79 inch
2005 and later models	
New	0.98 inch
Minimum	0.91 inch
Maximum disc thickness variation	0.0008 inch
Maximum disc/hub run-out (installed)	0.002 inch
Caliper piston diameter	2.13 inches

Rear drum brakes
Type	Leading and trailing shoes, with automatic adjusters
Drum diameter	
New	7.99 inches
Maximum	8.03 inches
Shoe width	1.42 inches
Wheel cylinder bore diameter	0.81 inch

Rear disc brakes
Minimum disc thickness	0.350 inch

Torque specifications
Ft-lbs (unless otherwise indicated)

Note: *One foot-pound (ft-lb) of torque is equivalent to 12 inch-pounds (in-lbs) of torque. Torque values below approximately 15 ft-lbs are expressed in inch-pounds, since most foot-pound torque wrenches are not accurate at these smaller values.*

ABS hydraulic unit bracket to body	
Models through 2004	18
2005 and later models	80 in-lbs
ABS hydraulic unit-to-bracket	84 in-lbs
ABS wheel sensor securing bolts	84 in-lbs
Brake pipe-to-master cylinder	
Models through 2004	156 in-lbs
2005 and later models	15
Brake pipe to hydraulic control unit	
Models through 2004	96 in-lbs
2005 and later models	156 in-lbs
Brake pipe unions	132 in-lbs
Front caliper guide bolts	21
Front caliper bracket bolts	98

Torque specifications (continued)

Ft-lbs (unless otherwise indicated)

Parking brake lever mountings	180 in-lbs
Master cylinder to servo mountings	180 in-lbs
Pedal bracket to servo mountings	17
Rear caliper bracket	41
Rear caliper guide bolts	26
Rear drum brake back plate/disc shield	49
Rear hub nut	173
Wheel cylinder mounting bolts	108 in-lbs
Wheel nuts	See Chapter 1
Wheel spindle mounting bolts	49
Yaw rate sensor to bracket	72 in-lbs
Yaw rate sensor bracket to body	48 in-lbs

1   General information

The braking system is of diagonally-split, dual-circuit design, with ventilated discs at the front, and drum brakes at the rear. Some models have rear disc brakes. The front calipers are of single sliding piston design, using asbestos-free pads. The rear drum brakes are of the leading and trailing shoe type, and are self-adjusting during foot-brake operation. The rear brake shoe linings are of different thicknesses, in order to allow for the different proportional rates of wear.

On models with rear disc brakes, the calipers are of a single-piston design with non-ventilated rotors, and the parking brake cables actuate the rear brakes by rotating the caliper piston.

The vacuum servo unit uses intake manifold vacuum (generated only when the engine is running) to boost the effort applied by the driver at the brake pedal and transmits this increased effort to the master cylinder pistons.

Pressure conscious regulator valves (PCRV's) are used on the rear brakes, to prevent rear wheel lock-up under hard braking. The valves are sometimes referred to as pressure control relief valves. On non-ABS models, they are attached to the master cylinder rear brake outlet ports; on models with ABS, they are located in the ABS hydraulic unit. On Wagon models without ABS there is a load sensing valve (LAV) for the rear wheels, which is connected to the rear suspension crossmember. It controls the brake fluid pressure to each of the rear wheels, depending on vehicle loading.

The parking brake is cable-operated, and acts on the rear brakes. The cables operate on the rear trailing brake shoe operating levers. The parking brake lever incorporates an automatic adjuster, which will adjust the cable when the parking brake is operated several times.

Where used, the anti-lock braking system (ABS) uses the basic conventional brake system, together with an ABS hydraulic unit installed between the master cylinder and the four brake units at each wheel. The hydraulic unit consists of a hydraulic actuator, an ABS brake pressure pump, an ABS module with built-in relay box, and two pressure-control relief valves. Braking at each of the four wheels is controlled by separate solenoid valves in the hydraulic actuator. If wheel lock-up is detected by one of the wheel sensors, when the vehicle speed is above 3 mph, the valve opens. Releasing pressure to the relevant brake, until the wheel regains a rotational speed corresponding to the speed of the vehicle. The cycle can be repeated many times a second. In the event of a fault in the ABS system, the conventional braking system is not affected. Diagnosis of a fault in the ABS system requires the use of special equipment, and this work should therefore be left to a dealer.

The traction control systems available for the Focus is the full speed traction control (TCS), sometimes called Spark Fuel Traction Control (SFTC). The systems are integrated with the ABS, and use the same wheel sensors. The hydraulic control unit has additional solenoid valves incorporated to enable control of the wheel brake pressure.

The TCS system is only active at speeds up to about 50 mph - when the system is active the warning light on the instrument panel illuminates to warn the driver. This uses controlled braking of the spinning driving wheel, when the grip at the driven wheels are different. The spinning wheel is braked by the ABS system, transferring a greater proportion of the engine torque through the differential to the other driven wheel, which increases the use of the available traction control.

The TCS system on Focus models also reduces the engine torque to improve directional stability. If the driving wheels are spinning, the ABS/TCS module calculates the required engine torque during traction control and sends this request to the engine PCM. This then calculates the required ignition timing and the number of fuel injectors to be deactivated in order to achieve the required engine torque.

The advantages of the TCS system are:

a) *Reduces the load on the braking system.*
b) *Reduces the load on the engine.*
c) *Improves directional stability.*
d) *Shortens reaction time.*
e) *Operates at all vehicle speeds.*

On the 2001 through 2004 Focus models, there is an Electronic Stability Program (ESP) available, this system supports the vehicle's stability and steering through a combination of ABS and traction control operations. The combined operation system is called AdvanceTrac. There is a switch on the center console, so that if required the system could be switched off. This will then illuminate the warning light on the instrument panel, to inform the driver that the AdvanceTrac is not in operation. The stability of the vehicle is measured by Yaw rate and Accelerometer sensors, which sense the movement of the vehicle about its vertical axis, and also lateral acceleration. Sensors in the steering system measure the driver input to the steering, and the actual direction of the vehicle. When discrepancies are noted, the system will alter the driving force at one or more wheels to correct for sideways movement or sliding incidents.

Note: *When servicing any part of the system, work carefully and methodically; also observe scrupulous cleanliness when overhauling any part of the hydraulic system. Always replace components (in axle sets, where applicable) if in doubt about their condition, and use only genuine factory replacement parts, or at least those of known good quality. Note the warnings given in 'Safety first!' and at relevant points in this Chapter concerning the dangers of asbestos dust and hydraulic fluid.*

2   Front brake pads - replacement

Refer to illustrations 2.2, 2.3a, 2.3b, 2.4, 2.5a and 2.5b

Warning: *Disc brake pads must be replaced on BOTH front wheels at the same time - never replace the pads on only one wheel, as uneven braking may result. Although genuine factory linings are asbestos-free, the dust created by wear of aftermarket pads may contain asbestos, which is a health hazard. Never blow it out with compressed air, and don't inhale any of it. DO NOT use petroleum-based solvents to clean brake parts; use brake cleaner or alcohol only. DO NOT allow any brake fluid, oil or grease to contact the brake pads or disc. Also refer to the warning at the start of Section 11 concerning brake fluid.*

Note: *Before starting work, wash the brake assembly with aerosol brake cleaner to protect yourself from brake dust, which might contain asbestos, a known carcinogen.*

1   Apply the parking brake. Loosen the front wheel nuts, then jack up the front of the vehicle and support it on axle stands. Remove the front wheels. Work on one brake assembly at a time, using the assembled brake for reference if necessary.

2.2 Pry the pad retaining clip from the caliper

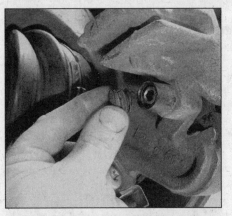

2.3a Pry the covers off to locate the caliper guide bolts . . .

2.3b . . . then loosen and remove the bolts

2.4 Remove the caliper, complete with brake pads

2.5a Unclip the inner pad from the piston . . .

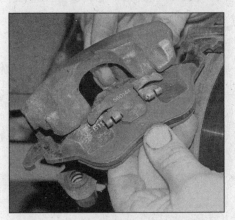

2.5b . . . then unclip the outer pad from the caliper

2 Using a flat-bladed screwdriver, pry the outer brake pad retaining clip from the caliper **(see illustration)**. Hold the clip with a pair of pliers as this is done, to avoid personal injury. Release the caliper's brake hose from the bracket at the strut.

3 Pry the plastic covers from the ends of the two guide pins then, using a 7 mm Allen wrench, unscrew the guide bolts securing the caliper to the carrier bracket **(see illustrations)**.

4 Lift the caliper from the disc **(see illustration)**, and support it on an axle stand to avoid straining the hydraulic hose.

5 Pull the inner pad from the piston in the caliper, then remove the outer pad from the caliper by sliding the pad out of the caliper with its securing clip, noting their installed positions **(see illustrations)**.

6 Wash all dust and dirt from the caliper, pads and disc with aerosol brake cleaner. Scrape any corrosion from the edge of the disc, taking care not to damage the friction surface.

7 Inspect the front brake disc for scoring and cracks. If a detailed inspection is necessary, refer to Section 4.

8 The piston must be pushed back into the caliper bore, to provide room for the new brake pads. Use a C-clamp to accomplish this. As the piston is depressed to the bottom of the caliper bore, the fluid in the master cylinder will rise slightly. Make sure that there is

sufficient space in the brake fluid reservoir to accept the displaced fluid, and, if necessary, siphon some off first. Any brake fluid spilled on paintwork should be washed off with clean water, without delay - brake fluid is also a highly-effective paint-stripper.
Warning: *Do not siphon the fluid by mouth; it is poisonous.*

9 Install the new pads using a reversal of the removal procedure, and tighten the guide bolts to the torque wrench setting given in the Specifications at the beginning of this Chapter.

10 On completion, firmly depress the brake pedal a few times, to bring the pads to their normal working position. Check the level of the brake fluid in the reservoir, and top-off if necessary.

11 Give the vehicle a short road test, to make sure that the brakes are functioning correctly, and to seat the new linings to the contours of the disc. New linings will not provide maximum braking efficiency until they have seated; avoid heavy braking as far as possible for the first hundred miles or so.

3 Front brake caliper - removal, overhaul and installation

Note: *Refer to the warning at the beginning of the previous Section before proceeding.*

Removal
Refer to illustrations 3.2 and 3.3

1 Apply the parking brake. Loosen the front wheel nuts, then jack up the front of the vehicle and support it on axle stands. Remove the appropriate front wheel.

2 Install a brake hose clamp to the flexible hose leading to the caliper **(see illustration)**. This will minimize brake fluid loss during subsequent operations.

3 Loosen the union on the caliper end of

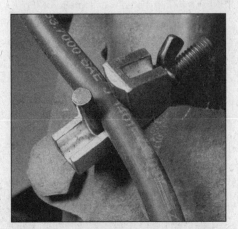

3.2 Brake hose clamp installed on the front brake hose

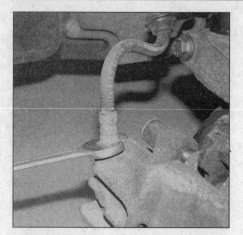

3.3 Loosen the brake hose at the caliper

3.15 Tighten the carrier bracket mounting bolts

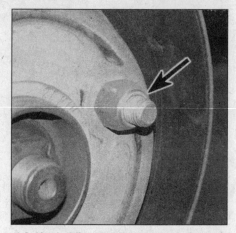

4.3 Nut holding the disc on firmly (arrow)

the flexible brake hose **(see illustration)**. Once loosened, do not try to unscrew the hose at this stage.

4   Remove the brake pads as described in Section 2.

5   Support the caliper in one hand, and prevent the hydraulic hose from turning with the other hand. Unscrew the caliper from the hose, making sure that the hose is not twisted unduly or strained. Once the caliper is detached, plug the open hydraulic fittings in the caliper and hose, to keep out dust and dirt.

6   If required, the caliper carrier bracket can be unbolted from the hub carrier.

Overhaul

Note: *Before starting work, check on the availability of parts (caliper overhaul kit/seals).*

7   With the caliper on the bench, brush away all traces of dust and dirt, but take care not to inhale any dust, as it may be harmful to your health.

8   Pull the dust cover rubber seal from the end of the piston.

9   Apply low air pressure to the fluid intake union, to eject the piston. Only low air pressure is required for this, such as is produced by a foot-operated tire pump. **Caution:** *The piston may be ejected with some force. Position a thin piece of wood between the piston and the caliper body, to prevent damage to the end face of the piston, in the event of it being ejected suddenly.*

10   Using a suitable blunt instrument, pry the piston seal from the groove in the cylinder bore. Take care not to scratch the surface of the bore.

11   Clean the piston and caliper body with brake cleaner, and allow to dry. Examine the surfaces of the piston and cylinder bore for wear, damage and corrosion. If the piston alone is unserviceable, a new piston must be obtained, along with seals. If the cylinder bore is unserviceable, the complete caliper must be replaced. The seals must be replaced, regardless of the condition of the other components.

12   Coat the piston and seals with clean

brake fluid, then manipulate the piston seal into the groove in the cylinder bore.

13   Push the piston squarely into its bore, taking care not to damage the seal.

14   Install the dust cover rubber seal onto the piston and caliper, then depress the piston fully.

Installation

Refer to illustration 3.15

15   Install the caliper by reversing the removal operations. Make sure that the flexible brake hose is not twisted. Tighten the mounting bolts and wheel nuts to the specified torque **(see illustration)**.

16   Bleed the brake circuit according to the procedure given in Section 11, remembering to remove the brake hose clamp from the flexible hose. Make sure there are no leaks from the hose connections. Test the brakes carefully before returning the vehicle to normal service.

---

4   Front brake disc - inspection, removal and installation

Note: *To prevent uneven braking, BOTH front brake discs should be replaced or reground at the same time.*

Inspection

Refer to illustrations 4.3, 4.4 and 4.5

1   Apply the parking brake. Loosen the relevant wheel nuts, jack up the front of the vehicle and support it on axle stands. Remove the appropriate front wheel.

2   Remove the front brake caliper from the disc with reference to Section 3, and undo the two caliper bracket securing bolts. Do not disconnect the flexible hose. Support the caliper on an axle stand, or suspend it out of the way with a piece of wire, taking care to avoid straining the flexible hose.

3   Temporarily install two of the wheel nuts to diagonally-opposite studs, with the flat sides of the nuts against the disc **(see illustration)**. Tighten the nuts progressively, to hold the disc firmly.

4   Scrape any corrosion from the disc. Rotate the disc, and examine it for deep scoring, grooving or cracks. Using a micrometer, measure the thickness of the disc in several places **(see illustration)**. The minimum thickness is stamped on the disc hub. Light wear and scoring is normal, but if excessive, the disc should be removed, and either reground by a specialist, or replaced. If regrinding is undertaken, the minimum thickness must be maintained. Obviously, if the disc is cracked, it must be replaced.

5   Using a dial gauge or a flat metal block and feeler gauges, check that the disc run-out 10 mm from the outer edge does not exceed the limit given in the Specifications. To do this, mount the measuring equipment, and rotate the disc, noting the variation in measurement as the disc is rotated **(see illustration)**. The difference between the minimum and maximum measurements recorded is the disc run-out.

6   If the run-out is greater than the specified amount, check for variations of the disc thickness as follows. Mark the disc at eight positions 45 degrees apart then, using a micrometer, measure the disc thickness at the eight positions, 15 mm in from the outer edge.

4.4 Use a micrometer to measure the thickness of the brake disc

4.5 Measure the disc run-out with a dial gauge

4.10 Remove the disc from the hub

5.2a Remove the dust cap . . .

If the variation between the minimum and maximum readings is greater than the specified amount, the disc should be replaced.

7   The hub face run-out can also be checked in a similar way. First remove the disc as described later in this Section, attach the measuring equipment, then slowly rotate the hub, and check that the run-out does not exceed the amount given in the Specifications. If the hub face run-out is excessive, this should be corrected (by replacing the hub bearings - see Chapter 10) before rechecking the disc run-out.

Removal

Refer to illustration 4.10

8   With the wheel and caliper removed, remove the wheel nuts which were temporarily installed in Step 3.

9   Mark the disc in relation to the hub, if it is to be reinstalled.

10   Remove the washer/retaining clip(s) (if equipped), and withdraw the disc over the wheel studs **(see illustration)**.

Installation

11   Make sure that the disc and hub mating surfaces are clean, then locate the disc on the wheel studs. Align the previously-made marks if the original disc is being reinstalled.

12   Install the brake caliper and carrier bracket with reference to Section 3.

13   Install the wheel, and lower the vehicle to the ground. Tighten wheel nuts to their specified torque.

14   Test the brakes carefully before returning the vehicle to normal service.

---

5   Rear brake drum - removal, inspection and installation

Note 1: *Refer to the warning at the beginning of Section 6 before proceeding.*

Note 2: *To prevent uneven braking, BOTH rear brake drums should be replaced at the same time.*

Removal

Refer to illustrations 5.2a and 5.2b

1   Chock the front wheels, release the parking brake and engage 1st gear (or P). Loosen the relevant wheel nuts, jack up the rear of the vehicle and support it on axle stands. Remove the appropriate rear wheel.

2   Remove the dust cap from the center of the drum, and remove the retaining nut **(see illustrations)**. This nut is very tight - use only high-quality, close-fitting tools, and take adequate precautions against personal injury when loosening it. **Note 1:** *The driveshaft/hub nut is of special laminated design, and should only be re-used a maximum of 4 times. (It is a good idea to mark the nut every time it is removed.) Obtain a new nut if necessary.* **Note 2:** *There is an alternative method if you are inspecting or replacing other brake/suspension parts and not replacing the drum. Remove the wheel spindle bolts from the back of the backing plate, then remove the drum and spindle assembly as a unit.*

3   If the drum will not pull off easily, make sure the parking brake cable is released fully, then use a suitable puller to draw the drum and bearing assembly off the stub axle.

4   With the brake drum removed, clean the dust from the drum, brake shoes, wheel cylinder and back plate, using brake cleaner or alcohol. Take care not to inhale the dust, as it may contain asbestos.

Inspection

Refer to illustration 5.5

5   Clean the inside surfaces of the brake drum, then examine the internal friction surface for signs of scoring or cracks. If it is cracked, deeply scored, or has worn to a diameter greater than the maximum given in the Specifications, then it should be replaced, together with the drum on the other side **(see illustration)**. If the drum is to be replaced, a press must be used to remove or install the hub on the drum.

6   Regrinding of the brake drum is not recommended.

5.2b . . . and remove the hub nut

Installation

7   The wheel bearings may have been damaged on drum removal; if necessary replace the bearings as described in Chapter 10.

8   Installation is a reversal of removal, tightening relevant bolts to their specified torque.

9   Test the brakes carefully before returning the vehicle to normal service.

5.5 Check the drum for wear

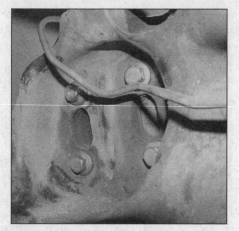

6.3a Undo the four bolts . . .

6.3b . . . and remove the
hub/drum assembly

6.4 Note the position of the springs

6.5a Unclip the brake shoe hold-down springs . . .

6.5b . . . and pull out the pins from the back plate

6   Rear brake shoes - replacement

*Refer to illustrations 6.3a, 6.3b, 6.4, 6.5a,
6.5b, 6.8, 6.9, 6.11, 6.12 and 6.14*
Warning: *Drum brake shoes must be renewed
on BOTH rear wheels at the same time - never
replace the shoes on only one wheel, as
uneven braking may result. Also, the dust created by wear of the shoes is a health hazard.
Never blow it out with compressed air, and
don't inhale any of it. An approved filtering
mask should be worn when working on the
brakes. DO NOT use petroleum-based solvents to clean brake parts; use brake cleaner
or alcohol only.*

1   Chock the front wheels, release the
parking brake and engage 1st gear (or P).
Loosen the relevant wheel nuts, jack up the
rear of the vehicle and support it on axle
stands. Remove the rear wheels. Work on
one brake assembly at a time, using the
assembled brake for reference if necessary.
2   Disconnect the ABS wiring connector (if
installed).
3   Remove the rear brake drum and hub
assembly by unscrewing the four bolts at the
rear of the hub assembly **(see illustrations)**.

This is to prevent any damage to the wheel
bearings on removal of the drum.
4   Note the installed position of the springs
and the brake shoes, then clean the components with brake cleaner, and allow to dry
(see illustration). Position a tray beneath the
back plate, to catch the fluid and residue.
5   Remove the two shoe hold-down
springs, use a pair of pliers to depress the
ends so that they can be withdrawn off the
pins. Remove the hold-down pins from the
back plate **(see illustrations)**.
6   Disconnect the top ends of the shoes
from the wheel cylinder, taking care not to
damage the rubber boots.
7   To prevent the wheel cylinder pistons
from being accidentally ejected, install a suitable elastic band or wire lengthways over the
cylinder/pistons. DO NOT press the brake
pedal while the shoes are removed.
8   Pull the bottom end of the brake shoes
from the bottom anchor **(see illustration)**
(use pliers or an adjustable wrench over the
edge of the shoe to lever it away, if required).
9   Pull the parking brake cable spring back
from the operating lever on the rear of the
trailing shoe. Unhook the cable end from the

cut-out in the lever, and remove the brake
shoes **(see illustration)**.
10   Working on a clean bench, move the
bottom ends of the brake shoes together, and
unhook the lower return spring from the
shoes, noting the location holes.
11   Pull the leading shoe from the strut and

6.8 Pull the brake shoe from the
bottom anchor

6.9 Use pliers to disengage the cable from the lever

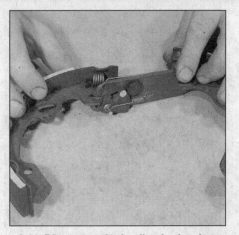

6.11 Disengage the leading brake shoe

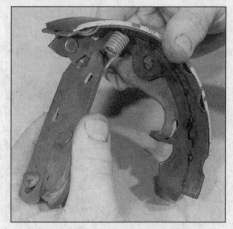

6.12 Disengage the adjustment strut

brake shoe adjuster **(see illustration)**, unhook the upper return spring from the shoes, noting the location holes.

12 Pull the adjustment strut to release from the trailing brake shoe, and remove the strut support spring **(see illustration)**.

13 If the wheel cylinder shows signs of fluid leakage, or if there is any reason to suspect it of being defective, inspect it now, as described in the next Section.

14 Clean the back plate, and apply small amounts of high-melting-point brake grease to the brake shoe contact points. Be careful not to get grease on any friction surfaces **(see illustration)**.

15 Lubricate the sliding components of the brake shoe adjuster with a little high-melting-point brake grease, but leave the serrations on the eccentric cam clean.

16 Install the new brake shoes using a reversal of the removal procedure, but set the eccentric cam at its lowest position before assembling it to the trailing shoe.

17 Before replacing the brake drum, it should be inspected as described in Section 5.

18 With the drum in position and all the securing bolts and nuts tightened to their specified torque, install the wheel. Then, carry

out the replacement procedure on the remaining rear brake.

19 Lower the vehicle to the ground, and tighten the wheel nuts to the specified torque.

20 Depress the brake pedal several times, in order to operate the self-adjusting mechanism and set the shoes at their normal operating position.

21 Make several forward and reverse stops, and operate the parking brake fully two or three times (adjust parking brake as required). Give the vehicle a road test, to make sure that the brakes are functioning correctly, and to seat the new shoes to the contours of the drum. Remember that the new shoes will not give full braking efficiency until they have seated.

7 Rear wheel cylinders - removal, overhaul and installation

Note: *Before starting work, check on the availability of parts (wheel cylinder, or overhaul kit/seals). Also bear in mind that if the brake shoes have been contaminated by fluid leaking from the wheel cylinder, they must be replaced. The shoes on BOTH sides of the*

vehicle must be replaced, even if they are only contaminated on one side. Be sure to order the correct parts, and be sure that the same size of wheel cylinder is installed on both sides, or uneven braking could result.

Removal

Refer to illustration 7.5

1 Remove the brake drum as described in Section 6, Steps 1 to 3.

2 Minimize fluid loss either by removing the master cylinder reservoir cap, and then tightening it down onto a piece of cellophane to obtain an airtight seal, or by using a brake hose clamp, a C-clamp, or similar tool, to clamp the flexible hose at the nearest convenient point to the wheel cylinder.

3 Pull the brake shoes apart at their top ends, so that they are just clear of the wheel cylinder. The automatic adjuster will hold the shoes in this position, so that the cylinder can be withdrawn.

4 Wipe away all traces of dirt around the hydraulic fitting at the rear of the wheel cylinder, then undo the union nut.

5 Unscrew the two bolts securing the wheel cylinder to the backing plate **(see illustration)**.

6.14 Grease the brake shoe contact points on the back plate

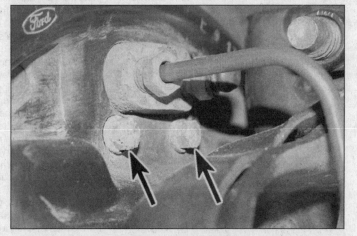

7.5 Loosen the brake pipe union nut, before removing the two securing bolts (arrows)

8.5 Remove the air filter housing

8.6 Release the wiring connectors from the base of the fusebox

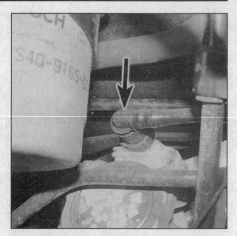

8.7 Release the supply hose (arrow) from the master cylinder

6   Pull the wheel cylinder from the backing plate so that it is clear of the brake shoes. Plug the open hydraulic unions, to prevent the entry of dirt, and to minimize further fluid loss while the cylinder is detached.

Overhaul

7   No overhaul procedures or parts were available at the time of writing, check availability of parts before dismantling. Replacing a wheel cylinder as a unit is recommended.

Installation

8   Wipe clean the backing plate and remove the plug from the end of the hydraulic pipe. Apply a small amount of RTV sealant around the wheel cylinder-to-backing plate surface. Install the cylinder onto the backing plate and screw in the hydraulic fitting nut by hand, being careful not to cross-thread it.

9   Tighten the mounting bolts, then fully tighten the hydraulic union nut.

10   Retract the automatic brake adjuster mechanism, so that the brake shoes engage with the pistons of the wheel cylinder. To do this, pry the shoes apart slightly, turn the automatic adjuster to its minimum position, and release the shoes.

11   Remove the clamp from the flexible brake hose, or the cellophane from the master cylinder (as applicable).

12   Install the brake drum with reference to Section 5.

13   Bleed the hydraulic system as described in Section 11. Providing suitable precautions were taken to minimize loss of fluid, it should only be necessary to bleed the relevant rear brake.

14   Test the brakes carefully before returning the vehicle to normal service.

---

8   Master cylinder - removal and installation

Warning: *Brake fluid is poisonous. Take care to keep it off bare skin, and in particular not to get splashes in your eyes. The fluid also attacks paintwork and plastics - wash off spills immediately with cold water. Finally,* brake fluid is highly flammable, and should be handled with the same care as gasoline.

Removal

Master cylinder

Refer to illustrations 8.5, 8.6 and 8.7

1   Exhaust the vacuum in the servo by pressing the brake pedal a few times, with the engine switched off.

2   Disconnect the negative battery cable. **Note 1:** *Before disconnecting the battery, refer to Chapter 5A, Section 1, for precautions.* **Note 2:** *On 2005 and later models, remove the battery (see Chapter 5A).*

3   Disconnect the low fluid level warning light multi-plug from the fluid reservoir. Unscrew the cap.

4   Draw off the hydraulic fluid from the reservoir, using an old battery hydrometer or similar. Alternatively raise the vehicle and remove the wheels. Loosen the front bleed nipples and drain the fluid from the reservoir. **Warning:** *Do not siphon the fluid by mouth; it is poisonous. Any brake fluid spilled on paintwork should be washed off with clean water, without delay - brake fluid is also a highly-effective paint-stripper.*

5   Lower the vehicle. Undo the securing bolts from the air filter housing and intake tube, then remove from the vehicle **(see illustration)**.

6   Disconnect the electrical connector from the auxiliary fusebox **(see illustration)**. Remove the retaining screw, and detach the fusebox from its bracket. Move the fusebox to the air filter housing position temporarily.

7   Release the clip and disconnect the fluid supply hose from the brake fluid reservoir to the master cylinder **(see illustration)**. Detach the hose from the firewall, keeping the end higher than the reservoir level, and plug or cap the hose, to prevent fluid loss or dirt entry.

8   Identify the locations of each brake pipe on the master cylinder. On non-ABS models, there are four pipes; the two rear brake pipes are attached to pressure-control relief valves on the master cylinder. On ABS models, there are only two pipes, which lead to the ABS hydraulic unit.

9   Place rags beneath the master cylinder to catch spilled hydraulic fluid.

10   Clean around the hydraulic fitting nuts. Unscrew the nuts, and disconnect the hydraulic lines from the master cylinder. If the nuts are tight, a split ring wrench should be used in preference to an open-ended wrench. Cap the end of the pipes and the master cylinder to prevent any dirt contamination.

11   On vehicles with TCS, disconnect the pressure sensors electrical connector.

12   Remove the master cylinder securing nuts, and withdraw the master cylinder from the studs on the servo unit.

13   Recover the gasket/seal from the master cylinder.

14   If the master cylinder is faulty, it must be replaced. At the time of writing, no overhaul kits were available.

Brake fluid reservoir

Refer to illustrations 8.16 and 8.17

15   The reservoir is not part of the master cylinder. Disconnect the electrical connector from the filler cap. Unscrew the cap, and using an old battery hydrometer or similar, empty the brake fluid. Install the cap.

16   Detach the wiring harness from the lower part of the reservoir **(see illustration)**.

8.16 Unclip the wiring harness (arrow) from the reservoir

8.17 Disconnect the electrical connector and remove the two screws (arrows)

9.3 Rotate the switch 45° to remove it

9.5 Remove the two bolts (arrows)

17   Remove the two securing screws from the reservoir and detach it from the firewall **(see illustration)**.

18   Release the clip and disconnect the fluid supply hoses for the brake and clutch fluid reservoir.

Installation

19   Installation is a reversal of the removal procedure, noting the following points:

a) *Clean the contact surfaces of the master cylinder and servo, and locate a new gasket on the master cylinder.*

b) *Install and tighten the nuts to the specified torque.*

c) *Carefully insert the brake pipes in the apertures in the master cylinder, then tighten the union nuts. Make sure that the nuts enter their threads correctly.*

d) *Fill the reservoir with fresh brake fluid.*

e) *Bleed the brake hydraulic system as described in Section 11.*

f) *Test the brakes carefully before returning the vehicle to normal service.*

9   Brake pedal - removal and installation

Removal

Refer to illustrations 9.3, 9.5, 9.6a, 9.6b, 9.7a, 9.7b, 9.8a, 9.8b and 9.9

1   Working inside the vehicle, move the driver's seat fully to the rear, to allow maximum working area.

2   Undo the four screws and pry out the retaining clip to remove the driver's side lower dash panel. Unclip the multi-plug from the trim panel. Disconnect the hood release cable, where applicable.

3   Disconnect the electrical connectors to the brake/clutch pedal switches. Remove the switches by turning them, then pulling them out of the pedal bracket **(see illustration)**.

4   Loosen the four retaining nuts on the pedal bracket assembly.

9.6a Remove the pedal pivot shaft bolt

5   Detach the clutch master cylinder, by unscrewing the securing bolts and unclipping from the pedal bracket **(see illustration)**.

6   Remove the clutch pedal pivot shaft nut, and slide the pivot shaft bolt out far enough to remove the clutch pedal. Release the return spring from the clutch pedal, and unclip the clutch actuator rod from the pedal

9.7a Remove the two clips . . .

9.6b Remove the clutch actuator rod, and release the return spring (arrow)

(see illustrations). (Make note of the position of the clutch pedal bushings and spacer on removal.)

7   Remove the two clips to release the brake pedal from the pedal assembly, the upper bracket bolt may need to be loosened **(see illustrations)**.

8   Depress the clip and remove the pin

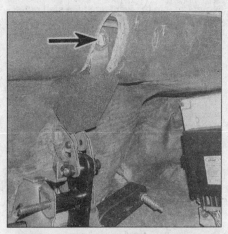

9.7b . . . and loosen the securing bolt (arrow) (dash panel removed for clarity)

9.8a Use screwdriver to depress clip . . .

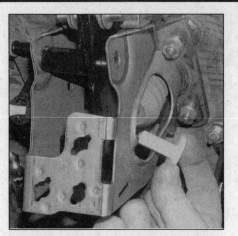

9.8b . . . and pull out the pin from the brake actuator rod

9.9 Pull out the pedal pivot shaft bolt

from the servo actuator rod **(see illustrations)**.

9   Slide the pivot shaft bolt out to remove the brake pedal **(see illustration)**. (Pry out the bushings from the brake pedal pivot to replace.) Replace the components as necessary.

Installation

10   Prior to replacing the pedal, apply a little grease to the pivot shaft, pedal bushings and actuator rods.

11   Installation is a reversal of the removal procedure, but make sure that the pedal bushings and actuator rods are correctly located.

12   Before installing the stop-light switch, pull the plunger on the switch out to its full extent. Depress the brake pedal, then install the switch in place on the bracket. Slowly release the brake pedal, and check the operation of the brake lights.

---

10   Hydraulic pipes and hoses - inspection, removal and installation

Note: *Refer to the warning·at the start of Section 11 concerning the dangers of brake fluid.*

Inspection

1   Jack up the front and rear of the vehicle, and support on axle stands. Making sure the vehicle is safely supported on a level surface.

2   Check for signs of leakage at the pipe unions, then examine the flexible hoses for signs of cracking, chafing and fraying.

3   The brake pipes should be examined carefully for signs of dents, corrosion or other damage. Corrosion should be scraped off, and if the depth of pitting is significant, the pipes replaced. This is particularly likely in those areas underneath the vehicle body where the pipes are exposed and unprotected.

4   Replace any defective brake pipes and/or hoses.

10.7 Unscrew the brake pipe fitting using a flare-nut wrench

Removal

Refer to illustrations 10.7, 10.9a and 10.9b

5   If a section of pipe or hose is to be removed, loss of brake fluid can be reduced by unscrewing the filler cap, and completely sealing the top of the reservoir with cellophane. Alternatively, the reservoir can be emptied (see Section 11).

6   To remove a section of pipe, hold the adjoining hose union nut with a wrench to prevent it from turning, then unscrew the union nut at the end of the pipe, and release it. Repeat the procedure at the other end of the pipe, then release the pipe by pulling out the clips attaching it to the body.

7   Where the fitting nuts are exposed to the full force of the weather, they can sometimes be quite tight. If an open-ended wrench is used, rounding of the flats on the nuts is not uncommon, and for this reason, it is preferable to use a flare-nut wrench **(see illustration)**, which will engage all the flats. If such a wrench is not available, self-locking pliers may be used as a last resort; these may well damage the nuts, but if the pipe is to be replaced, this does not matter.

8   To further minimize the loss of fluid when disconnecting a flexible brake line from a rigid pipe, clamp the hose as near as possible to

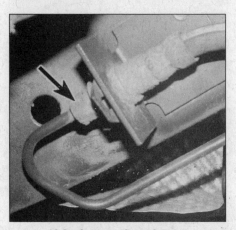

10.9a Loosen the union nut (arrow) before . . .

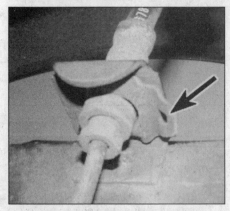

10.9b . . . pulling out the retaining clip (arrow)

the pipe to be detached, using a brake hose clamp or a pair of self-locking pliers with protected jaws.

9   To remove a flexible hose, first clean the ends of the hose and the surrounding area, then unscrew the union nuts from the hose ends. Remove the spring clip, and withdraw the hose from the serrated mounting in the support bracket. Where applicable, unscrew the hose from the caliper **(see illustrations)**.

10   Brake pipes supplied with flared ends

and union nuts can be obtained individually or in sets from dealers or accessory shops. The pipe is then bent to shape, using the old pipe as a guide, and is ready for installing. Be careful not to kink or crimp the pipe when bending it; ideally, a proper pipe-bending tool should be used.

Installation

11 Installation of the pipes and hoses is a reversal of removal. Make sure that all brake pipes are securely supported in their clips, and ensure that the hoses are not kinked. Check also that the hoses are clear of all suspension components and underbody fittings, and will remain clear during movement of the suspension and steering.
12 On completion, bleed the hydraulic system as described in Section 11.

11 Hydraulic system - bleeding

Refer to illustration 11.7
Warning: *Brake fluid contains polyglycol ethers and polyglycols that are poisonous. Take care to keep it off bare skin, and in particular not to get splashes in your eyes. Wash hands thoroughly after handling and if fluid contacts the eyes, flush out with cold running water. If irritation persists get medical attention immediately. The fluid also attacks paintwork and plastics - wash off spills immediately with cold water. Finally, brake fluid is highly flammable, and should be handled with the same care as gasoline.*
Note: *On vehicles with ABS, disconnect the negative battery cable (see Chapter 1).*
1 If the master cylinder has been disconnected and reconnected, then the complete system (all circuits) must be bled of air. If a component of one circuit has been disturbed, then only that particular circuit need be bled.
2 Bleeding should commence on the furthest bleed nipple from the master cylinder, followed by the next one until the bleed nipple remaining nearest to the master cylinder is bled last.
3 There are a variety of do-it-yourself 'one-man' brake bleeding kits available from auto parts stores, and it is recommended that one of these kits be used wherever possible, as they greatly simplify the brake bleeding operation. Follow the kit manufacturer's instructions in conjunction with the following procedure. If a pressure-bleeding kit is obtained, then it will not be necessary to depress the brake pedal in the following procedure.
4 During the bleeding operation, do not allow the brake fluid level in the reservoir to drop below the minimum mark. If the level is allowed to fall so far that air is drawn in, the whole procedure will have to be started again from scratch. **Note:** *On models equipped with ABS, if air enters the hydraulic unit, the unit must be bled using special test equipment. Only use new fluid for refilling, preferably from a freshly-opened container. Never re-use fluid bled from the system.*
5 Before starting, check that all rigid pipes

and flexible hoses are in good condition, and that all hydraulic unions are tight. Take great care not to allow hydraulic fluid to come into contact with the vehicle paintwork, otherwise the finish will be seriously damaged. Wash off any spilled fluid immediately with cold water.
6 If a brake bleeding kit is not being used, gather together a clean jar, a length of plastic or rubber tubing which is a tight fit over the bleed screw, and a new container of the specified brake fluid (see *Recommended lubricants and fluids*). The help of an assistant will also be required.
7 Clean the area around the bleed screw on the rear brake unit to be bled (it is important that no dirt be allowed to enter the hydraulic system), and remove the dust cap. Connect one end of the tubing to the bleed screw, and immerse the other end in the jar. This should be held at least a foot above the bleed nipple to maintain fluid pressure to the caliper **(see illustration)**. The jar should be filled with sufficient brake fluid to keep the end of the tube submerged.
8 Open the bleed screw by one or two turns, and have the assistant depress the brake pedal to the floor. Tighten the bleed screw at the end of the down stroke, then have the assistant release the pedal. Continue this procedure until clean brake fluid, free from air bubbles, can be seen flowing into the jar. Finally tighten the bleed screw with the pedal in the fully-depressed position.
9 Remove the tube, and install the dust cap. Top-off the master cylinder reservoir if necessary, then repeat the procedure on the opposite rear brake.
10 Repeat the procedure on the front brake furthest from the master cylinder, followed by the brake nearest to the master cylinder.
11 Check the feel of the brake pedal - it should be firm. If it is spongy, there is still some air in the system, and the bleeding procedure should be repeated.
12 When bleeding is complete, refill the master cylinder reservoir and install the cap.
13 On models with a hydraulically-operated clutch, check the clutch operation on completion; it may be necessary to bleed the clutch hydraulic system as described in Chapter 6.

12 Power brake booster - testing, removal and installation

Testing

1 To test the operation of the booster unit, depress the brake pedal four or five times to dissipate the vacuum, then start the engine while keeping the brake depressed. As the engine starts, there should be a noticeable give in the brake pedal as vacuum builds up. Allow the engine to run for at least two minutes, and then switch it off. If the brake pedal is now depressed again, it should be possible to hear a hiss from the booster when the pedal is depressed. After four or five applications, no further hissing should be heard, and the pedal should feel harder.

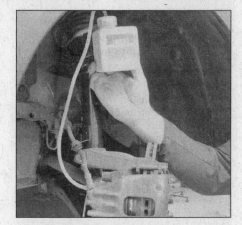
11.7 Hold the container up, to maintain fluid pressure

2 Before assuming that a problem exists in the booster unit itself, inspect the non-return valve as described in the next Section.

Removal

3 Refer to Section 8 and remove the master cylinder.
4 On vehicles with TCS, disconnect the electrical connector from the brake booster solenoid. On models with cruise control, remove the mounting screws at the firewall and set the cruise control actuator aside for access to the brake booster.
5 Release the cover on the hydraulic control unit and disconnect the electrical connector.
6 Remove the brake pipes to the hydraulic control unit. Cap the end of the pipes and the hydraulic unit to prevent any dirt contamination.
7 Remove the securing bolts from the hydraulic unit and remove from the vehicle.
8 Unclip the brake lines from the retaining clips on the firewall.
9 Remove the driver's lower dash panel for access to the brake pedal.
10 Depress the clip and remove the pin from the booster actuator rod, then remove the four nuts from the booster unit mounting bracket above the pedals.
11 Withdraw the booster unit from the firewall, and remove it from the engine compartment, taking care not to damage any other components.
12 Note that the booster unit cannot be disassembled for repair or overhaul and, if faulty, must be replaced.

Installation

13 Installation is a reversal of the removal procedure, noting the following points:
   a) *Refer to the relevant Sections/Chapters for details of replacing the other components removed.*
   b) *Compress the actuator rod into the brake booster, before replacement.*
   c) *Make sure the gasket is correctly positioned on the booster.*
   d) *Test the brakes carefully before returning the vehicle to normal service.*

13 Vacuum booster unit vacuum hose and non-return valve - removal, testing and installation

Removal

1   With the engine switched off, depress the brake pedal four or five times, to dissipate any remaining vacuum from the booster unit.

2   Disconnect the vacuum hose adapter at the booster unit, by pulling it free from the rubber grommet. If it is reluctant to move, pry it free, using a screwdriver with its blade inserted under the flange.

3   Detach the vacuum hose from the intake manifold connection, pressing in the collar to disengage the tabs, then withdrawing the collar slowly.

4   If the hose or the fittings are damaged or in poor condition, they must be replaced.

Testing

Refer to illustration 13.5

5   Examine the non-return valve **(see illustration)** for damage and signs of deterioration, and replace it if necessary. The valve may be tested by blowing through its connecting hoses in both directions. It should only be possible to blow from the booster end towards the intake manifold.

Installation

6   Installation is a reversal of the removal procedure. If installing a new non-return valve, ensure that it is installed the correct way.

14 Pressure-conscious regulator valve (non-ABS models) - removal and installation

Note: *Refer to the warning at the start of Section 11 concerning the dangers of brake fluid.*

Removal

Refer to illustration 14.1

1   On non-ABS models, the two pressure-conscious regulator valves are located on the master cylinder outlets to the rear brake circuits **(see illustration)**.

2   Unscrew the fluid reservoir filler cap, and draw off the fluid - see Section 11.

3   Position some rags beneath the master cylinder, to catch any spilled fluid.

4   Clean around the valve to be removed. Hold the valve stationary with one wrench, and unscrew the hydraulic pipe union nut with another wrench. Pull out the pipe, and bend it slightly away from the valve, taking care not to kink the pipe.

5   Unscrew the valve from the master cylinder and plug the master cylinder to prevent dirt contamination.

Installation

6   Installation is a reversal of the removal procedure. On completion, bleed the hydraulic system as described in Section 11.

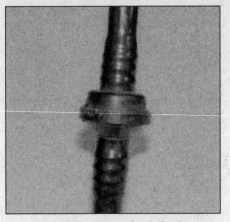

13.5 Non-return valve in brake vacuum hose

15 Electronic brake distribution (ABS models) - general information

1   In this system, the pressure conscious regulator valves are built into the ABS hydraulic unit, and electronic brake distribution is handled by a program addition to the ABS software.

2   Electronic brake force distribution (EBD) takes the place of the pressure-conscious regulator valves (PCRVs) and load-sensing valves (LAVs) used in the conventional braking systems.

3   Depending on traction and vehicle loading, the EBD function can come into operation during regular braking,

5   During the EBD operation, the brake force is determined by the wheel slippage. With conventional PCRVs or LAVs, the brake pressure or the vehicle speed controls the braking force.

16 ABS hydraulic unit - removal and installation

1   At the time of writing, no parts for the ABS hydraulic unit were available, and it must therefore be replaced as an assembly. Refer to the **Warning** at the start of Section 11 concerning the dangers of brake fluid.

Removal

2   Disconnect the negative battery cable. **Note:** *Before disconnecting the battery, refer to Chapter 5A, Section 1, for precautions.*

3   Disconnect the low fluid level warning light multi-plug from the brake fluid reservoir. Unscrew the cap. **Note:** *To release the electrical connector from the cap, pull back the tab and depress the two clips.*

4   Draw off the hydraulic fluid from the reservoir, using an old battery hydrometer or similar. Alternatively raise the vehicle and remove the wheels. Loosen the front bleed nipples and drain the fluid from the reservoir.

5   Disconnect the electrical connector from the auxiliary fusebox. Remove the retaining

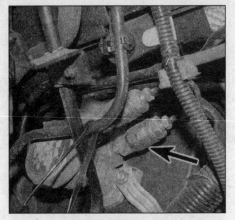

14.1 Pressure-conscious control relief valves (arrow)

screw, and detach the fusebox from its bracket. Move the fusebox to the air filter housing position temporarily.

6   On models with cruise control, disconnect the cruise control actuator electrical connector at the firewall. Remove the actuator mounting screws and set the actuator aside.

7   Release the cover on the hydraulic control unit and disconnect the electrical connector.

8   Undo the six brake pipes to the hydraulic control unit. Cap the end of the pipes and the hydraulic unit to prevent any dirt contamination. Unclip the brake lines from the retaining clips on the firewall.

9   Disconnect the brake pipes from the master cylinder.

10   Detach the wiring loom from the suspension tower.

11   Remove the securing bolts from the brake hydraulic unit, and withdraw from the firewall. Remove it from the engine compartment, taking care not to damage any other components.

Installation

12   Installation is a reversal of removal. Ensure that the multi-plug is securely connected, and that the brake pipe unions are tightened to the specified torque. On completion, bleed the hydraulic system as described in Section 11. **Note:** *If air enters the hydraulic unit, the unit must be bled using special test equipment.*

17 ABS wheel sensor - testing, removal and installation

Testing

1   Checking of the sensors is done before removal, connecting a voltmeter to the disconnected sensor multi-plug. Using an analog (moving coil) meter is not practical, since the meter does not respond quickly enough. A digital meter having an ac facility may be used to check that the sensor is operating correctly.

2   To do this, raise the relevant wheel, then disconnect the wiring to the ABS sensor and

connect the meter to it.

3   Spin the wheel and check that the output voltage is between 1.5 and 2.0 volts, depending on how fast the wheel is spun.

4   Alternatively, an oscilloscope may be used to check the output of the sensor - an alternating current will be traced on the screen, of magnitude depending on the speed of the rotating wheel.

5   If the sensor output is low or zero, replace the sensor.

Removal

Front wheel sensor

6   Apply the parking brake and loosen the relevant front wheel nuts. Jack up the front of the vehicle and support it on axle stands. Remove the wheel.

7   Unscrew the sensor mounting bolt from the hub carrier and withdraw the sensor.

8   Remove the sensor wiring loom from the support brackets on the front suspension strut and fenderwell.

9   Disconnect the multi-plug, and withdraw the sensor and wiring loom.

Rear wheel sensor

10   Chock the front wheels, and engage 1st gear (or P). Jack up the rear of the vehicle and support it on axle stands. Remove the relevant wheel.

11   Unscrew the sensor mounting bolt, located on the brake backing plate, and withdraw the sensor.

12   Disconnect the sensor wiring loom from the supports on the rear suspension arms.

13   Disconnect the multi-plug, and withdraw the sensor and wiring loom.

Installation

14   Installation is a reversal of the removal procedure.

18 Traction control/AdvanceTrac control components - removal and installation

Note: *This system uses the same components as the ABS and traction control system. The only additional components are the 'yaw rate' sensor and 'accelerometer sensor', which are mounted on the same bracket on the inner sill.*

Removal

1   Open the relevant door, then unclip the scuff plate trim from along the sill. Disconnect the negative battery cable (see Chapter 1).

2   Pull the carpet back to gain access to the sensors.

3   Undo the retaining bolt from the sensor bracket and detach it from the sill.

4   Disconnect the electrical connectors from the sensor. One connector is to measure the movement about the vehicles vertical axis (yaw rate) and the other is to measure the vehicle's lateral acceleration (accelerometer).

5   Undo the two retaining nuts, to remove

21.3 Disconnect the electrical connector from the switch

the yaw rate sensor from the bracket.

6   Unclip the accelerometer sensor from the bracket.

Installation

7   Installation is a reversal of the removal procedure.

19 Traction control system - general information

1   The Traction Control System is an expanded version of the ABS system. It is integrated with the ABS, and uses the same wheel sensors. It also uses the hydraulic control unit, which incorporates additional internal solenoid valves.

2   To remove the hydraulic unit or wheel sensors, carry out the procedures as described in Sections 16 and 17.

20 Brake light switch - removal, installation and adjustment

Removal

1   Disconnect the negative battery cable (see Chapter 1).

2   Undo the four screws and pry out the retaining clip to remove the dash lower panel. Unclip the multi-plug from the trim panel.

3   Disconnect the wiring connector from the brake light switch.

4   Rotate the switch clockwise by a quarter-turn, and withdraw it from the pedal bracket. (If the switch is installed in the upper part of the pedal bracket then rotate the switch counterclockwise to remove it.)

Installation and adjustment

5   With the switch removed, reset it by fully extending its plunger.

6   Depress the brake pedal and hold in this position, then install the stop-light switch to the mounting bracket.

7   With the switch securely clipped in position, release the brake pedal, and gently pull

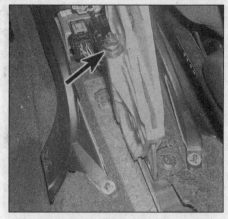

21.4 Undo the nut (arrow) to loosen the parking brake cable

it fully back to the at-rest position. This will automatically set the adjustment of the stop-light switch.

8   Reconnect the wiring connector and the battery, and check the operation of the switch prior to replacing the lower dash panel.

21 Parking brake lever - removal and installation

Removal

Refer to illustrations 21.3 and 21.4

1   Chock the front wheels, and engage 1st gear (or P). Disconnect the negative battery cable (see Chapter 1).

2   Remove the center console as described in Chapter 11.

3   Disconnect the electrical connector from the parking brake switch **(see illustration)**.

4   Undo the lock nut and loosen the parking brake adjusting nuts **(see illustration)**.

5   Unscrew the two mounting bolts securing the parking brake lever to the floor.

6   Withdraw the parking brake from inside the vehicle.

Installation

7   Installation is a reversal of removal.

8   When replacing the lever, it will be necessary to reset the mechanism, as follows.

9   Lift the parking brake lever up four notches, then tighten the adjustment nut until the slack in the cable has been taken up. Install the locking nut.

10   Check the operation of the parking brake several times before returning the vehicle to normal service.

22 Parking brake cables - removal and installation

Removal

Refer to illustrations 22.2, 22.3, 22.4, 22.6, 22.7a, 22.7b, 22.9 and 22.10

1   Chock the front wheels, and engage 1st gear (or P). Loosen the wheel nuts on the rel-

22.2 Unclip the parking brake boot

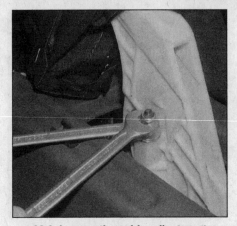

22.3 Loosen the cable adjustment

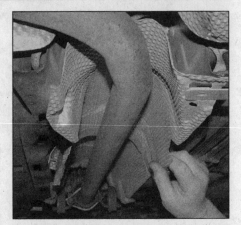

22.4 Move the heat shield along the exhaust

evant rear wheel, then jack up the rear of the vehicle and support it on axle stands. Fully release the parking brake lever.

2   Unclip the boot from around the hand-brake lever and remove **(see illustration)**.

3   Remove the locking nut and loosen the parking brake adjusting nut **(see illustration)**.

4   Working beneath the vehicle, unbolt the exhaust heat shield(s) from the underbody **(see illustration)**. Move them along the exhaust to gain access to the cables.

5   If required, release the exhaust system from the rubber mountings. Lower the exhaust system as far as possible, support-ing it on blocks or more axle stands.

6   Remove the relevant rear wheel and unclip the parking brake outer cable from its retaining clips **(see illustration)**.

7   Turn the cable through 90° to unhook the relevant cable from the equalizer bar. Lever the plastic cable guide from its bracket **(see illustrations)**.

8   On vehicles with ABS disconnect the brake system sensor.

9   Unclip the parking brake cable from the sleeve in front of the brake drum **(see illus-tration)**. On some models you may need to remove the rear brake shoes on the relevant side as described in Section 6, then remove the cable outer from the back plate by com-

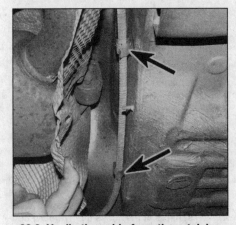

22.6 Unclip the cable from the retaining clips (arrows)

pressing the retaining lugs and pushing the cable through.

10   Unbolt the outer cable guide from the tie-bar, then disconnect it from its retaining clip **(see illustration)**. Withdraw the cable from beneath the vehicle.

Installation

11   Installation is a reversal of the removal procedure, noting the following points:

22.7a Twist the cable (arrow) to disengage

a)   *Adjust the cable as described in Sec-tion 21.*

b)   *Make sure that the cable end fittings are correctly located*

c)   *Check the operation of the parking brake. Make sure that both wheels are locked, then free to turn, as the parking brake is operated.*

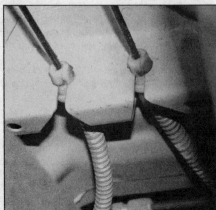

22.7b Release the cable guides from the bracket

22.9 Release the cable from the sleeve (arrow)

22.10 Remove the bolt (arrow) to release the cable guide

Chapter 10
Suspension and steering systems

Contents

Specifications

Tire size and pressure	See the decal at the rear of the driver's door jamb

Torque specifications
Ft-lbs (unless otherwise indicated)

Note: *One foot-pound (ft-lb) of torque is equivalent to 12 inch-pounds (in-lbs) of torque. Torque values below approximately 15 ft-lbs are expressed in inch-pounds, since most foot-pound torque wrenches are not accurate at these smaller values.*

Front suspension
Stabilizer bar clamp bolts
Models through 2005
Step 1 37
Step 2 52
2006 and later models 41
Stabilizer bar link nuts
Models through 2005 37
2006 and later models 41
Driveshaft/hub retaining nut .... See Chapter 8
Front subframe/crossmember
Models through 2004
Front bolts (two) 148
Rear bolts (four) 85
2005 and later models
Front bolts (two) 129
Rear bolts (four) 85
Insulator support bracket-to-transaxle center bolt 37
Lower arm balljoint-to-steering knuckle clamp bolt
Models through 2006 35
2007 and later models 46

Torque specifications

Ft-lbs (unless otherwise indicated)

Note: *One foot-pound (ft-lb) of torque is equivalent to 12 inch-pounds (in-lbs) of torque. Torque values below approximately 15 ft-lbs are expressed in inch-pounds, since most foot-pound torque wrenches are not accurate at these smaller values.*

Lower arm to subframe
   Models through 2004
      Step 1 (inner rear nut) 74
      Step 2 (inner rear nut) .... Tighten through further 60°
      Step 3 (outer rear nut) 89
      Step 4 (front bolt) 89
      Step 5 (front bolt) .... Tighten through further 90°
      Step 6 (front bolt) .... Check front bolt torque is between 125 and 170
   2005 models
      Step 1 (inner rear nut) 133
      Step 2 (outer rear nut) 89
      Step 4 (front bolt) 103
   2006 and later models
      Step 1 (front) 159
      Step 2 (inboard bracket nut) 118
      Step 3 (outboard bracket nut) 76
Suspension strut thrust bearing retaining nut
   Models through 2004 35
   2005 models 49
   2006 and later models 66
Suspension strut-to-knuckle pinch bolt
   Models through 2005 66
   2006 and later models 111
Suspension strut upper mounting nuts (three)
   Models through 2004 18
   2005 and later models 22

Torque specifications

Ft-lbs (unless otherwise indicated)

Rear suspension

Stabilizer bar clamp bolts
   Models through 2005 35
   2006 and later models 41
Stabilizer bar link to lower arm .... 132 in-lbs
Brake caliper bracket bolts 41
Brake caliper guide bolts 26
Crossmember mounting bolts 85
Shock absorber upper bolt (station wagon models) 85
Shock absorber upper nut (except station wagon) 13
Spindle/hub retaining bolts 49
Trailing arm front mounting bracket bolts 85
Upper arm mounting bolts 85

Steering

Flexible coupling-to-pinion shaft clamp bolt 18
Power steering pipe unions-to-valve body clamp plate bolt 17
Wheel nuts .... See Chapter 1
Steering column retaining locknuts .... 120 in-lbs
Steering column Torx bolt .... 120 in-lbs
Steering coupling-to-steering gear clamp bolt
   Models through 2004 26
   2005 and later models 22
Steering gear mounting bolts
   Models through 2006 59
   2007 and later models 47
Steering pump mounting bolts 17
Steering pump pressure line union 48
Steering wheel 37
Tie-rod end locknut 46
Tie-rod end balljoint-to-steering knuckle nut
   Models through 2005 35
   2006 models 30
   2007 and later models 26

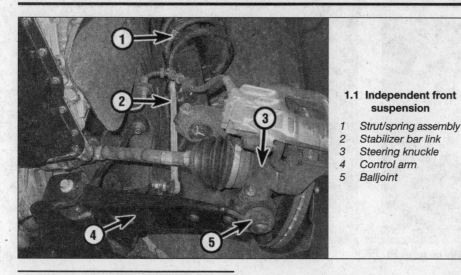

1.1 Independent front suspension

1   Strut/spring assembly
2   Stabilizer bar link
3   Steering knuckle
4   Control arm
5   Balljoint

1   General information

Refer to illustration 1.1

The independent front suspension is of MacPherson strut type, incorporating coil springs, integral telescopic shock absorbers, and a stabilizer bar **(see illustration)**. The struts are attached to steering knuckles at their lower ends, and the knuckles are in turn attached to the lower suspension arm by balljoints. The stabilizer bar is bolted to the rear of the subframe/crossmember, and is connected to the front suspension struts by links.

The fully independent rear suspension is a multi-link type. There are four arms on each side: one forged upper arm, two pressed-steel lower side arms, and a trailing arm. The trailing arm is of a one-piece pressed steel construction. The coil springs are separate from the shock absorbers and a rear stabilizer bar is installed on all models **(see illustrations)**.

A power steering type rack-and-pinion steering gear is used, together with a conventional column and telescopic coupling, incorporating a universal joint. The power steering has a relatively 'quick' rack with just 2.9 turns lock-to-lock and a turning circle of 35.75 feet. A power steering system fluid cooler is installed in front of the radiator on the crossmember.

When working on the suspension or steering, you may come across nuts or bolts that seem impossible to loosen. These nuts and bolts on the underside of the vehicle are continually subjected to water, road grime, mud, etc, and can become rusted or seized, making them extremely difficult to remove. In order to unscrew these stubborn nuts and bolts without damaging them (or other components), use lots of penetrating oil, and allow it to soak in for a while. Using a wire brush to clean exposed threads will also ease removal of the nut or bolt, and will help to prevent damage to the threads. Sometimes, a sharp blow with a hammer and punch will break the bond between a nut and bolt, but care must be taken to prevent the punch from slipping off and ruining the threads. Using a longer bar or wrench will increase leverage, but never use an extension bar/pipe on a ratchet, as the internal mechanism could be damaged. Actually *tightening* the nut or bolt slightly first, may help to break it loose. Nuts or bolts that have required drastic measures to remove them should always be replaced.

Since most of the procedures dealt with in this Chapter involve jacking up the vehicle and working underneath it, a good pair of axle stands will be needed. A hydraulic floor jack is the preferred type of jack to lift the vehicle, and it can also be used to support certain components during removal and installation operations.

Warning: *Never, under any circumstances, rely on a jack to support the vehicle while working beneath it. It is not recommended, when jacking up the rear of the vehicle, to lift beneath the rear crossmember.*

2   Steering knuckle and hub assembly - removal and installation

Removal

Refer to illustrations 2.2, 2.4, 2.7, 2.8, 2.9 and 2.10

1   Apply the parking brake. Remove the wheel cover from the relevant front wheel, and loosen (but do not remove) the driveaxle/hub nut. This nut is very tight - use only good quality, close-fitting tools, and take adequate precautions against personal injury when loosening the hub nut.

2   Loosen the three top strut nuts by five turns, but do not remove them **(see illustration)**. On 2005 and later models, loosen the nuts only four turns.

3   Loosen the front wheel nuts, jack up the front of the vehicle and support it on axle stands. Remove the front wheel.

4   Unscrew the tie-rod end balljoint nut, and detach the rod from the arm on the steering knuckle using a conventional balljoint removal tool **(see illustration)**. Take care not to damage the balljoint seal.

5   Remove the ABS sensor (if equipped) as described in Chapter 9.

6   Remove the brake caliper and brake disc as described in Chapter 9. Suspend the caliper from a suitable point under the fenderwell, taking care not to damage or strain the hose.

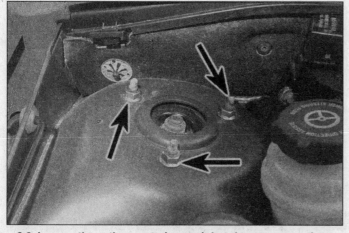

2.2 Loosen these three nuts (arrows), but do not remove them

2.4 Leave the nut on a couple of turns to save damaging the threads

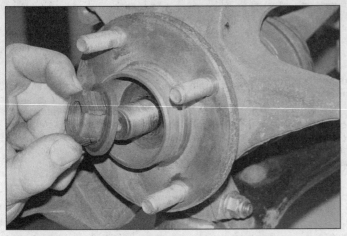

2.7 Unscrew the driveaxle/hub nut - the nut can only be re-used up to four times

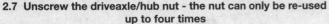

7   Unscrew and remove the driveaxle/hub nut **(see illustration)**. **Note:** *The nut is of special laminated design, and should only be re-used a maximum of 4 times. (It is a good idea to file a small notch on the nut every time it is removed.)* Obtain a new nut if necessary.

8   Note which way the lower arm balljoint clamp bolt is installed, then unscrew and remove it from the knuckle assembly **(see illustration)**. Lever the balljoint down from the knuckle; if it is tight, pry the clamp open using a large flat-bladed tool. Take care not to damage the balljoint seal during the separation procedure.

9   Pull the steering knuckle and hub assembly from the driveaxle splines **(see illustration)**. If it is tight, connect a universal puller to the hub flange, and withdraw it from the driveaxle. When the driveaxle is free, suspend it from a suitable point under the fenderwell, making sure that the inner constant velocity joint is not turned through more than 18 degrees. (Damage may occur if the joint is turned through too great an angle.)

10   Unscrew and remove the pinch-bolt securing the steering knuckle assembly to the front suspension strut, noting which way it is installed **(see illustration)**. Pry open the clamp using a wedge-shaped tool, and release the knuckle from the strut. If necessary, tap the knuckle downward with a soft-face mallet to separate the two components.

Installation

11   Locate the assembly on the front suspension strut. Insert the pinch-bolt with its head facing the same way as removal. Install the nut and tighten it to the specified torque.

12   Pull the steering knuckle/hub assembly outward, and insert the driveaxle to engage the splines in the hub. A special tool is available to draw the driveaxle into the hub, but it is unlikely that the splines will be tight. However, if they are, it will be necessary to obtain the tool, or to use a similar home-made tool.

13   Install the lower arm balljoint to the knuckle assembly, and insert the clamp bolt with its head facing the same way as on removal. Install the nut and tighten it to the specified torque.

14   Install the driveaxle/hub nut, and tighten it moderately at this stage. Final tightening of the nut is made with the vehicle lowered to the ground.

15   Install the brake caliper and brake disc as described in Chapter 9. Install the brake

2.8 Remove the bolt from the bottom balljoint

hose support bracket to the strut.

16   If equipped, install the ABS sensor as described in Chapter 9.

17   Reconnect the tie-rod end balljoint to the steering knuckle, and tighten the nut to the specified torque.

18   Install the front wheel, and lower the vehicle to the ground. Tighten the three top strut mounting bolts to the specified torque.

19   Tighten the driveaxle/hub nut and wheel nuts to their specified torque, then install the wheel cover.

---

3   Front hub and bearings - inspection and replacement

Inspection

1   The front hub bearings are non-adjustable, and are supplied already greased.

2   To check the bearings for excessive wear, apply the parking brake, jack up the front of the vehicle and support it on axle stands.

3   Grip the front wheel at the top and the bottom, and attempt to rock it. If excessive movement is noted, it may be that the hub

2.9 Carefully pull the driveaxle from the hub and support it on an axle stand

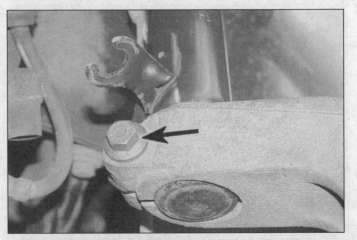

2.10 Steering knuckle to strut pinch-bolt (arrow)

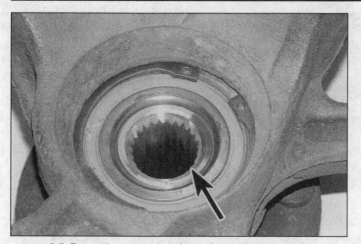

3.5 Press the center hub (arrow) out of the bearing

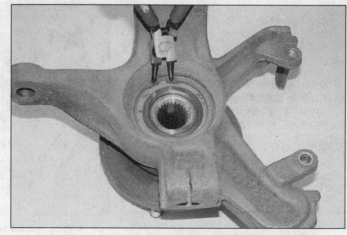

3.8 Remove the snap-ring from the steering knuckle

bearings are worn. Do not confuse wear in the driveshaft outer joint or front suspension lower arm balljoint with wear in the bearings. Hub bearing wear will show up as roughness or vibration when the wheel is spun; it will also be noticeable as a rumbling or growling noise when driving.

Note: *Removal of the front hub may damage the bearings, and render them unserviceable for future use. When replacing the hub, the bearing assembly must always be replaced.*

Replacement

Refer to illustrations 3.5 and 3.8

4   Remove the steering knuckle and hub assembly as described in Section 2.

5   The hub must now be removed from the bearing inner races. It is preferable to use a press to do this, but it is possible to drive out the hub using a length of metal tube of suitable diameter **(see illustration).**

6   Part of the inner race may remain on the hub, and this should be removed using a puller.

7   Note that when replacing the hub, the wheel bearing will have to be replaced also, as it may be damaged on removal.

8   Using snap-ring pliers, extract the snap-ring securing the hub bearing in the steering knuckle **(see illustration).**

9   Press or drive out the bearing, using a length of metal tubing of diameter slightly less than the bearing outer race.

10   Clean the bearing seating faces in the steering knuckle.

11   Using a length of metal tube of diameter slightly less than the outer race, press or drive the new bearing into the knuckle until it is fully located. Do not apply any pressure to the inner race.

12   Locate the snap-ring into the groove in the knuckle, taking care not to cover the wheel speed sensor with the snap-ring.

13   Support the inner race on a length of metal tube, then press or drive the hub fully into the bearing.

14   Install the steering knuckle and hub assembly as described in Section 2.

4   Front suspension strut assembly - removal and installation

Removal

Refer to illustrations 4.1, 4.2, 4.3a, 4.3b and 4.4

1   Disconnect the brake hose from the

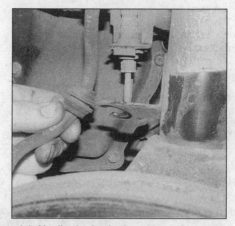

4.1 Unclip the brake hose from the strut

bracket on the strut **(see illustration).**

2   Remove the nut from the stabilizer bar link and disconnect it from the strut **(see illustration).** On models equipped with ABS, disconnect the wheel sensor wiring.

3   Unscrew and remove the pinch-bolt securing the steering knuckle assembly to the front suspension strut, noting which way it is installed. Lever the steering knuckle/hub assembly down and release it from the strut **(see illustrations).** If necessary, tap the

4.2 Remove the stabilizer bar link rod securing nut

4.3a Pry the hub assembly down . . .

knuckle downward with a soft-headed mallet to separate the two components. **Note:** *Support the steering knuckle/hub assembly when released from the strut, to prevent any damage to the driveshaft.*

4   Support the strut/spring assembly under the fenderwell, then remove the upper mounting nuts **(see illustration)**.

5   Lower the suspension strut from under the fenderwell, withdrawing it from the vehicle.

Installation

6   Installation is a reversal of removal. Making sure that all the relevant bolts are tightened to their specified torque.

5   Front suspension strut - overhaul

Refer to illustrations 5.3, 5.4, 5.5a, 5.5b, 5.5c, 5.5d and 5.9

Warning: *Before attempting to disassemble the front suspension strut, a tool to hold the coil spring in compression must be obtained. Do not attempt to use makeshift methods. Uncontrolled release of the spring could cause damage and personal injury. Use a high-quality spring compressor, and carefully follow the tool manufacturer's instructions provided with it. After removing the coil spring with the compressor still installed, place it in a safe, isolated area.*

4.3b . . . and disengage the strut

4.4 Remove the three upper mounting nuts

1   If the front suspension struts exhibit signs of wear (leaking fluid, loss of damping capability, sagging or cracked coil springs) then they should be disassembled and overhauled as necessary. The struts themselves cannot be serviced, and should be replaced if faulty; the springs and related components can be replaced individually. To maintain balanced characteristics on both sides of the vehicle, the components on both sides should be replaced at the same time.

2   With the strut removed from the vehicle (see Section 4), clean away all external dirt,

then mount it in a vise.

3   Install the coil spring compressor tools (ensuring that they are fully engaged), and compress the spring until all tension is relieved from the upper mount **(see illustration)**.

4   Hold the strut piston rod with an Allen key, and unscrew the thrust bearing retaining nut with a box-end wrench **(see illustration)**.

5   Withdraw the top mounting, thrust bearing, upper spring seat and spring, followed by the boot and the bump stop **(see illustrations)**.

5.3 Make sure the spring compressor tool is on securely

5.4 Loosen and remove the retaining nut

5.5a Remove the upper bearing and spring seat . . .

5.5b . . . then carefully remove the spring . . .

5.5c . . . followed by the boot . . .

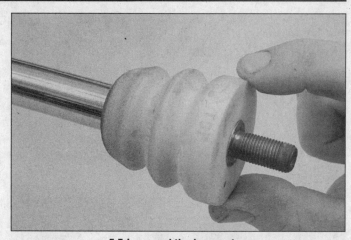

5.5d . . . and the bump stop

6   If a new spring is to be installed, the original spring must now be carefully released from the compressor. If it is to be re-used, the spring can be left in compression.

7   With the strut assembly now completely disassembled, examine all the components for wear and damage, and check the bearing for smoothness of operation. Replace components as necessary.

8   Examine the strut for signs of fluid leakage. Check the strut piston rod for signs of pitting along its entire length, and check the strut body for signs of damage. Test the operation of the strut, while holding it in an upright position, by moving the piston through a full stroke, and then through short strokes of 2 to 4 inches. In both cases, the resistance felt should be smooth and continuous. If the resistance is jerky, uneven, or if there is any visible sign of wear or damage to the strut, replacement is necessary.

9   Reassembly is a reversal of dismantling, noting the following points:

a) *Make sure that the coil spring ends are correctly located in the upper and lower seats before releasing the compressor* **(see illustration).**

b) *Check that the bearing is correctly installed on the piston rod seat.*

c) *Tighten the thrust bearing retaining nut to the specified torque.*

d) *The coil springs must be installed with the paint mark at the bottom.*

---

6   Front crossmember/stabilizer bar and links - removal and installation

---

Refer to illustrations 6.4, 6.5, 6.6, 6.8, 6.9a, 6.9b, 6.10 and 6.12

Removal

Note: *Before disconnecting the battery, refer to Chapter 5A, Section 1.*

1   Disconnect the battery negative cable.

2   Loosen the front wheel lug nuts. Apply the parking brake, jack up the front of the vehicle and support it on axle stands.

3   Center the steering wheel and lock it in position by removing the ignition key. Remove both front wheels.

4   Remove the tie-rod end balljoint nuts on both sides of the vehicle, and detach the rods from the arms on the steering knuckles using a conventional balljoint removal tool **(see illustration).** Take care not to damage the balljoint seals.

5   Remove the connecting link bottom ball-

5.9 Spring located in the lower seat (arrow)

joint nuts, and disconnect them from the stabilizer bar on both sides of the vehicle **(see illustration).** Use a balljoint removal tool if required, taking care not to damage the balljoint seal.

6   Disconnect the steering column shaft from the pinion extension; by removing the securing bolt at the lower part of the steering column the shaft will then pull apart **(see illustration).**

7   Remove the engine undertray, if equipped.

6.4 Remove the tie-rod end securing nut (arrow)

6.5 Remove the connecting link bottom balljoint (arrow)

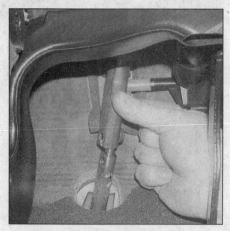

6.6 Remove the securing bolt and disconnect the steering column shaft

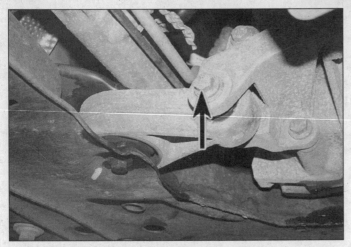

6.8 Remove the support bracket (arrow)

6.9a Loosen and remove the four rear crossmember bolts (arrows) . . .

8   Remove the bolt from the insulator support bracket on the rear of the transaxle unit **(see illustration)**.

9   Using a suitable jack, support the crossmember. Remove the six crossmember securing bolts **(see illustrations)**, and carefully lower. the crossmember just enough to gain access to the stabilizer bar clamps. There is a special tool to align the bolt holes in the crossmember on installation. If this is not available, mark the mounting points, so as to install them in the correct position.

10   Unscrew and remove the stabilizer bar mounting bolts from the crossmember on both sides of the vehicle **(see illustration)**.

11   Withdraw the stabilizer bar from the crossmember, taking care not to damage the surrounding components.

12   To remove the stabilizer bar connecting links from the strut assembly, remove the top balljoint nuts and detach from the strut bracket **(see illustration)**.

13   If the crossmember requires removing completely, remove the lower suspension arms and steering rack as described in Sections 7 and 20.

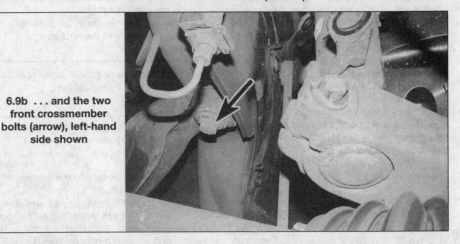

6.9b . . . and the two front crossmember bolts (arrow), left-hand side shown

Installation

14   When installing the stabilizer bar bushings make sure they are located correctly on the flats of the stabilizer bar with no lubricant.

15   Set the stabilizer bar to the design height setting of 3-7/8 inches and support it in that position.

16   Install the clamps to the stabilizer bar, installing the rear bolts first and tightening to Specifications. Then install the front bolts and tighten to Specifications. Further tighten the bolts in two stages as given in the Specifications.

17   Remove the stabilizer bar support for the design' height.

6.10 Remove the stabilizer bar securing bolts (arrows)

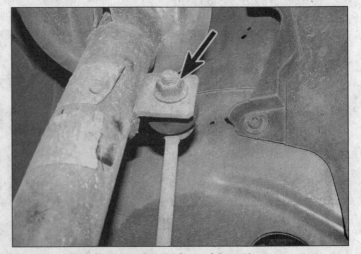

6.12 Remove the nut (arrow) from the upper connecting link balljoint

7.4a Remove the two rear mounting nuts (arrows) . . .

7.4b . . . then remove the front mounting bolt (arrow)

18 Jack the crossmember up, into the correct position on the chassis (using the aligning tool if available). Make sure the crossmember ball-bearing washers are installed correctly before tightening the new bolts.

19 Replace the crossmember bolts and tighten them to their specified torque.

20 Replacement is then a reversal of the removal procedure. Make sure that all the relevant bolts are replaced and tightened to their specified torque.

7 Front suspension lower arm - removal, overhaul and installation

Removal

Refer to illustrations 7.4a and 7.4b

1 Apply the parking brake, jack up the front of the vehicle and support it on axle stands. Remove the appropriate wheel.

2 Where applicable, remove the undertray from under the engine compartment and disconnect from the fenderwell.

3 Note which way the front suspension lower arm balljoint clamp bolt is installed, then unscrew and remove it from the knuckle

assembly. Pry the balljoint down from the knuckle; if it is tight, pry the joint open carefully using a large flat-bladed tool. Take care not to damage the balljoint seal during the separation procedure.

4 Unscrew and remove the lower arm rear mounting clamp nuts, also remove the front mounting bolt **(see illustrations)**.

5 Remove the lower arm from the subframe, and withdraw it from the vehicle.

Overhaul

6 Examine the rubber bushings and the suspension lower balljoint for wear and damage. At the time of writing the manual the balljoint and rubber bushings could not be replaced on the lower arm. Replace the complete lower arm if there is any wear or damage.

Installation

Note: *The bolts, nuts and bearing washers securing the lower arm to the subframe must be replaced with new ones after removal.*

7 Locate the lower arm on the subframe, and insert the front mounting bolt and nut. Install the clamp and nuts to the rear mount and tighten them in stages.

8 Install the front suspension lower arm balljoint to the knuckle assembly, and insert the clamp bolt with its head facing in the same direction as removal. Install the nut and tighten to the specified torque.

9 Install the wheel, and lower the vehicle to the ground. Making sure that all the relevant bolts are tightened to their specified torque.

8 Front suspension lower arm balljoint - replacement

Note: *If the lower arm balljoint is worn, the complete lower arm must be replaced. At the time of writing this manual, the balljoint could not be replaced separately from the lower arm.*

1 Remove and install the front suspension lower arm as described in Section 7.

9 Rear hub and bearings - inspection and replacement

Inspection

Refer to illustration 9.1

1 The rear hub bearings are non-adjustable **(see illustration)**.

2 To check the bearings for excessive wear, chock the front wheels, then jack up the rear of the vehicle and support it on axle stands. Fully release the parking brake.

3 Grip the rear wheel at the top and bottom, and attempt to rock it. If excessive movement is noted, or if there is any roughness or vibration felt when the wheel is spun, it is indicative that the hub bearings are worn.

Replacement

Refer to illustrations 9.5a, 9.5b, 9.6, 9.10, 9.13 and 9.16

4 Remove the rear wheel.

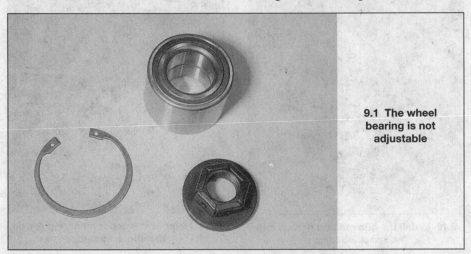

9.1 The wheel bearing is not adjustable

9.5a Remove the dust cap . . .

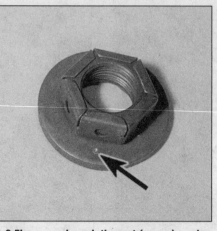

9.5b . . . and mark the nut (arrow) each time it is removed

9.6 Pull the brake drum from the stub axle

5   Tap off the dust cap and unscrew the hub nut **(see illustration)**. **Note:** *The nut is of special laminated design, and should only be re-used a maximum of 4 times. It is a good idea to mark the nut every time it is removed. Obtain a new one if necessary* **(see illustration)**.
6   Remove the rear brake drum **(see illustration)**. If the drum will not pull off easily, use a suitable puller to draw the drum and bearing assembly off the stub axle. On models with rear disc brakes, remove the caliper and rotor (see Chapter 9).

7   In stubborn cases, apply a little penetrating oil at the joint between the drum and the axle. A little heat from a propane torch on the inner edge of the drum may further loosen the bond.
8   Part of the inner race may remain on the stub axle, this should be removed using a puller.
9   Remove the ABS sensor ring from the hub/drum assembly (if equipped). This must be replaced when reinstalling.
10   Using snap-ring pliers, extract the snap-ring securing the bearing in the hub/drum **(see illustration)**.
11   Press or drive out the bearing, using a length of metal tubing of diameter slightly less than the bearing outer race.
12   Clean the bearing seating faces in the hub/drum.
13   Using the length of metal tubing, Press or drive the new bearing into the hub/drum until it is fully located **(see illustration)**. Do not apply any pressure to the inner race.
14   Locate the snap-ring into the groove in the hub/drum to secure the bearing in place.
15   Press the new ABS sensor ring onto the hub assembly slowly and squarely, as damage to the new ring will cause failure of the ABS system (if equipped).

16   Locate the new rear hub/drum and bearing assembly on the stub axle, then install the hub nut and tighten it to the specified torque **(see illustration)**. Keep rotating the hub assembly in the opposite direction when tightening the hub retaining nut to prevent damage to the bearing. **Note:** *On SVT models replace the stub axle whenever the bearing is replaced.*
17   Tap the dust cap fully onto the hub. If the dust cap was damaged on removal then a new one must be installed.
18   Install the rear wheel, and lower the vehicle to the ground. Tighten all bolts and nuts to their specified torque.

10   Rear shock absorber - removal, testing and installation

Removal
Sedan & Coupe models
Refer to illustration 10.2
1   Open the trunk or liftgate and remove the interior trim panel to gain access to the shock absorber top mounting nut.
2   Using an Allen key to hold the piston rod, remove the shock absorber upper

9.10 Remove the snap-ring

9.13 Use a threaded bar and a tube to press the bearing in

9.16 Install the hub nut and tighten it to the specified torque

10.2 Remove the upper mounting nut on the shock absorber

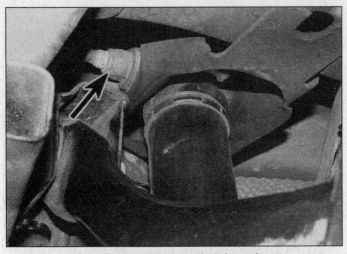

10.7a Remove the upper bolt (arrow) . . .

10.7b . . . and the lower bolt (arrow)

mounting nut **(see illustration)**.

3   Chock the front wheels, then jack up the rear of the vehicle and support it on axle stands. Remove the wheels as required.

4   Place a jack under the lower suspension arm/coil spring to support it. Unscrew and remove the shock absorber lower mounting bolt, then withdraw the shock absorber from under the vehicle.

Wagon models

Refer to illustrations 10.7a and 10.7b

5   Chock the front wheels, then jack up the rear of the vehicle and support it on axle stands. Remove the wheels as required.

6   On the left-hand shock absorber, release the exhaust from the rubber hanger, then undo the rear exhaust muffler heat shield bolts. Remove it from the vehicle, so as to gain access to the upper shock-mounting nut.

7   Place a jack under the lower suspension arm/coil spring to support it. Unscrew and remove the upper mounting bolt, then the lower mounting bolt **(see illustrations)**. Withdraw the shock absorber from under the vehicle.

Testing

8   Check the mounting rubbers for damage and deterioration. If they are worn, they may be able to be replaced separately from the shock absorber body (check the availability of parts).

9   Mount the shock absorber in a vise, gripping it by the lower mounting. Examine the shock absorber for signs of fluid leakage. Test the operation of the shock absorber by moving it through a full stroke, and then through short strokes of two to four inches. In both cases, the resistance felt should be smooth and continuous. If the resistance is jerky or uneven, the shock absorber should be replaced.

Installation

10   Installation is a reversal of the removal procedure, tightening the mounting bolts to

their specified torque. **Note 1:** *The supporting jack under the lower suspension arm/coil spring can be raised or lowered to install the shock absorber if required.* **Note 2:** *The final tightening of the mounting bolts must be carried out with the vehicle weight on the wheels. Alternatively, you can raise the rear suspension with the jack to simulate normal ride height, then tighten the fasteners to the torque listed in this Chapter's Specifications.*

---

11   Rear stabilizer bar and links - removal and installation

Note: *Before the final tightening of any components on the rear suspension, it must be set to the Design Height setting on both sides of the vehicle (see Step 9).*

Removal

Refer to illustrations 11.2 and 11.3

1   Remove the rear coil spring as described in Section 12.

2   Unscrew the nuts and bolts securing the stabilizer bar links to the rear lower arms, then remove the washers and bushings **(see illustration)**.

3   Unscrew the bolts securing the stabi-

lizer bar mounting clamps to the rear suspension crossmember **(see illustration)**; release the clamps (one each side), and withdraw the stabilizer bar from under the vehicle.

4   Examine the rubber bushings for the mounting clamps and links, and if necessary replace them. The links are available individually.

Installation

5   When installing the bushings to the stabilizer bar, make sure they are located correctly on the flats of the stabilizer bar with **no** lubricant (except water if required). Make sure the nipple is on the left-hand side of the bushing when installed.

6   Locate the stabilizer bar on the rear crossmember, then install the clamps and tighten the bolts to the specified torque.

7   Install the stabilizer bar links to the rear lower arms, together with the bushings and washers.

8   Carry out the procedures for the rear suspension Design Height setting (see below).

Suspension Design Height setting

9   Remove the rear coil springs as described in Section 12.

11.2 Remove the nut and bolt (arrow)

11.3 Rear stabilizer bar clamp bolts (arrows)

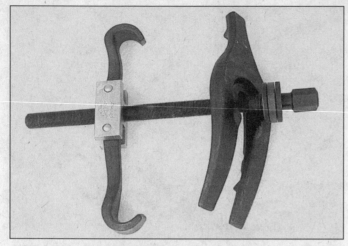

12.2 A typical aftermarket internal-type coil spring compressor: the hooked arms grip the upper coils of the spring, the plate is inserted between the lower coils, and when the nut on the threaded rod is turned, the spring is compressed

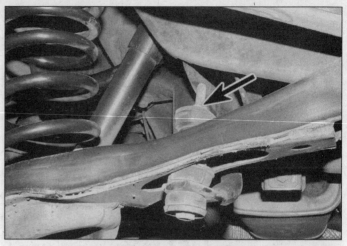

13.2 Remove the bolt (arrow) to disconnect the stabilizer bar

10   Use a jack to raise the lower arm until the fabricated spacer (113mm x 20mm for Sedan and Coupe, 187mm x 20mm for Wagon) can be put between the lower arm and crossmember in a vertical position, this is then the Design Height setting. (On the Sedan and Coupe it will be necessary to remove the bump-stop to locate the spacer vertically.)

11   When set in this position on both sides, all the rear suspension bolts can be tightened to their specified torques.

12   The spacers can then be removed and the coil springs installed as described in Section 12.

13   Install the rear wheels, and lower the vehicle to the ground.

12   Rear coil springs - removal and installation

Warning: *Before attempting to remove the rear suspension coil springs, a tool to hold the coil spring in compression must be obtained. Careful use of conventional coil spring compressors must be taken at all times to avoid personal injury.*

Removal

Refer to illustration 12.2

1   Chock the front wheels, then jack up the rear of the vehicle so the wheels are off the ground. Support the vehicle on axle stands. Remove the wheels as required.

2   Fit the coil spring compressor tool (ensuring that it is fully engaged), and compress the coil spring until all tension is relieved from the mount **(see illustration)**.

3   Withdraw the coil spring from under the vehicle, taking care to keep the compressor tool in full engagement with the coil spring.

4   If a new coil spring is to be installed, the original coil spring must be released from the compressor. If it is to be re-used, the coil spring can be left in compression.

Installation

5   Installation is a reversal of the removal procedure, but make sure that the coil spring is located correctly in the upper and lower seats. The coil springs must be installed with the paint mark at the bottom. **Note:** *If there is a rattle from the rear springs, check that a sleeve is installed to the top end of the coil spring. This sleeve can be purchased from a dealer.*

13   Rear suspension rear lower arm - removal and installation

Refer to illustrations 13.2, 13.3a and 13.3b

Removal

Note: *The bushings in the suspension arms cannot be replaced separately; replace the complete arm if there is any wear or damage.*

1   Remove the rear suspension coil spring as described in Section 12.

2   Remove the nut securing the stabilizer bar link to the lower arm **(see illustration)**.

3   Unscrew and remove the bolt securing the rear lower arm to the crossmember, and the bolt to the hub assembly **(see illustrations)**. **Note:** *On 2003 and later models, this*

13.3a Remove rear lower arm-to-crossmember bolt . . .

13.3b . . . and bolt-to-hub assembly (arrow)

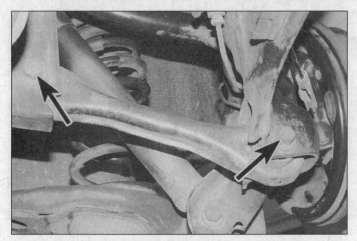

14.3 Remove the two mounting bolts (arrows)

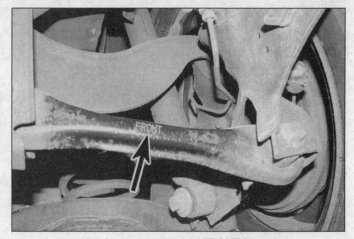

14.4 Lower arm marked FRONT (arrow)

bolt secures an eccentric that controls alignment of the rear lower arm. Before removal, make matching marks on the crossmember and eccentric.

4   Withdraw the rear lower arm from under the vehicle.

Installation

5   Installation is a reversal of the removal procedure. Delay fully tightening the lower arm mounting bolts, until the suspension Design Height setting procedure has been carried out as described in Section 11. The wheel alignment will also require checking (see Section 26).

14   Rear suspension front lower arm - removal and installation

Refer to illustration 14.3

Removal

Note: *The bushings in the suspension arms cannot be replaced separately; replace the complete arm if there is any wear or damage.*

1   Remove the rear suspension coil spring as described in Section 12. (This is to achieve the Design Height setting.)

15.3 Remove the two mounting bolts (arrows) - wagon model shown, other models similar

2   Unscrew and remove the bolt securing the front lower arm to the crossmember.

3   Unscrew and remove the bolt securing the front lower arm to the hub assembly **(see illustration)**, and withdraw the arm from under the vehicle.

Installation

Refer to illustration 14.4

4   Installation is a reversal of the removal procedure; make sure the arm (marked FRONT) is installed correctly **(see illustration)**. Delay fully tightening the lower arm mounting bolts, until the suspension Design Height setting procedure has been carried out as described in Section 11.

15   Rear suspension upper arm - removal and installation

Refer to illustration 15.3

Removal

Note: *The bushings in the suspension arms cannot be replaced separately; replace the complete arm if there is any wear or damage.*

1   Remove the rear suspension coil spring as described in Section 12. (This is to achieve

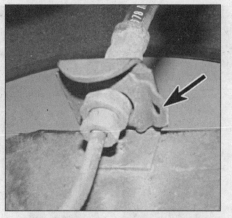

16.3 Loosen the brake line fitting and remove the securing clip (arrow)

the Design Height setting.)

2   Unscrew and remove the bolt securing the upper arm to the hub assembly.

3   Unscrew and remove the bolt securing the upper arm to the crossmember **(see illustration)**, and withdraw the arm from under the vehicle taking note of the way it was installed for reference on reassembly.

Installation

4   Installation is a reversal of the removal procedure, make sure the arm is installed the right way around. Delay fully tightening the upper arm mounting bolts, until the suspension Design Height setting procedure has been carried out as described in Section 11.

16   Rear suspension trailing arm - removal and installation

Removal

Refer to illustrations 16.3 and 16.9

1   Remove the rear suspension coil spring as described in Section 12.

2   Detach the parking brake cable guide from the tie-bar, and pull the cable clear of the tie-bar.

3   Install a brake hose clamp to the rear flexible brake hose, and disconnect the brake pipe union. Using a pair of pliers pull out the clip securing the brake pipe to the body **(see illustration)**. On 2002 and later models, release the clip securing the parking brake cable to the trailing arm.

4   Remove the rear brake drum/disc assembly as described in Chapter 9. On models with rear disc brakes, remove the rotor dust shield.

5   Unscrew and remove the bolt securing the lower part of the rear shock absorber to the trailing arm assembly.

6   Where applicable, release the ABS wheel sensor lead from the trailing arm.

7   Unscrew and remove the front and rear lower arm bolts from the trailing arm assembly.

8   Unscrew and remove the upper arm bolt from the trailing arm assembly.
9   Unbolt the trailing arm front mounting bracket from the underbody **(see illustration)**, and withdraw the assembly from under the vehicle.

Installation

10   Installation is a reversal of the removal procedure. Delay fully tightening all the mounting bolts, until the suspension Design Height setting procedure has been carried out as described in Section 11. Bleed the brake hydraulic system as described in Chapter 9.

---

17   Rear suspension crossmember - removal and installation

Removal

Refer to illustration 17.7
1   Remove the rear suspension coil springs as described in Section 12.
2   Support the hub assemblies on both sides of the vehicle using axle stands.
3   Remove the stabilizer bar as described in Section 11.
4   Remove the upper arm and lower arms as described in Sections 13, 14, and 15.
5   Detach and lower the exhaust system from its hanger, supporting it to prevent any damage.
6   Using a floor jack, support the crossmember.
7   Unscrew the mounting bolts (three bolts each side), and lower the crossmember to the ground **(see illustration)**.

Installation

8   Installation is a reversal of the removal procedure, noting the following points:
a)   *When raising the crossmember, note that locating pins are provided to ensure correct alignment.*
b)   *Delay fully tightening the suspension mounting bolts until the suspension Design Height setting procedure has been carried out as described in Section 11.*

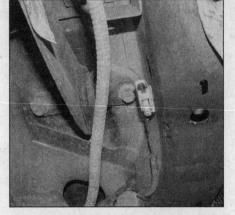

16.9 Remove the two front mounting bolts from the trailing arm

c)   *Tighten all bolts to the specified torque.*
d)   *Check, and if necessary adjust, the rear wheel toe setting as described in Section 26.*

---

18   Steering wheel - removal and installation

Warning: *All models are equipped with an airbag system. Make sure that the safety recommendations given in Chapter 12 are followed, to prevent personal injury.*

Removal

Refer to illustrations 18.5 and 18.6
1   Disconnect the negative battery cable (see Chapter 5). **Warning:** *Before proceeding, wait a minimum of 2 minutes, as a precaution against accidental firing of the airbag unit. This period ensures that any stored energy in the back-up capacitor is dissipated.*
2   Remove the airbag module (see Chapter 12). **Warning:** *Position the airbag module in a safe place, with the trim (upholstered) side facing Up as a precaution against accidental operation.*

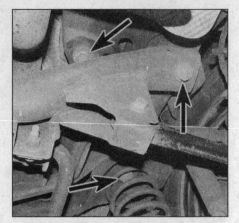

17.7 Rear crossmember bolts (arrows), left-hand side shown

3   Centralize the steering wheel so that the front wheels are in the straight-ahead position. Remove the keys and lock the steering in position.
4   Disconnect the speed cruise control electrical connector (if equipped).
5   Unscrew the retaining bolt from the center of the steering wheel. Mark the position of the steering wheel on the steering column shaft for installation **(see illustration)**.
6   Remove the steering wheel from the top of the column, while pushing the wiring connector through the hole, so the wiring stays in position on the steering column **(see illustration)**.

Installation

Warning: *If the airbag sliding contact has turned and become uncentered, center it following the procedure in Chapter 12.*
7   Make sure that the front wheels are still facing straight-ahead, then locate the steering wheel on the top of the steering column. Align the marks made during removal.
8   Install the retaining bolt and tighten it to the specified torque while holding the steering wheel. Do not tighten the bolt with the steering lock engaged, as this may damage the lock.

18.5 Hold the steering wheel while loosening the retaining bolt

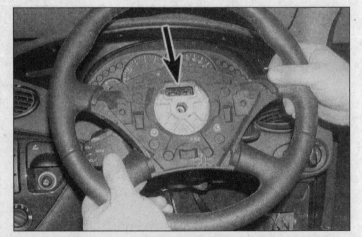

18.6 The wiring connector (arrow) stays in place

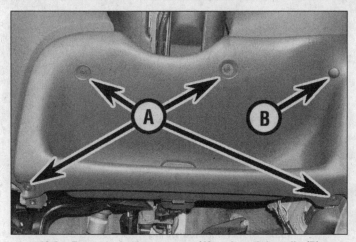

19.3a Remove the four screws (A) and retaining clip (B)

19.3b Withdraw the multi-plug from the trim

19.4a Unclip the upper shroud with a thin screwdriver (arrow) . . .

19.4b . . . then lift off the shroud

9   Reconnect the wiring connector(s) for the horn and airbag.
10   Locate the airbag module on the steering wheel as described in Chapter 12, then insert the securing screws and tighten them.
11   Reconnect the battery negative cable.

19   Steering column - removal, inspection and installation

Warning: *All models are equipped with an airbag system. Make sure that the safety recommendations given in Chapter 12 are followed, to prevent personal injury.*

Removal

Refer to illustrations 19.3a, 19.3b, 19.4a, 19.4b, 19.4c, 19.4d, 19.5, 19.6a, 19.6b, 19.8, 19.9, 19.10a and 19.10b

1   Disconnect the negative battery cable (see Chapter 5). **Warning:** *Before proceeding, wait a minimum of 2 minutes, as a precaution against accidental firing of the airbag unit. This period ensures that any stored energy in the back-up capacitor is dissipated.*
2   Remove the steering wheel as de-

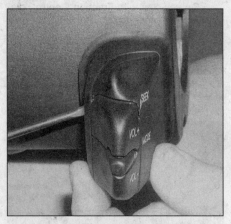

19.4c Unclip the remote from the lower shroud . . .

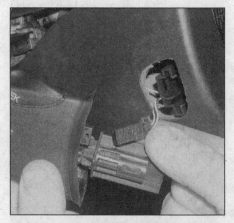

19.4d . . . and unplug the wiring connector

scribed in Section 18. Remove the airbag sliding contact as described in Chapter 12.
3   Remove the four screws and unclip the retaining clip to remove the dash panel below the steering column. Unclip the multi-plug from the trim panel **(see illustrations)**. On models so equipped, disconnect the hood release cable from the back of the panel and

disconnect the electrical connector from the diagnostic plug.
4   Lower the steering column locking lever. Remove the steering column upper shroud - release the two retaining clips with a thin-bladed screwdriver. Using the same screwdriver, unclip the radio control switch and disconnect the wiring connector **(see illustrations)**.

19.5 Unscrew the three screws from the lower shroud

19.6a Disconnect the wiring from the left . . .

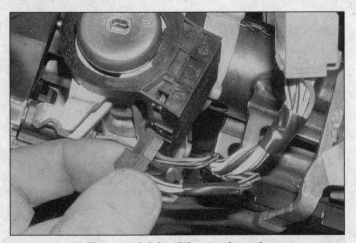

19.6b . . . and right of the steering column

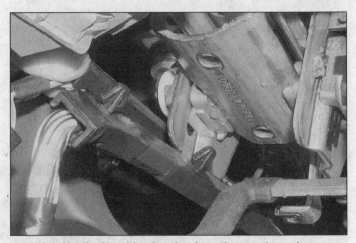

19.8 Unclip the wiring bracket from the steering column

5   Remove the three screws from the lower shroud and remove from the steering column **(see illustration)**.
6   Disconnect the electrical connectors from the right and left-hand side of the steering column switches **(see illustrations)**. On models so equipped, disconnect the anti-theft system transceiver.

7   On vehicles with Traction Control, disconnect the steering wheel rotation sensor electrical connector.
8   Release the locating clips to detach the wiring harness from the steering column **(see illustration)**.
9   Remove the securing bolt from the sleeve that joins the lower part of the steering

column to the steering rack **(see illustration)**.
10   Unscrew and remove the three steering column mounting locking nuts and one Torx bolt **(see illustration)**. Slide the column upward to disengage from the sleeve to the steering rack **(see illustration)**, and withdraw it from inside the vehicle.

19.9 Unscrew the bolt to disengage the column from the rack

19.10a Unscrew the three nuts and one Torx bolt (arrows) . . .

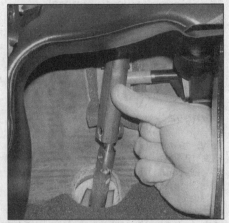

19.10b . . . then lift the column upward from the steering rack

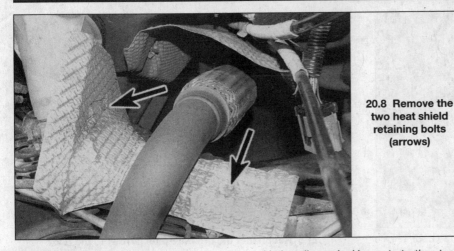

20.8 Remove the two heat shield retaining bolts (arrows)

Inspection

Note: *The first tests are performed with the column in the vehicle.*

11 With the steering lock disengaged, attempt to move the steering wheel up-and-down and also to the left-and-right without turning the wheel, to check for steering column bearing wear, steering column shaft joint play and steering wheel or steering column loose fasteners. The steering column cannot be repaired, if any faults are detected, install a new column.

12 Examine the height adjustment lever mechanism for wear and damage.

13 With the steering column removed, check the universal joints for wear, and examine the column upper and lower shafts for any signs of damage or distortion. Where evident, the column should be replaced as a complete assembly.

Installation

14 Installation is a reversal of removal, noting the following points:

a) Make sure the wheels are still in the straight-ahead position when the steering column is installed.

b) Install new locking nuts to the steering column mounting bracket.

c) Install a new pinch-bolt to the steering column sleeve, which joins to the steering rack.

d) Tighten bolts to their specified torque.

e) See Chapter 12 for the airbag sliding contact centering and installation procedure.

f) If the electronic stability program warning light (if equipped), comes on after installing the steering column, the system will need re-configuring at a dealer using specialized equipment.

20 Power steering rack - removal and installation

Removal

Refer to illustrations 20.8, 20.13a and 20.13b

1 Centralize the steering wheel so that the front wheels are in the straight-ahead position. Remove the keys and lock the steering in position.

2 From inside the vehicle, remove the securing bolt from the sleeve which joins the column to the steering rack.

3 Apply the parking brake, then jack up the front of the vehicle and support it on axle stands. Remove both front wheels.

4 Unscrew the tie-rod end nuts, and detach the rods from the arms on the steering knuckles using a conventional balljoint removal tool. Take care not to damage the balljoint seals.

5 Remove the connecting links from the struts and stabilizer bar, taking care not to damage the balljoint seals.

6 On models so equipped, remove the undershield from the engine.

7 Remove the bolt from the support bracket on the transaxle unit.

8 Unbolt and remove the heat shield from the steering rack (see illustration).

9 Remove the screw securing the hose support clamp to the housing on the steering gear pinion.

10 Position a container beneath the steering rack, then unscrew the bolt securing the power steering pipes to the steering rack. Identify the lines for position, then rotate the clamp, disconnect the pipes and check the O-ring seals for any damage. Allow the fluid to drain into the container. Cover the apertures in the steering rack and also the ends of the fluid pipes, to prevent the entry of dust and dirt into the hydraulic circuit.

11 Using a floor jack, support the front crossmember, and remove the six retaining bolts (see Section 6). There is a special tool to align the crossmember on reassembly. If this is not available, mark the mounting points, so as to install in the correct position.

12 Lower the crossmember, disconnecting the steering pinion drive and the floor seal from the steering column pinion housing. Remove the lower securing bolt from the steering column extension when visible.

13 Unscrew and remove the steering rack mounting bolts (see illustrations).

14 Withdraw the steering rack from the crossmember taking care not to damage any components on removal.

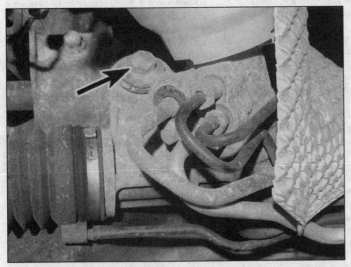

20.13a Remove the right-hand steering rack mounting bolt . . .

20.13b . . . and the left-hand mounting bolt (arrow)

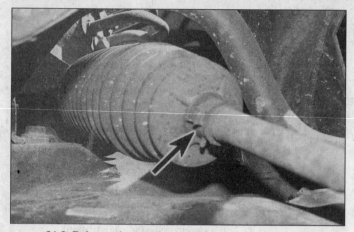

21.2 Release the retaining clip (arrow) from the boot

21.5 Reconnect the breather pipe (arrow) to the boot

15   With the steering rack removed, the bushings can be replaced in the housing. If the special tool is not available, use a long bolt with a metal tube and washers to press the new bushings into the housing. Make sure the bushings are installed to the correct depth.

Installation

16   Installation is a reversal of removal, noting the following points:

a) *Check the O-rings on the steering fluid pipes for damage, replace if necessary.*
b) *Make sure the pressure valve is correctly located in the valve body.*
c) *Check the steering column floor seal for damage. Make sure it is correctly located on the pinion housing.*
d) *Jack the crossmember up, into the correct position on the chassis using the aligning tool (if available). Make sure the crossmember ball-bearing washers are installed correctly, before tightening the bolts to their specified torque.*
e) *Replace the pinch bolt(s) in the steering pinion sleeve.*
f) *Fill and bleed the system with steering fluid as described in Section 22.*
g) *Check the front wheel alignment as described in Section 26.*

21   Power steering gear boots - replacement

Refer to illustrations 21.2 and 21.5

1   Remove the tie-rod end and its locknut from the tie-rod, as described in Section 25. Make sure that a note is made of the exact position of the tie-rod end on the tie-rod, in order to retain the front wheel alignment setting on installation.
2   Release the outer and inner retaining clips, and disconnect the boot from the steering gear housing **(see illustration)**.
3   Disconnect the breather from the boot, then slide the boot off the tie-rod.
4   Apply grease to the tie-rod inner joint. Wipe clean the seating areas on the steering gear housing and tie-rod.
5   Slide the new boot onto the tie-rod and

steering gear housing, and reconnect the breather **(see illustration)**.
6   Install new inner and outer retaining clips.
7   Install the tie-rod end as described in Section 25.
8   Have the front wheel alignment checked, and if necessary adjusted, at the earliest opportunity (refer to Section 26).

22   Power steering hydraulic system - bleeding

Warning: *Do not hold the steering wheel against the full lock stops for more than five seconds, as damage to the steering pump may result.*

1   Following any operation in which the power steering fluid lines have been disconnected, the power steering system must be bled, to remove any trapped air.
2   With the front wheels in the straight-ahead position, check the power steering fluid level in the reservoir and, if low, add fresh fluid until it reaches the MAX or MAX COLD mark. Pour the fluid slowly, to prevent air bubbles forming, and use only the specified fluid (refer to Chapter 1, *Recommended lubricants and fluids*).
3   Start the engine and slowly turn the steering from lock-to-lock.
4   Stop the engine, and check the hoses and connections for leaks. Check the fluid level and add more if necessary. Make sure the fluid in the reservoir does not fall below the MIN mark, as air could enter the system.
5   Start the engine again, allow it to idle, then bleed the system by slowly turning the steering wheel from side-to-side several times. This should purge the system of all internal air. However, if air remains in the system (indicated by the steering operation being very noisy), leave the vehicle overnight, and repeat the procedure again the next day.
6   If air still remains in the system, it may be necessary to resort to another method of bleeding, which uses a vacuum pump. Turn the steering to the right until it is near the stop, then attach the vacuum pump to the

fluid reservoir and apply vacuum. Maintain the vacuum for a minimum of 5 minutes, then repeat the procedure with the steering turned until it is near to the left stop.
7   Keep the fluid level topped-up throughout the bleeding procedure; noting that, as the fluid temperature increases, the level will rise.
8   On completion, switch off the engine, and return the wheels to the straight-ahead position. Check for leaks.

23   Power steering pump - removal and installation

Removal

1   Disconnect the negative battery cable (see Chapter 5).

2.0L Zetec-E models

Refer to illustrations 23.5 and 23.6

2   Remove the auxiliary drivebelt as described in Chapter 1.
3   Position a suitable container beneath the power steering pump, to catch any spilled fluid.
4   Remove the fluid cooler hose. Insert a special tool into the end of the hose along the pipe to release the locking tangs. Allow the fluid to drain into the container. On SVT models, refer to Chapter 11 and pull back the front of the right fenderwell liner and remove the lower headlight mounting bolt, for better access to the pump fluid lines and mounting bolts.
5   Loosen the clamp, and disconnect the fluid supply hose from the pump intake. Plug the hose, to prevent the ingress of dust and dirt **(see illustration)**.
6   Unscrew and remove the bolt securing the high pressure fluid line support to the pump mounting. Unscrew the union nut, and disconnect the high-pressure line from the pump **(see illustration)**. Allow the fluid to drain into the container. On some models, the high-pressure line may be equipped with a quick-disconnect connection. A simple tool (available at auto parts stores) is required to release the spring-lock coupling.

23.5 Disconnect the supply hose (arrow) from the pump

23.6 Disconnect the high pressure pipe (arrow)

24.6 The fluid cooler is positioned across the front of the radiator

7　Disconnect the power steering pressure (PSP) switch electrical connector by depressing the locking tab.

8　Unscrew and remove the four mounting bolts, and withdraw the power steering pump from its bracket. On most models, the lower bolts are best accessed from below. The pulley can be removed on the workbench, using an outside-jaw puller.

2.0L SPI models

9　Remove the accessory drivebelt (see Chapter 1).

10　A special tool is available to hold the power steering pump pulley during removal. If the tool is not available, use a strap-wrench to hold the pulley.

11　With the pulley secured, remove the center pulley bolt and the pulley.

12　Disconnect the power steering reservoir hose from the pump, allowing the fluid to drain into a suitable container.

13　Disconnect the power steering pressure hose from the pump, allowing the fluid to drain into a suitable container. Use two wrenches; a backup wrench to hold the fitting on the pump, the other to loosen the line fitting.

14　Remove the power steering pump mounting bolts (they are accessible only when the pulley is removed) and the pump.

15　On 2005 and later models, the pulley does not have to be removed to remove the four pump mounting bolts.

16　If the pulley is to be removed, a special tool is required, which also works as a pulley installer.

Installation

17　Installation is a reversal of removal, noting the following points.

a) Tighten the bolts and unions to the specified torque.

b) Where installed, the O-ring on the high-pressure outlet should be replaced. Use a special tool or a tapered tube to slide the new O-ring onto the pipe union.

c) Bleed the power steering hydraulic system as described in Section 22.

d) When replacing the pump, remove the power steering pressure switch and high pressure pipes, where installed, to the old pump.

24 Power steering fluid cooler - removal and installation

Removal

Refer to illustration 24.6

1　Refer to Chapter 3 and unbolt and set aside the coolant recovery tank. Detach the power steering reservoir from its retaining bracket, disconnect the hose and drain the fluid into a suitable container.

2　Unclip the hose from the retaining bracket.

3　Apply the parking brake, then jack up the front of the vehicle and support it on axle stands.

4　Unscrew the securing screws from the splash shield under the radiator and remove the shield. (Disconnect the temperature sensor electrical connector, if installed).

5　Remove the fluid cooler hose. Insert a special tool into the end of the hose along the pipe to release it. Allow the fluid to drain into the container.

6　Unscrew the fluid cooler securing bolts and remove the cooler from the vehicle **(see illustration)**.

Installation

7　Installation is a reversal of removal. Bleed the power steering hydraulic system as described in Section 22.

25 Tie-rod ends - replacement

Removal

Refer to illustrations 25.2 and 25.4

1　Apply the parking brake, then jack up the front of the vehicle and support it on axle stands. Remove the appropriate front wheel.

2　Loosen the locknut on the tie-rod by a

quarter-turn **(see illustration)**. Hold the tie-rod end stationary with another wrench engaged with the special flats while loosening the locknut.

3　Unscrew and remove the tie-rod end balljoint retaining nut.

4　To release the tapered shank of the balljoint from the steering knuckle arm, use a balljoint separator tool **(see illustration)** (if the balljoint is to be re-used, take care not to damage the dust cover when using the separator tool).

25.2 Loosen the locknut

25.4 Use a ball joint separator tool to release balljoint

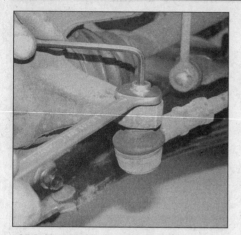

25.8 Use an Allen wrench to prevent the shank from turning

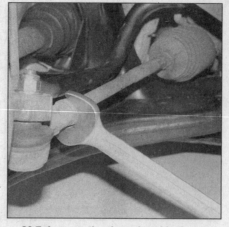

26.7 Loosen the tie-rod end lock nut

26.9 The rear wheel toe setting is adjusted with an eccentric bolt/washer at the inner end of each rear lower arm

5   Count the number of exposed threads visible on the inner section of the tie-rod, and record this figure.

6   Unscrew the tie-rod end from the tie-rod, counting the number of turns necessary to remove it. If necessary, hold the tie-rod stationary with self-locking pliers.

Replacement

Refer to illustration 25.8

7   Screw the tie-rod end onto the tie-rod by the number of turns noted during removal, until it just contacts the locknut.

8   Engage the shank of the balljoint with the steering knuckle arm, and install the nut. Tighten the nut to the specified torque. If the balljoint shank turns while the nut is being tightened, use an Allen wrench **(see illustration)** to hold the shank or press up on the balljoint. The tapered fit of the shank will lock it, and prevent rotation as the nut is tightened.

9   Now tighten the locknut on the tie-rod, while holding the tie-rod end as before.

10   Install the wheel, and lower the vehicle to the ground.

11   Finally check, and if necessary adjust, the front wheel alignment as described in Section 26.

---

26   Wheel alignment and steering angles - general information

Refer to illustrations 26.7 and 26.9

1   Accurate wheel alignment is essential to provide positive steering and vehicle control, and to prevent excessive tire wear. Before considering the steering/suspension geometry, check that the tires are correctly inflated, that the wheels are not buckled, and that the steering linkage and suspension joints are in good order, without slackness or wear.

2   Wheel alignment consists of four factors:

Camber is the angle at which the front wheels are set from the vertical, when viewed from the front of the vehicle. 'Positive camber' is the amount (in degrees) that the wheels are tilted outward at the top of the vertical.

Caster is the angle between the steering axis and a vertical line, when viewed from each side of the car. 'Positive caster' is when the steering axis is inclined rearward at the top.

Steering axis inclination is the angle (when viewed from the front of the vehicle) between the vertical and an imaginary line drawn through the suspension strut upper mounting and the lower suspension arm balljoint.

Toe setting is the amount by which the distance between the front inside edges of the wheels (measured at hub height) differs from the diametrically-opposite distance measured between the rear inside edges of the wheels.

3   With the exception of the toe setting, all other steering angles are set during manufacture, and no adjustment is possible. It can be assumed, therefore, that unless the vehicle has suffered accident damage, all the pre-set steering angles will be correct. Should there be some doubt about their accuracy, it will be necessary to seek the help of an alignment shop, as special gauges are needed to check the steering angles.

4   Two methods are available to the home mechanic for checking the toe setting. One method is to use a gauge to measure the distance between the front and rear inside edges of the wheels. The other method is to use a scuff plate, in which each front wheel is rolled across a movable plate which records any deviation, or scuff, of the tire from the straight-ahead position as it moves across the plate. Relatively-inexpensive equipment of both types is available from accessory outlets.

5   If, after checking the toe setting using whichever method is preferable, it is found that adjustment is necessary, proceed as follows.

6   Turn the steering wheel onto full-left lock, and record the number of exposed threads on the right-hand tie-rod. Now turn the steering onto full-right lock, and record the number of threads on the left-hand tie-rod. If there are the same number of threads visible on both sides, then subsequent adjustment can be made equally on both sides. If there are more threads visible on one side than the other, it will be necessary to compensate for this during adjustment.

Note: *After adjustment, there should be the same number of threads visible on each tie-rod. This is most important.*

7   To alter the toe setting, loosen the locknut on the tie-rod **(see illustration)**, and turn the tie-rod using self-locking pliers to achieve the desired setting. When viewed from the side of the car, turning the rod clockwise will increase the toe-in, turning it counterclockwise will increase the toe-out. Only turn the tie-rods by a quarter of a turn each time, and then recheck the setting.

8   After adjustment, tighten the locknuts. Reposition the steering gear boots to remove any twist caused by turning the tie-rods.

9   The rear wheel toe-setting may also be checked and adjusted. This setting is adjusted by turning the eccentric bolt/washer securing the rear lower arms to the rear axle crossmember **(see illustration). Note:** *Once the rear suspension bolts have been loosened, the suspension Design Height setting procedure has to be carried out as described in Section 11, before re-tightening.*

10   This bolt has to be loosened, then tightened up to 70 in-lbs. The eccentric bolt/washer can now be turned clockwise or counterclockwise to adjust the rear wheel alignment. When the wheel alignment is correct, the eccentric bolt/washer can be re-tightened back to Specifications.

11   The rear wheel toe-setting additionally requires alignment with the front wheels, therefore it would be best left to an alignment shop.

Chapter 11 Body

Contents

Specifications

Torque specifications

Ft-lbs (unless otherwise indicated)

Note: *One foot-pound (ft-lb) of torque is equivalent to 12 inch-pounds (in-lbs) of torque. Torque values below approximately 15 ft-lbs are expressed in inch-pounds, since most foot-pound torque wrenches are not accurate at these smaller values.*

Fender bolts	62 in-lbs
Hood hinge bolts to body	16
Hood hinge bolts to hood	84 in-lbs
Deck lid hinge bolts	16
Bumper mounting nuts	
Front	44 in-lbs
Rear	15
Door check strap-to-body bolts	16
Door check strap-to-door bolts	48 in-lbs
Door hinge-to-body bolts	26
Door hinge-to-door bolts	35
Door striker plate bolts	15
Front seat mounting bolts	21
Rear seat backrest catch retaining bolts	22
Rear seat hinge pins	15
Seat belt mounting bolts	
Front	39
Rear, center belts	41
Rear, outboard belts	28
Tailgate hinge-to-body bolts	16
Tailgate hinge-to-body nuts	72 in-lbs
Tailgate hinge-to-tailgate bolts	84 in-lbs
Wiper arm securing nuts	
Models through 2004	156 in-lbs
2005 and later models	18

1 General information

The bodyshell and underframe on all models feature variable thickness steel, achieved by laser-welded technology, and used to join steel panels of different gauges. This gives a stiffer structure, with mounting points being more rigid, which gives an improved crash performance.

An additional safety crossmember is incorporated between the A-pillars in the upper area of the firewall, and the instrument panel and steering column are secured to it. The lower firewall area is reinforced by additional systems of members connected to the front of the vehicle. The body side rocker panels (sills) have been divided along the length of the vehicle by internal reinforcement, this

functions like a double tube that increases its strength. All doors are reinforced and incorporate side impact protection, which is secured in the door structure. There are additional impact absorbers to the front and rear of the vehicle, behind the bumper assemblies.

All sheet metal surfaces that are prone to corrosion are galvanized. The painting process includes a base color that closely matches the final topcoat, so that any stone damage is not as noticeable. The front fenders are of a bolt-on type to ease their replacement if required.

Automatic seat belts are installed on all models, and the front seat safety belts are equipped with a pyrotechnic pretension seat belt buckle, which is attached to the seat frame of each front seat. In the event of a serious front impact, the system is triggered and pulls the stalk buckle downward to tension the seat belt. It is not possible to reset the tensioner once fired, and it must therefore be replaced. The tensioners are fired by an explosive charge similar to that used in the airbag, and are triggered via the airbag control module. The safety belt retractor, which is installed in the base of the B-pillar, has a device to control the seat belt, if the deceleration force is enough to activate the airbags.

Power doorlocks are available on certain models only. Where double-locking is installed, the lock mechanism is disconnected (when the system is in use) from the interior door handles, making it impossible to open any of the doors or the liftgate/decklid from inside the vehicle. This means that, even if a thief should break a side window, he will not be able to open the door using the interior handle. Models with the double-locking system are equipped with a control module located beneath the dash on the right-hand side. In the event of a serious accident, a crash sensor unlocks all doors if they were previously locked.

Many of the procedures in this Chapter require the battery to be disconnected. Refer to Chapter 5A, Section 1, first.

2 Maintenance - bodywork and underbody

The general condition of a vehicle's bodywork is the one thing that significantly affects its value. Maintenance is easy, but needs to be regular. Neglect, particularly after minor damage, can lead quickly to further deterioration and costly repair bills. It is important also to keep watch on those parts of the vehicle not immediately visible, for instance the underside, inside all the fenderwells, and the lower part of the engine compartment.

The basic maintenance routine for the bodywork is washing - preferably with a lot of water, from a hose. This will remove all the loose solids that may have stuck to the vehicle. It is important to flush these off in such a way as to prevent grit from scratching the finish. The fenderwells and underbody need washing in the same way, to remove any accumulated mud, which will retain moisture and tend to encourage rust. Paradoxically enough, the best time to clean the underframe and fenderwells is in wet weather, when the mud is thoroughly wet and soft. In very wet weather, the underframe is usually cleaned of large accumulations automatically, and this is a good time for inspection.

Periodically, except on vehicles with a wax-based underbody protective coating, it is a good idea to have the whole of the underframe of the vehicle steam-cleaned, engine compartment included, so that a thorough inspection can be carried out to see what minor repairs and renovations are necessary. Steam-cleaning is available at many garages, and is necessary for the removal of the accumulation of oily grime, which sometimes is allowed to become thick in certain areas. If steam-cleaning facilities are not available, there are some excellent grease solvents available that can be brush-applied; the dirt can then be simply hosed off. Note that these methods should not be used on vehicles with wax-based underbody protective coating, or the coating will be removed. Such vehicles should be inspected annually, preferably just prior to winter, when the underbody should be washed down, and any damage to the wax coating repaired. Ideally, a completely fresh coat should be applied. It would also be worth considering the use of such wax-based protection for injection into door panels, sills, box sections, etc, as an additional safeguard against rust damage, where such protection is not provided by the vehicle manufacturer.

After washing paintwork, wipe off with a chamois leather to give an unspotted clear finish. A coat of clear protective wax polish will give added protection against chemical pollutants in the air. If the paintwork sheen has dulled or oxidized, use a cleaner/polisher combination to restore the brilliance of the shine. This requires a little effort, but such dulling is usually caused because regular washing has been neglected. Care needs to be taken with metallic paintwork, as special non-abrasive cleaner/polisher is required to avoid damage to the finish. Always check that the door and ventilator opening drain holes and pipes are completely clear, so that water can be drained out. Chrome should be treated in the same way as paintwork. Windshields and windows can be kept clear of the smeary film that often appears, by the use of proprietary glass cleaner. Never use any form of wax or other body or chromium polish on glass.

3 Maintenance - upholstery and carpets

Mats and carpets should be brushed or vacuum-cleaned regularly, to keep them free of grit. If they are badly stained, remove them from the vehicle for scrubbing or sponging, and make quite sure they are dry before installation. Seats and interior trim panels can be kept clean by wiping with a damp cloth. If they do become stained (which can be more apparent on light-colored upholstery), use a little liquid detergent and a soft nail brush to scour the grime out of the grain of the material. Do not forget to keep the headlining clean in the same way as the upholstery. When using liquid cleaners inside the vehicle, do not over-wet the surfaces being cleaned. Excessive damp could get into the seams and padded interior, causing stains, offensive odors or even rot.

Caution: *If the inside of the vehicle gets wet accidentally, it is worthwhile taking some trouble to dry it out properly, particularly where carpets are involved. Do not leave oil or electric heaters inside the vehicle for this purpose.*

4 Minor body damage - repair

Repairs of minor scratches in bodywork

If the scratch is very superficial, and does not penetrate to the metal of the bodywork, repair is very simple. Lightly rub the area of the scratch with a paintwork renovator, or a very fine cutting paste, to remove loose paint from the scratch, and to clear the surrounding bodywork of wax polish. Rinse the area with clean water.

Apply touch-up paint to the scratch using a fine paint brush; continue to apply fine layers of paint until the surface of the paint in the scratch is level with the surrounding paintwork. Allow the new paint at least two weeks to harden, then blend it into the surrounding paintwork by rubbing the scratch area with a paintwork renovator or a very fine cutting paste. Finally, apply wax polish.

Where the scratch has penetrated right through to the metal of the bodywork, causing the metal to rust, a different repair technique is required. Remove any loose rust from the bottom of the scratch with a penknife, then apply rust-inhibiting paint to prevent the formation of rust in the future. Using a rubber or nylon applicator, fill the scratch with autobody glazing putty. If required, this paste can be mixed with cellulose thinners to provide a very thin paste that is ideal for filling narrow scratches. Before the paste in the scratch hardens, wrap a piece of smooth cotton rag around the top of a finger. Dip the finger in cellulose thinners, and quickly sweep it across the surface of the paste in the scratch; this will ensure that the surface of the paste is slightly hollowed. The scratch can now be painted over as described earlier in this Section.

Repairs of dents in bodywork

When deep denting of the vehicle's bodywork has taken place, the first task is to pull the dent out, until the affected bodywork almost attains its original shape. There is little point in trying to restore the original shape completely, as the metal in the damaged area will have stretched on impact, and cannot be reshaped fully to its original contour. It is better to bring the level of the dent up to a point that is about 3 mm below the level of the surrounding bodywork. In cases where the dent is very shallow anyway, it is not worth trying to pull it out at all. If the underside of the dent is accessible, it can be hammered out gently from behind, using a mallet with a wooden or plastic head. While doing this, hold a suitable block of wood firmly against the outside of the panel, to absorb the impact from the hammer blows and thus prevent a large area of the bodywork from being 'belled-out'.

Should the dent be in a section of the bodywork that has a double skin, or some other factor making it inaccessible from behind, a different technique is called for. Drill several small holes through the metal inside the area - particularly in the deeper section. Then screw long self-tapping screws into the holes, just sufficiently for them to gain a good purchase in the metal. Now the dent can be pulled out by pulling on the protruding heads of the screws with a pair of pliers.

The next stage of the repair is the removal of the paint from the damaged area, and from an inch or so of the surrounding 'sound' bodywork. This is accomplished most easily by using a wire brush or abrasive pad on a power drill, although it can be done just as effectively by hand, using sheets of abrasive paper. To complete the preparation for filling, score the surface of the bare metal with a screwdriver or the tang of a file, or alternatively, drill small holes in the affected area. This will provide a really good 'key' for the filler paste.

To complete the repair, see the Section on filling and respraying.

Repairs of rust holes or gashes in bodywork

Remove all paint from the affected area, and from an inch or so of the surrounding 'sound' bodywork, using an abrasive pad or a wire brush on a power drill. If these are not available, a few sheets of abrasive paper will do the job most effectively. With the paint removed, you will be able to judge the severity of the corrosion, and therefore decide whether to replace the whole panel (if this is possible) or to repair the affected area. New body panels are not as expensive as most people think, and it is often quicker and more satisfactory to install a new panel than to attempt to repair large areas of corrosion.

Remove all fittings from the affected area, except those which will act as a guide to the original shape of the damaged bodywork (e.g. headlight shells etc). Then, using tin snips or a hacksaw blade, remove all loose metal and any other metal badly affected by corrosion. Hammer the edges of the hole inwards, in order to create a slight depression for the filler paste.

Wire-brush the affected area to remove the powdery rust from the surface of the remaining metal. Paint the affected area with rust-inhibiting paint, if the back of the rusted area is accessible, treat this also.

Before filling can take place, it will be necessary to block the hole in some way. This can be achieved by the use of aluminum or plastic mesh, or aluminum tape.

Aluminum or plastic mesh, or glass-fiber matting, is probably the best material to use for a large hole. Cut a piece to the approximate size and shape of the hole to be filled, then position it in the hole so that its edges are below the level of the surrounding bodywork. It can be retained in position by several blobs of filler paste around its periphery.

Aluminum tape should be used for small or very narrow holes. Pull a piece off the roll, trim it to the approximate size and shape required, then pull off the backing paper (if used) and stick the tape over the hole; it can be overlapped if the thickness of one piece is insufficient. Burnish down the edges of the tape with the handle of a screwdriver or similar tool, to ensure that the tape is securely attached to the metal underneath.

Bodywork repairs - filling and respraying

Before using this Section, see the Sections on dent, deep scratch, rust holes and gash repairs.

Many types of bodyfiller are available, but generally speaking, those proprietary kits that contain a tin of filler paste and a tube of resin hardener are best for this type of repair. A wide, flexible plastic or nylon applicator will be found invaluable for imparting a smooth and well-contoured finish to the surface of the filler.

Mix up a little filler on a clean piece of card or board - measure the hardener carefully (follow the maker's instructions on the pack), otherwise the filler will set too rapidly or too slowly. Using the applicator, apply the filler paste to the prepared area; draw the applicator across the surface of the filler to achieve the correct contour and to level the surface. As soon as a contour that approximates to the correct one is achieved, stop working the paste - if you carry on too long, the paste will become sticky and begin to 'pick-up' on the applicator. Continue to add thin layers of filler paste at 20-minute intervals, until the level of the filler is just proud of the surrounding bodywork.

Once the filler has hardened, the excess can be removed using a metal plane or file. From then on, progressively-finer grades of abrasive paper should be used, starting with a 40-grade production paper, and finishing with a 400-grade wet-and-dry paper. Always wrap the abrasive paper around a flat rubber, cork, or wooden block - otherwise the surface of the filler will not be completely flat. During the smoothing of the filler surface, the wet-and-dry paper should be periodically rinsed in water. This will ensure that a very smooth finish is imparted to the filler at the final stage.

At this stage, the 'dent' should be surrounded by a ring of bare metal, which in turn should be encircled by the finely 'feathered' edge of the good paintwork. Rinse the repair area with clean water, until all of the dust produced by the rubbing-down operation has gone.

Spray the whole area with a light coat of primer - this will show up any imperfections in the surface of the filler. Repair these imperfections with fresh filler paste or glaze, and once more smooth the surface with abrasive paper. Repeat this spray-and-repair procedure until you are satisfied that the surface of the filler, and the feathered edge of the paintwork, are perfect. Clean the repair area with clean water, and allow to dry fully.

The repair area is now ready for final spraying. Paint spraying must be carried out in a warm, dry, windless and dust-free atmosphere. This condition can be created artificially if you have access to a large indoor working area, but if you are forced to work in the open, you will have to pick your day very carefully. If you are working indoors, dousing the floor in the work area with water will help to settle the dust that would otherwise be in the atmosphere. If the repair area is confined to one body panel, mask off the surrounding panels; this will help to minimize the effects of a slight mismatch in paint colors. Bodywork trim (e.g. chrome strips, door handles etc) will also need to be masked off. Use genuine masking tape, and several thicknesses of newspaper, for the masking operations.

Before commencing to spray, agitate the aerosol can thoroughly, then spray a test area (an old tin, or similar) until the technique is mastered. Cover the repair area with a thick coat of primer; the thickness should be built up using several thin layers of paint, rather than one thick one. Using 400-grade wet-and-dry paper, rub down the surface of the primer until it is really smooth. While doing this, the work area should be thoroughly doused with water, and the wet-and-dry paper periodically rinsed in water. Allow to dry before spraying on more paint.

Spray on the top coat, again building up the thickness by using several thin layers of paint. Start spraying at one edge of the repair area, and then, using a side-to-side motion, work until the whole repair area and about 2 inches of the surrounding original paintwork is covered. Remove all masking material 10 to 15 minutes after spraying on the final coat of paint.

Allow the new paint at least two weeks to harden, then, using a paintwork renovator, or a very fine cutting paste, blend the edges of the paint into the existing paintwork. Finally, apply wax polish.

Plastic components

With the use of more and more plastic body components by the vehicle manufacturers (e.g. bumpers. spoilers, and in some cases major body panels), rectification of more serious damage to such items has become a matter of either entrusting repair work to a specialist in this field, or replacing complete components. Repair of such damage by the DIY owner is not really feasible, owing to the cost of the equipment and materials required for affecting such repairs. The basic technique involves making a groove along the line of the crack in the plastic, using a rotary file in a power drill. The damaged part is then welded back together, using a hot-air gun to heat up and fuse a plastic filler rod into the groove. Any excess plastic is then removed, and the area rubbed down to a smooth finish. It is important that a filler rod of the correct plastic is used, as body components can be made of a variety of different types (e.g. polycarbonate, ABS, polypropylene).

These photos illustrate a method of repairing simple dents. They are intended to supplement *Body repair - minor damage* in this Chapter and should not be used as the sole instructions for body repair on these vehicles.

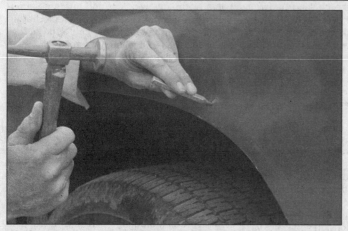

1 If you can't access the backside of the body panel to hammer out the dent, pull it out with a slide-hammer-type dent puller. In the deepest portion of the dent or along the crease line, drill or punch hole(s) at least one inch apart . . .

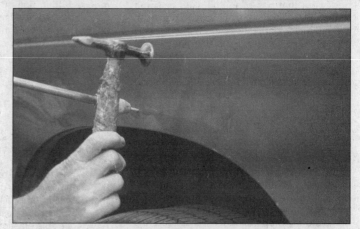

2 . . . then screw the slide-hammer into the hole and operate it. Tap with a hammer near the edge of the dent to help 'pop' the metal back to its original shape. When you're finished, the dent area should be close to its original contour and about 1/8-inch below the surface of the surrounding metal

3 Using coarse-grit sandpaper, remove the paint down to the bare metal. Hand sanding works fine, but the disc sander shown here makes the job faster. Use finer (about 320-grit) sandpaper to feather-edge the paint at least one inch around the dent area

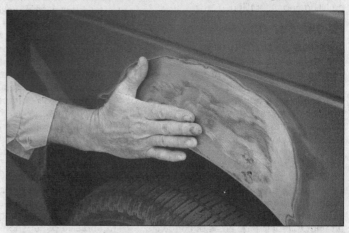

4 When the paint is removed, touch will probably be more helpful than sight for telling if the metal is straight. Hammer down the high spots or raise the low spots as necessary. Clean the repair area with wax/silicone remover

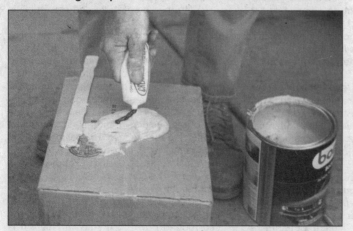

5 Following label instructions, mix up a batch of plastic filler and hardener. The ratio of filler to hardener is critical, and, if you mix it incorrectly, it will either not cure properly or cure too quickly (you won't have time to file and sand it into shape)

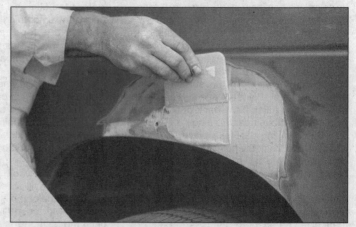

6 Working quickly so the filler doesn't harden, use a plastic applicator to press the body filler firmly into the metal, assuring it bonds completely. Work the filler until it matches the original contour and is slightly above the surrounding metal

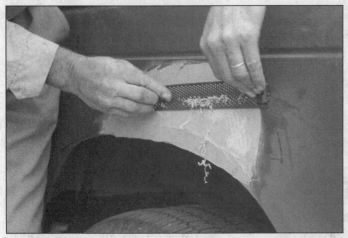

7 Let the filler harden until you can just dent it with your fingernail. Use a body file or Surform tool (shown here) to rough-shape the filler

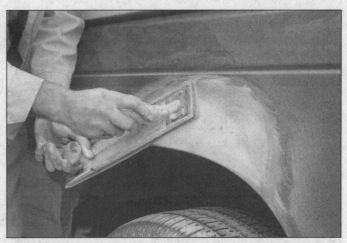

8 Use coarse-grit sandpaper and a sanding board or block to work the filler down until it's smooth and even. Work down to finer grits of sandpaper - always using a board or block - ending up with 360 or 400 grit

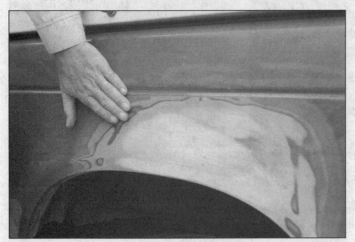

9 You shouldn't be able to feel any ridge at the transition from the filler to the bare metal or from the bare metal to the old paint. As soon as the repair is flat and uniform, remove the dust and mask off the adjacent panels or trim pieces

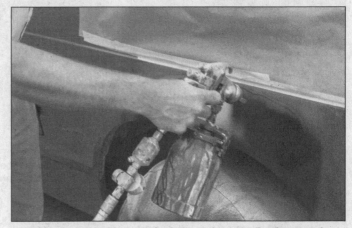

10 Apply several layers of primer to the area. Don't spray the primer on too heavy, so it sags or runs, and make sure each coat is dry before you spray on the next one. A professional-type spray gun is being used here, but aerosol spray primer is available inexpensively from auto parts stores

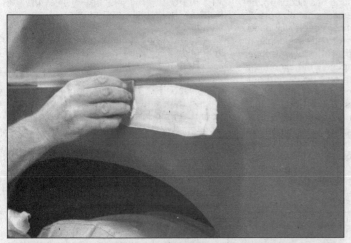

11 The primer will help reveal imperfections or scratches. Fill these with glazing compound. Follow the label instructions and sand it with 360 or 400-grit sandpaper until it's smooth. Repeat the glazing, sanding and respraying until the primer reveals a perfectly smooth surface

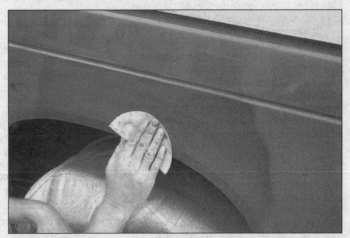

12 Finish sand the primer with very fine sandpaper (400 or 600-grit) to remove the primer overspray. Clean the area with water and allow it to dry. Use a tack rag to remove any dust, then apply the finish coat. Don't attempt to rub out or wax the repair area until the paint has dried completely (at least two weeks)

6.4a Disconnect the indicator wiring . . .

6.4b . . . and the foglight wiring

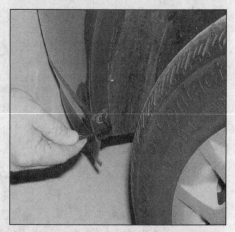

6.5a Remove the bumper-to-fenderwell lining screw . . .

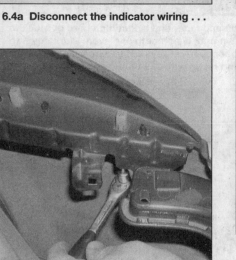

6.5b . . . and bumper-to-fender bolts

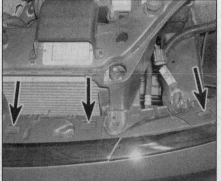

6.6a Release the bumper from the clips (arrows) . . .

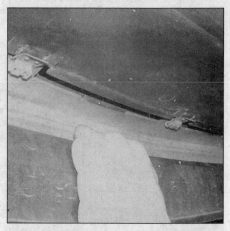

6.6b . . . and the lower cover trim clips

Damage of a less serious nature (abrasions, minor cracks etc) can be repaired by the DIY owner using a two-part epoxy filler repair material. Once mixed in equal proportions, this is used in similar fashion to the bodywork filler used on metal panels. The filler is usually cured in twenty to thirty minutes, ready for sanding and painting.

If the owner is replacing a complete component himself, or if he has repaired it with epoxy filler, he will be left with the problem of finding a suitable paint for finishing which is compatible with the type of plastic used. At one time, the use of a universal paint was not possible, owing to the complex range of plastics encountered in body component applications. Standard paints, generally speaking, will not bond to plastic or rubber satisfactorily. However, it is now possible to obtain a plastic body parts finishing kit that consists of a pre-primer treatment, a primer and colored top coat. Full instructions are normally supplied with a kit, but basically, the method of use is to first apply the pre-primer to the component concerned, and allow it to dry for up to 30 minutes. Then the primer is applied, and left to dry for about an hour before finally applying the special-colored top coat. The result is a correctly-colored compo-

nent, where the paint will flex with the plastic or rubber, a property that standard paint does not normally possess.

5 Major body damage - repair

Where serious damage has occurred, or large areas need replacement due to neglect, it means that complete new panels will need welding-in; this is best left to professionals. If the damage is due to impact, it will also be necessary to check completely the alignment of the bodyshell; this can only be carried out accurately by a bodyshop/frame alignment shop, using special jigs. If the body is left misarranged, it is primarily dangerous, as the car will not handle properly, and secondly, uneven stresses will be imposed on the steering, suspension and possibly transmission, causing abnormal wear or complete failure, particularly to items such as the tires.

6 Bumper covers - removal and installation

Note: *Headlamp washers are installed on some models; as the bumper is being removed, disconnect as required.*

Removal
Front bumper cover
Refer to illustrations 6.4a, 6.4b, 6.5a, 6.5b, 6.6a, 6.6b and 6.7

1   Apply the parking brake, jack up the front of the vehicle and support it on axle stands.

2   Remove the radiator grille as described in Section 7.

3   Remove the two front headlights as described in Chapter 12, Section 7.

4   Disconnect the wiring connectors from the indicator and foglight units **(see illustrations)**. On models so equipped, remove the radiator lower air deflector.

5   Remove the screws securing the fenderwell liners to the front bumper cover (each side), and the screws (each side) securing the bumper cover to the front fenders **(see illustrations)**. **Note:** *On some models, you may have to unbolt and remove the air intake tube and its splash shield to access screws in the left fenderwell.*

6   Release the securing clips from the top of the bumper cover, and the clips from the bottom of the bumper cover **(see illustrations)**.

7   With the help of an assistant to support

6.7 Disengage the locating pegs from the fender

6.10 Remove the fenderwell lining-to-bumper retaining screw

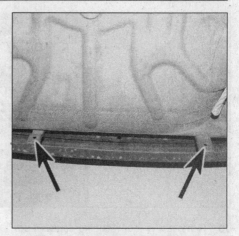

6.11 Remove the two retaining clips (arrows)

6.16a Open the left-hand compartment . . .

6.16b . . . and the right-hand compartment

6.17a Unscrew and remove the plastic trim . . .

one end of the bumper, withdraw the bumper forwards from the vehicle, at the same time pulling the sides away from the body to prevent damage to paintwork **(see illustration)**.

Rear bumper - except Wagon
Refer to illustrations 6.10 and 6.11

8   Chock the front wheels, jack up the rear of the vehicle and support it on axle stands. Open up the trunk or liftgate.

9   Remove the four retaining screws (nuts on later models) from the upper part of the bumper.

10   Remove the screws securing the fenderwell liners to the rear bumper **(see illustration)**.

11   Using a flat-bladed screwdriver, unclip the clips from the lower part of the bumper **(see illustration)**. On later models, the cover is secured by plastic pushpins.

12   On the Sedan model, unscrew the trims from inside the light units and remove. Remove the bumper securing nuts from behind the trims (three per side).

13   With the help of an assistant to support one end of the bumper, withdraw the bumper rearwards from the vehicle, at the same time pulling the sides away from the body to prevent damage to paintwork.

14   Disconnect the electrical connectors

from the rear foglight and reversing lamp, where installed.

Rear bumper - Wagon
Refer to illustrations 6.16a, 6.16b, 6.17a, 6.17b, 6.18, 6.19 and 6.20

15   Chock the front wheels, jack up the rear of the vehicle and support it on axle stands.

16   Open the liftgate, and open the two pockets on the side panels, one on the left

6.17b . . . then remove the bumper securing nut (arrow)

and one on the right **(see illustrations)**.

17   Remove the two screws from the top of the plastic First Aid kit holder, in the right-hand pocket, then unclip from the opening. Undo the bumper securing nut from behind the trim **(see illustrations)**.

18   Unclip the plastic tray from inside the left-hand pocket, and undo the bumper securing nut from behind the trim **(see illustration)**.

6.18 Unclip the plastic tray and remove the bumper securing nut (arrow)

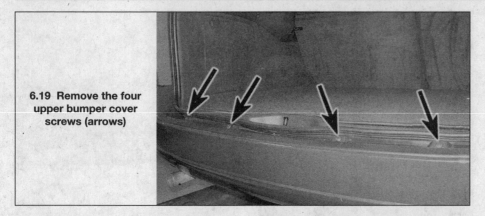

6.19 Remove the four upper bumper cover screws (arrows)

19   Remove the four retaining screws from the upper part of the bumper cover **(see illustration)**.
20   Remove the screws securing the fenderwell liners to the rear bumper cover **(see illustration)**.
21   Behind the fenderwell liners at each corner of the bumper cover, undo the securing nuts and also pull off the rubber bumpers (one on each side).
22   With the help of an assistant to support one end of the bumper, withdraw the bumper rearwards from the vehicle.

6.20 Remove the fenderwell lining-to-bumper retaining screw

Installation

23   Installation is a reversal of the removal procedure. Make sure that, where applicable, the bumper guides are located correctly. Check all electrical components that have been disconnected.

7   Radiator grille - removal and installation

Removal

Refer to illustrations 7.2 and 7.3
1   Support the hood in the open position.
2   Undo the four securing screws from the

7.2 Remove the air deflector

radiator air deflector and remove **(see illustration)**.
3   Disconnect the electrical connector at the turn signal lights. Undo the four securing screws from the radiator air deflector and remove it **(see illustration)**.
4   Lift out the grille from the front panel to remove.

Installation

5   Installation is a reversal of the removal procedure.

8   Hood - removal, installation and adjustment

Removal

Refer to illustrations 8.3a, 8.3b, 8.4a, 8.4b and 8.5
1   Open the hood, and support it in the open position using the stay.
2   Disconnect the negative battery cable (see Chapter 1).
3   Disconnect the windshield washer hoses from the bottom of the jets, and unclip from the hood **(see illustrations)**.
4   Disconnect the windshield washer wiring connector from the bottom of the jets, and unclip from the hood **(see illustrations)**.
5   To assist in correctly realigning the hood when installing it, mark the outline of the

7.3 Remove the four securing bolts (two on each side, arrow indicates one top bolt)

8.3a Pull the hose from the washer jet . . .

8.3b . . . and unclip it from the hinge

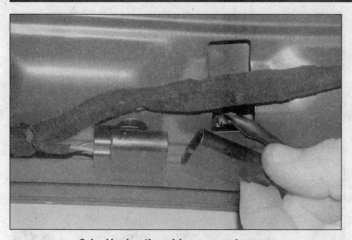

8.4a Unplug the wiring connectors . . .

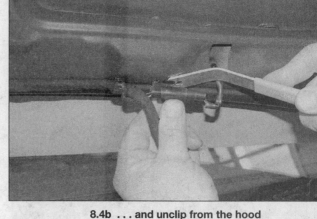

8.4b . . . and unclip from the hood

hinges with a soft pencil. Loosen the two hinge retaining bolts on each side **(see illustration)**.

6   With the help of an assistant, unscrew the four bolts, release the stay, and lift the hood from the vehicle.

Installation and adjustment

7   Installation is a reversal of the removal procedure, noting the following points:

 a) *Position the hood hinges within the outline marks made during removal, but if necessary alter its position to provide a uniform gap all around.*

 b) *Adjust the front height by repositioning the lock (see Section 9) and turning the rubber bumpers on the engine compartment front cross panel up or down to support the hood.*

---

9   Hood lock - removal, installation and adjustment

Removal

Refer to illustration 9.3

1   Open the hood and remove the air deflector panel in front of the radiator, then remove the radiator grille as described in Section 7.

2   Mark the position of the latch on the crossmember. Unscrew the two mounting bolts and remove the latch, unclipping it from the lock cylinder.

3   Disconnect the wiring connector from the lock assembly, as it is being removed **(see illustration)**.

4   Disconnect the cable from the back of the latch.

Installation and adjustment

5   Installation is a reversal of the removal procedure, starting by positioning the lock as noted before removal.

6   If the front of the hood is not level with the front fenders, the lock may be moved up or down within the mounting holes. After making an adjustment, raise or lower the rubber bumpers to support the hood correctly.

---

10   Door inner trim panel - removal and installation

Removal

Refer to illustrations 10.2a, 10.2b, 10.3a, 10.3b, 10.4, 10.5 and 10.6

Front

1   Disconnect the battery negative (ground)

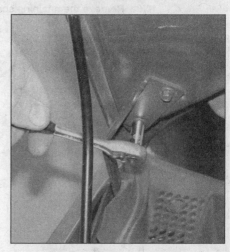

8.5 Remove the hinge bolts

lead (Chapter 5A, Section 1).

2   Insert a screwdriver into a hole under the door grab handle, then twist it to unclip the cover trim. Undo the two screws from behind the cover inside the door pull handle **(see illustrations)**.

3   Carefully pry out the plastic screw cover from the inner door handle cavity, using a small screwdriver. Remove the screw, and

9.3 Disconnect the wiring connector

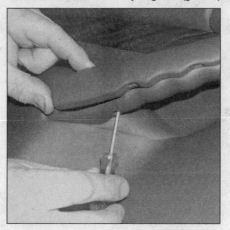

10.2a Unclip the grab handle trim . . .

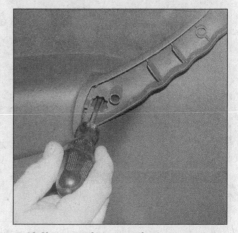

10.2b . . . and remove the two screws

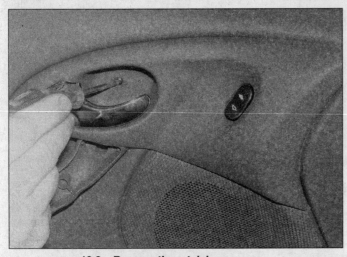

10.3a Remove the retaining screw . . .

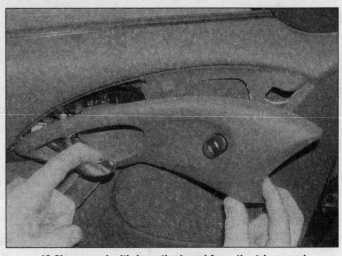

10.3b . . . and withdraw the bezel from the trim panel

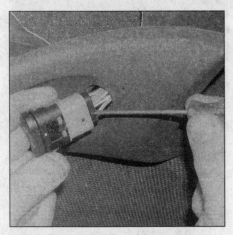

10.4 Disconnect the wiring connector

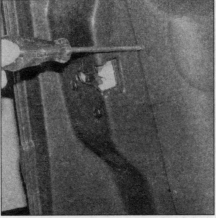

10.5 Remove all the retaining screws around the trim

then rotate upwards at the rear to remove from the vehicle (see illustration).

Rear

Refer to illustration 10.7

7   Carry out the procedures as described for the front doors, except on models equipped with manual (i.e., non-electric) rear windows, fully shut the window, and note the position of the regulator handle. Release the spring clip by inserting a clean cloth between the handle and the door trim. Using a 'sawing' action, pull the cloth against the open ends of the clip to release it, at the same time pulling the handle from the regulator shaft splines. Withdraw the handle (and, if installed, the spacer) and recover the clip (see illustration).

Installation

Refer to illustration 10.8

8   Installation is a reversal of the removal procedure. On the rear manual windows, install the retaining clip to the winder handle before installing the winder handle to the regulator shaft (see illustration).

ease the bezel from around the door handle (see illustrations).

4   Disconnect the wiring connector from the window operating switch (see illustration).

5   Working around the outer edge of the door inner trim panel, undo all the securing screws (see illustration). There are two at the front, two on the bottom, and two at the rear of the door. **Note:** *The number of screws varies with the year and model. Make sure all screws are removed before attempting to pull the door panel off.*

6   Pull the trim panel away from the door,

10.6 Lift the trim panel from the door

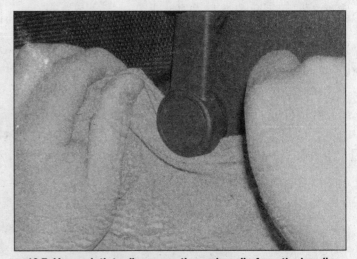

10.7 Use a cloth to disengage the spring clip from the handle

10.8 Position of the clip, before installing the handle

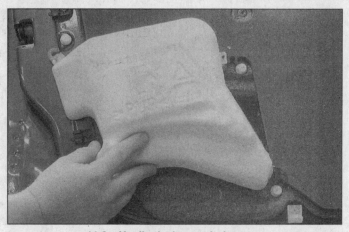

11.2a Unclip the impact bolster . . .

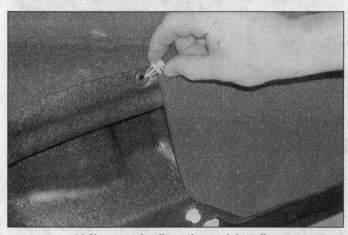

11.2b . . . and pull out the retaining clips

11.3a Remove the four screws . . .

11 Door window glass - removal and installation

Removal
Front
Refer to illustrations 11.2a, 11.2b, 11.3a, 11.3b, 11.4, 11.5, 11.6, 11.8 and 11.9

1   Remove the door inner trim panel as described in Section 10.

2   Rotate the side impact bolster counter-clockwise to remove it from its retaining clips, then pull out the retaining clips from the door panel **(see illustrations)**.

3   Remove the four screws from the speaker and remove from the door, disconnect the wiring as it becomes accessible **(see illustrations)**.

4   Detach the door release handle from the door by unclipping it from the front end, then slide the handle out in a forwards direction **(see illustration)**. (The door handle at this point can be left attached to the cable.)

5   Using a knife or scraper, cut through the butyl strip to enable the weather shield to be peeled back from the door panel. Take care not to damage the weathershield or door panel **(see illustration)**. (Do not touch the adhesive as re-bonding will be impaired.)

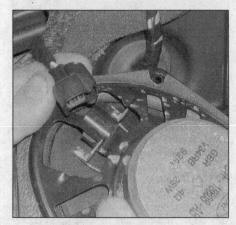

11.3b . . . and disconnect the wiring connector

11.4 Disengage the door release handle

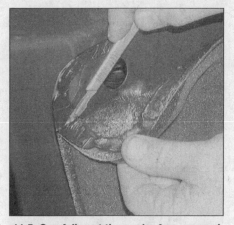

11.5 Carefully cut the sealer from around the weathershield

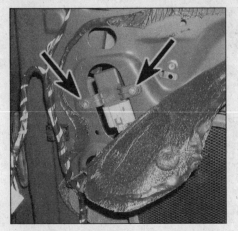

11.6 Remove the two screws (arrows)

11.8 Loosen the two bolts (arrows)

11.9 Lift the glass out from the door frame

11.11 Unclip the trim from the window frame

11.12a Loosen the two screws (arrows) . . .

11.12b . . . and lift the window glass runner out

6   On the driver's door only, undo the two retaining screws to remove the 'one-touch down' relay (if equipped) **(see illustration)**.

7   Temporarily install the window operating switch to its electrical connector.

8   Lower the window until the glass support bracket bolts align with the holes in the door panel,
then loosen the bolts in the support bracket

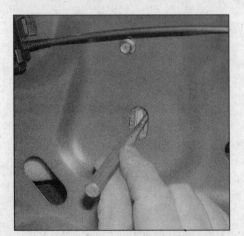

11.14 Align the sleeve/pin for removal

(see illustration). (Do not remove the bolts.)

9   Lift the window glass from the door while tilting it up at the rear, and withdraw it from the outside of the door frame **(see illustration)**.

Rear

Refer to illustrations 11.11, 11.12a, 11.12b, 11.14 and 11.17

10   Carry out the procedures as described in Steps 1 to 5 for the front door.

11   Unclip the triangular inner trim panel from the window frame **(see illustration)**.

12   Loosen the two retaining screws for the window runner guide, and lift up from inside the rear door opening to remove from door panel **(see illustrations)**.

13   Temporarily install the regulator handle on its splines, or the window operating switch to its electrical connector.

14   Lower the window until the glass support bracket securing sleeve/pin aligns with the hole in the door panel **(see illustration)**.

15   Using a punch, push out the pin in the securing sleeve, then push out the sleeve to release the window glass from the support bracket. Retrieve the pin and sleeve from inside the door for replacement.

16   Temporarily install the regulator handle

11.17 Lifting the glass out from the door frame

on its splines, or the window operating switch to its electrical connector to lower the window support bracket.

17   Lift the glass from the door while tilting it inwards, and withdraw it from the inside of the door **(see illustration)**.

Installation

Refer to illustration 11.18

18   Installation is a reversal of the removal procedure, making sure that the glass is correctly located in the support brackets. **Note:** *On the rear window, relocate the securing*

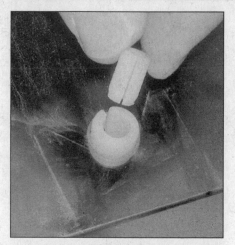

11.18 Press the sleeve/pin into the glass before installation

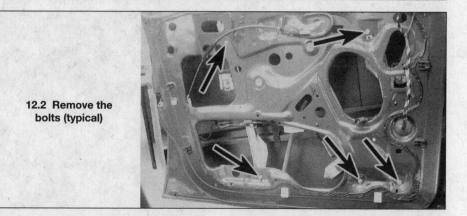

12.2 Remove the bolts (typical)

sleeve/pin in the window glass before installation **(see illustration)**, ensuring they project equally either side of the glass. Guide the window into the door so that the securing sleeve/pin locates into the window lifting support bracket. Lightly tap the top of the window to locate the sleeve/pin into the lifting support bracket.

12   Door window regulator - removal and installation

Removal

Front

Refer to illustrations 12.2, 12.3 and 12.4

1   Carry out the procedures to remove the window glass as described in Section 11, Steps 1 to 9. On later models with side impact airbags, remove the plastic cover over the side airbags.

2   Loosen and remove the regulator/electric motor mounting bolts **(see illustration)**.

3   Disconnect the wiring multi-plug from the window regulator motor **(see illustration)**.

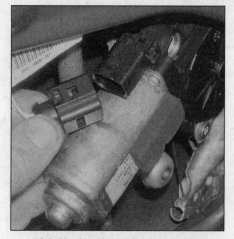

12.3 Unplug the wiring connector

4   Unclip the regulator cables from inside the door panel, then withdraw the window regulator mechanism downwards and out through the hole in the inner door panel **(see illustration)**.

Rear

Refer to illustrations 12.6 and 12.8

5   Carry out the procedures to remove the window glass as described in Section 11. On later models with side impact airbags, remove the plastic cover over the side airbags.

6   Loosen and remove the regulator and

12.4 Remove the front window regulator from the door

manual winder/electric motor mounting bolts **(see illustration)**.

7   On electric windows, disconnect the wiring multi-plugs from the window regulator motor.

8   Withdraw the window regulator mechanism from inside the door, through the hole in the inner door panel **(see illustration)**.

Installation

9   Installation is a reversal of the removal procedure.

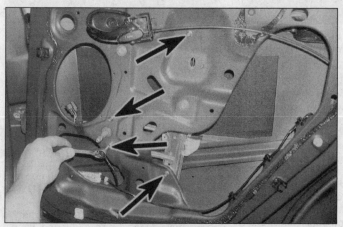

12.6 Remove the bolts (arrows) for manual windows (typical)

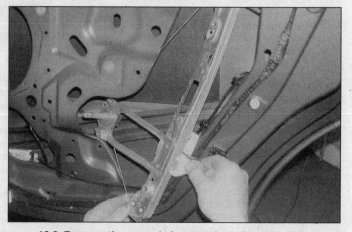

12.8 Remove the rear window regulator from the door

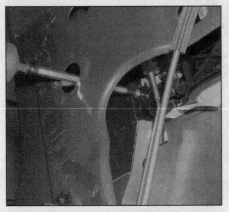

13.6a   Loosen the retaining screw . . .

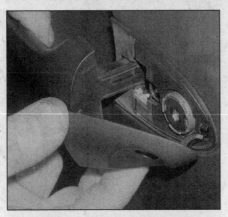

13.6b   . . . and remove the lock cylinder bezel

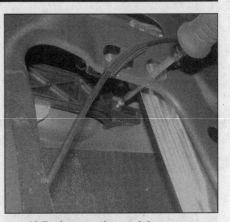

13.7a   Loosen the retaining screw

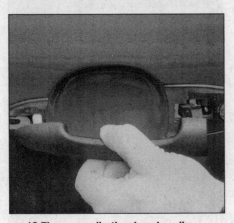

13.7b   . . . unclip the door handle . . .

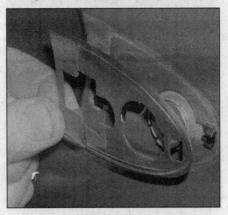

13.7c   . . . and remove the door handle seals

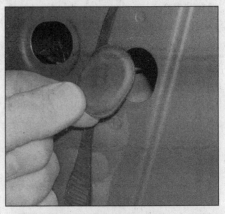

13.10   Remove the grommet to access the screw

13   Door handle and lock components - removal and installation

Warning: *Before working on any electrical components, disconnect the negative battery cable (see Chapter 1).*

Removal

Exterior handle - front

Refer to illustrations 13.6a, 13.6b, 13.7a, 13.7b and 13.7c

1   Remove the door inner trim panel as described in Section 10.

2   Rotate the side impact bolster counter-clockwise to remove it from its retaining clips, then pull out the retaining clips from the door panel.

3   Remove the four screws from the speaker and remove from the door, disconnect the wiring as it becomes accessible.

4   Detach the inner door release handle from the door by unclipping it from the front end, then slide the handle out in a forwards direction. (The door handle at this point can be left attached to the cable.)

5   Using a knife or scraper, cut through the butyl strip to enable the weather shield to be peeled back from the door panel. Take care not to damage the weather shield or door panel. (Do not touch the adhesive as re-

13.11a   Loosen the retaining screw (arrow) . . .

13.11b   . . . and unclip the outer bezel

bonding will be impaired.)

6   To remove the outer lock cylinder bezel, undo the retaining screw from the inside of the door handle assembly. **Note:** *You may have to remove a small plug to access this screw.* (It is not necessary to fully remove this screw.) Unclip and remove the bezel from the lock cylinder **(see illustrations)**.

7   Loosen but do not remove the screw from the inside of the door for the exterior handle. Slide the handle back, and pull out from the door. Unclip the door handle seals from the door panel **(see illustrations)**.

Exterior handle - rear

Refer to illustrations 13.10, 13.11a, 13.11b, 13.12a and 13.12b

8   Carry out the procedures as described for the front door exterior handle (Steps 1 to 5).

9   Unscrew the window runner guide from inside the rear door opening and remove from door panel.

10   Remove the grommet from the access hole on the inside of the door assembly **(see illustration)**.

11   Loosen the retaining screw through the access hole, to remove the outer door handle bezel **(see illustrations)**. (It is not necessary

13.12a Loosen the retaining screw . . .

13.12b . . . and unclip the door handle

13.14 Unclip the handle from the door

13.16 Unclip the outer cable, then release
the inner cable

13.19 Remove the lock mounting bolts

13.20 Withdraw the lock mechanism from
the door

to fully remove this screw.)

12   Loosen but do not remove the screw
from the inside of the door, for the exterior
handle. Slide the handle back, and pull out
from the door **(see illustrations)**. Unclip the
door handle seals from the door panel.

Interior handle
Refer to illustrations 13.14 and 13.16

13   Remove the door inner trim panel Section 10.

14   Detach the door release handle from the
door by unclipping it from the front end, then
slide the handle out in a forward direction
(see illustration).

15   Before you can remove the cable from
the handle, set the lever switch in the locked
position.

16   Using a thin-bladed screwdriver unclip
the outer cable locating clip, then release the
inner operating cable from the handle assembly **(see illustration)**.

Lock motor/module - front
*Refer to illustrations 13.19, 13.20, 13.21a,
13.21b, 13.22 and 13.24*

17   Remove the exterior handle as described
earlier in this Section.

18   Disconnect the electrical connector from
the door lock motor, using a small screwdriver
to release the retaining clip.

19   Loosen and remove the three Torx bolts
from the lock assembly at the rear edge of
the door **(see illustration)**.

20   Unclip the door lock/handle reinforcement bracket from the door panel. Maneuver

the assembly out through the door inner
frame, complete with the door lock mechanism **(see illustration)**.

21   With the door lock assembly on a work
top, unclip the trim from the back of the security shield then undo the two securing screws
to remove from the door lock assembly **(see
illustrations)**.

13.21a Unclip the cover . . .

13.21b . . . and remove the two
screws (arrows)

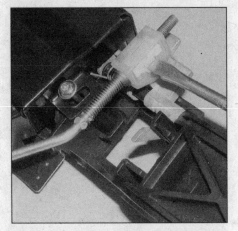

13.22 Pry out the locking clip (a new one may be needed)

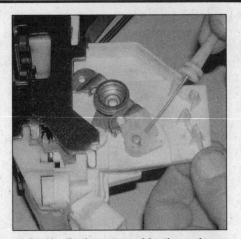

13.24 Unclip the outer cable, then release the inner cable

13.26 Release the locking tab

22   Release the adjustment locking clip from the remote control rod **(see illustration)**. Measure the amount of thread at the top of the rod before removing the clip as this will adjust the linkage on installation. (The clip may break on removal so a new one will be required.)

23   Unhook the connecting rod from the door lock cylinder lever, by turning it a quarter-turn.

24   Unclip the outer cable from the lock housing (note position of the outer cable in the lock housing), then turn the inner cable a quarter-turn to remove it from the door lock linkage **(see illustration)**.

Lock cylinder

Refer to illustrations 13.26 and 13.27

25   Remove the lock/module as described earlier in this Section.

26   Pry out the cylinder retaining tab from the handle reinforcement bracket, using a small screwdriver **(see illustration)**.

27   Insert the key, and turn it so that it engages the cylinder, then pull out the lock cylinder **(see illustration)**.

Lock motor/module - rear

Refer to illustrations 13.29, 13.30, 13.31, 13.32, 13.33 and 13.34

28   Remove the exterior handle as de-

13.27 Pull out the lock cylinder

13.29 Unscrew the lock mounting bolts

scribed earlier in this Section.

29   Loosen and remove the three Torx bolts, from the lock assembly at the rear edge of the door **(see illustration)**.

30   Unclip the door lock/handle reinforcement bracket from the door panel. Maneuver the assembly out through the door inner frame, complete with the door lock mechanism **(see illustration)**.

31   Disconnect the wiring connector from the door lock motor, using a small screwdriver to release the retaining clip **(see illustration)**.

32   With the door lock assembly on a work top, unclip the handle reinforcement bracket from the lock motor **(see illustration)**.

33   Remove the connecting rod/adjusting clip from the door lock assembly. Measure the amount of thread at the top of the rod

13.30 Remove the lock assembly from the door

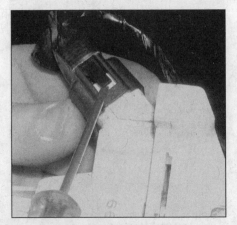

13.31 Unclip the wiring connector

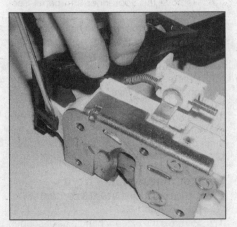

13.32 Unclip the bracket from the lock

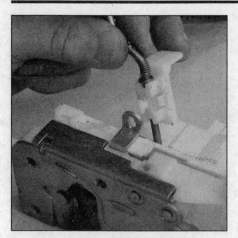

13.33 Disengage the clip from the lock lever

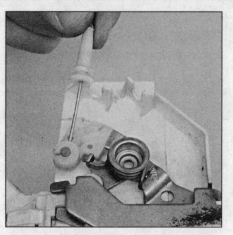

13.34 Unclip the outer cable, then release the inner cable

13.36a Remove the securing bolts . . .

before removing the clip as this will adjust the linkage on installation. Turn the rod/adjusting clip a quarter-turn to remove (**see illustration**).

34   Unclip the outer cable from the lock housing (note the position of the outer cable in the lock housing), then turn the inner cable a quarter-turn to remove it from the door lock linkage (**see illustration**).

Striker/contact switch

Refer to illustrations 13.36a and 13.36b

35   Using a pencil, mark the position of the striker/contact switch on the pillar.

36   Undo the mounting screws using a Torx key, and remove the striker/contact switch. Disconnect the wiring connector (**see illustrations**).

Check strap

Refer to illustrations 13.37, 13.38a and 13.38b

37   Using a Torx key, unscrew and remove the check strap mounting bolt from the door pillar (**see illustration**).

38   Pry the rubber grommet from the door opening, then unscrew the mounting nuts

and withdraw the check strap from the door (**see illustrations**).

Installation

Handles (exterior and interior)

39   Installation is a reversal of the removal procedure. (When installing operating cable, make sure the outer cable is located into the correct recess.)

Lock cylinder

40   Check that the retaining clip is installed correctly.

41   Align the grooves on the cylinder with the grooves on the reinforcement plate, then carefully push the cylinder into the handle until it engages the clip.

42   The remaining installation procedure is a reversal of removal.

Lock motor

43   Installation is a reversal of the removal procedure. (A new adjusting clip may need to be installed; do not fully clip together until the final adjustment is made.)

Striker

44   Installation is a reversal of the removal

13.36b . . . and disconnect the wiring connector

procedure, but check that the door lock passes over the striker centrally. If necessary, reposition the striker before fully tightening the mounting screws.

Check strap

45   Installation is a reversal of the removal procedure.

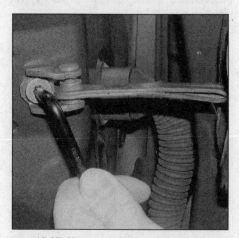

13.37 Unscrew the mounting bolt

13.38a Remove the rubber cover . . .

13.38b . . . and remove the check strap mounting nuts

14.2 Remove the mounting bolt

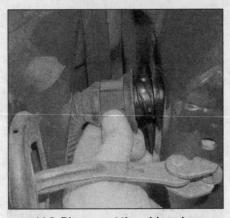

14.3 Disconnect the wiring plug

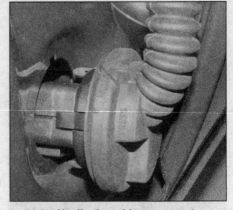

14.4a Unclip the rubber grommet . . .

14   Door - removal and installation

Removal

Refer to illustrations 14.2, 14.3, 14.4a, 14.4b and 14.5

1   Disconnect the negative battery cable (see Chapter 1).

2   Using a Torx driver, unscrew and remove the check strap mounting bolt from the door pillar **(see illustration)**.

3   On the front doors, disconnect the wiring connector by twisting it counterclockwise **(see illustration)**.

4   On the rear doors, unclip the rubber grommet and disconnect the wiring block connector **(see illustrations)**.

5   Using a Torx driver, loosen the retaining screws in the top and bottom hinges **(see illustration)**. On 2005 and later models, there are no retaining screws. Remove the hinge-to-body bolts to remove the door. Have an assistant help you with removal and make matching marks on the hinge and the body before removing the hinge bolts, so the original alignment can be maintained.

6   Carefully lift the door from the hinges.

Installation

7   Installation is a reversal of the removal procedure, but check that the door lock passes over the striker centrally. If necessary, reposi-

14.4b . . . and disconnect the wiring connector

tion the striker. When installing the wiring connector to the front doors, the line and the white dot on the connector should be in line.

15   Exterior mirror and glass - removal and installation

Removal

Refer to illustrations 15.2, 15.3 and 15.4

Mirror

1   Where electric mirrors are installed, dis-

14.5 Loosen the hinge setscrews

connect the negative battery cable (see Chapter 1).

2   Unclip the quarter bezel from the front of the window opening and remove it **(see illustration)**.

3   On manual mirrors, detach the adjustment lever by turning the rubber boot to disengage from the bezel **(see illustration)**.

4   On electric mirrors, disconnect the wiring multi-plug from the mirror control switch. Release the clip and detach the electrical connector to gain access to the retaining bolt **(see illustration)**.

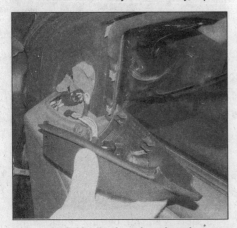

15.2 Unclip the mirror bezel

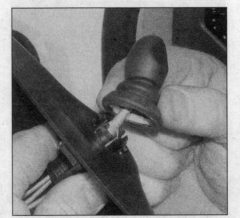

15.3 Turn the switch to disengage

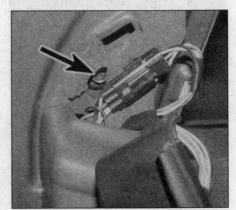

15.4 Unclip the wiring connector to access the mirror securing bolt (arrow)

15.6 Press the mirror glass in the direction of the arrow to remove

15.7 Disconnect the wiring connectors

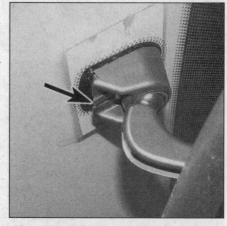

16.1a Lift up the retaining clip (arrow) . . .

5   Unscrew the mirror mounting bolt, then withdraw the mirror from the outside of the door. Recover the mirror seal as the wiring/ cable is being drawn through the rubber grommet.

Mirror glass

Refer to illustrations 15.6 and 15.7

6   Press the mirror glass from the inner side outwards and unclip from the retaining bracket **(see illustration).**
7   Withdraw the mirror glass and disconnect the wiring connectors for the heated mirrors **(see illustration).**

Installation

8   Installation is a reversal of the removal procedure. Take care not to drop the rubber grommet inside the door panel when removing the mirror, as the interior door trim will have to be removed to retrieve it.

16   Interior mirror - removal and installation

Refer to illustrations 16.1a and 16.1b

1   Lift up the retaining clip at the base of the mirror bracket, and slide the mirror

assembly upward off the mounting attached to the windshield **(see illustrations).**
2   Installation is the reversal of the removal procedure.

17   Trunk lid - removal and installation

Removal

Refer to illustrations 17.2, 17.3 and 17.7

1   Disconnect the negative battery cable (see Chapter 1), and open the trunk lid.
2   On the left-hand hinge, pull off the trim covering, and release the wiring on the hinge arm. Pry out the grommet to free the wiring **(see illustration).**
3   Remove the trim from inside the trunk lid **(see illustration).**
4   Disconnect the wiring at the connectors visible through the trunk lid inner skin opening.
5   Attach a length of strong cord to the end of the wires in the opening, to act as an aid to guiding the wiring through the lid when it is installed.
6   Pull the wiring harness through the trunk lid openings. Untie the cord, and leave it in

16.1b . . . and slide mirror upwards off the windshield mounting

place in the trunk lid for installing the wiring loom.
7   Using a small screwdriver, pry off the clips securing the struts to the trunk lid. Pull the sockets from the ball-studs, and move the struts downwards **(see illustration).**
8   Mark the position of the hinge arms with a pencil. Place rags beneath each corner of the trunk lid, to prevent damage to the paintwork.

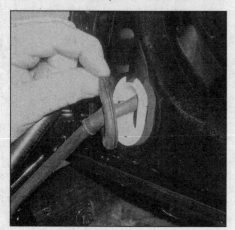

17.2 Pull the grommet out to remove the wiring

17.3 Remove the plastic screws and clips

17.7 Pry off clip to release the strut

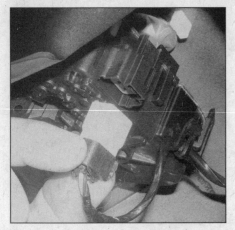

18.3 Unplug the wiring connector

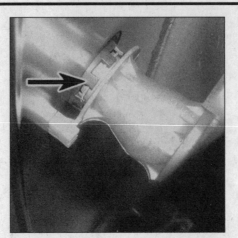

18.4a Unclip the lock cylinder surround (arrows from inside)

18.4b . . . and remove from the trunk lid

9   With the help of an assistant, unscrew the mounting bolts and lift the trunk lid from the car.

Installation

10   Installation is a reversal of the removal procedure, noting the following points:

a) *Check that the trunk lid is correctly aligned with the surrounding bodywork, with an equal clearance around its edge.*

b) *Adjustment can be made by loosening the hinge bolts, and moving the trunk lid within the elongated mounting holes.*

c) *Check that the lock enters the striker centrally when the trunk lid is closed.*

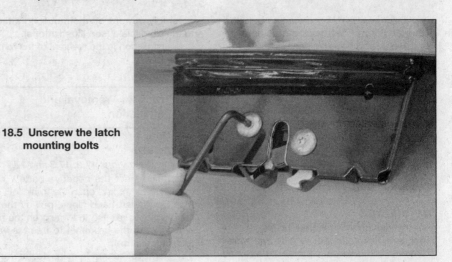

18.5 Unscrew the latch mounting bolts

18 Trunk lid lock components - removal and installation

Removal

Refer to illustrations 18.3, 18.4a, 18.4b, 18.5, 18.6a, 18.6b and 18.7

1   Disconnect the negative battery cable (see Chapter 1).

2   With the trunk lid open, undo the plastic screws from the trunk liner trim and remove.

3   Disconnect the wiring plug from the latch assembly **(see illustration)**.

4   Unclip the rubber grommet from around the lock cylinder on the inside of the trunk lid **(see illustrations)**.

5   Using a Torx wrench, unscrew the latch mounting screws, and withdraw the latch and lock cylinder **(see illustration)**. Disengage the latch cable end.

6   With the lock assembly on a suitable work bench; file down the lock cylinder housing to expose the spring and plunger **(see illustrations)**.

7   Remove the spring and plunger, then turn the lock cylinder and pull it out of the lock housing **(see illustration)**. (The spring is NOT used on installation.)

18.6a File down the lock cylinder housing (arrow) . . .

18.6b . . . and remove the spring and plunger

18.7 Turn lock cylinder to disengage it from the lock assembly

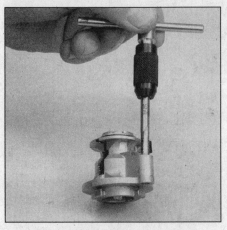

18.8a Use an M6 tap to cut a thread . . .

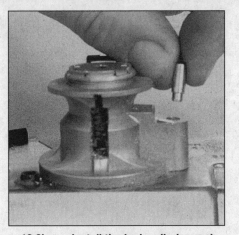

18.8b . . . install the lock cylinder, and insert the plunger . . .

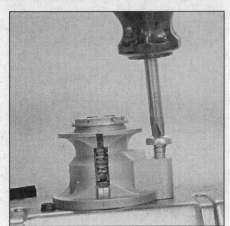

18.8c . . . then install the retaining screw, using Loctite sealer on the threads

19.3a Disconnect the wiring connector . . .

19.3b . . . and the rear washer pipe

19.4a On Hatchback models pull out the rear shelf cord posts . . .

Installation

Refer to illustrations 18.8a, 18.8b and 18.8c

8   Installation is a reversal of the removal procedure, noting when replacing the lock cylinder:

a) *Use an M6 tap to cut a thread in the lock cylinder housing, where the plunger had been removed* **(see illustration)**.

b) *Install the lock cylinder, then turn to locate into place.*

c) *Push the plunger into the hole, then install the retaining screw (M6 x 6.5mm) to secure the plunger* **(see illustrations)** *(use Loctite sealer on the threads).*

19   Liftgate - removal and installation

Removal

Refer to illustrations 19.3a, 19.3b, 19.4a, 19.4b, 19.6, 19.8, 19.9, 19.10 and 19.11

1   Disconnect the negative battery cable (see Chapter 1).

2   The tailgate may be unbolted from the hinges and the hinges left in position. Disconnect the electrical connector from the rear window defogger.

19.4b . . . then unclip the upper tailgate trim

3   Remove the two screws from the high-level rear brake light cover, and disconnect the bulbholder wiring and washer pipe **(see illustrations)**.

4   Undo the retaining screws, then unclip the tailgate trim. Carefully unclip the upper tailgate trims from around the rear screen. On Coupe models unclip the rear shelf cord

posts from the upper tailgate trims **(see illustrations)**.

5   Disconnect the wiring loom connectors through the tailgate inner skin opening including the ground wiring. Attach a strong, fine cord to the end of the wiring loom, to act as an aid to guiding the wiring through the tailgate when it is installed.

19.6 Unclip the rubber wiring grommet

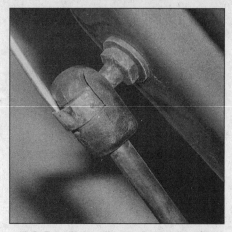

19.8 Pry off the clip to release the strut

19.9 Remove the two securing bolts (arrows)

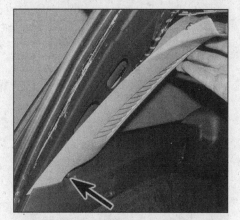

19.10 Remove the screw (arrow) and unclip the trim

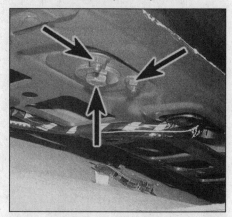

19.11 Remove the nuts and bolt (arrows) to remove the hinge

6   Pry the rubber grommet from the left-hand side of the tailgate opening **(see illustration)**, and pull out the wiring loom. Untie the cord, leaving it in position in the tailgate for guiding the wire through on installation.

7   Have an assistant support the tailgate in its open position.

8   Using a small screwdriver, pry off the clip securing the struts to the tailgate. Pull the sockets from the ball-studs, and move the struts downwards **(see illustration)**.

9   Unscrew and remove the hinge bolts (two per side) from the tailgate **(see illustration)**. Withdraw the tailgate from the body opening, taking care not to damage the paintwork.

10   If the hinges are to be removed from the roof panel, unscrew the retaining screws (one per side), from the bottom of the D-pillar trim panels **(see illustration)**. Unclip the trims from both sides and remove them from the pillars.

11   Carefully pull down the rear edge of the headliner for access to the nuts and bolts. Take care not to damage the headliner **(see illustration)**.

12   Unscrew the hinge mounting bolts and nuts from the rear roof panel.

Installation

13   Installation is a reversal of the removal procedure, but check that the tailgate is located centrally in the body opening, and that the striker enters the lock centrally. If necessary, loosen the mounting nuts and reposition the tailgate as required.

20 Support struts - removal and installation

Removal

Refer to illustrations 20.2a and 20.2b

1   Have an assistant support the tailgate, decklid or hood in its open position.

2   Pry off the upper spring clip securing the strut to the liftgate, decklid or hood, then pull

the socket from the ball-stud **(see illustrations)**.

3   Similarly pry off the bottom clip, and pull the socket from the ball-stud. Withdraw the strut.

Installation

4   Installation is a reversal of the removal procedure, making sure that the strut is installed the same way up as it was removed.

20.2a Use a thin screwdriver to release the securing clip . . .

21 Liftgate latch components - removal and installation

Removal

Latch assembly - Wagon

Refer to illustrations 21.2, 21.3, 21.4 and 21.5

1   Disconnect the negative battery (ground) cable (Chapter 5A, Section 1).

20.2b . . . then pull the strut off the ball-stud

21.2 Unclip the tailgate trim

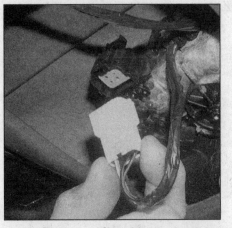

21.3 Disconnect the wiring connector from the lock

21.4 Unclip the outer cable, then release the inner cable

21.5 Remove the two securing bolts and remove the latch

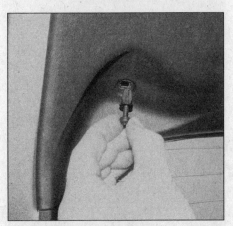

21.7 Remove the retaining screws from the tailgate trim

21.8 Disconnecting the wiring plug from the latch assembly

2   With the tailgate open, remove the two plastic screws and unclip the trim panel from the tailgate **(see illustration)**.
3   Disconnect the electrical connector from the tailgate lock assembly **(see illustration)**.
4   Disengage the operating cable from the rear of the lock cylinder. Unclip the outer cable, then rotate the cable to disengage the inner cable **(see illustration)**.

5   Remove the two lock securing bolts and remove the lock assembly, complete with the operating cable **(see illustration)**.

Latch assembly - Coupe
Refer to illustrations 21.7, 21.8, 21.9a, 21.9b and 21.10
6   Disconnect the negative battery cable (see Chapter 1).
7   With the tailgate open, undo the retain-

ing screws and unclip the trim panel from the tailgate **(see illustration)**.
8   Disconnect the electrical connector from the tailgate latch assembly **(see illustration)**.
9   Unclip the rubber grommet from around the lock cylinder on the inside of the tailgate **(see illustrations)**.
10   Using a Torx driver, unscrew the latch mounting screws, and withdraw the latch assembly **(see illustration)**.

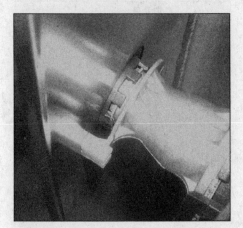

21.9a The rubber grommet is clipped onto the lock cylinder inside the tailgate . . .

21.9b . . . it can be lifted off after its tabs are unclipped from the opposite side

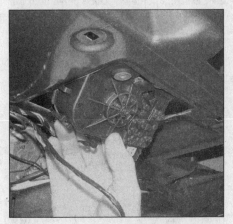

21.10 Remove the latch assembly from the tailgate

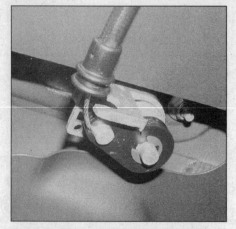

21.13 Unclip the outer cable, then release the inner cable

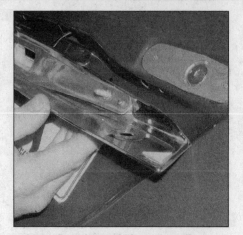

21.14 Pry trim away from the tailgate, after removing securing nuts

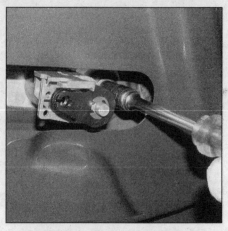

21.15 Undo the two securing nuts

21.16 Pry the lock cylinder from the tailgate

21.17a File down the lock cylinder housing (arrow) . . .

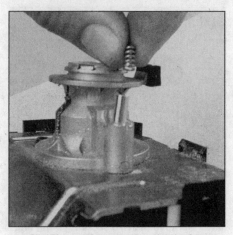

21.17b . . . then remove the spring and plunger

Lock cylinder - Wagon

Refer to illustrations 21.13, 21.14, 21.15 and 21.16

11   Disconnect the negative battery cable (see Chapter 1).

12   With the tailgate open, remove the two plastic screws and unclip the trim panel from the tailgate.

13   Disengage the operating cable from the rear of the lock cylinder **(see illustration)**.

14   Undo the three securing nuts from the rear number plate light trim and remove from the tailgate **(see illustration)**, disconnect the wiring connectors (if required) as they come into view. Double-sided sticking tape will be required on the ends of the trim for installation.

15   Loosen and remove the two lock cylinder securing nuts **(see illustration)**.

16   Pry the lock cylinder from the sealing gasket on the tailgate to remove it **(see illustration)**. Install a new sealing gasket when installing.

Lock cylinder - Coupe

Refer to illustrations 21.17a, 21.17b and 21.18

17   With the lock assembly removed (Steps 6 to 10), and on a suitable work bench,

file down the lock cylinder housing to expose the spring and plunger **(see illustrations)**.

18   Remove the spring and plunger, then turn the lock cylinder and pull out of the lock housing **(see illustration)**. (The spring is NOT used on installation.)

Installation

Refer to illustrations 21.19a and 21.19b

19   Installation is a reversal of the removal

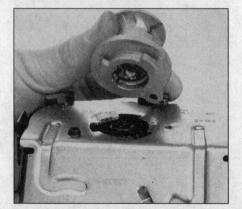

21.18 Turn the lock cylinder, to disengage it from the lock assembly

procedure, noting when installing the lock cylinder :

a) *Use an M6 tap to cut a thread in the lock cylinder housing, where the plunger had been removed **(see illustration)**.*

b) *Install the lock cylinder, then turn to locate into place.*

21.19a Use an M6 tap to cut a thread in the lock cylinder body

21.19b Put the plunger into the hole, then install the retaining screw

22.1 The interior light switch is built into the door latch

22.2 Clips and screws secure the trim panel

c) *Push the plunger into the hole* (see illustration), *then install the retaining screw (M6 x 6.5mm) to secure the plunger (use Loctite sealer on the threads).*

22 Power door lock system components - testing, removal and installation

Testing

Refer to illustration 22.1

1 The power door lock/alarm system incorporates a self-test function, which can be activated by operating one of the door interior light switches six times within 8 seconds (see illustration). During the check, the indicators will flash to acknowledge the input, then the indicators should flash every time a door, hood or liftgate is opened. If there is an alarm installed, then the horn will sound along with the indicators flashing. If the doors are double-locked, and the vehicle is equipped with interior sensors, the signal will occur when something is moved within the passenger compartment. A more comprehensive test can be made using a diagnostic scan tool.

Removal

Refer to illustrations 22.2 and 22.4

Central locking/alarm module

2 To remove the module, first remove the lower right A-pillar trim (see illustration). On 2003 and later models, remove the glove box instead of the kick panel (see Section 31).
3 Disconnect the negative battery cable (see Chapter 1).
4 Undo the securing screws, and remove the module from the bracket (see illustration).
5 Disconnect the wiring multi-plugs, and withdraw the module from inside the vehicle.

Door motors

6 This procedure is covered in Section 13.

Decklid/tailgate motor

7 Remove the lock as described in Section 18 or 21, as applicable.
8 Remove the two motor securing screws, then maneuver the motor assembly out from the body, disconnecting the wiring plug.

Installation

9 In all cases, installation is a reversal of the removal procedure.

23 Windshield and fixed windows - removal and installation

1 The windshield and rear window on all models are bonded in place with special mastic, as are the rear side windows. Special tools are required to cut free the old units and install replacements; special cleaning solutions and primer are also required. It is therefore recommended that this work is entrusted to a windshield replacement specialist.

24 Body side-trim moldings and adhesive emblems - removal and installation

Removal

1 Body side trims and moldings are attached either by retaining clips or adhesive bonding. On bonded moldings, insert a length of strong cord (fishing line is ideal) behind the molding or emblem concerned. With a sawing action, break the adhesive bond between the molding or emblem and the panel.
2 Thoroughly clean all traces of adhesive from the panel using methylated spirit, and allow the location to dry.
3 On moldings with retaining clips, unclip the moldings from the panel, taking care not to damage the paintwork.

22.4 Remove the screws and remove the module

Installation

4 Peel back the protective paper from the rear face of the new molding or emblem. Carefully fit it into position on the panel concerned, but take care not to touch the adhesive. When in position, apply hand pressure to the molding/emblem for a short period, to ensure maximum adhesion to the panel.
5 Replace any broken retaining clips before replacing trims or moldings.

25 Sunroof - removal, installation and adjustment

Note: *Sunroofs are not available on all models.*

Removal

Refer to illustration 25.2

Glass panel

1 Slide back the sun blind, and set the glass panel in the tilt position.
2 Remove the four securing screws (two

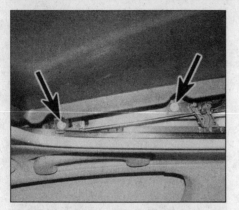

25.2 Remove the sunroof securing screws (arrows), two screws per side

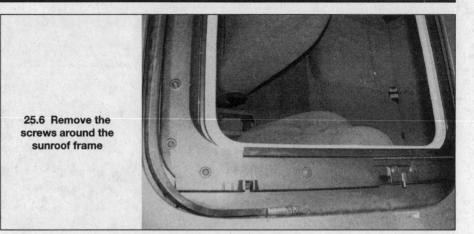

25.6 Remove the screws around the sunroof frame

per side) **(see illustration)**.
3   Lift up or remove the antenna, then lift the sunroof glass panel out from the vehicle.

Sun blind

Refer to illustration 25.6
4   Remove the glass panel as described in paragraphs 1 to 3.
5   Wind the roof opening mechanism to the rear, making sure the glass panel guides do not disengage from the guide rails.
6   Undo and remove the 16 screws from around the sun blind panel **(see illustration)**.
7   Slide the sun blind out from the guide rails, taking care not to disturb the cable guides in their runners. Prevent any ingress of dirt into the cable mechanism.

Installation

8   Installation is a reversal of removal. Lubricate the cables and guides on assembly.

Adjustment

Refer to illustration 25.11
9   The sunroof should operate freely, without sticking or binding, as it is opened and closed. When in the closed position, check that the panel is flush with the surrounding roof panel.

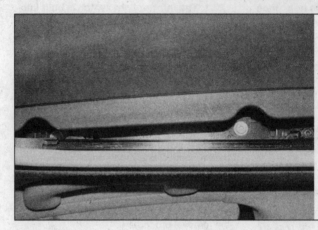

25.11 Loosen the screws to adjust the height of the glass panel

10   If adjustment is required, slide back the sun blind, but leave the glass panel in the closed position.
11   Loosen the rear securing screws (one per side). Adjust the glass panel up or down, so that it is flush at its back edge with the roof panel **(see illustration)**.
12   Loosen the front securing screws (one per side). Adjust the glass panel up or down, so that it is flush at its front edge with the roof panel.
13   Retighten the four securing screws.
14   Check the roof seal for wind noise and water leaks.

Checking

Drain tubes

Refer to illustrations 25.15, 25.16 and 25.17
15   There are four drain tubes, one located in each corner of the sunroof opening **(see illustration)**.
16   The front drain tubes go down the front A-pillars; remove the lower trim panel and electrical junction box or PCM to gain access to the drain tube **(see illustration)**.
17   The rear drain tubes go down the C-pillars; remove the rear side trims to gain access **(see illustration)**.

25.15 One of the front drain tubes (arrow)

25.16 Remove the electrical unit to check the drain tube

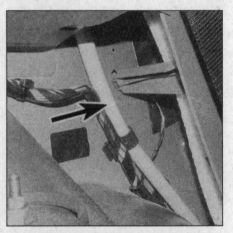

25.17 Rear drain tube (arrow)

26.3 Unclip the runner trim

26.4 Remove the seat mounting bolts

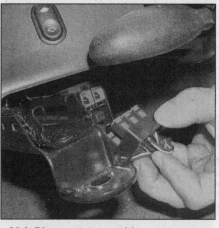

26.6 Disconnect any wiring connectors

26 Seats - removal and installation

Removal

Front seat

Refer to illustrations 26.3, 26.4 and 26.6

1   On models with electrically-operated or heated seats, or with side airbags, disconnect the negative battery cable, and position the cable away from the battery (see Chapter 5A, Section 1). **Warning:** *Where side airbags are installed, wait a minimum of 5 minutes before proceeding as a precaution against accidental firing of the airbag unit. This period ensures that any stored energy in the back-up capacitor is dissipated.*

2   Slide the seat fully backwards.

3   Remove the trim cover from the outer seat runner **(see illustration)**.

4   Undo the two front seat runner bolts and remove **(see illustration)**.

5   Slide the seat fully forwards, then undo the two rear seat runner bolts and remove.

6   On models with electrically-operated or heated seats, disconnect the various seat wiring multi-plugs from the seat base, noting their installed positions **(see illustration)**.

Rear seat cushion

Refer to illustration 26.8

7   On some models, unclip the plastic trim from the hinges at the front of each seat cushion.

8   Unscrew and remove the mounting bolts from the hinges **(see illustration)**, then withdraw the seat cushion from inside the vehicle.

Rear seat backrest

Refer to illustration 26.10

9   Remove the headrests, if installed, and fold the rear seat cushion forward (if not already removed). Remove the headrests and fold the backrest forward. Unbolt the center seatbelt anchor.

10   Undo and remove the four bolts from the rear of the backrest **(see illustration)**.

11   Release the rear backrest from the locating brackets, and withdraw the backrest from inside the vehicle.

Rear seat backrest catch and release cable

Refer to illustrations 26.12 and 26.13

12   Fold the seat backrest forward, unclip the cover from the backrest catch **(see illustration)**.

13   From inside the trunk, unclip the back-

26.8 Unbolt the rear seat cushion hinge

rest release cable from under the rear shelf **(see illustration)**.

14   Undo the backrest catch securing screws and remove the catch complete with the release cable. **Note:** *Most models have a catch rather than a cable.*

Installation

15   Installation is a reversal of the removal procedure, tighten the mounting bolts to the specified torque.

26.10 Remove the back seat retaining bolts

26.12 Unclip the cover to access the securing screws

26.13 Unclip the release cable from under the parcel shelf

27.2 Remove the lower seat belt bolt

27.3 Unclip the upper pillar trim

27.4 Remove the upper seat belt bolt

27 Seat belts - removal and installation

Warning: *Be careful when handling the seat belt tensioning device, it contains a small explosive charge (pyrotechnic device) similar to the one used to deploy the airbag(s). Clearly, injury could be caused if these are released in an uncontrolled fashion. Once fired, the tensioner cannot be reset, and must be replaced. Note also that seat belts and associated components that have been subject to impact loads must be replaced.*

Removal - front seat belt

1   Disconnect the negative battery cable, and position the cable away from the battery (see Chapter 1). **Warning:** *Before proceeding, wait a minimum of 5 minutes, as a precaution against accidental firing of the seat belt tensioner. This period ensures that any stored energy in the back-up capacitor is dissipated.*

4-door & 5-door models

Refer to illustrations 27.2, 27.3, 27.4, 27.5, 27.6 and 27.7

2   Undo and remove the bolt for the lower

27.5 Remove the screws from the lower trim panel

seat belt anchor **(see illustration)**.
3   Unclip the upper trim panel from the B-pillar, and pass the seat belt lower anchor through the trim panel **(see illustration)**.
4   Unscrew the Torx bolt securing the seat belt guide to the B-pillar **(see illustration)**.
5   Remove the two securing screws, then unclip the lower trim panel from the B-pillar **(see illustration)**.
6   Slide the guide loop forwards, then down to detach it from the pillar **(see illustration)**.

7   Unscrew the mounting bolt, and lift the seat belt reel unit to remove it from the base of the pillar **(see illustration)**.

3-door models

Refer to illustrations 27.8, 27.9a, 27.9b and 27.11

8   Undo the anchor rail bolt and slide the belt off **(see illustration)**.
9   Pry out the retaining clip, then unclip the upper trim panel from the B-pillar. Pass the

27.6 Slide the seat belt guide loop from the door pillar

27.7 Remove the mounting bolt and lift out the seat belt reel

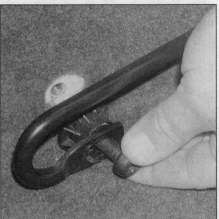

27.8 Remove the anchor rail bolt

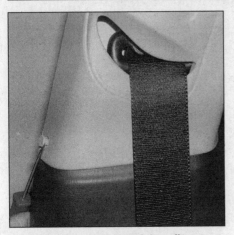

27.9a Pry out the retaining clip . . .

27.9b . . . and unclip the upper pillar trim

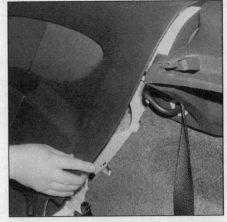

27.11 Remove the retaining clips and lift out the side trim panel

seat belt lower anchor through the trim panel **(see illustrations)**.

10   Unscrew the Torx bolt securing the seat belt guide to the B-pillar.

11   Remove the rear seat cushion and backrest as described in Section 26. Remove the two retaining clips and unclip the rear side trim panel, for access to the seat belt reel unit **(see illustration)**.

12   Unscrew the mounting bolt, and lift the seat belt reel unit to remove it from the base of the pillar. **Warning:** *There is a potential risk of the seat belt tensioning device firing during removal, so it should be handled carefully. Once removed, treat it with care - do not use chemicals on or near it, and do not expose it to high temperatures, or it may detonate.*

Removal - rear side seat belt

Wagon

Refer to illustrations 27.14 and 27.15

13   Fold the rear seat cushions forward, and unscrew the seat belt lower anchor bolt.

14   Fold the rear seat backrest forward. Undo the four securing screws from the luggage side cover trim, and unclip the cover trim from the seat belt reel unit **(see illustration)**.

15   Unscrew the mounting bolt securing the

27.14 Unclip the side trim from the luggage compartment

seat belt reel unit, and withdraw it from the vehicle **(see illustration)**.

3-door & 5-door models

Refer to illustrations 27.17, 27.18 and 27.19

16   Fold the rear seat cushions forward, and unscrew the seat belt lower anchor bolt.

17   From inside the trunk, undo the retaining

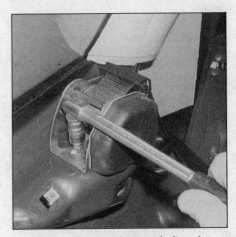

27.15 Remove the seat belt reel mounting bolt

screw from the seat belt reel cover trim **(see illustration)**.

18   Unclip the cover trim from around the seat belt reel **(see illustration)**.

19   Unscrew the mounting bolt securing the seat belt reel unit, and withdraw it from the vehicle **(see illustration)**.

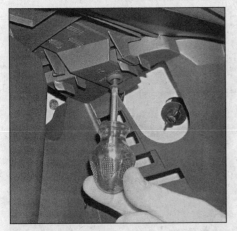

27.17 Remove the screw to release the seat belt reel cover

27.18 Unclip the cover trim

27.19 Remove the seat belt reel mounting bolt (arrow)

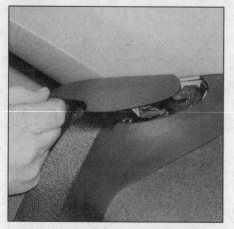

27.21 Unclip the seat belt trim cover

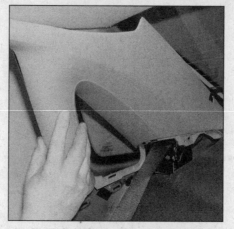

27.23 Unclip the upper trim panel

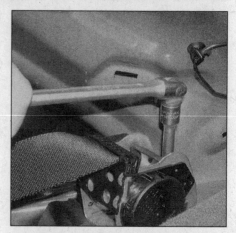

27.24 Remove the seat belt reel mounting bolt

Sedan

Refer to illustrations 27.21, 27.23 and 27.24

20   Fold the rear seat cushions forward, and unscrew the seat belt lower anchor bolt.

21   Fold the rear seat backrest forward, then unclip the small cover trim from the seat belt **(see illustration)**.

22   Undo the two securing screws from the C-pillar intermediate trim panel and unclip from around the seat belt reel unit.

23   Unclip the C-pillar upper trim panel, detaching it from the rear parcel shelf **(see illustration)**.

24   Unscrew the mounting bolt securing the seat belt reel unit, and withdraw it from the vehicle **(see illustration)**.

Removal - rear center seat belt

Wagon, 3-door & 5-door models

Refer to illustration 27.25

25   The center rear seat belt reel is attached to the rear seat backrest **(see illustration)**, but removal requires that the seat fabric be removed, so this operation should be referred to a dealer or competent specialist.

Sedan

Refer to illustrations 27.26 and 27.27

26   Fold the rear seat backrests forward,

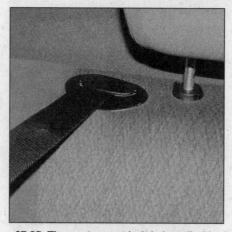

27.25 The center seat belt is installed in the backrest of the rear seat

27.26 Unclip the seat latch cover trim

then unclip the cover trims from the seat catches **(see illustration)**.

27   Unclip the cover trim from around the seat belt reel **(see illustration)**.

28   Slide the parcel shelf trim forwards to remove.

29   Unscrew the mounting bolt securing the seat belt reel unit to the parcel shelf, and withdraw it from the vehicle.

Removal - seat belt stalks

Refer to illustrations 27.30 and 27.31

30   The front seat belt stalks are bolted to the seat frame **(see illustration)** and can be removed after removing the front seat as described in Section 26.

31   The rear seat belt stalks can be removed by folding the rear seat cushions forward, then unscrewing the seat belt stalk anchor bolts **(see illustration)**.

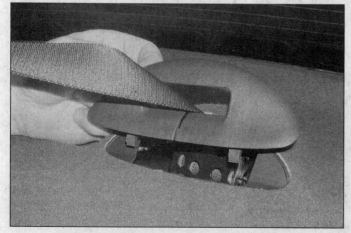

27.27 Unclip the trim from around the seat belt

27.30 Remove the mounting bolt on the seat frame

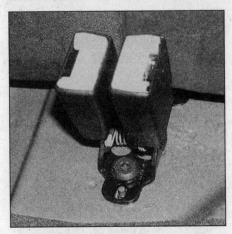

27.31 Unbolt the rear seat belt stalks

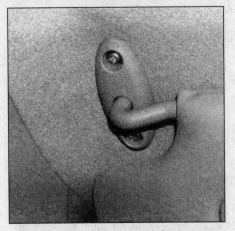

28.1 Remove the two retaining screws

28.3 Lift the plastic cover to remove the screw

Replacement

32   Installation is a reversal of the removal procedure, noting the following points:

a) *Tighten the mounting nuts and bolts to the specified torque.*
b) *Make sure the seat belt reel locating dowel is correctly positioned.*
c) *Install spacers in their correct position.*
d) *On 3-door models, make sure the anchor rail is located correctly.*

28 Interior trim panels - removal and installation

Note: *This section covers the removal and installation of the interior trim panels. It may be necessary to remove an overlapping trim before you can remove the one required. For more information on trim removal, look at relevant Chapters and Sections, where the trims may need to be removed to carry out any other procedures (e.g., to remove the steering column you will need to remove the shrouds).*

Removal

Sun visor

Refer to illustrations 28.1 and 28.3

1   Unscrew the mounting screws and

remove the visor **(see illustration)**.
2   Disconnect the wiring for the vanity mirror light, where installed.
3   Pry up the cover, unscrew the inner bracket mounting screws, and remove the bracket **(see illustration)**.

Passenger grab handle

Refer to illustration 28.4

4   Pry up the covers, then unscrew the mounting screws and remove the grab handle **(see illustration)**.

A-pillar trim

Refer to illustration 28.5

5   To remove the lower A-pillar trim, undo the two securing screws, and unclip from the vehicle complete with the instrument panel side trim **(see illustration)**.
6   Carefully press the A-pillar upper trim away from the retaining clips, and pull the trim upwards.
7   Release the phone microphone electrical connector from the upper trim clips (where installed).

B-pillar trim - Sedan and Wagon

Refer to illustrations 28.9 and 28.10

8   Unscrew the seat belt mounting bolt from its lower anchor point.

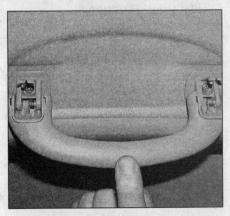

28.4 Lift the plastic covers to remove the screws

9   Carefully separate the upper trim from the lower trim, and unclip it from the B-pillar **(see illustration)**. Pass the seat belt lower anchor through the trim panel. On some models, you will have to remove a pushpin fastener at the bottom of the upper trim panel.
10   Undo the two securing screws from the lower trim panel, then unclip it from the B-pillar **(see illustration)**.

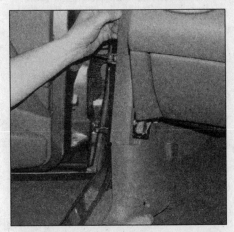

28.5 Remove the retaining screws and remove the trim

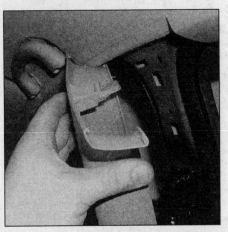

28.9 Unclip the upper trim from the B-pillar

28.10 Remove the two retaining screws from the lower trim

28.14 Remove the retaining screws from the rear side trim panels

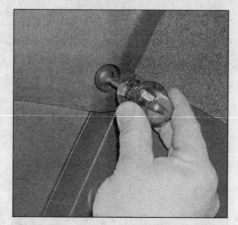

28.23 Remove the retaining screws from the lower side trim panels

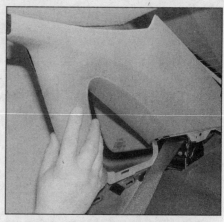

28.24 Unclip the upper trim panel

C-pillar trim - Hatchback
Refer to illustration 28.14

11   Remove the rear parcel shelf.
12   Fold the rear seat backrest cushion forwards.
13   Pry out the retaining clip, and remove the seat belt trim panel cover.
14   Undo the retaining screws from the parcel shelf support, disconnect the electrical connector from the interior light if installed **(see illustration)**.
15   Release the clips and locating tangs, and detach the upper trim.

C-pillar trim - Wagon
16   Remove the rear parcel shelf.
17   Fold the rear seat backrest forwards.
18   Unclip and remove the seat belt trim panel cover.
19   Undo the retaining screws from the parcel shelf support.
20   Unclip and remove the upper trim from the C-pillar.

C-pillar trim - Sedan
Refer to illustrations 28.23 and 28.24

21   Open the hatchback and fold the rear seat backrest cushion forward.
22   Unclip and remove the seat belt trim panel cover.

23   Undo the two securing screws, and remove the lower trim from around the seat belt reel unit **(see illustration)**.
24   Unclip the C-pillar upper trim panel, detaching it from the rear parcel shelf **(see illustration)**.

D-pillar trim - Wagon
Refer to illustration 28.25

25   Loosen and remove the securing screws from the luggage compartment side trim, then unclip the trim from the D-pillar **(see illustration)**.

Sill trim
Refer to illustration 28.26

26   Unclip the sill trims at each end from the pillar trims, and from the inner sill **(see illustration)**.

Steering column shrouds
27   To release the upper shroud from the lower shroud, insert a thin screwdriver into a hole at each side of the column (refer to Chapter 10 for illustrations). Lift the upper shroud from the column and unclip it from the bottom of the instrument panel.
28   Using a thin screwdriver unclip the radio control switch from the lower shroud.
29   Release the steering column height lever.

Undo the three securing screws from the lower shroud, and remove it from the column.

Lower dash panel
30   Undo the four securing screws from the lower panel and one retaining clip, and withdraw from the dash. Press out the wiring multi-plug from the panel.

Installation
31   Installation is a reversal of the removal procedure. Where seat belt fastenings have been disturbed, make sure that they are tightened to the specified torque. Replace any broken clips as required.

---

29   Center console - removal and installation

Removal
Manual transaxle models
Refer to illustrations 29.2, 29.4a, 29.4b, 29.5a, 29.5b, 29.7 and 29.8

1   Disconnect the negative battery cable (see Chapter 1).
2   Lift out the cup holders out from the front of the console, and undo the two retaining screws (one per side) **(see illustration)**.

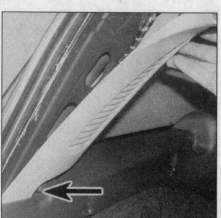

28.25 Remove the screw (arrow) and unclip the upper trim panel

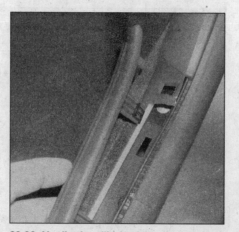

28.26 Unclip the sill trim from the inner sill

29.2 Lift out the cup holder and remove the screw

29.4a Lift out the rear ashtray . . . .

29.4b . . . and plastic screw cover, to remove the screw

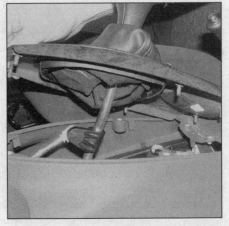

29.5a Unclip the shift lever trim panel from the console . . .

3   On some models pull the cup holder out from the rear of the console, and undo the securing screws.

4   Unclip the ashtray from the rear of the center console, then lift the cover to remove the securing screw from underneath **(see illustrations)**. **Note:** *Later models have a plastic cover instead of an ashtray*.

5   Unclip the shift lever trim panel from the center console, then unclip the boot from the trim panel leaving the boot on the shift lever **(see illustrations)**.

6   Remove the electrical connectors from any switches.

7   Unclip the parking brake boot from the center console and remove it from the parking brake lever **(see illustration)**.

8   Fully apply the parking brake lever to withdraw the center console from the vehicle **(see illustration)**.

Automatic transaxle models

9   This procedure is the same as given above for manual transmission models, except for the following.

10   Remove the screw on the side of the selector lever that secures the lever knob.

11   Using a screwdriver, carefully pry out the selector lever trim panel, and remove the selector lever knob and trim.

12   Detach and disconnect the wiring plugs inside the center console. Cut any cable-ties as necessary. **Note:** *On models with an armrest at the rear of the console, snap out the*

29.5b . . . then unclip the boot from the trim panel

trim panel at the rear of the armrest, then remove the screws and the armrest.

Installation

13   Installation is a reversal of the removal procedure.

30 Overhead console - removal and installation

Removal

Refer to illustrations 30.3 and 30.4

1   Disconnect the negative battery (ground)

29.7 Unclip the parking brake boot from the console

lead (Chapter 5A, Section 1).

2   On models with an electrically-operated sunroof, remove the sunroof switch (Chapter 12, Section 4).

3   On models with a manual sunroof, remove the sunroof handle, after undoing the securing screw **(see illustration)**.

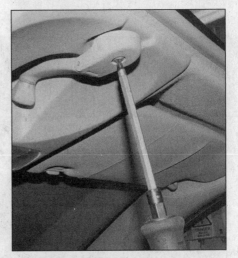

30.3 Remove the retaining screw and remove the sunroof handle

29.8 Withdraw the console over the shift lever and parking brake

30.4 **Carefully unclip the interior light**

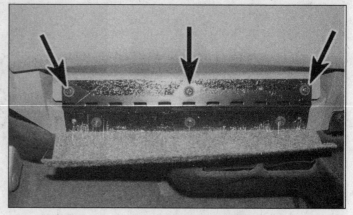

31.1 **Remove the three screws (arrows) to remove the glovebox lid**

4   Unclip the interior light and disconnect the electrical connector **(see illustration)**.
5   Undo and remove the retaining screws from the console and disengage from the roof panel. **Note:** *After the screws are removed, pull down on the console while pushing in on the sides to release the side clips, then move the console forward (toward the windshield) to release the rear clip.*

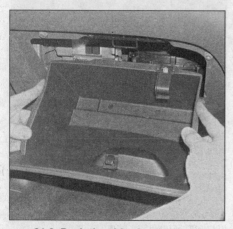

31.2 **Push the sides in to remove the glovebox**

Replacement

6   Installation is a reversal of the removal procedure.

---

31   Glovebox - removal and installation

Removal

Refer to illustrations 31.1 and 31.2
1   Pull back the carpet trim (where installed), and undo the three retaining screws from the glovebox hinge **(see illustration)**.
2   Withdraw the glovebox by pushing in at both sides **(see illustration)**.

Installation

3   Installation is a reversal of the removal procedure, making sure that the glovebox is located correctly before tightening the screws.

---

32   Instrument panel - removal and installation

Warning: *Before disconnecting the battery, refer to Chapter 5A, Section 1. The covered vehicles are equipped with airbags. See*

Chapter 12 for move information on the air-bag system.
Note: *Removal of the instrument panel is a complex procedure, involving the disconnection of a number of electrical connectors and the removal of many (sometimes hidden) plastic fasteners, some of which may break during removal. This is not a recommended procedure for the average home mechanic.*

Removal

Refer to illustrations 32.3, 32.4, 32.7, 32.10, 32.11, 32.12a, 32.12b, 32.12c, 32.13, 32.14 and 32.15
1   Disconnect the negative battery cable (see Chapter 1). Wait five minutes for the air-bag system to disable. **Warning:** *Failure to disable the airbag system could result in airbag deployment and personal injury (see Chapter 12).*
2   Remove the center console as described in Section 29.
3   Release the two retaining clips from the rear of the air ducting under the center console and remove it from the heater housing **(see illustration)**.
4   Remove the four securing screws from the lower center dash trim and remove the trim from the dash panel **(see illustration)**.
5   Remove the steering column (Chap-

32.3 **Lift off the air ducting**

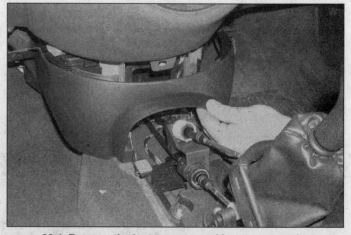

32.4 **Remove the instrument panel lower center trim**

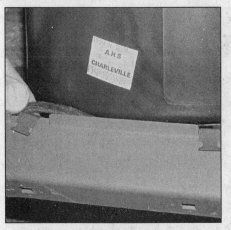

32.7 Unclip the wiring harness

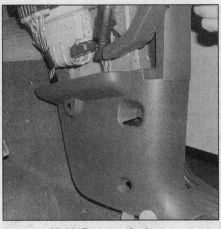

32.10 Remove the lower A-pillar trim panels

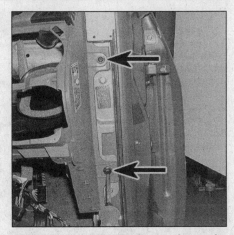

32.11 Remove the two screws (arrows)

32.12a Use pliers to pull out the bolt . . .

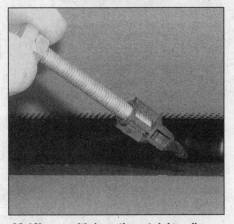

32.12b . . . withdraw the retaining clip . . .

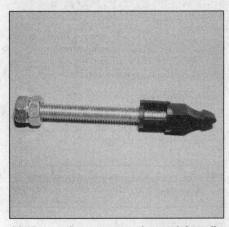

32.12c . . . then unscrew the retaining clip from the bolt for installation

ter 10). Remove the instrument cluster (see Chapter 12).

6   Remove the radio/cassette player and, where applicable, the passenger airbag, as described in Chapter 12.

7   Remove the glovebox (Section 31). Unclip the wiring loom from the lower area of the glovebox opening **(see illustration)**.

8   Remove the heater control panel (Chapter 3).

9   Remove the main headlight control switch (Chapter 12, Section 4).

10   Remove the securing screws/clips from the lower side trim panels, at the base of the A-pillars on each side of the vehicle. Unclip and remove the trim panels to gain access to the instrument panel side-mounting screws **(see illustration)**.

11   Unscrew the instrument panel side-mounting screws (two per side) **(see illustration)**.

12   Screw a bolt into the retaining clip in the air vent, in the top of the dash (there are three retaining clips, one in the center and one at

each side). When the bolt is tight in the retaining clip, pull on the bolt to remove the clips **(see illustrations)**. Carefully lever the upper part of the dash panel from its position. **Note:** *Some models use a one piece trim strip across the air vent instead of the three clips.*

13   Unscrew the dash center-mounting screw from behind the heater control panel **(see illustration)**.

14   Unscrew the two screws from behind the instrument panel **(see illustration)**.

32.13 Remove the instrument panel center-mounting screw (arrow)

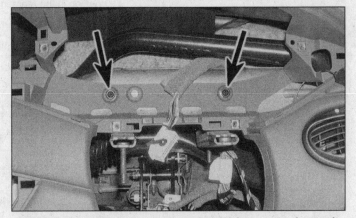

32.14 Remove the instrument panel mounting screws (arrows)

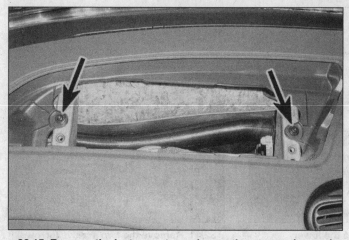

32.15 Remove the instrument panel mounting screws (arrows)

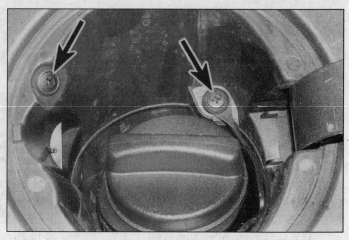

34.2 Remove the two retaining screws (arrows)

15   Unscrew the two screws from behind the passenger airbag **(see illustration)**.
16   Withdraw the instrument panel from the firewall, and out from the vehicle.

Installation

17   Installation is a reversal of the removal procedure. On completion, check the operation of all electrical components.

---

33   Fenderwell liner - removal and installation

Removal
Front
1   Apply the parking brake. If the wheel is to be removed (to improve access), loosen the wheel nuts. Jack up the front of the vehicle and support it on axle stands. Remove the front wheel.
2   Unscrew the screws securing the liner to the inner fenderwell panel.
3   Remove the screws securing the liner to the outer edge of the fenderwell and bumper. Withdraw the liner from under the vehicle.

Rear
4   Chock the front wheels, and engage 1st gear (or P). If the wheel is to be removed (to

improve access), loosen the wheel nuts. Jack up the rear of the vehicle and support it on axle stands. Remove the rear wheel.
5   Remove the screws securing the liner to the outer edge of the fenderwell and bumper.
6   Remove the clips securing the liner to the inner fenderwell, and withdraw the liner from under the vehicle.

Installation
7   Installation is a reversal of the removal procedure. If the wheels were removed, tighten the wheel nuts to the specified torque.

---

34   Fuel filler door and lock cylinder - removal and installation

Removal
Refer to illustrations 34.2 and 34.4
1   Remove the fuel filler neck as described in the relevant part of Chapter 4.
2   Remove the retaining screws in the plastic housing around the filler neck **(see illustration)**.
3   Carefully twist the filler door and plastic housing from the vehicle and pull it from the opening in the rear fender.

34.4 Use a screwdriver to release the locking tabs, then pull out the filler-door lock cylinder

4   If required, the filler door lock can be removed from the door - take care, as the door is made of plastic **(see illustration)**.

Installation
5   Installation is a reversal of removal.

Chapter 12
Chassis electrical system

Contents

Specifications

Fuses

Refer to the wiring diagrams at the end of this Chapter

Note: *Fuse and relay ratings, numbering, labeling and circuits are liable to change from year to year. Consult the owner's manual for your vehicle, or consult a dealer for the latest information.*

Torque specifications

Ft-lbs (unless otherwise indicated)

Note: *One foot-pound (ft-lb) of torque is equivalent to 12 inch-pounds (in-lbs) of torque. Torque values below approximately 15 ft-lbs are expressed in inch-pounds, since most foot-pound torque wrenches are not accurate at these smaller values.*

Horn unit mounting bracket bolt	108 in-lbs
Windshield wiper motor bolts	72 in-lbs
Wiper arm nuts:	
Front	18
Rear	15
Wiper lever nut on front wiper motor	15

---

1 General information

Warning: *Before carrying out any work on the electrical system, read through the precautions given in 'Safety first!' at the beginning of this manual.*

The electrical system is of 12-volt nega-tive ground type. Power for the lights and all electrical accessories is supplied by a lead-acid battery that is charged by the alternator.

This Chapter covers repair and service procedures for the various electrical compo-nents not associated with the engine. Infor-mation on the battery, alternator and starter motor can be found in Chapter 5A; the igni-tion system is covered in Chapter 5B.

All models are equipped with a driver's airbag, which is designed to prevent serious chest and head injuries to the driver during an accident. A similar bag for the front seat pas-senger is also available. The electronic control module for the airbag is located under the center console inside the vehicle. It contains two frontal impact sensors, a crash sensor, and a safety sensor. The crash sensor and safety sensor are connected in series, and if they both sense a deceleration in excess of a predetermined limit, the electronic airbag control module will operate the airbag. The airbag is inflated by a gas generator, which forces the bag out of the module cover in the center of the steering wheel. A coiled spring, that is able to 'wind-up' and 'unwind' as the steering wheel is turned, maintains the electronic contact at all times.

As an option, some models can be equipped with side airbags, which are built into the sides of the front seats. The intention of the side airbags is principally to offer greater passenger protection in a side impact. The side airbags are linked to the 'front' airbags, and are also controlled by the electronic control module under the center console, but are triggered by side-impact sensors located under the carpet and sill trims inside the vehicle.

All models are equipped with an ignition immobilizer, which is built into the key and ignition lock. An alarm system is an option. On vehicles with alarms, the horn is located on the left-hand side of the luggage compartment, or on Wagon models, it is on the right-hand side.

Some models are equipped with a headlight leveling system, which is controlled by a knob on the dash. On position 0, the headlights are in their base position, and on position 5, the headlights are in their maximum inclined angle.

It should be noted that, when portions of the electrical system are serviced, the negative battery cable should be disconnected, to prevent electrical shorts and fires. **Warning:** *When disconnecting the battery for work described in the following Sections, refer to Chapter 5A, Section 1.*

2 Electrical troubleshooting - general information

Note: *Refer to the precautions given in 'Safety first!' before starting work. The following tests relate to testing of the main electrical circuits, and should not be used to test delicate electronic circuits (such as engine management systems, anti-lock braking systems, etc), particularly where an electronic control module is used. Also refer to the precautions given in Chapter 5A, Section 1.*

General

1 A typical electrical circuit consists of an electrical component, any switches, relays, motors, fuses, fusible links or circuit breakers related to that component, and the wiring and connectors which link the component to both the battery and the chassis. To help to pinpoint a problem in an electrical circuit, wiring diagrams are included at the end of this Chapter.

2 Before attempting to diagnose an electrical fault, first study the appropriate wiring diagram, to obtain a complete understanding of the components included in the particular circuit concerned. The possible sources of a fault can be narrowed down by noting if other components related to the circuit are operating properly. If several components or circuits fail at one time, the problem is likely to be related to a shared fuse or ground connection.

3 Electrical problems usually stem from simple causes, such as loose or corroded connections, a faulty ground connection, a blown fuse, a melted fusible link, or a faulty relay (refer to Section 3 for details of testing relays). Visually inspect the condition of all fuses, wires and connections in a problem circuit before testing the components. Use the wiring diagrams to determine which terminal connections will need to be checked in order to pinpoint the trouble spot.

4 The basic tools required for electrical fault finding include a circuit tester or voltmeter (a 12-volt bulb with a set of test leads can also be used for certain tests); an ohmmeter (to measure resistance and check for continuity); a battery and set of test leads; and a jumper wire, preferably with a circuit breaker or fuse incorporated, which can be used to bypass suspect wires or electrical components. Before attempting to locate a problem with test instruments, use the wiring diagram to determine where to make the connections.

5 To find the source of an intermittent wiring fault (usually due to a poor or dirty connection, or damaged wiring insulation), a 'wiggle' test can be performed on the wiring. This involves wiggling the wiring by hand to see if the fault occurs as the wiring is moved. It should be possible to narrow down the source of the fault to a particular section of wiring. This method of testing can be used in conjunction with any of the tests described in the following sub-Sections.

6 Apart from problems due to poor connections, two basic types of fault can occur in an electrical circuit - open-circuit, or short-circuit.

7 Open-circuit faults are caused by a break somewhere in the circuit, which prevents current from flowing. An open-circuit fault will prevent a component from working.

8 Short-circuit faults are caused by a 'short' somewhere in the circuit, which allows the current flowing in the circuit to 'escape' along an alternative route, usually to ground. Short-circuit faults are normally caused by a breakdown in wiring insulation, which allows a feed wire to touch either another wire, or a grounded component such as the bodyshell. A short-circuit fault will normally cause the relevant circuit fuse to blow.

Finding an open-circuit

9 To check for an open-circuit, connect one lead of a circuit tester or the negative lead of a voltmeter either to the battery negative terminal or to a known good ground.

10 Connect the other lead to a connector in the circuit being tested, preferably nearest to the battery or fuse. At this point, battery voltage should be present, unless the cable from the battery or the fuse itself is faulty (bearing in mind that some circuits are live only when the ignition switch is moved to a particular position).

11 Switch on the circuit, then connect the tester lead to the connector nearest the circuit switch on the component side.

12 If voltage is present (indicated either by the tester bulb lighting or a voltmeter reading, as applicable), this means that the section of the circuit between the relevant connector and the switch is problem-free.

13 Continue to check the remainder of the circuit in the same fashion.

14 When a point is reached at which no voltage is present, the problem must lie between that point and the previous test point with voltage. Most problems can be traced to a broken, corroded or loose connection.

Finding a short-circuit

15 To check for a short-circuit, first disconnect the load(s) from the circuit (loads are the components which draw current from a circuit, such as bulbs, motors, heating elements, etc).

16 Remove the relevant fuse from the circuit, and connect a circuit tester or voltmeter to the fuse connections.

17 Switch on the circuit, bearing in mind that some circuits are live only when the ignition switch is moved to a particular position.

18 If voltage is present (indicated either by the tester bulb lighting or a voltmeter reading, as applicable), this means that there is a short-circuit.

19 If no voltage is present during this test, but the fuse still blows with the load(s) reconnected, this indicates an internal fault in the load(s).

Finding a ground fault

20 The battery negative terminal is connected to 'ground' - the metal of the engine/transmission unit and the vehicle body - and most systems are wired so that they only receive a positive feed, the current returning via the metal of the car body. This means that the component mounting and the body form part of that circuit.

21 Loose or corroded mountings can therefore cause a range of electrical faults, ranging from total failure of a circuit, to a puzzling partial failure. In particular, lights may shine dimly (especially when another circuit sharing the same ground point is in operation), motors (e.g., wiper motors or the radiator cooling fan motor) may run slowly, and the operation of one circuit may have an apparently unrelated effect on another.

22 Note that on many vehicles, ground straps are used between certain components, such as the engine/transmission and the body, usually where there is no metal-to-metal contact between components, due to

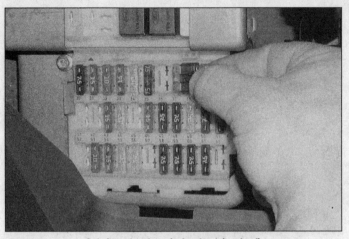

3.1 Interior fuse/relay box (typical)

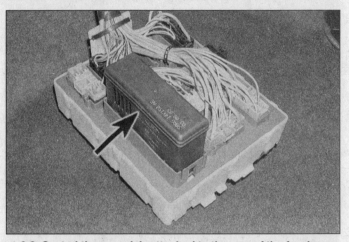

3.2 Central timer module attached to the rear of the fusebox

flexible rubber mounts, etc.

23   To check whether a component is properly grounded, disconnect the battery (refer to Chapter 5A, Section 1) and connect one lead of an ohmmeter to a known good ground point. Connect the other lead to the wire or ground connection being tested. The resistance reading should be zero; if not, check the connection as follows.

24   If an ground connection is thought to be faulty, disassemble the connection, and clean both the bodyshell and the wire terminal (or the component ground connection mating surface) back to bare metal. Be careful to remove all traces of dirt and corrosion, then use a knife to trim away any paint, so that a clean metal-to-metal joint is made.

25   On reassembly, tighten the joint fasteners securely; if a wire terminal is being installed, use serrated washers between the terminal and the bodyshell, to ensure a clean and secure connection.

26   When the connection is remade, prevent the onset of corrosion in the future by applying a coat of petroleum jelly or silicone-based grease, or by spraying on (at regular intervals) a proprietary water-dispersing lubricant.

3   Fuses, relays and timer module - testing and replacement

Refer to illustrations 3.1, 3.2, 3.3, 3.4 and 3.7
Note: *It is important to note that the ignition switch and the appropriate electrical circuit must always be switched off before any of the fuses (or relays) are removed and replaced. If electrical components/units have to be removed, the battery ground lead must be disconnected. When reconnecting the battery, reference should be made to Chapter 5A.*

1   Fuses are designed to break a circuit when a predetermined current is reached, in order to protect components and wiring which could be damaged by excessive current flow. Any excessive current flow will be due to a fault in the circuit, usually a short-circuit (see Section 2). The main central fusebox, which also carries some relays, is located inside the vehicle behind a small removable cover at the left end of the instrument panel, below and to the left of the steering column **(see illustration)**.

2   A central timer module (CTM) is located in the back of the main central fusebox **(see illustration)**. This module contains the time

control elements for the heated rear window, interior lights and intermittent wiper operation (front and rear). The module also activates a warning buzzer/chime when the vehicle is left with the lights switched on, or if a vehicle equipped with automatic transmission is not parked with the selector in position P.

3   The auxiliary fusebox is located in the engine compartment **(see illustration)**, against the firewall next to the air cleaner, and is accessed by unclipping and removing the cover. The auxiliary fusebox also contains some relays.

4   Each circuit is identified by numbers on the main fusebox and on the inside of the auxiliary fusebox cover. Reference to the wiring diagrams at the end of this Chapter will indicate the circuits protected by each fuse. The best way to check the fuses is with a test light. Check for power at the exposed terminal tips of each fuse. If power is present at one side of the fuse but not the other, the fuse is blown. A blown fuse can also be identified by visually inspecting it **(see illustration)**. Plastic tweezers are attached to the auxiliary fusebox to remove and install the fuses. To remove a fuse, use the tweezers provided to pull it out of the holder, then slide the fuse sideways from the tweezers.

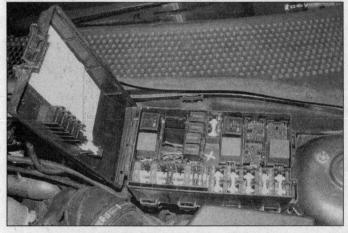

3.3 Auxiliary fusebox under the hood

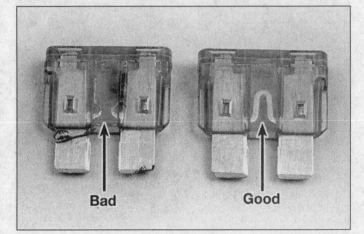

Bad   Good

3.4 When a fuse blows, the element between the terminals melts

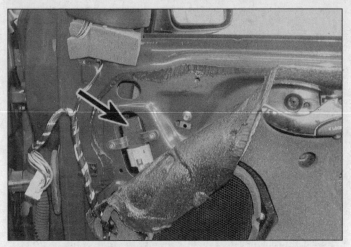

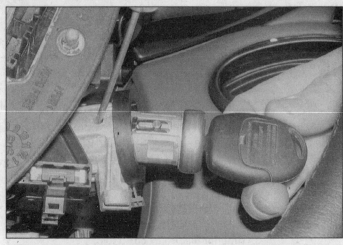

3.7 'One touch down' window relay in the driver's door

4.2 Depress the locking plunger and withdraw the lock

5   Always replace a fuse with one of an identical rating. Never substitute a fuse of a higher rating, or make temporary repairs using wire or metal foil; more serious damage, or even fire, could result. The fuse rating is stamped on top of the fuse. Never replace a fuse more than once without tracing the source of the trouble.

6   Note that if the vehicle is to be stored for a long period, there is a 'battery saver' relay installed in the central fusebox to prevent the electrical components from discharging the battery.

7   Relays are electrically-operated switches, which are used in certain circuits. The various relays can be removed from their respective locations by carefully pulling them from the sockets. Some of the relays in the fuse boxes have a plastic bar on its upper surface to enable the use of the tweezers. The locations and functions of the various relays are given in the specifications **(see illustration)**.

8   If a component controlled by a relay becomes inoperative and the relay is suspect, listen to the relay as the circuit is operated. If the relay is functioning, it should be possible

to hear it click as it is energized. If the relay proves satisfactory, the fault lies with the components or wiring of the system. If the relay is not being energized, then either the relay is not receiving a switching voltage, or the relay itself is faulty. (Do not overlook the relay socket terminals when tracing faults.) Testing is by the substitution of a known good unit, but be careful; while some relays are identical in appearance and in operation, others look similar, but perform different functions.

---

4   Switches - removal and installation

Warning: *Always disable the airbag system before working in the vicinity of any airbag system components (see the Warning in Section 25, Step 1).*

Removal

Ignition switch and lock barrel
Refer to illustrations 4.2, 4.3a, 4.3b, 4.4a and 4.4b

1   Remove the steering wheel covers and

the lower dash panel (see Chapter 10).

2   Insert the ignition key, and turn it to the accessory position. Using a small screwdriver or twist drill through the hole in the side of the lock housing, depress the locking plunger and withdraw the lock barrel **(see illustration)**.

3   The switch which is on the opposite side of the steering column, may be removed by disconnecting the. multi-plug, then use a screwdriver to release the switch retaining tabs at the top and bottom **(see illustrations)**.

4   On models with the PATS ('Safeguard') immobilizer, remove the immobilizer transceiver from around the lock barrel by disconnecting the wiring plug and removing the securing screw **(see illustrations)**.

Direction indicator and windshield wiper multi-function switches
Refer to illustrations 4.5 and 4.6

5   Release the steering column upper shroud from the lower shroud by inserting a thin screwdriver into a hole at each side of the column. Lift the upper shroud from the column and unclip from the bottom of the

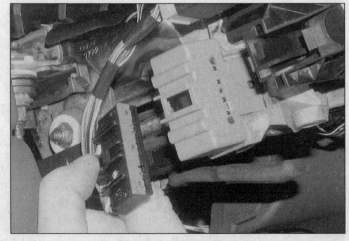

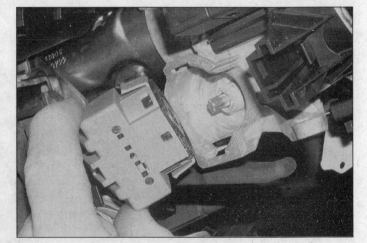

4.3a Disconnect the multi-plug . . .

4.3b . . . and unclip the switch

4.4a Disconnect the wiring connector . . .

4.4b . . . and unscrew this screw (arrow) to remove

4.5 Unclipping the upper shroud

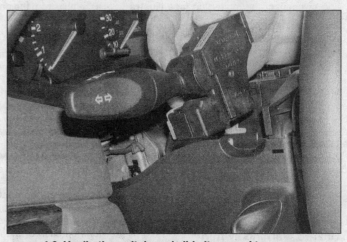

4.6 Unclip the switch, and slide it upward to remove

4.8 Remove the bezel retaining screw

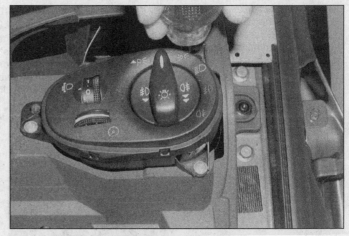

4.9 Remove the three switch mounting screws

instrument panel **(see illustration)**.

6   Depress the plastic tab at the top of the switch with a screwdriver. Lift the switch assembly from the steering column, disconnecting the switch multi-plug on removal **(see illustration)**.

Main light, auxiliary foglight and rear foglight combination switch

Refer to illustrations 4.8, 4.9 and 4.10

7   Remove the four retaining screws and pry out the one securing clip, to remove the driver's side lower dash panel.

8   Remove the retaining screw from the bottom of the light switch bezel/air vent and unclip from the dash **(see illustration)**.

9   Unscrew the three mounting screws from the switch unit **(see illustration)**.

10   Withdraw the switch from the dash panel

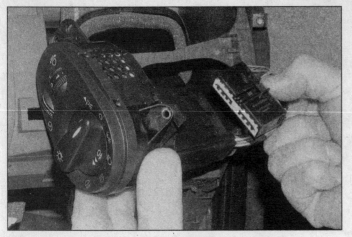

4.10 Disconnect the multi-plug on removal

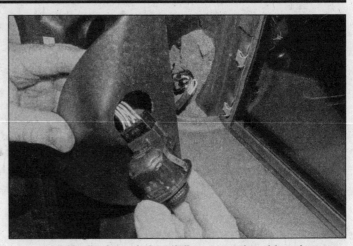

4.14 Unclip the switch and disconnect the wiring plug

and disconnect the multi-plug **(see illustration)**.

Instrument light rheostat

11   Carry out the procedures as described in Steps 7 to 10.

Headlight aim adjustment control

12   Carry out the procedures as described in Steps 7 to 10.

Door mirror control switch

Refer to illustration 4.14

13   Carefully pry the mirror bezel from the doorframe.

14   Disconnect the multi-plug and withdraw the switch from the bezel **(see illustration)**.

Hazard warning switch

Refer to illustration 4.16

15   Remove the radio/cassette player as described in Section 21.

16   Remove the four securing screws from inside the radio/cassette player opening **(see illustration)**, then carefully unclip the heater control panel from its three retaining clips in the dash.

17   Remove the retaining screws from the rear of the switch, withdraw the switch

assembly from the panel, then disconnect the multi-plug.

Horn switch

Warning: *Before carrying out any work on airbags, read through the precautions given in Section 25.*

18   Remove the airbag unit from the steering wheel as described in Section 25.

19   Disconnect the wiring connectors from the contact plate, releasing the locking tangs to remove.

20   Carefully lift out the four wedges, located in the pegs for the contact plate under the airbag.

21   Lift the contact plate off the locating pegs and remove from the airbag unit. **Note:** *There are four springs under the contact plate (one on each of the locating pegs). Note the position of the four springs before installing the contact plate.*

Radio remote control switch

Refer to illustration 4.23

22   Some models have optional radio control switches on the steering column. Release the upper shroud from the lower shroud, by inserting a thin screwdriver into a hole at each side of the column. Lift the upper shroud from

the column and unclip from the bottom of the instrument panel.

23   Depress the retaining lug at the rear of the radio switch and withdraw it from the lower shroud **(see illustration)**, then disconnect the wiring connector.

Cruise control switches

24   Refer to Section 19.

Electrically-operated window switches

Refer to illustrations 4.25 and 4.26

25   Carefully pry out the plastic screw cover from the inner door handle cavity, using a small screwdriver. Remove the screw, and ease the bezel from around the door handle **(see illustration)**.

26   Depress the retaining lug and unclip the window operating switches from the bezel **(see illustration)**, disconnect the wiring connector.

Electrically-operated sunroof switch

27   Pry out the switch with a screwdriver, using a cloth pad to prevent damage to the trim.

28   Disconnect the multi-plug and remove the switch.

4.16 Remove the four retaining screws

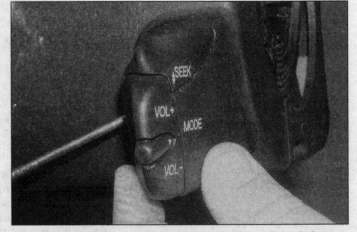

4.23 Use a thin screw driver to unclip the radio switch

4.25 Unscrew the screw and remove the bezel

4.26 Unclip the switch from the bezel

Parking brake-On warning switch

Refer to illustration 4.30

29   Remove the center console as described in Chapter 11.

30   Disconnect the wiring connector and remove the securing screw to remove the switch from the parking brake lever mounting bracket **(see illustration)**.

Overdrive mode switch (automatic transmission models)

31   The overdrive switch is located on the gear selector lever, for further information (refer to Chapter 7B).

Heated windshield and rear window switch

Refer to illustration 4.35

32   Remove the radio/cassette player as described in Section 21.

33   Remove the four securing screws from inside the radio/cassette player opening, then carefully unclip the heater control panel from its three retaining clips in the dash.

34   Disconnect the wiring connectors from the switches as the control panel is being removed.

35   Remove the securing screws from the rear of the panel, and withdraw the switch assembly **(see illustration)**.

Seat height adjustment switch

Refer to illustration 4.37

36   Push the switch out from the trim, at the bottom of the seat cushion on the front seats.

37   Disconnect the multi-plug to disengage the switch **(see illustration)**.

Heated front seat switch

38   Remove the center console as described in Chapter 11.

39   Disconnect the electrical connector from the switch, then press the switch out from the console.

Traction control system (TCS) switch

40   Remove the center console as described in Chapter 11.

41   Disconnect the electrical connector from the switch, then press the switch out from the console.

4.30 Disconnect the wiring terminal and remove the screw

Courtesy light door switch

Refer to illustration 4.43

42   Open the door, then using a pencil, mark the position of the door striker/contact switch on the pillar.

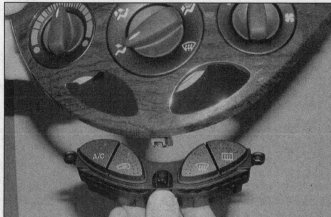

4.35 Switches come off as a complete assembly

4.37 Release the tang to disengage the multi-plug

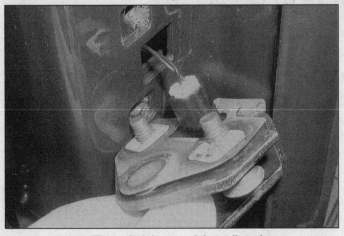

4.43 The switch is part of the striker plate

4.47 Press out the trunk switch

43   Unscrew the two securing screws to remove the striker/contact switch, then disconnect the electrical connector **(see illustration)**.

Trunk/liftgate opening switch

Refer to illustration 4.47

44   Lower the steering column locking lever and release the retaining clips with a thin-bladed screwdriver to remove the steering column upper shroud (Chapter 10).

45   Remove the upper retaining screws from the instrument panel surround, then unclip it from the dash.

46   As the surround is withdrawn, remove the electrical connector from the luggage compartment release switch and trip computer (if equipped).

47   Press the switch out from the surround **(see illustration)**.

Trunk light switch

48   Removing the switch will entail removing the lock components to gain access to the switch and its wiring plug - refer to the relevant Sections of Chapter 11 for lock removal details.

49   The switch is part of the lock assembly,

and at the time of writing could not be purchased separately.

Fuel cut-off switch

Refer to illustration 4.50

50   The switch is located behind the driver's side kick panel/lower A-pillar trim **(see illustration)**. Refer to Chapter 4A.

Air conditioning and air recirculation switch

51   Remove the radio/cassette player as described in Section 21.

52   Remove the four securing screws from inside the radio/cassette player opening, then carefully unclip the heater control panel from its three retaining clips in the dash.

53   Disconnect the wiring connectors from the switches as the control panel is being removed.

54   Remove the securing screws from the rear of the panel, and withdraw the switch assembly **(see illustration 4.35)**.

Installation

55   Installation of all switches is a reversal of the removal procedure.

5   Bulbs (exterior lights) - replacement

1   Whenever a bulb is replaced, note the following points:

a)   *Switch off all exterior lights.*

b)   *Remember that if the light has just been in use, the bulb may be extremely hot.*

c)   *Always check the bulb contacts and holder, ensuring that there is clean metal-to-metal contact between the bulb and its connections. Clean off any corrosion or dirt before installing a new bulb.*

d)   *Wherever bayonet-type bulbs are installed, ensure that the contact(s) bear firmly against the bulb terminals.*

e)   *Always ensure that the new bulb is of the correct rating and that it is completely clean before installing it; this applies particularly to headlight/foglight bulbs.*

f)   *Do not touch the glass of halogen-type bulbs (headlights, front foglights) with your fingers, as this may lead to rapid blackening and failure of the new bulb; if the glass is accidentally touched, clean it with rubbing alcohol.*

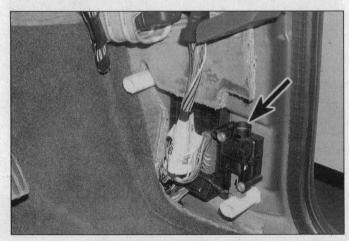

4.50 Fuel cut-off switch (arrow)

5.2 Unclip the headlight rear cover

5.3 Disconnect the wiring plug from the bulb

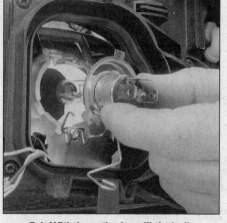

5.4 Withdraw the headlight bulb

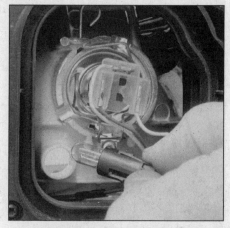

5.7 Withdraw the sidelight bulb

g) If replacing the bulb does not cure the problem, check the relevant fuse and relay with reference to the Specifications, and to the wiring diagrams at the end of this Chapter.

Headlight

Refer to illustrations 5.2, 5.3 and 5.4

Caution: *Halogen gas-filled bulbs are under pressure and may shatter if the surface is scratched or the bulb is dropped. Wear eye protection and handle the bulbs carefully, grasping only the base. Do not touch the surface of the bulb with your fingers because the oil from your skin could cause it to overheat and fail prematurely. If you do touch the bulb surface, clean it with rubbing alcohol.*

2   At the rear of the headlight unit, release the clip and remove the cover for access to the bulb **(see illustration)**.

3   Disconnect the wiring plug from the rear of the bulb **(see illustration)**.

4   Release the wire clip securing the bulb, and remove the bulb. Note how the tabs fit in the slots on the rear of the headlight **(see illustration)**.

5   Install the new bulb using a reversal of the removal procedure. Have the headlight beam alignment checked as described later in this Chapter. **Note:** *The park light bulb is also in the headlight housing, and is replaced in the same manner as the headlight bulbs.*

Front sidelight

Refer to illustration 5.7

Note: *On most models the sidelight is mounted in the front fender. Reach behind the fender to remove the bulbholder for bulb access. On later models, the sidelights are located in the bumper cover (at the sides). Remove the bulbholder from below.*

6   At the rear of the headlight unit, release the clip and remove the cover for access to the bulb.

7   Pull the bulbholder out from the rear of the headlight unit **(see illustration)**. Pull the wedge-type bulb from the bulbholder.

8   Install the new bulb using a reversal of the removal procedure.

Front turn signal

Refer to illustrations 5.9, 5.11 and 5.13

Note: *On some models, the front turn signal is in the grille. Open the hood and reach behind the grille to remove the bulbholder from the back of the turn signal. On later models, the turn signal and park light bulbs are accessed at the back of the headlight housing.*

9   Remove the screw located in the front direction indicator unit **(see illustration)**.

10   Withdraw the front direction indicator light unit from the bumper assembly.

11   Rotate the bulbholder counterclockwise,

5.9 Remove the light unit retaining screw

and withdraw it from the light unit **(see illustration)**.

12   Twist the bulb counterclockwise, and remove it from the bulbholder.

13   Install the new bulb using a reversal of the removal procedure, but before installing the retaining screw, make sure the light unit is located correctly **(see illustration)**.

5.11 Removing the bulbholder from the light unit

5.13 Locate the peg on the light unit (arrow)

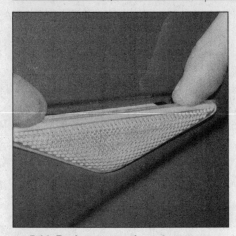

5.14 Push repeater down to remove

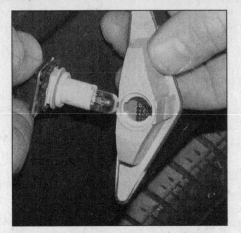

5.15 Remove the bulbholder from the repeater

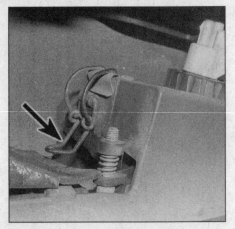

5.18a Unclip the spring clip (arrow) . . .

Direction indicator side repeaters

Refer to illustrations 5.14 and 5.15

14   Slide the side repeater assembly downwards, and remove it from the front fender **(see illustration)**.

15   Turn the bulbholder counterclockwise, and disconnect it from the repeater unit **(see illustration)**.

16   Pull the wedge-type bulb from the holder.

17   Install the new bulb using a reversal of the removal procedure.

Front foglight

Refer to illustrations 5.18a, 5.18b, 5.19 and 5.20

18   Remove the bolts and pushpins to remove the splash shield apron under the front bumper cover. Release the retaining spring from the rear of the foglight unit and disconnect the wiring connector **(see illustrations)**.

19   Twist off the rear cover from the light unit, and disconnect the wiring terminal **(see illustration)**.

20   Release the wire clip, and take out the bulb, noting how it's installed **(see illustration)**.

21   Install the new bulb using a reversal of the

5.18b . . . and disconnect the wiring connector

removal procedure. An adjustment screw is located at the bottom corner of the light unit.

Rear foglight/back-up light (Hatchback)

Refer to illustration 5.23

Note: *This optional light is not installed on*

5.19 Disconnect the terminal from the bulb

most models. On later models, the backup lights are located in the rear light unit (see Step 26).

22   To remove the rear light unit push down the clip at the rear of the light unit, and withdraw from the bumper.

23   Turn the bulbholder counterclockwise to remove from the light unit **(see illustration)**.

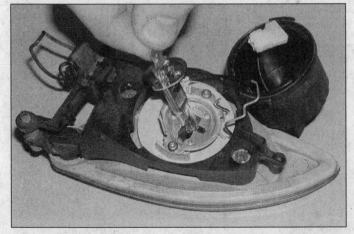

5.20 Release the clip and withdraw the foglight bulb

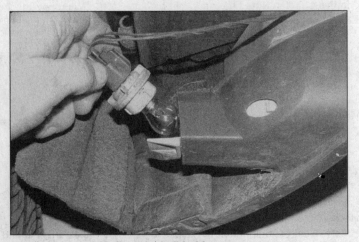

5.23 Turn the bulbholder to remove

5.26a Remove the rear light retaining screw . . .

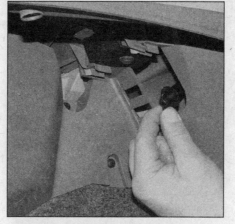

5.26b . . . and the plastic retaining nut inside the luggage compartment

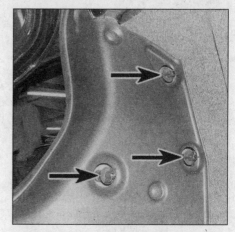

5.27 Unscrew the three plastic retaining nuts (arrows)

24   Depress and twist the bulb counter-clockwise to remove it from the bulbholder.

25   Install the new bulb using a reversal of the removal procedure. Make sure that the light unit is located correctly.

Rear light cluster

Refer to illustrations 5.26a, 5.26b, 5.27, 5.28, 5.30, 5.31 and 5.32

26   On Hatchback models, open the liftgate. Remove the securing nut from the inside of the light cluster, and the securing screw, on the outside of the light cluster **(see illustrations)**.

27   On Sedan models, open the luggage compartment. Remove the three turn-fasteners from the rear light cluster **(see illustration)**.

28   On Wagon models, open the liftgate. Undo the two securing screws from the side of the light cluster and unclip the light unit outwards to remove **(see illustration)**.

29   Carefully remove the light cluster from the vehicle.

30   On Wagon and Sedan models, lift the retaining clips to separate the bulbholder from the light cluster **(see illustration)**.

31   On Hatchback models, twist the appro-priate bulbholder counterclockwise and pull it

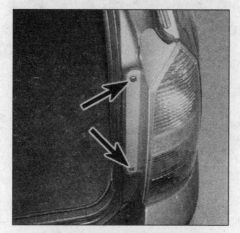

5.28 Remove the two retaining screws (arrows)

out from the light cluster **(see illustration)**.

32   Depress and twist the appropriate bulb counterclockwise to remove it from the bulb-holder **(see illustration)**.

33   Install the new bulb using a reversal of the removal procedure. Make sure that the rear light cluster is located correctly.

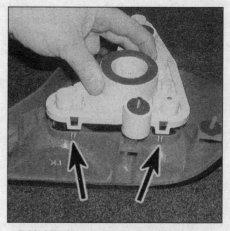

5.30 Lift the retaining clips (arrows) to release the bulbholder

License plate light

Refer to illustrations 5.34 and 5.35

34   Insert a flat-bladed screwdriver in the recess on the left of the license plate light, and carefully pry out the light unit **(see illus-tration)**.

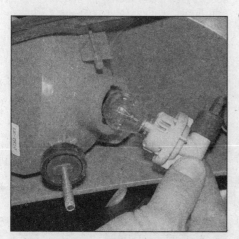

5.31 Twist the bulbholder to release it from the light unit

5.32 Push in and twist the bulb counterclockwise to remove it

5.34 Pry out the license plate light unit

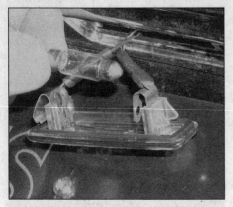

5.35 Withdraw the bulb from the license plate light

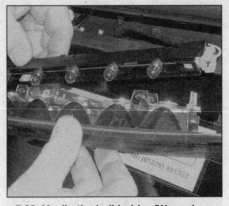

5.39 Unclip the bulbholder (Wagon) . . .

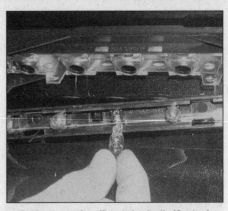

5.40 . . . and pull out the bulb (Sedan)

35   Release the bulb from the contact springs (see illustration).
36   Install the new bulb using a reversal of the removal procedure. Make sure that the tension of the contact springs is sufficient to hold the bulb firmly.

High-level brake-light

Refer to illustrations 5.39 and 5.40

37   On Hatchback and Wagon models, unscrew the two securing screws and remove the light cover.
38   On Sedan models, open the luggage compartment and remove the carpet trim from behind the light unit.
39   Unclip the bulbholder from the reflector (see illustration).
40   Pull out the relevant wedge-type bulb from the holder (see illustration).
41   Fit the new bulb, and install the light unit using a reversal of the removal procedure.

---

6   Bulbs (interior lights) - replacement

1   Whenever a bulb is replaced, note the following points:

a) *Make sure the light is turned off. Also, when working near airbag system components, disable the airbag system (see the Warning in Section 25, Step 1).*

6.2a Pry out the front interior light to remove it

b) *Remember that if the light has just been in use, the bulb may be extremely hot.*
c) *Always check the bulb contacts and holder, ensuring that there is clean metal-to-metal contact between the bulb and its hot and ground connections. Clean off any corrosion or dirt before installing a new bulb.*
d) *Wherever bayonet-type bulbs are installed, ensure that the contact(s) bear firmly against the bulb terminals of the connector.*
e) *Always ensure that the new bulb is of the correct rating and that it is completely clean before installing it.*

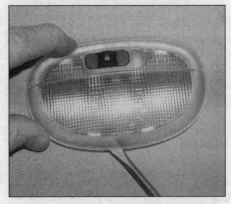

6.2b The rear interior light is also removed by prying

Interior/map reading lights

Refer to illustrations 6.2a, 6.2b, 6.3a, 6.3b, 6.3c and 6.4

2   Ensure that the interior light is switched off by locating the switch in its correct position. Using a small screwdriver, carefully pry out the light assembly at the side opposite the switch (see illustrations).
3   Disconnect the wiring connector, then lift up and unclip the reflector from the light unit. Release the bulb from the contact springs (see illustrations).
4   If map reading lights are installed, bulbholders are installed each side of the reflec-

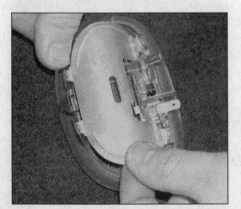

6.3a Unclip the reflector from the rear interior light . . .

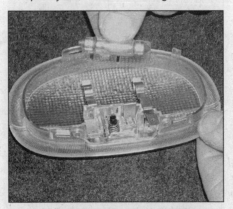

6.3b . . . and remove the bulb

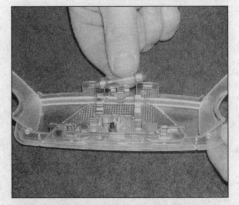

6.3c Removing the bulb from the front interior light

6.4 Remove the bayonet fitting bulb from the map reading light

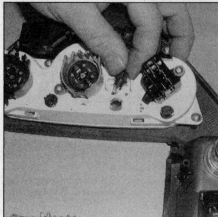

6.15 Turn the bulbholder to remove

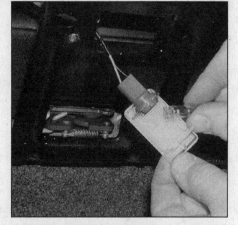

6.17 Pull the bulb straight out to remove it

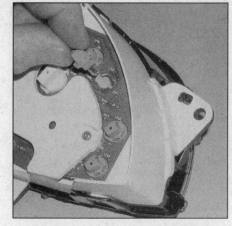

6.7 Turn the bulbholder to remove

tor. Remove the bayonet installed on bulbs by twisting them out of their holders **(see illustration)**.

5   Install the new bulbs using a reversal of the removal procedure. Make sure that the tension of the contact springs is sufficient to hold the bulbs firmly.

Instrument cluster illumination and warning lights

Refer to illustration 6.7

6   Remove the instrument cluster as described in Section 10.

7   Twist the bulbholder counterclockwise to remove it **(see illustration)**.

8   Install the new bulbholder using a reversal of the removal procedure.

Hazard warning light

9   Remove the switch as described in Section 4.

Main headlight/foglight switch illumination

10   Remove the light switch as described in Section 4.

Automatic transmission selector panel illumination

11   Pry out the panel from around the selector lever on the center console.

12   Disconnect the bulbholder and pull out the wedge-type bulb.

13   Install the new bulb using a reversal of the removal procedure.

Clock illumination

Note: *On later models, the clock illumination bulb is not readily replaceable. The clock may have to be removed and taken to a dealer or automotive electrician for bulb replacement.*

14   Remove the clock as described in Section 12.

Heater control/fan switch illumination

Refer to illustration 6.15

15   Remove the heater control panel as described in Chapter 3. To remove the bulb from the rear of the panel twist the bulbholder and pull out **(see illustration)**.

Luggage compartment light

Refer to illustration 6.17

16   With the light switched off (the battery negative cable disconnected), pry out the light using a small screwdriver.

17   Pull the wedge type bulb straight out to remove it **(see illustration)**.

18   Install the new bulb using a reversal of the removal procedure.

Cigar lighter illumination

Refer to illustrations 6.20a and 6.20b

19   Remove the heater control panel as described in Chapter 3.

20   Unclip the bulbholder from the rear of the cigar lighter, and pull out the bulb **(see illustrations)**.

21   Install the new bulb using a reversal of the removal procedure.

6.20a Unclip the bulbholder . . .

6.20b . . . and remove the bulb

7.3 Unscrew the lower headlamp mounting bolt (arrow)

7.6a Unscrew the upper mounting bolts . . .

7.6b . . . and remove the headlamp, disconnecting the wiring

7 Exterior light units - removal and installation

Note: *The headlight housing is an expensive component to replace. If one of the mounting tabs on the housing is broken, the housing can be repaired (rather than replaced) with a kit available at your dealer parts department.*

1 Before removing any light unit, note the following points:

a) *Ensure that the light is switched off.*
b) *Remember that if the light has just been in use, the bulb and lens may be extremely hot.*

Headlight unit

Refer to illustrations 7.3, 7.6a and 7.6b

2 Apply the parking brake, jack up the front of the vehicle and support it on axle stands.
3 From under the vehicle (with one screw from the plastic fendershield removed and the plastic pulled back for access), remove the headlamp bottom securing bolt **(see illustration)**. On later models, remove the air cleaner housing in the fenderwell to access the back of the left headlight housing. Remove the lower radiator splash apron to access the lower headlight housing bolt.

4 Lower the vehicle and, with the hood supported in its open position, remove the radiator grille as described in Chapter 11.
5 Disconnect the wiring multi-plug for the headlight unit.
6 Unscrew the mounting bolts from the top of the headlight unit, and withdraw the unit from the front of the vehicle **(see illustrations)**.
7 Installation is a reversal of removal. Have the headlight alignment checked as described in the next Section.

Front direction indicator

8 Remove the screw located in the front direction indicator unit.
9 Withdraw the front direction indicator light unit from the bumper assembly.
10 Rotate the bulbholder counterclockwise, and withdraw it from the light unit. Alternatively, the wiring plug can be disconnected from the bulbholder, leaving the bulb in position. Remove the light unit (for illustrations, see bulb replacement in Section 5).
11 Installation is a reversal of removal.

Direction indicator side repeaters

12 Slide the side repeater assembly downwards, and remove it from the front fender **(see illustration 5.14).**

13 Turn the bulbholder counterclockwise, and disconnect it from the repeater unit **(see illustration 5.15).**
14 Install the new repeater using a reversal of the removal procedure.

Front foglight

Refer to illustrations 7.15 and 7.16

15 Working behind the front bumper, release the retaining clip from the rear of the foglight unit, and remove the foglight unit **(see illustration)**.
16 Twist off the rear cover from the light unit, and disconnect the wiring connector **(see illustration)**.
17 Release the wire clip, and take out the bulb.
18 Installation is a reversal of the removal procedure. An adjustment screw is located at the bottom corner of the light unit.

Rear foglight/back-up light (Hatchback)

Refer to illustrations 7.19a and 7.19b

Note: *The rear fog light is not installed on all models.*

19 Push the clip up under the rear of the light unit, then press the light unit out from the bumper **(see illustrations)**.

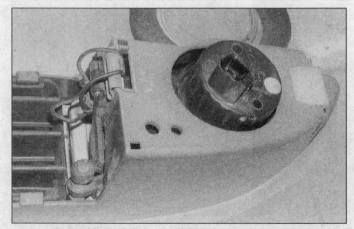

7.15 Retaining clip located at the rear of the bumper

7.16 Disconnect the wiring from the foglight

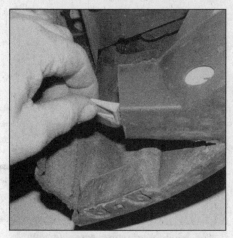

7.19a Unclip the rear light unit . . .

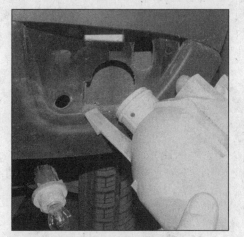

7.19b . . . and remove from the rear bumper

7.29 Unclip the license plate light

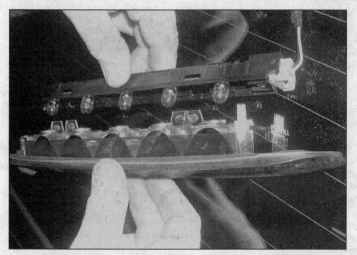

7.34 Unclip the bulbholder from the reflector (Wagon)

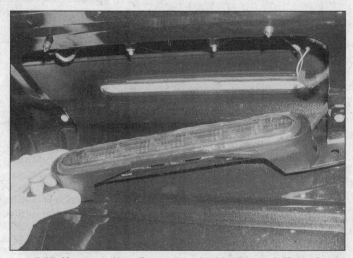

7.35 Unscrew the reflector from inside the trunk (Sedan)

20   Disconnect the wiring connector. Turn the bulbholder counterclockwise to remove from the light unit.

21   Install the new light unit using a reversal of the removal procedure. Make sure that the light unit is located correctly.

Rear light cluster

22   On Hatchback models, with the liftgate open, remove the securing nut from the inside of the light cluster, and the securing screw on the outside of the light cluster (see illustrations 5.26a and 5.26b).

23   On Sedan models, from inside the luggage compartment, remove the three turn-fasteners from the rear of the light cluster (see illustration 5.27).

24   On Wagon models, with the liftgate open, remove the two securing screws from the side of the light cluster (see illustration 5.28).

25   Carefully remove the light cluster from the vehicle.

26   On Wagon and Sedan models, lift the retaining clips to separate the bulbholder from the light cluster (see illustration 5.30).

27   On Hatchback models, twist the bulb-holders counterclockwise and pull out from the light cluster (see illustration 5.31).

28   Install the new light cluster unit using a reversal of the removal procedure. Make sure that the rear light cluster is located correctly.

License plate light assembly

Refer to illustration 7.29

29   Insert a flat-bladed screwdriver in the recess on the left of the license plate light, and carefully pry out the light unit (see illustration).

30   Release the bulb from the contact springs.

31   Install the new light unit using a reversal of the removal procedure.

High-level brake-light

Refer to illustrations 7.34 and 7.35

32   On Hatchback and Wagon models, unscrew the two securing screws and remove the light cover.

33   On Sedan models, open the luggage compartment and remove the carpet trim from behind the light unit.

34   Unclip the bulbholder from the reflector and disconnect the wiring (see illustration).

35   On Sedan models, unscrew the securing screws inside the trunk lid from the light unit and remove it from the vehicle (see illustration).

36   Install the new light unit using a reversal of the removal procedure.

---

8   Headlight and front foglight beam alignment - checking and adjustment

---

Refer to illustrations 8.3 and 8.4

1   Accurate adjustment of the headlight or front foglight beams is only possible using optical beam-setting equipment. This work should therefore be carried out by a service station with the necessary facilities.

2   Temporary adjustment can be made after replacement of a bulb or light unit, or as an emergency measure if the alignment is incorrect following accident damage.

3   To adjust the headlight aim, turn the adjustment screws on the top of the headlight

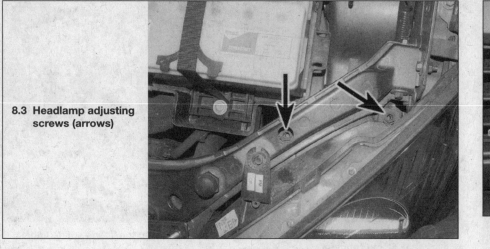

8.3 Headlamp adjusting screws (arrows)

8.4 Foglight adjusting screw (arrow)

unit to make the adjustment **(see illustration)**. (One of the screws is for vertical alignment, and the other one is for horizontal alignment.) **Note:** *On most models (without headlight leveling motors) the horizontal aim of the headlights is not adjustable.*

4   Adjustment of the front foglight beam is carried out using the small screw visible at the bottom corner of the surround trim **(see illustration)**.

5   Before making any adjustments to the settings, it is important that the tire pressures are correct, and that the vehicle is standing on level ground with no additional load in the vehicle.

6   Bounce the front of the vehicle a few times to settle the suspension. Ideally, somebody of average size should sit in the driver's seat during the adjustment, and the vehicle should have half a tank of fuel.

7   If the vehicle is equipped with a headlight beam leveling system, set the switch to the 0 position before making any adjustments.

8   Whenever temporary adjustments are made, the settings must be checked and if necessary reset by a qualified shop as soon as possible.

9   Headlight leveling motor - removal and installation

Note: *Not all models are equipped with headlight leveling motors.*

Removal
Refer to illustrations 9.3, 9.4 and 9.5

1   Make sure the beam adjustment switch is in the 0 position.

2   Remove the headlight unit as described in Section 7.

3   Unscrew and remove the securing screws from the cover on the rear of the headlight unit **(see illustration)**.

4   Turn the headlight leveling motor from its bayonet fitting, then unclip the motor spindle balljoint from its socket and pull out from the headlight reflector **(see illustration)**.

5   Disconnect the wiring multi-plug from the motor as it is removed from the headlight unit **(see illustration)**.

Installation
Refer to illustration 9.6

6   Installation is a reversal of the removal procedure, noting the following points:

9.3 Remove the rear headlamp cover

a) *Make sure the beam adjustment switch is still in the 0 position.*

b) *Check that the adjuster balljoint engages in its socket correctly **(see illustration)**.*

c) *On completion, test the operation of the system, and have the beam alignment checked as described in Section 8.*

9.4 Turn the motor to withdraw it from the headlamp

9.5 Disconnect the motor wiring plug

9.6 Recess to locate the balljoint

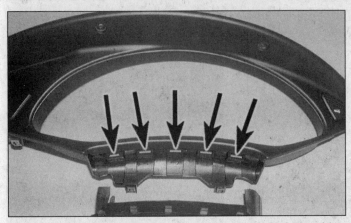

10.3a The upper steering shroud clips into the slots (arrows) in the instrument cluster bezel

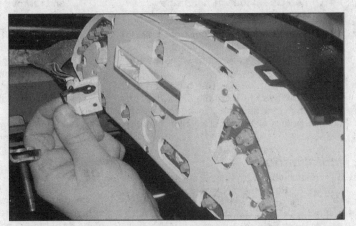

10.3b Unclip the instrument cluster bezel

10.5 The instrument cluster is secured by four screws (arrows)

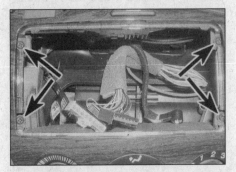

10.6 Disconnecting the multi-plug from the instrument cluster

10 Instrument cluster - removal and installation

Warning 1: *The instrument cluster must be kept in the upright position, to avoid silicone liquid leaking from the gauges.*
Warning 2: *Always disable the airbag system before working in the vicinity of any airbag system components (see the Warnings in Section 25).*

Removal

Refer to illustrations 10.3a, 10.3b, 10.5 and 10.6

1   Disconnect the negative battery cable (see Chapter 5).
2   Lower the steering column locking lever and release the retaining clips with a thin-bladed screwdriver to remove the steering column upper shroud (Chapter 10). On 2005 models, refer to Chapter 11 and remove the under-dash panel to access one bolt securing the bottom of the cluster bezel.
3   Remove the upper retaining screws from the instrument cluster bezel, then unclip it from the dash **(see illustrations)**.
4   As the surround is withdrawn, remove the electrical connector from the luggage compartment release switch and trip computer (where equipped).

5   Unscrew the four mounting screws from the instrument cluster assembly **(see illustration)**.
6   Disconnect the multi-plug(s) from the rear of the instrument cluster, as it is withdrawn from the dash **(see illustration)**.

Installation

7   Installation is a reversal of the removal procedure.

11 Instrument cluster components - removal and installation

Warning: *The instrument panel must be kept in the upright position, to avoid silicone liquid leaking from the gauges.*

The instrument panel should not be stripped, as no components were available at the time of writing. In the event of a faulty gauge, remove the instrument cluster as described in Section 10, and take it to a dealer for diagnosis. If a warning light or an illumination bulb has failed, remove the bulb-holder by twisting it counterclockwise and pulling it out from the instrument cluster. The wedge type bulb can then be pulled out from the holder.

12 Clock - removal and installation

Removal

Refer to illustration 12.3

1   Disconnect the negative battery cable (see Chapter 5).
2   Remove the radio/cassette player as described in Section 21. Pull out and remove the ashtray.
3   Remove the four securing screws from inside the radio/cassette player opening, then carefully unclip the heater control panel from its three retaining clips in the dash **(see illustration)**.

12.3 Unscrew these four screws (arrows) to remove the panel

13.2a The horns are located behind the bumper on the left-hand side

13.2b Disconnect the wiring connector and remove the bolt (arrow)

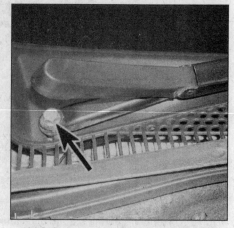

14.3 Loosen the wiper arm retaining nut (arrow)

4   Disconnect the multi-plugs from the rear of the control panel (where required). Remove the two retaining screws and withdraw the clock.

5   On some models, the bulb can be removed by twisting it counterclockwise; on others, the clock should be taken to a dealer or automotive electrical specialist for bulb replacement.

Installation

6   Installation is a reversal of the removal procedure. Reset the clock on completion.

---

13 Horn - removal and installation

Removal

Refer to illustrations 13.2a and 13.2b
Note: *On most models there are two horns.*

1   Apply the parking brake, jack up the front of the vehicle and support it on axle stands.

2   Disconnect the electrical connector(s) from the horn terminal **(see illustrations)**.

3   Unscrew the mounting bolt(s), and withdraw the horn with its mounting bracket from under the vehicle .

Installation

4   Installation is a reversal of the removal procedure. Tighten the horn unit mounting bolt to the specified torque, making sure the mounting bracket is located correctly.

---

14 Wiper arms - removal and installation

Removal

Refer to illustrations 14.3 and 14.5

1   Disconnect the negative battery cable (see Chapter 5).

2   With the wiper(s) 'parked' (i.e., in the normal at-rest position), mark the positions of the blade(s) on the screen, using a wax crayon or strips of masking tape.

3   With the hood open (for the front wipers), lift up the plastic cap from the bottom of the wiper arm, and loosen the nut one or two turns **(see illustration)**.

4   Lift the wiper arm, and carefully release it from the taper on the spindle by moving it from side-to-side.

5   Completely remove the nut, and withdraw the wiper arm from the spindle **(see illustration)**.

Installation

6   Installation is a reversal of the removal procedure. Make sure that the arm is installed in the previously-noted position before tightening its nut to the specified torque.

---

15 Windshield wiper motor and linkage - removal and installation

Removal

Refer to illustrations 15.3, 15.4, 15.5, 15.6, 15.7a, 15.7b, 15.9, 15.10a and 15.10b

1   Disconnect the negative battery cable (see Chapter 5).

2   Remove the wiper arms (Section 14).

3   Release the cowl grille panel from just in

14.5 Remove the wiper arm from the spindle

front of the windshield, by prying off the caps and unscrewing the retaining screws **(see illustration)**. On 2005 and later models, the cowl grille is retained by clips only. Remove the left panel first.

4   Unclip the small stay from the firewall, and disconnect the wiper motor multi-plug **(see illustration)**.

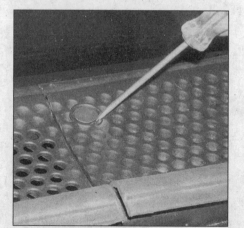

15.3 Pry off the screw cap, then remove the cowl grille screws

15.4 Unclip the stay and move it to one side

15.5 Wiper motor/linkage mounting bolts (arrows)

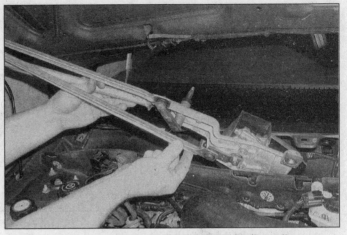

15.6 Withdraw the assembly from the firewall

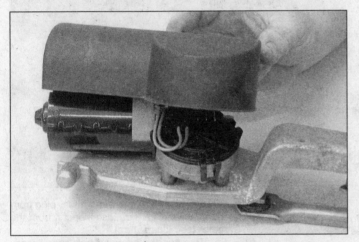

15.7a Unclip the wiper motor cover . . .

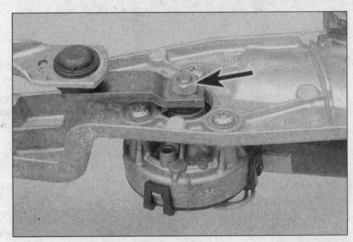

15.7b . . . and remove the nut (arrow) - note the position of the arm for installation

5   Unscrew the three mounting bolts securing the wiper motor and linkage to the firewall **(see illustration)**.
6   Withdraw the wiper motor, complete with the linkage, from the firewall **(see illustration)**.
7   Unclip the cover from the wiper motor, and mark the position of the motor arm on the mounting plate. Unscrew the center nut from the wiper motor spindle **(see illustrations)**.
8   Remove the three securing screws, and separate the motor from the mounting plate.
9   If the linkages need to be removed, use a flat-bladed screwdriver to lever the ball and sockets apart **(see illustration)**.
10   The wiper arm spindles can be removed by unclipping the snap-ring, then lift off the washer and slide the spindle from the wiper linkage **(see illustrations)**.

15.9 Carefully pry the linkage to release the ball and socket

15.10a Unclip the snap-ring, remove the washer . . .

15.10b . . . and slide the spindle from the linkage

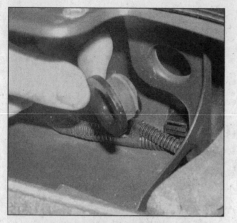

15.11a Make sure the grommet is installed in the firewall

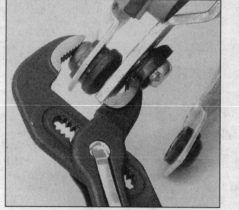

15.11b Press the ball and socket firmly together

16.4 Disconnect the wiper motor multi-plug

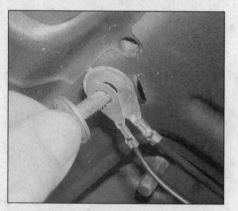

16.5 Remove the bolt to release the ground terminal

16.6 Wiper motor mounting bolts (Wagon)

Installation

Refer to illustrations 15.11a and 15.11b

11   Installation is a reversal of the removal procedure, noting the following points:

a) *Tighten the wiper motor mounting bolts to their specified torque.*

b) *Make sure that the wiper motor is in its 'parked' position before installing the motor arm, and check that the wiper linkage is in line with the motor arm.*

c) *When installing the wiper motor and linkage to the firewall, make sure the rubber grommet is in place to locate the wiper motor in the firewall (see illustration).*

d) *Use a pair of pliers to press the ball and sockets firmly together (see illustration).*

e) *Use grease to lubricate the wiper spindle and linkages when re-assembling.*

---

16   Liftgate wiper motor assembly - removal and installation

Removal

Refer to illustrations 16.4, 16.5, 16.6, 16.7 and 16.8

1   Disconnect the negative battery cable (see Chapter 5).

2   Remove the liftgate wiper arm as described in Section 14.

3   Remove the liftgate inner trim panel by unscrewing the securing screws, then pull the trim off its retaining clips.

4   Release the wiper motor multi-plug from the retaining clip, then disconnect it from the motor (**see illustration**).

5   Remove the securing bolt and disconnect the wiper motor ground lead (**see illustration**).

6   Unscrew the three mounting bolts, and remove the wiper motor from inside the liftgate (**see illustration**).

7   Unscrew the retaining screws to remove the mounting plate from the motor. If necessary, remove the rubber mounts for replacement (**see illustration**).

8   The rubber grommet can be removed from the rear window by first pulling out the plastic sleeve, then pull out the grommet (**see illustration**).

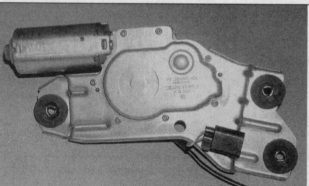

16.7 Wiper motor, showing mounting bracket retaining screws and rubber mounts

16.8 Pull out the plastic sleeve, so as to remove the rubber grommet

17.6a Undo the two retaining screws . . .

17.6b . . . and lower the fusebox to remove

17.7 Timer module attached to the rear of the fusebox

Installation

9   Installation is a reversal of the removal procedure. Make sure that the wiper motor is in its 'parked' position before installing the wiper arm.

---

17 Auxiliary warning system - general information and component replacement

---

1   Models through 2002 have a Central Timer Module (CTM), which is located in the back of the central fusebox. This module controls the timed features in the vehicle and also the acoustic signals. On later models, a GEM (Generic Electronic Module) is used that incorporates a number of previously separate functions, including the warning and timing functions. The GEM module is accessed after removing the glove box (see Chapter 11).

Functions of the CTM standard version

a) *Intermittent wiper, front and rear.*
b) *Windshield washer with wiper function, front and rear.*
c) *Heated rear window and windshield.*
d) *Entry illumination.*
e) *Power saving relay.*
f) *Lights-on warning chime.*
g) *Acoustic signal from trip computer module, anti-theft warning system/double locking module and airbag module.*

Additional functions for vehicles with automatic transmission

a) *Safety belt warning.*
b) *Reverse gear warning.*
c) *Ignition key warning.*
d) *Gear lever not in park position.*

2   Some models are equipped with an auxiliary warning system. This has a washer reservoir level warning light and also a frost warning light.

Component replacement

3   The following Steps describe brief removal procedures for the auxiliary warning system components. Disconnect the negative battery cable before commencing work

(see Chapter 1). Installation procedures are a reversal of removal.

Central Timer Module (CTM)

Refer to illustrations 17.6a, 17.6b and 17.7

4   Open the glovebox, press both sides of the glovebox in to release from the dash.
5   Hinge the glovebox downward to gain access to the fusebox.
6   Undo the two securing bolts from the fusebox, and remove it downward from the dash bracket **(see illustrations)**.
7   Pull the timer module from the back of the fusebox **(see illustration)**.

Display module

8   Remove the instrument cluster bezel, referring to Section 10.
9   Disconnect the multi-plug from the trip computer, then release the trip computer from the instrument panel surround.

Low air temperature warning sender unit

The location of the sender unit may vary on the age of the vehicle (the front bumper or the door mirror are the more usual places used).
10   If installed in the front bumper, remove the bumper as described in Chapter 11.
11   Unclip the sender unit from the bumper and disconnect the multi-plug.
12   If installed in the door mirror, remove the mirror as described in Chapter 11.

Low washer fluid switch

13   Remove the washer reservoir as described in Section 20.
14   Disconnect the multi-plug from the washer fluid reservoir.
15   Using a screwdriver, lever out the switch from the reservoir.
16   After installing the switch, refill the reservoir (see Chapter 1).

---

18 Anti-theft alarm system - general information

Refer to illustrations 18.3, 18.6 and 18.10

1   As an option, all models can be equipped with an active anti-theft alarm system, which

protects all doors, including the hood and trunk lid/liftgate. It is activated when the vehicle is locked, either with the key or remote transmitter. When the alarm has been activated, the horn will sound for 30 seconds and the indicators will operate for 5 minutes. The system will then reset, to an armed state, so that if there is another intrusion it will be activated again.

2   All models are equipped with a Passive Anti-theft System (or PATS), which is fully passive in operation and requires no procedure to arm or disarm the system. The PATS circuit is separate from the alarm, meaning that the car is immobilized even if the alarm is not set. This function is incorporated in the engine management PCM to prevent the vehicle from starting.

3   The PATS transceiver unit surrounds the ignition switch **(see illustration)**, and it 'reads' the code from a microchip in the ignition key to activate, and deactivate. This means that any replacement or duplicate keys must be obtained through a dealer - any cut locally will not contain the microchip, and will therefore not disarm the immobilizer. If an incorrect code, or no code is received then the PCM will immobilize the engine.

18.3 Wiring connector for the transceiver unit

18.6 The central locking/security module (models through 2002)

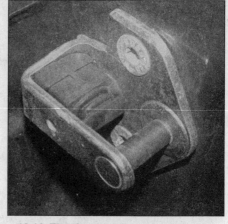

18.10 The door catch incorporates the interior light switch

4   The radio/cassette unit is incorporated into the alarm system - if an attempt is made to remove the unit while the alarm is active, the alarm will sound.

5   The movement sensors on the system consist of two ultrasonic units, located in the B-pillars, incorporating transmitters and receivers. The receivers check that the echo frequency matches the original frequency. If there is any significant difference, the system triggers the alarm.

6   The Central locking/Central Security Module (CSM) has five versions of module depending on vehicle specification:

1) *Central locking.*
2) *Central locking and remote control.*
3) *Central locking, double locking and remote control.*
4) *Central locking, double locking, remote control and alarm system.*
5) *Central locking, double locking, remote control and alarm system with infrared interior scanning.*

This module is mounted on a bracket beneath the right-hand side of the dash at the bottom of the A-pillar **(see illustration)**.

7   If the liftgate or decklid are opened using the key or remote transmitter, the alarm will not activate due to an inhibit switch built into to the lock. This suppresses the alarm system until the liftgate or decklid is closed again.

8   The remote central door locking is operated by radio frequency, and can be operated from approximately 30 feet. The key has three buttons, depending on the sequence of the buttons pressed, it will lock and unlock the doors, arm the alarm, and also lock and unlock the liftgate.

9   The alarm system (if equipped) has its own horn. On Hatchback and Sedan models, it is located on the left-hand side of the luggage compartment; on Wagon models, it is located on the right-hand side of the luggage compartment.

10   The CSM incorporates a self-test function, to activate this the ignition must be in the OFF position. Operate one of the door light switches **(see illustration)** six times within eight seconds, once the self-test mode has been entered the module will sound the horn and the hazard lights will flash once to acknowledge the input. The horn should

sound, and hazard lights flash every time a door, hood or liftgate is opened. If the doors are double locked, and interior scanning is installed, the signal will occur when something is moved within the passenger compartment. A more comprehensive test can be made using a diagnostic tester, used by a dealer.

11   The following are inputs to the CSM that can be tested while in the self-test mode:

a) *Remote transmitter.*
b) *Hood switch.*
c) *Driver's door interior light switch.*
d) *Passenger door interior light switch.*
e) *Liftgate interior light switch.*
f) *Driver's door lock motor set/reset switch.*
g) *Passenger's door lock motor set/reset switch.*
h) *Liftgate anti-theft inhibit switch.*
i) *Integrated lock/unlock switches within power door lock actuator.*
j) *Ignition switch.*
k) *Radio disconnect trigger.*
l) *Liftgate release switch.*

19 Cruise control system - general information and component replacement

1   Cruise control is available as an option on certain models.

2   The system is active at road speeds above 30 mph, and comprises:

a) *Electronic speed control servo.*
b) *Driver-operated switches.*
c) *A speed control cable.*
d) *Brake and clutch pedal switches.*
e) *Vehicle speed sensor.*

3   The driver-operated switches are mounted on the steering wheel, and allow the driver to control the various functions.

4   The vehicle speed sensor is mounted on the transmission, and generates pulses that are fed to the speed control unit.

5   The brake light switch, brake pedal switch and (when applicable) clutch pedal switch are used to disable the cruise control system. The brake light switch is activated when the brake pedal is applied gently, and the brake pedal switch is activated when the

brake pedal is applied forcibly.

6   An indicator light on the instrument panel is illuminated when the system is in operation.

7   The following Steps describe brief removal procedures for the cruise control system components. The negative battery cable should be disconnected before commencing work (see Chapter 1). Installation is a reversal of removal.

Steering wheel switches

8   Remove the airbag unit from the steering wheel as described in Section 25.

9   Disconnect the wiring plugs, noting the location of each plug and how the wiring is routed for installation.

10   Remove the two screws on each side securing the operating switches, and remove them as required from the steering wheel.

Brake and clutch pedal switches

11   Remove the four retaining screws and pry out the one securing clip, to remove the driver's side lower dash panel.

12   Disconnect the wiring connectors from the clutch switch, brake pedal switch and brake light switch.

13   To remove the clutch and brake pedal switches, twist them to release from the pedal assembly.

14   Installation is the reverse of removal. To ensure correct operation of the brake pedal switches, reset the switch by fully extending its plunger. Depress the pedal and hold the pedal in this position, clip the switch securely into position and gently raise the pedal to the at-rest position. This will automatically set the position of the switch.

Speed control actuator

15   On all models except 2.3L and 2005 and later 2.0L, loosen the two retaining clamps and remove the air intake duct, from between the air cleaner and the throttle body.

16   Disconnect the actuator cable from the throttle linkage on the throttle housing, by releasing the inner cable end fitting from the

20.1 Mounting bolt for filler neck (arrow)

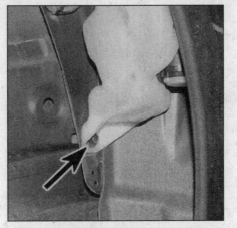

20.4a Remove the mounting bolts (arrow indicates lower bolt) . . .

20.4b . . . and slide the bottle out of the slot in the inner fender (arrow)

segment and unclipping the outer cable from the bracket. **Note:** *On SVT models, remove the shield from the throttle body for access to the cable ends.*

17   Disconnect the actuator multi-plug, then unscrew the actuator mounting bolts, and remove the actuator from the firewall (at the left fenderwell on later models).

18   Remove the four securing bolts to remove the actuator from its bracket.

19   Depress the actuating cable cap locking arm, and remove the cap by turning it counterclockwise.

20   Gently raise the cable retaining lug by a maximum of 1/32-inch, and push the cable end out of the slot in the pulley.

21   When replacing, make sure that the cable end locks into the slot in the pulley.

22   To locate the cable cap onto the actuator pulley, keep the cable taut and in the pulley groove, and pull the throttle linkage end of the cable to draw the cable cap onto the pulley.

23   To install the cable cap, keep the cable taut and the pulley still, then install the cable cap tabs into the actuator slots; turn the cap clockwise until the locking arm locates on the locking stop. **Note:** *Incorrect assembly of the cable onto the pulley may result in a high idle speed. Check that the throttle lever is in its idle position after installing the actuator.*

20   Windshield/liftgate washer system components - removal and installation

Removal

Washer reservoir and pump

Refer to illustrations 20.1, 20.4a, 20.4b, 20.5, 20.6 and 20.7

1   Open up the hood, and remove the securing bolt for the washer bottle filler neck **(see illustration)**. Pull the filler neck up, to disengage it from the washer reservoir.

2   Apply the parking brake and loosen the left-hand front wheel nuts. Jack up the front of the car and support it on axle stands. Remove the front wheel.

3   Remove the retaining screws, and release the fenderwell liner as necessary for access to the reservoir. On 2005 models, remove the drivebelt splash shield beneath the vehicle, then remove the bolts and set aside the air-conditioning accumulator (without disconnecting any hoses) to access the 2 bolts securing the washer bottle.

4   Unscrew the mounting bolts, and slide the reservoir forwards to release it from the inner fender panel **(see illustrations)**.

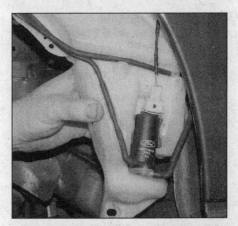

20.5 Disconnect the washer hoses and wiring from the washer pump

5   Disconnect the washer hoses and wiring connector from the washer pump as the reservoir is being removed **(see illustration)**. (Anticipate some loss of fluid by placing a container beneath the reservoir.)

6   Pull the windshield washer pump, and (where applicable) the headlight washer pump, from the reservoir **(see illustration)**.

7   Remove the rubber seal/filter to clean it out and check for damage **(see illustration)**.

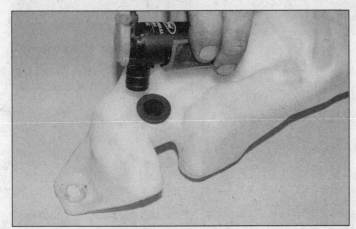

20.6 Pull out the washer motor

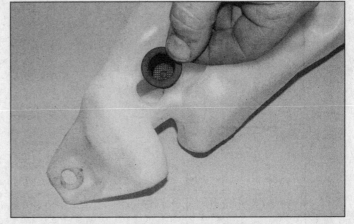

20.7 Check that the filter is not blocked

20.9a Disconnect the wiring connector for the jet heater (if equipped) . . .

20.9b . . . then carefully pry the jet from the hood

20.10 Remove the retaining screws from the high-level brake-light

Washer jet (windshield)

Refer to illustrations 20.9a and 20.9b

8   With the hood supported in its open position, carefully disconnect the washer tube from the bottom of the jet.

9   Where necessary, disconnect the wiring for the jet heater. Pry the jet out from the hood, taking care not to damage the paint-work **(see illustrations)**.

Washer jet (rear window)

Refer to illustrations 20.10 and 20.11

10   On Hatchback and Wagon models, undo the two securing screws and remove the high-level brake-light unit **(see illustration)**.

11   Pull the washer tube from the jet **(see illustration)**. (Check with a dealer to find if the washer jet is available separately from the rear light lens.)

Headlight washer jet (if equipped)

12   Remove the front bumper as described in Chapter 11.

13   Disconnect the washer tube from the base of the jet.

14   Pull off the jet retaining clip/screw and withdraw the jet from the bumper.

Installation

15   Installation is a reversal of the removal procedure, noting the following points:

a) *In the case of the screen washer jets, press them in firmly until they are fully engaged.*

b) *After installing the headlight washer jet, install the front bumper as described in Chapter 11.*

c) *When reinstalling the washer reservoir, lubricate the grommet with a water-based lubricant.*

---

21   Radio/cassette player (Audio Unit) - removal and installation

Refer to illustration 21.1

Note: *Special tools are required to remove the audio unit on models prior to 2005. The tools can be obtained inexpensively in most auto parts stores.*

1   A Keycode anti-theft system is featured in the audio unit, if the unit and/or the battery is disconnected, the audio unit will not function again on reconnection until the correct security code is entered. Details of this procedure are given in the Audio Systems Operating Guide supplied with the vehicle when new, with the code itself being given in a Radio Passport and/or a Keycode Label at the same time. Some units have a detachable front bezel that can be removed when the vehicle is not in use **(see illustration)**. The RDS/EON audio units also allow the registration of the vehicle, or the Vehicle Identification Number (VIN) to be entered into the memory.

2   For obvious security reasons, the re-coding procedure is not given in this manual - if you do not have the code or details of the correct procedure, but can supply proof of ownership and a legitimate reason for wanting this information, the vehicle's selling dealer may be able to help.

3   Note that these units will allow only ten attempts at entering the code - any further attempts will render the unit permanently inoperative until it has been reprogrammed by the dealer themselves. At first, three consecutive attempts are allowed; if all three are incorrect, a 30-minute delay is required before another attempt can be made. Each of any subsequent attempts (up to the maximum of ten) can be made only after a similar delay.

Removal

Refer to illustrations 21.6 and 21.7

4   Disconnect the negative battery cable (see Chapter 5).

5   On models through 2004, in order to release the audio unit retaining clips, the U-shaped tools must be inserted into the special holes on each side of the unit. If possible, it is preferable to obtain purpose-made tools from an audio specialist, as these have

20.11 Pull the washer hose from the washer jet

21.1 Press the securing button to release the bezel

21.6 Using the U-shaped tools to remove the radio

21.7 Disconnect the multi-plugs and antenna lead

22.5 There are three mounting screws on each side of the CD changer (arrows)

cut-outs that snap firmly into the clips so that the unit can be pulled out.

6   On models through 2004, lightly push the U-shaped tools outwards as the audio unit is being removed **(see illustration)**. Pull the unit squarely from its opening, or it may jam.

7   On 2005 and later models, pry out the center instrument panel trim panel, then remove the four screws securing the audio unit.

8   With the audio unit withdrawn, disconnect the power supply, ground, antenna and speaker leads **(see illustration)**. Where applicable, also detach and remove the plastic support bracket from the rear of the unit. Audio units on 2005 models are removed by removing the bezel and four mounting screws.

Installation

9   Installation is a reversal of removal. With the leads reconnected to the rear of the unit, press it into position until the retaining clips are felt to engage. Where applicable, reactivate the unit by entering the correct code in accordance with the maker's instructions.

22 Compact disc autochanger - removal and installation

Note: *The 6000 RDS/EON is a radio and single disc CD player, and can be removed as described in Section 21.*

1   A compact disc (CD) player autochanger is available as an optional extra, which is compatible with the 5000 RDS/EON radio cassette player. This autochanger is mounted under the passenger front seat and can hold 6 compact discs. Later models have an optional system with a 6-CD unit in the instrument panel.

Removal

Refer to illustration 22.5

2   The negative battery cable should be disconnected before commencing work.

3   The CD autochanger unit is mounted in a bracket below the front passenger's seat. **Warning:** *If the seats are equipped with side-impact airbags, read the warnings in Section 25 of this Chapter before removal.*

4   Remove the front passenger seat as described in Chapter 11.

5   Remove the unit mounting screws (three each side), and disconnect the wiring plug **(see illustration)**. Slide the player out of the brackets below the seat, and remove it from the car.

Installation

6   Installation is a reversal of the removal procedure.

23 Speakers - removal and installation

Removal

Refer to illustrations 23.2 and 23.3

1   Remove the front or rear door trim panel as described in Chapter 11.

2   Unscrew the four cross-head screws, and withdraw the speaker from the inner panel **(see illustration)**.

3   Disconnect the electrical connector from the speaker **(see illustration)**.

Installation

4   Installation is a reversal of the removal procedure.

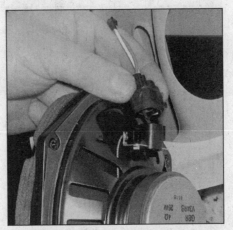

23.3 Disconnecting the speaker wiring connector

23.2 Rear speaker on 3-door model

24 Radio antenna - removal and installation

Removal

Refer to illustrations 24.1, 24.2 and 24.3

1   If just the antenna mast is to be removed, this can be unscrewed from the base from outside **(see illustration)**.

24.1 Unscrew the antenna mast from the base

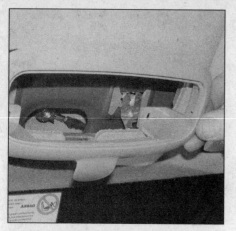

24.2 Withdraw the interior light bezel

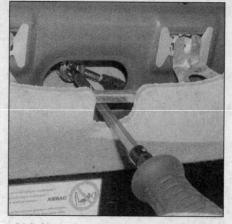

24.3 Undo the antenna mounting screw

25.3 Unscrew the airbag mounting bolts

2   To remove the antenna base, pry out the interior light and remove the two retaining screws from the light bezel **(see illustration)**.

3   Unscrew the retaining screw from the base of the antenna **(see illustration)**, disconnect the antenna lead, and remove the base and gasket from outside.

Installation

4   Installation is a reversal of the removal procedure.

25   Airbag units - removal and installation

Warning 1: *Handle any airbag unit with extreme care, as a precaution against personal injury, and always hold it with the cover facing away from the body. If in doubt concerning any proposed work involving an airbag unit or its control circuitry, consult a dealer or other qualified specialist.*

Warning 2: *Stand any airbag in a safe place with the cover uppermost, and do not expose it to heat sources in excess of 212°F.*

Warning 3: *Do not attempt to open or repair an airbag unit, or check it with an ohmmeter, or apply any electrical current to it. Do not*

use any airbag unit which is visibly damaged or which has been tampered with.

Driver's airbag

Refer to illustrations 25.3 and 25.4

1   Disconnect the negative battery cable (see Chapter 5). **Warning:** *Before proceeding, wait a minimum of 5 minutes, as a precaution against accidental firing of the airbag unit. This period ensures that any stored energy in the back-up capacitor is dissipated.* On 2005 and later models, also pull out the RCM (Restraint Control Module) fuse from the interior fuse box.

2   Rotate the steering wheel so that one of the airbag mounting bolt holes (at the rear of the steering wheel boss) is visible above the steering column upper shroud.

3   Unscrew and remove the first mounting bolt **(see illustration)**, then turn the steering wheel 180° and remove the remaining mounting bolt.

4   Carefully withdraw the airbag unit from the steering wheel far enough to release its clips, then disconnect the wiring multi-plugs and remove it from inside the vehicle **(see illustration)**. Stand the airbag in a safe place with the cover uppermost as soon as possible.

5   Installation is a reversal of the removal procedure.

Passenger's airbag

Refer to illustrations 25.7a, 25.7b, 25.8, 25.9a and 25.9b

6   Disconnect the negative battery cable (see Chapter 5). **Warning:** *Before proceeding, wait a minimum of 5 minutes, as a precaution against accidental firing of the airbag unit. This period ensures that any stored energy in the back-up capacitor is dissipated.*

7   Using a flat-bladed tool, release the clips on the airbag module trim cover. Start at the outer edge and work your way around, carefully disengaging the trim from the dash, and hinge up towards the windshield **(see illustrations)**. On 2003 and later models, remove the glove box (see Chapter 11) and set aside the defroster duct to access the airbag mounting screws.

8   Remove the four airbag unit mounting screws, and withdraw the unit from the dash **(see illustration)**.

9   Disconnect the wiring multi-plug from the airbag unit as it comes into view. A long-nosed pair of pliers may be required to release the connector **(see illustrations)**.

10   Installation is a reversal of removal.

25.4 Disconnect the airbag wiring multi-plug

25.7a Work around the trim to unclip the trim from the dash . . .

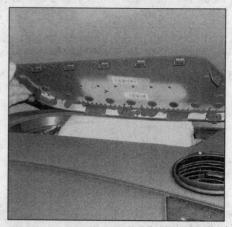

25.7b . . . then hinge the trim towards the windshield to access the airbag

25.8 Undo the four mounting bolts (models though 2002 shown)

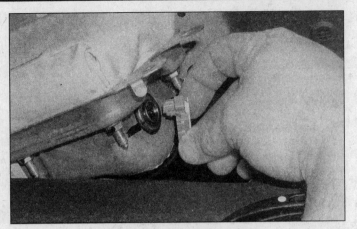

25.9a Disconnect the wiring plug . . .

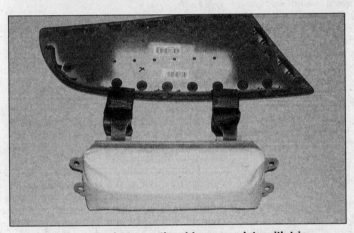

25.9b . . . and remove the airbag complete with trim

26.4 The airbag control module is located under center console

Side airbag

11 The side airbag units are built into the front seats, and their removal requires that the seat fabric be removed. This work should be left to a dealer or other qualified repair shop.

26 Airbag control module - removal and installation

Removal

Refer to illustration 26.4

1 Disconnect the negative battery cable (refer to Chapter 5A, Section 1). **Warning:** *Before proceeding, wait a minimum of 5 minutes, as a precaution against accidental firing of the airbag unit. This period ensures that any stored energy in the back-up capacitor is dissipated.*

2 Remove the center console and air ducting as described in Chapter 11.

3 Press the retaining lugs and disconnect the multi-plug(s) from the module.

4 Unscrew the mounting bolts and remove the module from the vehicle **(see illustration)**.

Installation

5 Installation is a reversal of the removal procedure.

27 Airbag sliding contact - removal and installation

Removal

1 Remove the driver's airbag unit as described in Section 25.

2 Disconnect the horn switch wiring connector.

3 If equipped, disconnect the multi-plugs for the cruise control switches.

4 Remove the steering wheel and column shrouds as described in Chapter 10.

5 Detach the steering column multi-function switches by depressing the plastic retaining tabs with a flat-bladed screwdriver.

6 Using a small screwdriver, release the two retaining tabs, then remove the sliding contact from the steering column. Note the position of the spacing collar within the center of the sliding contact.

Installation

Refer to illustration 27.7

7 Installation is a reversal of the removal procedure, noting the following points:

a) *Make sure that the front wheels are still pointing straight-ahead.*

b) *The sliding contact must be installed in its central position, with the special alignment marks aligned and the arrow mark to the top* **(see illustration).** *To center the sliding contact, turn the hub of the sliding contact by hand couterclockwise until it stops (don't apply too much force, or you could damage it), then turn it clockwise 2-1/2 turns and align the arrow mark on the hub with the "V" mark at the top of the housing.*

c) *Make sure the spacing collar is installed.*

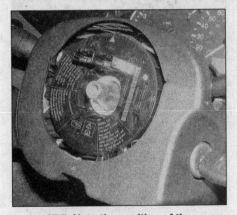

27.7 Note the position of the sliding contact

28 Electric seat components - removal and installation

Warning: *If airbags are installed, de-power them (see Section 25, "Airbag units - removal and installation") before removing the front seats.*

Heated seats

1   If heated seats are installed, both driver's and front passenger seats have heating elements built into the seat cushion and backrest.
2   No repairs can be made to the heating elements without dismantling the seat and removing the seat fabric - therefore this work should be left to a dealer or other specialist.
3   The heated seat switches are removed as described in Section 4.
4   For further diagnosis of any problems with the system, refer to Sections 2 and 3, and to the wiring diagrams at the end of this Chapter.

Seat adjustment components

Refer to illustration 28.8
5   Only the driver's seat is equipped with seat adjustment motors, on the highest specification models.
6   To gain access to the motors, remove the driver's seat as described in Chapter 11.
7   The motors are bolted to a mounting frame, which in turn is bolted to the seat base. Before removing a motor, trace its wiring back from the motor to its wiring plug, and disconnect it.
8   Remove the roll-pins from the motor mounting adjusting bar, and remove from the seat base **(see illustration)**.
9   Installation is a reversal of removal. It is worth periodically greasing the worm-drive components and seat runners, to ensure trouble-free operation.

28.8 The seat adjustment motor is secured by roll-pins (arrows)

10   The seat adjustment switches are removed as described in Section 4.
11   For further diagnosis of any problems with the system, refer to Sections 2 and 3, and to the wiring diagrams at the end of this Chapter.

29 Cigarette lighter - removal and installation

Removal

Refer to illustrations 29.3, 29.4 and 29.5
1   Disconnect the negative battery cable (see Chapter 5).
2   Remove the heater control panel as described in Chapter 3.
3   Release the retaining clips inside the cigarette lighter insert, and slide it out from the plastic panel **(see illustration)**.
4   Push the plastic surround out to release it from the control panel **(see illustration)**.
5   To remove the bulb, unclip the bulbholder from the plastic surround **(see illustration)**.

Installation

6   Installation is a reversal of the removal procedure.

30 Wiring diagrams - general information

Since it isn't possible to include all wiring diagrams for every year covered by this manual, the following diagrams are those that are typical and most commonly needed.

Prior to troubleshooting any circuits, check the fuse and circuit breakers (if equipped) to make sure they're in good condition. Make sure the battery is properly charged and check the cable connections (see Chapter 1).

When checking a circuit, make sure that all connectors are clean, with no broken or loose terminals. When unplugging a connector, do not pull on the wires. Pull only on the connector housings themselves.

29.3 Unclip and slide out the metal insert

29.4 Release the plastic bezel from the panel

29.5 Unclip the bulbholder from the plastic surround

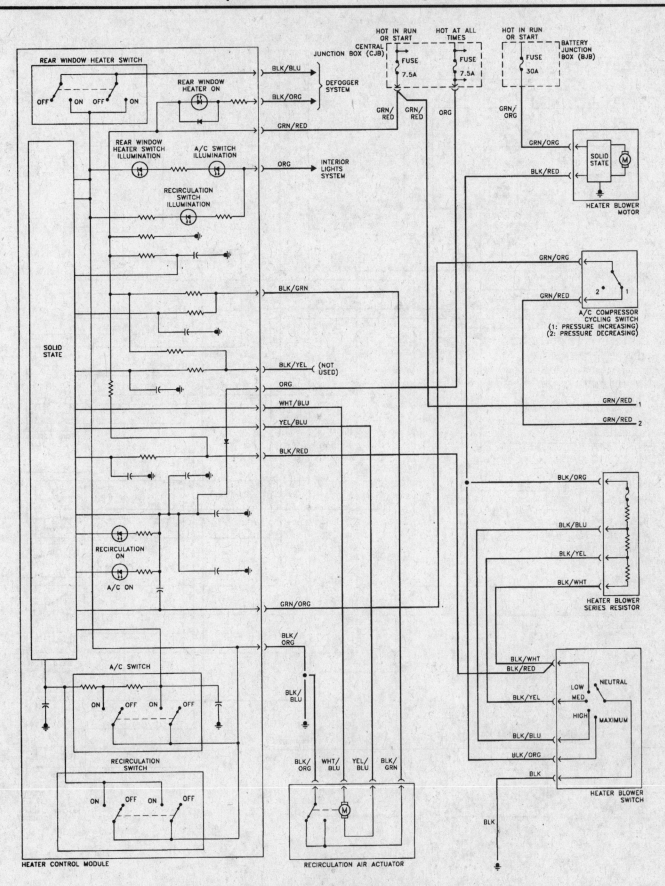

Typical air conditioning and heating system (1 of 2)

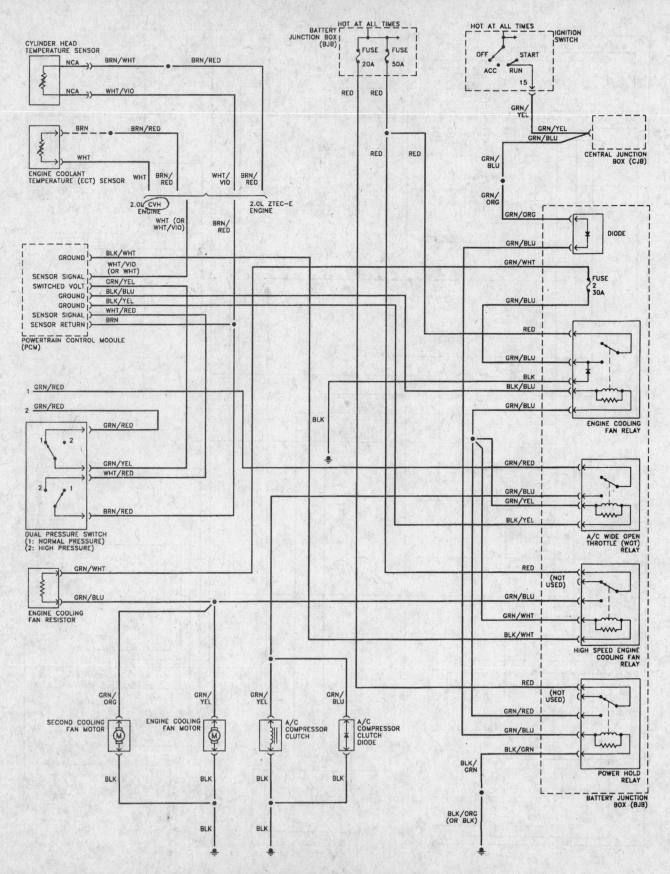

Typical air conditioning and heating system (2 of 2)

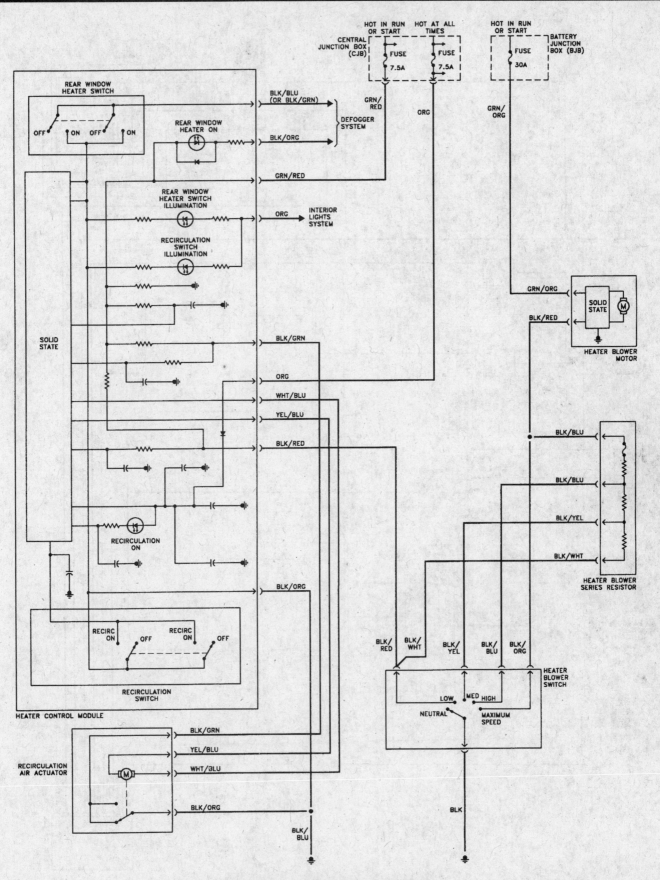

Heater system (without air conditioning)

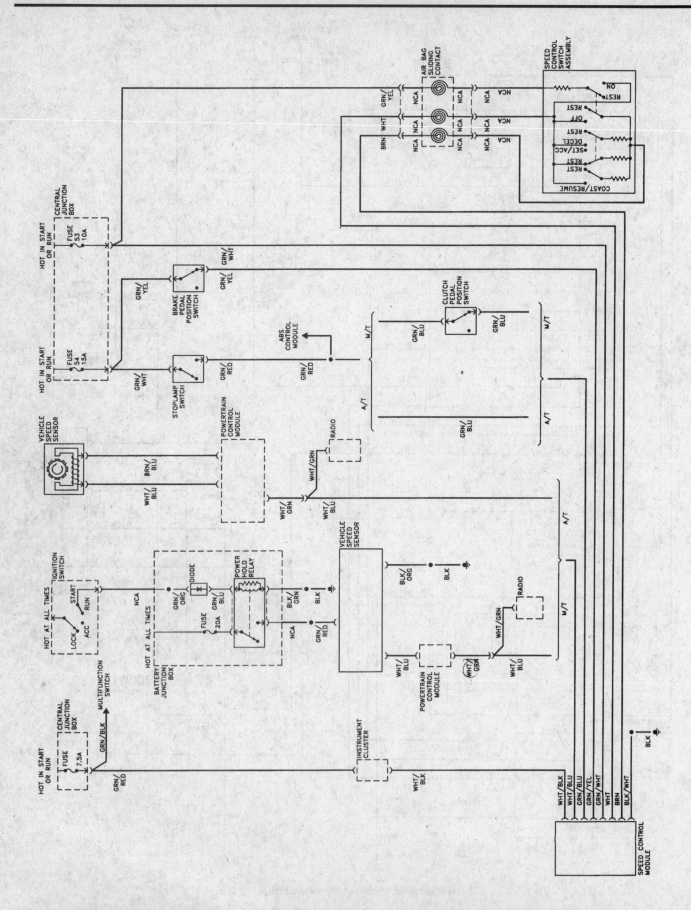

Cruise control system

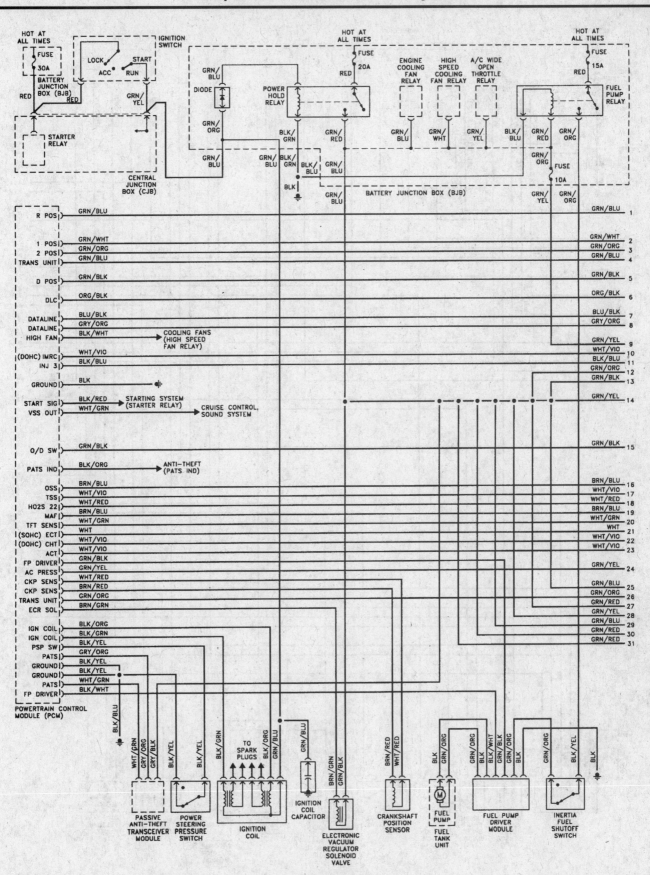

Typical engine control system (1 of 3)

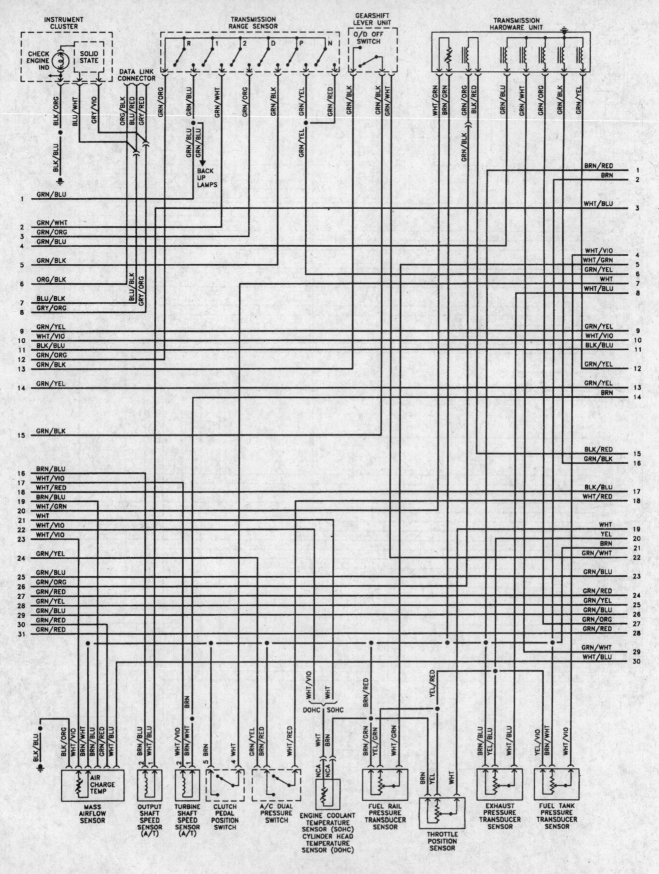

Typical engine control system (2 of 3)

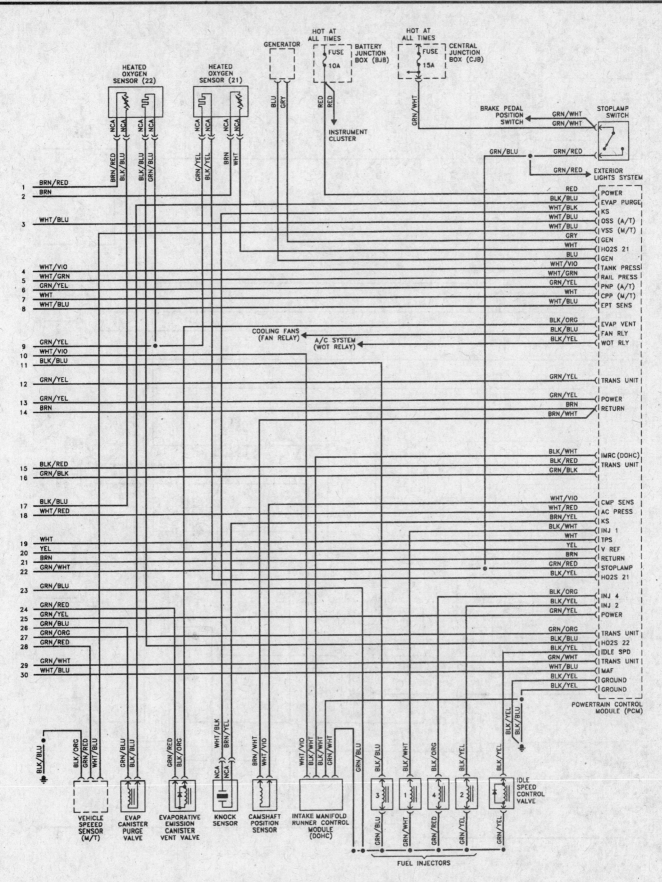

Typical engine control system (3 of 3)

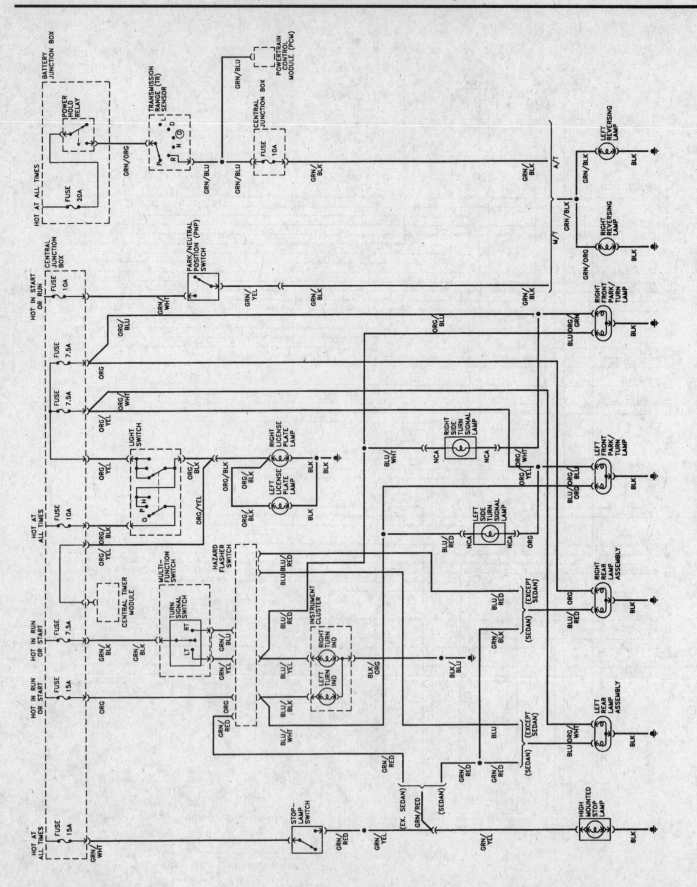

Exterior lighting system

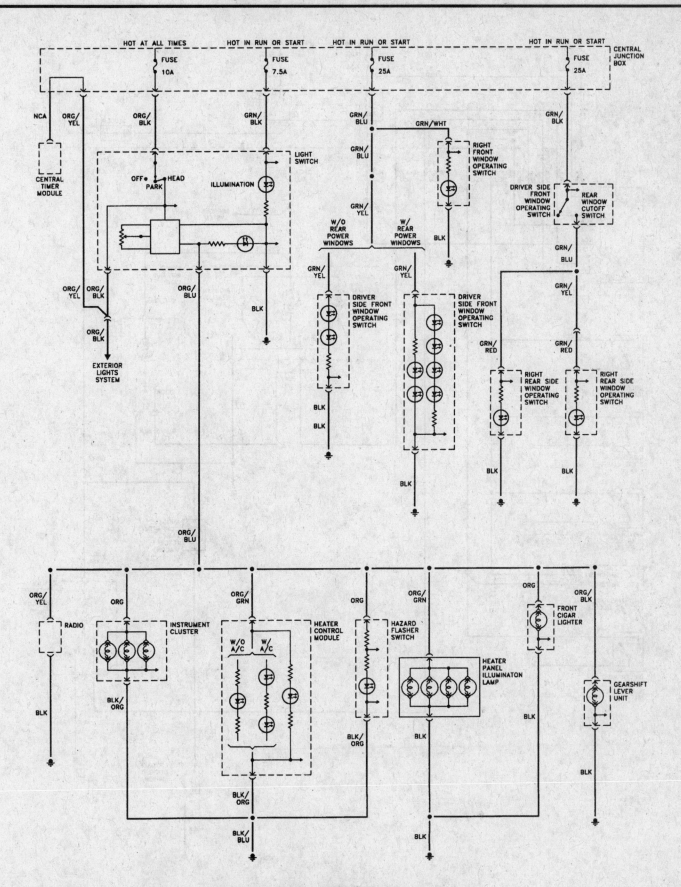

Instrument panel and switch illumination system

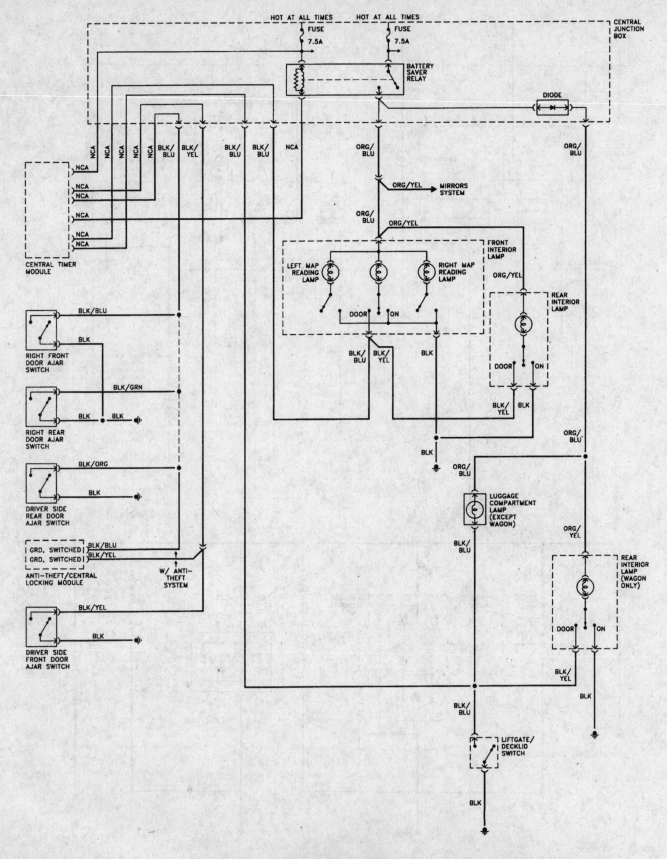

Interior lighting system

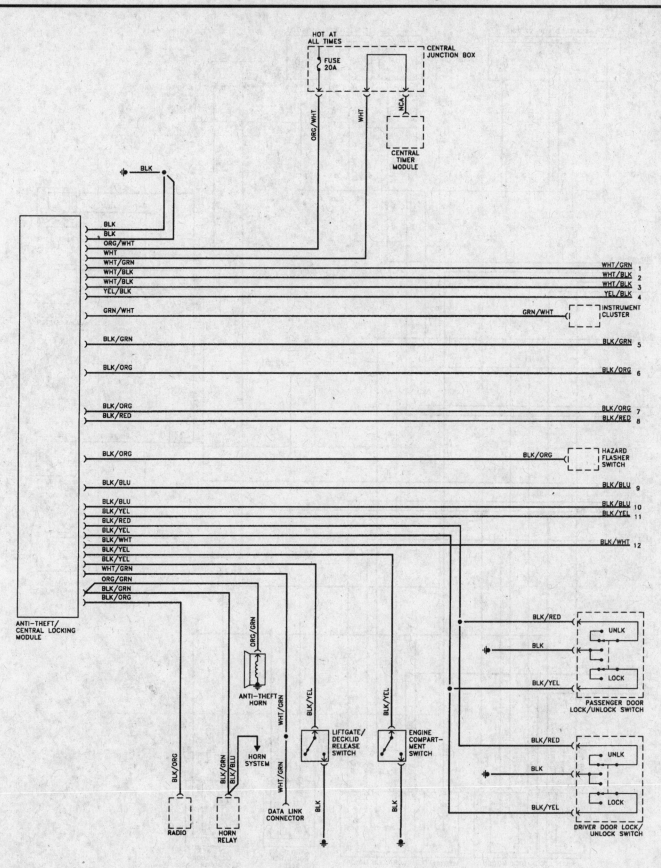

Power door lock system - with anti-theft (1 of 2)

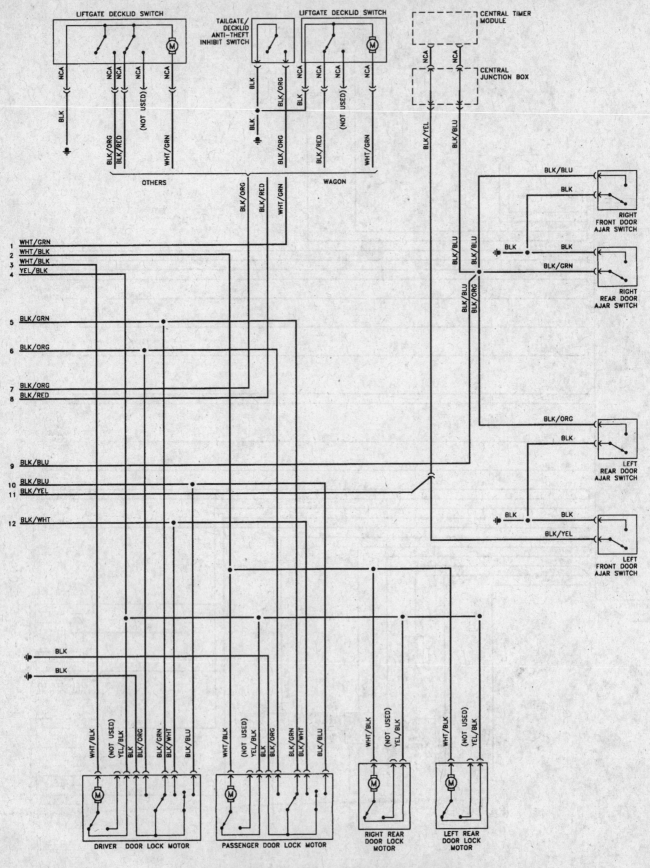

Power door lock system - with anti-theft (2 of 2)

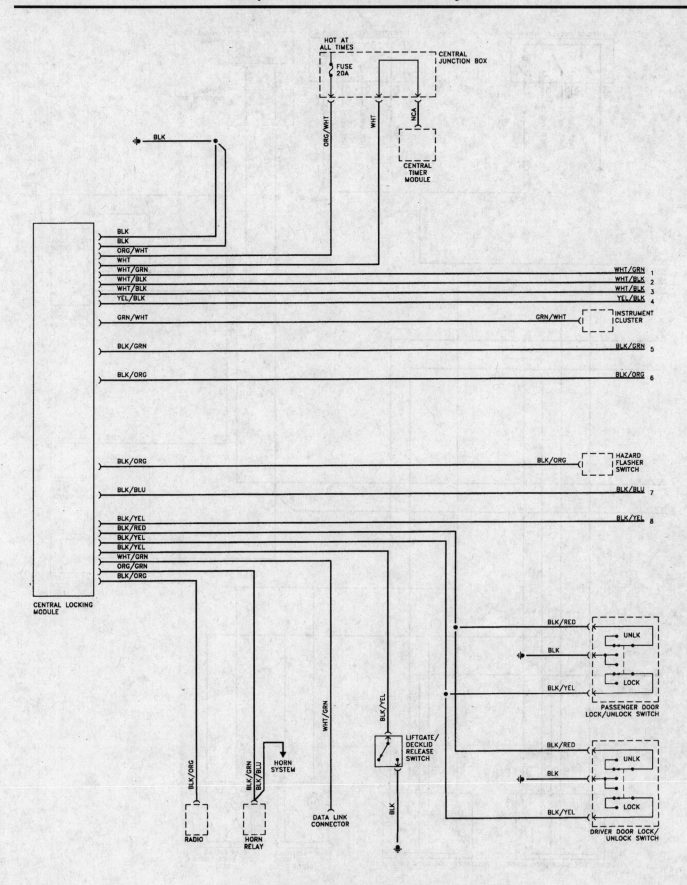

Power door lock system - without anti-theft (1 of 2)

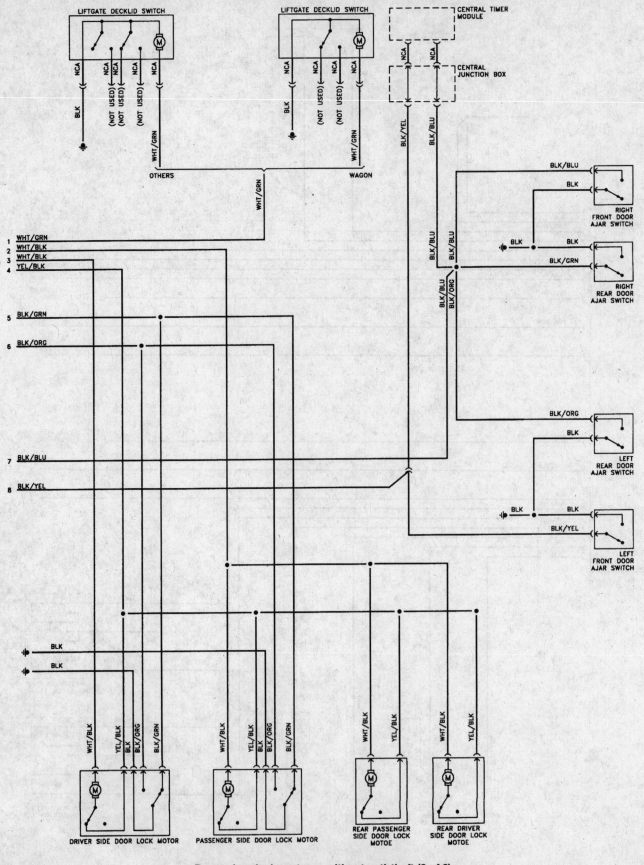

Power door lock system - without anti-theft (2 of 2)

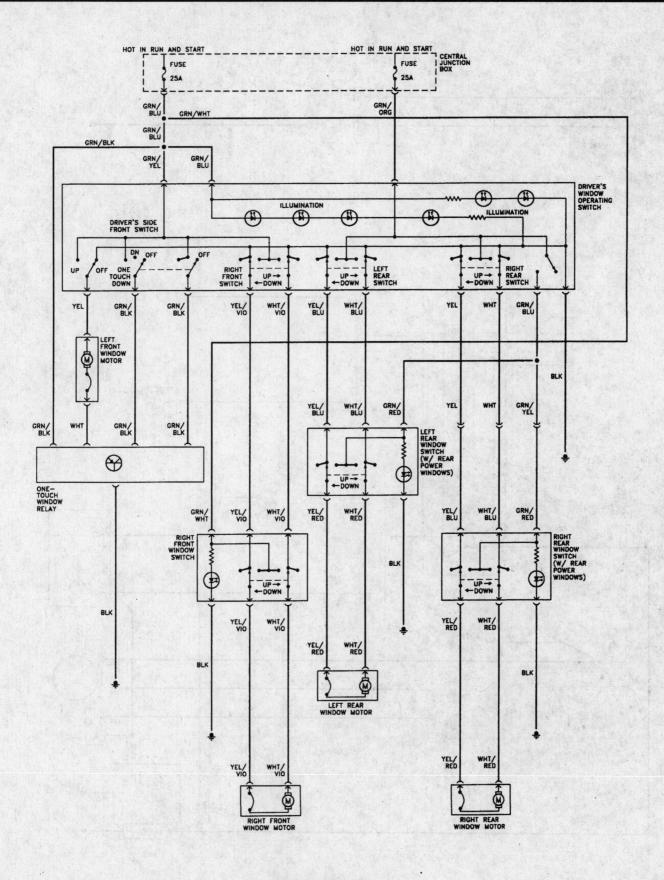

Power window system

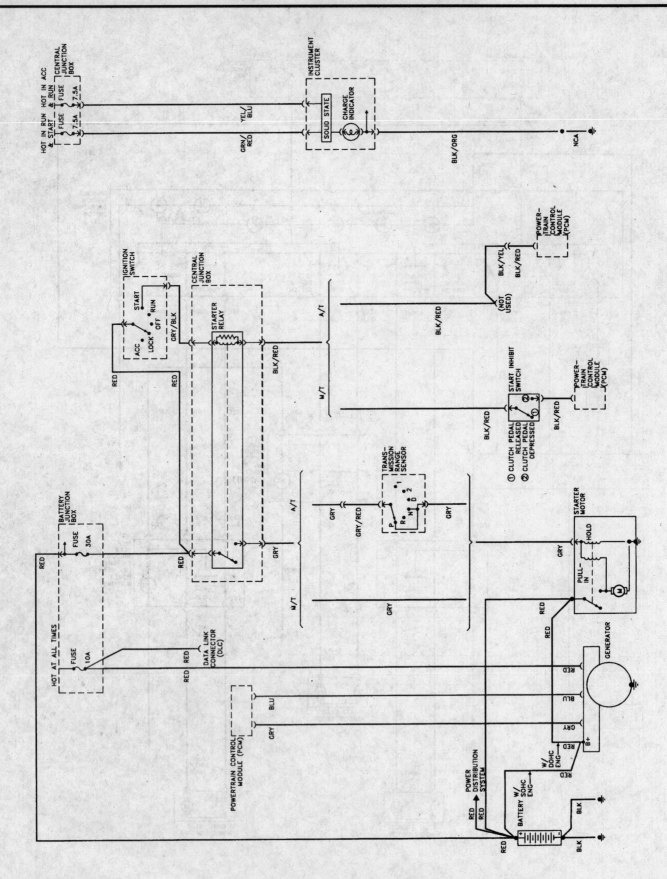

Starting and charging system

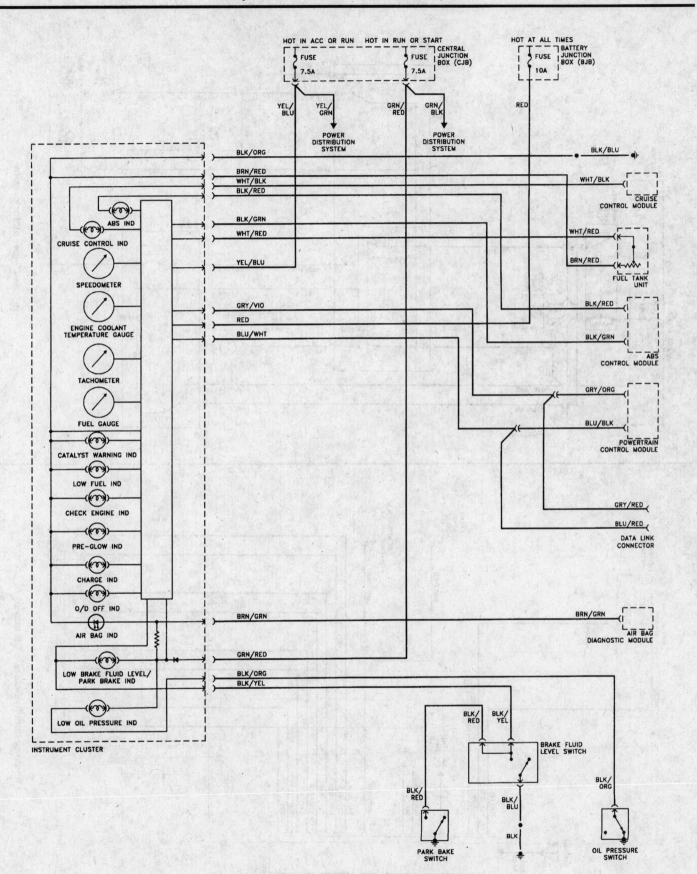

Instrument panel gauges and warning lights system

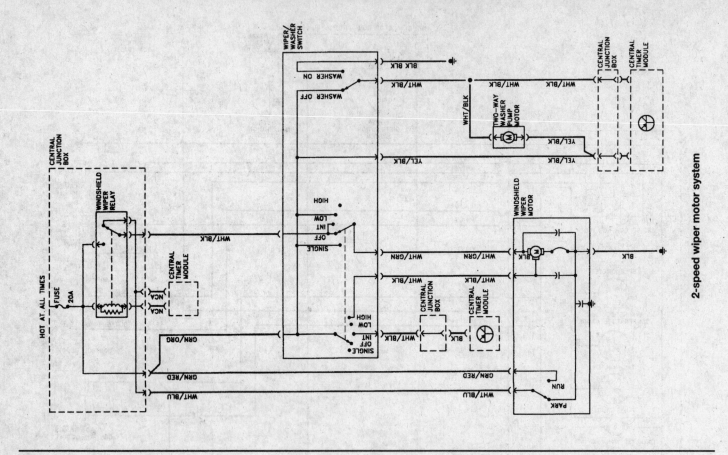

2-speed wiper motor system

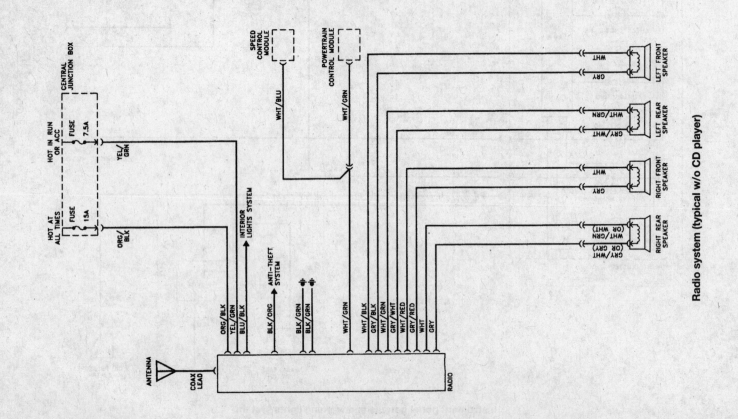

Radio system (typical w/o CD player)

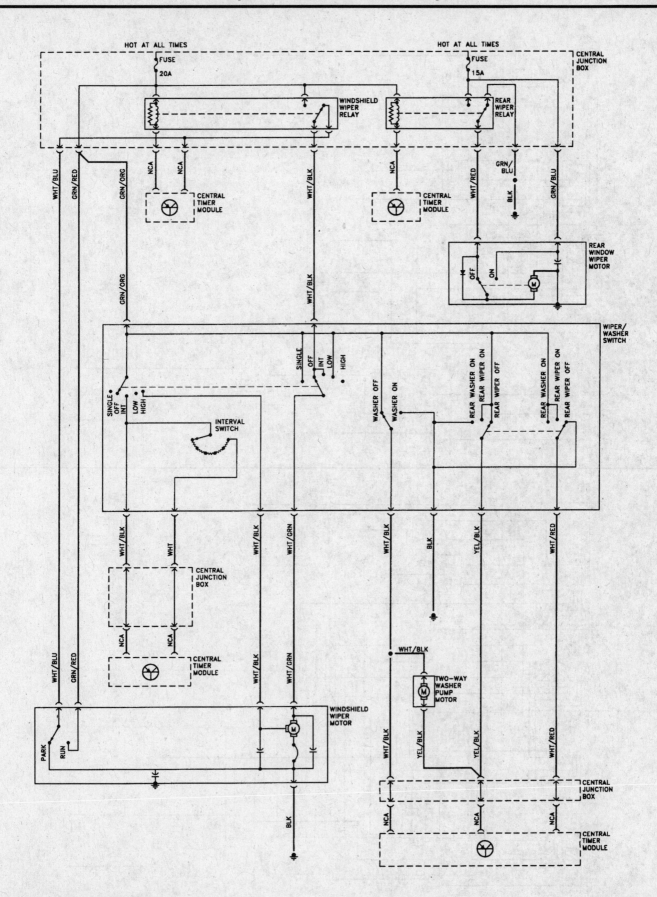

Intermittent wiper motor system

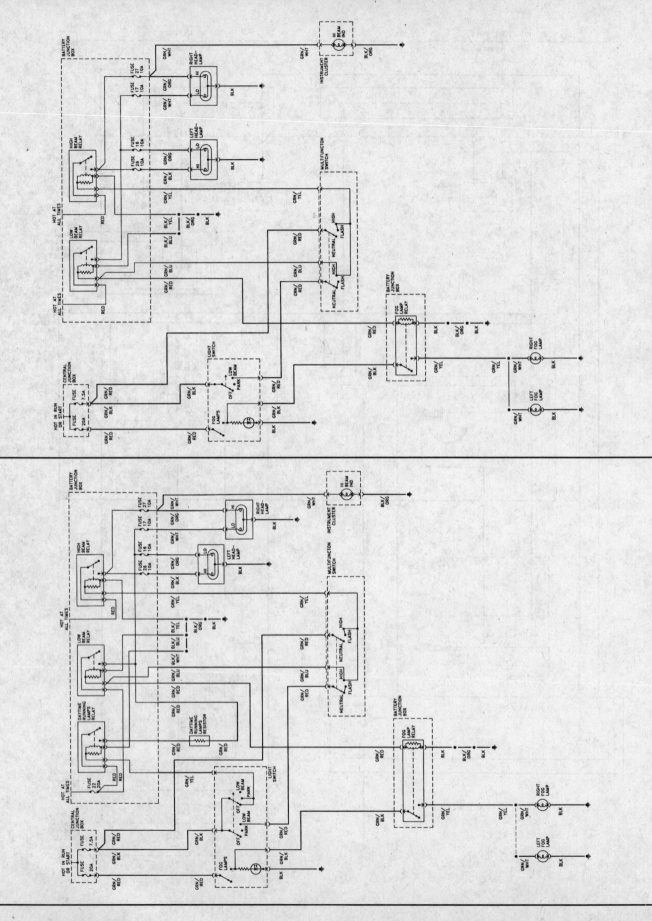

Headlight system (without Daytime Running Lights, w/o HID lamps)

Headlight system (with Daytime Running Lights, w/o HID lamps)

Index

A

B

Haynes Automotive Manuals

NOTE: If you do not see a listing for your vehicle, consult your local Haynes dealer for the latest product information.

HAYNES XTREME CUSTOMIZING
- **11101** Sport Compact Customizing
- **11102** Sport Compact Performance
- **11110** In-car Entertainment
- **11150** Sport Utility Vehicle Customizing
- **11213** Acura
- **11255** GM Full-size Pick-ups
- **11314** Ford Focus
- **11315** Full-size Ford Pick-ups
- **11373** Honda Civic

ACURA
- **12020** Integra '86 thru '89 & Legend '86 thru '90
- **12021** Integra '90 thru '93 & Legend '91 thru '95

AMC
- **Jeep CJ** - see JEEP (50020)
- **14020** Mid-size models '70 thru '83
- **14025** (Renault) Alliance & Encore '83 thru '87

AUDI
- **15020** 4000 all models '80 thru '87
- **15025** 5000 all models '77 thru '83
- **15026** 5000 all models '84 thru '88

AUSTIN-HEALEY
- **Sprite** - see MG Midget (66015)

BMW
- **18020** 3/5 Series not including diesel or all-wheel drive models '82 thru '92
- **18021** 3-Series incl. Z3 models '92 thru '98
- **18022** 3-Series, E46 chassis '99 thru '05, Z4 models '03 thru '05
- **18025** 320i all 4 cyl models '75 thru '83
- **18050** 1500 thru 2002 except Turbo '59 thru '77

BUICK
- **19010** Buick Century '97 thru '05
  - Century (front-wheel drive) - see GM (38005)
- **19020** Buick, Oldsmobile & Pontiac Full-size (Front-wheel drive) '85 thru '05
  - Buick Electra, LeSabre and Park Avenue; Oldsmobile Delta 88 Royale, Ninety Eight and Regency; Pontiac Bonneville
- **19025** Buick Oldsmobile & Pontiac Full-size (Rear wheel drive)
  - Buick Estate '70 thru '90, Electra '70 thru '84, LeSabre '70 thru '85, Limited '74 thru '79 Oldsmobile Custom Cruiser '70 thru '90, Delta 88 '70 thru '85, Ninety-eight '70 thru '84 Pontiac Bonneville '70 thru '81, Catalina '70 thru '81, Grandville '70 thru '75, Parisienne '83 thru '86
- **19030** Mid-size Regal & Century all rear-drive models with V6, V8 and Turbo '74 thru '87
  - **Regal** - see GENERAL MOTORS (38010)
  - **Riviera** - see GENERAL MOTORS (38030)
  - **Roadmaster** - see CHEVROLET (24046)
  - **Skyhawk** - see GENERAL MOTORS (38015)
  - **Skylark** - see GM (38020, 38025)
  - **Somerset** - see GENERAL MOTORS (38025)

CADILLAC
- **21030** Cadillac Rear Wheel Drive all gasoline models '70 thru '93
  - **Cimarron** - see GENERAL MOTORS (38015)
  - **DeVille** - see GM (38031 & 38032)
  - **Eldorado** - see GM (38030 & 38031)
  - **Fleetwood** - see GM (38031)
  - **Seville** - see GM (38030, 38031 & 38032)

CHEVROLET
- **24010** Astro & GMC Safari Mini-vans '85 thru '03
- **24015** Camaro V8 all models '70 thru '81
- **24016** Camaro all models '82 thru '92
- **24017** Camaro & Firebird '93 thru '02
  - **Cavalier** - see GENERAL MOTORS (38016)
  - **Celebrity** - see GENERAL MOTORS (38005)
- **24020** Chevelle, Malibu & El Camino '69 thru '87
- **24024** Chevette & Pontiac T1000 '76 thru '87
  - **Citation** - see GENERAL MOTORS (38020)
- **24027** Colorado & GMC Canyon '04 thru '06
- **24032** Corsica/Beretta all models '87 thru '96
- **24040** Corvette all V8 models '68 thru '82
- **24041** Corvette all models '84 thru '96
- **10305** Chevrolet Engine Overhaul Manual
- **24045** Full-size Sedans Caprice, Impala, Biscayne, Bel Air & Wagons '69 thru '90
- **24046** Impala SS & Caprice and Buick Roadmaster '91 thru '96
  - **Impala** - see LUMINA (24048)
  - **Lumina** '90 thru '94 - see GM (38010)
- **24048** Lumina & Monte Carlo '95 thru '05
  - **Lumina APV** - see GM (38035)
- **24050** Luv Pick-up all 2WD & 4WD '72 thru '82
  - **Malibu** '97 thru '00 - see GM (38026)
- **24055** Monte Carlo all models '70 thru '88
  - **Monte Carlo** '95 thru '01 - see LUMINA (24048)
- **24059** Nova all V8 models '69 thru '79
- **24060** Nova and Geo Prizm '85 thru '92
- **24064** Pick-ups '67 thru '87 - Chevrolet & GMC, all V8 & in-line 6 cyl, 2WD & 4WD '67 thru '87; Suburbans, Blazers & Jimmys '67 thru '91
- **24065** Pick-ups '88 thru '98 - Chevrolet & GMC, full-size pick-ups '88 thru '98, C/K Classic '99 & '00, Blazer & Jimmy '92 thru '94; Suburban '92 thru '99; Tahoe & Yukon '95 thru '99
- **24066** Pick-ups '99 thru '06 - Chevrolet Silverado & GMC Sierra '99 thru '06, Suburban/Tahoe/ Yukon/Yukon XL/Avalanche '00 thru '06
- **24070** S-10 & S-15 Pick-ups '82 thru '93, Blazer & Jimmy '83 thru '94,
- **24071** S-10 & Sonoma Pick-ups '94 thru '04, Blazer & Jimmy '95 thru '04, Hombre '96 thru '01
- **24072** Chevrolet TrailBlazer & TrailBlazer EXT, GMC Envoy & Envoy XL, Oldsmobile Bravada '02 thru '06
- **24075** Sprint '85 thru '88 & Geo Metro '89 thru '01
- **24080** Vans - Chevrolet & GMC '68 thru '96
- **24081** Chevrolet Express & GMC Savana Full-size Vans '96 thru '05

CHRYSLER
- **25015** Chrysler Cirrus, Dodge Stratus, Plymouth Breeze '95 thru '00
- **10310** Chrysler Engine Overhaul Manual
- **25020** Full-size Front-Wheel Drive '88 thru '93
  - **K-Cars** - see DODGE Aries (30008)
  - **Laser** - see DODGE Daytona (30030)
- **25025** Chrysler LHS, Concorde, New Yorker, Dodge Intrepid, Eagle Vision, '93 thru '97
- **25026** Chrysler LHS, Concorde, 300M, Dodge Intrepid, '98 thru '03
- **25027** Chrysler 300, Dodge Charger & Magnum '05 thru '07
- **25030** Chrysler & Plymouth Mid-size front wheel drive '82 thru '95
  - **Rear-wheel Drive** - see Dodge (30050)
- **25035** PT Cruiser all models '01 thru '03
- **25040** Chrysler Sebring, Dodge Avenger '95 thru '05
  - **Dodge** Stratus '01 thru 05

DATSUN
- **28005** 200SX all models '80 thru '83
- **28007** B-210 all models '73 thru '78
- **28009** 210 all models '79 thru '82
- **28012** 240Z, 260Z & 280Z Coupe '70 thru '78
- **28014** 280ZX Coupe & 2+2 '79 thru '83
  - **300ZX** - see NISSAN (72010)
- **28018** 510 & PL521 Pick-up '68 thru '73
- **28020** 510 all models '78 thru '81
- **28022** 620 Series Pick-up all models '73 thru '79
  - **720 Series Pick-up** - see NISSAN (72030)
- **28025** 810/Maxima all gasoline models, '77 thru '84

DODGE
- **400 & 600** - see CHRYSLER (25030)
- **30008** Aries & Plymouth Reliant '81 thru '89
- **30010** Caravan & Plymouth Voyager '84 thru '95
- **30011** Caravan & Plymouth Voyager '96 thru '02
- **30012** Challenger/Plymouth Saporro '78 thru '83
- **30013** Caravan, Chrysler Voyager, Town & Country '03 thru '06
- **30016** Colt & Plymouth Champ '78 thru '87
- **30020** Dakota Pick-ups all models '87 thru '96
- **30021** Durango '98 & '99, Dakota '97 thru '99
- **30022** Dodge Durango models '00 thru '03 Dodge Dakota models '00 thru '04
- **30023** Dodge Durango '04 thru '06, Dakota '05 and '06
- **30025** Dart, Demon, Plymouth Barracuda, Duster & Valiant 6 cyl models '67 thru '76
- **30030** Daytona & Chrysler Laser '84 thru '89
  - **Intrepid** - see CHRYSLER (25025, 25026)
- **30034** Neon all models '95 thru '99
- **30035** Omni & Plymouth Horizon '78 thru '90
- **30036** Dodge and Plymouth Neon '00 thru '05
- **30040** Pick-ups all full-size models '74 thru '93
- **30041** Pick-ups all full-size models '94 thru '01
- **30042** Dodge Full-size Pick-ups '02 thru '05
- **30045** Ram 50/D50 Pick-ups & Raider and Plymouth Arrow Pick-ups '79 thru '93
- **30050** Dodge/Plymouth/Chrysler RWD '71 thru '89
- **30055** Shadow & Plymouth Sundance '87 thru '94
- **30060** Spirit & Plymouth Acclaim '89 thru '95
- **30065** Vans - Dodge & Plymouth '71 thru '03

EAGLE
- **Talon** - see MITSUBISHI (68030, 68031)
- **Vision** - see CHRYSLER (25025)

FIAT
- **34010** 124 Sport Coupe & Spider '68 thru '78
- **34025** X1/9 all models '74 thru '80

FORD
- **10355** Ford Automatic Transmission Overhaul
- **36004** Aerostar Mini-vans all models '86 thru '97
- **36006** Contour & Mercury Mystique '95 thru '00
- **36008** Courier Pick-up all models '72 thru '82
- **36012** Crown Victoria & Mercury Grand Marquis '88 thru '06
- **10320** Ford Engine Overhaul Manual
- **36016** Escort/Mercury Lynx all models '81 thru '90
- **36020** Escort/Mercury Tracer '91 thru '00
- **36022** Ford Escape & Mazda Tribute '01 thru '03
- **36024** Explorer & Mazda Navajo '91 thru '01
- **36025** Ford Explorer & Mercury Mountaineer '02 thru '06
- **36028** Fairmont & Mercury Zephyr '78 thru '83
- **36030** Festiva & Aspire '88 thru '97
- **36032** Fiesta all models '77 thru '80
- **36034** Focus all models '00 thru '05
- **36036** Ford & Mercury Full-size '75 thru '87
- **36044** Ford & Mercury Mid-size '75 thru '86
- **36048** Mustang V8 all models '64-1/2 thru '73
- **36049** Mustang II 4 cyl, V6 & V8 models '74 thru '78
- **36050** Mustang & Mercury Capri all models Mustang, '79 thru '93; Capri, '79 thru '86
- **36051** Mustang all models '94 thru '04
- **36052** Mustang '05 thru '07
- **36054** Pick-ups & Bronco '73 thru '79
- **36058** Pick-ups & Bronco '80 thru '96
- **36059** F-150 & Expedition '97 thru '03, F-250 '97 thru '99 & Lincoln Navigator '98 thru '02
- **36060** Super Duty Pick-ups, Excursion '99 thru '06
- **36061** F-150 full-size '04 thru '06
- **36062** Pinto & Mercury Bobcat '75 thru '80
- **36066** Probe all models '89 thru '92
- **36070** Ranger/Bronco II gasoline models '83 thru '92
- **36071** Ranger '93 thru '05 & Mazda Pick-ups '94 thru '05
- **36074** Taurus & Mercury Sable '86 thru '95
- **36075** Taurus & Mercury Sable '96 thru '05
- **36078** Tempo & Mercury Topaz '84 thru '94
- **36082** Thunderbird/Mercury Cougar '83 thru '88
- **36086** Thunderbird/Mercury Cougar '89 and '97
- **36090** Vans all V8 Econoline models '69 thru '91
- **36094** Vans full size '92 thru '05
- **36097** Windstar Mini-van '95 thru '03

GENERAL MOTORS
- **10360** GM Automatic Transmission Overhaul
- **38005** Buick Century, Chevrolet Celebrity, Oldsmobile Cutlass Ciera & Pontiac 6000 all models '82 thru '96
- **38010** Buick Regal, Chevrolet Lumina, Oldsmobile Cutlass Supreme & Pontiac Grand Prix (FWD) '88 thru '05
- **38015** Buick Skyhawk, Cadillac Cimarron, Chevrolet Cavalier, Oldsmobile Firenza & Pontiac J-2000 & Sunbird '82 thru '94
- **38016** Chevrolet Cavalier & Pontiac Sunfire '95 thru '04
- **38017** Chevrolet Cobalt & Pontiac G5 '05 thru '07
- **38020** Buick Skylark, Chevrolet Citation, Olds Omega, Pontiac Phoenix '80 thru '85
- **38025** Buick Skylark & Somerset, Oldsmobile Achieva & Calais and Pontiac Grand Am all models '85 thru '98
- **38026** Chevrolet Malibu, Olds Alero & Cutlass, Pontiac Grand Am '97 thru '03
- **38027** Chevrolet Malibu '04 thru '07
- **38030** Cadillac Eldorado '71 thru '85, Seville '80 thru '85, Oldsmobile Toronado '71 thru '85, Buick Riviera '79 thru '85
- **38031** Cadillac Eldorado & Seville '86 thru '91, DeVille '86 thru '93, Fleetwood & Olds Toronado '86 thru '92, Buick Riviera '86 thru '93
- **38032** Cadillac DeVille '94 thru '05 & Seville '92 thru '04
- **38035** Chevrolet Lumina APV, Olds Silhouette & Pontiac Trans Sport all models '90 thru '96
- **38036** Chevrolet Venture, Olds Silhouette, Pontiac Trans Sport & Montana '97 thru '05
  - **General Motors Full-size Rear-wheel Drive** - see BUICK (19025)

GEO
- **Metro** - see CHEVROLET Sprint (24075)
- **Prizm** - '85 thru '92 see CHEVY (24060), '93 thru '02 see TOYOTA Corolla (92036)

(Continued on other side)

Haynes North America, Inc., 861 Lawrence Drive, Newbury Park, CA 91320-1514 • (805) 498-6703

Haynes Automotive Manuals (continued)

NOTE: If you do not see a listing for your vehicle, consult your local Haynes dealer for the latest product information.

40030 Storm all models '90 thru '93
Tracker - *see SUZUKI Samurai (90010)*

GMC
Vans & Pick-ups - *see CHEVROLET*

HONDA
42010 Accord CVCC all models '76 thru '83
42011 Accord all models '84 thru '89
42012 Accord all models '90 thru '93
42013 Accord all models '94 thru '97
42014 Accord all models '98 thru '02
42015 Honda Accord models '03 thru '05
42020 Civic 1200 all models '73 thru '79
42021 Civic 1300 & 1500 CVCC '80 thru '83
42022 Civic 1500 CVCC all models '75 thru '79
42023 Civic all models '84 thru '91
42024 Civic & del Sol '92 thru '95
42025 Civic '96 thru '00, CR-V '97 thru '01, Acura Integra '94 thru '00
42026 Civic '01 thru '04, CR-V '02 thru '04
42035 Honda Odyssey all models '99 thru '04
42037 Honda Pilot '03 thru '07, Acura MDX '01 thru '07
42040 Prelude CVCC all models '79 thru '89

HYUNDAI
43010 Elantra all models '96 thru '01
43015 Excel & Accent all models '86 thru '98

ISUZU
Hombre - *see CHEVROLET S-10 (24071)*
47017 Rodeo '91 thru '02; Amigo '89 thru '94 and '98 thru '02; Honda Passport '95 thru '02
47020 Trooper & Pick-up '81 thru '93

JAGUAR
49010 XJ6 all 6 cyl models '68 thru '86
49011 XJ6 all models '88 thru '94
49015 XJ12 & XJS all 12 cyl models '72 thru '85

JEEP
50010 Cherokee, Comanche & Wagoneer Limited all models '84 thru '01
50020 CJ all models '49 thru '86
50025 Grand Cherokee all models '93 thru '04
50029 Grand Wagoneer & Pick-up '72 thru '91 Grand Wagoneer '84 thru '91, Cherokee & Wagoneer '72 thru '83, Pick-up '72 thru '88
50030 Wrangler all models '87 thru '03
50035 Liberty '02 thru '04

KIA
54070 Sephia '94 thru '01, Spectra '00 thru '04

LEXUS
ES 300 - *see TOYOTA Camry (92007)*

LINCOLN
Navigator - *see FORD Pick-up (36059)*
59010 Rear-Wheel Drive all models '70 thru '05

MAZDA
61010 GLC Hatchback (rear-wheel drive) '77 thru '83
61011 GLC (front-wheel drive) '81 thru '85
61015 323 & Protegé '90 thru '00
61016 MX-5 Miata '90 thru '97
61020 MPV all models '89 thru '94
Navajo - *see Ford Explorer (36024)*
61030 Pick-ups '72 thru '93
Pick-ups '94 thru '00 - *see Ford Ranger (36071)*
61035 RX-7 all models '79 thru '85
61036 RX-7 all models '86 thru '91
61040 626 (rear-wheel drive) all models '79 thru '82
61041 626/MX-6 (front-wheel drive) '83 thru '92
61042 626 '93 thru '01, MX-6/Ford Probe '93 thru '01

MERCEDES-BENZ
63012 123 Series Diesel '76 thru '85
63015 190 Series four-cyl gas models, '84 thru '88
63020 230/250/280 6 cyl sohc models '68 thru '72
63025 280 123 Series gasoline models '77 thru '81
63030 350 & 450 all models '71 thru '80

MERCURY
64200 Villager & Nissan Quest '93 thru '01
All other titles, see FORD Listing.

MG
66010 MGB Roadster & GT Coupe '62 thru '80
66015 MG Midget, Austin Healey Sprite '58 thru '80

MITSUBISHI
68020 Cordia, Tredia, Galant, Precis & Mirage '83 thru '93

68030 Eclipse, Eagle Talon & Ply. Laser '90 thru '94
68031 Eclipse '95 thru '01, Eagle Talon '95 thru '98
68035 Mitsubishi Galant '94 thru '03
68040 Pick-up '83 thru '96 & Montero '83 thru '93

NISSAN
72010 300ZX all models including Turbo '84 thru '89
72015 Altima all models '93 thru '04
72020 Maxima all models '85 thru '92
72021 Maxima all models '93 thru '04
72030 Pick-ups '80 thru '97 Pathfinder '87 thru '95
72031 Frontier Pick-up '98 thru '04, Xterra '00 thru '04, Pathfinder '96 thru '04
72040 Pulsar all models '83 thru '86
Quest - *see MERCURY Villager (64200)*
72050 Sentra all models '82 thru '94
72051 Sentra & 200SX all models '95 thru '04
72060 Stanza all models '82 thru '90

OLDSMOBILE
73015 Cutlass V6 & V8 gas models '74 thru '88
For other OLDSMOBILE titles, see BUICK, CHEVROLET or GENERAL MOTORS listing.

PLYMOUTH
For PLYMOUTH titles, see DODGE listing.

PONTIAC
79008 Fiero all models '84 thru '88
79018 Firebird V8 models except Turbo '70 thru '81
79019 Firebird all models '82 thru '92
79040 Mid-size Rear-wheel Drive '70 thru '87
For other PONTIAC titles, see BUICK, CHEVROLET or GENERAL MOTORS listing.

PORSCHE
80020 911 except Turbo & Carrera 4 '65 '89
80025 914 all 4 cyl models '69 '76
80030 924 all models including Turbo '76 thru '82
80035 944 all models including Turbo '83 thru '89

RENAULT
Alliance & Encore - *see AMC (14020)*

SAAB
84010 900 all models including Turbo '79 thru '88

SATURN
87010 Saturn all models '91 thru '02
87011 Saturn Ion '03 thru '07
87020 Saturn all L-series models '00 thru '04

SUBARU
89002 1100, 1300, 1400 & 1600 '71 thru '79
89003 1600 & 1800 2WD & 4WD '80 thru '94
89100 Legacy all models '90 thru '99
89101 Legacy & Forester '00 thru '06

SUZUKI
90010 Samurai/Sidekick & Geo Tracker '86 thru '01

TOYOTA
92005 Camry all models '83 thru '91
92006 Camry all models '92 thru '96
92007 Camry, Avalon, Solara, Lexus ES 300 '97 thru '01
92008 Toyota Camry, Avalon and Solara and Lexus ES 300/330 all models '02 thru '05
92015 Celica Rear Wheel Drive '71 thru '85
92020 Celica Front Wheel Drive '86 thru '99
92025 Celica Supra all models '79 thru '92
92030 Corolla all models '75 thru '79
92032 Corolla all rear wheel drive models '80 thru '87
92035 Corolla all front wheel drive models '84 thru '92
92036 Corolla & Geo Prizm '93 thru '02
92037 Corolla models '03 thru '05
92040 Corolla Tercel all models '80 thru '82
92045 Corona all models '74 thru '82
92050 Cressida all models '78 thru '82
92055 Land Cruiser FJ40, 43, 45, 55 '68 thru '82
92056 Land Cruiser FJ60, 62, 80, FZJ80 '80 thru '96
92065 MR2 all models '85 thru '87
92070 Pick-up all models '69 thru '78
92075 Pick-up all models '79 thru '95
92076 Tacoma '95 thru '04, 4Runner '96 thru '02, & T100 '93 thru '98
92078 Tundra '00 thru '05 & Sequoia '01 thru '05
92080 Previa all models '91 thru '95
92081 Prius all models '01 thru '08
92082 RAV4 all models '96 thru '05
92085 Tercel all models '87 thru '94
92090 Toyota Sienna all models '98 thru '02
92095 Highlander & Lexus RX-330 '99 thru '06

TRIUMPH
94007 Spitfire all models '62 thru '81
94010 TR7 all models '75 thru '81

VW
96008 Beetle & Karmann Ghia '54 thru '79
96009 New Beetle '98 thru '05
96016 Rabbit, Jetta, Scirocco & Pick-up gas models '75 thru '92 & Convertible '80 thru '92
96017 Golf, GTI & Jetta '93 thru '98 & Cabrio '95 thru '98
96018 Golf, GTI, Jetta & Cabrio '99 thru '02
96020 Rabbit, Jetta & Pick-up diesel '77 thru '84
96023 Passat '98 thru '01, Audi A4 '96 thru '01
96030 Transporter 1600 all models '68 thru '79
96035 Transporter 1700, 1800 & 2000 '72 thru '79
96040 Type 3 1500 & 1600 all models '63 thru '73
96045 Vanagon all air-cooled models '80 thru '83

VOLVO
97010 120, 130 Series & 1800 Sports '61 thru '73
97015 140 Series all models '66 thru '74
97020 240 Series all models '76 thru '93
97040 740 & 760 Series all models '82 thru '88
97050 850 Series all models '93 thru '97

TECHBOOK MANUALS
10205 Automotive Computer Codes
10206 OBD-II & Electronic Engine Management Systems
10210 Automotive Emissions Control Manual
10215 Fuel Injection Manual, 1978 thru 1985
10220 Fuel Injection Manual, 1986 thru 1999
10225 Holley Carburetor Manual
10230 Rochester Carburetor Manual
10240 Weber/Zenith/Stromberg/SU Carburetors
10305 Chevrolet Engine Overhaul Manual
10310 Chrysler Engine Overhaul Manual
10320 Ford Engine Overhaul Manual
10330 GM and Ford Diesel Engine Repair Manual
10333 Building Engine Power Manual
10340 Small Engine Repair Manual, 5 HP & Less
10341 Small Engine Repair Manual, 5.5 - 20 HP
10345 Suspension, Steering & Driveline Manual
10355 Ford Automatic Transmission Overhaul
10360 GM Automatic Transmission Overhaul
10405 Automotive Body Repair & Painting
10410 Automotive Brake Manual
10411 Automotive Anti-lock Brake (ABS) Systems
10415 Automotive Detailing Manual
10420 Automotive Electrical Manual
10425 Automotive Heating & Air Conditioning
10430 Automotive Reference Manual & Dictionary
10435 Automotive Tools Manual
10440 Used Car Buying Guide
10445 Welding Manual
10450 ATV Basics
10452 Scooters, Automatic Transmission 50cc to 250cc

SPANISH MANUALS
98903 Reparación de Carrocería & Pintura
98904 Carburadores para los modelos Holley & Rochester
98905 Códigos Automotrices de la Computadora
98910 Frenos Automotriz
98913 Electricidad Automotriz
98915 Inyección de Combustible 1986 al 1999
99040 Chevrolet & GMC Camionetas '67 al '87 Incluye Suburban, Blazer & Jimmy '67 al '91
99041 Chevrolet & GMC Camionetas '88 al '98 Incluye Suburban '92 al '98, Blazer & Jimmy '92 al '94, Tahoe y Yukon '95 al '98
99042 Chevrolet & GMC Camionetas Cerradas '68 al '95
99055 Dodge Caravan & Plymouth Voyager '84 al '95
99075 Ford Camionetas y Bronco '80 al '94
99077 Ford Camionetas Cerradas '69 al '91
99088 Ford Modelos de Tamaño Mediano '75 al '86
99091 Ford Taurus & Mercury Sable '86 al '95
99095 GM Modelos de Tamaño Grande '70 al '90
99100 GM Modelos de Tamaño Mediano '70 al '88
99106 Jeep Cherokee, Wagoneer & Comanche '84 al '00
99110 Nissan Camioneta '80 al '96, Pathfinder '87 al '95
99118 Nissan Sentra '82 al '94
99125 Toyota Camionetas y 4Runner '79 al '95

Over 100 Haynes motorcycle manuals also available

10-07

Haynes North America, Inc., 861 Lawrence Drive, Newbury Park, CA 91320-1514 • (805) 498-6703